Possible Ways to Reduce Project Cost or Bid Price

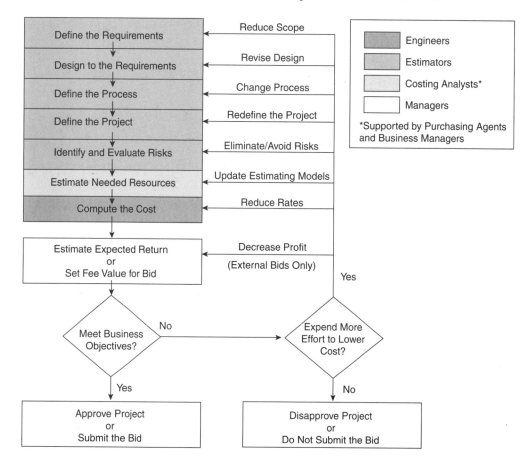

Estimating Software-Intensive Systems

Estimating Software-Intensive Systems

Projects, Products, and Processes

Richard D. Stutzke

♦♦Addison-Wesley

Upper Saddle River, NJ • Boston • Indianapolis • San Francisco
New York • Toronto • Montreal • London • Munich • Paris • Madrid
Capetown • Sydney • Tokyo • Singapore • Mexico City

Carnegie Mellon
Software Engineering Institute

The SEI Series in Software Engineering

The publisher offers excellent discounts on this book when ordered in quantity for bulk purchases or special sales, which may include electronic versions and/or custom covers and content particular to your business, training goals, marketing focus, and branding interests. For more information, please contact:

U. S. Corporate and Government Sales
(800) 382-3419
corpsales@pearsontechgroup.com

For sales outside the U. S., please contact:

International Sales
international@pearsoned.com

Visit us on the Web: www.awprofessional.com

Library of Congress Number: 2004116955

ISBN: 0-201-70312-2
Text printed in the United States on recycled paper at Courier in Westford, Massachusetts.
First printing: April 2005

Contents

Preface

Software-intensive systems include the following:

- In-house systems for accounting, production control, and e-business
- Applications sold commercially in the mass market ("shrink-wrapped products")
- Large, complex, "one-of-a-kind" military, industrial, and commercial systems

Projects to develop and maintain software-intensive systems can involve the following:

- Designing, building, testing, and distributing software components
- Selecting and purchasing commercial software and hardware components
- Configuring and, in some cases, designing hardware
- Training and supporting users

Practitioners who develop, manage, procure, or operate software-intensive systems need to estimate and measure the resources needed to perform such activities. They also need to calculate costs, set bid prices, and evaluate cost and price. Some practitioners also need to estimate and measure the usage of computer resources, product quality (defects), and the effectiveness and efficiency of production processes.

The Book

To meet these needs, this book describes *practical, proven estimating techniques* that are simple and easy to use. Numerous examples show how to apply the techniques correctly. One example shows how to construct, calibrate, and use a complete cost model for software maintenance. The book explains how to use Microsoft Excel to build estimating and tracking tools. It provides implementation guidance and aids (checklists, templates, and spreadsheets). Boxes in each chapter provide details on specific topics. A "Recommended Reading" section at the end of each chapter directs readers to sources of additional information. Appendixes provide supplemental information, including acronyms and an extensive glossary.

You can use computer-based tools to generate an estimate in a few minutes. Remember, however, that estimation is more than clever techniques, parametric models, and tools. *The greatest challenge for an estimator is deciding where to start when faced with a blank sheet of paper.* For example, during a proposal, engineers, managers, planners, and estimators must quickly gain an understanding of the user's problem and requirements, the structure of the solution, and the process needed to design, build, and deliver that solution.

This book describes ways to help readers quickly "get their arms around" a product or system that they have never seen before. It also provides guidance on selecting appropriate estimating techniques and tools based on the type of resource and project phase.

This book discusses measurement and data collection so that readers can obtain accurate data to track progress, prepare updated estimates, and calibrate estimating models. For example, it describes different measures of software size, including use case points, function points, and source lines of code. The book describes earned value measurement and provides practical suggestions to address the particular needs of large projects related to status tracking and cost accounting.

This book covers a wide range of topics and techniques. To help you quickly find information, the book has 27 chapters, organized into five parts:

1. The Essentials
2. The Details
3. Closing the Feedback Loop
4. Handling Large Projects
5. Estimating Products and Processes

This book is relevant to both small and large projects using either agile or plan-driven production processes. Much of the material applies to criteria in process maturity models and to earned value measurement. Table P-1 shows the relevance of specific chapters and appendices to each of these areas. The book also addresses internal Information Technology applications, mass market shrink-wrapped products, and complex systems as detailed in Table P-2. Table P-3 shows the applicability of the material to individuals having specific job responsibilities.

Table P-1 *Relevance to Process Type*

#	Title	Agile Methods	Plan Driven Methods	Process Maturity Models	Earned Value Measures
	Part 1 - The Essentials				
1	Introduction	X	X	X	X
2	Planning a Warehouse Inventory System	X	X	X	
3	A Basic Estimating Process: The Linear Method	X	X	X	X
4	Measurement and Estimation	X	X	X	X
5	Estimating Techniques	X	X	X	X
6	Estimating Annual Maintenance Costs	X	X		
	Part 2 - The Details				
7	Preparing to Estimate (Precursors of Estimation)	X	X	X	X
8	Estimating Software Size: The Basics	X	X	X	
9	Estimating Software Size: The Details	X	X	X	
10	Production Processes (Project Life Cycles)	X	X	X	X
11	Bottom-Up Estimating and Scheduling	X	X	X	X
12	Top-Down Estimating and Allocation	X	X	X	
13	Parametric Models		X	X	
14	Estimating Risk Reserves	X	X	X	X
15	Calculating Cost and Price: The Basics	X	X	X	X
	Part 3 - Closing the Feedback Loop				
16	Collecting Data: Basics	X	X	X	X
17	Tracking Status	X	X	X	X
18	Updating Estimates	X	X	X	X
19	Consolidating and Applying Your Knowledge	X	X	X	
	Part 4 - Handling Large Projects				
20	Crafting a WBS		X	X	X
21	Earned Value Measurement		X	X	X
22	Collecting Data: Details			X	X
23	Calculating Cost and Bid Price				X
	Part 5 - Estimating Products and Processes				
24	Determining Product Performance			X	
25	Determining Product Quality			X	
26	Measuring and Estimating Process Performance			X	
27	Ranking and Selecting Items	X	X	X	
	Appendixes				
A	Roles and Responsibilities for Estimation	X	X	X	X
B	Measurement Theory and Statistics			X	
C	Measures of Estimation Accuracy			X	
D	Summation Formulas for Series				
E	Excel for Estimators	X	X	X	

Table P-2 *Relevance to Product Type*

#	Title	Internal IT Application	Mass Market Product	Large Complex System
	Part 1 - The Essentials			
1	Introduction	X	X	X
2	Planning a Warehouse Inventory System	X	X	X
3	A Basic Estimating Process: The Linear Method	X	X	X
4	Measurement and Estimation	X	X	X
5	Estimating Techniques	X	X	X
6	Estimating Annual Maintenance Costs	X	X	X
	Part 2 - The Details			
7	Preparing to Estimate (Precursors of Estimation)	X	X	X
8	Estimating Software Size: The Basics	X	X	X
9	Estimating Software Size: The Details	X	X	X
10	Production Processes (Project Life Cycles)	X	X	X
11	Bottom-Up Estimating and Scheduling	X	X	X
12	Top-Down Estimating and Allocation	X		X
13	Parametric Models	X		X
14	Estimating Risk Reserves	X	X	X
15	Calculating Cost and Price: The Basics	X	X	X
	Part 3 - Closing the Feedback Loop			
16	Collecting Data: Basics	X	X	X
17	Tracking Status	X	X	X
18	Updating Estimates	X	X	X
19	Consolidating and Applying Your Knowledge			
	Part 4 - Handling Large Projects			
20	Crafting a WBS			X
21	Earned Value Measurement			X
22	Collecting Data: Details			X
23	Calculating Cost and Bid Price			
	Part 5 - Estimating Products and Processes			
24	Determining Product Performance	X	X	X
25	Determining Product Quality	X	X	X
26	Measuring and Estimating Process Performance		X	
27	Ranking and Selecting Items	X	X	X
	Appendixes			
A	Roles and Responsibilities for Estimation	X	X	X
B	Measurement Theory and Statistics			
C	Measures of Estimation Accuracy			
D	Summation Formulas for Series			X
E	Excel for Estimators			

Table P-3 *Relevance to Job Responsibilities (part 1 of 2)*

#	Title	System & Software Engineer	Project or Technical Manager	Product Manager	Govt Program Manager	Acquisition or Cost Analyst	Process Improve. Specialist
	Part 1 - The Essentials						
1	Introduction	X	X	X	X	X	X
2	Planning a Warehouse Inventory System	X	X	X	X	X	
3	A Basic Estimating Process: The Linear Method	X	X	X	X	X	X
4	Measurement and Estimation	X	X		X	X	X
5	Estimating Techniques	X	X	X	X	X	X
6	Estimating Annual Maintenance Costs	X	X	X	X	X	
	Part 2 - The Details						
7	Preparing to Estimate (Precursors of Estimation)	X	X	X	X	X	X
8	Estimating Software Size: The Basics	X	X	X	X		X
9	Estimating Software Size: The Details	X	X	X	X		X
10	Production Processes (Project Life Cycles)	X	X	X	X	X	X
11	Bottom-Up Estimating and Scheduling		X	X	X	X	X
12	Top-Down Estimating and Allocation		X	X	X	X	X
13	Parametric Models		X	X	X		X
14	Estimating Risk Reserves		X	X	X		X
15	Calculating Cost and Price: The Basics		X	X	X	X	X
	Part 3 - Closing the Feedback Loop						
16	Collecting Data: Basics	X	X	X	X	X	X
17	Tracking Status	X	X	X	X	X	X
18	Updating Estimates	X	X	X	X	X	X
19	Consolidating and Applying Your Knowledge		X	X	X		X

Table P-3 *Relevance to Job Responsibilities (part 2 of 2)*

#	Title	System & Software Engineer	Project or Technical Manager	Product Manager	Govt Program Manager	Acquisition or Cost Analyst	Process Improve. Specialist
	Part 4 - Handling Large Projects						
20	Crafting a WBS		X		X	X	X
21	Earned Value Measurement		X		X	X	X
22	Collecting Data: Details		X		X	X	X
23	Calculating Cost and Bid Price		X		X	X	X
	Part 5 - Estimating Products and Processes						X
24	Determining Product Performance	X	X	X	X		
25	Determining Product Quality	X	X	X	X		X
26	Measuring and Estimating Process Performance		X	X	X		X
27	Ranking and Selecting Items	X	X	X	X	X	X
	Appendixes						X
A	Roles and Responsibilities for Estimation	X	X	X	X	X	X
B	Measurement Theory and Statistics	X	X	X	X		X
C	Measures of Estimation Accuracy		X	X	X	X	X
D	Summation Formulas for Series	X					
E	Excel for Estimators	X	X	X	X	X	X

The CD-ROM

To help you quickly apply new techniques, the book has a CD-ROM with templates, spreadsheets, short "Notes" on specific topics, and examples showing how to use the features of Microsoft Excel to analyze, plot, and manage data. This will help you build your own tools for estimating and tracking. The CD-ROM also contains the references I used in preparing this book. These include books, journal articles, and conference proceedings. The bibliography is in Rich Text Format so that you can search it with a document editor. The CD-ROM also lists related web sites. (I have generally restricted my web references to established organizations such as official government organizations and professional societies. Universities and companies are less certain but sometimes are the only source of information.)

The Web Site

The book's Web site, *http://sw-estimation.com*, supplements the book by providing updated information, more Notes, and additional spreadsheets, as well as the errata for the book. This information is *cross-indexed* to the book. The web site also has links to relevant web sites, including professional organizations and tool vendors.

The Benefits

This book will enable you to start preparing better estimates immediately. You can use the techniques, templates, tools, and implementation guidance to define a *disciplined and repeatable process* to produce accurate and complete estimates for your projects, products, and processes. This book also provides you with a *foundation to tackle new estimating situations* in the future.

Dick Stutzke
Huntsville, Alabama
December, 2004

Dedication

To my colleagues and students.

Acknowledgements

Many people provided information, suggestions, criticisms, and support that helped make this a better book. My many professional colleagues generously shared their knowledge and ideas. These include Barry Boehm and his colleagues at the USC Center for Software Engineering: Winsor Brown, Ray Madachy, Brad Clark, Sunita Chulani, and Chris Abts. Don Reifer generously shared ideas on the audience, content, and structure of this book. Wolf Goethert at the SEI reviewed early drafts of the book and provided information and reports. Brad Tyler and I co-authored the original description of the Linear Method in April 1990 that was the basis for Chapter 3. Ken Powers and members of the SAIC Business Automation Team (Boyce Beech, Robin Brasher, George Sumners, and Tommy Guerin) provided technical assistance and practical suggestions for developing many of the book's spreadsheets. Robert "Mutt" Suttles helped with graphics. Over the years, teaching software engineers and managers has helped me understand their needs and the fundamental concepts at a deeper level. Many students have encouraged me to write this book. Gordon Wright and Neil Marple, instructors for SAIC's estimating courses, also shared ideas and student feedback. Bill Craig, Fred Reed, and the staff of the U.S. Army Research Development and Engineering Command, Aviation and Missile RDEC, Software Engineering Directorate provided the opportunity to apply estimating and measurement techniques to a wide range of software-intensive systems over the past 12 years. Other colleagues who contributed in various ways include Carol Dekkers, Tom DeMarco, George Bozoki, Dan Ligett, Richard Thayer, Jim Magnusson, Lloyd Mosemann, Jerry

Obenour, Scott Donaldson, Stan Siegel, and Barbara Hitchings. John Fodeh shared his spreadsheet of the Waterman error trending model, which became TRENDX.XLS. Laura Zuber provided FPLEDGER.XLS, which became FP.xls. Martin Stutzke provided an example of a Monte Carlo simulation written in Excel VBA. Extra special thanks to Sharon Gaetano for continuing support.

Various individuals reviewed parts of the book and provided valuable comments. Early reviewers included Wolf Goethert, Harry Delugach, Steve Tockey, Brad Tyler, Chuck Connell, and Gary Thomas. Kathy Hedges reviewed several early chapters and provided detailed suggestions. Reviewers of the first draft (May 2004) included Mike Tarrani, Tom McGibbon, Kelly Butler, Jim Brosseau, Ron Lichty, and two anonymous reviewers. Ron Lichty's 40 pages of detailed comments were especially helpful, and led to a restructuring of the book. Dick Fitzer of SAIC reviewed the final manuscript.

Peter Gordon, my editor at Pearson Education, guided me, provided sage advice, and never lost hope over the many years it took to produce this book. (Thanks to Anita Carleton and Kim Caputo for recommending Peter.) The Pearson Education production staff in Boston and Indianapolis completed a lot of quality work in a short time.

Many SAIC employees shared their knowledge as we worked together on various proposals and projects. Certain individuals deserve special mention. Tony Jordano sponsored the development and update of SAIC's estimating courses over the years, which provided me the opportunity to test and hone my ideas. Rod Roberts provided encouragement and support throughout the project. Ken Powers provided tips on using Microsoft Office and helped debug VBA macros on numerous occasions. Mary Ellen Harris promptly obtained numerous reprints and researched obscure citations. The Redstone Scientific Information Center provided access to technical books and journals.

Most importantly, I would like to thank my indispensable assistant, Sue Totten. Sue prepared charts for SAIC's estimating courses, my conference presentations, and technical reports. She formatted numerous drafts of this book and prepared many of the original line drawings. She suggested improvements to the book and to our processes. Sue maintained configuration control over the many drafts of courses, papers, and book chapters. She worked late on many days, and asked what she could do next to help. She acted as my alter ego, handling many routine duties so I had more time to write. Throughout the entire ordeal, Sue retained her sense of humor. (At one point, I thought I would have to rename the book *Unser Kampf.*) Sue, I could not have done it without you!

About the Author

Dr. Richard D. Stutzke has more than 40 years experience with software development and project management in the military and industry, including scientific, embedded real time, and commercial systems. He has authored more than fifty papers and articles on software estimation and management. In 1989, he established Science Applications International Corporation's Corporate Software Process Group and led it for two years. Since then, he has focused on defining integrated processes for developing software-intensive systems and managing their development and operation.

Part I

The Essentials

Chapter 1

Introduction

Estimation and measurement are important for designing, building, modifying, and operating all types of products and for delivering many types of services. This chapter identifies the types of quantities that you must be able to estimate and measure and explains why estimation is inherently difficult. Software is difficult to describe, build, and measure, making estimation even more difficult. The number of systems and products with software content continues to increase. Therefore, more and more people need techniques to estimate software-intensive systems. Estimation must be a continuing process because all estimates have uncertainty, and because many things change during a project. This chapter describes a feedback control system that links measurement and estimation to produce better estimates over time.

1.1 Reasons to Estimate and Measure

Projects exist to design, build, and test products and to provide associated services to customers. (Sometimes the buyer is not the end user. In this case, the term *customer* refers to both.) Products include hardware, software, documents, and operational data. (Operational data includes anything the product needs to operate. Some examples are configuration files, tax tables, catalogs, price lists, and customer records.) Services include installation, check out, and user training. (See the box "Product, System, or Service?".) Projects have a definite beginning and end, and therefore operate for a finite period of time.[1] Processes describe and organize the project's activities. Performing these activities consumes project resources.

Product, System, or Service?

Many authors, me included, tend to use the words *system* and *product* interchangeably. There are some subtle distinctions, however. The word *system* usually implies a unique collection of hardware and software, which a single organization owns and operates. One example is a firm's custom-built warehouse management system. Another example is a single integrated system for nationwide air traffic control. The word *product* usually implies that several unrelated individuals own and independently operate copies of an item, possibly configuring their copy to meet their particular needs. Both products and systems contain hardware, software, and operational data, and have users who need training and support. Therefore, for estimation purposes, there is no substantial difference between systems and products.

Some organizations operate systems or copies of a product solely to deliver services, such as retailing and banking. Many of the activities involved in delivering services are the same as those performed for systems and products, and so many of the same measurement and estimation techniques apply.

As you encounter the words *product*, *system*, and *service* in this book, interpret them in your particular context. If you are a commercial software developer or a manufacturer of consumer products, you think of a product. If you are a contractor building one-of-a-kind systems, you think of a system. If you are a service provider, you think of services.

---

[1] Some "projects" deliver services on a continuing basis. Examples are product maintenance (especially providing user support) and user training. Such projects still have a specified "period of performance."

Good estimates are key to project (and product) success. Estimates provide information to make decisions, define feasible performance objectives, and plans. Measurements provide data to gauge adherence to performance specifications and plans, make decisions, revise designs and plans, and improve future estimates and processes. Table 1-1 shows reasons to estimate and measure products, projects, and processes. Engineers use estimates and measurements to evaluate the feasibility and affordability of proposed products, choose among alternate designs, assess risk, and support business decisions. Engineers and planners estimate the resources needed to develop, maintain, enhance, and deploy a product. Project planners use the estimated staffing level to identify needed facilities (offices, furniture, computers). Planners and managers use the resource estimates to compute project cost and schedule, and to prepare budgets and plans. Estimates of product, project, and process characteristics also provide "baselines" to gauge progress during the course of a project. Managers compare estimates (the cost and schedule baselines) and actual values to detect deviations from the project plan and to understand the causes of the variation. For products, engineers compare estimates (the technical baseline) to observed performance to decide if the product meets its functional and performance requirements. Process capability baselines establish norms for process performance. Managers use these norms to control the process, and to detect compliance problems. Process engineers use capability baselines to improve the production processes.

Bad estimates affect everyone associated with a project: the engineers and managers (and their families), the customer who buys the product, and sometimes even the stockholders of the company responsible for delivering the software. Incomplete or inaccurate resource estimates for a project mean that the project may not have enough time or money to complete the required work. (A project whose cost has been greatly underestimated cannot be saved by technical wizards, nor by a superhuman manager.) If the computer hardware is undersized, incompletely specified, or both, this could result in inadequate capacity or unacceptable performance. (I have seen customers specify product performance values that were very difficult or even impossible for any developer to achieve. Engineers should be able to estimate the feasible limits, and the increased cost and risk associated with approaching target values that are near these limits.) Incorrect estimates of product quality and dependability can affect the product's acceptability, safety, commercial success, and operating costs.

Table 1-1 *Reasons to Estimate and Measure*

Product Size, Performance, and Quality
• Evaluate feasibility of requirements.
• Analyze alternative product designs.
• Determine the required capacity and speed of hardware components.
• Evaluate product performance (accuracy, speed, reliability, availability).
• Quantify resources needed to develop, deploy, and support a product.
• Identify and assess technical risks.
• Provide technical baselines for tracking and controlling.
Project Effort, Cost, and Schedule
• Determine project feasibility in terms of cost and time.
• Identify and assess project risks.
• Negotiate achievable commitments.
• Prepare realistic plans and budgets.
• Evaluate business value (cost versus benefit).
• Provide cost and schedule baselines for tracking and controlling.
Process Capability and Performance
• Predict resource consumption and efficiency.
• Establish norms for expected performance.
• Identify opportunities for improvement.

These examples show that "software" estimators must deal with many different quantities. This book addresses all the quantities of interest for a complete software-intensive system or product: hardware, software, operational data, user support and training, plus all the resources needed to develop, test, and install the hardware and software for these systems. You may not deal with some of these quantities for your particular types of projects and products. Pick what you need and skip the rest.

1.2 Specific Quantities to Estimate and Measure

Table 1-2 identifies the types of quantities that you must be able to estimate and measure to design products, prepare plans, and evaluate processes. The Software Engineering Institute's Capability Maturity Model-Integrated for Systems/Software Engineering (CMMI-SE/SW) identifies these same quantities.[2]

Table 1-2 *Quantities of Interest*

Project
• Effort (activities)
• Staff (number, skill and experience, turnover)
• Time (phases, schedule milestones)
• Effort (direct and indirect)
• Costs (labor and nonlabor)
• Computer resources used for development and test
• Performance (capacity, accuracy, speed, response time)
• Quality (conformance to requirements, dependability)
• Price and total ownership cost
• Size or amount (created, modified, purchased)
Process
• Effectiveness
• Efficiency
• Flexibility

Different individuals focus on particular quantities. Project resources, costs, time, and money are primarily of interest to managers, financial analysts, and, of course, the customer who pays for the product. Computer resources include the processor, main memory, mass storage, network, and peripherals. Developers use computers to develop and test software, so computer resource usage may affect project costs.

Product performance and quality are of interest to engineers and users. Performance has both static and dynamic aspects. For example, providing a large data storage capacity increases hardware costs. Slow throughput may increase the user's operating costs. Quality includes providing useful (or specified) functions to the user with a level of dependability that is adequate for the particular

---

[2] The Software Engineering Institute's Capability Maturity Models (SEI CMMs) define best practices for defining, planning, controlling, and improving products, processes, and projects. In particular, the CMMs identify many quantities that should be estimated, measured, and tracked.

application. (Dependability might refer to access security, operator safety, data integrity, or system reliability. Specifications should clearly state which interpretation to use.)

Later chapters describe ways to estimate each quantity. Unfortunately, "good" estimates of these quantities are difficult to obtain. The following three sections explain why.

1.3 The Nature of Estimation

The verb *estimate* means to produce a statement of the approximate value of some quantity that describes or characterizes an object. (The noun *estimate* refers to the value produced.) The *object* can be an artifact (e.g., software module, hardware part or assembly, or document) or an activity (e.g., planning, testing, or installing). You make an estimate because you cannot directly measure the value of the quantity because

- The object is inaccessible (e.g., it is in continuous operational use).
- The object does not yet exist.
- Measurement would be too expensive or dangerous.

For existing objects (artifacts or activities), you may estimate the values directly, or you may compute the values using the values of other characteristics that can be directly measured (or at least more easily estimated). If you have historical data from similar objects, you can use it to help you estimate, either by scaling the historical values or by building estimation models. The computation might be simple, such as effort equals size divided by productivity. (But even this is not as simple as it might appear. Chapter 4, "Measurement and Estimation," explains why.) You may use a (mathematical) model to compute the values of the desired quantities. A model is a function plus a procedure for using it. Every model is an approximation. As George E. P. Box says, "All models are wrong but some are useful." [Box, 1979] This means that the estimated value will contain errors due to both the measurements and the model(s) used.[3]

Estimating becomes more difficult for an object that has not yet been built, or has never been built, or for an activity that has never been performed. There is nothing to be measured, either directly or indirectly. This is the usual situation faced by estimators for new products and systems. In many cases, the product requirements, design details, process activities, and the people who will perform the activities are not known at the time the estimate is being prepared.

---

[3] Measurement theory gives guidance on the correct forms of measures and models. Statistics helps account for uncertainties due to measurement errors and imperfect knowledge of the form of a model. Appendix B, "Measurement Theory and Statistics," provides details.

The estimator must predict the future. Three things typically occur when predicting the future: omissions, uncertainties, and change.

1.3.1 Omissions

The estimator may fail to identify all the elements that contribute to the estimate, as well as key underlying assumptions. The estimator must rely on features specified by buyers or product managers, and on information provided by designers and managers. Unfortunately, buyers do not always know all the features that they want. Specifications written in natural language are imprecise and subject to interpretation by the reader. To further complicate the situation, there are sometimes several stakeholders (buyer, end user, operator, and maintainer), all with slightly different views of the system. Designers interpret user needs and written requirements from their own unique perspective. Lack of domain knowledge may also cause designers to oversimplify or omit functions. Managers may supply incorrect rates for labor, inflation, and other key financial parameters.

This sin of omission leads to low estimates (a bias).[4] The chances of omission increase as products and projects become larger and more complex. Over time, the omissions are discovered, and the estimated value increases. Figure 1-1 illustrates typical behavior for the estimated amount of some quantity such as the number of requirements, the software size, or the project effort versus elapsed time, expressed as a fraction of the project's total time (relative time). The growth is finite because any project ultimately ends. Usually, the growth rate decreases as the end of the project approaches, causing the curve to flatten on the right end. The flatness on the left end arises for two reasons. First, the team does not immediately discover the omissions because there is a delay as they get oriented to the project, product, and processes. Second, the external environment has not yet had time to change significantly.

1.3.2 Uncertainty

Estimates are based on incomplete or imperfect knowledge about the properties of objects and the values of these properties. There are three possible cases:

1. Property is identified and the value is known accurately (or at least within a narrow range).
2. Property is identified but the value is unknown (or possibly known within a wide range).
3. Property is not identified (and so the value is unknown).

---

[4] Ignorance and conservatism can also lead to wild guesses that are far larger than the correct values. Low estimates predominate, however.

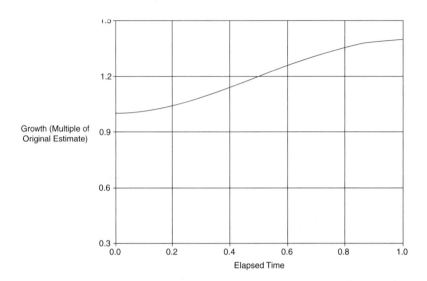

Figure 1-1   *The estimated amount typically increases*

Case 1 also includes the case where the "known" value is actually incorrect.

The uncertainty (probable error) in the estimated value usually decreases over time because the estimator obtains more detailed information about the problem. (This assumes, of course, that the estimator makes use of the new information.) Figure 1-2 illustrates how the amount of error in an estimated quantity typically decreases with time. The estimator learns more as the project unfolds. (The amount of uncertainty will only decrease if the rate of learning is greater than the rate of change occurring in the product's requirements and design, and the project's processes and staffing.) The uncertainty decreases slowly at first because the staff requires some time to understand the problem domain, the project goals, the customer's needs, and the product design. After the participants become oriented, they then start to provide information that can be used to reduce the uncertainty in the estimate.

Barry Boehm published a similar curve for project cost estimates in Figure 21-1 of [Boehm, 1981, page 311]. (He calls it the funnel curve.) His figure shows the types of information that become available as the project proceeds. Figure 1-3 illustrates this using terms you will encounter in later chapters. This information decreases the uncertainty in the cost estimate. As an example, for a new development project, at the end of detailed design phase, the team has identified and described all of the modules in the product. (Chapter 10, "Production Processes (Project Life Cycles)," describes software project life cycles.) However, they have also expended ~50% of the project resources (effort, time), and the uncertainty is still about ±10%. To get a "perfect" estimate with no uncertainty, you must complete the project![5] The project team expends effort on analysis and design to obtain the more detailed information, and so decrease the uncertainty in the estimates.

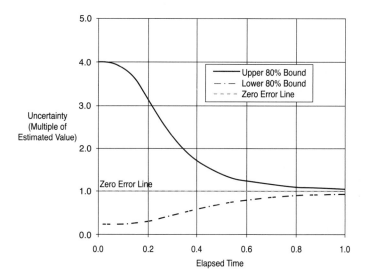

Figure 1-2   *Estimation uncertainty typically decreases with time*

The key lesson from Figure 1-3 is this: In estimation, you get what you pay for. This principle applies to other estimated quantities as well, not just to cost. During initial project definition or proposal preparation, engineers, managers, planners, and estimators must quickly gain an understanding of the following:

- The user's problem and requirements
- The structure of the solution
- The process needed to design, build, and deliver that solution

The dilemma that estimators and managers face is how to obtain as much information as possible given limited resources (time and money). A major factor that reduces the uncertainty is prior experience building similar products and delivering similar services. (See Section 1.4.) Regardless of how much time and effort you expend to prepare your initial estimate, however, there is still the problem of change.

---

[5] Because time reporting and cost accounting systems are never perfect, however, you actually never know the total effort and cost precisely. This means the curve does not really converge to a point! Chapter 22, "Collecting Data: Details," explains the causes of inaccuracy.

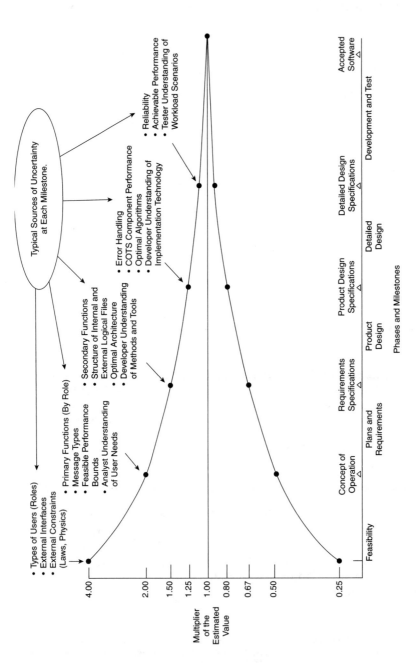

Figure 1-3 *Estimating accuracy increases with time (assuming no requirements volatility)*

1.3.3 Change

Assumptions associated with the product, project, and process may (and usually do) change during the course of the project. In addition, other external factors may also change. These include required product features, interfaces to other systems, regulatory requirements, and enterprise business objectives. So even the "identified and known" quantities may change! A further complication is that most of the changes are not predictable.

Buyers, users, and designers all learn as the job progresses. If the buyer provided written requirements, one typical result is that the buyer tries to reinterpret the meaning of the written requirements. (This is a big risk for developers of custom systems working under fixed-price contracts.) The external environment also changes as the job progresses. This environment includes laws, regulations, business rules, interfaces to other systems, and even the technology and tools used by the developers. These types of changes apply to all types of development projects: software, hardware, and systems. The amount of change is proportional to the duration of the project. In addition, hardware production projects encounter changes in the characteristics and prices of parts and materials, and in worker productivity (often quantified by a learning curve).

Changes to product requirements or design become more expensive as the project proceeds. This is especially true for software-intensive systems. Barry Boehm collected the data on costs to correct requirements errors as a function of the project phase for several software development projects. Figure 1-4 summarizes his results. The solid line represents plan-driven development and illustrates that requirements errors cost approximately 100 times more to correct after the system is in operation than when the error is corrected at the start of the project (during requirements analysis). The dashed line represents decreased penalties for agile development. Figure 1-5 shows similar data from Siemens [Paulisch, 1993]. Requirements errors cost 20 times more to correct when detected during field use than when detected early during requirements analysis. (KDM stands for thousands of German marks.) Both of these figures reflect "plan-driven" processes that follow a sequence of stages. (Chapter 10 describes plan-driven processes and "agile processes," which are specifically designed to greatly reduce the cost penalty for late detection.) Certain types of systems typically experience large amounts of change. The next two sections describe these systems.

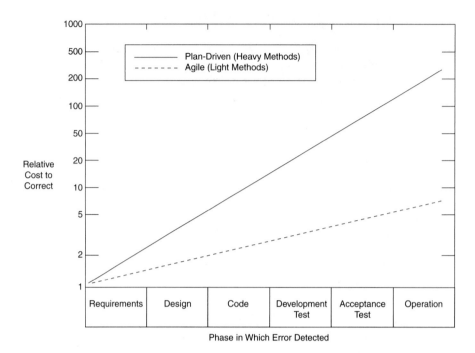

Figure 1-4   *Changes become more expensive as the project proceeds*
(Adapted from Figure 4-2 in [Boehm, 1981, page 40])

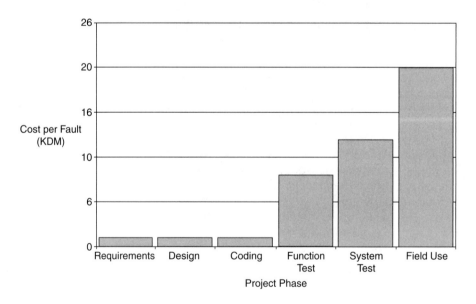

Figure 1-5   *Cost per fault versus project phase*

1.4 Unprecedented Systems

Lack of knowledge is the primary cause of estimation errors. This section examines the different levels of ignorance, describes a real-life example, and summarizes the impacts of ignorance on estimates.

1.4.1 Precedentedness As Predictor of Success

In 1988, an Air Force study group examined a number of successful and unsuccessful software development projects [Beam, 1989]. Their goal was to identify criteria that could predict project success. Although they focused on software projects, their results apply regardless of the type of product or system that is to be built or modified. They concluded that if a system is "precedented," there is a good chance of building it successfully. According to Richard Sylvester and Marilyn Stewart [Sylvester, 1994], a precedented system meets three criteria:

1. The requirements are consistent and well understood.
2. A feasible system architecture[6] that can satisfy the requirements is known.
3. All participants have worked together previously to develop a similar system.

Any system that fails to meet one or more of these criteria is "unprecedented" to some degree. Unprecedented systems are risky to build and difficult to estimate.

The three criteria are listed in order of decreasing estimation uncertainty and project risk. In Criterion 3, the lowest-risk situation, the requirements are understood and a known, feasible architecture exists. The only uncertainty is how well all participants (the stakeholders) can work together and coordinate their efforts. The stakeholders include buyers and developers. (For large, custom systems, the buyer and the end user may be distinct, and may or may not belong to the same organization. For commercial, "shrink-wrapped" products, the buyer is also the user.)

In Criterion 2, a proven system architecture is known to have adequate capabilities to meet the functional and performance requirements of the product. If there is no known architecture that will meet the requirements, however, the designers may not understand the areas of the system that represent a high-risk in terms of product performance or production. Also, they may not understand

---

[6] You can think of the system architecture as a template that describes a technical solution. The system architecture identifies all major hardware and software components, their functions and interfaces, and the constraints and rules that govern their interactions.

the relationships between various system components and so the impact of such dependencies on project cost and schedule. This means that they are unable to accurately assess trade-offs and risks. (This is often the case for systems that utilize new technologies.) Failure to satisfy Criterion 2 represents a higher risk than Criterion 3 because without a proven architecture, the developers cannot possibly have any experience building a system of that type. Thus, Criterion 3 is also not satisfied.

If Criterion 1 is not met, the project has the highest risk of the three cases because requirements are the main driver of project cost and schedule. Usually, the buyers and developers understand some, possibly most, of the requirements. (These are the "identified knowns.") They may not, however, completely understand other requirements. In addition, there may be missing, incomplete, inconsistent, or ambiguous requirements. The stakeholders may realize the existence of these problems. On the other hand, they may be unaware that these problems exist. (These two cases are the "identified unknowns" and the "unidentified unknowns," respectively.) Such problems mean that the stakeholders do not really know all of the functional and performance requirements for the system. In addition, they are also unable to identify areas of ambiguity, inconsistency, or incompleteness. This is the highest risk situation because inadequate requirements necessarily imply that no similar product has ever been built before and therefore no feasible architecture has been identified and proven for this particular system. As noted for Criterion 2, this also means that the team cannot possibly have experience in producing a similar system. For this reason, poor requirements constitute the highest degree of risk for an unprecedented system because the project fails to meet all three of the criteria. (Requirements growth and volatility increase these problems, leading to the behavior shown in Figure 1-1.)

Organizations differ in their experience with particular application domains, product types, technologies, tools, and processes. Therefore, what is unprecedented for one organization may be precedented for another.

1.4.2 The Humber Bridge Project

Even well-established fields can encounter unprecedented situations and experience project failures. Because engineers have constructed bridges for more than 2,000 years, you might think that bridge construction would be a well-understood engineering discipline. However, when the engineers attempt to use new technologies, scale up proven designs, or build atop poorly understood soil, they can encounter problems similar to those of a software project. Victor Bignell and Joyce Fortune describe the problems encountered by the builders of the Humber Bridge in Chapter 3 of [Bignell, 1984]. The Humber Bridge is the world's largest single-span suspension bridge. Initial plans for the bridge were prepared in the 1930s. The project was chartered by the Humber Bridge Act passed in 1959, but the project languished until sufficient political support could be obtained. Detailed design finally started in 1971. Construction work started in July 1972. The planned completion date was 1976. After surmounting many problems with the soil, steel shortages, and accidents, the first car actually crossed the bridge in June 1981. (This is a schedule slip of 100%.)

The construction costs also increased, as shown in Figure 1-6. In early 1969, the estimated cost of the bridge was £23,000,000. Because of the various problems encountered during the project, construction lasted five years longer than originally planned. The final construction cost of the bridge calculated in August 1981 was £91,000,000, an increase of 296%. (The total debt was actually £145,000,000, consisting of £91,000,000 in construction costs and £54,000,000 in interest costs.) Bignell and Fortune also document huge cost increases for other large projects having a "high development content" (i.e., unprecedented systems). They cite values of 50% for petrochemical plants, 140% for North Sea oil drilling projects, 210% for some nuclear power plants, and 545% for the development of the Concorde aircraft.

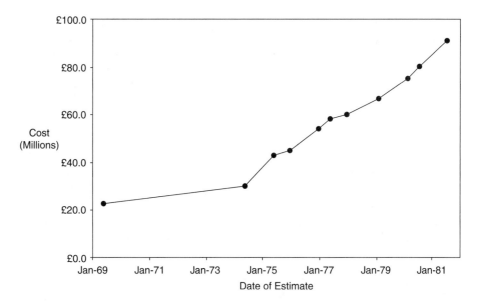

Figure 1-6 *Humber Bridge costs (excluding interest)*

Estimates for unprecedented systems display the same types of behavior described in Section 1.3, but the amount of growth and uncertainty is much larger than for precedented, well-understood systems. These projects therefore frequently experience significant growth in project cost and schedule, as shown for the Humber Bridge. The next section looks at an archetypal unprecedented system: software.

1.5 Why Software Is Especially Hard to Estimate

The fairy tale about the emperor's new clothes provides a good analogy for software. In this fairy tale, unscrupulous tailors claim to use magic thread to weave invisible clothes for the emperor. The tailors appear to work industriously for a long time, and incur great costs. All is apparently going well until delivery finally occurs! Software products are similar to the emperor's clothes because

- The requirements are hard to state precisely.
- The product is essentially invisible until it is finished.
- The product is hard to measure (intangible).
- The product's acceptability depends on the customer's taste.

Software products include commercial applications ("shrink-wrapped products"), software-intensive systems, and embedded systems. A software-intensive system is one in which software, databases, computers, and networks provide most of the system's functionality. Examples are an organization's accounting system and an e-business website. An embedded system is composed of hardware and software, and hardware performs the primary functions, with software providing data processing and control. Embedded systems usually operate in real time. Embedded systems are often safety critical (e.g., a fly-by-wire aircraft).

Software-intensive systems are complex. They contain many components that interact with one another, and with the system's external environment. One reason that software is complex is that designers use software to overcome hardware deficiencies. System complexity is driven to the software. Specifying requirements for a complex system is a wicked problem, one that is so complex and has so many related entities that there is no definitive problem specification [Rittel, 1973]. The true nature of the problem only emerges as a solution is developed.

To develop software, engineers transform customer requirements into a design, transform the design into working code, and then test the code. During this sequence of transformations, engineers create, share, and revise a series of increasingly detailed, abstract mental models. Due to the poor requirements, system complexity, and unprecedentedness, engineers make many mistakes.[7] Approximately half of software development effort is typically spent finding and removing defects. These activities all require creativity and analytical thinking. Therefore, the main factor driving software development costs is human effort.

---

[7] Poor requirements and product complexity are not the only reasons that projects fail. Some others are poor processes, lack of skilled workers, and poor management.

Many factors affect programmer productivity, and so the project's effort, cost, and schedule. Tom DeMarco notes the following important characteristics of software development [DeMarco, 2001]:

- Individual productivity varies over a wider range than in other technical disciplines.
- Creative processes are difficult to plan.
- People can only think so fast.

This last comment means that there is a lower limit on development time. Typically, for any project, dependencies between certain tasks lead to a minimum possible time to accomplish all the necessary tasks. Furthermore, most of today's software systems and products are too complex for one person to handle. Therefore, teams of people must collaborate to produce most software-intensive systems. This means that interpersonal relations, group dynamics, and communication skills play an important role in software development. In addition, contention for key resources (people, equipment, or facilities) always lengthens the schedule, as do holidays. These characteristics make estimating software development effort difficult.

Because software is intangible, it is difficult to see, measure, and control. One of the objectives of software development methods (and associated tools) is to capture descriptions of the product's requirements and design early in the project, and so make the product visible. These descriptions enable managers and customers to assess status. More importantly, however, programmers need these descriptions to communicate their abstract models and to coordinate their work. Software designs are complex, however, and so is the notation used to represent these designs. If the notation is easy to use, it is incomplete (i.e., some essential information is not recorded). If the notation is complete, it is complex and so is difficult and expensive to use. Even with rather complex notations, it is not possible to capture all of the information needed to generate executable code. The result is flawed, incomplete representations of the product that is to be built, leading to flaws in the final product.

Software, hardware, and system development projects encounter essentially the same types of management problems. Because software is invisible, however, problems are harder to detect. Because software components are closely coupled, a problem in one component often "ripples" and so a small problem can rapidly "snowball." Managers need an "early warning system" to detect problems early. Estimation and measurement play a key role, as explained in the next section.

1.6 A Practical Approach

Initial estimates are inaccurate because of imperfect knowledge, incorrect assumptions, and omissions. The estimator's knowledge of the product, project, and process improves with time, as illustrated by the funnel curve in Figure 1-3. However, some characteristics of the product, project, and process will change as time passes. To cope with change, you must update estimates throughout a project. Therefore, estimation inevitably is (or should be) a continuing process.

1.6.1 The Feedback Process

You must use a feedback process to track and control project tasks, product characteristics, and production processes. Although this book focuses on project estimates, the same process applies to estimates of product size, performance, and quality, and to estimates of production processes. During a project, you collect and compare measurements of quantities to their target values (baselines) to detect any deviations. If the deviations exceed the expected random variation based on historical norms, or exhibit an adverse trend, managers and engineers must perform actions to correct the cause of the deviations. You can also use the data you collect to prepare more accurate estimates.

This iterative process has two feedback loops, shown in Figure 1-7. The inner loop (Loop 1) periodically updates estimates during the course of a project based on new information and actual measurements. (You may use different techniques to prepare these updated estimates than you used to prepare the initial estimate.) This loop accommodates any changes that occur and increases the accuracy of your reference baselines. The outer loop (Loop 2) updates estimating relations and models after one or more projects have been completed. You analyze the historical measurements and refine your estimating relations and models to increase estimation accuracy for future projects. This captures your organization's actual demonstrated performance. Measurements play an important role in both loops.

1.6.2 How Accurately Must You Estimate?

Estimation and measurement support by the project manager's feedback control loop. A natural question is how accurately must you estimate (to establish the baseline) and measure (to determine the current state of the process). The short answer is "accurately enough so that you can control the production processes." The necessary accuracy depends on project goals, financial or business risk, the time needed to make decisions (or to convey information between the developers and the buyer, end user, or product manager), and other factors.

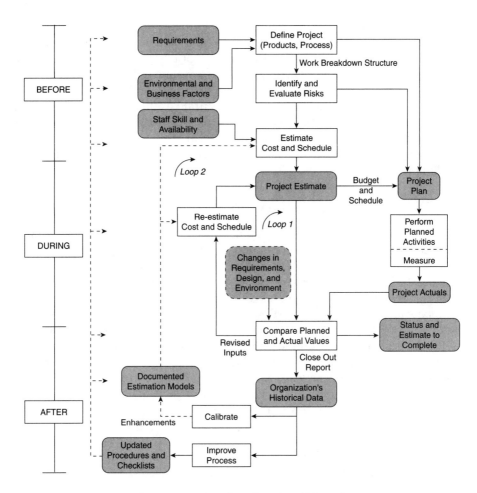

Figure 1-7 *Total estimation life cycle*

Steve McConnell makes some insightful comments in an editorial titled "Sitting on the Suitcase" [McConnell, 2000]. First, he notes that the purpose of a project estimate is not to make a perfect prediction of a project's cost and schedule. Due to the inevitable changes, you seldom end up with the same project that you originally estimated anyway. Second, he states that a project estimate should be "sufficiently accurate" to allow the project manager to control the project to meet its business objectives. The required estimation accuracy depends on how well your feedback control systems work and on the needs of the project. Typically, ±20% is adequate for project cost and schedule. Accuracy goals typically tighten as the end of a project approaches because there is less time to correct problems.

As Steve McConnell observes, estimation determines feasible intended targets so that the project's feedback control system can guide the project to the desired targets. (The "targets" can be project, product, or process characteristics. They are the project's technical, cost, and schedule baselines.) The estimates of various quantities are (moving) targets, so you must update them as illustrated in Loop 1 in Figure 1-7. Finally, reasonably accurate estimates are necessary but not sufficient for project success. During a project, the project manager must ensure that none of the assumptions and constraints underlying the estimate are violated. I tell my students that the project team makes the estimate a self-fulfilling prophecy!

1.6.3 Ways to Improve Estimation Accuracy

Table 1-3 summarizes the three ways that you can improve estimation accuracy. You need to obtain certain information before you can prepare an estimate, which I call the "precursors of estimation."[8] Devote as much time as possible to defining the job and use this information to prepare the initial estimate. Then collect measurements and track progress during the project, and use the information to prepare an updated estimate. (Either this will be a more accurate estimate for the original job or it will reflect the new situation in which the project now finds itself!) Collect data from multiple completed projects and use it to improve your organization's estimating processes and tools. The following chapters address all three items shown in the table.

Table 1-3 *Ways to Improve Estimation Accuracy*

Before Starting the Project
• Understand product requirements and architecture.
• Choose a suitable production process and supporting tools.
• Use a mix of estimating techniques, models, and historical data.
• Produce the estimate in a disciplined way.
During the Project
• Collect actual measurements (costs, performance, progress).
• Watch for violations of the estimating assumptions.
• Watch for changes in key factors (software size, turnover).
• Update the estimate with the latest information.
After the Project
• Collect final measurements.
• Analyze data and lessons learned.
• Capture the new information (calibrate models, update checklists).
• Improve the estimating process (procedures, new tools, training).

---

[8] Fred Heemstra proposes similar preconditions in [Heemstra, 1992].

1.7 Recommended Reading

Frederick Brooks provides an insightful and humorous description of software engineering in [Brooks, 1995]. His Chapter 16 describes the essential nature of software, amplifying my discussion in Section 1.5 of this chapter. For more on the challenges of developing software, see [Glass, 1998], [Yourdon, 1997], [DeMarco, 1995], [DeMarco, 1999], and [Gibbs, 1994]. Peter DeGrace and Leslie Hulet Stahl discuss wicked problems encountered with software [DeGrace, 1990].

The Standish Group published data on software project failures in the "CHAOS Report" (1994), plus a follow-up report titled "Unfinished Voyages." You can download both from http://www.standishgroup.com/sample_research. Victor Bignell and Joyce Fortune describe failures of large systems, including the Humber Bridge Project, in [Bignell, 1984]. For descriptions of other failures in engineering see [Petroski, 1992], [Adams, 1991], and [Spector, 1986].

1.8 Summary

Estimation and measurement play an important role in creating and maintaining products and systems, and in delivering services. Stakeholders use estimates and measurements to evaluate feasibility, analyze alternatives, predict performance, determine the amount of resources needed to perform project activities, and evaluate the business value of a proposed product or project. Good estimates also provide the information needed to negotiate achievable commitments (targets) and to prepare plans, budgets, and schedules. Good estimates require time and money. In estimation, you get what you pay for.

Estimates are uncertain because they predict the future. You may also estimate characteristics of objects that you cannot measure directly. Using past experience from similar products or activities provides the most accurate estimates. Unprecedented systems provide the greatest challenge to estimators because there is little or no prior experience. Unprecedented systems have

- Incomplete or poorly understood requirements.
- Unknown or unproven product architecture (a template for a feasible solution).
- Inexperienced stakeholders (especially the development team).

These characteristics cause estimators to overlook components and activities; make invalid assumptions; and incorrectly estimate the characteristics of the product, process, and project. The most challenging unprecedented systems have all three characteristics. Many software-intensive systems are unprecedented to some degree due to their abstract nature, complexity, and intangibility, and to the rapid evolution of technology and tools. Software has a great deal of "newness," and so software products, projects, and processes are especially difficult to estimate.

The unprecedented nature of software-intensive systems and products, the knowledge-intensive nature of software development, and the rapid evolution of the hardware and software technology used to construct them present estimators with two significant challenges:

1. Inadequate or missing knowledge of
    *   Product requirements
    *   Product architecture (feasibility and performance)
    *   Software technology (components, industry standards)
    *   Capability and maturity of methods and tools
    *   Production processes
    *   Developers' skills
    *   The interactions of all stakeholders

2. Rapid and unpredictable changes in
    *   User requirements
    *   External interfaces
    *   Product architecture and design
    *   Software technology (components, industry standards)
    *   Development and test tools
    *   Personnel (turnover)

All estimation methods and techniques must address these challenges.[9]

The project team transforms product requirements into a working product that meets the needs of the end user. Software development requires substantial mental effort, and so human labor is the main factor driving software development costs.

Because all estimates have biases and uncertainties, here are two tips for presenting and reviewing estimates:

1. Estimators should always state assumptions and provide uncertainty ranges.
2. Managers and reviewers should always ask how large the uncertainty is!

Feedback control enables you to reach desired targets for projects, products, and processes even if

- You don't know everything.
- You make errors in estimation/modeling.
- Things change.

Estimation and measurement support two feedback loops to plan and manage projects. Estimates help determine whether the targets for product, project, and process characteristics are feasible and help set realistic target values. The project team uses these target values to design the product and plan the project. Change inevitably occurs during a project, so the project team uses measurements to assess status and prepare updated estimates. Comparing measurements and updated estimates with the target values enables the project team to adjust their activities to meet the targets. Estimates and measurements must be accurate enough to enable the project team to control their activities in order to achieve the planned targets. You can use measurement data to estimate future products, projects, and processes. You can use the data directly, or you can analyze it to create more accurate estimating models. Analysis also provides insights to improve your estimating, measurement, and production processes.

Parts I through IV of this book focus on the estimation and measurement of project-related characteristics. (Chapter 8, "Estimating Software Size: The Basics," and Chapter 9, "Estimating Software Size: The Details," in Part II address the estimation and measurement of software size, because it determines project effort.) Part II also describes methods to estimate project resources (effort, cost, and time). Part III addresses the collection and use of measurements to track progress, update estimates, and improve your estimating process. Part IV specifically addresses estimation and measurement for large projects. Part V covers the estimation and measurement of product performance, product quality, and process performance, completing the coverage

---

[9] Some items listed under the first item are not repeated under the second item because I assume that these items are reasonably stable during the course of a project. This may not be true for your project!

of quantities identified in the SEI's CMMI. The appendixes summarize concepts, challenges, and approaches for these quantities, provide references to textbooks, and present some simple techniques and examples.

Chapter 2

Planning a Warehouse Inventory System

Planning identifies all deliverable products and services, describes the products, and defines the process to make the products and deliver the services. This chapter describes a simple example that illustrates the types of items that a good estimating method should identify. I have used this example for more than 15 years in my estimating classes. Even though the example is of necessity short and the solution is incomplete, it shows how to get something written down. Putting something on paper helps the participants communicate with one another, and so obtain a better understanding of the overall job. The documentation also establishes a basis to elaborate, refine, and revise the estimate. (You will always need to refine your estimate as your understanding of the requirements and design improves, or because the requirements and the design change.) The example reveals topics that must be addressed to prepare better estimates. The following chapters cover these topics.

2.1 Warehouse Inventory Management System

You are asked to prepare an estimate for a computerized *warehouse inventory management system* (WIMS). Your organization has received a short *statement of work* (SOW) from the XYZ Corporation, shown in Figure 2-1. (Some organizations call the SOW the *scope of work*.) This SOW is short to reduce the time that the class spends on the exercise. In actual practice, you will usually receive a more lengthy description of the customer's requirements, with a longer SOW listing all the tasks to be performed, and possibly a detailed product specification.

STATEMENT OF WORK

The XYZ Corporation is buying an inventory control system for its warehouses located in Los Angeles, Chicago, New York City and London. We are soliciting bids to provide this system, which also includes a software maintenance capability to be located in Los Angeles. The bidder must deliver the following items:

1. One "computer set" per site consisting of computer, peripherals, software, and user manuals. All computers shall be linked electronically via telephone lines to permit rapid exchange of inventory and shipping data.

2. Source code for all applications programs developed by the bidder.

3. Software maintenance tools, such as compilers, etc.

4. Installation and checkout of the system at each site.

5. Training of operators at each site plus the maintenance staff (who are located at XYZ's corporate headquarters in Los Angeles).

The bidder is also required to present monthly status briefings in Los Angeles.

Figure 2-1 *SOW from the XYZ corporation*

The engineers in your organization have analyzed the customer's requirements and investigated possible solutions. They have designed a solution and documented it in the memo reproduced in Figure 2-2. Again, this solution is shorter than you would have in practice, but it suffices to convey all the important teaching points.

TECHNICAL NOTE

TO: The Cost Estimator
FROM: Software Development Department
SUBJECT: Development Plan for the XYZ Inventory Control System

We have analyzed the job and have devised the following design solution. The computing needs are modest and only one operator needs access in each warehouse. We will put one (1) computer workstation in each warehouse. We have selected the vendor's standard package "SP #2", which includes a computer, terminal, 10 GB hard disk, laser printer, the UNIX operating system and UNIX utilities which include all communications software. (This is a package deal at a great price.) The computers at all sites will be connected via dedicated modems running at 56.8 Kbps. We will connect the four operational sites in a ring configuration to provide assured communications if a single link fails. We will use the uunet protocol (supported by the STD_PKG utilities) for intersite communications. (The uunet utilities handle store-and-forward of messages to sites in the ring.) We will connect the maintenance system to the individual warehouse systems via a dial-up link as needed to permit on-line troubleshooting and to download software upgrades.

We will implement the software using the Oracle Relational Data Base Management System (RDBMS). All applications will be written in SQL. Reports will be generated using SQL*FORMS. We will write the control and communication routines in C.

We estimate that the following items must be produced:

Number	Description
11	Menus
22	Data input screens (forms)
13	Reports
3	Main programs (stocking, shipping, and monthly billing reports)

We will do the work in San Diego. It will take about four (4) months. We will develop on the Sun system, which will be subsequently delivered to the maintainers. Installation at each site will take one week each. We will send a trainer and a software expert to each site to do the installation.

We estimate that each main program needs 50 pages of documentation. We will provide 16 hours of training for the operators and 40 hours of training for the software maintainers.

Figure 2-2 *Technical note from the Development department*

The class identifies the types of items (the "elements") to include in the estimate and the number ("count") of objects of each type. For example, one element is the standard package. The project must deliver five copies of the standard package (Chicago, Los Angeles, New York, London, plus the maintenance facility located in Los Angeles).

2.2 Recording the Information

You tabulate the elements identified and their counts using a spreadsheet, as illustrated in Table 2-1. The first column shows categories of elements. These categories help to organize the estimate and facilitate my explanations of the various items. (The end of this section suggests another way to organize the information.) The second column lists the names of the elements. The third column lists the number (count) of the element. The fourth column is titled Notes. Notes provide a precise way to reference supplemental information at varying levels of detail. See the box "Capturing Details." Some items may require no explanation at all. For example, in Table 2-1 under Commercial Off-The-Shelf (COTS) products, the C compiler and linker require no explanation (although you might specify the vendor's name and model number). Under Applications Software, however, the element labeled Menus has a short note stating "simple item selections" to indicate the (assumed) complexity of the menus. (It also references Risk 5.) Some elements require more extensive explanations. For example, under the COTS Products, the Standard Package has a reference to Note 1. Referring to Table 2-2, Note 1 states that the engineers have decided to supply a fifth system for the maintainers.

Capturing Details

You need a flexible way to record explanations, questions, and potential risks as they occur to you. *Notes* can include assumptions, estimating rationale, and the basis of estimate (such as references to sources of historical data, textbooks, or other reports). *Questions* may arise as you assemble and analyze the quantities in the estimate. You often identify *potential risks* as you prepare an estimate.

You can record such textual information in a spreadsheet. One way is to wrap the text in the Notes column. (Appendix E, "Excel for Estimators," explains how to format text in a worksheet cell.) If you must enter large amounts of text, however, I find it better to record the information in separate Microsoft Word documents. Within each document, I have a set of numbered items or paragraphs. This enables me to succinctly refer to the numbered blocks of text in the Notes column of the spreadsheet as Note 1, Question 6, or Risk 4.

Table 2-1 *Initial Spreadsheet for WIMS Estimate*

Category	Elements	Number	Notes
COTS Products	Standard package SP #2	5	Note 1, Risks 1 and 2
	One-year warranty	5	Ques 1
	C compiler and linker	1	
	Oracle runtime license	4	Ques 2
	Oracle development license	1	Ques 2
	Oracle maintenance license	4	Ques 3
	Cable sets	5	
	56.8 kbps direct-connect modems	8	Figure 1, Ques 4
	56.8 kbps dial-up modems	5	Ques 5 and 6
Applications SW	Menus	11	Simple item selections, Risk 5
	Input screens	22	Complex structure
	Reports	13	Predefined content, Risk 4
	Main programs	3	
	Backup/restore	1	Ques 7 and 8
Documents	User manual	1	Ques 9, Risk 5
	Operator manual	1	Ques 10
	Training course (charts, notes)	1	
	Installation plan	1	Note 2, Ques 11

(continued)

Table 2-1 *Initial Spreadsheet for WIMS Estimate (continued)*

Category	Elements	Number	Notes
Documents	Maintainer document	1	
	Design document	1	
	Acceptance test plan	1	Note 3, Ques 12
Consumables	8.5" × 11" paper (boxes)	5	
	Printer toner cartridges	5	
	Backup tapes	30	
	Document reproduction	?	Ques 9
	Shipping and insurance	?	Risks 2 and 3
Trips Notation used is: *Location (# days)* (# people)*	Kickoff meeting (LAX) 1*3	3	Ques 13
	Status meetings (LAX) 3*3	6	Note 4
	Install and train (USA) 3*2	6	Notes 2, 4, and 5 Ques 14 and 15
	Install and train (UK) 1*2	2	Notes 2, 4, 5, and 6, Ques 14 and 15
	Acceptance test (LAX) 1*2	2	Note 3, Ques 12, Ques 15
Level of Effort Tasks	Status meetings	10 p-days	
	Write training courses	40 p-days	
	Deliver training	80 p-days	(5 systems, 2 days each)
	Plan acceptance tests	20 p-days	Note 5
	Plan installation	20 p-days	Note 2
	Build and demonstrate prototype	60 p-days	
	Develop test database	15 p-days	
	Initialize operational DB?	? p-days	Ques 14
	Configuration control (CM)	5 p-days	
	Independent reviews (QA)	5 p-days	
	Integration and testing	10 p-days	
	Site preparation and installation	2 p-days	

Table 2-2 *Notes for the WIMS Estimate*

1. We include a fifth system for the maintainers.
2. Installation will be performed at each site in turn. Each site will be activated "standalone" and the operators trained. After all sites are operating, we will use the trained operators at each site to activate the communications network.
3. We want to ensure that acceptance testing is well thought out to avoid problems. We have provided enough effort to allow thorough planning. This will pay off later.
4. Each trip is two people for two days, from San Diego to Los Angeles. We have four technical interchange meetings (TIMs) plus a kickoff plus a closeout. (We will do closeout at the same time as the acceptance test at Los Angeles.)
5. Trips were estimated assuming two persons per trip. The durations are as follows: Install in Chicago and New York = 5 days. Install and train all the operators and maintainers in Los Angeles = 10 days. Install in London = 10 days (due to travel time).
6. Round-trip business class airfare to London is about $5K.

Putting the information into three documents makes it easier to convey information to different individuals who are responsible for specific areas. The explanatory notes help the people who write the estimating rationale and justify the values shown in the spreadsheet (Table 2-1). Engineers respond to the questions to provide the additional information needed to complete the estimate. Separating the questions from the explanatory material makes it easier for the engineers to focus on the questions and for the estimator to extract the answers. Similarly, recording all risks in a single document helps manage them in a systematic way.

The important thing is to write something down. Whether you record it as a question, an assumption, or a risk does not matter initially. By writing it down, you or others can review and analyze the item. Then you can decide whether your engineers can answer the question, whether you should ask the customer for additional information, or whether you should plan to avoid or mitigate the risk in some way.

You can also use figures to document the estimate. Consider the number of modems listed under COTS Products. The engineers provided the WIMS network architecture diagram shown in Figure 2-3. (In Table 2-1, this is called Figure 1 in the Notes for the modems.) This is a "key diagram" for the system. (Chapter 7, "Preparing to Estimate (Precursors of Estimation)," discusses other key diagrams.) It shows the communications network that links the sites of the

warehouse inventory management system. This diagram shows that the engineers have decided to connect the four warehouses using dedicated modems
and a ring network. (This design provides an alternate routing in the event that
one of the links fails.) In addition, each of the warehouses, plus the maintenance facility, has a dial-up modem to allow maintenance programmers to dial
in to individual sites to diagnose problems and to update software. (This
design means that the maintenance facility can only connect to one warehouse
at a time. This may or may not be a significant limitation of the proposed
design.) Based on this diagram, you can see that you need eight direct-connect
modems and five dial-up modems. (A more modern architecture would use a
high-speed network to link the sites, with a web server at each site, giving the
maintainers and operators continuous access. It could use the Internet or,
if security is a concern, an intranet. Whatever the design, a diagram of the
network architecture will help you count the required modems, routers, and
communications lines.)

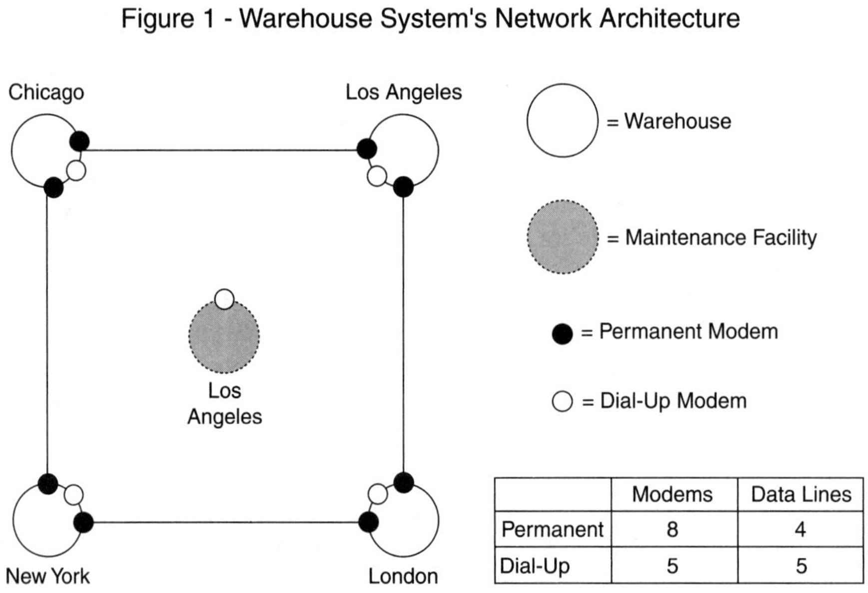

Figure 1 - Warehouse System's Network Architecture

Figure 2-3 *WIMS network architecture diagram*

2.3 Discussion of the Example

This section discusses some of the items in Table 2-1 to show how writing the elements down in a structured way helps you prepare better estimates.

Under COTS Products, the element "Oracle runtime license" has a question, Question 2. Referring to Table 2-3, you see that this question involves the basic Oracle license. You need to determine whether the license includes all the components that the engineers will need, such as a structured query language (SQL) capability, a graphical user interface, a report generator, etc. Question 3 does not actually identify the need for an Oracle maintenance license. It does, however, indicate an unresolved issue about the scope of the services to be provided, specifically the support that your organization must provide after delivery. Writing this down as a question ensures that you will not forget it.

Table 2-3 *Questions for WIMS Estimate*

1. Are we providing a warranty? If we buy the hardware and use it to develop the system, how do we transfer the warranty to the buyer? (Our use of the equipment will consume some of the warranty time.)
2. Does the basic Oracle license include *all* the components you will need (SQL interface, forms generator, report generator, etc.)?
3. Is this a turnkey system or must we provide maintenance for some period after delivery? Are we to provide post-delivery support (for example, a "help desk")? If so, we will need to maintain a working computer system in San Diego to diagnose problems and make repairs. The overseas time difference means we will have to have two shifts to man the help desk! (You may need multilingual technical staff to support foreign users.)
4. Does the customer supply the modems or must we provide them? For our estimate, we have assumed that we must provide the modems. Who provides the phone lines? Who pays for the line charges during development? (These decisions affect our cost.)   When will the lines be needed? If the customer provides the communications lines, when will they be made available to us? Will they be available 24 hours per day or only during specified times? (This could affect test schedules.) Installing the lines is a long-lead-time item.
5. Is the same software used at all sites? One issue here is data formats (dates, floating point numbers). More importantly, will each site use the same menus and screens or not? (See Risks 4 and 5.)
6. Does "four months" mean four persons-months or four calendar-months? If the latter, how many people will be working on this job? Is the project manager's direct labor included or not? Does this include documentation, installation, and site testing?

(continues)

Table 2-3 *Questions for WIMS Estimate (continued)*

7. Does the standard package include a tape drive? (We need one to perform backup and recovery.)
8. What are the reliability requirements for the system? (Maybe we need to purchase uninterruptible power supplies, etc.)
9. How many copies of documents are needed at each site? How large and formal are these documents? Can we use a contractor format? The number of different documents and their formality needs to be determined or, if this is not possible, specified via a contract Term and Condition and/or a pricing assumption.
10. What Oracle documents are needed at each site? (We will have to purchase these.)
11. Regarding Note 2, can we install at each site in turn? (Is this technically feasible?) If so, will the customer accept this?
12. When does "delivery" occur? This needs to be formalized!
13. Would the customer agree to hold the meetings via teleconference? (This would reduce our travel costs.)
14. We can save costs if we do all the training in one location. Could we propose to the customer that all users be brought to Los Angeles and trained there? This approach ensures that everyone receives exactly the same training and also gives the outside staff a chance to see the headquarters. This would lower our bid and simplify our logistics.
15. Must we convert the customer's existing operational data and load it into the new system? (This could be expensive if there is a large amount of data.) Must we process the same operational data with both the old and new systems, and compare results? (It may be hard to get identical results due to errors in the old system.) If we must run our new system alongside the old system for weeks or months, this will be expensive. The acceptance test strategy needs to document whether or not we will perform such activities. We must also include any such activities in our estimates.

Table 2-1 also shows a question relating to the modems, Question 4. Table 2-3 shows that Question 4 really consists of several questions relating to the communications lines. If you must provide them, you will have to include the necessary costs in your estimate. You will also have to include tasks in your development plan to order and install these lines so that they will be available when needed. (Installation of communications lines is often a long-lead-time item.) On the other hand, if the customer provides the communications lines, you need to explicitly state three key things. First, you must specify the *characteristics of the line* (type, speed). Second, you must specify the *activation date* that you will first need the lines to support testing and checkout. (Instead of a specific calendar date, you can specify a relative date such as "90 days after product design review" or "6 calendar-months after contract award.") Third, you need to specify the times that you will need access during the work-day (and on weekends and holidays if appropriate). See the box "The Price of Free Computer Time."

The Price of Free Computer Time

I once worked on a project where the customer provided us with free computer time on a large mainframe computer located in its facility. The problem was that we were granted access only *after* working hours when the customer's employees had gone home. Besides impacting our sleep schedule, this had the added disadvantage that there was no one available to answer our questions. We were forced to wait until the next day for answers, slowing our progress. Obviously a similar situation could arise if the XYZ Corporation will be supplying access to its existing communications lines.

You should define your needs, constraints, and assumptions because they have a major effect on project costs and risks. If you are developing a system under contract to an external buyer, you can use *contract terms and conditions* (called *Ts and Cs*) to document such things. For this case, you would specify the type and number of lines, the date when you first expect the lines to be made available, and the hours during the work-day (and on weekends and holidays) when you will be given access to the lines. Using terms and conditions is one way to communicate your estimating assumptions. From a legal standpoint, terms and conditions establish a basis to negotiate compensation later if the customer does not meet its commitments, either by failing to provide the lines by the date needed, or access during the specified times during the day.

In Table 2-1 under Applications Software, more analysis is needed. The elements shown were simply taken from the memo provided by the engineers. I have added one important item, however: the backup and restore capability. This is essential for an operational system, and yet it is often overlooked in customer specifications and sometimes even by the software developers themselves. This requires more than merely archiving copies of data. Specifically, there needs to be some way to restore the database to a known state. This can be especially difficult if multiple sites are involved. ("The Operational Concept," described in Chapter 7, addresses such concerns.)

Table 2-1, under Documents, identifies user manuals, operator manuals, and course materials. The obvious question to ask (Question 9) is, what is the number of copies needed at each site? More important, however, is how large and formal these documents are. In many government procurements, extremely detailed documentation is required for the product. Another question is whether you can use "contractor format" for these documents. This means a format of your own choice, in contrast to a government or industry standard. Most organizations have standard formats defined as part of their standard process. These cost less to produce than customer-specified formats. If it is not possible to determine this prior to submitting your offer, you could use a contract term and condition stating that you will negotiate the details of the documentation before signing the final offer. (On the other hand, you could document your estimating or pricing assumptions as described in Section 3.6.) Another question (Question 10) involves the number of copies of documents for the COTS products because you will have to purchase these from the Oracle Corporation.

Table 2-1, under Consumables, lists some typical items that will be needed. The question on document reproduction also refers to Question 9, which relates to the number of copies of documents needed at each site and the size (number of pages) of each document.

The estimating team also begins to identify and document possible risks. The reason for including an overseas installation (London) in this example is that there are often unanticipated difficulties associated with doing business in any foreign country. These may include travel costs, laws and regulations, environmental differences (electrical power), and even different working hours (midday siestas) and holidays. Table 2-4 illustrates some of the typical risks that you might encounter overseas. Risk 1 deals with electrical voltage and frequency. Other environmental conditions are less obvious. See the box "When Ordinary COTS Hardware Failed." Risks 2 and 3 are cited in the Note for Shipping and Insurance under Consumables in Table 2-1. See the box "When Ordinary COTS Software Cannot Be Used." Risk 3 notes that costs for express shipping are higher and delivery times are longer than for domestic shipping. (Notes 5 and 6 in Table 2-2 already address overseas travel costs, which are higher than domestic travel costs.) There may also be costs for customs duties and freight handling.

Table 2-4 *Overseas Risks for WIMS Estimate*

1. The electrical power source in Europe is 50 Hertz, 220 volts. The power connectors are also different. Will the proposed computer equipment handle this?
2. There may be export restrictions on the COTS packages and/or computer hardware (for example, encryption algorithms in Microsoft Access). We may need export licenses or permits, which could take a long time to obtain. (This will also entail additional costs.)
3. Federal Express costs are very expensive for overseas shipments (hundreds of dollars per 10 kilograms) and take two days, not one. There may be additional costs for customs duties, reshipping, and freight forwarding.
4. Data formats are different. For calendar dates, the United States uses mm/dd/yy, whereas Europe uses dd/mm/yy. For floating point numbers, the use of commas and decimal points is interchanged between the United States and Europe.
5. If the overseas personnel speak a different language, we will have to translate messages, menu items, reports, help files, and all the user documentation. (We may need separate spelling checkers for American English and British English!)

When Ordinary COTS Hardware Failed

On one project, we had to provide laser printers for use in a hot and dry desert environment. We bid and purchased standard laser printers distributed in the United States. We discovered that these failed at the site. We had to locate a vendor in Europe who provided modified units especially designed for use in desert conditions. Obviously, these printers were more expensive than the typical models purchased in the United States. We were able to solve the problem, but we did not anticipate the increased costs.

When Ordinary COTS Software Cannot Be Used

One company I know used a commercial database product to build a system for an overseas customer. It turned out that this particular product, which was widely available within the United States, used encryption algorithms that could not be shipped overseas due to export restrictions. The firm had to contact an overseas vendor and obtain the export version of the product and use it to deliver the system.

More subtle problems may arise with overseas installations. Data formats are often different. For example, the United States and Europe interchange commas and decimal points in floating point numbers. For calendar dates, the United States and Europe both use the Gregorian calendar, but the United States uses the format mm/dd/yy, whereas Europe uses dd/mm/yy. That is, European dates go day, month, year, whereas United States dates go month, day, year. (See the box "Dates in the Moslem Calendar.") For the warehouse inventory management system, this might mean that you have to develop two versions of each screen layout and each report format, one for use in the United States warehouses and one for use in the London warehouse.

Dates in the Moslem Calendar

The date-conversion problems become harder in non-European countries. Many Moslem nations use the Hijrah calendar. The first day of the first year occurs on 15 July 622 A.D. in the Gregorian calendar. (The Hijrah year has 354 days divided into 12 months, with an extra day added to the last month 11 times every 30 years.) Systems used for commercial business in these countries must report dates using this particular calendar. If the XYZ Corporation also had a warehouse located in the Middle East, you would have to handle this date conversion.

Another potential requirement is to report monetary values in the country's local currency, and possibly in other currencies as well. The system in London might have to track prices in pounds, euros, and U.S. dollars, for instance. (Handling the daily changes in currency exchange rates has a major impact on the design.)

If the personnel operating the system in the foreign country speak a different language, especially if the language uses different alphabets (e.g., Cyrillic, Chinese, or Japanese) and languages that are written and read right to left, instead of from left to right like Indo-European languages. This can have several cost impacts:

- *Design*. The system must be able to display menu items, report titles, and information in each of the specified languages.
- *Displays*. Special display hardware and software may be needed.
- *Text conversion*. You will have to translate error messages, menu items, report titles, help files, and the user documentation.
- *Test cases*. You must test the displays and reports in each language.
- *Personnel*. You must hire developers and testers who know the languages.

Some development tools enable you to easily modify software for use in foreign countries with different alphabets and keyboard layouts. Choosing such tools will reduce development effort, but may increase costs for tools and equipment.

Travel is often an important contributor to costs. The Trips section in Table 2-1 identifies various trips based on their purpose. Each trip has associated notes to indicate the destination, the number of people traveling, and the duration of the trip. (This is a typical set of questions that you need to ask when estimating travel expenses.) The trips within the United States and the trips to London are entered as separate elements because the overseas trips take longer and cost more. Notes 4 through 6 in Table 2-2 record the details that affect the amount of travel required. These really depend on assumptions about system installation, the location and frequency of technical interchange meetings with the customer, and customer training. For example, can you train all of the customer's users at a single site (Los Angeles) or must you train people at each particular site? Training all the users in one location could reduce your costs. Therefore, you might want to propose to train all operators and users in the XYZ Corporation's Los Angeles office. (See Note 14 in Table 2-3.) This is a win-win situation because you reduce your travel costs, labor costs, and the total project costs. In addition, the XYZ Corporation may obtain an intangible benefit. Training all operators and users together ensures that all will learn the same things, and should help to build a coordinated team. This will help when installing the system at each site, and will facilitate the interactions between the sites after the system becomes operational. Although Note 14 suggests a better approach for training the users, the Trips section of Table 2-1 shows trips to "Install *and train*." The team will need to make a decision and update the documentation accordingly.

The last category shown in Table 2-1 is *Level of Effort* (LOE) tasks, which the team must perform to complete the project. The list shown is not complete but serves to illustrate the types of items that you need to include.

Table 2-1 organizes the data into six categories. The box "Structure the Estimate to Fit the Customer's SOW" describes another way to organize the estimate.

Structure the Estimate to Fit the Customer's SOW

Grouping the items as they are listed in the customer's SOW offers some advantages. First, it directly ties your estimated costs to the deliverable items and services requested by the customer. Second, this traceability helps the customer evaluate competing bids. To facilitate evaluation, the customer may even specify the format of the estimate, asking for the information in both printed form (hard copy) and in machine-readable form (soft copy), and often provide spreadsheet templates as part of the solicitation package. This makes it easy for the customer to load estimates from multiple bidders and perform various analytical comparisons.

For large government and commercial procurements, the customer often specifies *in detail* how the bidders' estimates must be decomposed and presented. The customer often provides a work breakdown structure (WBS), described in Chapters 11, "Bottom-Up Estimating and Scheduling," and 20, "Crafting a WBS," which is a hierarchical decomposition of a project's products and services. The customer also provides descriptions of each element in the WBS. (This is called the WBS dictionary.) The customer usually specifies the upper levels of the WBS hierarchy, and the developer then decomposes these into lower-level tasks, providing the necessary descriptions and associated resource and cost estimates.

This example does not analyze the risks in detail. Step 7 of the Linear Method described in Chapter 3, "A Basic Estimating Process: The Linear Method," identifies risks and the actions to eliminate, mitigate, or accept each identified risk. You would then include estimates of effort, costs, and terms and conditions to address these risks.

Virtually all students make one tacit assumption during the class exercise that could lead to a serious underestimate. The estimate presented previously assumes that there is only one warehouse in each city, and that only one system is needed per warehouse. The system complexity and the project costs would be much higher if there were multiple warehouses at multiple locations in each city. Figure 2-3, the network diagram, is a possible way of making visible your assumption that there is only a single site in each of the four cities. In addition, the documented estimate indicates the number of computer systems, modems, and cable sets based on the assumption of one warehouse per city, plus one maintenance facility located in Los Angeles. If you conveyed such estimating assumptions to the customer and the customer accepted them during the negotiation process, you would logically expect that the customer would call this mistake to your attention so that you could revise your design and your estimate.

One way to avoid making incorrect assumptions is to visit the customer's site prior to submitting a bid. The box "Ignorance Is Expensive" describes the results of an incorrect assumption. If you cannot make a site visit, you can possibly locate someone who has been there and can provide information. Lacking either of these options, you have to rely on your documented estimate to stimulate a dialogue with the customer *before* you complete the negotiations for the project. If the customer had the opportunity to inform you but did not do so, the documented estimate could provide a legal basis for negotiating an equitable adjustment later. Hopefully it will never come to this. See the box "Ignorance Is Expensive."

Ignorance Is Expensive

Our firm did a project more than 25 years ago to automate a factory that produced rifle ammunition. No one visited the site. Instead, the design team used scaled engineering drawings of the facility's floor plan to estimate the distances between the various rooms, and so determined the lengths of cables to connect the sensors, data concentrators, and computers. The team proceeded to assemble the hardware, build all of the cables, and write the software in our Huntsville facility. The team conducted a factory acceptance test there and determined that everything worked correctly. Then they shipped everything to the customer's plant. Arriving there they found that the walls between adjacent processing lines were 12 inches of solid concrete. (This prevented any explosions from propagating to adjacent work areas.) They had assumed that the walls were the usual wood-and-plaster construction, and so had intended just to drill holes through them and run the cables. Because this was not possible, they had to purchase a large amount of additional wire and construct the necessary cables onsite to connect the various devices. This caused the project to overrun in both cost and schedule.

2.4 Doing Better: A Planning Workbook

Having all participants identify and record items on a list helps ensure that nothing gets overlooked. The list also helps to communicate the team's understanding of the entire job, and also indicate who is responsible for providing various items. The list covers two types of information:

- Project Products (deliverables and nondeliverables)
- Major Resources (equipment, tools, and facilities)

Project products include *all* deliverable *and* nondeliverable items and services that you must produce to complete the project. These include reports, databases, design documents, converted data, user training, development and test tools, prototypes, and test articles. The customer's list of required deliverables is a start. Certain work products are associated with specific project life cycles, as described in Chapter 10, "Production Processes (Project Life Cycles)." The project's defined process also identifies many items. (Just look at the artifacts and activities.) Some of these items are "permanent" (e.g., a user manual or a design document) and others are "transient" (e.g., monthly cost and status reports). In addition, a project may need additional items. Software development has prototypes. Hardware development has mockups, brass boards, prototypes, and units needed for destructive testing. All of these require resources to produce, which is why they are of interest to estimators.

Major Resources include unusual, expensive, or hard-to-obtain equipment, tools, and facilities. Collecting such items on a *single* list helps ensure that nothing gets overlooked. Identify objects furnished by the customer so they can be included in the contract's terms and conditions or the estimating assumptions. Loaned items may have to be reserved in advance. One example is block time in a special test facility, which may have to be reserved months or years in advance. Leased or purchased items contribute to the project's estimated costs.

TIP: Don't forget to include labor costs associated with obtaining and tracking the items. Tracking a large number of customer-furnished items located at multiple sites can be a full-time job. Tracking components and assemblies that are incorporated into the final product may also be necessary.

The book's CD-ROM has a spreadsheet called "Planning Workbook" with four worksheets. You can use it to list deliverables, materials, consumables, and trips. Figure 2-4 shows an excerpt from the "Materials" worksheet. The first three rows record the project name, the author, and the date that the worksheet was prepared. (The header of the spreadsheet also captures the filename, worksheet name, the date and the time, and the page number. (Appendix E, "Excel for Estimators," explains how to label a spreadsheet.) The printed figure shows slight shading in some of the cells. In the actual spreadsheet, these cells are pale green, which is my convention to indicate cells where the user enters information.

Row 4 contains the column titles. The item names in column A form the checklist to guide the user. The description of each item is optional and so is not shaded. In each row, enter the number of items needed, if any. Entering a number in column C causes the cells in that row in columns D through I to turn pale green, prompting the user to enter data in one or more of these columns. For each item (row), you should indicate whether you already have the item, will obtain the item from the customer, intend to buy the item, intend to build the item, or will borrow or lease the item. (You actually enter the number of items obtained from each source.) Column I indicates whether the item will take a long time to obtain (Yes or No).[1] Use Column J to enter optional numbered notes providing additional information.

The main categories in column A are computer hardware, communications, computer software, facilities, and training. By definition, all items shown on this particular sheet are standard catalog items that can be purchased from a vendor. (The Deliverables worksheet identifies all the custom items that the developer must design and build. The Consumables worksheet indicates all items that the developer will need to deliver products and services. The Trips worksheet records any trips.)

The actual spreadsheet has many more rows, and covers projects that

- Purchase and configure hardware and software components.
- Configure, design, code, build, and test hardware and software components.
- Manufacture hardware components.
- Build facilities to house these components.
- Provide, create, generate, or convert operational data.
- Install the components and data in the facilities.
- Train and support the users.

Just remove the items that you do not need and add any other items that you do need.

---

[1] Rows 2 and 3 of column I contain the values Y and N, which are used to display the pull-down list in the cells of column I. See the discussion of data validation in Appendix E.

	A	B	C	D	E	F	G	H	I	J
1	Project Name:									
2	Prepared By:								Y	
3	Date Prepared:								N	
4	Item	Description (Name, Model, Part Number)	# Needed	# Have	# From Cust.	# To Buy	# To Build	# To Borrow or Lease	Long Lead Item?	Note
5	**COTS Computer Hardware**									
6	Desktop Computers									
7	Servers									
8	Display Monitors									
9	Keyboards									
10	Mice									
11	Modems									
12	LAN Cards									
13	Printers									
14	Other Special Peripherals									
15	Cables									
16	Racks									
17										
18	**Communications**									
19	Telephone Lines									
20	Modems									
21	Local Area Network Cards									
22	Router									
23	Firewall									
24	Purchase Web Address (URL)									
25										
26	**COTS Computer Software**									
27	Operating System									
28	Relational Data Base Mgt. System									
29	Other:									
30										
31	**Facilities (Provide Sketch of Layout)**									
32	Offices									
33	Laboratory Space: Square Feet =									
34	Special Electrical Wiring?									
35	Desks									
36	Chairs									
37	Tables									
38										
39	**COTS Training for Users**									
40	Course Title and # Students:									
41										
42	*End of Formulas*	*Last Line*								

Figure 2-4 *Excerpt of the Materials worksheet*

You can use this workbook to prepare estimates and to document commitments and assumptions. For a small project, this may be all you need. For large projects, these worksheets help you to prepare the *bill of materials* (BOM), which lists all items that must be purchased during the project.

2.5 Recommended Reading

Rodney Stewart identifies five questions for each item you have identified that will help you characterize the item and produce a better plan:

1. What is it? (process, product, project, or service)
2. What does it look like? (nature and scope, number, size, attributes)
3. When is it to be available? (delivery date, other key dates, long lead items)
4. Who will do it? (department, skills needed)
5. Where will they do it? (location affects costs and shipping time)

I added the information in parentheses to clarify the intent of the questions. Size may refer to weight, number of software modules, power, and the like. Attributes may include accuracy, speed, power, safety, and material type.

2.6 Summary

The estimated resources and costs for a project depend on how you intend to do the job. A dialog between engineers, managers, customers, and estimators leads to a better understanding of the job (product, process, and project), and so to more complete estimates. The example in this chapter illustrates the benefit of *writing something down*, either as text, as spreadsheet, or a diagram, so that others can *review and discuss* it. The various notes and diagrams help the engineers, customers, and estimators communicate. (Chapter 7 describes more key diagrams.) During the class exercise, students see the benefits of having multiple people review the documented estimate. There is often a lot of discussion about the estimating assumptions and rationale, questions, and risks. This quickly improves the estimate as people point out missing items, double counting, and bad assumptions. Over the years, students have uncovered new items to add to the solution. (It is still not complete, of course.)

This example reveals that to prepare good estimates you need the following:

1. A basic process to identify items and to validate these items and their estimated amounts
2. Standard formats to record various types of information
3. Ways to measure characteristics, sizes, and amounts
4. Techniques to estimate characteristics, sizes, and amounts

5. Techniques to quantify the uncertainty in estimated and measured values

6. Systematic ways to identify all items to include in the estimate

Chapter 3 describes a basic estimation process, identifies types of resources and costs, and provides forms and templates to help you document your estimates. The process also addresses validation of the estimates. Chapter 4, "Measurement and Estimation," identifies the types of project resources and how to measure them. Chapter 5, "Estimating Techniques," describes estimation techniques. Chapter 7, "Preparing to Estimate (Precursors of Estimation)," describes how you can systematically identify all the items that you need to estimate.

Chapter 3

A Basic Estimating
Process:
The Linear Method

You must estimate values for many kinds of quantities as you specify, choose, and design products and systems; plan and manage projects to build, deploy, and maintain them; and control and improve the associated production processes. Good estimates are critical to the success of these endeavors.

This chapter describes a simple process to prepare estimates for products, projects, and processes. Section 3.1 defines criteria for "good" estimates and estimation methods. Such methods produce well-documented estimates, but also achieve other important objectives. Section 3.2 defines the types of project resources that you must estimate. Section 3.3 describes the important concept of proxy-based estimation. Section 3.4 describes the Linear Method, which is a series to steps to document and refine an estimate. Section 3.5 provides guidance for using the Linear Method. Section 3.6 presents a short example that shows the need to document your estimates and identifies what you should record. Section 3.7 describes several forms that you can use to record your various estimates. (All are provided on the CD-ROM.) Section 3.8 explains how to manage all your information. Section 3.9 recommends additional reading. Section 3.10 summarizes the chapter's key points.

3.1 Criteria for "Good" Estimates

A "good method" produces a "good estimate" for *all* the quantities you need without exceeding the resources allocated for estimation.

The primary requirement for the method is to provide a value for some quantity with a "known and appropriate level of accuracy." All estimates, by their very nature, have errors. The key questions are

- How certain are you that the estimated value has some particular accuracy?
- How much accuracy do you really need?
- How much accuracy are you willing to pay for?

The accuracy of an estimated value depends on two things: The inherent accuracy of the estimating technique or model that you choose, *and* any errors in the input parameter values. Some techniques and models have better accuracies than others.[1] It is usually not possible, however, to attain this accuracy in practice because of errors in the input parameter values. To reduce the errors in the input values, you can define and structure the estimation process, use historical data, and train the people who prepare the estimates. As Chapter 2, "Planning a Warehouse Inventory System," showed, having multiple reviews of an estimate is a good way to detect omissions and inconsistencies.

The second question relates to the amount of risk associated with "bad" estimates. For example, an underestimate of processor resource utilization may lead to buying computer hardware that has insufficient capacity. An underestimate of project costs may lead to a cost overrun. For firms that competitively bid projects, an overestimate is undesirable because it may cause the buyer to award the job to another bidder.

The second question also relates to how well the organization can control its production processes. Extremely precise estimates are worthless if you cannot control the process. There is an old adage about measuring a board with a micrometer, and then cutting it with an axe. Sometimes rough estimates are acceptable.

The third question deals with the resources (e.g., time and money) available to prepare the estimate. You get what you pay for! Sometimes there is no time to do a precise estimate, even though you may know how to obtain it. You need to know such constraints so that you do not choose a time-consuming and expensive estimating method.

---

[1] Appendix C, "Measures of Estimation Accuracy" describes several accuracy measures used for evaluating estimating techniques and models.

Table 3-1 lists mandatory, desirable, and practical criteria for good estimation methods.

Table 3-1 *Criteria for a "Good" Estimation Method*

Mandatory Capabilities
• Identify the key factors to consider
• Produce a well-documented estimate (scope, assumptions, values, uncertainties)
• Validate the documented estimate
• Approve the estimate (accept it as a baseline)
Desirable Capabilities
• Support refinement of estimates as project proceeds (estimate to complete)
• Promote better understanding of the contributing factors (sensitivity analysis)
• Provide a means to organize and preserve experience
• Support refinement and extension of the method
Practicality
• Fits characteristics of application domain and product
• Fits the organization's business process and previous experience
• Provides acceptable accuracy given available resources (effort, time, money)
• Is accepted by all stakeholders (credibility)
• Uses input data that is readily available when needed
• Resists erroneous inputs (validity and sanity checks)
• Doesn't require unnecessary paperwork

Mandatory. The method must help the participants identify the key factors that affect the estimated values and the uncertainty in these values. In addition, the method should help identify missing information. For example, a good method to estimate project costs should identify all the necessary products and services that are to be delivered. It should also identify all project tasks used to produce these items and the resources needed by the project team. Chapter 2 illustrated the benefits of a documented estimate. (Section 3.6 provides more specific guidance.)

Validation checks the accuracy, completeness, and consistency of the estimated values. (Note that you lack the information to do this unless the estimate is documented.) *Accuracy* includes checking the calculations for errors. Have someone check your calculations! You can also compare estimated values to historical data for similar items, possibly scaling the values to adjust for differences. *Completeness* means that no items have been omitted. *Consistency* means that measured and estimated values of a quantity have the same definition, and so allows meaningful comparison. (These definitions include units of measure, the time interval covered, the activities included, and the work products included. Section 4.2 provides a detailed example.) Consistency also involves relationships between estimated quantities. For example, the productivity value may assume highly capable and experienced workers, but the labor rate may assume new college graduates with no experience.

Validation also identifies *redundant items*, which are of two types. *Duplicated items* arise due to the overlap or multiple counting of estimated items. This usually happens because the scopes of the individual elements (components, tasks, etc.) being estimated are not well defined. *Extra items* may be added by the engineers and estimators, but are not required for the product, project, or process. (This is called "gold-plating." Requirements traceability is one way to detect this.) *Redundancy is a particular problem when separate groups of people estimate parts of a product or portions of a project.*

The stakeholders must approve the documented estimate and accept it as a *baseline* for subsequent planning of the project. Often, the validation and approval are accomplished together using reviews.

Desirable Capabilities. The estimation method should allow you to refine the estimate as the project proceeds. For cost and schedule, these are called the *estimate to complete* (ETC). It should also promote a better understanding of the elements and factors that can contribute to the estimated value of a particular quantity. A good method should organize and preserve your experience by capturing proven techniques, estimating relations, and productivity values.

The method should be extensible for two reasons. First, you want to accommodate changes in product technology, development processes, and project characteristics. Second, you want to incorporate improvements as you learn. For example, calibration uses historical data to adjust estimating equations and models to fit your particular environment (product line, process, project constraints) so that it produces more accurate estimates of the desired quantities. You can also improve the method by revising checklists, adding reviews, or automating certain calculations.

Practicality. The estimation method should be relevant to your particular environment, dependable, and affordable. Environment includes the application domain, product line, organization, and customer. The method should provide acceptable accuracy within constraints of time and money. Stakeholders should accept the method as credible. (Accuracy and stakeholder acceptance could possibly be considered Mandatory requirements.) It should also use input data that is available at the time you want to prepare the estimate, or data that can be easily estimated. Ideally, this input data should be a byproduct of the production activities. For example, one input to a method might be the number of use cases identified during requirements definition. Dependable means that the method resists erroneous inputs. (Reviews are one way to accomplish this.) Computing the same value using two different techniques is also recommended. Many automated tools check input values for valid ranges and for consistency with each other. Any method should not require unnecessary paperwork. Less paperwork and automation makes a method more affordable in terms of effort, time, and cost.

You should consider all of these criteria when selecting an estimation method. Section 13.10 gives specific guidance on selecting techniques, models, methods, and tools.

3.2 Types of Resources

Members of the project team must identify and estimate the resources needed for each project task. Table 3-2 shows the types of resources.[2] *Materials* are existing items purchased from a catalog, and are listed in the bill of materials. *Subcontracted* items are configured or custom built by another firm, and incorporated in the product, or they may be services such as site preparation and training. Subcontracted items have labor content and provide deliverables, which are described by a statement of work (SOW). Workers use consumables during the production process. Examples include paper, disks, telephone calls, shipping, and rented equipment. (The distinction between consumable resources and their corresponding costs is often blurred. Many estimators refer to the consumable *resources* as other direct costs, or ODCs.) Travel is also a consumable resource, but estimators often handle it as a separate item because it is a major cost for many projects. See note N01, "Nonlabor Items," for guidance on identifying these items.

---

[2] Time is also a resource. Chapter 11, "Bottom-Up Estimating and Scheduling," discusses scheduling. Chapter 12, "Top-Down Estimating and Allocation," discusses simple ways to estimate the duration of a project.

Table 3-2 *Types of Project Resources*

Nonlabor
• *Materials*—Catalog items incorporated in the delivered product
• *Subcontracted items*—Custom products and services provided by an outside firm
• *Consumables*—Items consumed during production
• *Travel*—Travel and lodging (a consumable, but often itemized separately)
Labor
• *Core Activities*—Produces the product and provides services
• *Support Activities*—Assists the people who perform the core activities

Labor consists of core activities and support activities. Core activities produce the primary product and its associated documentation and include analysis, design, coding, fabrication, integration, and testing. Core activities may also include data conversion, product installation and configuration, user training, and manufacturing copies of the product. These "additional" activities depend on the product type and customer needs. Support activities provide the infrastructure needed by the people who perform the core activities. These activities include configuration management, quality assurance, project management, and business support functions such as accounting. (Some organizations consider one or more of these to be core activities.)

3.3 Proxy-Based Estimation

You can estimate the amount of resources for many types of activities and artifacts using a linear relationship. Examples include computers, cables, and commercial-off-the-shelf (COTS) licenses. Similarly, engineers and managers identify the trips required, specifying the purpose, destination, number of people traveling, and the duration.

Other resources are not discrete items. To estimate the amount of these resources, you relate some measurable characteristic of the item (a proxy) to the amount of resources needed to produce it. This proxy corresponds to the "size" of the item. You specify, estimate, or measure the size of the item, and then multiply by a *production coefficient* (pc) or divide by a *productivity* (P) to get the amount:

Amount = Size*Production coefficient = Size/Productivity

Or in symbols:

$$A = S*pc = S/P$$

The size is some measurable characteristic that you estimate or specify. For any particular quantity, the production coefficient is the reciprocal of the productivity ($P = 1/pc$). You will encounter both. Paying attention to the units of measure, however, prevents confusion. The units of measure should always cancel out in your estimating calculations, leaving the correct units for the estimated quantity. See the box "Dimensional Analysis."

Dimensional Analysis

Many metrics of interest to estimators have dimensional units (also called engineering units, units of measure, or simply units). The measured value for each of these quantities consists of a numeric value and associated dimensional units. You often receive data in nonstandard units (person-months) and so must convert the data into standard units (person-hours). The calculations can become confusing when you must combine various measures. Consistency and correctness are important. (The loss of the Mars Climate Orbiter in 1999 was attributed to an interface between two components using inconsistent units.) You can use dimensional analysis to ensure that converted measurements, mathematical equations, and parametric models are correct.

Dimensional analysis is a technique to ensure that all terms on both sides of an equation have the same units of measure. (You cannot add apples and oranges.) For each term, write down the units of each quantity in the term, and cancel out identical units that appear in both the numerator and denominator. (Singular and plural units are equivalent; e.g., page/pages and person/people.) Do this for each term in the expression. When you are done, all terms should have the same units.

For example, suppose that you must convert a document productivity from units of pages/person-month to lines/person-hour. Assume that you have measured the following conversion factor:

$$C_{Size} = 50 \text{ lines/page}$$

and have determined the size of a person-month:

$$C_{Effort} = 152 \text{ person-hours/person-month} = 152 phr/PM$$

You are given the productivity 300 pages/PM. Convert this value to units of lines/phr as follows:

$$\text{Productivity[lines / phr]} = \text{Productivity [pages / PM]} * C_{Size} / C_{Effort}$$
$$= \frac{(300 \text{ pages / PM})(50 \text{ lines / page})}{(152 \text{ phrs / PM})}$$

To explicitly show the units of a quantity, I enclose the units in square brackets. The value and the units of measure for the quantity are both shown in the calculation. The units of pages cancel, as do the units of PM, giving the following:

Productivity [lines/phr] = 300 lines*50/152 phr = 98.7 lines/phr

As a second example, suppose that you define the following:

E = effort [phr]
S = size [lines]
P = productivity [lines/phr]

Suppose that an estimator uses the equation E = S*P. This is clearly incorrect because

E = S*P = [lines]*[lines/phr] = [lines]²/phr ≠ phr

The correct equation is this:

$$E = S / P = \frac{\text{lines}}{\text{lines / phr}} = \text{phr}$$

The incorrect equation arose because the estimator confused *productivity* and *production coefficient*, which are reciprocals of each other.

In science and engineering, you must also handle *equivalent units*, which are combinations of units that *reduce* to the same basic measures. For example, physics uses mass, length, and time. One joule of energy equals one kilogram * (meter/sec)² and also equals one newton * meter. Such equivalent units are called "commensurate units."

3.4 The Linear Method: A Simple Process[3]

This section describes a simple, versatile method that uses proxy-based estimation. You can use this method in many different ways for all types of projects. For small projects, it is the only estimation method that you will need. For larger projects, the Linear Method can augment other estimation methods such as parametric models and project planning tools. For example, parametric models (described in Chapter 13, "Parametric Models") estimate the effort and schedule for many of the activities involved in producing a product. These models do not, however, estimate costs associated with travel (airfare, lodging, meals) or the purchase of materials such as COTS components or hardware.

Defining some standard terminology helps to describe the steps of the Linear Method. The term *element* denotes any item (thing) that must be produced or service (activity) that must be performed, whether deliverable or nondeliverable. A deliverable item might be a data entry screen in a software application, a hardware assembly, or a document. A nondeliverable item might be a computer program that generates special test data. (Such programs are often called *tooling*.) A deliverable service could be converting operational data. A nondeliverable service is an (internal) activity, such as configuration management. For estimating purposes, an *element* is anything that you have to expend resources to produce or provide.[4]

A *count* is the number of units of a particular element that must be produced. For example, the application developers may have to design and implement 100 data entry screens. You can also use a size measure (proxy) in place of the count.

A *production coefficient* measures the amount of a resource needed to produce one unit. The resources can be effort, raw materials, or money. For example, the resources might be cable, connectors, and the effort to assemble the cables. For knowledge—intensive work, the most important resource is effort. For example, it might require 50 person-hours of effort for a programmer to design, code, and test a single data entry screen.

Table 3-3 defines the 10 steps of the Linear Method. The following paragraphs explain each step in turn.

---

[3] Brad Tyler and I first recorded this method in a short document titled "Guide to Estimating and Costing Small Projects" in April 1990. It has stood the test of time, and we still use it.

[4] I considered other terms such as units, types, entities, objects, things, components, tasks, and activities. All are used in other contexts, however. Element, denoting a thing or activity, seemed like the best choice

Table 3-3 *10 Steps of the Linear Method*

1. Identify the types of elements.
2. Estimate the number of elements (counts) of each type.
3. Estimate the production coefficient for each element.
4. Tabulate the counts and production coefficient.
5. Refine and validate the table entries.
6. Include environmentals (support activities, consumables).
7. Identify and estimate risks.
8. Write down your results and rationale.
9. Convert counts to cost.
10. Obtain an independent review.

Step 1. Identify the types of the (estimating) elements that you must develop, produce, or provide. These types include the following:

- Computer programs
- Operational databases
- Screens
- Reports
- User manuals
- User training
- Custom tooling
- Prototypes
- Data conversion
- Technical support

Use the above list as a starting point to develop your own list of elements suited to your particular product line, application domain, or service offering. To identify the types of elements, you can look in several places:

- Customer specification (described in Chapter 7)
- Statement of work (SOW) (described in Chapter 2)
- List of required product features (described in Chapters 7 and 8)
- Product architecture (described in Chapters 7 and 9)

- Product design documents (described in Chapter 10)
- Development process (described in Chapter 10)
- Work breakdown structure (described in Chapters 11 and 20)
- Contract data requirements list (CDRL) (described in Chapter 20)
- Contract line items (CLINs) (described in Chapter 20)

During Step 1, do not worry about identifying redundant items. A later step will consolidate the list of element types. To help identify deliverable items, ask your customer or experienced project managers. For formal government or commercial solicitations, ask your contracts or legal department for help. They are skilled in reading contractual documents that identify deliverable items. (Sometimes these items are hidden in the most unexpected places! Tasks may be identified in a specification. Product requirements may be stated in a task in the SOW.) Consult with experienced developers and engineers to identify non-deliverables. If your organization has a standard production process, it will identify work products such as plans, design documents, and reviews. Subject matter experts can also help you identify both deliverables and nondeliverables.

Step 2. Estimate the number of elements of each type. This number is the count. You do *not* estimate the cost of the elements in this step. The goal is to keep the estimation of resources clearly separated from the estimation of costs associated with obtaining these resources. In this step, the counts are engineering guesses and represent preliminary values. (Later steps crosscheck and validate these values.) To determine the values for the counts, you can use historical data, analogies, and past experience if these are available. You will produce hard numbers for a firm commitment in Step 5.[5] A variation is to reorder the steps to obtain a unique, nonredundant list of types *before* you estimate the sizes (counts). In practice, however, you often discover more items as you try to count and estimate, and so it is not too important to reorder the steps. (See the description of Step 5.) Either way, you will end up iterating.

Step 3. Estimate the production coefficient for each element. For knowledge-intensive work, the most important resource is labor. If you develop hardware systems or install computer systems, however, you will also be interested in materials and consumables. Actual historical data provides the best possible source of production coefficients. Even if the data represents elements that are not identical to the one being estimated, you can use techniques such as scaling (described in Section 5.2) to adjust the values in a disciplined, organized way.

---

[5] A possible refinement at this point is to use the PERT technique described in Section 5.3. In this technique, you record the smallest possible, most likely, and largest possible values for each count.

Step 4. Tabulate the elements, their counts, and the production coefficients. Do this using a spreadsheet such as the one shown in Figure 3-1 for labor. The left column indicates the element type. The next column indicates the count for that type of element. The third column shows the production coefficient, measured here in person-hours per element produced. The next column shows the total effort for that element in person-hours. Even though the goal is to estimate resources, the last column shows the row cost because managers often like to get a feel for the associated costs. To convert labor resources to costs in this step, you might use average labor rates for the organization or negotiated bid rates. This particular spreadsheet assumes an average loaded labor cost of $50 per person-hour to convert the total effort to an approximate cost. Also provide totals for the last two columns. In this figure, the total effort is 2,174 person-hours and the cost is approximately $109,000.

TIP: Placing totals and other computed quantities at the *top* of the spreadsheet allows you to easily add more values by dragging formulas down the spreadsheet, providing a more useful tool.

Project:	Sample		Column Totals	
Author:	R. Jones		Effort	Cost
Date Prepared:	21-Dec-04		2,174	$108,700.00
Hourly Labor Rate:	$50.00			
Element	Count	Production Coefficient (phrs/unit)	Row Total (phrs)	Row Cost ($)
Messages	19	48	912	$45,600.00
Filters	3	16	48	$2,400.00
Screens	5	40	200	$10,000.00
Plots	3	8	24	$1,200.00
Files	5	16	80	$4,000.00
Board Interface	1	160	160	$8,000.00
COTS Interface	3	40	120	$6,000.00
Modules	30	8	240	$12,000.00
Pages of Engr. Documents	100	1	100	$5,000.00
Pages of User Manual	50	1	50	$2,500.00
Site Installation	6	40	240	$12,000.00
Last Line				

Figure 3-1 *Sample labor spreadsheet*

TIP: If you want to provide a form or template with a fixed number of rows, mark the row immediately following the last row having your formulas and formatting. I typically color the row and type "Last Line" in one of the columns. (The only drawback to this approach is that when you print the sheet, all pages up to and including the one containing the last line will print out. You can select how many pages to print, however.)

Step 5. Refine and validate the table entries: elements, counts, and production coefficients. This is the step where you identify any redundant or missing types of elements. (If you discover any missing types, repeat Steps 1 through 4 to add them to the estimate.) You also adjust the counts and production coefficients if necessary. It is important to use as many sources of information as possible in this step. There are several possible ways to do this. You can compare the elements, counts, and production coefficients with historical data, possibly adjusting it using scaling techniques (described in Section 5.2). You can ask experienced engineers and subject matter experts to review the information for completeness and consistency. Having the information expressed in an organized, written form such as the spreadsheet shown in Figure 3-1 helps structure the review process and makes it easier to assess the completeness, consistency, and correctness of the items shown.

Step 6. Consider the *environmentals*, which are other support activities and consumables. The objective of this step is to identify other resources that are associated with producing the elements identified in the tabulation. Examples might be support activities, office equipment, shipping charges, telephone and network charges, office supplies, travel, and special tools and equipment. These depend on the process (e.g., the amount of configuration management and quality assurance required). (Chapter 10, "Production Processes [Project Life Cycles]," describes various production processes.) Historical data often proves useful in identifying these additional resources. Also, many environmental influences are ingrained in your historical production coefficients.

There are three approaches to record the resources for environmentals. First, you can list them directly, adding them as distinct items to the tabulation (spreadsheet). Second, you can apply a "tax" on the previously estimated resources. For example, you might define a *loading rate* for engineering labor to account for quality assurance services. (Chapter 15, "Calculating Cost and Price: The Basics," discusses loading rates.) Third, you can adjust the productivity coefficients. For example, you might increase historical production coefficients from projects where an outside department performed quality assurance so that the adjusted production coefficient includes effort for quality assurance. (Chapter 15 explains direct and indirect charges so that you will know how to do such adjustments when necessary.) The customer, organizational policies, or cost accounting guidelines may dictate the particular approach that you use for a particular resource (or type of element).

The key advice for Step 6 is to *look for the differences* from past projects or products. Differences are a good clue that your project may be heading into uncharted territory, where environmentals may consume more resources. Use historical data to help identify the differences.

Step 6 may identify additional items or activities tied to the production process. One example is assemblies used for destructive testing. (You should already have identified materials and purchased items in Steps 1 and 2.)

Step 7. Estimate the resources needed to address risks. A *risk* is an uncertain event or condition that, if it occurs, will have a positive or negative effect on the project, product, or process. For example, the capacity of the proposed computer platform(s) may not be adequate to handle the customer's operational workload. If this turns out to be true, you might have to buy computers with more capacity, causing the project's costs to increase. To offset the impact of this risk, you might want to estimate a reserve to cover the cost of more capable computers. Another example might be loss or damage to an expensive computer during shipping. To cover this risk, you might buy insurance. (You would record the cost of the insurance in Step 6.) Alternatively, the engineers may decide to specify more powerful computers in the first place, increasing the bid price.

So, in Step 7, you list potential risks and estimate the resources needed to avoid (prevent) or mitigate them.[6] This may be difficult for large projects since there are many types of risks. Chapter 14, "Estimating Risk Reserves," describes how to estimate risk reserves and provides checklists to help you identify potential risks. (The intervening chapters cover the estimation of project, product, and process quantities to provide the foundation to address the risks associated with each quantity.) For this example, assume that you have a similar spreadsheet listing risks and have estimated a "risk reserve" for each. Also assume that these reserves total $15,000.

Step 8. Write down the estimate in an organized way. This includes a list of items, their associated estimated values, the basis of estimate (e.g., sources of historical productivity data), assumptions, and supporting rationale. The objective is to collect everything in one place. "Everything" includes notes, reports, printouts, and disks. Often most of the information is captured in machine-readable form. This makes it easy to archive the estimate. (It also makes it easy to update the estimate later when things change.) To help you, Section 3.8 describes a project estimation notebook.

---

[6] You can avoid or mitigate some risks at no cost using contract terms and conditions, as explained in Section 2.3.

Step 9. Convert all the counts to (approximate) costs. In most companies, resource estimators are not authorized to compute official (binding) costs. I include this step only because managers who review the estimates want to see estimates in monetary terms. The discussion of Figure 3-1 in Step 4 showed how to do this for labor. Figure 3-2 shows how to do this for materials and sub-contracts (M&S) and other direct costs (ODCs), which are the consumables. This spreadsheet has a new column, Size of an Element, so that you can record estimates of document sizes and the duration of trips. To convert nonlabor resources to costs in this step, use published airfares, catalog prices, historical data, etc. For example, you can obtain historical production coefficients for items such as document copying (cost per page). Ask your accounting department for help. For the example shown in Figure 3-2, the total estimated cost is $39,750.

		Project:	Sample					
		Author:	R. Jones				TOTAL =	$39,750.00
		Date Prepared:	21-Dec-04					
	Element		Size Unit	Size of One Element	Number of Elements	Total Elements	Coefficient (Cost/Element)	Row Cost ($)
M&S	*Hardware:*							
	Computer			1	6	6	$2,000.00	$12,000.00
	Comm Board			1	6	6	$500.00	$3,000.00
	Printer			1	1	1	$300.00	$300.00
	Software:							
	Plot Package			1	6	6	$150.00	$900.00
	Math Library			1	6	6	$200.00	$1,200.00
	Window Library			1	6	6	$350.00	$2,100.00
	Compiler			1	1	1	$500.00	$500.00
ODCs	*Reproduction:*							
	Engineering Docs		pages	100	2	200	$0.05	$10.00
	User Docs		pages	50	8	400	$0.05	$20.00
	Trips:							
	R-T Airfare			1	10	10	$1,500.00	$15,000.00
	Per Diem		days	5	10	50	$50.00	$2,500.00
	Car		days	5	10	50	$40.00	$2,000.00
	Consumables:							
	Diskettes (10/box)		boxes	1	5	5	$20.00	$100.00
	Paper (10 K pages/box)		boxes	1	4	4	$30.00	$120.00
	Last Line							

Figure 3-2 *Sample spreadsheet for materials and ODCs*

Using the risk reserve from Step 7, the total estimated cost for the project is as follows:

$108,700	Labor costs
$ 39,750	Materials, subcontracts, consumables
$ 15,000	Risk reserve
$163,450	Total project cost

Step 10. Obtain an independent review from inquisitive, helpful skeptics. Experienced managers and senior engineers are good choices. For small projects, the reviewer might just be your supervisor or department manager who would just examine the documented estimate (values, assumptions, rationale, etc.). For large or especially important projects, reviews are more formal and involve more people. For a formal review, you must often prepare a presentation, and may have to provide answers to a standard list of review questions. (Formal reviews often specify standard forms, templates, or plots.) To obtain the most benefit from this review, expose uncertainties. Possibly one of the expert reviewers can help you resolve them, or can identify sources of useful historical data.

TIP: You should also review project scope and estimating assumptions at the start of a project. The scope of the project includes the deliverables, and the estimated effort, cost, and time. Sometimes the developer and customer may renegotiate the scope. If so, the project team should update all estimates and plans to reflect the renegotiated scope. Failure to do so can lead to a "death march project" [Yourdon, 1999]. You should also confirm that all of the estimating assumptions are satisfied when the project starts. For example, if your estimates assume that developers will have high-performance development tools, but they only receive a few old personal computers with simple tools, you should re-estimate the development effort, costs, and time and then renegotiate the project's commitments.

3.5 Using the Linear Method

The Linear Method is simple, but flexible. This section describes some useful details.

3.5.1 Estimating Support Effort

Estimating the effort for support activities is usually done as follows. First estimate the effort needed to perform each production activity. These activities include analysis, design, code, test, data conversion, and user document preparation. Do not forget to add effort for writers, technical editors, librarians, subject matter experts (SMEs), consultants, and other workers with special skills if needed. Then sum these estimates to get the "core" effort. Then calculate the effort for each support activity directly by multiplying the core effort by an appropriate percentage:

Core Effort	=	Engineering Effort
CM Effort	=	F_{CM} * Core Effort
QA Effort	=	F_{QA} * Core Effort
PM Effort	=	F_{PM} * Core Effort

where the F_i are the percentages for the support activities of configuration management (CM), quality assurance (QA), and project management (PM).

An alternative set of rules is as follows:

Core Effort	=	Effort for all production activities
CM Effort	=	f_{CM} * Core Effort
QA Effort	=	f_{QA} * (Core Effort + CM Effort)
PM Effort	=	f_{PM} * (Core Effort + CM Effort + QA Effort)

Here, the last three equations compute the effort for the support activities as a percentage of the cumulative effort. For example, the quality assurance effort is based on the core effort *plus* the configuration management effort because the quality assurance activity must monitor both the engineers and the configuration management personnel. Similarly, the project management effort is based on the sum of the effort for the other three categories because the manager must supervise *all* of the other personnel working on the project. The f_i are analogous to the F_i used in the preceding equations (but have different values, of course). Each organization has its particular conventions and determines the values from its own historical data. If you are responsible for preparing estimates of this type, you should consult with the appropriate personnel in your organization for advice.

Here are some typical rules of thumb for the amount of support effort needed to support the core activities, expressed as a percentage of the core effort:

- Management effort is 5% to 15%.
- Administrative and clerical effort is 5% to 10%.
- Effort to maintain a software environment[7] is 2% to 4%.
- Configuration management effort is 2% to 8%.
- Quality assurance effort is 5% to 15%.

Choose values at the high end of the range if the product is complex, many organizations are involved, business risk is high, and the product is mission critical or safety critical. If a team has *separate* development and test environments, include 2% to 4% for each one.

---

7 The suite of desktop computers, servers, and tools used to develop and test software.

3.5.2 Performing Sensitivity Analysis

The rows with the largest totals contribute the most to the total estimated value. These influential rows are the "resource drivers." Estimation errors in these rows will cause the most damage. The errors can be in the count, the production coefficient, or both. For example, in Figure 3-1 the labor for Messages is 912 person-hours, about 42% of the total effort. A 10% error in the production coefficient (or in the count) will affect the total estimated effort by 91 person-hours, or 4%. Engineers, estimators, and reviewers should pay particular attention to the resource drivers.

To reduce the total cost of the project, the resource drivers provide the greatest opportunity. The estimate assumed that every message would be designed and coded from scratch. Instead, suppose that the engineers choose a different development process. In this process, they will design and implement a "message class," which is a common template for all 19 message types. Using this template, they can quickly create instances that represent each individual message type. Suppose that it takes 200 person-hours to develop the message class, and 20 person-hours to analyze one message and create an instance. The total development effort is now 580 person-hours (= 200 + 19*20). Choosing a new process reduces the estimated cost by 332 person-hours (= 912 − 580), and reduces the total estimated effort by 15%. This simple example shows how product design, production processes, and estimation are intertwined. You will see this again in Chapter 7 (the precursors of estimation) and Chapter 15 (calculating costs).

If you use a spreadsheet to record your estimates, it is easy to perform a sensitivity analysis on multiple quantities, counts, and production coefficients. Just change the value and recalculate to see the effect of the change. You can also use statistical measures such as the mean and standard deviation to perform sensitivity analyses. There are some commercial tools, such as Crystal Ball, that allow the user to specify probability distributions for various values. The tool then iteratively performs many recalculations, choosing the values for each iteration using the specified probability distributions. (This is called the Monte Carlo technique.)

3.5.3 The Assumption of Linearity

The Linear Method assumes a *linear* estimating relation: resource amount equals amount produced times production coefficient. (Alternatively, you could say that resource equals amount produced divided by the productivity.) This assumption may not be valid for some quantities. For example, in purchasing hardware items from a vendor, you often receive a price discount if you buy more than some number of units. For software development or other knowledge-intensive activities, productivity *decreases* as the amount of product increases. (The production coefficient increases.) The reason is that more people are involved, increasing the effort needed to communicate information and coordinate concurrent activities. This phenomenon is called the "diseconomy of scale."

Productivity also depends on many other factors as illustrated in Table 3-4. Some increase it, and others decrease it. For example, programming productivity is lower for complex algorithms than for simple algorithms. Parametric cost (effort) estimation models (described in Chapter 13) quantify the effects of such factors on productivity. In the Linear Method, these effects are included in the organization's historical productivity data for "similar" projects. If a project is not very similar, however, you can use parametric models to adjust historical productivity data to account for the differences. See the box "Using Parametric Models to Adjust Productivity."

Table 3-4 *Factors Affecting Productivity*

Product
• Complexity (application domain, product functions)
• Requirements quality (completeness, stability)
• Amount of reuse
Process
• Amount of engineering documentation
• Use of peer reviews (reduces rework costs)
• Formality and frequency of reviews
• Degree of automation (design and test tools)
Project
• Number and stability of organizations involved (customer, developer, subcontractor, supplier)
• Quality of staff (skill, experience)
• Experience working as a team
• Schedule pressure

Using Parametric Models to Adjust Productivity

Several parametric models estimate software development effort and time and the distribution of these quantities by project phase and activity. The model builder chooses tables, equations, and rules that capture the influence of (input) parameters on the output values. A parametric model to estimate software development effort accounts for factors that affect the productivity of the development team such as those shown in Table 3-4. Product size is the most important parameter. In effect, such a model calculates an "average productivity" given all the factors, and divides it into the size to obtain the estimated effort. (The models are not actually this simple, of course.) Because labor accounts for most of the software development cost, the project cost is proportional to the effort. Thus, many software estimators refer to a "cost model" even though it actually estimates effort.

You can use a parametric model to adjust historical productivity values as follows. Suppose that a parametric model, M, estimates development effort, EDEV, as a function of size, S, and some set of parameters, {p}:

$$EDEV = M(S, \{p\})$$

Let subscript H denote known historical data, and subscript N denote parameters for a new project. Then you can scale the historical productivity, P_H, using the following:

$$\frac{P_N}{P_H} = \frac{S_N / M(S_N, \{p_N\})}{S_H / M(S_H, \{p_H\})}$$

or

$$P_N = P_H * S_N * M(S_H, \{p_H\}) / [S_H * M(S_N, \{p_N\})]$$

3.5.4 Handling Uncertainty

To focus on the essentials of each step, the description in Section 3.4 did not explicitly mention recording the uncertainty in the input and output values. You should of course do this. Section 5.2 explains how to use ranges or statistical measures. The PERT technique, described in Section 5.3, is also very useful. You may also have statistical measures (mean, standard deviation) for historical production coefficients. Section 5.5 shows how to use the mean and standard deviation to estimate the probability of errors of various sizes.

3.6 Documenting Your Estimates

Documenting an estimate enables you to

- Understand the scope, constraints, and assumptions.
- Interpret the estimated value(s).
- Critically review the results.
- Re-create the estimate (possibly with modified assumptions and inputs).
- Communicate important information to all stakeholders.

Good documentation can prevent cost overruns by definitizing vague requirements. See the box "Stating the Assumed Scope."

Stating the Assumed Scope

Several years ago I advised a project that was to build a new system. Among other tasks, the team had to estimate the effort to "train all the users" on the new system. We documented the estimating assumptions that would form the basis of our estimate. We stated that

1. The students would already be able to use the organization's standard desktop environment (operating system and office automation tools).

2. Each student would require 8 contact-hours of classroom instruction.

3. The class size would be 20 students per session.

4. A single instructor would teach each session.

5. The instructor would need an additional 8 person-hours to prepare the classroom and handle administrative details for each session.

6. There were 300 users to be trained. (We based this number on our knowledge of the customer's organization.)

7. The customer would pay all student costs (labor and travel expenses).

Our historical data showed that the production coefficient to develop course materials for the type of training planned was 20 person-hours per contact-hour. We thus estimated a total effort of 160 person-hours to develop the training materials (= 20*8).

To estimate the effort needed to deliver the sessions, we first calculated that we would have to offer 15 training sessions (= 300/20). Based on our assumptions, the single instructor would require 16 person-hours to teach a single session. The total instructor effort for course delivery was thus 240 person-hours (= 15*16).

The total estimated effort for user training was 400 person-hours (= 160 + 240). We also added costs for copying and binding student notes. We submitted our bid and the customer awarded us the contract.

We started the project to develop the system and train the users. Approximately six months into the project, the customer informed us that they now thought that 1,000 people would use the new system and so would have to be trained. We responded by computing the effort to deliver 35 (= 700/20) additional sessions and renegotiated the price. If we had not documented our estimating assumptions, and instead had just said, "We will train all of your users for 400 person-hours," then legally we would have had no recourse to charge for the increased scope. We would have lost a significant amount of money, corresponding to the cost of delivering the additional 560 person-hours. This is 140% above the amount of effort in the original bid.

Note the careful use of units of measure in this example. These units of measure include course, session, person-hours, and contact-hours.

Table 3-5 summarizes the components of a well-documented estimate, dividing them into directives and results. *Directives* refer to the information that you need to begin to prepare the estimate.[8] *Scope and objectives* indicate the purpose of the estimate, the quantities to be estimated, and the required accuracy. For example, you might be asked to estimate the effort for a small in-house project to develop a prototype. If so, you need only estimate the approximate effort required, and the project team will then use the value as a "not-to-exceed" target, reducing features if necessary. *Conditions* apply to the estimate itself. For example, the customer or your managers may direct that you must provide an answer within 10 working days, or spend no more than 40 person-hours to prepare the estimate. *Constraints* apply to the item(s) whose characteristics you are to estimate. These may come from the customer, the engineers, or managers. For example, customers often specify the project's target completion date.

---

[8] You actually need even more information before you can begin to prepare an estimate. See "The Precursors of Estimation" in Chapter 7.

Table 3-5 *Criteria for a Well-Documented Estimate*

Directive
• Scope and objectives
• Conditions
• Constraints
Results
• Assumptions
• References (models, tools, historical data)
• Input values
• Output values
• Potential risks and unknowns
• Key factors and sensitivities

You must also record all of the "results" of the estimation process. *Results* include your *estimating assumptions* and *references* to estimating techniques and models, and also to the sources of historical data used for productivity values, model calibration, analogies, and comparisons. See the box "Basis of Estimate." Be alert to identify and record new assumptions as you prepare the estimate. *Inputs* include the independent variables and characteristics that determine the (dependent) estimated value. (You can view estimating as a function.) Using the example from Section 3.3, the values of size and productivity determine the estimated effort. (Note that engineers and other participants may actually provide some assumptions and input values to the estimator. Thus, the term *results* is a bit of a misnomer.) Record the estimated values for all inputs *and* the uncertainty in these values.

Basis of Estimate

A basis of estimate (BOE) provides estimated values for various quantities *and* justifications for these values. Here are several possible justifications, listed in order of *decreasing* desirability and credibility:

1. Documented prior experience with a similar task

2. Documented prior experience with a similar task but adjusted by mathematical scaling or judgment

3. Magnitude of effort and documented productivity rates

4. Level of effort (LOE) based on experience

5. Industry standard estimating models and productivity factors

6. Task decomposition

7. Estimator experience

8. Best engineering judgment

Documented prior experience means quantitative historical data. These particular justifications apply to estimating effort, the key resource for knowledge-intensive products. Many also apply to justifying estimates of other resources such as materials and consumable items. Note that *historical data* is the most credible, with *adjusted historical data* the second most credible. This is another motivation to collect historical data. (Chapter 4, "Measurement and Estimation," describes quantitative techniques for adjusting historical data.)

Outputs include the estimated value(s) *and* the (estimated) uncertainty in these values. For example, you could give a simple range of the estimated value (high, low), a standard deviation, or some other statistical measure described in the note Appendix B, "Measurement Theory and Statistics." Estimators should report the estimated values and the uncertainties in these values to stakeholders and decision makers. Too often I see estimators provide a single value (a point estimate). For example, an estimated effort of "1,000 person-hours" does not tell you much (even if the estimator has documented the scope, assumptions, etc. as described previously). Is the estimated value "(1000 ± 50) person-hours" or is it "(1000 ± 500) person-hours?" The decision maker will react quite differently to these two estimates.

Record the units of measure for historical data, inputs, and outputs. This is especially important if the units are different from your organization's standards. For example, some firms use a different number of person-hours in a person-month for particular bids depending on customer directives and competitive considerations. Finally, describe any conversion of units that you performed for historical productivity values.

Record potential risks and unknowns as well. Section 2.3 gives some examples. (Chapter 14 describes types of risks.) *Identify key factors* that have a large influence on the estimated value(s). It is often a good idea to *perform a sensitivity analysis* to quantify the effects of changes to, or errors in, these key factors.

All of this documentation can be expensive. Do not expend resources preparing unneeded documentation. Here are three tips.

TIP 1: Focus on the information that you would need to re-create the estimate.

TIP 2: Use information that you collect or generate as you prepare the estimate. To save time and effort, you can record the inputs as screen dumps, redlined memos, and so forth.

TIP 3: Use standard forms to ensure that you collect all the necessary information. (You can automate many forms as Word documents, Excel spreadsheets, web pages, and so forth.) The Project Profile form (described in Section 16.3.1) is a good way to collect project and product information. You can use this information later to identify data from similar projects to use for reviewing new estimates, analogy estimation, and calibrating estimation models. The next section gives examples.

3.7 Standard Forms

The CD-ROM contains the following standard forms, implemented as Excel spreadsheets, to help you apply the Linear Method:

- Labor (by task)
- Labor allocation (by month or period)
- Purchased items (materials)
- Other direct costs (supplies, rent)
- Travel

These are shown in Figures 3-3 through 3-7. Later chapters describe additional forms that you can use as well.

The top six rows of each form contain the same information: project name, project task, the name of the person completing the form, the date completed, phone number, and the person who approves of the form and the date of approval. You can tailor this to meet your needs.

Figure 3-3 shows labor by task. Each row of the table in Figure 3-3 shows the effort for a specific task or activity, decomposed by firms and labor categories for each firm. Here, each firm has three labor categories (indicated by the column headings LCx, where x can be some combination of letters or numbers). The total effort (person-hours) for the task is in the column at the right. One disadvantage of this form is that it does not show the time phasing of the effort. Figure 3-4 shows the activity for a single task, with each labor category on a separate line. The effort (in person-hours) for each labor category is shown by month during the year. You can choose which of the two formats best suits your needs.

Projects often purchase a number of items. Figure 3-5 shows the bill of materials, which contains items purchased for incorporation into the delivered product. The form indicates the date that you need the item. This is important information for the person who actually places the order because some items take a long time to obtain. (Vendors often do not begin fabricating expensive or custom-built items until they receive a legally binding purchase order. Some items are *not* available off the shelf. Vendors usually quote delivery times as calendar-days after receipt of order [ARO].)

Figure 3-6 shows a form for other direct costs. These are similar to purchased materials. You could use the bill of materials form to identify items that you will purchase such as paper and supplies. As Figure 3-6 shows, however, items such as rent, leasing fees, and services often are tied to a time interval (period of performance). Thus, you might want a separate form for such expenses.

Figure 3-7 is a travel worksheet showing the origin and destination using international airport codes, which are convenient shorthand. It also shows the number of scheduled trips, the number of persons per trip, and the length of each trip in days. (The Planning Workbook mentioned in Chapter 2 is an alternative format for travel.)

You must also capture the rationale and justification. (See the box "Basis of Estimate" in Section 3.6.)

Project:							Name:		
Task:							Date:		
							Phone:		
						Approved By:			
						Date:			
Labor by Task (Person-Hours)									
		Firm #1			Firm #2			Firm #3		Total Person-Hours	Note (Optional)

Task or WBS #	Task or Activity	LC1	LC2	LC3	LCA	LCB	LCC	LCX	LCY	LCZ	Total Person-Hours	Note (Optional)
	Build the Widget	50.0	30.0		25.0		40.0				95.0	
	Test the Widget		20.0		15.0			45.0	12.0		92.0	

Figure 3-3 *Labor estimation worksheet*

Project:									Name:				
Task:									Date:				
									Phone:				
									Approved By:				
									Date:				
Labor Allocation (Person-Hours by Calendar-Month)													

Task or WBS #	Position Title	Labor Grade	Year	Jan	Feb	Mar	Apr	May	Jun	Jul	Aug	Sep	Oct	Nov	Dec	Total Person-Hours	Note (Optional)
			TOTALS:	220	180	150	100	60	60	0	0	0	0	0	0	770	
	Engineer	02	2005	140	120	110	60	20	20							470	
	Manager	02	2005	80	60	40	40	40	40							300	

Figure 3-4 *Labor allocation worksheet*

Project:					Name:		
Task:					Date:		
					Phone:		
*Cost Source Codes:	WQ - Written Quote	EE - Engr. Estimate			Approved By:		
	VQ - Verbal Quote	GS - GSA Catalog			Date:		
	CA - Catalog	PO - Purchase Order					
					TOTAL =	$12,000.00	
Bill of Materials							

Task or WBS #	Description	Vendor	Part #	Date Needed	Quantity	Unit Cost	Total Cost	Cost Source*	Note (Optional)
	Computer	XYZ	123-456	11-Feb-01	6	$1,500.00	$9,000.00	WQ	30 days ARO
	Laser Printer	ABC	789-10	14-Feb-01	3	$1,000.00	$3,000.00	VQ	

Figure 3-5 *Bill of materials worksheet*

Project:						Name:				
Task:						Date:				
						Phone:				
*Cost	WQ - Written Quote		EE - Engr. Estimate			Approved By:				
Source	VQ - Verbal Quote		GS - GSA Catalog			Date:				
Codes:	CA - Catalog		PO - Purchase Order							
						TOTAL =	$13,250.00			

			Other Direct Costs							
Task or WBS #	Description	Period Covered		Size Unit	Quantity	Unit Cost	Total Cost	Cost Source*	Note (Optional)	
		From Date	To Date							
	Boxes of Printer Paper (20 lb.)	4-Jan-01	4-Dec-01	Box (5000 Shts)	50	$45.00	$2.250.00	CA		
	Lease 1000 Square Feet of Office Space	4-Jan-01	4-Dec-01	$/month	11.0	$1,000.00	$11,000.00	WQ		

Figure 3-6 *Other direct costs worksheet*

Project:				Name:		
Task:				Date:		
				Phone:		
				Approved By:		
				Date:		

			Travel Worksheet			
Task or WBS #	Origin	Destination	# Round Trips	# Persons per Trip	# Days per Trip	Date	Purpose
	HSV	COS	5	2	2	Monthly	Monthly Status Meeting
	HSV	JFK	1	5	2	14-Jan-01	Inspect Customer's Facility

Figure 3-7 *Travel worksheet*

3.8 Managing Your Information

Estimators, engineers, and managers generate many documents and spreadsheets related to estimates corresponding to different designs, processes, and assumptions. As changes and updates occur, new versions of these will appear. It is critical to label all information associated with an estimate because you may have pages and files associated with different estimates in your work area. To manage all of this information, you should

- Date/time stamp everything.

    Put a date and time stamp on *every* page of *every* document and *every* worksheet of *every* spreadsheet. Use default templates to do this so that you do not forget! Appendix E, "Excel for Estimators," describes how to label spreadsheets and documents.

- Collect everything in a "project estimation notebook."

Establish a project estimation notebook to collect the information in an organized way. This helps ensure that a complete set of information is captured and promotes consistency across an organization. Table 3-6 identifies possible items to include in the project estimation notebook and provides a starting point that you can adapt to your particular needs. If desired, you can also specify the forms, templates, or spreadsheets can be used to record certain types of information. (Use the spreadsheets on the CD-ROM supplied with this book.)

Table 3-6 *Project Estimation Notebook*

Tabs	Contents
Project Data	Description of project
	Application, sponsor
	Schedules
	Memos (redirection, changes)
Product Description	Baselines used to prepare the estimates
	Specification (functional and performance requirements)
	Design (architecture, components)
	Basis for size estimates
Submitted Estimates	Data for all submitted estimates
	Ground rules and assumptions
	Methods and models used
	Historical data used for calibration
	Input data and printouts
	Historical log listing all estimates
Risk Analysis	Critical parameters, risk summaries
	Potential impacts and contingency plan
	(additional tasks or terms and conditions)

3.9 Recommended Reading

Barry Boehm presents criteria for evaluating a software cost model in [Boehm, 1981, page 476]. Section 29.8 of [Boehm, 1981] evaluates COCOMO 1981 against these criteria. Lionel Briand and Isabella Wieczorek define a set of criteria that extend Boehm's 10 criteria [Briand, 2001]. Table 3-7 summarizes their criteria.

Table 3-7 *Expanded Evaluation Criteria for Resource Estimation Models**

Estimation Model
• Predictive accuracy ("quality")
• Inputs required
• Completeness (types of resources estimated)
• Uncertainty information (point value, uncertainty range, or probability distribution)
• Calibration
• Interpretability (meaningful to practitioners, "constructiveness")
Estimation Method
• Assumptions
• Repeatability (objectivity of model's inputs, defined steps of method)
• Complexity (number and difficulty of steps performed)
• Automation of modeling (tools for model building)
• Transparency (algorithms and rationale documented)
Application
• Potential uses (prediction, benchmarking, trade studies, or risk assessment)
• Generalizability (to different development environments)
• Comprehensiveness (level of detail for phases, activities, and resources)
• Availability of estimates (at different stages of a project)
• Automation (tool support)

*Based on Table 4 in [Briand, 2001]

Barry Boehm describes a seven-step estimation process in Chapter 21 of [Boehm, 1981]. Mike Cotterell and Bob Hughes describe an 11-step process in Chapter 2 of [Cotterell, 1995].

Robert Grady and Deborah Caswell describe a simple estimation process in [Grady, 1987]. They show how their data collection forms evolved as they learned, improving their process. David Peeters and George Dewey discuss sources of estimating bias in [Peeters, 2000]. Albert Lederer and Jayesh Prasad give nine management guidelines for better cost estimating in [Lederer, 1992]. Catherine Tilton and Konstantinous Triantis address systems engineering cost estimation [Tilton, 1994].

3.10 Summary

The Linear Method provides a way to prepare estimates in a disciplined and repeatable way. It is adequate for a small project or for one iteration of an agile method. It provides a way to estimate quantities that parametric estimation models do not address.

The Linear Method meets the criteria in Table 3-1 and produces the documentation identified in Table 3-5. You can easily update estimates, analyze the effects of uncertainty in estimated values, and identify the factors having the most influence (sensitivity analysis).

You can adapt the Linear Method to your needs. Use the worksheets presented in Sections 3.4 and 3.7 as a starting point. You can capture past experience in checklists and production coefficients.

Chapter 4

Measurement and Estimation

Measurement provides the foundation for estimation. Chapter 3, "A Basic Estimating Process: The Linear Method," explained how to estimate amounts of resources using size and production coefficients, but avoided precise definitions of the quantities. In estimation, sloppy definitions can kill you! The devil is in the details. This chapter covers the essentials of measurement to keep you out of trouble. This chapter defines "good" measurements and describes the process to collect valid data. It also provides simple forms and spreadsheets that you can use to begin collecting data. (Chapter 16, "Collecting Data: Basics," covers data collection and provides improved forms.)

Section 4.1 discusses reasons to measure. Section 4.2 describes measures of size and productivity in some detail. These are extremely important quantities in their own right because they are often misunderstood and misused. In addition, however, Section 4.2 provides a concrete example of the issues that you must confront in defining meaningful metrics. Later sections refer to this example when describing abstract concepts. Section 4.3 defines criteria for "good" measurements. Section 4.4 explains operational definitions. Section 4.5 discusses how you choose what to measure. Section 4.6 recommends sources of additional information. Section 4.7 summarizes the key points of the chapter.

4.1 Reasons to Measure

You use measurements to

- Control your projects.
- Understand your business and your processes.
- Estimate future projects more accurately.

Tom DeMarco said it best: "You cannot control what you cannot measure." Measurements help you assess and report the status of products, processes, and projects. You see where you are now. By collecting a series of measurements over time, you can identify trends and predict where you are going. By analyzing trends and comparing your predictions to known thresholds, you can get early warning of problems. Differences between planned (reference) values and the corresponding actual values (measurements) provide "control signals" to control processes. Reference values and thresholds depend on plans, and on process capability baselines, which are quantitative expectations of achievable performance. Establishing these baselines is an important part of operating a quantitatively managed process (CMMI Level 4). For details, see [Florac, 1999].

Measurements are essential to the scientific method. Science and engineering have made significant strides in the past two centuries by applying the scientific method to obtain a quantitative understanding of physical phenomena and processes. Laboratory experiments measure tangible objects to determine their properties and behavior and to confirm theories. The social sciences have been hampered because they deal with quantities that are difficult to define and measure. It is difficult to apply the scientific method to software development processes for three reasons. First, it is hard to quantify the size of the software product and the progress of the development team. (You can usually measure the cost expended by the team but not the amount of useful work done.) Martin Shepperd observes that software has some "transcendental attributes" such as complexity and quality that are very difficult to define [Shepperd, 1995, page 12]. He points out that software engineers have not really achieved a shared understanding of these attributes and how they are quantitatively measured. Second, if a project is very large in scope (cost and time), it is too expensive and risky to experiment, or to conduct full-scale pilot projects. Often, you have to take whatever data you can get and try to use it as best you can. Third, even if you can collect data under controlled conditions, it is difficult to obtain enough data to obtain a statistically meaningful sample. Large projects take years to complete. Meanwhile, the technologies, methods, and tools change rapidly, often on a time scale of 12 to 18 months. For these reasons, software engineers will probably never achieve a quantitative under-standing of their discipline to the degree obtained by engineering disciplines that can conduct laboratory experiments [Card, 1990, page 118].[1]

Measuring provides insights to improve the performance of processes and products. Both qualitative and quantitative historical data are useful. You can use qualitative experience and "lessons learned" to revise procedures, check-lists, and templates. (One purpose of this book is to share my lessons learned, checklists, templates, and tools.) You can use quantitative data to calibrate cost estimating relations (CERs) and estimating models. You can also use quantita-tive historical data to justify and defend your estimates.

4.2 Measuring Size and Productivity (Direct and Indirect Measures)

Size and productivity play an important role estimating software development effort, but are often misunderstood and misused, leading to serious estimation errors. Because effort dominates software project costs, such errors can be expensive. This section explains possible pitfalls.

Consider this simple cost estimate:

Effort [phr]   = Size [sizel]/Productivity [sizel/phr]
                 = (9,500 sizel)/(1.2 sizel/phr) = 7,917 phr

Cost [$]   = Effort [phr]*Loaded Labor Rate [$/phr]
                 = (7,917 phr) ($50/phr) = $396K

where the square brackets enclose the units of measure. (Section 3.3 explained units of measure.) For generality, the units of software size are "size elements" or "sizels." (Chapters 8, "Estimating Software Size: The Basics," and 9, "Esti-mating Software Size: The Details," discuss software size and define several measures of software size.) Note that you estimate the cost in two distinct steps. First, you use the size and productivity to estimate the amount of resources (effort). Second, you convert the resource amount into cost using the loaded labor rate, which is a production coefficient (resources per unit of product pro-duced). Some people estimate cost in a single step using a "productivity" mea-sured in dollars per line of code. This is very dangerous because the dollar

---

[1] The German Fraunhofer Institute for Experimental Software Engineering (IESE) is working to collect precisely defined data under controlled conditions. In 1998, the University of Maryland established a Fraunhofer Center in the United States. In 2000, the National Science Foundation established the Center for Empirically Based Software Engineering (CeBASE), which involves sev-eral universities and the Fraunhofer Center-Maryland. The goal of these programs is to establish an empirical basis for software engineering. For details, see the references at the end of this chapter.

value includes assumptions about labor rates, which vary from project to project and from year to year. For example, labor rates usually increase every year due to inflation. In the 1970s, software cost about $10 per source line to produce. In the 1990s, software cost several times that amount to produce. Using a dollar value locks your estimating technique into historical data that may be obsolete. Keep estimating separate from costing. Use productivity in sizel/phr and then apply a loaded labor rate expressed as dollars per phr. (Chapter 15, "Calculating Cost and Price: The Basics," discusses labor costs, loading, and cost escalation.)

The productivity and the labor rate are usually correlated, however, because both depend on the developer's skill and experience. Hiring better people increases productivity, reducing the estimated effort, but increases the cost. Usually, however, the gain in productivity is larger than the increase in labor cost so there is a net decrease in the total cost. For example, if $60/phr people have a productivity of 1.6 sizel/phr, the effort is only 5,938 phr and the cost is $356K.

To obtain accurate estimates of software development effort, you need precise definitions of size and productivity. This turns out to be easier said than done. The next subsections explain why.

4.2.1 Measuring Size

Table 4-1 lists some items whose size you might need to estimate or measure. It lists the item, possible size measures, and possible aids to help estimate the value. (Chapter 8 describes some aids for estimating software size.)

Consider the first item in the table, software size. Users perceive size in terms of external characteristics such as screens, reports, and master files. Developers can measure size in terms of the objects that they must design, build, and test: use cases, screens, reports, master files, modules, or tables. (Developers may also measure size in terms of the source lines of code that they write). Operators are interested in the size in bytes because they must purchase or allocate memory and disk resources for the program. Every person has a different way to measure software size.[2]

The definition of a size measure can affect estimated values and the interpretation of historical values. For example, there are many possible definitions of a source line of code, and so a particular software program can actually have many different sizes. (See the box "What Is a Line of Code?") People often

---

[2] This is like the parable about several blind people who have never seen an elephant but are asked to describe one. Each person feels a part of the elephant and then describes what the elephant is like. One person feels the tail, and says that it is like a rope. Another feels the leg, and states that it is like a tree. A third feels the trunk, and reports that it is like a snake. There are many possible views of a system.

quote values without stating the underlying definitions, leading to problems. For example, Section 4.2.2 shows how the size definition affects the calculated productivity value.

Table 4-1 *Possible-Sized Items*

Item	Size Measures	Possible Aids
Software	Number of use cases, screens, reports, business rules, files, tables; number of modules, function points, lines of code, bytes	Operational concept, user stories, product design (architecture, hierarchy)
Database	Number of distinct record types, number of distinct field types comprising each record type, field length, number of fields of a given type in each record type, number of instances of each record type	Information model or entity relation diagram
Document	Number of pages (text, figures, tables), number of words, number of copies required	Document list, plus description of each document (scope, audience)
User training	Contact hours, number of students, number of locations, class size, number of sessions taught	Course list plus descriptions (learning objectives, audience)
Hardware components	Counts, physical dimensions	Bill of materials, drawing, blueprints
Requirements	Number of "shall" verbs, features, change requests, problem reports	Specifications, interviews, site survey
Test cases	Number of features, operating modes, events	Requirements list, state transition diagrams, event trace diagrams, use cases, scenarios

---

What Is a Line of Code?

Definitions for a line of code vary widely. Thus, a particular program can have many different sizes:

- 1,000 PSLOC (physical lines)

- 850 NCSL (Noncomment [physical] source lines)

- 700 LSLOC (Logical source lines of code [statements])

Physical lines measure the number of end-of-line delimiters in the text file. (Note that this number includes blank lines added to improve readability.) But, you might exclude comments, giving the second value. You could count logical statements in the particular programming language by counting statement delimiters, giving logical source lines of code. Noncomment source lines is defined as all physical lines that are not comment lines.[3] Depending on the particular programming language, logical statements or constructs may extend over several physical lines, and/or multiple logical statements can be on a single physical line. Thus, the number of logical statements may be greater than or less than the number of physical source lines. Most languages allow comments to appear on the same physical line as a logical statement. Should these lines be counted as both logical statements and comments or not? Finally, the size (in any of the three measures) depends on the developers' design and coding style. You must consider these questions when defining your size measure. (Section 9.8 gives a detailed definition.)

Table 4-1 shows a similar difference of perspectives for measuring database size, documents, and training courses. The first two size measures for a database (record types and field types) relate to the number of unique data elements that the engineer must design and implement. Use them if you want to estimate the development effort. The remaining database size measures relate to the number of instances of that record that will be created and stored when the system is operating. Use them if you want to estimate the amount of effort to enter records, or the amount of disk storage needed. For documents, the number of original pages of manuscript determines the author's effort. (See the box "Measuring Document Size.") The number of copies of a particular document determines printing and distribution costs. For training courses, the number and duration (contact-hours) primarily determine the development effort. The course duration, number of students, and number of sessions to be taught determine the delivery costs.

---

[3] This definition still includes blank lines in the count.

Measuring Document Size

To estimate the effort to create and edit documents, you can measure document size in words, lines, bytes, or pages of text. Pages of text is not a good measure because the amount of information contained on the page (and thus the amount of effort taken to write that information) depends on the font size, the page margins, and the line spacing. Still, text pages is often used. You should distinguish between text pages, tables, and figures because each has a different characteristic productivity.

An alternative approach is to define a conversion factor to obtain "equivalent pages of text." For example, one table may equal 5 text pages, one figure may equal 7 text pages, and one illustration or drawing may equal 12 text pages. This approach gives a single size measure for documents that you can use to compute productivity. Note that this size is larger than the actual number of pages in the document. (Section 8.4 describes the difference between delivered size and "processed" size.)

Generalizing from these examples, the key points are as follows:

- There are several possible size measures for any particular object.
- The choice of a particular definition depends on how you intend to use the (measured or estimated) value.

Thus, there is no single "correct" measure of software size, whatever units of measure you choose. Future examples in this chapter measure size in "size units," denoted by "sizel." You can substitute your particular choice. (Software size is so important for estimators that two chapters of this book address it. Chapter 8 describes a sizing process, and how to account for growth and volatility. Chapter 9 defines several measures of software size and provides advice on how to estimate size values.)

4.2.2 Measuring Productivity

Productivity is defined as the amount of product produced divided by the resources expended. This definition seems simple and straightforward. But how do you determine the productivity value for a team or for an organization? You cannot measure productivity directly. Instead, you directly measure size, S, and effort, E, and then divide them. (Productivity is measured indirectly.) Definitions become very important in obtaining the correct values. Different definitions can yield productivity values that differ by factors of 10 or more. The following paragraphs explain how this can happen.

You have already seen that there are several possible definitions for the "size" unit (logical statements, physical lines with comments, and physical lines without comments). Using the values of 1,000; 850; and 700 from the example in the box "What Is a Line of Code?" in the preceding section, choosing the wrong definition for lines of code can give errors as large as 43% (= [1,000 − 700]/700).

4.2.3 Measuring Effort

Always measure effort in person-hours, not person-months, because the number of person-hours in a person-month varies by organization (and sometimes within different departments of the same organization). The amount of vacation and sick leave included in the organization's benefit plan affects the number of person-hours in a person-month. For example, assume that you receive historical productivity data measured in sizel per person-month (PM). Suppose that this data is based on 160 phr/PM, but you incorrectly assume that it was 154 phr/PM. If so, your estimated effort will be low by 4% (= 6/154). Measuring productivity in sizel/phr avoids this particular problem.

Agreeing on the units of measure is not sufficient to define what the effort value means. Engineers distinguish software development activities such as analyzing, designing, coding, and testing, arranging these activities into a project life cycle having a sequence of phases. The early phases gather and analyze information about user needs, product requirements, and alternative designs. Later phases design, build, and test the product. These engineering activities actually overlap to some degree during the project life cycle. Support activities include project management, configuration management, and quality assurance, and occur throughout a project.

The activities included affect the measured effort, which affects the calculated productivity. Does the effort include the support activities or not? In addition, corporate accounting data may not show all the effort expended for the activities. For example, unpaid overtime is often not reported. This means that the reported effort will be low, the productivity will be too high, and every future job will be underestimated. This dooms the staff to similar amounts of overtime on the next project! The lesson: measure and report all hours worked, paid and unpaid.

The phases included in the measured effort also affect the apparent productivity as shown in Figure 4-1. This chart shows three quantities plotted versus time. The x-axis shows time, which increases toward the right. This example uses a waterfall life cycle, defined in Chapter 10, "Production Processes (Project Life Cycles)." The triangles at the bottom indicate the milestones:

SOP: Start of project (The project is authorized and receives resources.)

SRR: Software requirements review (Requirements baselined. Plans updated.)

PDR: Product design review (Architecture and test strategy completed.)

UTC: Unit test complete (All code is completely written.)

IOC: Initial operational capability (Product is delivered.)

The top plot shows the cumulative effort expended by the staff versus time. I assume constant staffing to keep the example simple. Thus, the cumulative effort increases linearly with time. The center plot shows the cumulative amount of completed code reported versus time. Early in the project, no software is produced because the engineers are analyzing requirements and choosing the architecture. During the product design phase, which ends with the product design review (PDR), the life cycle architecture is defined so some interface code and service routines can be built. Most of the code, however, is developed after the product design review. Code production ideally stops at the unit test complete (UTC) milestone when the programmers complete unit testing.[4] In practice, however, a small amount of code is added after UTC because testing usually discloses some missing features.

The bottom plot shows the apparent productivity versus time, computed as the cumulative size divided by the cumulative effort at the corresponding time. If you only measure from the start of the project until PDR, the apparent productivity is low. Note that the apparent productivity peaks at UTC and then declines. The reason is that the team is producing tiny amounts of additional code after UTC, but is expending large amounts of effort to integrate, test, and correct the product. This causes the denominator to increase, decreasing the apparent productivity.

Many other factors associated with the product, process, and project (which include personnel) also influence the productivity for "knowledge-intensive" work. Chapter 13, "Parametric Models," discusses how to quantify the effects of such factors.

Many managers use productivity values to estimate effort and decide how many programmers to assign to a project. As you have just seen, just using a particular value without understanding it can be very dangerous. Capers Jones even mentions the "paradox" of using lines of code as productivity indicators [Jones, 1986]. He notes that high-level programming languages enable programmers to produce a given amount of product functionality using fewer lines of source code than when they use a low-level programming language. Thus, apparent productivity expressed in lines per person-hours appears to decrease as the level of the programming language increases. For an extensive discussion of programming productivity, see [Jones, 1986].

---

[4] On small projects, developers retain custody of their code after the UTC milestone, and actively participate in integration and testing. On large projects, programmers relinquish control of their code. Then an independent team integrates and tests the code. The code is under formal configuration control. Developers must check out their code modules to repair problems found by the testers.

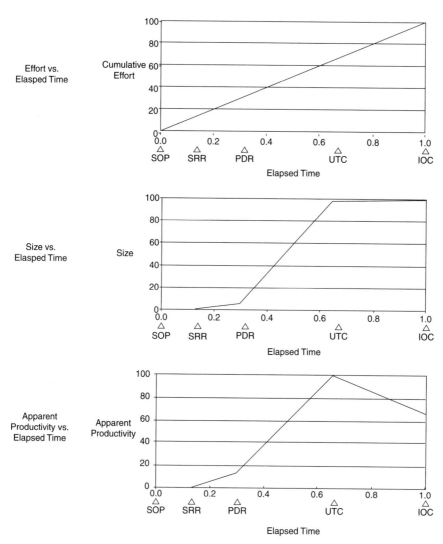

Figure 4-1 *Apparent productivity varies*

There is one last potential problem. Suppose that you have carefully defined all the units of measure, the types of code included in the product, and the project's phases and activities, and that you have used these to collect accurate historical data for several projects. If you want to use this data to estimate a new project, you must ensure that the new project will use the same definitions.[5] The same applies if you want to compare your data with data from

---

[5] You can adjust the historical data to compensate for some of the differences. See Sections 5.2 and 12.1.

another project. You need to be consistent. Comparing historical data from different organizations requires extreme care because organizations may use different definitions for size, and include different activities in the reported effort. (See the discussion of direct and indirect charges in Chapter 15.)

Table 4-2 gives a checklist to help you review productivity data.

Table 4-2 *Checklist to Review Productivity Data*

1. What types of software are included in the reported size?
2. What is the definition of size?
3. What programming language was used?
4. What project life cycle was used?
5. What phases of the life cycle model are covered by the reported effort?
6. What activities of the life cycle model are covered by the reported effort?
7. How many person-hours are in a person-month?
8. Does the reported effort include uncompensated overtime?
9. How formal was the development process?
10. For *all* of the above questions, did each project use the *same* definition, value, life cycle, formality, etc.?

4.3 Criteria for "Good" Measures

Table 4-3 lists five criteria for "good" measures. Adequate precision means that the measured value is recorded to a level of detail that is consistent with the accuracy that is achievable and that is needed by the stakeholder. (This is also called resolution or granularity.) Decision makers need adequate resolution to draw conclusions and observe trends. (See the next paragraph on forecasting.) For example, a measure of project status with only two possible values—"Doing Fine" and "Has Failed"—lacks enough resolution to be useful. Dependable means that all the values in a set of samples are measured consistently. (Validity and consistency mean that you can trust the data values.) Dependability also means that any operations you perform on the measured values will produce correct results.[6] Timely means that the stakeholder receives the data soon enough to make decisions affecting the product, project, or process.

---

[6] This refers to measurements scales and the allowed transformations associated with each. See Appendix B, "Measurement Theory and Statistics."

For example, suppose the metrics analyst tells the project manager in December that "Your March data shows that your project is headed for trouble." The manager responds, "Yes, it was canceled last August." Affordable relates to the funnel curve in Chapter 1, "Introduction." You can get an accurate estimate of a project's total cost if you perform the entire project as part of the estimation process, but this is neither affordable nor timely. If a measure satisfies these criteria it will be useful and valuable to a stakeholder.

To use metrics for control, they must meet the first six criteria in Table 4-3, and must also meet two additional criteria: predictability and controllability. Predictability means that you must be able to predict (or forecast) quantities of interest at future times using the measured values to some acceptable level of accuracy.[7] This might be as simple as extrapolating a trendline. On the other hand, it may involve complicated mathematical and statistical models.

Table 4-3 *Criteria for Good Metrics*

Criteria	Definition
Relevance	Represents the characteristic of interest.
Accuracy	Faithfully represents the amount or degree of that characteristic.
Adequate Precision	The level of detail needed by user is achievable.
Dependable	Values are measured consistently. Mathematical operations "work" as expected.
Timely	User receives values in time to act on them.
Affordable	The value of the information exceeds the cost of obtaining it.
Predictability	Adequately accurate forecasts of future values are possible.
Controllability	Actions exist that can influence the measured value.

---

[7] Forecasting and estimating are very similar. I distinguish them as follows. Forecasting involves predicting future values of a measure based on observed trends. Estimating involves predicting values from a static population of possible values. The population represents uncertainty due to the influences of various factors. If a *future* project belongs to the same population, however, you can use statistical techniques to estimate values for that project.

Controllability means that control actions performed by managers and engineers influence the characteristic of interest. It does little good to collect measures of things that you cannot control. (So why do you measure the weather I wonder? The answer is that weather forecasts help us to plan our activities to avoid potential risks.)

To control a process you must determine how "good" the measured object (product, project, or process) is doing at some particular time. To do this, you must compare an observed value to some "target value." The target value comes from customer requirements, project plans and estimates, or capability baselines based on historical data obtained for similar objects. The target value may be an upper or a lower bound. The observed value (at the specified time) may be measured, forecasted, or even estimated.

4.4 Operational Definitions

> "Any measurement is the result of applying a procedure. An operational definition puts communicable meaning into a concept."
> —W. Edwards Deming

The definition of a metric (or measure) must cover assumptions, scope, units of measure, and the conditions of measurement. The conditions are important to ensure that different people will obtain the same measured value for a quantity (within the error inherent in the particular measurement technique). Operational definitions, first described by W. Edwards Deming, focus on how the measurement is actually collected [Deming, 1986]. The concept says that if you know how the value was collected, then you know what the measured value means.[8] Operational definitions also ensure consistency and repeatability because they contain the rules for collecting and reducing the data values. The Software Engineering Institute has provided operational definitions for effort, time, defects, and size. See note N04, "Software Engineering Institute Measurement Reports."

Figure 4-2 illustrates a template to define a measure of "problems" reported for a software product. This particular example is adapted from Figure 4-1 in [Florac, 1992]. (I simplified his example by removing the criteria relating to value and array counts.) The two-page checklist shows various characteristics of a problem. For each characteristic, you indicate whether that characteristic is

---

[8] This is not totally true, as the preceding discussion of measurement theory explains. The empirical relations determine the scale type [Fenton, 1996, page 53].

Included or Excluded in the count of a problem. The first page shows many possible activities that could find and report a problem. As shown by the checkmarks, problems are only counted if they arise from software development activities. This particular definition thus excludes any problems reported after the product enters operational service. (Whether this suits your analysis needs or not, the checkmarks in the list clearly convey what types of problems are included in the count.) The Finding Mode, at the bottom of the first page, indicates that problems found by static analysis or by dynamic testing will be included. Any problem report that lacks complete information (such as the Finding Mode) is excluded from the count.

The second page has fields that characterize the type of problem. Criticality relates to the effect of the problem on the safety and performance of the system in operational service. Urgency deals with how important it is to fix the problem quickly. During testing, certain problems "crash" the system and prevent the testers from exercising any other tests. Developers must correct such problems immediately to allow testing to continue. If a problem report fails to provide a value for criticality or urgency, then it is excluded from the count.

The problem count includes both open and closed problem reports. It also includes the type of problem. Typically, this is not determined until an analyst has reviewed the problem and determined the cause of the error. The checkmarks in the Included column show that the focus is on problems in engineering documents, code, or user documents. Errors related to test cases or other causes are excluded. Also, problems caused by hardware, operating system software, user mistakes, and requests for new features are all excluded from the count. Clearly, the focus of this particular definition is on software-related problems arising during development. If a problem report lacks information or cannot be reproduced, then it is excluded from the count. Finally, duplicate problems are excluded. The definition shown in this figure essentially defines a "validated unique software problem report" for any work product that is directly related to the software.

For other types of measure, you may need to specify the required accuracy (and so the precision or number of significant digits). This might depend on the duration of the measurement. For example, if you are measuring the average arrival rate of transactions at a server, you need to specify which transactions are counted and how long to count. You must also specify other conditions affecting the measurement, including when to count (day of week, and time of day), the system configuration, the number of users, and the operational workload. (Such issues are important for measuring product performance.) You may also need to specify the measuring instrument, such as a particular code counting tool. To count network traffic, you might specify a particular model of network analyzer, how it is connected, and its configuration (operating modes and control settings).

Problem Count Definition Checklist		
Software Product ID [Example V1 R1]		
Definition Identifier: [Problem Count A]	Definition Date [01/01/05]	
Attributes/Values		
Finding Activity	**Include**	**Exclude**
Inspections of:		
Operational Concept	✔	
Requirements	✔	
Product Design	✔	
Detailed Design	✔	
Code	✔	
User Documentation	✔	
Test Procedures	✔	
Formal Reviews of:		
Operational Concept	✔	
Project Plans	✔	
Requirements	✔	
Product Design	✔	
Detailed Design	✔	
Test Plans	✔	
Test Results		
Module or Class	✔	
Component	✔	
Integration Test	✔	
System Test	✔	
Field Test	✔	
Formal Acceptance Test	✔	
Independent Verification and Validation	✔	
Customer Support		
Production/Deployment		✔
Installation		✔
Operation		✔
Undetermined		
Value not Identified		✔
Finding Mode	**Include**	**Exclude**
Static (Non-Operational)	✔	
Dynamic (Operational)	✔	
Value not Identified		✔
Criticality	**Include**	**Exclude**
1st Level (Catastrophic)	✔	
2nd Level (Key Function Fails, No Workaround)	✔	
3rd Level (Key Function Fails, Have Workaround)	✔	
4th Level (Minor Function Fails)	✔	
5th Level (Cosmetic)	✔	
Value Not Identified		✔
Urgency	**Include**	**Exclude**
1st (Immediate Action Required)	✔	
2nd (Next Scheduled Build)	✔	
3rd (Before Final Delivery)	✔	
Value Not Identified		✔

(continues)

Problem Status	Include	Exclude
Open	✔	
Recognized		
Evaluated		
Resolved		
Closed	✔	
Problem Type	**Include**	**Exclude**
Software Defect		
Requirements Defect	✔	
Design Defect	✔	
Code Defect	✔	
User Document Defect	✔	
Test Case Defect		✔
Other Work Product Defect		✔
Other Problems		
Hardware Problem		✔
Operating System Problem		✔
User Mistake		✔
New Requirement/Enhancement		✔
Undetermined		
Not Repeatable/Cause Unknown		✔
Value Not Identified		✔
Uniqueness	**Include**	**Exclude**
Original	✔	
Duplicate		✔
Value Not Identified		✔

*Adapted from Figure 4-1 in [Florac, 1992]

Figure 4-2 *Example problem count definition checklist*

If the measure is derived (indirect), you must also specify the rules for computing it from directly measured (fundamental) quantities. For example, productivity equals size (in some unit of measure) divided by effort (in some unit of measure). Your definition for effort must indicate which phases and activities are included. For a checklist, see [Goethert, 1992]. Effort is the hardest quantity to capture. If you do not collect uncompensated overtime, the productivity value will be too high. A standardized work breakdown schedule (WBS; defined in Chapters 11, "Bottom-Up Estimating and Scheduling," and 20, "Crafting a WBS") provides a good template to collect effort and cost data consistently. (Chapter 22, "Collecting Data: Details," explains how to use the WBS to collect such data.)

4.5 Choosing Useful Measures

No single set of measures will meet the needs of every organization. Thus, you should select measures appropriate for your organization's products and production processes. Your choice of measures will also change over time as you learn. You will identify new measures and will discard others. (After you have learned a lesson and drawn the conclusion, you do not need to collect additional evidence.)

The problem is that there are many stakeholders involved in any project, and each wants certain measurement data. Figure 4-3 identifies potential stakeholders and the data that each needs. At the lowest, most detailed level, software engineers, administrative assistants, testers, and other support personnel collect the raw data. Managers and administrators summarize the data, often on a weekly, monthly, or quarterly basis, and pass it to higher levels in the management hierarchy (e.g., to the program manager and to more senior managers). The pyramid shape shows that the amount of data examined at each level decreases as you ascend the hierarchy. The day-to-day practitioners want details. Upper managers want monthly summaries. Senior managers may receive quarterly summaries, and are especially interested in alerts of adverse trends and emerging problems.

With so many individuals requiring different kinds of data, it could become very expensive to collect everything that is requested. The key is to collect only data that is really needed. Victor Basili and David Weiss defined a way to do this called the Goal-Question-Metric (GQM) Method [Basili, 1984].[9] Figure 4-4 illustrates their concept. Suppose that your organizational goal is to produce products at a low cost. You then identify one or more questions whose answers will determine whether you have achieved this particular goal. For this example, you might want to know the productivity of your production process. To answer each question, you must identify specific measures (metrics) that you must define, collect, and analyze. In this particular example, you would need to collect size and effort in order to compute the productivity. (Size and effort are directly measured. The productivity is calculated from the measured values and so is an indirect measurement.) For another example, see the box "Applying GQM to Estimation Accuracy."

---

[9] The software engineering community often uses "metric" to refer to a measured quantity, a measure. A measurement is the value of that quantity.

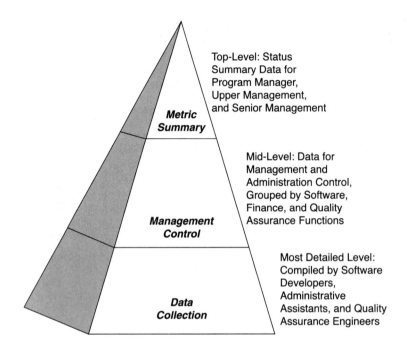

Figure 4-3 *Metrics hierarchy*

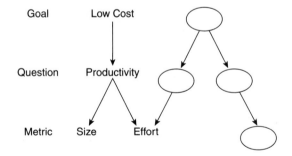

Figure 4-4 *The three levels of the GQM Method*

Applying GQM to Estimation Accuracy

Martin Shepperd discusses the GQM Method in [Shepperd, 1995]. On page 152, he discusses how to establish the current accuracy of project effort estimates. To determine whether this goal has been achieved, you must answer three questions:

Q1:		**How accurate are typical estimates at present?**
	M1:	Estimated project effort
	M2:	Actual project effort
Q2:		**Are estimates more accurate for new development or for maintenance projects?**
	M1:	Estimated project effort
	M2:	Actual project effort
	M3:	Project type (new or maintenance)
Q3:		**How does project manager experience influence estimation accuracy?**
	M1:	Estimated project effort
	M2:	Actual project effort
	M4:	Number of years as a project manager

For each question, you must collect either two or three metrics. Some metrics are used to answer more than one question. For example, metric M1, the estimated project effort, and metric M2, the actual project effort, are used in answering all three questions.

4.6 Recommended Reading

ISO/IEC Standard 15939:2001, "Software Measurement Standard," defines a measurement information model and a measurement process model. The Practical Software Measurement handbook, defined by the U.S. Department of Defense, explains how to implement ISO/IEC 15939. Practical software measurement is based on actual experience, and so provides a good source of proven techniques and tools. Practical Software Measurement (PSM) assumes that successful measurement requires two things. First, you must identify the information needs of the managers and decision makers. Second, you need a structured and repeatable process for performing measurements, analyzing the data, and reporting the results. For more information, see note N02, "Practical Software Measurement." The best reference on Practical Software Measurement is [McGarry, 2002].

The Software Engineering Institute used concepts from ISO/IEC 15939 and PSM to define the measurement and analysis process area of the integrated capability maturity model (CMMI). Note N03, "SEI CMMI Measurement and Analysis," identifies requirements for measurement processes. William Florac and Anita Carleton identify possible software-related measures, and discuss selecting, collecting, and analyzing metrics in [Florac, 1999]. The Software Engineering Institute has several useful reports on software measurement, and workers there applied operational definitions to software in the early 1990s. For details, see note N04, "SEI Measurement Reports." Also see Section 2.2 in the book by William Florac and Anita Carleton [Florac, 1999], especially Sections 2.2.3 and 2.2.4. Donald McAndrews explains how to establish a software measurement process in [McAndrews, 1993].

Robert Grady and Deborah Caswell provide useful checklists and guidance on implementing a practical metrics program [Grady, 1987]. Robert Grady also has a later book on the subject [Grady, 1992].

Rini van Solingen and Egon Berghout provide a detailed guide for applying the GQM method [van Solingen, 1999]. They also provide four detailed case studies that are directly applicable to software development projects. These case studies address the measurement of reliability, reviews and inspections, effort, and interruptions.[10] Robert Grady also provides examples of the GQM method for maximizing customer satisfaction, minimizing engineering effort and schedule, and minimizing defects [Grady, 1992]. [Park, 1996] addresses goal-driven measurement, and is especially recommended.

The Joint Industry/Government Parametric Estimating Handbook, sponsored by the U.S. Department of Defense, is an excellent handbook that addresses data collection and analysis, as well as other estimating topics [ISPA, 1999].

IEEE Standard 1045 provides an excellent discussion of various software and document size measures [IEEE Std 1045, 1992].

---

[10] Interruptions break the developer's flow of thought and so reduce productivity and introduce errors. For more on this effect, see "Peopleware" [DeMarco, 1999].

4.7 Summary

Measurements are important to determine how a project is proceeding and to collect historical data needed to estimate future projects. This data can also help the organization improve its processes. Precise, consistent definitions are essential for all quantities that you measure and estimate. Standard definitions make meaningful communication possible. The particular definition of measure of some quantity depends on your goals and objectives, measurement scales, the processes for collecting and analyzing data, and affordability. The definition of a metric (or measure) must cover assumptions, scope, units of measure, and the conditions of measurement. The conditions are important to ensure that different people will obtain the same measured value for a quantity (within the error inherent in the particular measurement technique).

The examples of size and productivity show how estimation and measurement are closely linked. You can measure a quantity, such as size, in different ways. Your choice of the quantity to measure (and the accuracy and frequency of reporting) depends on the needs of the various stakeholders and on your intended use of the measurement. You must balance the benefit gained from measurements against the costs of obtaining the measurements.

Many organizations use "operational definitions" that focus on how the measurement is actually collected. If you know how the value was collected, you know what the measured value means. Operational definitions also ensure consistency and repeatability because they contain the rules for collecting and reducing the data values.

There are many stakeholders involved in any project, and each wants certain measurement data. There are a potentially large number of possible measures. However, it costs money to define, collect, store, analyze, and report measurement data. To reduce costs, you can use the Goal-Question Metric (GQM) Method to identify why each measurement is needed. (Some measurements can be used to answer multiple questions.)

Templates and forms can help you implement a cost-effective and useful metrics program to support estimating and tracking. Forms and procedures structure the collection process, ensuring that complete and consistent data is collected for every project. Automation also promotes consistency, reduces collection costs, and increases accuracy (by immediately detecting data entry errors).

This chapter provides the information you need to start measuring. This supports the CMMI's Measurement and Analysis Process area, which is Level 2 in the staged representation. Later chapters use measurement data for the following:

- Tracking the characteristics of projects, products, and processes
- Updating estimates
- Calibrating, updating, or building estimation models

Without data you are just another person with an opinion!

Chapter 5

Estimating Techniques

This chapter describes simple techniques that you can use to estimate a wide range of quantities for projects, products, and processes. You can implement these using paper forms, templates, or spreadsheets. These techniques are basic building blocks that you can use to create estimating models, methods, and processes. After reading this chapter, you can immediately start using these techniques to start producing better estimates. The following chapters show you how to apply these to estimate specific quantities such as product size and project effort.

Section 5.1 describes the Delphi technique. Sections 5.2 through 5.6 describe various techniques. The sections also provide examples showing the use of each technique. The CD-ROM contains the spreadsheets for each example. Section 5.7 gives recommended reading, and Section 5.8 provides a summary.

5.1 Expert Judgment: The Delphi Technique

Expert judgment techniques tend to be informal and qualitative in nature, even though they often produce quantitative results. The main source of information is the estimator's memory of past projects, products, or processes. Although the experts may consult historical records to refresh their memories, these techniques do not use historical data in an organized way, even though they may perform quantitative calculations.

The difficulty with expert judgment methods is that the results are no better than the participants involved. Every individual has incomplete recall and may even have biases. For example, a developer may recall that she took six calendar-months to write the code for a particular subsystem, but may not recall that she worked an average of 50 hours per week during this six-month period. (For example, the hours worked per week are usually high just before the "gold master" disk is cut for a shrink-wrapped product, raising the average.) If so, this represents an underestimate of 25% (= 10/40). Hopefully, the experts chosen to estimate particular quantities are experienced and have good memories of relevant products, projects, or processes.

Expert judgment techniques do have some advantages, however. Experts are often able to assess whether the new object is representative of similar objects developed in the past. They are also good at identifying exceptional circumstances, major differences, and interactions between the projects, tasks, and system components. Biases can arise if there are external influences exerted on the estimator. See the box "Guesstimating Techniques."

Guesstimating Techniques

Barry Boehm describes two "guessestimating" techniques: Price-to-Win and Parkinsonian estimation [Boehm, 1981, pages 336-337]. In the Price-to-Win technique, the estimate is based solely on external influences such as the customer's desired price or the performance capabilities promised by a hardware vendor. Generally, the estimator produces an estimate without regard to any real facts related to the characteristics of the product, project, or process. For example, if the bidder has information about the price that the customer is prepared to pay, then the bidder submits a bid value slightly less than the desired price. This often wins the bid. Unfortunately, the price has no correlation to the products and services that must be delivered, often leading to a cost overrun for the project. Similarly, the engineers (or customers) may specify the capacity of computer hardware based on catalog descriptions, instead of on an analysis of the system's resource usage or consideration of current technology.

Parkinsonian estimation is based on C. Northcote Parkinson's famous law (1955) that states "work expands to fill the time available for its completion" [Parkinson, 1957]. Parkinsonian estimation is similar to Price-to-Win in that an external expectation or constraint exerts a tremendous influence on the value produced by the estimator. For example, suppose that a development team has five people and their manager wants to obtain enough work to keep the team employed for the next year. Thus, the manager estimates the effort for the new project as five person-years. This approach can either overestimate or underestimate the required effort. In the case of an overestimate, the customer pays too much. In the case of an underestimate, the developer will lose money.

The Delphi technique is an organized way to help a group of informed experts achieve a consensus on an estimated value. The original technique arose from work done at the RAND Corporation in the late 1950s [Helmer, 1959] and matured in the following decade [Dalkey, 1963]. It is an iterative process consisting of a series of rounds. In each round, every expert in the group anonymously and independently estimates the value of an item. No person knows the values provided by other persons. This removes peer pressure and political bias. At the end of each round, the estimators receive feedback based on all of the estimated values for that round. The feedback tends to filter out extreme opinions and values, leading to convergence on the value.

You can use the Delphi technique to estimate many kinds of quantities such as the sizes of software modules, the amount of effort required to perform a task, or the value for a model's input parameters. Model developers sometimes use the Delphi technique to estimate the values of effort multipliers used in parametric models before any empirical data is available. (Boehm and his colleagues describe an interesting approach to combine expert judgment data and empirical data using a Bayesian algorithm in Chapter 4 of [Boehm, 2000].)

You implement the Delphi technique as follows: Select a group of knowledgeable experts and provide them with information relevant to the quantity to be estimated such as descriptions of software modules or project tasks. It is important to provide clear descriptions of the "nature and scope" of each item to be estimated. For example, you might provide a short description of the product architecture (Section 7.6) or the WBS dictionary (Sections 11.1 and 11.2).

Each expert in the group produces a series of estimated values for a particular quantity. Figure 5-1 shows a form to submit estimated values for a set of items such as modules or tasks. The left column lists the items to be estimated. The center column contains the estimated value for each item. (You could alternately ask for multiple values [e.g., lowest, most likely, and highest]. See Section 5.3.) The last column allows the estimator to submit written notes explaining his/her estimating rationale for the value recorded.

Project Name:	Sample	
Quantity:	Module Size	
Units of Measure:	Use Case Points	
Round #:	2	
Estimated By:		
Date:		
Item Name	**Estimated Value**	**Notes and Comments**
First Item		
Second Item		

Figure 5-1 *Delphi form for individual estimator*

A Facilitator summarizes the set of estimates received from all of the estimators for the round. Figure 5-2 illustrates a typical tabular summary suitable for estimates of several items. The left column lists the items. The next four columns summarize the estimated values. This particular table shows the smallest value and the largest value reported by the estimators, as well as the average and the standard deviation. (You could also show the median, mode, or other statistics. The median is perhaps better than the average because it is less sensitive to extreme values. The utility of various statistical measures depends on the number of estimators. See Appendix B, "Measurement Theory and Statistics.") The rightmost column references any notes or remarks that the Facilitator wants to share with the estimators. For example, the Facilitator could summarize comments or rationale provided by the various estimators. You can use spreadsheets to automate some of the data collection and summarization. (Barry Boehm shows a graphical summary suitable for displaying values for a single quantity in Figure 22-1 of [Boehm, 1981].)

The Facilitator then provides the summary data to the estimators prior to the start of the next estimation round. Each expert then independently estimates a new set of values. The feedback causes the estimated values to converge as the iteration continues. The values of a particular quantity typically stabilize in three or four iterations. There may still be some variation in the values.[1]

---

[1] To monitor convergence you could plot the mean value with error bars based on the standard deviation for each round. This becomes difficult if there are many items being estimated. If, however, you are estimating values of the same quantity for all the items, then you can total the data, and take the square root of the sum of the variances to get the standard deviation for the sum. Then plot this value. For example, you could plot the total size of the software versus iteration to see whether convergence is occurring. The plot in Figure 17-6 provides an example for estimated size versus time.

Project Name:	Sample					
Quantity:	Module Size					
Units of Measure:	Use Case Points					
Round #:	2				**Summary of the Round**	
# of Estimators:	4					
Item Name	**Min Value**	**Max Value**	**Mean**	**Std Dev**	**Coef Var**	**Summary Notes and Comments**
First Item	11	20	14	4.1	0.29	A Comment
Second Item	8	23	17	7.0	0.41	0

Figure 5-2 *Summary of estimation round*

There are two versions of the Delphi technique, distinguished by the type of feedback provided. In both versions, the Facilitator prepares summaries such as the one shown in Figure 5-2. The estimators remain anonymous. In Narrow-Band Delphi, the estimators never meet face to face. Instead they only receive copies of the summary for each estimation round. In Wide-Band Delphi, the Facilitator provides the summary information, and then the estimators meet face to face to discuss the results and their rationale. In both versions, the estimators individually estimate values for the next round in private. Narrow-Band Delphi is useful when the estimators are geographically dispersed. The Facilitator can use electronic mail or facsimile transmission to exchange data with the estimators. Wide-Band Delphi requires the estimators to be collocated (or to have access to a video or audio teleconferencing capability). On proposals, I have used a single-pass Wide-Band Delphi technique. I provide a description of all the items (e.g., software modules) to the estimators who then fill out the estimation form. Then we all meet face to face, review the summary data, and proceed down the list, item by item, arguing and coming to a consensus on the spot.

The Delphi technique provides an important benefit: It sharpens the definitions of the "nature and scope" of the items being estimated. For example, in estimating the size of software modules, estimators may clarify where the error handling logic resides (some in each module or all in one module).[2] The team revises the module descriptions appropriately, and the estimators use these for the next round. *One benefit of good estimating techniques is improved understanding of the product, processes, and project.*

---

[2] This is an architectural decision.

5.2 Additive and Multiplicative Analogies

Quantitative analogy techniques are a simple way to adjust historical values. You can use these when you have only a single historical data point. (Section 5.5 describes an analogy technique that uses multiple values.)

In analogy estimation, estimators or experts crudely quantify "how much different" the value of the new object is relative to the value of a known object. You can express the differences as percentages or as actual amounts (measured in some units). For example, the estimator states "Based on my experience, I think that this module is 30% larger than the similar module that we developed last year." To estimate the differences, experts can use the Delphi technique (narrow- or wide-band), past experience, or some other technique. You can apply the estimated differences additively or multiplicatively to the known reference point. You can use the additive technique with ordinal, ratio, or absolute measurement scales. You can use the multiplicative technique (also called ratio scaling) for values represented by the ratio or absolute measurement scales.

Although simple, these two quantitative analogy techniques are an improvement over the basic Delphi technique. Using the Delphi technique, the estimators provide only one number for the quantity with little or no supporting details.[3] Using the quantitative analogy techniques, the estimators provide estimates for multiple subquantities, often with supporting rationale, and that contribute to or influence the quantity of interest. You then combine these values to produce the estimated value for the quantity. Dividing the estimate in this way makes the various contributors and influences visible and so open to discussion and refinement. Also, the resulting value may be more accurate because the errors in the estimated values of the subquantities may tend to cancel one another out.

In terms of structuring the estimation process, quantitative analogy techniques lie between the pure Delphi technique and more quantitative methods such as algorithmic analogy estimation (Section 5.6) and the analytic hierarchy process (Section 27.4). Although simple, quantitative analogy techniques provide a way to state and crudely quantify assumptions and to investigate the uncertainty in the estimated value.

5.2.1 Additive Analogy

Barry Boehm describes "analogy estimation" in Section 22.3 of [Boehm, 1981]. This is based on an estimating technique described by Ray Wolverton that tries to identify similarities and differences between projects [Wolverton, 1974]. The

---

[3] A refinement is to agree on a *range* of values. You can also use the PERT technique, described in Section 5.3, in conjunction with the Delphi technique.

estimator adds or subtracts small amounts from a known (historical) value to calculate the estimated value for the new object. Randall Jensen describes a similar technique called "relative comparison" [Jensen, 1991].

To illustrate the additive analogy technique, assume that you know that the size of a previously completed software product is 230 size elements ("sizels"). Engineers have analyzed the requirements for a new product and determined that there will be more user display screens, increasing the amount of code required by 15%. In addition, they now plan to use a commercial relational database management system (RDBMS) and think that this will reduce the amount of code by 40%. These percentages are expressed with respect to the size of the reference object. This gives the absolute amounts, measured in sizels:

Reference size	230.0	
Additional displays	34.5	(= 230*0.15)
Less data management	−92.0	(= 230*0.4)
Estimated size	172.5 sizel	

(I show four digits of precision only to help you trace the calculations. The data only justifies two digits.)

You can also use the additive analogy technique if the engineers provide estimates of the estimated lines of code added and deleted instead of estimated percentages of the reference size. For this example, suppose they say: "Add 35 sizel for the displays" and "Subtract 92 sizel for the database." The estimated size is then 175 sizel (= 230 + 35 – 90). (This minor difference is due only to the truncation used to obtain the values of 35 and 92.)

5.2.2 Multiplicative Analogy (Ratio Scaling)

Ratio (or multiplicative) scaling applies to a quantity that can be represented by a ratio or absolute measurement scale. Many cost models use such scaling to account for the influence of cost drivers. As an example, choose the same estimated values used previously. Apply the two values multiplicatively to compute the estimated size:

Estimated Size = 230*1.15*0.60 = 158.7 sizel

Compare this result to the preceding result of 172 sizel. Why is this answer different? The answer is that you are not applying the scaling values to the same reference object. The preceding multiplicative expression in effect says to increase the size by 15% (times 1.15), and then reduce the resulting size (= 230*1.15 = 264.5) by 40% (= 264.5*0.6). That is, the 40% decrease is applied to the inflated value of 264.5, not to the reference value of 230. This removes 105.8 sizel (= 264.5*0.4). In the additive example, the 40% removed only 92 (= 230*0.4). This explains the observed difference of 13.8 sizel (= 172.5 – 158.7), which equals 105.8 minus 92.0. This illustrates the importance of the choice of scale. The additive analogy technique measures all adjustments relative to the same reference value. The multiplicative analogy technique applies adjustments to a "current" reference obtained by applying the previous adjustments. To see the difference more clearly, let x and y denote two adjustments. The adjustment factors for the two techniques are as shown here.

Technique	Equation	Example
Additive	$(1 + x + y)$	$1 + 0.15 - 0.40 = 0.75$
Multiplicative	$(1 + x)*(1 + y) = 1 + x + y + x*y$	$(1.15)*(0.6) = 0.69$

The multiplicative equation is greater than the additive equation by $-x*y$. For the preceding example, the difference is 0.06 (= 0.15*0.40). Applied to the base size of 230 sizel, the size difference is 13.8 sizel.

This simple comparison shows that the interpretation (effect) of the input values and the computed results both depend on the equations used in the estimating model. Stated another way, different models will produce different estimated values for the same quantity. You need to understand whatever model you are using. This includes the units of measure, scope, assumptions, and the estimating equations. (This is unfortunately not possible for many commercial parametric models because their proprietary internal equations are not published.)

5.2.3 Proportionality Relations

A special type of ratio scaling is a proportionality relation. William Roetzheim gives the following relation between development effort and time for software development projects [Roetzheim, 1988, page 217]:

$$E_2/E_1 = (T_2/T_1)^2$$

where E_i and T_i denote the effort and time for project i, respectively. If you have historical data for project 1, and can estimate the effort for project 2, you can compute the time for project 2, assuming that the products, projects, and processes are similar, using the following formula:

$$T_2 = T_1*(E_2/E_1)^{0.5}$$

The exponent of 1/2 is appropriate for rapid application development projects. Larger projects use an exponent of 1/3. The exponent is 1 for projects that use constant staffing. (An example in Chapter 12, "Top-Down Estimating and Allocation," computes the phase duration for constant staffing.)

5.2.4 Calculating the Uncertainty

You can also quantify the uncertainty in the estimated value if you have ranges for the estimated differences. Suppose that the engineers in the preceding example say that the increase due to the display screens is in the range 15% to 20%, and the decrease due to the RDBMS is in the range 35% to 40%. The lowest value is a size decrease of 25% (= 15 – 40). The highest value is a decrease of 15% (= 20 – 35). Using these values, you estimate the size to be 172 to 196 sizel.[4]

The box "Estimating the "Error in Effort" provides another example.

Estimating the Error in Effort

You can also handle ranges in both size and productivity when estimating effort. Assume that you have completed a single project for an application domain that was new to the team (an "unprecedented" system) and the effort expended was 10,000 phr. You want to estimate the effort for a new project to build a similar system for the same application domain. You estimate that the size of the new system will be 10% to 30% larger than the size of the completed system. (Chapters 8, "Estimating Software Size: The Basics," and 9, "Estimating Software Size: The Details," give better methods to estimate sizes.) You expect that the productivity of the team will increase by 20% to 25% because the team members are now familiar with the application domain, the development methods, and the development tools. You can estimate a range of effort values for the new project using simple scaling:

Low = 10,000*1.1/1.25 = 8,800 phr
High = 10,000*1.3/1.20 = 10,833 phr

because effort equals size divided by productivity.

---

[4] The lowest value is the sum of the minimum values. The highest value is the sum of the maximum values. You must use the correct signs. The decreases are *negative* numbers. Thus, the minimum value of the decrease is –40, and not –35. The minimum value of the increase is +15. The lowest value is thus +15 + (–40) or –25.

If you are combining a set of estimated values and can assume that the errors in the estimates are independent, the preceding calculation overestimates the error because it assumes that the errors always reinforce each other. In practice, some cancellation will probably occur. (Some errors will be positive and others negative.) Suppose that the engineers provide a mean and a standard deviation for each of the two quantities. The variance of the result is just the sum of the variances of the contributing factors.[5] For this case, Var(Size) = Var(Display) + Var(RDBMS). The variance is the square of the standard deviation. Suppose that you receive these values:

Display size increase: Mean = 15%, Standard deviation = 5%
RDBMS size decrease: Mean = 40%, Standard deviation = 10%

As before, the estimated size is 172 sizel, with a fractional error of 11% (= SQRT(5^2 + 10^2)). Because this represents one standard deviation, the estimated size has a 68% probability of lying between 153 and 191 (= 172*(1 ± 0.11)). This is a wide range, but at least it indicates the degree of confidence in the estimated value.

5.2.5 Improving the Analogy Estimation Technique

You can improve the analogy estimation technique in two ways. First, you could establish an algorithm (such as a look-up table) to associate quantitative difference values with estimated qualitative values of particular factors. (Many parametric cost models do exactly this for their cost drivers.) They associate numeric values with a particular rating value, and then use these values to adjust the base estimate up or down. Second, you could determine the percentages by using the PERT technique or the Delphi technique.

5.3 Program Evaluation and Review Technique (PERT)

Lockheed and the U.S. Navy developed the Program Evaluation and Review Technique (PERT) in the late 1950s. Lawrence Putnam and Anne Fitzsimmons applied it to software in 1979 [Putnam, 1979] and [Putnam, 1980].

The PERT technique uses additional information from the estimator to produce a better estimate. The estimator provides three estimates for the quantity of interest: the lowest possible value, the most likely value, and the highest possible value, denoted by L, M, and H, respectively. (The basic mathematics assumes that these estimates are unbiased, and that L and H correspond to the

---

[5] This calculation assumes that each quantity contributes equally to the result. This is a special case of the Law of Propagation of Errors. See Note N06 "Propagation of Errors" or consult any statistics textbook for details. One reference is Section 5.7 in [Mandel, 1964].

minus and plus three-sigma limits of the distribution.) Using these three values, the PERT technique calculates the expected value, E, and the standard deviation, σ, using the following equations:

$$E = (L + 4 * M + H)/6$$
$$\sigma = (H - L)/6$$

E represents the estimate of the average value. These equations are very simple to apply in practice, leading to widespread use by estimators. Even if the underlying assumptions are not exactly satisfied, the technique does provide some indication of the degree of uncertainty in the estimator's mind. The key indicator is to look at the ratio σ/E. (Statisticians call this ratio the "coefficient of variation.") A large value of this ratio indicates a high degree of uncertainty on the part of the estimator.[6]

You can easily implement the PERT technique using a spreadsheet. All items on a worksheet must have the same units of measure if you intend to calculate a total and its standard deviation. (Prepare a separate worksheet for each set of items having the same units of measure.) For example, to estimate the sizes of a set of software modules, you would list each module on a separate row of the spreadsheet. The columns of the spreadsheet would be the module's name, the lowest value, the most likely value, the highest value, the expected value (the mean), the standard deviation (σ), and the ratio of (σ/E). Figure 5-3 shows an example with four modules, identified in the left column. The next three columns contain the three estimated size values for each module. The last three columns show the values calculated by the PERT equations. Use the following formulas to calculate the total value and the standard deviation of this total:

$$E_{TOTAL} = \sum_i E_i \qquad \text{where } E_i = (L_i + 4 * M_i + H_i)/6$$

$$\sigma_{TOTAL} = \left[\sum_i \sigma_i^2\right]^{\frac{1}{2}} \quad \text{where } \sigma_i = (H_i - L_i)/6$$

These equations assume that each estimate is independent of the others. That is, they belong to different random distributions. This means that the variance of the total value is computed by adding the variances of each estimate, computed using the preceding formula. The standard deviation is then the square root of the total variances. Do not compute the standard deviation of the total by summing the columns to obtain L_{total} and H_{total}, and then using these values in the equation for σ.

---

[6] Boehm notes that people's "most likely" estimates tend to cluster toward the "lower limit" [Boehm, 1981, p. 320]. This leads to an underestimation bias. To offset this, some estimators alter the weights: E = (L + 3*M + 2*H)/6.

Project:				Name:							
Task:				Date:				*Size Estimation Worksheet*			
				Phone:				*Version 3.1*			
Item Type: Modules											
Units of Measure: UFPs				Approved By:							
				Date:							
	Estimation Information			Values for the Entire Set:	27.8	1.14	4.1%				
								Calculated Values			
Task or WBS #	Item Name	Lowest	Most Likely	Highest	Assumptions and Rationale (or Note)	Expected Value	Standard Deviation	Coefficient of Variation	Fraction of Total	Asymmetry	
	Component ABC	7.00	8.00	9.00		8.00	0.33	4%	29%	1.00	
	Component DEF	3.00	5.00	6.00		4.83	0.50	10%	17%	0.50	
	Component GHI	6.00	7.00	9.00		7.17	0.50	7%	26%	2.00	
	Component JKL	5.00	8.00	10.00		7.83	0.83	11%	28%	0.67	

Figure 5-3 *Example of PERT technique results*

5.4 An Example: Using PERT Values

The following example shows the power of the PERT technique. Suppose that you are to review the sample module size estimate shown in Figure 5-4. I have included another measure called "skew" in the last column, defined as follows:

$$Skew = (H - M)/(M - L)$$

Which values in this table are suspicious and why? There are actually several difficulties with the values shown in this chart. I discuss each in turn.

Project:				Name:							
Task:				Date:			Size Estimation Worksheet				
				Phone:			Version 3.1				
	Item Type:	Modules									
	Units of Measure:	Sizes		Approved By:							
				Date:							
				Values for the Entire Set:	184.0	16.85	9.2%				
	Estimation Information					Calculated Values					
Task or WBS #	Item Name	Lowest	Most Likely	Highest	Assumptions and Rationale (or Note)	Expected Value	Standard Deviation	Coefficient of Variation	Fraction of Total	Asymmetry	
	Component ABC	6.00	8.00	10.00		8.00	0.67	8%	4%	1.00	
	Component DEF	7.00	8.00	9.00		8.00	0.33	4%	4%	1.00	
	Component GHI	1.00	8.00	15.00		8.00	2.33	29%	4%	1.00	
	Component JKL	130.00	150.00	230.00		160.00	16.67	10%	87%	4.00	

Figure 5-4 *Sample size estimate*

- *Total size.* The best estimate for the total system size is 184 sizel, with a standard deviation of 16.8 sizel, which is about 9% of the total. Assuming that the estimated values are normally distributed, the true size of the system will lie between the following values for the given probability:

# Std Dev	Probability (%)	Minimum	Maximum
1	68.3	167	201
2	95.4	150	218
3	99.7	133	235

- *Degree of understanding.* The ratio of the standard deviation to the average size is the coefficient of variation, and indicates the estimator's confidence in the estimated value. I informally call this ratio the "uncertainty" of the estimate. (A wider range [H–L] gives a larger standard deviation and so a larger ratio, indicating higher uncertainty.) The Data Collection module seems to be the best understood because its uncertainty is only about 4%. The Executive and Report Generation modules have uncertainties (8% and 10%, respectively) comparable to that of the Data Collection module, and so all three modules are probably understood at roughly the same level. The Algorithms module, however, has an uncertainty of 29%. Clearly it is not very well understood. You should direct the analysts to examine this module in greater detail.

- *Uniformity of the partitioning.* The sizes of the modules relative to the total (the "fraction of total" column) are also interesting. It shows that the Report Generator module accounts for about 87% of the total size of the system. Modules constituting such a large fraction of the total size are disturbing because a small fractional error in the estimated size can have large impact on the total size, and thus on the effort to develop the system. It is generally a good idea to decompose such large pieces into smaller pieces and estimate the size of each piece separately because the errors tend to cancel, giving less error in the total size. (This analysis also results in greater understanding of the components.) The goal is to partition the system so that the sizes of the pieces are roughly equal.

- *Asymmetry of limit values.* Our concern about the Report Generator module increases because of the asymmetry of the Low and High values relative to the Most Likely (central) value. The Low value is only 13% below the Most Likely value, while the High value is 53% above it. This seems to indicate that the analysts know that the module cannot be lower than 130 sizel with some confidence, but are unsure just how large the module can be. This large gap between the Most Likely and the Highest estimated sizes of the component signals a lack of confidence (i.e., a lack of understanding of the component). The skew parameter provides a quick way to identify such asymmetries. If you assume that L, M, H define a triangular probability distribution (see Section 5.5), then skew indicates the ratio of probabilities that the true value is above or below M. For example, if skew = 4, then there is approximately an 80% probability $[= 4/(4 + 1)]$ that the true value lies above M. You can also show that there is a 39% probability that the true value will exceed the expected value E (called "Average" in the table), which is computed using $(L + 4*M + H)/6$. When checking PERT estimates, you should pay more attention when skew > 1 because this indicates a higher probability of underestimating the quantity of interest.

Underestimating the system's size is of concern because it can lead to underestimating the cost (and schedule) of the project. The development effort is roughly proportional to the amount of code to be produced (i.e., the total size). The cost is primarily determined by the programming labor (effort) and so is also proportional to the total estimated size. Obviously, you could greatly reduce the chance of an overrun by basing cost estimates on an inflated estimate for the total size of the software. The challenge is to weigh the risk of a cost overrun (due to underestimating the size of the system) against the risk of losing the work (due to setting the cost so high that the customer cannot afford it or that another competitor has a lower cost). Section 5.5 gives an example.

5.5 Using the PERT Values to Estimate Risk Reserve

If you can estimate the mean, μ, and standard deviation, σ, you can estimate the degree of risk involved in an estimate. (One way to obtain μ and σ is to use the PERT technique.) Assume that you have estimated several modules and obtained the total values shown in Figure 5-4. Assume that the error in the total size follows a normal distribution as shown in Figure 5-5. The peak of this distribution lies at the expected value, E. The width of the curve is determined by the standard deviation, σ. Set the bid value, B, to the expected (mean) value, μ, plus some multiple, t, of the standard deviation, σ: $B = \mu + t^*\sigma$. If $t = 1$, $B = \mu + \sigma$. For a one-tailed normal distribution, the probability that the actual value will lie below the value B is 0.84 (= 0.50 + 0.34). This means that the size of the system is less than or equal to 201 sizel (= 184 + 17) 84% of the time. Because effort is directly proportional to size, and cost is directly proportional to effort, you can use this information to set a "safe" bid price. The project suffers a cost overrun only if the actual size turns out to be above the value used for the bid. (This ignores other possible causes of cost overruns.) A good manager can typically influence the project cost by 20%; it should be feasible to complete the project for the cost estimated using the size of 201 sizel. (This is obviously overly simplified, but conveys the concept.)

Table 5-1 shows how to choose a safe value given any desired probability. For example, choose a size of ($\mu + 1.3^*\sigma$) if you want to have a 90% probability of not exceeding that size value. Because the normal curve falls off rapidly, a small increase in bid price "buys" a lot of confidence. For example if $\sigma/\mu = 0.1$, choosing a size of ($\mu + \sigma$) increases the size (and the cost) by only 10%, but increases the probability by 34%. See the box "Choosing the Right Value."

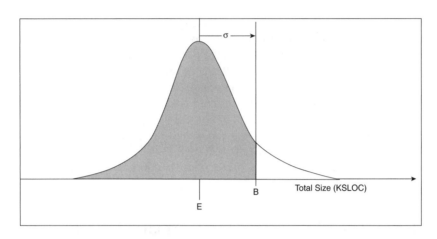

Figure 5-5 *Probability distribution for total size*

Table 5-1: *Choosing a "Safe" Value*

Size Value	Probability That the Size Will Not Exceed the Size Value
μ	50%
μ + 0.5σ	59%
μ + 0.8σ	79%
μ + 1.0σ	84%
μ + 1.3σ	90%

Choosing the Right Value

I once helped a team estimate the effort for a large number of project tasks. We used the PERT technique and followed the procedure just described. We provided several values to the manager: the expected value, the one-sigma value, the 90% value, and so forth. The manager, used to receiving a single number from the engineers, asked, "But which value should I use?" My reply was, "You have to decide the amount of risk that you want to accept, and then choose a value."

You might question the use of the normal distribution. Fortunately, various theorems in probability theory state that the distribution of the sum of many independent random variables will approach a normal distribution as the number of terms in the sum increases. In practice, the convergence is often very rapid. The most famous result is the central limit theorem and applies to independent variables with identical distributions whose expected value and variance are finite. Other limit theorems do not require identical distributions but instead require some condition that guarantees that none of the variables exerts "a much larger influence" than the others. (Two examples are the Lindberg condition and the Lyapunov condition. See http://en.wikipedia.org/wiki/Central_limit_theorem.) Thus, in practice, even if some of the variables in the sum do not have the same distribution, the distribution of the sum is still very close to normal. The error from this approximation is small compared to the goal of achieving ±20% estimation accuracy. The central limit theorem says that you can add up quantities of the same type and know that the sum or their average value is normally distributed. If you partition a product or project into multiple pieces and estimate some quantity (software size, task effort, durations, or costs), you can safely assume a normal distribution to calculate uncertainties. These results explain the widespread use of the normal distribution.

Triangular Distributions

In real life, it is very unusual for values to lie outside plus or minus three standard deviations from the mean value. For this reason, estimators often use a triangular distribution, which looks like this:

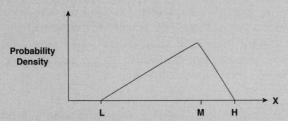

The probability is zero for $x < L$ and $x > H$. This distribution has

Mode $= M$

Mean $= (L + M + H)/3$

Variance $= (L_2 + M_2 + H_2 - L{*}M - L{*}H - M{*}H)/18$

Choosing a triangular distribution allows you to compute many results in closed form. Paul Garvey provides many examples [Garvey, 2000].

5.6 Algorithmic Analogy Estimation

Algorithmic analogy estimation (AAE) produces quantitative results in a repeatable way using data from multiple objects that have similar characteristics. The quantitative analogy techniques described in Section 5.2 used only a single data point. The quantitative analogy and the AAE techniques are better than expert judgment because they use the available historical data in a quantitative way. AAE is useful if you have a database containing, say, the software development effort for a number of completed projects. You can then use AAE to estimate the development effort for a new project. Similarly, you could have historical size data for a number of systems belonging to a particular product family, and could use AAE to estimate the size of a new system.

Adrian Cowderoy and John Jenkins described one of the first structured approaches for using analogies for estimation [Cowderoy, 1988]. Strictly speaking, for software and system estimation, the analogies apply to objects in the same problem domain. This is more properly called case-based reasoning [Vicinanza, 1990]. Such techniques can produce quantitative estimates even when you only have categorical (nominal scale) data. This is often the case early in a project.

5.6.1 General Concept

Algorithmic analogy estimation (AAE) uses a set of historical data points for objects in some domain of interest. Each data point consists of N attributes that characterize an object, one of which is the quantity that you want to estimate. To estimate this quantity for a new object, you specify the values of $(N - 1)$ attributes for that object, and the algorithm searches the set of data points to locate the M points that are "closest" to the attribute values that you specify. The algorithm then "averages" the values of the quantity for the M points to produce the estimate.

For example, you might have data on completed projects, and want to estimate total effort. The $(N - 1)$ attributes must relate in a "significant way" to the quantity. The AAE technique is very general. You can choose any set of characteristics and any quantity of interest. Possible attributes could be application type, programming language, software size, and average staffing level. (The attributes can have different measurement scales.)

Details of the AAE Technique

There are two main activities: define the method, and apply the method to estimate the value for a new object. Seven steps define the method:

1. Define a data set (a set of characteristics plus the quantity of interest).

2. Define measures for each characteristic and for the quantity.

3. Collect data sets for multiple existing instances.

4. Validate the data. (Discard any bad values.)

5. Define an algorithm to measure the degree of similarity between instances.

6. Define an algorithm to select the "nearest neighbor(s)" for the new instance.

7. Define an algorithm to use the value(s) for the "neighbor(s)" to calculate the value for the new instance.

Three steps estimate the value for a new instance using the defined method:

1. Specify (estimate) the characteristics of the new object.

2. Locate and select the desired number of nearest neighbors.

3. Combine the values from the neighbors to get the estimated value.

In Step 2, you can optionally examine the selected data points to decide whether any are inappropriate. If so, you can discard these points to improve the estimated value. (This combines the expert judgment technique with algorithmic analogy estimation.) You can also use a range of values for each input characteristic to obtain a set of estimated output values. You can use statistics to evaluate these values. Fuzzy logic is another possibility.

When defining an algorithmic analogy estimation model, you must choose characteristics of the particular object (project, module, etc.) that are able to depict significant differences among the various projects. That is, the attributes should be correlated with the quantity of interest. Even though a characteristic is correlated with the quantity of interest, however, it still may not be possible to exploit that relationship to produce an estimate. For example, if one of the characteristics is the "quality of management," and every manager rates his or her management ability as "high," then this attribute will provide no help in trying to explain the different cost values observed for a project. (This is called co-linearity of the data. See Section 5.4.2 in [Boehm, 2000].) You must precisely define the units of measure for all the characteristics and quantities, and ensure that all the projects in the data set use the same definitions for metrics and attributes. (Steps 2–4 address these concerns.)

5.6.2 Example

Figure 5-6 shows a spreadsheet that demonstrates the algorithmic analogy estimation technique. This example assumes that project effort is a function of three variables: size (in KSLOC), complexity (CPLX), and performance (PERF):

$$\text{Effort} = 3*(\text{Size}^{1.10})*(\text{CPLX}^{0.5})*(\text{PERF}^{0.333})$$

Column E gives the true value of the effort for each project. Column F gives the "actual" reported effort for 10 reference projects. The actual effort equals the true effort times a random multiplier to represent measurement errors.

	A	B	C	D	E	F	G	H	I	J	K	L
1								Distance				
2		Size	CPLX	PERF				Threshold				
3	Weights:	3.0	2.0	1.0				7.50				
4												
5					E_true	E_est	% Error				Sums	
6	New Project:	8.0	3	2	64.46	76.03	17.9%		4		1.70	129.27
7												
8										Selected	Weight	Weighted
9	Project ID	Size	CPLX	PERF	E_true	E_act	% Error	DIST		Ref.	(1/Distance)	Ref. Values
10										Values		
11	1	1.5	3	2	10.22	12.13	18.6%	11.26				
12	2	2.4	3	4	21.60	15.31	-29.1%	9.90				
13	3	5.3	2	5	45.40	46.00	1.3%	5.73	X	46.00	0.17	8.02
14	4	7.1	4	3	74.72	77.76	4.1%	2.33	X	77.76	0.43	33.37
15	5	8.6	3	2	69.80	71.42	2.3%	1.04	X	71.42	0.96	68.72
16	6	11.8	5	4	160.75	142.41	-11.4%	7.44	X	142.41	0.13	19.15
17	7	16.2	4	5	219.47	301.35	37.3%	14.58				
18	8	23.8	1	2	123.48	152.44	23.4%	27.51				
19	9	32.5	3	4	379.52	484.98	27.8%	42.48				
20	10	37.1	2	1	225.92	239.12	5.8%	50.43				
21												
22												
23												
24												
25												
26												
27		End of Formulas										

Figure 5-6 *Algorithmic analogy estimation technique*

The parameters for the new project are in cells B6, C6, and D6. The spreadsheet calculates a weighted distance between each reference project and the new project using

$$DIST = SQRT\ [\ B*(\$B\$6 - \$B_i)^2 + C*(\$C\$6 - \$C_i)^2 + D*(\$D\$6 - \$D_i)^2\ ]$$

where i denotes the ith reference project, and B, C, and D are the relative weights for each parameter (stored in cells B3, C3, and D3, respectively). These weights also convert the units of measure, whatever they are. The weighting function for this example is simply 1/DIST.

The spreadsheet selects projects whose distance from the new project is less than or equal to a distance threshold (in cell H3). The X in column I indicates the projects selected. Cell I6 gives the number of reference projects selected. The estimated effort equals the sum over the selected projects of each project's weight times its actual effort, divided by the sum of the weights. The two values are in cells L6 and K6, respectively. The estimated effort is in cell F6. The error is 18% for this case.

The CD-ROM describes some additional implementation details. These handle the cases where a reference project has parameters exactly equal to the new project, giving a distance of zero, and the case where no reference project lies within the threshold distance.

5.7 Recommended Reading

Barry Boehm discusses estimation methods and their strengths and weaknesses in Chapter 22 of [Boehm, 1981]. He notes that every method has its own particular strengths and weaknesses. For this reason it is a good idea to select techniques or methods with complementary strengths and weaknesses. Barry Boehm provides a brief description of the PERT technique in Section 21.4 (pages 318–320) of [Boehm, 1981].

There are many books and articles on the Delphi technique (also called the Delphi method in much of the literature). One is [Linstone, 1975]. Also see Section 22.2 in [Boehm, 1981]. Robert Hughes describes expert judgment for software applications in [Hughes, 1996].

You can find good overviews of the Delphi technique at these websites:

http://www.iit.edu/~it/delphi.html

http://www.tcdc.com/dmeth/dmeth5b.htm

http://www.unomaha.edu/~unoai/avn8120/tools/definitions/
delphitechnique.html.

Martin Shepperd and Chris Schofield have automated the analogy estimation process for project effort. Their "ANaloGy software Estimation tooL" (ANGEL) operates on a PC [Shepperd, 1997]. The ANGEL tool examines the data and tries to identify the best set of drivers for the quantity of interest by successively trying combinations of drivers to see which combination gives the least average error. This automatically produces the "best" estimation model. To learn more about the ANGEL project and obtain a free copy of the ANGEL tool, see the Bournemouth University website (http://dec.bmth.ac.uk/ESERG/ANGEL).

Chapter 13, "Parametric Models," covers another important estimating technique. Note 05, "Soft Methods," describes techniques that, in effect, combine parametric models, analogy estimation, and case-based reasoning. Note N06, "Propagation of Errors," explains how to combine the errors in individual quantities to obtain the total error in a calculated quantity.

5.8 Summary

This chapter described simple, general-purpose techniques for estimating various types of quantities. The Linear Method described in Chapter 3, "A Basic Estimating Process: The Linear Method," can use one or more of these techniques to estimate various quantities. For the warehouse inventory system example, you might use the PERT technique to estimate the number of display screens required. You might use algorithmic analogy estimation to estimate total project effort as a cross-check on values estimated using other techniques.

A key need is to provide an organized and systematic way to partition the estimating problem so that you can apply the various techniques where appropriate. Chapter 7, "Preparing to Estimate (Precursors of Estimation)," describes how to divide the objects whose characteristics you want to estimate into pieces so that you can apply appropriate techniques, CERs, models, and so on. to each piece. Then the following chapters show you how to apply these to estimate specific types of quantities. All chapters provide examples and implementation guidance.

Chapter 18, "Updating Estimates," discusses how to select estimating techniques based on the type of resource and the phase of your project. Chapter 19, "Consolidating and Applying Your Knowledge," discusses how you can apply the book's techniques and tools in your organization.

Chapter 6

Estimating Annual Maintenance Costs

This chapter shows how to use the Linear Method to develop a simple model to estimate the annual costs for maintaining a software product. Although many parametric models address this topic, they only focus on a small part of the problem: adding, changing, and deleting lines of code from the existing product. The first section describes the maintenance process. This identifies the activities that consume effort. Subsequent sections describe how to build and calibrate the model, and to use it to update the estimates. The chapter concludes by showing how you can improve the model, and use insights from the model to reduce the maintenance costs.

6.1 The Maintenance Process

Industry often refers to "software maintenance." A more correct term is *software sustainment* because software is not maintained in the same way that hardware is maintained. When hardware fails, the repairperson replaces the failed part with an identical but functioning part. In addition, preventive maintenance is often a significant expense for hardware. This includes activities to protect equipment from corrosion, and to replace worn-out components such as bearings. When software fails, however, the software engineer does not replace the defective code with an identical piece of code but instead must modify the code to remove the design defect that caused the failure [Brooks,

1995, p. 121]. In addition, a large part of software "maintenance" involves enhancing the product throughout its operational life. After making any changes, no matter how minor, software engineers retest the product to verify that the changes have the intended effect and cause no undesirable effects.[1]

Table 6-1 shows the four distinct types of activities that consume effort during software sustainment. E. Burton Swanson classified software repair into the first three types shown [Swanson, 1976]. He classified changes to external interfaces as adaptive maintenance, however. The other gray area is changes to externally imposed business rules (e.g., tax tables). If these are easy, they are considered adaptive. If they require major changes, they could be viewed as enhancements.

Table 6-1 *Allocation of Software "Maintenance" Effort*

Type	Examples
Correct	Correct design and coding errors
Perfect	Improve human factors (ease of use)
	Improve performance (tuning)
	Delete unneeded capability
	Improve maintainability (refactoring)
Adapt	Respond to platform changes (upgrades, porting)
	Respond to COTS changes (COTS refresh)
Enhance	Add new capability (functions, interfaces)
	Respond to external changes (business rules, data tables, interfaces)

An industry adage for large, custom systems is that 30% of the system's total life cycle cost is expended to achieve the initial operational capability. "Maintenance" consumes the other 70%. Examples are command and control systems and financial systems. If software is embedded in a consumer product (e.g., toaster or DVD player), then 95% of the total life cycle cost is typically allocated to the first (and only) release, with the remaining 5% spent on customer support.

To develop an estimation model, you must first understand the underlying production process. Many textbooks describe processes that develop a totally new product. Sustainment operates in a cyclic fashion, producing a series of

---

[1] The testing effort depends on the scope of the changes and the degree of risk associated with shipping a defective product. For example, you would expect that a safety-critical product would be tested extensively after any modifications.

releases. Although development and sustainment both involve analyzing, designing, coding, integrating, testing, and installing, these activities differ in significant ways. These differences affect estimation.

Table 6-2 shows the characteristics of sustainment. Requirements come from many sources and arrive over time. Constrained resources limit the number of repairs and enhancements implemented in a particular release. Deployment can be expensive if there are many users or many sites. The potential for adverse side effects can be high for complex systems. The probability that fixing a defect introduces a new defect is 20%–50% [Brooks, 1995, p. 122]. Product size and complexity also increase with time, decreasing the productivity of maintenance programmers [Lehman, 1985, p. 168]. Another problem that affects customer support costs (and defect counting) is that not all users install a new release at the same time. Some users never install the release because they do not use the corrected features and do not want to risk disrupting their current working system [Adams, 1984].

Table 6-2 *Characteristics of Software Sustainment*

Requirements arrive over time: • Users report problems.   • Owner requests enhancements.   • The underlying platform (server, operating system, database) changes.
Not all "problems" are software defects: • Duplicate reports.   • Hardware failures.   • Confusing manuals.   • External cause (e.g., electrical spike).   • Suggested enhancements (new features).
The architecture and design exist but will evolve: • A small staff must understand it all.   • Design documentation may help or mislead.
The owner may decide not to correct all known defects: • Cost or time constraints (design, code, test, deploy).   • Adequate workarounds may exist.   • Risk (potential adverse side effects).
The user may not install the new release: • Adequate workarounds may exist.   • Risk (potential adverse side effects).   • Cost or time too high.

Figure 6-1 shows the five main activities of the software sustainment process.

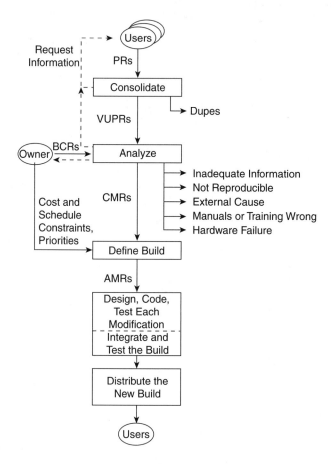

Figure 6-1 *The sustainment process*

Table 6-3 defines the names of variables that will appear in the maintenance cost model described later. The following pages define all of these variables. (The figure only shows some of these variables.) Users submit problem reports and possibly requests for enhancements. These requests can arrive in various forms.[2] Thus, the sustainment organization must establish a standard way to identify, log, and track every request, regardless of its source. I use the term *problem report* (PR) to describe information received from the users. The owner

---

[2] Possible names for problem reports include problem change request, software trouble report, bug report, discrepancy report, and baseline change request. (Baseline change request usually refers to a new or modified requirement, not to a problem.)

of the system submits requests for enhancements, which I call *baseline change requests* (BCRs). Analysts receive duplicate reports of some problems. Also, problem reports may describe software problems, hardware failures, user errors, incomplete or erroneous documentation, or even enhancements (because the users do not know the product's original requirements). Some problem reports are incomplete or illegible.[3] (Baseline change requests hopefully have none of these problems.) For these reasons, engineers have to "screen" all problem reports. (Screening is the analog of requirements analysis for new development.) From an estimation perspective, screening has two distinct steps: consolidation and analysis.

Table 6-3 *Data Types Related to Sustainment*

Acronym	Definition	Comments
PR	Problem report	Anomaly, failure, unexpected behavior, suggestion (e.g., perfective changes).
VUPR	Validated unique problem report	The problem is completely described. All duplicate reports are removed.
BCR	Baseline change request	Enhancement or repair submitted by owner (or possibly the sustainer). Includes new features plus adaptive and perfective changes.
APCR	Analyzed problem/ change request	A VUPR or BCR that has been analyzed and categorized.
CMR	Candidate modification	Description of changes to correct a defect (VUPR) or add a feature (BCR).
AMR	Approved modification request	Change selected for implementation in the next build or version.
VUSD	Validated unique software defect	A valid defect in the fielded software (a corrective change).

6.1.1 Consolidation and Analysis

Consolidation removes the incomplete and illegible PRs, and produces validated unique problem reports (VUPRs). It also collects metrics (number of duplicates, and possibly the sites submitting reports).

---

[3] The operational definition of a software problem report in Figure 4-2 addressed all these concerns.

Analysis examines each VUPR and decides on its disposition. Some are rejected, either because they lack sufficient information, because the problem is not reproducible, or because it is considered insignificant and not worthy of implementation. (If the analysts have a heavy workload, they may defer some problem reports.) Analysis classifies each remaining VUPR based on its cause(s), and identifies possible ways to correct the problem. A single VUPR may indicate multiple problems. (Consolidation could generate separate VUPRs, one per problem if you choose to define your process this way.) A particular problem may require multiple changes. For example, to correct a frequent user error you might add data validation code (a perfective repair), add or rewrite the text in user manuals and help files, and update training materials. Figure 6-1 illustrates some of these options.[4] Analysis also examines each baseline change request to identify possible ways to add the requested capability. Analysis estimates the approximate cost and schedule to make the modification (including regression testing and related documentation updates). In some cases, analysts may validate the change, possibly by prototyping. The engineers actually code the change and execute it in a testbed to ensure that they have correctly identified the cause, and that their proposed correction will work. This can make analysis very expensive. (But it also reduces the effort to implement changes once the owner and the sustainer have defined the content of the new build. See below.) Analysis accumulates a set of candidate modification requests (CMRs).

A "critical problem" may arrive at any time and may trigger an "emergency build." Such problems usually involve errors that could cause severe damage, loss of life, or mission failure. Thus, consolidation and analysis must occur continuously, even when the team is producing a new build. While a build is in progress, however, some organizations only screen ("triage") the incoming problem reports to identify the critical ones, deferring consolidation and analysis of the remaining problems until later.

6.1.2 Defining a Build

Analysis of VUPRs and BCRs produces a set of candidate modifications. At some point, the owner directs the team to produce a new release (a build). For some systems, releases occur at regular intervals such as every 12 months. The engineers must define the build content and write a plan to produce the build.

---

[4] For tracking, you will want to distinguish the effect (symptoms), the root cause, and the actions taken (the disposition). The figure only shows the disposition. See the "Recommended Reading" section for sources giving possible categories.

The software engineers determine which CMRs to include in a build, based on constraints and priorities specified by the owner. (Actually, these are only the CMRs related to the software and its documentation.) Sometimes they perform a trade-off analysis to balance the modifications (fixes, new capabilities), cost, and schedule. To estimate sustainment projects, the engineers must adjust the requirements (the build content) to fit the constraints on cost and/or time. Cost constraints are based on the owner's budget. Schedule constraints may arise from the need to synchronize the release with other projects or planned outages, to comply with statutory requirements, or to correct a potentially catastrophic problem. Once negotiated with the owner, the team records the build content, which is usually just a list of the approved modification requests (AMRs). See the box "Types of Releases."

Types of Releases

Some organizations distinguish major releases, minor releases, and patches based on the type of changes that they contain. A major release provides new features. A minor release primarily corrects bugs. A patch only corrects a few very serious bugs. Developers and vendors often use numbering to distinguish the type of release. The following table illustrates the typical release content (type of changes) and numbering.

Type of Change	Release Type		
	Major	Minor	Patch
Enhance	Yes		
Adapt	Yes	Maybe	
Perfect	Yes	Maybe	
Correct (minor)	Maybe	Yes	
Correct (serious)			Yes
Numbering	1.0	1.1	1.1.1

The distinction between minor releases and patches depends on the type of system. If there are many copies of a product, or if it is installed in locations worldwide, deploying a new version may be extremely expensive and time-consuming. For these systems, it makes sense to limit the number of releases by grouping changes to produce periodic releases (e.g., annually). If an error might jeopardize operator safety or mission accomplishment, however, the organization will ship an unscheduled patch release. For consumer software, however, many vendors post patches on a website for users to download. Since distribution is inexpensive, vendors post patches often, a typical example being patterns for virus checkers. The distinction between patches and minor releases disappears. (Users of commercial products must usually pay for major releases.)

There are two approaches to determine the build content, which I call "batch" and "continuous." In the batch approach, the owner and developer jointly analyze the set of candidate modifications and negotiate the ones that will be implemented (the build content) based on business needs, priority, cost, and schedule. Table 6-4 illustrates a set of candidate modifications in priority order. Analysis produces the estimated effort for each change. Suppose that the customer has only 1,000 person-hours of effort available. The cumulative effort for the three highest priority changes is 850 person-hours. Nominally, this would terminate the list of approved modification requests (AMRs). However, the customer may also direct that the fifth item be included since it is only an additional 100 person-hours. In addition, adding the seventh item increases the total effort to only 1,050 person-hours, slightly over the 1,000 person-hour budget. Given the uncertainty in the estimates, the owner and the developer will probably agree to implement the changes indicated with the asterisks in the last column. This defines the build content.

The continuous approach to defining build content has the benefit of providing a partially completed build that can be quickly completed and deployed. In this approach, the owner and the developer examine each individual candidate modification request (CMR) when they receive it from the analyst. Then they either approve or reject it. If approved, the developer implements the modification, and the modifications accumulate in a "rolling baseline" that contains all the modifications implemented to date. (Another approach is to produce a file of patches that generates the new baseline when applied to the current baseline.) At some point, the owner directs the developer to ship the latest baseline as a new release. At this point, the developer completes integration testing and regression testing, and then ships the product to the users. By deferring integration and regression testing until the end, the "continuous" process differs from the "code and fix" life cycle described in [McConnell, 1996, Section 7.1, page 140ff]. In the code and fix process, several programmers independently make changes to the product. This often leads to problems because they fail to coordinate their activities. In addition, if each programmer runs regression tests for their changes, this means that the developers repeat the same regression tests multiple times, increasing the effort expended.

Table 6-4 *Determining the Build Content*

Priority	Description of Change	Estimated Effort (phr)	Cumulative Effort (phr)	Included Next Build
1	Correct calculation of parabolic trajectories	300	300	*
2	Correct azimuth calculation for sensor type 3	150	450	*
3	Change thrust model for missile type D-7	400	850	*
			——— 1000 phr Available ———	
4	Add sensor type 7	500	1,350	
5	Install error check of user-supplied sensor coordinates	100	1,450	*
6	Restructure modules X, Y, Z	600	2,050	
7	Expand azimuth format to F10.3 in "Look Angle Report"	100	2,150	*

6.1.3 Producing and Deploying a Build

The engineers execute the build plan, performing detailed design, coding, unit testing, integration, functional testing, regression testing, and acceptance testing. Detailed design and possibly coding may take little effort if the analysts performed prototyping when preparing the candidate modification request.

The engineers or production personnel reproduce products and package them for shipment. For some systems, they may also install and check out the product at a user site. These activities are essentially the same as for projects that develop new products.

6.1.4 Where Are the "Defects?"

The preceding process description defined many objects (in Table 6-3) but which object corresponds to the "real" defects? A "defect," like a "line of code," has many possible definitions. To illustrate this, consider two more quantities. First, analyzed problem change requests (APCRs) are the sum of VUPRs and BCRs. You can categorize APCRs by symptom, root cause(s), or disposition. Omitting illegible or rejected VUPRs, you might classify candidate modification requests (CMRs) by the type of work product involved:

CSMR   Candidate software modification request

CHMR   Candidate hardware modification request

CCMR   Candidate courseware modification request (training materials)

CDMR   Candidate document modification request (manuals)

Note that correcting some problems may require modifying multiple work products; code, user documentation, and courseware. Analogously, you can count the accepted modification requests (ASMR, AHMR, ACMR, and ADMR). Second, validated unique software defects (VUSDs) are the bugs in the software. (One question is whether a "defect" is only corrective, or also includes perfective and adaptive modifications. The analysts need to determine the true number of VUSDs based on your definition.) Analysts may fail to count some legitimate defects (whatever the definition) due to illegible or incomplete PRs, or to problems that they cannot reproduce. The programmers only repair a subset of the VUSDs due to limited resources, the ability of users to easily work around the problem, or because the defect is cosmetic (e.g., a misspelled menu title). The workload of the software team depends on the number of approved modification requests (AMR) (and other factors such as the difficulty of the modification and the experience of the team).

The estimation model in the next section addresses only software sustainment, and assumes that other departments handle hardware, courseware, and document modifications. For simplicity, the model uses CMR and AMR to refer to CSMR and ASMR, respectively.

6.2 Building the Estimation Model

You can use the preceding model of the sustainment process to construct a model to estimate annual sustainment costs. The approach is to define a linear estimating model for each of the activities. Table 6-5 lists the six sustainment activities. Potential parameters that affect each activity's effort or cost appear below that activity.

Table 6-5 *Sustainment Activities and Possible Cost Factors*

1. Sustain "core competency"   • Amount of software   • Staff knowledge and skills   • Facilities and tools
2. Consolidate problem reports   • Amount of defects in release (size * defect density)   • Amount of multiple reporting (# sites, usage profiles)   • Detection efficiency
3. Analyze unique problem reports and baseline change requests   • Amount of multiple reporting (# sites, usage profiles)   • Number of new or changed requirements or external interfaces   • Anticipated upgrades to the platform (hardware, middleware)   • Suggested improvements
4. Define a release (the build content)   • Urgency of modifications   • Compatibility of modifications   • Resource constraints (time, money)   • Political pressure
5. Produce the build   • Build "size"   • Amount, clarity, and structure of code   • Formality of process   • Amount of regression testing   • Resource constraints
6. Deploy the new version   • Level of involvement   • # systems   • # sites   • # users (if provide training)

Activity 1 is different from the other activities because it provides the "core competency" needed to sustain a software-intensive system or product. Software sustainment is analogous to firefighting. To be ready to fight a fire at any time, a town must have trained firefighters, provide them with equipment, and house them in a facility. Similarly, the organization responsible for sustainment must provide a "core competency" of skilled individuals who know the system, have the necessary skills and tools to diagnose and correct problems, and house them in a facility. Having "firefighters" trained and ready to respond is mandatory for any system that performs life-critical functions, or that operates continuously (e.g., plant process control or an e-commerce website).

The type of individuals needed for sustainment depends on the particular software-intensive system. These individuals might include the following:

- Software engineers (repair, update, and test the software)
- Hardware engineers (perform preventive maintenance, repair equipment, upgrade equipment)
- Subject matter experts (provide specialized knowledge)
- User support technicians (train and assist users)
- Team support (supervise, handle administrative tasks)

Each individual's typical activities are shown within the parentheses. You will obviously need software engineers. You usually need hardware engineers and equipment technicians to support the computer platforms, peripherals, networks, and specialized hardware components. You may also need subject matter experts to provide specialized knowledge in domains such as inertial guidance, trajectory computation, or federal tax regulations. (You may have to hire these experts full-time to ensure that they are available when needed.) You may also need supervisors and administrative support, but these people may be included in the overhead costs for the workers already mentioned.

As a simple example, focus only on the software engineers and their associated support staff. You will need to specify a "support productivity," the amount of code that one programmer can understand well enough to be able to diagnose problems and make repairs quickly and correctly. The precise value depends on the type of system, its complexity, the quality of the code and its associated documentation, and the capabilities of the available automated tools. For this example, assume that one full-time person can support 50,000 lines of source code (SLOC). Also assume that you must sustain 230 KSLOC of software. If so, then you will need 4.6 full-time software engineers [= 230 KSLOC/(50 KSLOC/person)]. Assuming 152 person-hours/person-month (= 1,824 person-hours/person-year), 4.6 full-time people can deliver 8,390 person-hours during the year.[5] They expend effort performing the other activities listed in the table.

---

[5] If you cannot assign part-time people to a team, then you round up to five full-time software engineers, who could provide 9,120 person-hours per year.

If the effort for these activities exceeds 8,390 person-hours, then you will have to add additional software engineers. The workload depends on the number of problem requests analyzed, the amount of code modified, and other factors. Assume that the workload depends only on the number of modifications made. Figure 6-2 illustrates the basic situation. The core team can handle some number of modifications. When the number exceeds this limit, you must add more software engineers to the team.

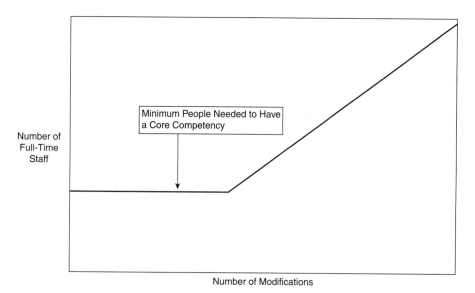

Figure 6-2 *Saturation of the core team*

Figure 6-3 shows the spreadsheet to estimate each of the six activities, plus three additional support activities (configuration management, quality assurance, and project management). This uses a linear estimation model to estimate the annual effort for each activity. (Later subsections discuss how to improve the estimates for the activities.) The spreadsheet uses assumed counts and production coefficients for each activity. Column A gives the activity number. Column B describes the activity. Activities 3 and 5 have subactivities below them shown in italics. (See below.) The next four columns implement the linear estimation model. Column C is the estimated number of units "processed" during the year (the count). (Section 6.5.1 provides advice on estimating the counts.) Column D is the units of measure for the estimated counts.[6] Column E is the

_____

[6] Although the Linear Model does not explicitly show the units of measure, I included them in column D to stress that the estimates use different measures of size. The earlier sections defined these measures.

production coefficient in person-hours per unit of measure. Column F is a flag used to facilitate calculating subtotals. Column G is the total estimated effort for each activity or subactivity. Column H records the estimating assumptions, supporting rationale, and any additional explanations needed. Note the large number of assumptions needed to calculate even this simple estimate. All of these assumptions are (or should be) based on historical data. (If you expect differences in the coming year, you can adjust the historical values using the scaling techniques described in Chapter 5, "Estimating Techniques.") This implies that you will need to collect several types of measurements to produce a documented estimate.

	A	B	C	D	E	F	G	H
1	Activity	Description	Estimated Units	Units of Measure	Production Coefficient		Total	Comments
2	1	Maintain Core Competency	230.0	KSLOC	0.02		8,390	Unrounded FTE staff. Assume 152 phrs/person-month.
3								
4	2	Consolidate Problem Reports	444.0	PR	11.40	1	5,062	Assume 10 sites submit 3.7 PRs per calendar-month each.
5	3	Analyze Unique Requests	139.9	CMR		1	3,956	Candidate modications to software, hardware, document and courses.
6		User Requests =	124.3	VUPR	27.20		3,382	Assume 72% are duplicates.
7		Organization Requests =	15.6	BCR	36.80		574	Assume 1.3 BCRs per calendar-month. All BCRs are unique.
8	4	Define Build Content	1.0	phrs	120.00	1	120	Assume one build during the year. Three people for one week.
9	5	Produce and Test the Build	42.0	ASMR	N/A	1	3,508	Assume that 50% of the CMRs are software-related, and that 60% of these are approved for implementation.
10		Software Modifications =	42.0	ASMR	65.00		2,728	Assume each modification will require 65 phrs of effort for design and coding.
11		Product Testing =	42.0	ASMR	15.00		630	Assume each modification will require 15 phrs of effort for testing.
12		Regression Testing =	1.0	Build	150.00		150	Assume fixed amount for full test suite.
13	6	Ship New Version to Users	10.0	Site	10.00	1	100	Have 10 sites. Assume that the site administrator installs, with 10 hours of phone support from our engineers per site.
14					Subtotal =		12,745	This exceeds 8,390 so need more engineers.
15	7	Configuration Management	Sum of 2–6	%	5	1	637	
16					Subtotal =		13,383	
17	8	Quality/Assurance	Sum of 2–7	%	7	1	937	
18					Subtotal =		14,319	
19	9	Project Management	Sum of 2–8	%	12	1	1,718	
20					Total =		16,038	Person-hours
21								
22		PHRS per PM =	152.0		Average FTE =		8.8	Total Full-Time People
23							7.0	Total Full-Time Software Engineers and Testers
24							1.8	Total Full-Time Support Staff

Figure 6-3 *Estimate of annual sustainment effort*

The basic calculations are straightforward. For example, Activity 3, analyze unique requests, has two subactivities. The first analyzes the validated unique problem reports received from the users. Of the 444 problem reports received, the estimator assumes that 72% of these are duplicates, based on historical information. This gives 124.3 validated unique problem reports submitted by the users during the year. Analysis must also examine requests received from the organization that owns the system or product. (This could be a corporate department or a government project office.) The estimator assumes that the baseline change requests received from the organization are all unique, and that historical data shows an average arrival rate of 1.3 BCRs per calendar-month. This gives an estimate of 15.6 BCRs per calendar-year. Column E shows that the effort to analyze each type of request (VUPR and BCR) is different. Multiplying the counts by their corresponding production coefficients gives the totals shown in column G in italics. Summing these gives the total estimated effort for Activity 3, shown in column G, row 5.

Proceeding in this way for the other activities gives the total estimated effort of 12,745 person-hours for the first six activities. This exceeds the 8,390 person-hours available from the "core competency" staff, and so the organization will need to provide more engineers in order to sustain this particular system.

The last three activities support the engineering activities. For simplicity, this example estimates the effort for each activity as a percentage of the total effort for the preceding activities.[7] The configuration management effort is 5% of the total engineering effort (12,745 person-hours) and equals 637 person-hours. Totaling these two values gives 13,383 person-hours. The quality assurance effort is 7% of this total, amounting to 937 person-hours. Similarly, the project management effort is 12% of the preceding subtotal, amounting to 1,718 person-hours. The total estimated effort is 16,038 person-hours. Assuming 152 person-hours per-person month gives 8.8 total full-time people to support this particular product. (Of these, 7.0 are software engineers and testers.)

Figure 6-4 shows the corresponding cost estimates. Columns A and B repeat the information shown on the "Effort" worksheet. Column C gives the total effort from column G of the "Effort" worksheet. Column D shows the loaded labor rates for the personnel assigned to perform the particular activity. (A loaded labor rate includes fringe benefits and possibly other costs. See Chapter 15, "Calculating Cost and Price: The Basics.") Column E shows the product of the effort and the labor rate in dollars. (Activity 1 has no associated cost because the "core competency" team is included in the effort estimated for Activities 2 through 6.) The total labor cost amounts to slightly more than $1.2 million.

---

[7] The rationale for this approach is that the particular activity supports all of the activities shown above it. Configuration management supports the engineers. Quality assurance monitors the work of the engineers and the configuration management specialists. The project manager must supervise the engineers, the configuration management specialists, and the quality-assurance specialists. There are other ways of calculating this. See Section 3.5.1.

To prepare a complete annual budget you need to include Other Direct Costs (ODCs) for items such as office space, computers, tools, and consumables (paper, disks, office supplies, and pizza).[8] This example multiplies an annual ODC rate by the number of full-time equivalent people (7.0 engineers and 1.8 support people). The costs to upgrade office automation software products are included in the ODC rates for the support staff and the software engineers and testers. (The latter have a higher ODC rate, however, due to upgrades of their software tools.) This estimate assumes that there are no costs for preventive maintenance of any hardware in the development and test facility.

	A	B	C	D	E	F
1	Activity	Description	Total Effort (phrs)	Loaded Labor Rate ($/phr)	Labor Cost ($)	Comments
2	1	Maintain Core Competency	8390.4	N/A		This cost included in Activities 2 through 6.
3	2	Consolidate Problem Reports	5051.5	$75.00	$379,620	
4	3	Analyze Unique Requests	3955.6	$75.00	$296,669	
5	4	Define Build Content	120.0	$75.00	$9,000	
6	5	Produce and Test the Build	3508.1	$75.00	$263,106	
7	6	Ship New Version to Users	100.0	$70.00	$7,000	
8	7	Configuration Management	637.3	$60.00	$36,236	
9	8	Quality Assurance	936.8	$65.00	$60,890	
10	9	Project Management	1718.3	$90.00	$154,648	
11						
12				Total Labor Costs =	$1,209,170	
13						
14		Total Staff =	8.8	ODCs/pyr		
15		Support Staff =	1.8	$6,300.00	$11,372	The annual Other Direct Cost per person includes office space, computers, office tool licenses, and consumables.
16		Software engineers and testers =	7.0	$7,700.00	$53,804	Includes the same costs as the support staff, phs annual support for 4 software tools.
17				Other Direct Costs =	$65,176	
18				Total Annual Cost =	$1,274,345	This is the (point) estimate.
19				Fee Rate =	10%	Omit this if this is an internal project.
20				Profit =	$127,435	
21				Total Price =	$1,401,780	This is the amount quoted to the customer.

Figure 6-4 *Estimate of annual sustainment costs*

Row 17 shows that the total estimated cost for the assumed scope of work is slightly over $1.27 million. This is the amount quoted for an in-house support organization. If the sustainment organization performs the work for an external customer, however, then you would add profit to the total estimated cost. This example applies a fee rate of 10% to the total cost, giving a total price of $1.4 million.

---

[8] ODCs also include travel. This example assumes that the administrators at the user sites will install the new releases. Thus, this example includes no travel costs.

These two worksheets, plus supporting assumptions and historical data, provide a documented cost estimate for annual sustainment of the product. You can extend this example. First, you can also use a Linear Model to estimate the number of equipment technicians and hardware engineers based on the number of systems to be supported. You can also factor in planned equipment upgrades and installations of the product at new user sites. Second, this example does not show any costs associated with user support in the form of training programs or technical support (help desk). If you were sustaining a commercial product, then you would want to add the estimated costs for these activities. (Alternatively, this estimate may assume that another department provides user support and will submit its own budget.)

This example estimated the software modifications (Activity 5) using the number of AMRs. In some organizations, developers estimate the total number of source lines of code added and changed, and divide by a productivity value. Customers often analyze proposed budgets by calculating the apparent productivity based on the estimated effort. For discussion, assume that the software engineers will process 23 KSLOC of code (= 10% of the product's total size). If so, their productivity is 6.7 SLOC/phr (= 23,000 SLOC/3,508 phr). The external customer, however, sees a total labor budget of 16,038 phr, which gives an apparent productivity of 1.43 SLOC/phr (= 23,000 SLOC/16,038 phr), 4.6 times lower. To evaluate competing bids correctly, the customer must understand the particular definition of "productivity" being used. The apparent productivity is a poor measure of sustainment process performance because the total effort (or labor cost) depends on multiple size values.

This example illustrates what I call a "federated cost model." You use several models, each having a different size measure (and possibly other different parameters as well) to estimate effort for various activities, and then add the values to obtain the total.

6.3 Calibrating the Model

Table 6-6 identifies the historical data that you must collect to calibrate the sustainment cost model. These three types of data are size, effort, and cost. You must define procedures to collect, validate, and store this data.

Table 6-6 *Calibration Data for Software Sustainment Estimates*

Size by type (counts):
<ul><li># PRs received</li><li># VUPRs analyzed</li><li># BCRs analyzed</li><li># VUSDs found (indicates product quality)</li><li># VUSDs implemented</li><li># BCRs implemented</li><li>Size of the release (in SLOC for this example)</li><li># Modules "touched" (optional)</li></ul>
Effort by activity:
<ul><li>Consolidation</li><li>Analysis</li><li>Production (design, code, and test)</li><li>Configuration management</li><li>Quality assurance</li><li>Management and build definition</li></ul> Costs by type: <ul><li>Labor</li><li>ODCs</li><li>Travel (if required)</li></ul>

6.4 Tracking and Updating

You can use a spreadsheet to estimate expected arrivals by month if desired. If so, you can also use the spreadsheet during the year to track the original estimates (plan values) against actual values. You can extrapolate the trend to detect potential problems. For example, Figure 6-5 shows a "Time History" worksheet for estimating and tracking the number of problem reports received each month. (This number determines the effort for Activity 2 in the preceding example.) This example has actual problem report data entered through July. This worksheet fits a line to the actual data points, and uses the slope and intercept to estimate future values. Summing the actual values reported to date and the estimated values for the remainder of the year gives an updated estimate of the year's total problem reports. The original estimate assumed 444 problem reports. The predicted value is 461. (The cell containing the estimated total is shaded to indicate that the value exceeds the original estimate.) The team may need to request more resources! Figure 6-6 plots the estimated and actual arrivals by month for this example. It also shows linear trendline. (Appendix E, "Excel for Estimators," explains how to add trendlines to a plot.) You can use similar spreadsheets to estimate and track the other counts used to estimate the sustainment effort and costs.

	A	B	C	D	E	F
1	Project:	Example				
2	Prepared By:	S. Smith				
3	Date Prepared:	10/7/2004				
4						
5		**Problem Reports**				
6	**Month**	**Estimated**	**Actual**	**Comments**	**Index**	**Value**
7	Jan	35	32		1	32.00
8	Feb	35	35		2	35.00
9	Mar	35	34		3	34.00
10	Apr	35	36		4	36.00
11	May	35	38		5	38.00
12	Jun	35	37		6	37.00
13	Jul	39	39	Increase due to planned release of new version.	7	39.00
14	Aug	39			8	40.00
15	Sep	39			9	41.04
16	Oct	39			10	42.07
17	Nov	39			11	43.11
18	Dec	39			12	44.14
19						
20		*Total To Date =*	251	Intercept at Index = 1 is		31.714
21				Slope is		1.0357
22		**Totals =**	**444**	**461**	**<= = Estimated Total for Year**	

Figure 6-5 *Analysis of problem reports through July*

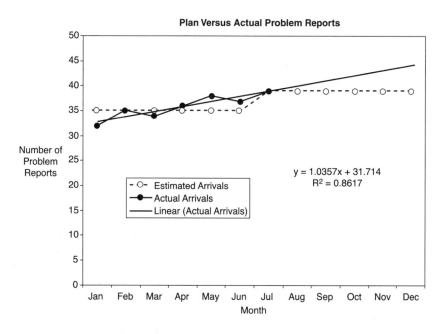

Figure 6-6 *Plot of problem reports versus month*

6.5 Improving the Estimation Model

This section illustrates ways to improve the accuracy of estimated sustainment costs. It also suggests ways to change the process to reduce the costs.

6.5.1 Predicting PR Arrival Rate

Figure 6-7 shows that the mix of changes occurs over time. You can use such information to develop more accurate predictions of the arrival rate of problem reports. Specifically, you estimate the arrival rate of each type of report using a different model, and then add them up. The topmost gray line is the total arrival rate (e.g., the number of change requests received per calendar-month).

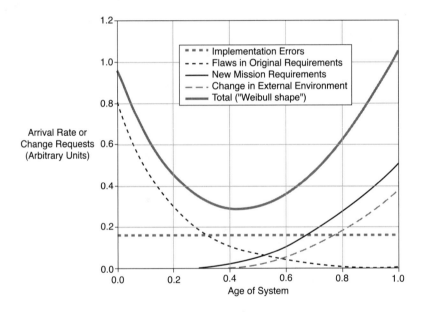

Figure 6-7 *Sources of change requests versus time*

When planning support for a product, consider that support costs usually increase every time that a new release goes to the users. One reason is that the technical support staff must continue to support users of the old product, as well as users of the new product (assumed here to be new customers, not exist- ing customers that transitioned from the old version). The main cause, however, is that users find some of the features unfamiliar and so require addi- tional help. Many organizations have a special department that acquires large data processing systems. People in this department represent the users but do not always understand the users' true needs. (This is why you should identify all stakeholders and elicit requirements from them.) When this happens, the delivered product, no matter how well engineered, does not meet the needs of all the users. This results in a sudden increase in problem reports and change requests. If you know the release schedule, and especially if you know that a particular future release will involve major changes to the product's capabilities, then you should account for this in your estimates by increasing the expected number of problem reports for that period, and increasing the effort allocated for repair and enhancement of the product. Figure 6-8 shows a saw tooth curve that illustrates the typical behavior in the number of problem reports received per month for a complex, software-intensive system that takes years to procure. Examples include air traffic control and military command and control systems. The exact shape of the curve depends on how many new customers purchase the product. If the product is very popular, then the number of customers rapidly increases, and so the number of problem reports may increase with time. Figure 6-9 shows the cumulative effects for three releases of a commercial product. Not all users install the new version simultaneously. (In fact, some never do.)

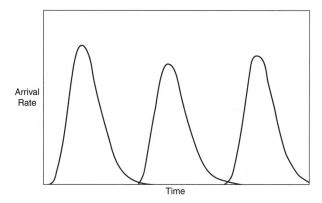

Figure 6-8 *Predicted problem report arrivals for three releases: Plot 1*

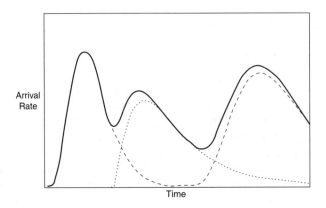

Figure 6-9 *Predicted problem report arrivals for three releases: Plot 2*

6.5.2 Allocating Effort

You need to allocate software engineering effort differently for maintenance, as illustrated in Figure 6-10. This is idealized, but representative. "Support" here means configuration management, quality assurance, and project management. "Screening" includes logging, consolidating, and analyzing problem reports and requests, and is excluded from the other "production and support" activities. Screening is done continuously in order to detect "emergency fixes" (life-threatening problems), or new requirements that may affect the current build content. For example, a customer may demand inclusion of a new requirement. Some organizations add another continuous task (under "screening") for "customer support," which could include answering phone calls, operating a help desk, and delivering user training courses. (Use past experience with the customer(s) to estimate how much effort is required. Some customers demand more support than others.) Developers may also provide some technical support to customers and users. If so, don't forget to reduce the average availability of the programming team when estimating the build schedule. (Chapter 12, "Top-Down Estimating and Allocation," explains how to use average availability when estimating project schedules.) Finally, the allocation of effort between production and screening changes if the programmers do some detailed design and coding of fixes as part of analyzing VUPRs.

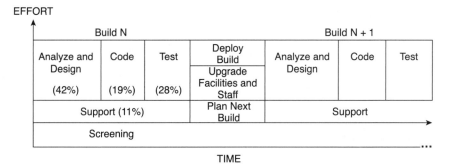

Figure 6-10 *The allocation of sustainment effort (idealized)*

6.5.3 Targeting the Troublemakers

Metrics can help you manage the sustainment process and reduce costs. Typically, the 80/20 rule applies to software sustainment. For whatever reason, 20% of the modules seem to generate 80% of the problem reports. Tracking which modules are changed when implementing each approved modification request (problem request report or enhancement request) enables you to identify which modules require frequent changes. If the module is "error-prone," you can decide to redesign or recode it so that it will not fail so often. If a module requires frequent updates, you might redesign it to make updating easier. As an example, suppose that a business program stores tax-withholding rates as hard coded IF/ELSEIF statements. You could redesign the code to load these values from a data file or a database table. This allows a database administrator to make the updates instead of a programmer. (Analysts should identify such frequently modified information at the start of a project. It does not always happen, however.)

6.5.4 Including Uncertainty

The Linear Model provides a single estimated value for each quantity. You can include uncertainty using the PERT technique described in Chapter 5. You can also obtain a mean and standard deviation for each quantity of interest if you obtain estimates from multiple sources and combine them, or if you use multiple historical data points to determine your production coefficients.

6.5.5 Improving Your Measurements

You can classify PRs, VUPRS, and VUSDs by type to obtain (1) a better understanding of the sources of problems, and (2) to provide a basis for more accurate estimates. For example, you might classify VUPRs to indicate the general
cause of the reported problem:

- Software problem
- Hardware problem
- User error (due to deficient documents or training)
- User abuse (e.g., pounding on the computer, causing a disk crash)
- Environment problem (power surge)
- External interface problem (other system changed)
- No cause identified
- New requirement (proposed enhancement)

Many software metrics books decompose software problems ("defects") into
categories such as data type mismatch, incorrect data initialization, error in
control logic, error in placement or formatting of information, error in timing,
and violation of design and coding standards. (The recommended reading for
this chapter identifies sources for several schemes.) Similarly, you might subdivide hardware problems based on the type of assembly or component that
failed.

User errors arise because of incomplete, inconsistent, or ambiguous information, or ignorance. For example, a product may function correctly according to
its specifications. The user may misuse the product, however, because there is
an error in the user documentation. (It may say "Click button B" when it
should have said "Click button C.") Both the software and the documentation
may be consistent, but the user may not have read it. (This may indicate that
the user-training program is deficient. Perhaps the training course did not
cover the use of that particular feature.) Such information provides the sustainment organization with valuable insight into how to improve product
deliverables (software, documents, and training courses) and how to instruct
technical support representatives to handle common types of problems. I distinguish misuse from abuse. See the box "An Example of User Abuse."

Environmental problems refer to conditions that cause the system to fail but are
outside of your control. Examples include power surges, immersion in water,
excessively high or low temperatures, and noise on communications circuits.
(A well-designed system should be able to defend itself against garbled trans-
missions, but sometimes extremely unlikely situations occur.) External interfaces are similar, and occur when another system changes an interface such as
a message format.

Resolving a particular problem may require changes to multiple work products (e.g., code, manuals, and training courses). Thus, deciding what to track is not easy. There are many ways to classify problem reports. First, decide what you want to know. Then use the Goal-Question-Metric (GQM) method, described in Chapter 4, "Measurement and Estimation," to decide how to collect the information you need.

An Example of User Abuse

Our firm once built a small desktop training device for the military. Each device had switches and displays that represented the control panel for the system, and had a single board computer and hard disk located inside. We built, tested, and shipped dozens of these units to the training facility. Over the next few months, we received three problem reports complaining about poor reliability: The hard disks had crashed. The cause turned out to be user abuse. The students often fell asleep during class. To awake them, the instructor walked over and slammed his fist on the top of the device, causing a head crash in the disk drive. One solution to the problem would have been to retrain the instructor. Instead, we located ruggedized disk drives and installed them in special shock mountings. (Sometimes it is better to retreat than to confront the real problem.)

6.6 Recommended Reading

Thomas Pigoski covers software maintenance in depth in [Pigoski, 1997]. He discusses processes, planning, metrics, tools, resources, and organization. He provides case studies for software transition and for metrics, including the lessons learned. He speculates on the future of software maintenance, including the impacts of object-oriented technology and commercial off-the-shelf products. He also provides a list of available resources (organizations, conferences, periodicals, and Internet).

Shari Lawrence Pfleeger examines software maintenance in Chapter 11 of [Pfleeger, 1998]. She describes different types of systems, defines roles and responsibilities, identifies maintenance challenges, and discusses factors that affect maintenance effort. Her discussions of impact analysis, automated tools, and "rejuvenation" techniques are especially interesting. Ian Sommerville briefly covers software maintenance in Chapter 32 of [Sommerville, 2004]. Barry Boehm covers estimation for software maintenance in Chapter 30 of

[Boehm, 1981]. Kurt Welker and Paul Oman discuss software maintainability metrics [Welker, 1995].

Robert Secord, Daniel Plakosh, and Grace Lewis address modernizing legacy systems, an aspect of software maintenance [Seacord, 2003]. Chapter 16 of [STSC, 2003] gives a good overview of software sustainment.

The most complete source for defining defects is the "IEEE Standard Classification for Software Anomalies" [IEEE 1044, 1993]. It describes the classification of a problem as a series of four activities: recognition, investigation, action, and disposition, providing a structure to identify information that you might want to collect. The standard also provides examples of classification schemes for activities, project phases, causes, and the like. This is a good source to identify possible options.

Norman Fenton and Shari Lawrence Pfleeger discuss factors to consider when defining problems, failures, faults, and changes in Section 5.2 of [Fenton, 1997]. This is a good high-level introduction. They also discuss IEEE Standard 1044.

Robert Grady and Deborah Caswell identify three categories of software defects in Figure 9-4 of [Grady, 1987, page 124]. Their categories are programming defect, user interface/interaction, and operating environment. These loosely correspond to corrective, perfective, and adaptive repairs, respectively. Robert Grady categorizes the sources of software defects by project phase in Figure 11-5 of [Grady, 1992, page 128]. He based his model on an early version of IEEE Standard 1044. He describes a defect in terms of its origin, type, and "mode," which characterizes the type of failure (missing, unclear, wrong, changed, or better way). In his Appendix B, Grady stresses the need to collect additional project information in order to interpret the types and causes of defects.

Orthogonal defect classification (ODC) uses defect data to locate problems in process phases and to evaluate product quality [Chillarege, 1992]. Engineers collect and analyze defect information at two different times: when a tester finds a defect, and when the programmer completes the repair. Several software companies use ODC. For more information see http://www.research .ibm.com/softeng/ODC/ODC.HTM.

William Florac and Anita Carlson provide an operational definition of defects using a checklist shown in Figure 2.10 of [Florac, 1999, pages 33-34]. Their Figure 6.2 (page 150) lists these software defect types: function, interface, timing, algorithm, checking, assignment, build/package, and documentation, which are based on Table 2.11 of [Humphrey, 1995]. Watts Humphrey provides a log to record defects and instructions for completing it in Tables 2.8 and 2.9 of [Humphrey, 1995, pages 45-47].

6.7 Summary

This chapter described how to build a model to estimate the annual budget for sustaining software. The first step was to understand the sustainment process itself. Diagramming the data flow provided an overall picture of how the process operates. You can use the inputs to each activity to identify "size" parameters that affect the effort needed to perform that activity. Historical data played an important role in determining the productivity values for each activity, even if you cannot identify other factors that might affect the productivity. (The text mentioned some factors for each activity that may affect the productivity.) If the sustainment organization is stable, however, the main variation in effort is the workload. This allows you to use historical productivity values plus estimates of the workload to calculate the required effort.

Although simple, this model is more complete than models that only address the software production activities. In fact, the example showed that gauging the efficiency of the sustainment process in terms of lines of code per person-hour could be misleading. The underlying reason is that *different measures of size drive the effort for the various activities*. To estimate the effort for the entire process requires what I call a *federated estimation model*, one composed of multiple models, each contributing estimates for a particular subprocess.

Part 2

The Details

Chapter 7

Preparing to Estimate (Precursors of Estimation)

The greatest challenge for an estimator is deciding where to start when faced with a blank sheet of paper. The warehouse problem described in Chapter 2, "Planning a Warehouse Inventory System," illustrated how to develop estimates by identifying "pieces" (product components, delivered services, and project tasks), and then estimating the resources needed to buy or build each piece, and to perform each activity. This chapter describes specific ways to systematically decompose products, processes, and projects into pieces. Then you can apply the estimating techniques described in Chapter 5, "Estimating Techniques," to these pieces.

Section 7.1 defines the "precursors to estimation." Without these, it is impossible to produce an accurate estimate. Section 7.2 explains how to quickly understand the overall job using "key diagrams." Section 7.3 explains how the operational concept can help estimators identify the user's needs, constraints, and outside influences. Section 7.4 addresses how to identify products and services. Section 7.5 discusses product requirements. Section 7.6 discusses the product architecture. Section 7.7 addresses project considerations that affect how the products are produced. (Chapter 10, "Production Processes (Project Life Cycles)," describes types of production processes, and how each meets customer needs and project constraints.) Section 7.8 gives recommended reading. Section 7.9 summarizes the chapter's key points.

7.1 The Precursors of Estimation

You cannot create estimates out of thin air (although some managers and customers seem to expect this). You need certain types of information. It is obvious that

- You cannot estimate the size, performance, or quality of a product if you cannot describe the product and its characteristics.
- You cannot estimate the development resources (effort, time, materials, and supplies) needed to build the product if you cannot describe the production process.
- You cannot estimate project costs and schedule without some understanding of your organization's business rules, financial objectives, legal constraints, and potential risks.

Before you can prepare any project estimate, you must understand the six "precursors of estimation":

- Customer's needs and operational environment
- Products and services to be delivered
- Production process to be used
- Project goals and constraints
- Estimate's purpose and constraints
- Applicable estimating techniques and tools

These precursors establish the context for the estimate: the data and assumptions that you must have to use the estimating techniques.

Without this context, estimates are just meaningless numbers. This chapter addresses the first two precursors. Chapter 10 addresses the third. Chapter 15, "Calculating Cost and Price: The Basics," addresses the fourth. In particular, business and legal aspects can have important impacts on project cost, schedule, and risks. The fifth refers to the desired accuracy and the resources available to prepare the estimate. These affect the techniques and methods you choose. The sixth may seem obvious, but Chapter 13, "Parametric Models," gives examples of misusing parametric estimation models.

7.2 How to Understand the Overall Job: The Key Diagrams

All participants in the estimating process need an integrated understanding of the "overall job," which includes the customer's needs, the product's structure, the development process, and the project's constraints and business objectives. Section 4.2.1 mentioned the parable about several blind people observing an elephant for the first time. Each person reported a different perception. This parable also typifies the problem of describing a complex product or system that you must estimate. For complex products and large projects, no single person understands all of the pieces that go together to create the product and to run the project. Engineers, project managers, accountants, lawyers, buyers, and users all view a product and a project from different perspectives. As Gerry Weinberg says, "There are many views of a system. All are equally correct" [Weinberg, 2001]. These different views provide valid, complementary ways to structure the elements of the job to facilitate planning, estimating, and tracking. These different views also facilitate communication between the various participants.

I find that every project has four or five "key diagrams" that capture this essential information. These "diagrams" may be system data flow diagrams, hardware layouts, the floor plan of a facility, or a depiction of the production process that shows activities, phases, and milestones. The "diagrams" may also be lists of tasks, deliverables, constraints, or risks, or they may be tables of transaction types or operating modes. The key diagrams serve as a basis to start planning and estimating the project. (Later sections illustrate this.) When reviewing estimates, I find that teams that cannot provide this integrated view of what they are trying to accomplish usually produce very poor estimates.

The specific diagrams are different for each project so I cannot give you a standard list. Instead, this chapter describes several examples. Your team needs to recognize the diagrams that are useful to describe your particular project, product, and process. It is hard to identify all the key diagrams at the start of the planning process. Usually, the key diagrams naturally emerge as the team learns more about the application and solution domains. (Various analysis methods help the team elicit, digest, and consolidate the information and usually include specific diagrams and tables to represent the information.)

Hint 1: Pretend that you must describe your proposed project to a senior decision maker and that you will only have 30 minutes to do it. This means that you only have time to explain four or five charts. These are the key diagrams. (Some people mention an "elevator speech" where you ride in an elevator with the senior decision maker and so must convey your important points in only two or three minutes. I think that software-intensive systems are more complex and you should be allowed at least 30 minutes to explain what you are trying to accomplish!)

Hint 2: To identify the key diagrams, look at what people are actually using. During a proposal or early planning, some diagrams (lists, tables, or figures) become the focus of discussions and may appear in different places in a draft proposal or planning documents. The team repeatedly refers to these key diagrams because they capture the essence of the problem.

Hint 3: Keep your charts short! Each "key diagram" is only a page or two long, even for a large project. (You can supplement them with detailed documents on larger projects.) Each chart should only have a simple diagram or a short list of items. A good way to format this is to provide one chart with the diagram or list, accompanied by a page of explanatory text. (If you use a tool such as Microsoft PowerPoint, include the text in the Speaker Notes section. Then the information can be printed on a single piece of paper, with the itemized list or diagram on top, and the explanatory text below it.)

Figure 7-1 shows the relation between user requirements and other deliverable items. For estimation, the user requirements drive the operational needs, as captured in the operational concept. The operational concept drives product requirements, which drive functions. Functions drive size. Size drives effort. Effort drives cost and schedule. (In some cases, a specified cost or schedule may constrain the product requirements that the project can implement.) If the user does not specify the product requirements, the estimator must depend on analysts and engineers to elicit the true requirements for the system from the stakeholders, whoever they may be.

The operational concept describes the structure of the user's organization (e.g., departmental responsibilities) and the business objectives (the purpose of the enterprise). The designers examine the operational concept to identify the system requirements. Then they devise a product architecture, which identifies the hardware, software, and data components of the system. The product architecture also affects the content and form of the user manuals. The user manuals, the business' policies and procedures, and the knowledge and skill of the users influence the training courses that must be developed. The training courses "program" the users so that they can use the business process and the capabilities provided by the product. Although not shown in the figure, the developer may also have to deliver additional services such as system installation and data conversion. These arise from the activities needed to activate the new system, especially if the organization must transition from an existing system.

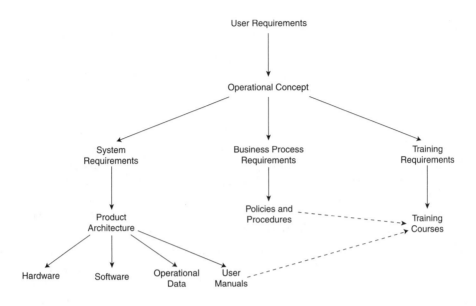

Figure 7-1 *Requirements fan out*

A good approach is to define an operational concept, then the product vision, and then a requirements list. (See the following sections.) These documents are key to producing a good initial estimate. They also record the initial estimating assumptions, product requirements, and project scope, providing the basis to detect and manage change and to control the scope of the job.

7.3 The Operational Concept

The operational concept describes the environment in which the system will operate, and explains how various types of users, external systems, and the system will function together to accomplish the "mission" of the organization or enterprise.[1] Many software products perform obvious, "easily understood" functions and so an operational concept is unnecessary. Examples include shrink-wrapped applications and websites. Others are larger and more complex, and so an operational concept is useful. Examples include internal corporate Information Technology systems, business-to-business intranets, and

---

[1] Fred Heemstra provides essentially the same view, which he calls the "prerequisites for software cost estimation." He identifies characteristics of the product, process, production personnel, the production organization, and the user organization, plus the availability of estimation techniques and tools. For details, see [Heemstra, 1992].

business-to-business customer (e-business) applications.[2] An operational concept is most useful for understanding large unprecedented systems (many classes of users, external stakeholders, functions, and modes of operation). If your products are "simple" and/or well understood, then you can skip this section. Other readers will find the operational concept a useful tool to understand the objects to be estimated. [3]

The operational concept is a key document for estimators because it assigns specific functions of the business process (i.e., the sociotechnical system) to the automated system, and other functions to human beings (or possibly other external systems). This assignment directly affects the sizes of the items that you must estimate. The product's requirements and design affect the software size, which in turn affects the development effort. The manual activities affect the effort to write user documentation and training materials.

The operational concept conveys important information to various people who are involved with buying, using, and building the system. Each person has specific interests as shown in Table 7-1. For example, the facility manager also needs to evaluate the system's impact on the overall organization's operation (processes, other systems, facilities) and coordinate the introduction of the new (or modified) system.

Table 7-1 *Information Needs Vary by Role*

Role	Primary Interest(s)
Customers and buyers	Purchase cost, operating costs, affordability
Users and operators	Capabilities, dependability, ease of use
Facility managers and maintainers	Operating and support costs, modifiability, performance, dependability
System and software engineers	Feasibility, design constraints, features, build versus buy

---

[2] The operational concept (Ops concept or OpsCon) is also called the *concept of operations* (ConOps). Both terms are used interchangeably. Note, however, that some manufacturers use the term concept of operations to denote the *technical* principles of operation of a system or device. (Other vendors call this document the "principles of operation.") To avoid possible confusion, I prefer to use the term *operational concept*, consistent with the SEI's CMMI. The INternational Council On Systems Engineering (INCOSE) and the Institute of Electrical and Electronic Engineers (IEEE) both use the term *concept of operations*, however.

[3] Not all of these are simple, of course.

Role	Primary Interest(s)
System implementers	Roles, data structures, data flow, functions, modes
Testers	Scenarios and operational data
Development managers	Risks, development cost and time

Table 7-2 summarizes the essential elements of the operational concept as described by Richard Fairley and Richard Thayer [Fairley, 1997]. The operational concept is written from a user standpoint and is nontechnical. The initial, high-level operational concept should be brief. Describe processes (data flows, activities) to help clarify the purpose of the system, and identify processing threads. List the roles that will use the system and the functions that each must perform. (You can use this information to identify needed functions, and so estimate the amount of software that must be developed. Chapter 8, "Estimating Software Size: The Basics," gives an example.) Describe the assumed knowledge and skills for each role, and the staffing concept (number of workers by role and shift). Describe the general characteristics of the (computing) system.

Table 7-2 *Essential Elements of an Operational Concept*

A description of the needs that motivate development of a new system or modification of an existing system
Modes of operation for the proposed system
User classes (roles) and user characteristics
Operational features of the proposed system
Priorities among proposed operational features
Operational scenarios for each operational mode and class of user
Limitations of the proposed approach

The operational concept should state how often the system is used. Designing a system that will be used 24 hours per day, seven days per week presents additional challenges in design, cut over, and maintenance compared to a simple system that is activated "on demand" to perform some sort of batch processing. The operational concept should identify the major operating modes of the system. For example, a system might perform a large volume of processing at the end of every month when invoices are generated, stressing the system. Describing possible operational scenarios for the system is an excellent way to understand what users need to accomplish and how they will use the system to do it. Operational scenarios are called "use cases" in the newer software development methods. These are one way to size the product (discussed in Chapter 9, "Estimating Software Size: The Details") and to identify meaningful test cases.

System engineers allocate the user's mission requirements to people and to the system. People need procedures and must be trained. The system must be designed, built, tested, and deployed. Each alternative has associated costs. System engineers must evaluate trade-offs involving costs, performance, and risk. For example, should you provide a highly automated system that can be operated by semi-skilled (and inexpensive) workers, or should you provide a "bare bones" system to be operated by expert users? Estimates of performance, costs, schedule, and risks play an important role in such trade studies. See Part III, Fundamentals of Engineering Economics, in [Boehm, 1981]. Also see Don Reifer's book that describes how to prepare a business case [Reifer, 2002].

A context diagram is often useful as well. A context diagram depicts the boundary and external interfaces of a system. It is drawn as a single circle, labeled with the name of the system, with directed lines (arrows) on the exterior of the circle indicating data flows to and from external entities, which are shown as rectangles (called "terminators"). Context diagrams are used in structured analysis as the starting point for stepwise decomposition of the system's data flows.

7.4 Identifying Products and Services

Developers and estimators must identify all products and related services. Otherwise, how can you know what to estimate? The level of description varies depending on the size of the project and the customer's desires. For example, a developer of commercial products might just use a short project charter, a list of tasks, or a SOW (Statement Of Work or Scope Of Work). The U.S. government uses very formal descriptions. The basic elements of a SOW are

- Deliverables
- Project constraints
- Product acceptance criteria
- Customer-furnished items

You must identify all items to be delivered by a project. These items can be tangible things or services. The box "Types of Deliverables" identifies categories of items and examples for each category. (Also refer to the planning checklist described in Section 2.4.) The customer specifies the number or amount of each item. The customer may also specify the delivery date for each deliverable. You may receive dates for draft and final versions of each document. You may receive the "build sequence" for product releases. This indicates capabilities needed (delivered) tied to specific dates. (This assumes that the chosen project life cycle produces multiple releases.) Large projects integrate the delivery dates with the milestones of the project life cycle. For documents, the customer may specify how large and formal each document must be. If not, you can delimit the scope of each document by specifying the purpose, intended audience, and size (number of pages) in estimating assumptions or proposals. Alternatively, cite industry or government standards that describe each document.

Types of Deliverables

Product or system (as defined in the product specification)
    Hardware components
    Software components

Databases (if applicable)
    Operational data (e.g., parts catalog or customer accounts)
    Calibration/support
    User training scenarios and associated data

Documents (product-related)
    User manual
    Installation manual
    Maintenance manual (how to perform preventive maintenance, report problems, make repairs, and use specific tools)
    Top-level design (architecture description: components, allocation of functions, and interactions)
    Version description document
    Design and coding guidelines

Documents (project-related)
    Status reports
    Trade studies
    Plans and schedules
    Metrics

Services
    Trade studies
    System installation
    Database conversion
    Packing and shipping

> Site installation
> User/operator training
> Perform maintenance (preventive, repairs, enhancements)
>
> Meetings and reviews
> Status meetings
> Milestone reviews (requirements, design, test)
> Demonstrations

The customer may also specify project constraints. These may include the following:

- Total funding (or funding profile by year)
- Time limits (especially any key milestones.)
- Regulatory requirements (foreign offsets, health and safety certification)
- Enterprise policies (e.g., CMMI compliance)
- Development life cycle (defines milestones and reviews)

Some possible key "external" milestones are demonstrations, synchronize with other projects, or meet satellite launch windows. Key "internal" milestones may be formal reviews or the dates when funds either become available or expire.

Some customers specify the criteria for product acceptance. These include the types of testing required. Examples include functional, regression, user, stress, environmental, and field tests. Commercial developers often perform developer tests, alpha tests, and beta tests. If the customer fails to specify these criteria, you should state how you intend to demonstrate that the product is acceptable.

This is a good time to identify any customer-furnished items that you will need. Project success often depends on items furnished by the customer. The development team may need documents, hardware, software, databases, and expertise (access to subject matter experts). State when you will need each item. If you must go to the customer's site to install and test the system, also consider the following:

- Access to special networks (Internet, intranet)
- Work areas with furniture, network access, and telephones

Specify when you will need access to these (start and end dates, and the times during this period).

TIP: Document your needs in contract terms and conditions or a memorandum of agreement (MOA).

7.5 Product Requirements

The complexity of the product determines how detailed the requirements must be. This section describes a simple product vision, a requirements list, and a more detailed product specification.

7.5.1 Product Vision

The *product vision* provides a high-level description of the product's requirements. It supplements the operational concept, and is written from a user perspective. The product vision bounds the scope of the product by succinctly describing what the product is, and what the product is not. Table 7-3 summarizes the components of the product vision. The name of the product should be descriptive, and any acronyms should be defined. The purpose should indicate the business objective that is supported. The capabilities indicate what the product is supposed to do. These are the "minimum essential" features and functions needed to make the product acceptable or successful. Tie the functions to specific user roles, and state them in the user's vernacular. For example, the product vision may identify specific types of transactions to be handled, and state that every transaction will be validated immediately upon input. (You can record details as user stories, use cases, or operational scenarios.) External interfaces identify other systems, other organizations and departments, and any unusual peripherals such as sensors and actuators. Performance could include the maximum number of transactions to be handled per day. Critical characteristics indicate what the system must not do, how well it performs its functions, or how "dependably" it performs the functions. For example, an important characteristic might be to ensure operator safety. Design constraints specify the target computing platform, the implementation language, commercial off-the-shelf (COTS) components, and reused components. They might also state the desire to construct portions of the product for later reuse, and the need for compatibility with other products. Assumptions indicate decisions that affect scope, unknowns, or potential risks. (As in the warehouse problem, you can prepare a list of risks and a list of questions to accompany the product vision. These lists provide a way to collect additional information.)

Table 7-3 *Components of the Product Vision*

Product name
Product purpose (one sentence)
Capabilities included: • User roles • Functions or features • External interfaces
Capacity and performance
Critical characteristics (e.g., dependability)
Design constraints: • Platform • COTS or reused components • Programming language
Assumptions and risks

The product vision should be short, no longer than three or four pages. This forces people to focus on what the "minimum essential" capabilities are. (My preference is to limit it to a single page.) If the product is large, you may need to describe multiple products and multiple services. I recommend, however, that each of these be described in one page or less, listing no more than 10 items (features and constraints) per product. Focus on the most important "minimum essential" characteristics of each product or service to be delivered.

TIP: To better define product scope, you can distinguish three types of capabilities:

- Required (specifically included)

- Undesired (specifically excluded)

- Desired (optionally included)

All of these items should be short phrases or a single sentence in a list. You should indicate what the product "is" and what the product "is not." This helps avoid misunderstandings later! You may also indicate "desired capabilities" that will be implemented if time and resources permit. The requirements list, described next, extends this by assigning a priority to each requirement in the list. This helps distinguish the *must have* from the *nice to have*. "The best is the enemy of the good (enough)."

The product vision guides the team without excessive detail, channeling their creative energies in the same general direction. This allows the team to innovate and adapt its designs within broad, commonly agreed constraints. The product vision also records the developers' understanding of the customer's requirements, and the proposed product that will meet these requirements. Providing the product vision to the customer early in the project exposes problems before substantial resources have been expended. (I know of one large project that did not discover a fundamental disagreement over the interpretation of requirements until the middle of acceptance testing, two years after the start of the project. The developers had to work for another six months to correct the problem. It was an expensive mistake.)

7.5.2 The Requirements List

The requirements list is a numbered list of the product's requirements or features. For a small project, the requirements list may be fairly short, no more than a page or two. Projects to build large systems usually have a formal specification that may be hundreds of pages long. Your project must decide what level of detail is appropriate.

The requirements list is the primary input to the design team, and to the testers, who will determine whether the product meets the (acceptance) requirements. The requirements list controls the evolution of the entire product or system. (Larger projects use a requirements traceability matrix or RTM instead.) You (or your customer) will usually discover additional requirements as the project proceeds. Thus, you should establish configuration control of the list.

For the estimator, the requirements list makes the requirements visible so that you can count them. You can determine whether the total is growing. If the engineers maintain the date for each change to a requirement, plus the date it was first added, you can also track volatility. (This requires a database or a tool. It is difficult to keep track of the dates and revised text using only a spreadsheet.)

Figure 7-2 shows a simple spreadsheet for recording product requirements. The heading of the requirements list has the name of the product, the name of the person who prepared the list, the date it was prepared or last updated, and optionally an approval. The body of the list is a set of individual requirements. Each requirement consists of an identifier, a text statement, and some keywords to facilitate accessing requirements based on characteristics such as category, priority, and so forth. (See next paragraph.) Optionally, you may include a few "key diagrams." (Reference these diagrams in a text statement contained in the requirements list to maintain traceability.)

PROJECT NAME:				PREPARED BY:	
PRODUCT NAME:				DATE:	
	F	M		PHONE:	
	I	D			
	P	O		APPROVED BY:	
	N			DATE:	
	D				
	M				

Reqmt #	Type	Priority	Description (Requirement, Feature, Function)	Source (Optional)	Notes and Comments
123			Calculate the employee's gross wages	IRS Code 123.4	This is a comment

Figure 7-2 *A simple requirements list*

One way to organize this list is to identify five types of requirements:

- Functional requirements
- Interface requirements (users and external systems or devices)
- Performance requirements (capacity, accuracy, and speed)
- Nonfunctional requirements (dependability)
- Design and construction requirements (implementation constraints)
- Maintenance and support requirements (optional)

The box "Product Requirements" discusses each of these. Using such categories also helps elicit information from the user and developer. This leads to a better understanding of the system, how it will be built, and what resources will be required. It also allows you to count the number of requirements in each category.

Product Requirements

Functional requirements are derived from the operational concept that meets the user's business or mission needs.

Interface requirements identify external systems or devices with which the product must interface. Specify peripherals and external systems and provide details such as the type of hardware connectors and communications protocols.

Performance requirements include static and dynamic characteristics such as maximum storage (number of records or rows in a database, number of bytes of disk storage) and accuracy, speed, and throughput. Some specifications have two values for a key parameter: Must meet (minimum acceptable) and goal (achieve if possible).

Nonfunctional requirements apply to the product as a whole. Examples include dependability (reliability, availability, security, safety, as appropriate), maintainability, extensibility, and other "ilities."

Design and construction constraints ensure that the product will be compatible with existing products, or with the skills of the maintenance staff. For example, the customer may want the product to run on a particular computing platform. (The "platform" is whatever the developer assumes is taken as a "given," stable foundation. The developer builds the product on top of the platform.) For many software-intensive systems, the platform consists of commercial off-the-shelf (COTS) components such as the computer, peripherals, the operating system, a relational database management system (RDBMS), communications packages, and device drivers.

Design and construction constraints can include the target platform, development platform (sometimes divided into the software engineering environment and the software test environment), and specific COTS or customer-furnished items that must be used or that will be supplied, for example, a commercial RDBMS. (Note that choosing a Windows environment implies an architecture.) Related design constraints (which are also "key computer resources") may include the number of available card slots in the motherboard, available ports (by type: USB, IEEE 488, RS 232, etc.), types and numbers of peripherals (dual video card, high-resolution graphics card). You should also identify any obsolete cards or software versions (operating system, COTS products, compilers, linkers) that must be used.

Maintenance and support requirements for software might include the need to periodically defragment disks. For hardware components, they might include the need for preventive maintenance (e.g., cleaning and lubrication).

Priority is another important characteristic. For example, is the requirement "must have," "desirable," or "if resources permit"? Priority ratings may be hard to obtain, but will help you to prune the list of features. (Use one of the ranking techniques described in Chapter 27, "Ranking and Selecting Items.") Another characteristic is "urgency." You can use it to decide which features to assign to a particular release if the product will be delivered in increments.

7.5.3 The Product Specification

The product specification formally defines the desired product. The key areas to cover in a product specification are as follows:

- Product Requirements
- Acceptance Criteria
- Requirements Priorities
- Clarifications

Product requirements include functional requirements, interface requirements, performance requirements, nonfunctional requirements, design and construction constraints and, optionally, maintenance and support requirements.

Acceptance criteria essentially say "Satisfy all requirements contained in the product specification." They may define specific types of tests that the developer must perform. The developer should create and maintain a requirements traceability matrix (RTM) that links the requirements, design elements, and test cases. This ensures that all requirements are allocated to one or more design elements, and that each requirement has been tested.

Requirements priorities are useful because not all requirements have equal business value. For the customer, priority has two aspects: value to the user ("importance") and urgency (when needed). All requirements do not have equal value to the end user. For example, 20% of the system's specified functions may provide 80% of the business value to the system's users. To select requirements with a reasonable return on investment, you can ask developers to rate the difficulty (amount of implementation effort) of each requirement. (Do not ask for precise estimates, only categories such as Easy [cheap], Medium, and High [expensive].) The best requirements have high business value and are easy to implement. Chapter 27 describes techniques to prioritize requirements, and to balance value and cost.

Clarifications define any words or phrases that are unusual or subject to misinterpretation. Use a project glossary, attached to the specification. This ensures that all readers agree on the meaning of words and phrases.

You can state requirements more precisely by giving lists and examples. For example, you might list all of the communication protocols that a system must handle. For user manuals, you can provide a sample document description (outline and number of pages). You might also want to add notes stating what the system will not do. (This is another way to delimit the scope of the product.)

7.6 Product Architecture

The product architecture describes the product that will meet the requirements. The product architecture captures top-level design assumptions about the system. This is important for both engineers and estimators. Engineers use the architecture as a guide during detailed design and coding to identify and describe the pieces that will be implemented by an individual or a small team. The architecture ensures that the engineers are all decomposing consistently. For estimators, the product architecture is one way to partition a system so that you can identify the pieces that must be constructed. You can then count these pieces or estimate their sizes. (Chapter 9 provides an example.) A good architecture can reduce the amount of software that must be designed, coded, and tested, and improves the quality of the product.

As shown in Table 7-4, the product architecture identifies major components, their functions and interfaces, and the constraints and rules that govern their interactions. The choice of platform, middleware, and other application-specific COTS components is an important architectural decision. The choice of platform and COTS components is often coupled because certain application packages only run on a particular platform. Estimators need to know whether the engineers intend to buy, build, or modify existing components because each of these options has a different associated cost. The choice of programming language, methods, and tools is often tied to the architecture as well, and this also affects development costs.

Table 7-4 *Definition of Product Architecture**

Components: Both Hardware and Software
• Platform (computer hardware and operating system)
• Peripherals (keyboard, mouse, display, sensors, actuators)
• Software components
• COTS and reused components (relational database, middleware)
Structure and Relationship of Components
• Interconnection of hardware components
• Allocation of functions to software components (nature and scope)
• Allocation of software components to hardware components
• Internal software interfaces
• Interfaces to external systems
Interaction Rules and Constraints
• Communications and information passing
• Resource sharing
• Control and synchronization of processing
• Error handling
• User interaction (GUI, help functions)
• Measurement system (units of measure, coordinate systems, gravity model)
• Basic data types (date, time, identifiers, etc.)

*Based on [Shaw, 1996].

Architectural services implement the interaction rules. These services are the glue that allows components to transfer data and coordinate their activities. My definition of "product architecture" adds the last two items shown in Table 7-4 because they are vitally important for many software-intensive systems. There should be a single, consistent set of units for measuring quantities such as length, angles, time, mass, force, voltage, current, and money. (Mixing metric and British engineering units led to the destruction of a Mars lander.) The architecture should specify a set of standard coordinate systems to express orientation and motion. The architecture should identify a set of basic data types associated with the application and solution domains. Some typical examples are date, time, identifiers (e.g., Social Security number), vectors (for position and velocity) expressed in a specified coordinate system, and design elements (queues, linked lists, and trigonometric functions).

Identifying and implementing common services, functions, and data types reduces the total amount of code to be written, understood, and maintained. This reduces the development and testing effort.[4] In addition, such elements are good candidates for components that can be reused in future systems belonging to the same or similar product lines. Typically, engineers identify these "basic services" as the design progresses. As new elements become apparent, the engineers should revise the design and code as necessary to incorporate them (retrofit or refactor). Estimators should include some effort for this! The box "Architecture, Top-Level Design, and Detailed Design" clarifies the distinction between these three objects and provides an example of each.

Architecture, Top-Level Design, and Detailed Design

- Architecture: A template that solves a computing problem

"A single module will detect, log, and report (display) errors."

- Top-level design: A named instance of a template

"The module name is ERRMON. It will handle communications faults."

- Detailed design: The fully described instance

"The list of specific error conditions (and response actions) follows:

(1) If [checksum (sent) ≠ checksum (computed)], then request retransmission.

(2) Additional items..."

Pictures or diagrams can help depict an architecture. Software development methods use various diagrams for data flows, state transitions, and other views of the system. Architecture diagrams help identify support functions that are necessary for the system to operate, but that are usually not apparent to the user or operator of the system. This helps prevent underestimating the software size. Chapter 8 provides examples.

Figure 7-3 shows some simple drawings of the product architecture that can help estimators identify missing components and functions. The type of picture

---

[4] I once analyzed software for a fighter aircraft and discovered four separate implementations of the same coordinate transformation. Each had been independently designed, coded, tested, and documented by different teams. (This was not immediately obvious because each team used different mathematical symbols.)

to use depends upon the application. On the left, the sketch shows an application that has a graphical user interface, connected to some application modules, and ultimately to a local area network interface. The right half of the figure shows a product partitioned into five types of components. The application, in the center, is supported by a number of service routines. These include the user interface, data management services, and the operating system services, and communications services to handle external interfaces.

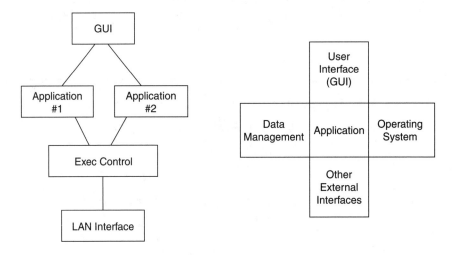

Figure 7-3 *Simple pictures help identify software components*

7.7 Project Goals and Constraints

A project provides resources (people, equipment, tools, and facilities) for the processes that build products and deliver services. Every project has start and completion dates, and begins when the project team receives authorization and funding from a customer or other sponsor.

Project goals are the "success criteria" for the project. They indicate what the project must do (targets) and may indicate things that the project should not do (constraints). Typical goals are a specified completion date and a maximum project cost. (The distinction between a target and a constraint is somewhat arbitrary. You can view a specified completion date as a target or a constraint.)

An external constraint might be the need to comply with regulatory requirements relating to product certification or licensing. An internal constraint is the
organization's business rules for calculating costs. (Chapter 15 describes rules
to calculate various costs.)

Project goals affect how you plan and manage a project, the process used to
develop the products, and what resources are available for the project. For
example, the project may have to prepare additional documents to support the
licensing of a safety critical product, which increases costs. Chapter 10 discusses how project goals can affect the choice of project life cycle. Cash flow,
discussed in Chapter 15, may affect how you define and schedule incremental
releases.

Project success is actually multifaceted and involves characteristics of both the
products and the project shown in Table 7-5. The product vision addresses the
first two. The project goals address the last two. Project planners and estimators often face multiple conflicting goals for these four characteristics. Table
7-6 illustrates the relative priorities of these goals for four different products,
shown in decreasing importance for each product. For a factory process control
system, capability is the most important and, arguably, schedule is the least
important. (Note that cost for this type of product includes operating costs and
savings due to the use of the automated system.) For a commercial product,
schedule might be the most important because the developer wants to ship the
product by a specified date to meet a market window (e.g., the Christmas buying season). A project to build a planetary probe will have schedule as its most
important goal because favorable launch opportunities only occur every few
years. Cost is, arguably, the least important goal for these projects. Finally, for
scientific data analysis, quality (correctness of the computed values) is the most
important, followed by capability (sophisticated data reduction algorithms and
plotting capabilities), followed by cost, and then by schedule. Estimators must
often provide numbers to support the analysis of different alternatives with
respect to such goals. Chapter 13 describes how you can use parametric models to evaluate trade-offs between conflicting goals. Chapter 27 discusses ways
to rank alternatives. Opportunity costs, discussed in Chapter 15, may also
affect the decision to choose one project over another.

Table 7-5 *The Dimensions of Project Success*

Product Capability
• Functions
• Performance
Product Quality
• Residual Defects (reliability)

(continues)

Table 7-5 *The Dimensions of Project Success (continued)*

Project Cost
• Development • Operations • Maintenance
Project Schedule
• Fixed end date (market window, planetary conjunction) • Floating end date

Table 7-6 *Projects Prioritize the Success Criteria Differently*

Factory Process Control System
• Capability (performance, automated features) • Quality (dependability, fail safe) • Costs (development, operations, savings) • Schedule (end of fiscal year)
Commercial Product
• Schedule (market window) • Cost (selling price) • Capability (features, performance) • Quality (dependability, ease of use)
Space Probe
• Schedule (launch window) • Quality (reliability, fault tolerance, fail operational) • Capability (functions, reprogrammability en route) • Costs (develop, test, flight operations, data analysis)
Scientific Data Analysis
• Quality (correctness) • Capability (data analysis algorithms, plots) • Cost (develop tool versus analyze data) • Schedule (end of research grant)

7.8 Recommended Reading

Richard Fairley and Richard Thayer describe the concept of operations in [Fairley, 1997]. They also explain processes for developing and maintaining the operational concept. Appendix A of their paper gives an outline for the document. The Institute of Electrical and Electronic Engineers (IEEE) publishes a standard for concept of operation documents [IEEE Std 1362, 1998]. Their URL is http://www.ieee.org. The International Council on Systems Engineering (INCOSE) provides access to various system engineering standards at http//www.incose.org/stc/stc_library.htm.

Steve McConnell discusses feature set control in Chapter 14 of [McConnell, 1996]. He provides good advice on "creating a minimal specification" (p. 323ff), identifying some alternatives to the vision statement.

In the early 1990s, researchers began to study ways to define architectural styles and representations. For more details, see the book by Mary Shaw and David Garlan [Shaw, 1996], and the books by Paul Clements and his colleagues [Clements, 2002], [Clements, 2003], and [Bass, 2003]. An article by Gregory Rochford and colleagues closely mirrors my thinking [Rochford, 1997]. One Web reference is an article by Mark J. Gerken on research directions in software architecture. The URL is http://www.dacs.dtic.mil/awareness/newsletters/tech-news 2-3/research.html.

7.9 Summary

Before you can prepare any project estimate, you must understand the six "precursors of estimation":

- Customer's needs and operational environment
- Products and services to be delivered
- Production process (project life cycle) to be used
- Project goals and constraints
- Estimate's purpose and constraints
- Applicable estimating techniques and tools

These precursors establish the context for the estimate: the data and assumptions that you must have to use the estimating techniques. Without this context, estimates are just meaningless numbers. The first four precursors provide a way to identify the objects to be estimated. All of these affect the partitioning of a project into tasks that you can estimate, schedule, and track.

Many individuals participate in producing products and delivering services. Each person has his or her own particular perspective, and possesses specific domain knowledge that is not known to the other participants. Diagrams concisely convey important information and help the engineers, the customer, and estimators communicate. Every system, product, project, or process has certain "key diagrams" that capture essential features of the object represented. The objects depicted depend on the particular product, organization, and process.

Four complementary views help the entire team gain an integrated understanding of the product(s), production processes, and the overall project:

- Operational concept
- Product vision
- Product architecture
- Project goals

The operational concept is the first step in defining the scope of the overall system. It identifies which mission functions are done manually and which are done by the product's hardware and software. The manual functions require user documentation and training. The automated functions tie directly to the product's requirements and design, and so to the software size. This allocation affects project cost and risk. The product vision identifies the functional and performance requirements for the product, external interfaces, user interfaces, and possibly details related to the product design, use, and maintenance. (The requirements list and product specification elaborate the product vision.) The product architecture describes the overall form of the product, especially any purchased or reused components. The project goals identify the schedule for product delivery, also identify any business requirements related to profitability, cash flow, regulatory approvals, and risks. (Chapter 10 describes a fourth view of the production process, also called the project life cycle.)

Project planners and estimators must identify all the resources that are needed to perform the production process. The complementary views described in this chapter provide a structured way to identify product components, process activities, project tasks, and other items that you must estimate. These views provide a foundation to develop checklists that you can use to prepare estimates, or to review estimates made by others. The next two chapters describe how to use these views to estimate software size.

Chapter 8

Estimating Software Size: The Basics

There are many possible definitions of product size, each suited to a particular purpose. (In Section 4.2, Table 4.1 identified possible-sized items and their units of measure.) Section 4.2 also discussed how to use size and productivity to compute the effort needed to produce code, data, and documents, and to deliver services such as training. When a project is completed, it is possible (but not necessarily easy) to measure the amount of product delivered and the resources consumed and so compute the (historical) productivity. To estimate software development effort, the challenge is estimating the amount (size) of software that must be produced.

This chapter and the next describe ways to help you estimate the size of a software product. Section 8.1 describes the basic process, criteria for a "good" software size measure, and explains why there is a spectrum of possible size measures, each suited for a particular purpose, and each offering advantages and disadvantages. Section 8.1 also explains why it is difficult to identify all of the software "pieces" that you must include in your estimate. Section 8.2 shows how to identify the software "pieces" using the operational concept described in Chapter 7, "Preparing to Estimate (Precursors of Estimation)." Section 8.3 describes measures of hardware size. Section 8.4 describes how to include growth and volatility in size estimates, regardless of which size measure you choose. Section 8.5 covers measuring and tracking growth and volatility. Section 8.6 gives implementation guidance for managing size. Section 8.7 gives recommended reading. Section 8.8 summarizes the key points of this chapter.

Chapter 9, "Estimating Software Size: The Details," addresses specific size measures, proceeding from "external" characteristics of the product to "internal" characteristics related to the actual code. The size measures include stories, use cases, function points, and lines of source code. Chapter 9 also covers sizing for reused code and commercial off-the-shelf (COTS) components. Together, these two chapters give you the knowledge to choose a size measure appropriate for your needs, and simple procedures and checklists to help you identify the items whose size you will estimate.

8.1 The Sizing Process

Table 8-1 shows the recommended process for estimating size. Steps 1 and 2 are the focus of this chapter and Chapter 9. Step 3 uses estimating techniques explained in Chapter 5, "Estimation Techniques," plus sizing models for reused code (described in Section 9.10) and COTS components (described in Section 9.11). Step 4 is part of the Linear Method, described in Chapter 3, "A Basic Estimating Process: The Linear Method."

Table 8-1 *Basic Process to Estimate Size*

1. Define your size measure.

2. Identify all items to be built.
  • Delivered capabilities (by build)
  • Tools for testing and data conversion?
  • Prototypes?

3. Estimate size of the items using
  • Expert judgment (experience)
  • Analogy (historical data)
  • Converting counts to size
  • (Reverse backfiring, PDL scaling, CERs based on past projects)
  • Sizing models (new, reused, breakage)

4. Add up sizes of like items.

5. Validate the results:
  • Compare values computed using different methods.
  • "Graybeard" review (sanity check).
  • Investigate items having high σ/E.
 	
Repeat Steps 2-4 as appropriate.

8.1.1 Choosing a Size Measure

The characteristics of a "good" size measure are as follows:

- It is correlated to the development effort expended by the engineers.
- It is independent of the technology used and the production process.
- It can be estimated early in the project.
- It can be estimated easily (cheap and fast).
- It can be precisely counted later using automated tools.

Estimators have defined various software size measures that meet some subset of these goals. No size measure meets them all, however, so you must depend on judgment and opinion. The usefulness of a particular size measure depends on the completeness and precision of its definition. Operational definitions, discussed in Chapter 4, "Measurement and Estimation," are best but are not always feasible. The last criterion, automated counting, is useful to objectively validate the hypothesized correlation, and to calibrate conversion factors and size estimation models. The final size can be measured in terms of classes, modules, script files, or lines of code.

Different software size measures become available as a project proceeds, as shown in Figure 8-1.[1] The level of product decomposition increases as the project proceeds. Initially, the stakeholders may only have a product vision and a short list of features. When the operational concept is available, it becomes possible to identify scenarios (user stories), use cases, and then a more complete list of features. These can be refined in terms of screens, reports, and collections of related data. (These are used to count application points and function points.) After the architecture and top-level design are chosen, estimators can identify and count components of various types (modules, files, and data tables). Finally, the engineers can estimate the size of each software component. Different size measures reflect this progression. (Chapter 9 follows this progression in explaining various size measures.)

In practice, experienced engineers bidding precedented systems already have a good idea of the requirements, architecture, and even some existing components that will be reused, or that can at least serve as a basis for analogy estimation. During a proposal, the team actually performs some initial requirements analysis and product design to provide enough detail to produce the best possible size estimate given the time available. They can still overlook items, however. The problem is worse for unprecedented systems. The next section explains why.

---

[1] Lawrence H. Putnam, Sr. and Ware Meyers show a similar spectrum of size measures in Figure 4.7 of [Putnam, 1992, p. 84].

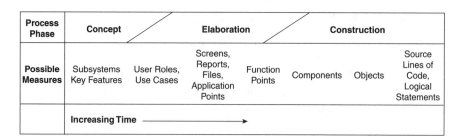

Process Phase	Concept		Elaboration		Construction		
Possible Measures	Subsystems Key Features	User Roles, Use Cases	Screens, Reports, Files, Application Points	Function Points	Components	Objects	Source Lines of Code, Logical Statements
	Increasing Time ⟶						

Figure 8-1 *The spectrum of software size measures*

8.1.2 The Nature of the Problem

Software is like an iceberg: Most of its components are not immediately perceived, yet all of these components are essential to provide a working system. Only 10% or so of an iceberg is visible above the water line. Similarly, for software, perhaps 20% of the system's functions are apparent to the buyer and users, who usually focus on the "mission functions" directly tied to the user's day-to-day operations. For a commercial business, these would be functions such as entering orders, shipping, and billing. For a radar system, these would be functions such as scanning an area for targets, and tracking the path of detected targets. The primary functions of the software system are like the tip of an iceberg.

Figure 8-2 shows the "software iceberg" for a complex, custom-built, software system. Such systems are "worst case" because the software may handle unusual hardware devices, real-time process control, error detection, and failover.[2] To create a complete product, however, you also need support functions that enable the system and its users to perform the mission functions. These might include periodic but infrequent reports (year-end close), aperiodic database updates (such as tax tables), radar calibration, and user assistance (help files and possibly computer-based training). Both the purchaser and the developer often overlook installation aids that facilitate the transition of the system to the end users. Even though these may be used only once to convert operational databases, and compare results during dual operations, engineers must still expend resources to develop, test, and document them.

---

[2] Similar "hidden" components exist for hardware. Many of the items shown in Figure 8-1 are also needed for developing hardware systems. Some support or assist in performing the mission functions. Examples are subsystems for electrical power conditioning and cooling. Some are used to build the product. Examples are tools, dies, and alignment fixtures for assembly. Some are needed to install and repair the product.

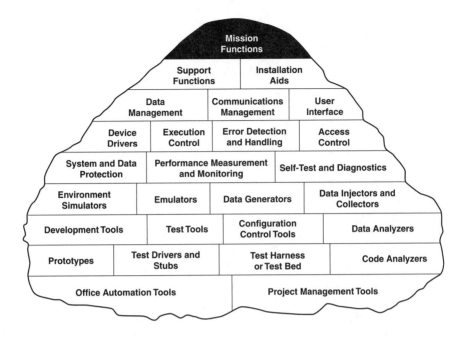

Figure 8-2 *The software iceberg*

The next two levels in the iceberg show typical architectural services that are needed by the mission and support functions. Some of these may reside within the platform's operating system, a commercial database management system, or other commercial off-the-shelf (COTS) components that are integrated with the custom code. (These components are sometimes called "middleware.") I show them because you must build these services for some systems (e.g., real-time embedded systems), and this requires resources.[3] Database management software protects data by enforcing relational integrity, journalizing transactions, periodic archiving, and so forth. Communications management handles ports, modems, and network connections. User interfaces manage the keyboard, mouse, display, and possibly other specialized peripherals. Operating systems include device drivers for various types of peripherals and the ability to control the execution of processes (scheduling, resource management, and synchronization of multiple threads). Operating systems often provide some error detection and handling, as well access control and user authentication. (User interface services may also perform user authentication.) Operating sys-

---

[3] Even though some of these functions are purchased as COTS components, engineers must still expend effort to select and configure these components, integrate them with the other code, and test them. They may also have to write "glue code" to affect the interface. See Section 9.12.

tems and additional products provide various forms of protection (e.g., virus detection).

Operators and system administrators often perform activities that are not apparent to most users. The system must provide functions to support backup and recovery, performance measurement and monitoring, self-test, and diagnostics. The operating system and other middleware components may provide such capabilities. Engineers may, however, have to develop additional, application-specific capabilities to perform these functions. Testers may need environment simulators, emulators for devices and peripherals, test data generators, and data injectors and collectors. For example, to measure performance, an environmental simulator may apply a "standard workload" to stimulate the system in a known and controlled way.

The lower layers of the figure show additional tools to support the developers of the system. Development tools allow software engineers to edit, compile, link, and debug code. Test tools help execute integrated code and analyze the results. Most of these tools are COTS products. However, engineers may still need to build some custom tooling such as compilation scripts and special code analyzers. Other custom code that supports development and test includes prototypes, test drivers and stubs, and a test harness or test bed. The developer can usually purchase code analyzers, office automation tools, and project management tools. However, some projects may need to configure or customize these.

Overlooking the types of functions shown in the "iceberg" leads to the "sin of omission," causing the estimated size of the system to be too low. This problem exists regardless of what size measure you are using. Use the iceberg as a checklist to identify software that you must build.

How bad is the iceberg problem? For embedded systems, the support software is often overlooked. Figure 8-3 plots the support software size versus the mission software size for 14 military systems. The average size of the support software is nearly twice that of the mission software. Ignoring the support software means that the total size will be low by a factor of three. (There is a large variability in this ratio, however. The coefficient of variation is 0.64.) Some authors report that the support software is three to five times larger than the mission software.

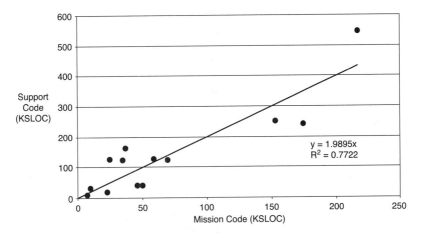

Figure 8-3 *Size comparison*

8.1.3 Ways to Identify All the Pieces

To identify all the software components, you must first understand the purpose of the product, how it will be used, and its top-level conceptual design (the architecture). The precursors of estimation, described in Section 7.1, provide you with much of this information. Have several people participate. Use the operational concept, the product vision, and the product architecture to provide a structure to help organize their efforts. Historical size data is also helpful for analogies and sanity checks.

You can use various "key diagrams," described in Chapter 7, to identify the pieces. Which diagram is best depends on the type of product. Figure 8-4 identifies useful key diagrams ("primary aids") versus time.

Process Phase	Concept		Elaboration		Construction		
Possible Measures	Subsystems Key Features	User Roles, Use Cases	Screens, Reports, Files, Application Points	Function Points	Components	Objects	Source Lines of Code, Logical Statements
Primary Aids	Product Vision, Analogies	Operational Concept, Context Diagram	Specification, Feature List		Architecture, Top Level Design	Detailed Design	Code
	Increasing Detail ⟶						

Figure 8-4 *Primary aids to estimate software size*

8.2 Example: Using the Operational Concept

The operational concept is (or should be) available early in a project. The top layers in the iceberg of Figure 8-2 generally correspond to the types of functions identified in the operational concept. Thus, you can use the operational concept to define a set of checklists, tied to user roles, that provide a systematic way to identify the functions performed by a system. This gives a template to identify and organize the system's functions. This section describes two such checklists.

Table 8-2 shows the system's functions in two dimensions: role and frequency of execution. This is suited to user stories, use cases, and operational scenarios. (See the box "User Stories and Agile Estimation.")

Table 8-2 *Functions (Stories) by Role and Execution Frequency*

Frequency of Execution	Roles	
	End User	*System Administrator*
Daily	Post new transactions Enroll new customers Make adjustments (corrections)	Run daily backup Update virus checker Monitor system workload Monitor firewall activities
Monthly	Prepare invoices	Run monthly backup
Quarterly	Prepare quarterly report Prepare quarterly tax statement	None
Annually	Prepare fiscal year reports Perform year-end close	Prepare annual equipment inventory
On Demand	Update business rules Update tax tables	Add new users Change user privileges Update COTS software

User Stories and Agile Estimation

Agile methods, described in Chapter 10, "Production Processes (Project Life Cycles)," produce software by rapidly evolving a product through a sequence of iterations, each lasting only a few weeks. Many agile projects plan their work based on "user stories." Each user story describes how the system is supposed to work to accomplish some particular business. Users write each story on an index card. These cards are tokens in the planning process or the "planning game." (This process is similar to the cards-on-the-wall method described in Chapter 11, "Bottom-Up Estimating and Scheduling.") Users assign a business value to each story. Software engineers estimate the cost of implementing the functionality required by the story. (To help estimate the effort, some agile methods prepare use cases to formalize the user stories.) Then the users evaluate the cost/benefit ratio for each story to decide whether they want the developers to implement it. Based on available resources and time constraints, the developers and users negotiate which stories will be included in the next release of the software.

For large systems, the analog of user stories is operational scenarios, which are often included in the operational concept.

Systems engineers often focus on the functions that a system performs. You can also use the operational concept to identify the software functions that must be developed, including prototypes and custom tools to support development and test. Each role identified in the product's operational concept uses different types of software functions. As shown in Table 8-3, these include application functions, operational functions, and software implementation functions. Some of the functions are more "externally visible" than others. The functions listed near the top of the list are external. The functions near the bottom of the list are more internal. Typically, the customer specifies the external functions as deliverables. The internal functions may be optionally deliverable based upon the customer's desires. The "transition support" category refers to special tools for one-time use to convert data needed to cut over to a new system and activate it.

The right half of the table shows three roles: the end user, the operator, and the programmer. As indicated by the Xs in the right half of the table, each role perceives different types of functions. The key point of the table is that no single person associated with the software product is aware of all of the functions that the product performs. (Recall the story of the blind men attempting to describe an elephant. Each person perceives a different part of the whole.)

Table 8-3 *Functions by Role*

Activity	Types of Functions	End User	Roles Operator	Programmer
Conduct Business or Perform Mission*	Primary application	X		
	Secondary application	X		
Operation and Support*	Backup & Recovery		X	
	Performance Monitoring		X	
	Self-Test & Diagnostics		X	
	Data Conversion		X	
Software Construction	Development Tools			X
	Test Tools			X
	Other Custom Tools			X
	Learning Aids (prototypes)			X
	Transition Support			X

*These can be subdivided by Continuous, Periodic, and On Demand.

You can use Table 8-3 as a checklist to help identify all software functions that need to be implemented. However, a more detailed decomposition increases your understanding, and will help you identify more functions. One way you can subdivide the functions is by the type of function (mission, support, transition) and when they are performed: continuously, periodically, or on demand. Figure 8-3 showed this for a business data processing application. A continuous (daily) function would be posting transactions that arrive daily. Periodic functions would correspond to the preparation of monthly, quarterly, and yearly reports. On-demand functions would be adding new business clients and updating business rules such as tax tables. Table 8-4 illustrates this decomposition for plant process control systems. (For details, see [Stutzke, 1992].) You could also decompose the roles. For example, you could split "end user" into departments or roles within departments, and then identify the functions needed by each one. (Appendix A, "Roles and Responsibilities for Estimation," identifies some possible roles to use.) List common functions used by multiple roles in a separate column called "Shared" to prevent double counting! You can use similar checklists to identify hardware items. See Section 8.3.

Checklists provide a structure to elicit information from prospective users. The elicitation process may generate a large list of requirements. You can use the techniques described in Chapter 27, "Ranking and Selecting Items," to prune the list and prioritize the requirements. You should use the information that you collect to refine your checklists and so improve your future estimates. Context diagrams, mentioned in Section 7.3, are also helpful in eliciting requirements.

Table 8-4 *Software to Be Developed*

Mission Functions (Plant Process Control)
• Data collection and validation
• Data smoothing and reduction
• Process monitoring (alarm generation)
• Data display
• Decision support and predictions
• Command generation

(continues)

Table 8-4 *Software to Be Developed (continued)*

Support Functions
• System performance monitoring and reporting
• Maintenance of parameters, tables and rules
• Software maintenance (see development support)
• Training and exercise
Transition Functions (Single Use)
• Data conversion (forward and backward)
• Data validation
System Services
• Display management
• User assistance (online help, error handling)
• Data management (especially if distributed)
• Communications (interprocess, intersystem)
• Access control (authorization)
• Process management (startup, workload control)
• Reliability (failover, backup, recover)
Development Support
• Edit, compile, link
• Code analysis
• Configuration management
• Document generation
• Component libraries (source code)
Test Support
• Test drivers and stubs
• Test data capture and analysis
• Stimulators
• Regression test tools and test cases
User Support
• Converted data
• Sample data and scenarios
• Simulators
• Computer-based training

Learning Aids for Developers
• Experimental prototypes (design trades)
• Benchmarking tools (performance prediction)
Tooling*
• Code generators
• Consistency checkers
• Custom code metrics tools
• Design data management (ICASE tools)
• Document production

*These may be purchased as COTS, but will require effort to install, configure, and check out.

8.3 Sizing Hardware

You can also use the operational concept and the roles to identify hardware components, as illustrated in Table 8-5. The "Diagnostic Tools" may also help isolate faults. Some systems contain built-in self-test and some degree of fault-isolation capabilities. If so, these tools might move up to the "System" area. Workers on the production line use the "Test Tools and Equipment," which are custom built, along with the production tooling. The production and test processes may affect the number of items required. Obvious examples are prototypes and copies used for destructive testing. Each role probably needs specialized documents and training courses as well. The estimator works with other members of the estimating team to identify all of the items.

In contrast to software development, where the labor is the primary cost, hardware estimates are often expressed in dollars. The cost of materials and ODCs (facilities, tooling, consumables, etc.) is often a significant part of the total cost. The dollars should be expressed with respect to a particular fiscal or calendar-year. For example, "USD 1999" might indicate a cost measured in U.S. dollars for the calendar year 1999.

Different size measures are used to estimate the costs of developing and producing various types of hardware. The weight (in pounds) is often used for aircraft and spacecraft. The power consumption (in watts) is sometimes used for electronic equipment, especially avionics.

Table 8-5 *A Checklist to Identify Hardware Items*

Activity	Types of Items	User	Trainer	Maintainer	Logistician	Producer	Designer	Tester
Operations	Installed Systems (number by location)	X	X		X			
	Crew Trainers	X	X		X			
	Line Replaceable Units	X		X	X			
Deployment and Support*	Spare Parts			X	X			
	Diagnostic tools (measure, test)			X	X	?	X	
	Special tools (for dis-assembly, alignment, etc.)			X	X	?		
Production	Assemblies					X		
	Production tooling (jigs, fixtures, dies, machines)					X		
	Test tools and equipment					X	?	X
Initial Development (First Unit)	Prototypes		?				X	
	Test articles							X

Figure 8-5 shows an example for "spacecraft development costs" (actually, production coefficients) based on NASA data [Hamaker, 2001]. This figure shows production coefficients in kilodollars (for some unspecified year) per pound to develop Earth-orbital spacecraft, crewed spacecraft, planetary spacecraft, and engines. The median and mean values are shown for each type of object. For spacecraft, the mean value is always larger than the median value, indicating that a few extremely high values have influenced the mean.[4] The error bars for the median value are the minimum and maximum values reported. The error bars for the mean value are plus and minus one standard deviation. As shown by the error bars, the variation in the average costs is substantial, making these average values suitable only for very rough estimates. The data does seem to indicate, however, that crewed spacecraft cost slightly more than twice (2.2) as much to develop as unmanned Earth-orbital spacecraft. Spacecraft that must be capable of autonomous operation for extended periods of time cost approximately four (3.8 to 4.1) times as much to develop as an Earth-orbital spacecraft. Interestingly, engines are more expensive to develop than any kind of spacecraft.

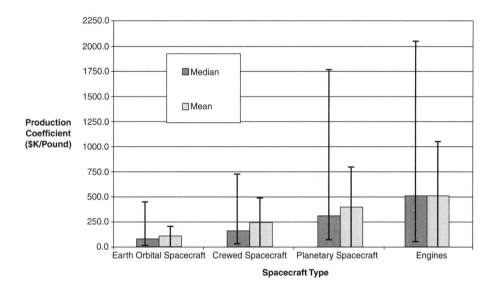

Figure 8-5 *A categorization of spacecraft development costs*

---

[4] The asymmetry of the distribution determines the relative sizes of the median, mode, and mean. See Appendix B, "Measurement Theory and Statistics."

8.4 Accounting for Size Growth and Volatility

Regardless of which size measure you choose, the estimated size often grows during a project. This is especially true for software because it is so hard to describe. For long-duration projects, you can account for the size increase using a growth parameter, G:

$$Size_{Final} = (1 + G)*Size_{Initial}$$

Capers Jones states that an average growth rate is 1%/calendar-month. If so, a 15 calendar-month project would have G = 15%. This is a worst case value. In practice, any project must freeze requirements at some point, and then finish building and testing the product. For large projects, this typically occurs halfway through the project.[5] Thus, a better estimate for G in the preceding example is G = (15/2)*1% = 7.5%. You must decide what value is appropriate for your project.

You can directly measure G using the following:

$$G = (Size_{Final} - Size_{Initial})/Size_{Initial}$$

where $Size_{Final}$ is the final delivered size and $Size_{Initial}$ is the initial estimated size excluding any adjustments for growth or volatility. For estimating effort, however, you want to include the effects of volatility, which causes revision of any work products already completed by the developers. (The number of work products affected by volatility and growth increase with time. The rework effort is larger for projects that produce many formal documents.)

If you assume that effort is proportional to size,

$$Effort = Size/Productivity$$

you can directly measure the final productivity:

$$P_{Final} = Size_{Final}/Effort_{Final}$$

where $Size_{Final}$ is the delivered size, which equals $(1 + G)*Size_{Initial}$. This gives:

$$P_{Final} = [(1 + G)*Size_{Initial}]/Effort_{Final}$$

This enables you to separate the effect of growth. The effects of volatility are hidden within the value of P_{Final}, however.

---

[5] Agile methods, described in Section 10.2, build a product by performing a series of iterations, each lasting a few weeks. During each iteration, the requirements are frozen.

You can directly measure the effect of volatility, V, on the effort using the production coefficient, pc

$$V = (pc_{Final} - pc_{Initial})/pc_{Initial}$$

Because productivity = $P = 1/pc$, this is equivalent to

$$V = (P_{Initial}/P_{Final}) - 1$$

and so

$$P_{Final} = P_{Initial}/(1 + V)$$

where $P_{Initial}$ is the value used for your initial estimate and is assumed to exclude the effects of volatility. (It may include the effects of other factors such as product complexity or programmer experience.)

These definitions allow you to write

$$
\begin{aligned}
Effort_{Final} \quad &= Size_{Final}/P_{Final} \\
&= (1 + G)*(1 + V)*Size_{Initial}/P_{Initial} \\
&= (1 + G + V + GV)*Effort_{Initial} \\
&\approx (1 + G + V)*Effort_{Initial}
\end{aligned}
$$

where the last expression assumes that G and V are small (e.g., a few percent). These expressions depend on two assumptions: (1) Effort equals the (initial) size divided by the (initial) productivity, and (2) the (initial) productivity value excludes the effects of volatility. You should distinguish growth and volatility because you can measure them directly, and so can estimate their values for future projects. (If you expect G and V to be large, you should include the cross term G*V in the equation.)

To summarize, there are two software sizes:

PSize = Processed Size = Initial Size*(1 + G + V)
DSize = Delivered Size = Initial Size*(1 + G)

where G is the expected growth and V is the expected volatility, both expressed as a fraction of the original estimated size. G and V increase the size used to estimate the effort, while only G increases the size of the delivered product. (These values are often expressed as percentages. Remember that a value of 12% is entered as 0.12 in the preceding equations.)

The values for G and V depend on the customer, the stability of the external environment, the precedentedness of the system, the experience of the development team, the capability of the development process, and the type of software. The values of G and V are often subjective, and so this simple model may look like a way to include an arbitrarily large "fudge factor" in your estimate. As your organization collects historical data and gains experience, however, you can estimate more objective values for G and V. You also can make estimates using a range of values for G and V. You can also treat the values of G and V as risk items.

You can refine the basic model by specifying different growth and volatility values for different software components or subsystems, for successive development intervals, or both. See note N07, "Refinements for Growth and Volatility."

8.5 Tracking Size

Whenever the estimated or actual (processed) size exceeds the estimated value that was the basis for the original project cost and schedule commitments, there will be a cost problem.

8.5.1 Tracking Growth and Volatility

As Tom DeMarco says, "You can't control what you can't measure." [DeMarco, 1982]. Tracking size allows you to proactively manage project scope. Tracking both size growth and volatility provides insight into the cause of the changes. Are new requirements being discovered or are the requirements being revised? To handle the changes, you can freeze the requirements baseline, or negotiate increased resources (effort, cost, and schedule), or do both.

Just maintaining a numbered list of requirements can provide a way to detect growth and volatility. Figures 8-6 and 8-7 illustrate this point. Figure 8-6 shows the growth and volatility values observed at several times during a project. (Elapsed time is expressed in relative units, that is, normalized to standard initial and final milestones.) The growth is the number added minus the number deleted in the preceding period. The volatility is just the number of changes in the preceding period. The values shown are percentages with respect to the original number of requirements. (Using percentages and relative times makes it easy to compare data from different projects.) Shortly after the project starts, there is significant growth and volatility. These decrease with time as the customer and engineers understand the product better and reach mutual agreement on the product requirements.

Figure 8-7 shows the impact of growth and volatility on the amount of analysis, design, and construction work done by the engineers (top line) and the size of the product delivered to the customer (bottom line). The increased engineering work is the sum of the requirements added, changed, and deleted. The increase in size of the product delivered to the customer is the sum of requirements added, minus the sum of requirements deleted. For this example, the total increase in size was 7.4%, whereas the extra work (assumed to be proportional to the engineering size) increased by 31.2%. This example underscores the two different definitions of size. You can make similar plots for the values (counts) of other proxy objects used to estimate product size and development effort.

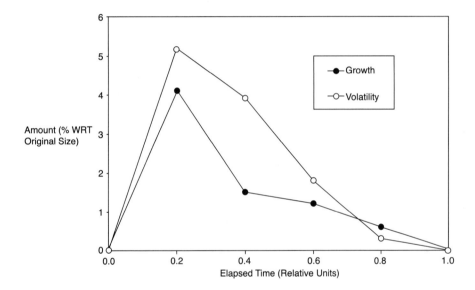

Figure 8-6 *Growth and volatility values for a hypothetical project*

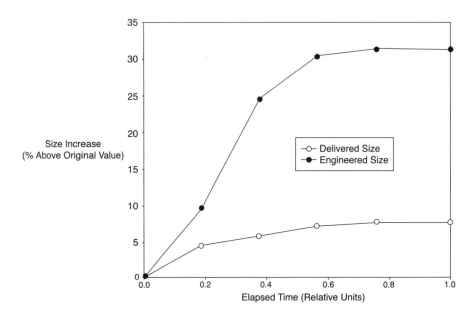

Figure 8-7 *Two sizes versus time*

8.5.2 The Migration of Reused Code

A subtle problem that increases development effort, costs, and schedule is the "migration" of reused code. As a project proceeds, the percentage of reuse usually decreases, sometimes considerably. (Optimism fades with time as the team performs more detailed analysis and confronts the real world.)

Figure 8-8 shows an example of typical behavior observed during a project. The figure shows estimated sizes versus time (in relative units) for all code (new plus reused), the reused code (modified plus copied), and the copied code (reused unmodified).[6] This example uses actual sizes measured in thousands of source lines of code (KSLOC), but you can obviously use any size measure. Because these are actual sizes, each type of code has a different characteristic productivity.[7] During the course of the project two things happen. First, new requirements and discoveries by the project team cause the product's size to grow, as indicated by the increase in the total size (solid) line. Second, as the team learns more about the reused code, they typically discover that less code

---

[6] Richard E. Fairley suggested tracking these quantities.

[7] Section 9.10 explains how to calculate "equivalent sizes" so you can use the same productivity value for all types of code.

can be reused than originally estimated. This decrease usually occurs for both the copied code (reused "as is") and the modified code. (This particular example assumes that the original estimated amount of reused code does not change.) In addition, some of the reused size also "migrates" to the other types over time. This example assumes that each time the sizes are re-determined (estimated or, later, measured), two-thirds of the loss of "unmodified" code migrates into "modified" code, and the remaining one-third of the loss must be replaced by "new" code. All of the code lost from the "modified" category becomes "new" code. These particular assumptions mean that the total estimated amount of reused code does not change, and so the total estimated size of the software, excluding growth, remains constant. (This is indicated in the figure by the faint horizontal gray line at the value original value of 225 KSLOC.)

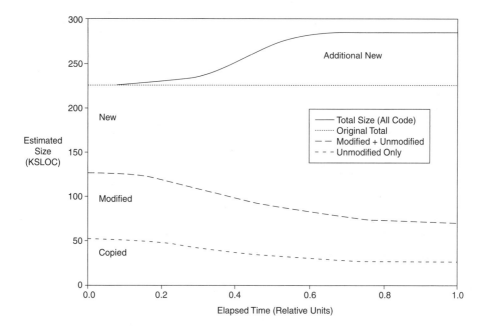

Figure 8-8 *Typical size trends*

The initial estimates for this project were 100, 75, and 50 KSLOC, for new, modified, and copied code, respectively. At the end of the project, the corresponding values are 216, 43, and 25 KSLOC. The total size growth was 60 KSLOC (= 285 – 225) or 27%. The amount of reused code decreased 24 KSLOC (= 50 – 26) or 48%. The amount of modified code decreased 32 KSLOC (= 75 – 43) or 43%.

This migration has implications for the estimated effort because the code "migrates upward" to regions where the code requires more effort to produce. (This assumes that the productivity for modified code is higher than that for new code.) For example, the amount of new code increases from the original estimate. One reason is the growth from external causes. The other is the migration of reused code into new code. For this particular example, 56 KSLOC of reused code eventually migrated into new code.[8]

Table 8-6 illustrates how to estimate the cost impact for this particular example. Column 1 shows the type of code. "New" means the size without the external growth, which is shown separately as "Growth." Column 2 shows representative production coefficients for each type of code. Columns 3 and 4 give the original and final estimated sizes, and columns 5 and 6 give the corresponding estimated effort. The migration of reused code increases the effort by 21% (= [187 − 155]/155). Overall, the effort increased by 59% (= [247 − 155]/155). Migration of reused code accounts for 35% of the increase. Code migration can cause a significant cost (and schedule) overrun!

Table 8-6 *Migration of Reused Code Increases Costs*

Type of Code	Production Coefficient (phr/SLOC)	Original Size (KSLOC)	Final Size (KSLOC)	Original Effort (Kphr)	Final Effort (Kphr)
New	1.0	100	156	100	156
Modified	0.6	75	43	45	26
Unmodified	0.2	50	26	10	5
Growth	1.0	0	60	0	60
Totals Without Growth		225	225	155	187
Totals With Growth		225	285	155	247

TIP: Track the amount of code by type versus time during a project to help manage risk associated with imperfect knowledge of (and undue optimism about) reused code. A decrease in either the "unmodified" or "modified" amounts signals a cost overrun.

---

[8] You could plot the *equivalent sizes*, defined in Section 9.10, which are directly proportional to the development effort. Essentially, the equivalent size equals the product of the actual reused size, which may decrease due to migration, and an Adaptation Adjustment Multiplier (AAM), which may increase due to better understanding. Such competing effects make the shapes of the curves harder to predict. Using actual sizes makes it easier to understand the essential phenomenon.

If you observe several projects, you may be able to identify recurring patterns. For example, you may be able to determine means and standard deviations for the changes in each type of code. You may even be able to devise functions that approximate the time behavior of these values. For an example, see [Stutzke, 2000].

8.5.3 Measuring and Tracking Size: An Example

This section describes the size growth observed for a simple analysis program, and explains how you can use such information to estimate growth and volatility.

The program was a small decision support tool that incorporated simple business rules. The programmer implemented an initial working version of the program based on the business rules supplied. Testing revealed, however, that in certain cases these rules gave incorrect results. (The rules provided did not cover certain situations.) The programmer then determined additional rules, and the criteria to choose among the various rules. (This is analogous to discovering that the domain of a mathematical function must be partitioned into regions, or discovering that a system has multiple modes of operation, each of which performs different functions.) After the algorithm had been strengthened, a few cosmetic features were added to improve the user interface. The program progressed through 11 versions. The final size of this application was approximately 275 physical source lines of code, excluding blank lines.

Figure 8-9 shows the size growth of the source code relative to the size of the initial working version (version 1). Overall, the code doubled in size, primarily due to the discovery of fundamental weaknesses in the original algorithm, plus adding the ability to export data to a file. (The growth was 101%.) The curve has three regions with large increases. The first region spans versions 2 and 3. The second region spans versions 5, 6, and 7. The third region spans versions 10 and 11. The size increase from version 2 to version 3 was due to code added to (1) write results to a file for exporting data to a spreadsheet (72%), and (2) do minor cleanup of the decision logic in the algorithm (28%). Thus, 72% of the increase was due to a new functional requirement. The size increase from version 5 to version 6 was due to three changes: (1) provide additional information on the operator's display (22%), (2) write additional data fields to the output file (23%), and (3) correct the algorithm to handle deficiencies discovered in testing (55%). The size increase from version 6 to version 7 was due to two changes: (1) adding still more additional fields to the output file (20%), and (2) completely restructuring the algorithm so it would handle all cases (80%). The size increase from version 10 to version 11 was due to providing code to allow the user to specify a specific step size (100%).

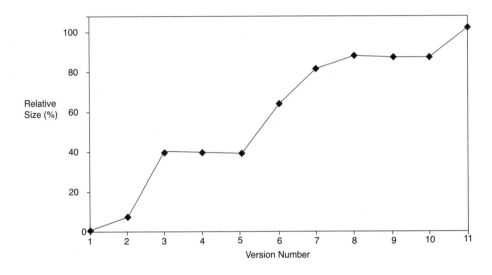

Figure 8-9 *Size growth relative to the first version*

To gain additional insight, I counted the numbers of lines of various types that were added to each release. The tool counted physical source lines of code, subdivided by data declarations (which includes type definitions and object declarations), computations, and comments. (Lines containing computations that also contained a comment were only counted as computations. The tool had no ability to distinguish what I call "mixed" lines, ones that contain both computations and comments. The tool also did not identify lines that were changed. This prevented analyzing volatility.)

Version 1 had 16% data declarations, 12% comments, and 72% computations. Version 11 had 16% data declarations, 11% comments, and 73% computations. Figure 8-10 shows the composition of each release in terms of the three line types. The relative percentages of data declarations, computations, and comments are essentially constant for all the versions. This suggests that the sizes of the three line types increased at essentially the same rate. If this result holds true for other types of programs, then the ratios can be used to estimate total size based on estimates of, say, the size of the computational code. (This is similar to the approaches of Herron and of Gaffney, described in Section 9.6.2.) For example, suppose that computations are 75% of the total, and that analysis of the requirements identifies the amount of code (SLOC, UFPs, etc.) needed to do the computations. Given the estimated size for the computations, the total size is 1.38 (= 1/0.725) times the size of the computational code. (If you do not include comments, the factor is 1.16 [= 0.84/0.725].)

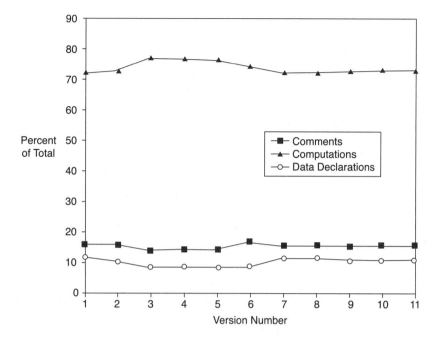

Figure 8-10 *Composition by version*

8.6 Implementation Guidance

This section provides implementation guidance for estimating size. This guidance applies to all size measures.

8.6.1 Manage All the Requirements

Requirements are the key driver of size and hence effort. Remember that "requirements" can be features, functions, reports, data entry screens, or modules. Document the requirements so that all stakeholders can "see" them and so that you can count them. Use tools to record and manage the requirements. You can use a simple numbered list, possibly stored in a spreadsheet or a simple database. For more complex systems, you can use commercial tools to manage requirements and maintain traceability between requirements and the product components that are responsible for satisfying these requirements.

8.6.2 Avoiding Size Bias

Estimated sizes depend on the skill and experience of the individual estimator. This may lead to overestimation or underestimation of the size of the work product that another individual will eventually produce. You can take six actions to increase the accuracy of size estimates:

1. Carefully specify the boundary of the application.
2. Carefully define the "nature and scope" of each item whose size will be estimated. For example, the product architecture briefly describes each component.
3. Define detailed rules for estimating size. (Function point analysis, described in Section 9.5, is one example. FPA also requires the estimator to specify the boundary of the application before estimating the size.)
4. Provide estimators with historical size data measured for similar work products built using the same design guidelines and coding standards. This data provides a known reference point to anchor the estimated value.
5. Train developers to become better estimators by estimating a module's size before they build it, measuring the size afterward, comparing the two values, and using this information to improve their estimating ability. (The Personal Software Process does this [Humphrey, 1995].)
6. Use the Delphi technique to avoid biases from an individual estimator.

8.6.3 Managing Size Growth and Volatility

Size growth and volatility are important because they impact development effort, cost, and time. Some size growth and volatility is expected because early estimates of the project are based upon limited information. You cannot totally control growth and volatility, but you can manage it. You can

- Use key diagrams to identify all items.
- Have knowledgeable people prepare estimates.
- Negotiate firm cutoff dates for changes to requirements.
- Negotiate firm cutoff dates for upgrading COTS components.
- Explicitly include estimates for growth and volatility.
- Re-estimate periodically.
- Track estimates over time.

The first two items provide better information on which to base the size estimates. The next two items stop changes to requirements and commercial off-the-shelf components after some specified time or milestone. See note N08,

"Managing the Volatility of Externally Supplied Components." Estimation plays a role in the last three activities. Including estimates for growth and volatility forces all stakeholders to confront the issue. You should re-estimate sizes periodically during the course of a project, typically at the completion of major project phases or milestones.

8.7 Recommended Reading

Bob Hughes discussed the measurement of software size in Chapter 6 of [Hughes, 2000]. Norman Fenton and Shari Lawrence Pfleeger discuss measures of software size from the perspective of measurement in Chapter 7 of [Fenton, 1997]. IEEE Standard 1045, "Software Productivity Metrics," defines growth and volatility in more detail, and provides an informative discussion of size measures and productivity measures for software and documents. Watts Humphrey addresses size estimation in Chapter 5 of [Humphrey, 1995]. In particular, he discusses the use of fuzzy logic to estimate size in Section 5.2.

8.8 Summary

There are many possible measures of software size. This chapter addressed the size that is used to estimate software development effort. Most software size measures relate to proxies, entities that can be identified early and whose size correlates with the final development effort. This "size" can be larger than the size of the delivered software due to volatility and breakage.[9]

The main challenge in software sizing is to ensure that you have identified all the modules in the product. To estimate size, you must first identify all of the software to be built. To do this, you must understand the purpose of the product, how it will be used, and its top-level conceptual design (the architecture). The precursors of estimation, described in Section 7.1, provide you with much of this information. This chapter explained how to use key diagrams to identify modules and components. Decompose the job, requirements, features, and product to the level at which you intend to do the sizing. (This level is often based on the time and resources available.) If you understand certain parts of a product well, you do not need to decompose these parts as deeply. (Hopefully you have some historical data for such parts!) Have several people participate. Use the operational concept, the product vision, and the product architecture to

---

[9] Breakage is the amount of previously delivered software that must be modified to prepare a subsequent release.

organize their efforts. The resulting detail gives you better understanding, helps identify omissions, and also gives more accuracy (because errors tend to cancel out). Historical size data is also helpful for analogies and sanity checks.

Regardless of your choice of size measure, growth and volatility cause the final value to be larger than the initial value. (Growth only affects the delivered size.) Reused components usually require less effort than new components, but in extreme cases can require more effort. The portion of size contributed by reused components may decrease during a project as optimism fades and reality sets in.

There are many possible ways to define software size in terms of application objects. Some approaches use information that is available in the early conceptual phase of a project, whereas others use information available only in later design phases. The trade-off, of course, is that estimating later increases estimation accuracy, but costs more and takes longer to obtain. This is the funnel curve in Figure 1-3. The next chapter defines several measures of software size.

Chapter 9

Estimating Software Size: The Details

This chapter describes specific measures of software size used to estimate software development effort. These size measures reflect either "external" characteristics of the product or "internal" characteristics of the actual code. The size measures include stories, use cases, function points, and lines of source code. This chapter also covers sizing for reused code and commercial off-the-shelf (COTS) components. This is a long chapter because there are many measures of software size. Most readers will not be interested in every size measure described in this chapter. Just select the sections relevant to your needs and skip the rest.

9.1 Requirements

The earliest description of a product is usually its requirements, which identify the product's functions, features, and capabilities. One possible way to estimate the size of the product is to count requirements. Some authors advocate counting the number of sentences containing the word *shall* in the specification. I do not recommend this approach because sentences with the word *shall* can require widely varying amounts of effort to implement. For example, adding the sentence "The system shall operate in real-time, responding to all inputs within 10 milliseconds" will greatly increase the complexity and cost of the software.[1]

The preceding chapter described a simple list of requirements, features, or functions. Section 8.2 also described operational scenarios and user stories. Although each capability so identified may require a different amount of effort to implement, at least the product's capabilities are documented, providing a basis for tracking requirements growth and volatility, and for assessing impact on the product and the project. (You should document and track size estimates regardless of the size measure you choose. This is part of documenting the estimate, one of the steps of the Linear Method described in Chapter 3, "A Basic Estimating Process: The Linear Method.")

If your team writes the requirements, you can use standardized keywords or phrases to provide more uniformity. These can serve as proxies. Phrases such as *add a record, update a record, display a record*, and *delete a record* are used to describe actions and functions. This is a better approach than simply counting the *shalls* in a specification because the proxies deal with specific functionality that must be developed. The "action phrases" are "closer" to the code. If you associate a size with each function, you can use a tool to count the number of occurrences of each phrase in the text, multiply the counts by the corresponding size value, and sum the values to obtain an estimate of the product's total size.

Requirements are still a crude way to quantify the functionality of a software product. The following sections describe some better ways. Essentially, these ways partition requirements into standardized categories that (hopefully) correlate with the required development effort.

---

[1] A refinement on counting *shalls* is to count imperatives such as *shall, must, is required to, are applicable, is to, are to, will, should*, and the like. The Automated Requirement Measurement (ARM) tool from NASA's Software Assurance Technology Center does this and more. See http://satc.gsfc.nasa.gov/tools/index.html.

9.2 UML-Based Sizing and Use Case Points

One approach is to use the products of analysis as a basis for early reliable measures of size. Several authors have considered Unified Modeling Language (UML) because it is emerging as an industry standard. See the box "Unified Modeling Language."

Unified Modeling Language

Unified Modeling Language (UML) brings together elements of several object-oriented modeling approaches. The main authors are Grady Booch (developer of the Booch method), James Rumbaugh (co-developer of the Object Management Technique, OMT), and Ivar Jacobson (inventor of use cases). The first version of UML was released in 1996. Analysts and developers use UML to specify, visualize, and document models of problems and systems. UML defines approximately two dozen diagrams. The language is evolving into a full method. For details see one of the many textbooks on UML. One is by the three originators of UML [Booch, 1999]. Bruce Douglass describes how to apply UML to real-time embedded systems [Douglass, 1998].

There has been some interest in generating code directly from the UML description.[2] If it is ever possible to eventually build "executable UML," the lowest-level objects directly manipulated by software engineers will be the UML elements, making these elements an ideal basis for estimating effort.

UML provides a standard notation, and some software development tools can capture the diagrams. Thus, at end of project it may be possible to automatically measure the various components contributing to the size measure. To use this for estimation, however, you must be able to relate the objects identified during early analysis to the final count of all objects implemented. You need to define an "expansion ratio." This is difficult, however, because modern development tools use prebuilt components to provide some of the functionality. Each tool provides and uses different types of components. This means that the value of the expansion ratio will have to depend on the tool (language, method, underlying architecture, and level of reusable components).

---

[2] This requires supplementing the UML diagrams with formal specifications. One possibility is Object Constraint Language, proposed by the Object Management Group, http://www.omg.com. Also see the Project Technology website, http://www.projtech.com.

A use case is one of the components of UML. A use case employs diagrams and text to capture the high-level interactions between an actor (the user or an external system) and the system being analyzed. The main elements of a use case are the purpose (business goal or action to be achieved), the actor(s) involved, the context, and the "scenario," which is a sequence of events. The use case records the main sequence needed to achieve the goal, and also includes alternate sequences to represent exceptional situations. Events may convey data, and so the use case identifies the information that is passed between the actor and the system. Use cases do not capture nonfunctional requirements, nor are they simply a functional decomposition of the system. Because they capture functions and data in user terms, they provide a possible way to size software during requirements analysis.

Use case points (UCPs) are a metric to estimate effort for projects [Karner, 1993]. Geri Schneider and Jason Winters describe how to estimate size in use case points in Chapter 10 of their book [Schneider, 2001]. The basic scheme was developed by Gustav Karner, and is shown in Table 9-1.

Table 9-1 *Steps to Count Use Case Points*

1. Identify the actors and assign a weight based on how they interact with the system of interest:

Actor Type	Description of Interface	Weight
Simple	Another system via a defined application programming interface (API)	1
Average	Another system via a protocol, or a person via a text-based terminal	2
Complex	A person interacting via a graphical user interface (GUI)	3

2. Sum the weights for the actors in all use cases to obtain the unadjusted actor weight, UAW.

3. Identify use cases, and assign a complexity to each use case based on the number of transactions or scenarios that each use contains:

Complexity	# of Transactions	Weight
Simple	1–3	5
Average	4–7	10
Complex	8 or more	15

Alternatively, you can use "analysis classes" to estimate the use case complexity. See [Schneider, 2001, page 152].

4. Sum the weights for all the use cases to obtain the unadjusted use case weight, UUCW.

5. Sum UAW and UUCW to obtain the size in unadjusted use case points (UUCPs).

6. Adjust for the technical complexity of the product by rating the degree of influence of each of 13 factors. The ratings range from 0 to 5; 0 means that the factor is irrelevant for the project; 5 means that it is essential. The 13 factors and their associated weights are

Factor	Description	Weight
T1	Distributed system	2
T2	Response or throughput performance objectives	2
T3	End-user efficiency	1
T4	Complex internal processing	1
T5	Reusable code	1
T6	Easy to install	0.5
T7	Easy to use	0.5
T8	Portable	2
T9	Easy to change	1
T10	Concurrent	1
T11	Includes security features	1
T12	Provides access for third parties	1
T13	Special user training facilities are required	1

7. For each factor, multiply the degree of influence by the weight, and sum the products to obtain the technology sum, TSUM. Use the weights shown in the table in the preceding step.

8. Compute the technical complexity factor, TCF, using

    $TCF = 0.6 + 0.01*TSUM$

    This formula is similar to one used to calculate adjusted function points, except the coefficients are 0.6 and 0.1, instead of 0.65 and 0.01.

(continues)

Table 9-1 *Steps to Count Use Case Points (continued)*

9. Adjust for the "environment," which addresses the skills and training of the staff, precedentedness, and requirements stability. (This is really an adjustment for the productivity of the project team and is unrelated to the product's characteristics.) There are eight factors:

Factor	Description	Weight
F1	Familiar with Rational Unified Process	1.5
F2	Application experience	0.5
F3	Object-oriented experience	1
F4	Lead analyst capability	0.5
F5	Motivation	1
F6	Stable requirements	2
F7	Part-time workers	−1
F8	Difficult programming language	−1

10. Rate each factor's influence from 0 to 5, with 3 denoting "average." For factors F1 through F4, 0 means no experience in that area, and 5 means expert. For factor F5, 0 means no motivation, and 5 means high motivation. For factor F6, 0 means extremely unstable requirements and 5 means unchanging requirements. For factor F7, 0 means no part-time staff, and 5 means all part-time staff. For factor F8, 0 means an easy-to-use programming language, and 5 means a very difficult programming language. Note that the last two weights are negative.

11. For each factor, multiply the degree of influence by the weight, and sum the products to obtain the environment sum, ESUM.

12. Compute the environmental factor, EF, using

    $EF = 1.4 - 0.03*ESUM$.

13. Compute the size in (adjusted) Use Case Points (UCPs) using

    $UCP = UUCP*TCF*EF$

Using a productivity value determined from your organization's data, you can compute the effort to implement the application. Karner suggested a production coefficient of 20 person-hours/UCP [Karner, 1993]. Schneider and Winters observe that the environmental factors gauge the team experience and project stability, which are independent of the product's characteristics. Thus, they use the environmental factors to determine the production coefficient [Schneider, 2001, page 157]. They call the product of the factor's weight and its rating the "extended value." They count the number of factors in F1 through F6 whose extended values are below 3, and count the number of factors in F7 and F8 whose extended values are above 3. If the sum of these two numbers is less than or equal to 2, they recommend a production coefficient of 20 person-hours/UCP. If the sum is 3 or 4, then use 28 person-hours/UCP. If the total exceeds 4, this indicates a challenging project. They recommend revising the project parameters to make it easier. For example, the planners might decide to hire staff who have more experience. This will change some of the environmental characteristics and so lower the sum below 4. If this is not possible, they suggest using a value of 36 person-hours/UCP for the production coefficient.

9.3 Application Points

Another approach is to count objects such as screens and reports. These objects are "closer" to the work done by developers. The basic assumption is that the effort needed to implement objects of a particular type is more uniform than the effort needed to implement textual requirements or use cases. This approach meshes well with projects that use Integrated Computer-Aided Software Engineering (ICASE) environments to develop software. These environments include a repository of pre-built components and a set of tools. Software engineers use the tools to configure existing components, build new components, and integrate and test components. (This development process is sometimes called application composition.) The tools include editors, compilers, linkers, and high-level tools such as graphical user interface (GUI) builders. The programmers directly manipulate screens, reports, and components so these seem like a good choice for a size measure to estimate effort.

Rajiv D. Banker and his colleagues define a simple measure called object points for sizing software built in ICASE environments [Banker, 1991]. They based their measure on the numbers of screens, reports, and business rules.

Barry Boehm and his co-workers adapted object points for use in COCOMO II's application composition effort estimation model but made two changes [Boehm, 2000, page 193ff]. First, they added a rating scale to estimate the team's productivity based on the capability and maturity of the ICASE environment and on the developers' capability and experience. Second, they changed the name from object points to application points to avoid confusion with sizing metrics developed by other researchers. (Section 9.7 discusses object-oriented size measures.)

Table 9-2 shows the COCOMO II application point size estimation procedure. First, the estimator identifies the screens, reports, and algorithms (called third generation language [3GL] components). Second, the estimator uses simple tables to classify each type of object by complexity based on characteristics such as number of data tables and number of views. A second table maps the complexity to a numerical weight. Third, the estimator adds up the weights for all objects identified, and then adjusts the total for the amount of reuse, REUSE, expressed in percent. (Remember that 10% corresponds to a value of 0.1.) This gives the size in new application points, NAP. Finally, the estimator determines the productivity of the team from another table. Dividing the size by the productivity gives the estimated effort. For details, see [Boehm, 2000]. The Application Point Method has not been validated, but you may want to try it.

Table 9-2 *COCOMO II Application Point Estimation Procedure (reproduced from Figure 5.1 in [Boehm, 2000])*

1. Assess application counts. Estimate the number of screens, reports, and 3GL components that will comprise this application. Assume the standard definitions of these objects in your ICASE environment.

2. Classify each object instance into simple, medium, and difficult complexity levels depending on values of characteristic dimensions. Use the following scheme:

For Screens				For Reports			
	# and Source of Data Tables				# and Source of Data Tables		
Number of Views Contained	Total < 4 (< 2 srvr < 3 clnt)	Total < 8 (2/3 srvr 3-5 clnt)	Total 8+ (> 3 srvr > 5 clnt)	Number of Sections Contained	Total < 4 (< 2 srvr < 3 clnt)	Total < 8 (2–3 srvr 3-5 clnt)	Total 8+ (> 3 srvr > 5 clnt)
<3	Simple	Simple	Medium	0 or 1	Simple	Simple	Medium
3–7	Simple	Medium	Difficult	2 or 3	Simple	Medium	Difficult
≥8	Medium	Difficult	Difficult	4+	Medium	Difficult	Difficult

3. Weight the number in each cell using the following scheme. The weights reflect the relative effort required to implement an instance of that complexity level:

Object Type	Complexity Weight		
	Simple	Medium	Difficult
Screen	1	2	3
Report	2	5	8
3GL component			10

4. Calculate the application point count, APC, by adding all the weighted object instances.

5. Estimate the fraction of APC, REUSE, that you expect to provide by reusing existing components. Compute the new application points to be developed using NAP = ACP*(1 – REUSE).

6. Determine the productivity rate, PROD [NAP / person-month], using the following table:

Developers' experience and capability		Very Low	Low	Nominal	High	Very High
ICASE maturity and capability		Very Low	Low	Nominal	High	Very High
PROD		4	7	13	25	50

7. Compute the estimated development effort: EDEV [person-months] = NAP / PROD.

The application point method focuses on the effort associated with the construction of the user interface (screens and reports). It tacitly assumes that the data repository exists. This is true for many legacy systems. A back-office mainframe hosts a large complicated database that no one has the time or temerity to reengineer. (These databases often consist of many flat files and are not relational.) The Object Point and Application Point Methods were developed for such environments and so omit the effort needed to engineer the database. Data from one of our development projects indicates that approximately one-third of the total development effort was expended engineering the database. This means that the Object Point and Application Point Methods may underestimate the total effort by 50% or so (= [1.00 – 0.67]/0.67). The weights associated with the various object characteristics may need to be revised. For more details see [Stutzke, 2000].

You can use the object/application point approach fairly early in a project. One problem, however, is that the development difficulty (effort) for a particular type of object depends on the particular technology and tools being used (Microsoft Access, Oracle, Visual Basic, Powerbuilder, Delphi, or whatever.). This makes it hard to define a basic size measure that correlates with development effort that is independent of technology. (Perhaps this dependence can be factored into the productivity. This just transfers the dependencies into another parameter, however.)

9.4 Web Objects and Internet Points

New size measures are emerging for web development, but no standard size measure exists. This section describes two such measures.

The most obvious object that developers define and manipulate is web pages. David Cleary defines "Web-points" by considering the number, size, and complexity of HTML pages [Cleary, 2000]. The complexity is based on the size of each page in words and the combined number of hyperlinks into and out of the page plus the number of nontextual elements on the page. Table 9-3 shows the criteria used to assign complexity ratings to static HTML pages. The intervals for word count and link count were determined based on data from Charismatek Software Metrics Pty Ltd. Each page is assigned a size in web-points based on its complexity: Low (4), Average (6), and High (7). Summing the sizes of all Web pages gives the amount to be produced. Dividing by a productivity gives the effort. Cleary cites a value of 0.5 web-points/person-hour. Of course, this particular value depends on the phases and activities included, the skill of the developers, and the other usual factors.

Table 9-3 *Complexity Ratings for HTML Pages*

| Word Count | Link Count (In, Out, and Nontextual | | |
	0–5	6–15	>15
0–300	Low	Low	Avg
301–500	Low	Avg	High
> 500	Avg	High	High

Donald Reifer addresses more than just text and links. He identifies the following objects in Table 3 of [Reifer, 2000]:

- Building blocks (fine-grained components and widgets)
- Web components (applets, agents)
- COTS components (including wrapper code)
- Graphics files (templates, diagrams, images)
- Multimedia files (text, audio, video, 3D objects, but no graphics files)
- Source code (HTML, XML, SQL, and wrappers for COTS, etc.)
- Scripts
- Application points

Reifer counts the number of objects of each type, and then uses a complexity weighting (low, average, and high) analogous to that used in function points. He uses the resulting size, measured in "web objects," in a parametric model to estimate effort and duration. See [Reifer, 2000] for details.

Another approach is to identify objects associated with the client or the server, and subdivide these by type. Section 3.3 described proxies, quantities that you can identify and count early, and that are correlated to the amount of development effort. Possible proxies for web development are:

- Client
  - Web pages
  - Scripts and stored procedures
  - Applets
- Server
  - Active Server Pages
  - Queries
  - Data tables (ILF, EIF)
  - Graphics (images, diagrams)
  - Multimedia clips (audio, video, text)

You can purchase some of these objects as prebuilt components. If so, they will not contribute to the development effort. (Section 9.11 discusses commercial off-the-shelf [COTS] components.)

9.5 Function Points

Function points, defined by Allan J. Albrecht in 1979, are a software size measure designed to meet three goals:

- Gauge delivered functionality in terms users can understand
- Be independent of technique, technology, and programming language
- Give a reliable indication of software size during early design

9.5.1 The Counting Rules

Function point analysis (FPA) quantifies product functionality in terms of five externally visible system elements, called *function types*, that are readily understood by both users and developers:

EI: External input
EO: External output

EQ: External query

ILF: Internal logical file

EIF: External interface file

The International Function Point Users Group (IFPUG) maintains precise definitions for each function type. (The above terms are the 1990 IFPUG nomenclature that is now in general use. Albrecht originally used different terminology.) Function point analysis (FPA) is also called function point counting because the analyst counts the items of each type.

Figure 9-1 shows the relation of the five function types to the system itself. The figure also shows "algorithms," which are used in feature point counting, described later. Both users and other applications can submit inputs and queries, and can receive outputs. The following paragraphs briefly define the five function types.

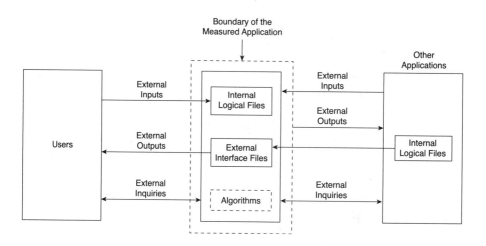

Figure 9-1 *Function types used in function point counting*

An *external input* (EI) is a related group of user data or control information that enters the boundary of the application and adds or changes data in an internal logical file, or is used to perform some function or calculation. An input is considered to be unique if it has different data or format, or if it requires different processing. Examples of inputs are data entered from a screen or form, data read from a magnetic strip, or data obtained from a digital or analog sensor.

An *external output* (EO) is a related group of user data or control information that leaves the boundary of the application. An output is unique if it has different data or format, or if it requires different processing. Examples of outputs are reports, invoices, error messages, or commands to an actuator.

An *external query* (EQ) is a related group of user data or control information that enters the boundary of the application and generates an immediate output of a related group of user data or control information. A query is a set of selection criteria that are used to extract information from an existing database. A query does not add or change data in the database. A query is unique if it has different data or format, or if it requires different editing or sorting in order to produce its results. Examples of queries are requests for a specific data record, a selection menu and the resulting response, a request for all records in the database that satisfy some specified set of selection criteria, or a help request and the resulting help information. (Version 4.0 of the IFPUG counting rules revised the way that help requests and error messages are counted.)

An *internal logical file* (ILF) is a user-identifiable group of logically related data or control information that (1) resides within the boundary of the application, and (2) is maintained and used by the application. The group of data or control information meets a specific business requirement and is maintained by the application itself (via adds, changes, and deletes). Examples of internal logical files are information on a set of employees, information on a set of billing records, state information used to control processing, or a view of data from a database. Note that not every file or database table within an application is considered to be an internal logical file.

An *external interface file* (EIF) is a user-identifiable group of logically related data or control information that (1) resides outside of the application boundary, and (2) is used by the application for some of its processing. An experienced user would identify the data as fulfilling a specific business requirement of the application. The only difference between internal logical files and external interface files is that some other application is responsible for maintaining the information in the external interface file. The application of interest only reads this information.

Function point counting is a type of Linear Method. The analyst (estimator) defines the application boundary and describes the system in general terms. Then the analyst counts the instances of each function type.[3] Next, the analyst determines the "complexity" of each instance based on the rules for each function type. Function point counting defines three complexity levels: low (L), average (Avg), and high (H). Complexity is based on the number of data element types (DETs), record element types (RETs), and file types referenced (FTRs). The analyst uses the values of these types in lookup tables to determine the complexity of each instance. These rules make function point counting complicated. Then the analyst uses another lookup table to assign a numeric value (weight) to each object based on its function type and complexity. In 1985,

---

[3] The function point community refers to the analysts as "counters." I use "analyst" to avoid confusion with automated tools.

Capers Jones proposed a simplified size measure called feature points. Feature points all have average complexity, making them easier to count. (Feature point counting also identifies a sixth data type, algorithms, to account for complex calculations.) Table 9-4 shows the weights for both function points and feature points.

Table 9-4 *Weights for Function Points and Feature Points*

Function Types	IFPUG Function Points (1984)			SPR Feature Points (1985)
	Low	Avgerage	High	
Input	3	4	6	4
Output	4	5	7	5
Inquiry	3	4	6	4
Internal logical files	4	10	15	7
External interface files	5	7	10	7
Algorithm	None			3

For each function type and complexity level, the analyst multiplies the count by the corresponding weight. Summing the results for all 15 pairs (5 function types and 3 complexity levels) gives the total number of unadjusted function points (UFPs) for the software product. The analyst adjusts this total to account for the general system characteristics (GSCs) of the product. Table 9-5 lists the 14 GSCs defined by IFPUG, and some of the main factors considered in assigning a value.[4] Each factor is rated based on its "degree of influence" (0 = no influence, up to 5 = strong influence). Summing these 14 ratings gives the total degree of influence (TDI), which is used to compute value adjustment factor (VAF), as follows:

$$TDI = \sum_{i=1}^{14} Rating_i$$

and

$$VAF = 0.65 + 0.01*TDI$$

---

[4] Some of these characteristics appear very similar to one another based on the factors considered. For a discussion, see Chapter 9 in [Garmus, 2001]. To avoid introducing variations in the size due to subjective judgments of the characteristics' values, the trend is to use only UFPs.

Applying the value adjustment factor gives the software size in adjusted function points (AFPs):

Size (AFP) = VAF*Size (UFP)

The VAF can increase or decrease the size by no more than 35%. The "dynamic range" of the size adjustment is 2 (= 1.35/0.65).[5]

Table 9-5 *General System Characteristics*

Characteristic	Considerations
Data communications	Batch versus interactive
Distributed data processing	Client/server, real-time process control
Performance	Response time, throughput
Heavily used configuration	Security or timing considerations
Transaction rate	Batch, online, real time
Online data entry	Interactive data entry and control
End-user efficiency	User interface, multilingual support
Online update	Updates to internal logical files
Complex processing	Control logic, numeric calculations
Reusability	Parameterized to permit customization by user
Installation ease	Conversion of operational data
Operational ease	Startup, backup, recovery, unattended operation
Multiple sites	Differences in hardware and software environments
Facilitate change	Ad hoc queries, table-driven logic

The IFPUG counting manual defines three types of count: development, enhancement, and application. The application count corresponds to the value perceived by the end user. See the box "Value Versus Cost." Here are the calculations for each type of count:

---

[5] If a system has subsystems or applications that differ in performance, dependability, or business constraints, count each one separately. Calculate a value adjustment factor based on that subsystem's characteristics to adjust its size, and use the adjusted size to estimate the resources to develop that subsystem. Add the estimates to obtain the total for the entire project, and add resources for system integration and testing, management, and coordination.

Development size: VAF*(UFP + CFP)

Enhancement size: VAFA*(ADD + CHGA + CFP) + VAFB*DEL

Application value: VAFA*(UFPB + ADD + CHGA – CHGB – DEL)

where

ADD   = Unadjusted function points added to the product

CFP   = Converted function points

CHGA = Unadjusted function points changed, evaluated after enhancement

CHGB = Unadjusted function points changed, evaluated before enhancement

DEL   = Unadjusted function points deleted from the product

UFP   = Unadjusted function points to be developed

VAF   = Value adjustment factor

VAFA = Value adjustment factor, evaluated after the enhancement

VAFB = Value adjustment factor, evaluated before the enhancement

---

Value Versus Cost

Function point counting distinguishes the amount of functionality ("value") provided to the end user from the amount of functionality ("size") built by the developer. If you modify a software product, the new value to the end user is the original size, plus the added functionality, minus the deleted functionality. The developer, however, expends effort to add, change, and delete code. In simple terms, the two views of size are

End user value = Original size + Added – Deleted

Developer size = Added + Changed + Deleted

This is another example showing that the use of the measure affects its definition. If the amounts added and deleted are the same, the value is unchanged. The developer's effort can be arbitrarily large, however.

9.5.2 Estimating Effort

Function point counting only produces the (functional) size of the software product. To estimate the development effort, each organization must determine a productivity value based on measurements of their particular production process (the activities, phases, development environment, staff capabilities, etc.). Dividing the adjusted function point count by the productivity gives the required development effort. Although function point practitioners address only size, dividing the size by productivity (called "delivery rate" or "rate of delivery" in the function point community) gives the effort.[6]

Although function point size is defined to be independent of the language used for implementation, the developers' productivity depends on the "language level." This is how you account for the lower productivity when writing assembly code. Figure 2.2 on page 59 of [Jones, 1997] shows ranges of productivity values (in function points per staff month) for various types of languages. However, all of the usual warnings about defining productivity still apply. You should measure the productivity for your own organization.

The next section gives an example of how a function point count is performed. Section 9.6 describes ways to speed the counting process. You can also apply the PERT technique to function point counts by putting the counts for each object type onto three separate lines. Then calculate the expected value and standard deviation for each line, and multiply them by the object's weight. Then sum the expected values and the variances for all of the lines. The CD-ROM has a spreadsheet to do this.

9.5.3 Example of a Function Point Count

This section shows how to calculate the size and effort for the development of a new online order entry subsystem for the warehouse project described in Chapter 4, "Measurement and Estimation." Figure 9-2 shows the context diagram for the system. First, the estimator analyzed the requirements and formulated a high-level view of the system. Next, the estimator identified the 18 objects, shown in Table 9-6 grouped by the five function types. Table 9-7 shows the weights applied to each object, producing a total of 164 unadjusted function points. Table 9-8 shows the degree of influence estimated for each of the 14 general system characteristics, giving a total degree of influence (TDI) of 44. The value adjustment factor, VAF, is

$$VAF = 0.65 + 0.01*TDI = 0.65 + 0.01*44 = 1.09$$

The adjusted size is 179 (adjusted) function points (= 164*1.09). Suppose that the development organization has determined a productivity of 20 phr per (adjusted) FP for the chosen implementation language, target platform, and development environment. Then the estimated effort is 3,575 phr (= 179 FP * 20 phr/FP). (Productivities can easily vary by a factor of 10 or more. Calibration with your own historical data is essential!)

---

[6] Function point counters use the terms *delivery rate* and *production rate*, which are misnomers because *rate* implies time, not effort. These are really production coefficients. This terminology is important to know, however, if you want to look up data in books dealing with function point counting.

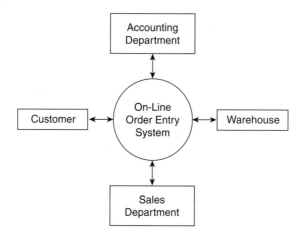

Figure 9-2 *Context diagram for the inventory system*

Table 9-6 *Identified Objects for the Online Order Entry System*

Inputs
• Customer data
• Order (includes shipping address)
• Item size and quantity
• Payment arrangements (includes billing address)
• Remarks
Outputs
• Order confirmation
• Picking ticket
• Invoice
• Shipping label
• Inventory reports
• Sales reports
• Accounts payable report
• Back-order summary report
Queries
• Order status
• Customer information
• Product information

Internal Logical Files
• Product catalog • Customers • Orders • Invoices
External Interface Files
• Rate table (sales taxes and shipping rates)

Table 9-7 *Calculation of the Unadjusted Size (UFP)*

Description	Low	Average	High	Total
Input	$6 \times 3 = 18$	$7 \times 4 = 28$	$2 \times 6 = 12$	58
Output	$2 \times 4 = 8$	$3 \times 5 = 15$	$3 \times 7 = 21$	44
Query	$3 \times 3 = 9$	$2 \times 4 = 8$	$1 \times 6 = 6$	23
Internal User Data Group	$2 \times 7 = 14$	$2 \times 10 = 20$	$\times 15 =$	34
External User Data Group	$1 \times 5 = 5$	$\times 7 =$	$\times 10 =$	5
		Total unadjusted function points = UFP =		164

Table 9-8 *Degree of Influence for the General System Characteristics*

Characteristic	DI
Data communications	4
Distributed data processing	4
Performance	4
Heavily used configuration	3
Transaction rate	4
Online data entry	5
End-user efficiency	4
Online update	5
Complex processing	3

(continues)

Table 9-8 *Degree of Influence for the General System Characteristics (continued)*

Characteristic	DI
Reusability	1
Installation ease	2
Operational ease	4
Multiple sites	0
Facilitate change	1
Application characteristics sum = AC = 44	

9.5.4 Advantages and Disadvantages of Function-Based Sizing

A major benefit of function point counting is that it facilitates the dialogue between the user of the system and the developer. The developer understands the method and this provides a means to negotiate project scope. (See note N12, "Using Function Points to Manage Scope Creep.")

Function point size estimates are generally claimed to be accurate within ±10% if the estimators are trained and experienced. The United Kingdom Software Measurement Association (UKSMA) performed an Inter-Counter Consistency Checking Experiment (ICCE) [Rule, 1998]. The data indicates that "experienced" function point counters (with more than four years of practice) demonstrated a variance of approximately ±10%, whereas "inexperienced" function point counters demonstrated a variance of approximately ±23%. These stated errors apply only to the size of the product. Errors in the productivity value used to compute the effort will increase error in the estimated effort. (The accuracy of the ICCE effort data was no better than ±20%.)

Function point counting cannot take place until the requirements are reasonably well understood and the high-level design of the system is known. Based on the funnel curve shown in Figure 1-3, you would expect that function point counting would provide more accurate estimates since it has more information about the software product. Basically, the method requires careful analysis of the proposed system. In my opinion, if you perform a similar level of careful analysis, then estimates using other size measures (including source lines of code) can be just as accurate.

The main disadvantage of function points is that they must be counted manually. This is expensive. The effort to count function points depends on the skill of the person doing the counting.

Skill Level	Rate (FP/phr)
Beginner	25
Experienced	60
Skilled	75
Professional	125

Also, function point counting only gives the (functional) size of a software product. It does not estimate development effort or time, nor allocate these to phases and activities. You must use historical data for your particular development process to determine productivity values. Some functions are easier to implement than others. On some projects it may take 10 times more effort to import data than to export it [Stensrud, 1998]. The reason is that the programmers must design and implement a great deal of data validation logic. In such cases, it might be appropriate to increase the weights for EIs and EIFs. Such situations blurs size and productivity. Where do you draw the line between the two? There is a deeper issue. A single set of weights may not be adequate both to size software to estimate development effort, and to value the utility of the resulting software. What if some functions are easy to develop but are of great value to a user?

There are some other concerns with functional size measurement. Norman Fenton and Shari Pfleeger provide a summary in [Fenton, 1997, pages 262-265]. Table 9-9 categorizes the main concerns. Various international groups update the definitions as technology advances. It might be possible to calibrate the weights using data. (Section 9.6.1 provides an example for the weights of the Dutch Method.) The formula to compute the value adjustment factor mixes ratio scale (the counts) and ordinal scale (the characteristic ratings) quantities, which violates the rules of measurement theory. (See [Fenton, 1997].) You can avoid the subjective general system characteristics and the value adjustment factor calculation by using only unadjusted function points. If you do use the general system characteristics, it might be better to separate user-perceived complexity and internal system complexity. [Kitchenham, Pfleeger, and Fenton suggest viewing function points as a vector representing different aspects of functionality, rather than a single number Kitchenham, 1995]. This is similar to Tom DeMarco's suggestion of keeping measures of function size and data size separate [DeMarco, 1982].) The process issues really involve the funnel curve. It you want to estimate early, you have less detailed information, and so less accuracy. One reason that initial counts are less than the final counts is that the initial description does not describe the final delivered product. (This is the growth and volatility issue.) Despite these concerns, function points are a useful measure of software size for many estimators.

Table 9-9 *Some Concerns with Function Points*

Element Definitions
• The definitions need clarification and interpretation for new types of software.
• Analysts sometimes fail to classify inputs, outputs, queries, and "logical files" consistently even with detailed rules.

Element Weights for Unadjusted Function Point
• The weights are subjective, and based on Albrecht's experience. They may not be appropriate for other product types and development environments.
• The weights may be different for "value" and for "development effort."

General System Characteristics (GSC)
• The Likert ratings are subjective.
• They mix user-perceived complexity and internal system complexity. (It might be better to separate these aspects.)

Value Adjustment Factor (VAF) and Adjusted Function Points (AFP)
• Assigning all ratings as Average (= 3) gives VAF = 1.07, not 1.0, as you expect.
• Using VAF does not significantly improve the accuracy of the estimated effort.
• The calculation of AFP mixes measurements from ratio and ordinal scales.

Process Issues
• You cannot count function points very early. (You must have a high-level design.)
• Initial counts are sometimes much less than the final counts of the delivered product.

9.6 Simplified Ways to Count Function Points

This section describes some fast, approximate methods to count function points early in a project when there is little detailed information.

9.6.1 Early Function Point Counting (The Dutch Method)

The Netherlands Software Metrics Association (NESMA) publishes guidelines for counting function points very early in the product life cycle. NESMA defines three types of function point counts: Detailed, Estimated, and Indicative, which are summarized in Table 9-10. The detailed count is performed the same way as the IFPUG count, except that the adjustment for general system characteristics is not used. The estimated count uses default values for the complexity ratings. The indicative count uses only the number of data objects (ILF and EIF) and assumes average values for the associated transactions. Specifically, for each ILF there are approximately three EIs (to add, change, and delete information in the ILF), two EOs, and one EQ. For every EIF there are approximately one EO and one EQ. Using the IFPUG weights gives

One ILF = 3*4 + 2*5 + 1*4 + 1*10 = 36
One EIF = 0*4 + 1*5 + 1*4 + 7 = 16

The official NESMA values are actually chosen to be 35 and 15, respectively.

NESMA compared the accuracy of these three counting methods using a database of 100 projects. They observed close agreement between the detailed and estimated counts. The indicative and detailed counts were also correlated, but showed more dispersion as you would expect. For additional details, see the NESMA website, http://www.nesma.nl. This site also has tutorial materials on function points in general.

Table 9-10 *NESMA's Three Function Point Counting Methods*

Detailed Count (identical to IFPUG Function Points)
• Count the occurrences of all object types (EI, EO, EQ, ILF, EIF)
• Rate the complexity of each occurrence
• Calculate the total unadjusted function point count
Estimated Count (similar to Feature Points)
• Count the occurrences of all object types (EI, EO, EQ, ILF, EIF)
• Rate the complexity of every data object (ILF, EIF) as Low
• Rate the complexity of every transaction object (EI, EO, EQ) as Average
• Calculate the total unadjusted function point count
Indicative Count (the "Dutch Method")
• Count the occurrences of only data object types (ILF, EIF)
• Calculate the total unadjusted function point count using   Size (UFP) = 35*(# ILFs) + 15*(#EIFs)

As an example, repeat the count for the warehouse inventory system described earlier. The detailed count is the same as before, which has 164 UFPs. The estimated count gives

EI	15*4	=	60
EO	8*5	=	40
EQ	6*5	=	24
ILF	4*7	=	28
EIF	1*5	=	5
			Total 157 UFP

The indicative count gives

ILF	4*35	=	140
EIF	1*15	=	15
			Total 155 UFP

Before you use such approximations, have a certified function point counter produce an accurate count for several of your software products. This will also provide the number of ILFs and EIFs in each product so you can use a regression fit to obtain values for the two size coefficients, Size(ILF) and Size(EIF), that are appropriate for your applications. These fitted values replace the default values of 35 and 15. The equation to fit is

Total size = (# ILFs)*Size(ILF) + (# EIFs)*Size(EIF)

To illustrate how to fit the weights, I generated sizes in unadjusted function points for 12 projects. The total size was calculated using ILF*40 + EIF*10, where ILF and EIF were uniformly distributed over the ranges [2, 10] and [0, 6], respectively. Then, I multiplied the total size by a random value uniformly distributed over the interval [0.7, 1.3]. Table 9-11 shows the results using the official NESMA weights (the "Dutch values") of 35 and 15, which give a mean magnitude of relative error of 21%. Fitting using Excel's Solver gives weights of 47.1 and 15.0, and MMRE 15%. Figure 9-3 plots the estimated sizes for both sets of weights versus the true size (computed without any error). Calibrating improved the performance slightly ($R^2 = 0.72$ versus $R^2 = 0.82$).

Table 9-11 *Results Using the Default NESMA Weights*

Solution:	35.0	15.0		70595.0		21.2%
						MMRE
		Average =	280.3	230.8	-49.4	
		Std Dev =	125.8	81.1	61.3	
Project	ILF	EIF	UFP (actual)	UFP (calc)	Residual	MRE
1	3	2	176	135	-41.0	0.233
2	2	3	126	115	-11.0	0.087
3	5	2	281	205	-76.0	0.270
4	7	2	382	275	-107.0	0.280
5	4	5	217	215	-2.0	0.009
6	9	1	434	330	-104.0	0.240
7	3	0	90	105	15.0	0.167
8	8	0	368	280	-88.0	0.239
9	6	1	300	225	-75.0	0.250
10	6	3	288	255	-33.0	0.115
11	9	3	504	360	-144.0	0.286
12	6	4	197	270	73.0	0.371

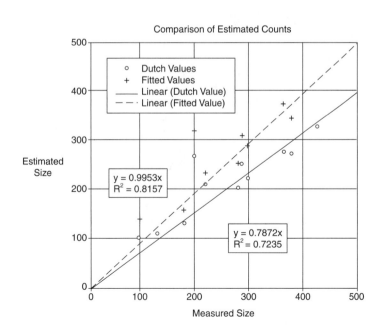

Figure 9-3 *Comparison of estimated counts*

9.6.2 Scaling Approaches (Herron, Gaffney)

David Herron proposes a similar approach, as reported in [Jones, 1991, pp. 101-102]. Herron observes that particular types of applications seem to be driven by certain object types. For example, accounting systems seem to be driven by inputs and file structures. He also notes that some characteristics of the product are known with more accuracy earlier in a project than others are. For example, analysts can usually identify the ILFs and EIFs early. Herron suggests measuring the ratios between the sizes of the function point object types for a particular type of application. For example, you might measure

Object Type	% of Size (in UFP)
EI	20
EO	25
EQ	15
ILF	35
EIF	5

If the developers analyze the ILFs first, this might provide a reasonably accurate count of the ILFs. You can then estimate the size of each remaining type of object using the observed percentages. The total size of the product in UFP is given by

Total size = (Object count)*(Object weight)/(% of total)

As an example, if the analysts identify 15 ILFs, these represent 150 UFPs (using a weight of 10, corresponding to an average complexity value). The total size is 429 UFP (= 15*10/0.35). The estimated size of the EIs is 86 UFPs (= 429*0.20). Values for the other object types can be estimated similarly. (This approach is similar to the Dutch Method described previously.) You can refine the size estimate for the ILFs by subdividing by complexity and using the appropriate weights. For example, suppose the analysts subdivide the 15 ILFs as follows:

ILF Complexity	# of ILFs	Weight	Contribution
Low	3	7	21
Average	7	10	70
High	5	15	75

ILF Total = 166 UFPs

Then use 166 in place of 150 in the preceding calculation.

If the analysts identify two parameters early on, say the numbers of ILFs and EIFs, you can use both to obtain a weighted average. If 5 EIFs are identified, this gives 35 UFPs (again assuming Average complexity) and a total size of 700 UFPs (= 5*7/0.05). Using this estimate of the total size to estimate the size of the EIs gives 140 UFPs (= 700*0.20). These two estimates (86 and 140) differ by 50% or so. A possible approach is to use the average of these two values to estimate "likely" values, and the values themselves to indicate upper and lower limits. (These are approximate limits but will serve to indicate the degree of uncertainty in the estimated values.)

Key point: All of these calculations are based on historical data, poor though it may be. Even a little data can go a long way toward improving your estimates.

John Gaffney describes an approach that is similar to Herron's approach [Gaffney, 1996]. Gaffney shows how to estimate the software development effort using only the numbers of inputs and outputs. He reports that his estimates were as accurate as estimates based on function points. Gaffney speculates that his "simplified function point estimation method" apparently works because the data used to compute the function point size is redundant.

Gaffney actually analyzed three sets of data using six linear and five nonlinear models that related effort to various independent variables. The baseline model used UFPs and had the form: Effort = A + B*(# of UFPs). The best performing model had the form: Effort = A + B*(# of EIs) + C*(# of EOs). Another model had the form: Effort = A + B*(# of Files), which is similar to the Dutch Method, except that the ILFs and EIFs are combined. Table 9-12 indicates the performance of these three models against Gaffney's three data sets. (The three rows of values beside each model correspond to his data sets 1, 2, and 3.) Gaffney's work provides empirical evidence that simple methods to estimate software size may perform surprisingly well.

Table 9-12 *Performance of Simplified Effort Estimation Models**

Model Form	Sample Correlation	% of Variability Explained
A + B(# of UFPs)	0.95	89.5
	0.76	58.5
	0.93	87.0
A + B(# of EIs) + C*(# of EOs)	0.95	89.8
	0.81	65.1
	0.91	82.1

(continues)

Table 9-12 *Performance of Simplified Effort Estimation Models* (continued)*

Model Form	Sample Correlation	% of Variability Explained
A + B(# of EIs + # of EOs)	0.90	81.6
	0.63	39.7
	0.90	80.7
A + B*(# of Files)	0.73	62.0
	0.46	20.9
	0.81	80.7

*The values shown are from [Gaffney, 1996].

Manfred Bundschuh reports similar results [Bundschuh, 1998] and [Bundschuh, 1999]. In [Bundschuh, 1999], he reports that the third model shown in Table 9-12 (EIs plus EOs) gave size estimates that were within 15% to 20% of the complete, detailed function point counts, based on data from 40 projects. For additional data and discussion see his papers.

9.6.3 Backfiring

Capers Jones of Software Productivity Research developed a technique in 1984 called "backfire" counting to estimate the size of existing legacy systems by counting the lines of code in the software product and then multiplying by a language-specific conversion factor. This method only provides moderate accuracy but makes it very easy to count legacy systems. (The backfiring technique is another example of proxy-based estimation described in Section 3.3. The proxy for function points is lines of code.)

Backfiring uses conversion values, expressed in logical statements per (unadjusted) function point, for the programming language used to write the legacy code. Some backfire conversion values are

Language	Logical Statements per Function Point
C	128
C++	53
COBOL	105
Ada 1983	71
Ada 1995	49

These backfire values are based on the IFPUG Version 3 function point definitions. (In 1994, IFPUG revised the counting rules, causing the sizes to become
slightly smaller.) Table 2.15 in [Jones, 1991, p.76] lists values for 50 languages.
Software Productivity Research maintains a table of conversion values for over
300 languages. To purchase the latest copy of the "Programming Languages
Table" see the SPR website at http://www.spr.com.

To illustrate the use of backfiring, suppose that you have an existing application written in C++ whose size is measured with a line counter to be precisely
156,237 physical source lines of code (PSLOC). You want to estimate the size of
this application in IFPUG 4.0 unadjusted function points. To do this you must
convert PLSOC to logical statements (LSTMT), LSTMT to IFPUG 3.0 UFPs
(UFP3), and finally IFPUG 3.0 unadjusted function points to IFPUG 4.0 unadjusted function points (UFP4). Each step of the conversion introduces some
error. Suppose that you have determined the following conversion values and
their associated errors.

Quantity	Value	Error (%)	Units	Source
Source size	156,237	0	PSLOC	Count of C++ code
Conversion 1	0.924	8	LSTMT/PSLOC	Historical data
C++ backfire value	53	15	LSTMT/UFP3	Backfire table
Conversion 2	0.8	10	UFP4/UFP3	Table 8-15

The errors are the coefficient of variation (one standard deviation divided by
the average value), expressed in percent. Using these values, the size is

$$Size(UFP4) = 156{,}237 * 0.924 * (1/53) * (1/0.8) = 3{,}405 \text{ UFP4}$$

Using the law of propagation of errors, described in note N06, the coefficient of
variation, CV, is

$$CV^2 = (0)^2 + (0.08)^2 + (0.15)^2 + (0.10)^2 = 0.039$$

which gives CV = 20%. So the estimated size is 3,405 ± 681 UFP4s. Assuming
that the errors are normally distributed, there is a 68% probability that the size
will lie between 2,724 and 4,806 UFP4s.

Different design and coding styles for a particular programming language will
affect the backfire value. Thus, there is really no single value for a particular
language. Unfortunately, most of the published tables do not give a range for
the number of statements. There are published sources giving observed ranges

in the backfire values [Jones, 1996] and [Jones, 1997]. Table 9-13 lists the data from [Jones, 1996]. The low and high values represent the lowest and highest values reported to Capers Jones. For widely used languages, he obtained many values, and so you can assume that these values represent approximate three-sigma values. Figure 9-4 shows a plot of the mean conversion values versus the language level. The error bars represent the low and high values. (For points having the same language level, the lower values, and the upper values, are averaged.) There is a large amount of variation. For rough estimates, the three-sigma values (in logical statements per IFPUG 3.0 UFPs) can be approximated by

Low value   = 180/LL
Mean value = 320/LL
High value   = 460/LL

where LL is the language level. (Better fits to the data in the table are possible but are not justified.) The coefficients for the one-sigma values are 273 and 367 for the low and high values, respectively. These correspond to a Coefficient of Variation of ±15%.

Table 9-13 *Range of Backfire Conversion Ratios**

Language	Language Level	Logical Statements per FP		
		Low	Mean	High
1st generation + basic assembly	1.0	210.0	320.0	475.0
Macro Assembly	1.5	130.0	213.0	300.0
C and BASIC (interpreted)	2.5	65.0	128.0	167.5
2nd generation, FORTRAN, ALGOL, COBOL, CMS, JOVIAL	3.0	67.2	107.0	156.7
Pascal	3.5	50.0	91.0	125.0
3rd generation, PL/1, Modula 2	4.0	60.0	80.0	115.0
Ada 1983	4.5	60.0	71.0	80.0
LISP, FORTH	5.0	26.0	64.0	82.5
Quick BASIC	5.5	38.0	58.0	90.0
C++	6.0	30.0	53.0	125.0
Ada 1995	6.5	28.0	49.0	110.0
Database Default	8.0	25.0	40.0	75.0

Language	Language Level	Logical Statements per FP		
		Low	Mean	High
Visual Basic (Windows), APL	10.0	15.0	32.0	41.0
Smalltalk	15.0	15.0	21.0	40.0
Program Generator Default	20.0	9.0	16.0	25.0
SQL	27.0	7.0	12.0	15.0
Spreadsheet Default	50.0	3.0	6.0	9.0

*Reprinted from [Jones, 1996] with permission of the Cutter Consortium.

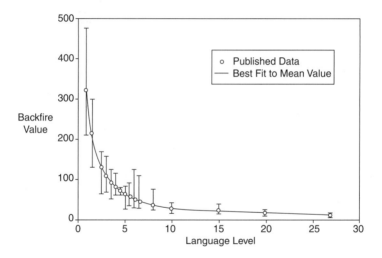

Figure 9-4 *Plot of conversion ratios versus language level*

The Software Productivity Research (SPR) backfire values are widely cited. Other organizations publish similar data, however, and corresponding values differ significantly. For example, Table 9-14 shows a comparison of some backfire values from SPR and from the David Consulting Group (DCG). (The SPR values are converted to IFPUG 4 values using Jones's value of 0.8.) Neither set of values is necessarily "more correct" because coding styles, and so forth, may affect the number of source lines.

Table 9-14 *Variation of Backfire Values*

Language	SPR (IFPUG 3)	SPR (IFPUG 4)	DCG (IPFPUG 4)
Basic Assembly	320	256	575
Macro Assembly	213	170	400
C	128	102	225
C++	53	42	80
COBOL 74	107	86	220
COBOL 85	107	86	175
Pascal	91	73	160
Java	53	42	80

TIP: To use backfiring in your organization, you should

1. Have a certified function point counter count some of your software products.
2. Measure the size of these same products in logical statements (or whatever size measure you desire).
3. Use this data to determine your conversion value (and the associated uncertainties).

9.7 Object-Oriented Size Measures

Objects are entities that persist in the world modeled by a software program, which includes both the application domain and the solution domain. Application objects can be physical things, roles, and events. Some examples are purchase orders, invoices, missile trajectories, messages, buyers, sellers, and project milestones. Solution objects are associated with the implementation of the software product itself. Examples are queues, linked lists, state transition matrices, and routing tables. Ultimately, developers represent the objects in software using "classes," components that encapsulate all the information (data, functions, and state) about a particular object.

There are two primary challenges to defining suitable object-oriented size measures. First, most analysis and design methods include a large number of elements, many of which convey equivalent or overlapping information. For example, Unified Modeling Language (UML) has approximately two dozen diagrams (elements) depicting classes, states, use cases, communication (collaboration), and sequencing (event trace). There are too many UML elements to use them all, plus some of the same information is recorded in multiple elements. The challenge is deciding which elements to use.

The second challenge is the trade between detail (and so accuracy) and timeliness. (This is the funnel curve again.) Object-oriented analysis and design methods can be applied to both the application domain (the requirements) and the solution domain (the architectural elements and software components). The trick to obtaining a useful size measure is to stay near the application side, and not drift too far toward the solution (implementation) side. For example, one approach is to identify application objects early in a project, and then "expand" the number of application objects to obtain the total number of application and solution objects. (This is similar to the scheme proposed by David Herron described earlier.) Some size measures use characteristics that are not available until detailed design has been completed. Such methods are not too practical for the early estimation of size, but they do have other uses.[7]

To meet these challenges, a good size measure should

- Base the size measure on the products of logical design (design elements).
- Hide the effects of implementation methods in the productivity.
- Use only a subset of the elements produced during analysis.

There is not yet a standard object-oriented size measure. Note N09, "Object-Based Size Measures," describes some of the proposed measures.

9.8 Defining Source Lines of Code (SLOC)

Many organizations measure software size in source lines of code (SLOC) because automated tools can objectively and precisely measure its value once the software exists. (You must still estimate the size early in a project.) There is no standard definition for a source line of code.

A precise definition of a "line of code" must address many factors. You must decide whether you are counting "physical source lines" (carriage returns or line feeds) or "logical source lines" (statements in the source language). A single logical statement may extend over multiple physical lines, and a single

---

[7] The situation is not so clear-cut, however. Depending on the "depth" of the decomposition, "objects" can be external (application domain) or internal (solution domain). Various object-oriented size measures lie along the spectrum.

physical line may contain several logical statements. Size in one measure can be greater than or less than size in the other, sometimes by factors of four or five. In addition, physical lines may include or exclude comments.[8] Compiler directives may copy segments of library code or expand macros "in line," inflating the size of the source code, but consuming little programmer effort. Capers Jones discusses similar considerations [Jones, 1991, pages 48–53].

Code may originate from different sources as illustrated in Figure 9-5. In addition, programmers can manipulate existing code in different ways, as shown in the shaded portions on the right of the figure. Some authors use the alternate terms for the categories shown in Figure 9-5. These follow the equal signs:

Programmed = New, custom, built from scratch, developed, developmental

Generated   = Produced by a tool from high-level specifications or designs

Converted   = (Automatically) translated

Copied   = (Re)used "as is," (reused) unmodified, reused verbatim

Modified   = Adapted, leveraged

Removed   = Deleted

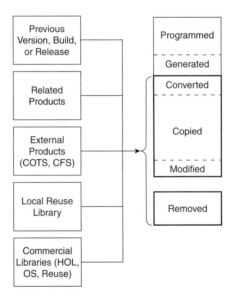

Figure 9-5 *Relation between sources of reused code and production activities (adapted from [Park, 1992])*

---

[8] Counting statements is more difficult than counting physical lines (carriage returns or line feeds) because the counting tool must parse the programming language.

9.8.1 The SEI Operational Definition

An operational definition is a set of rules that specifies exactly how to determine a measured value. Table 9-15 summarizes factors needed to completely specify a source line of code, and is adapted from templates in [Park, 1992], [Shepperd, 1995, page 12], and [Fenton, 1997, page 30]. The entity measured indicates the scope of the definition. You must specify what types of source code are to be counted. Regarding the counting rules, you must specify whether each type of line is to be included in the count or excluded from the count. The table lists many items, but the list is actually incomplete. Robert Park developed a five-page checklist of items needed to specify a "line of code" [Park, 1992, Figure 5-2]. The COCOMO II model uses this scheme to define its "line of code" measure.[9]

Table 9-15 *Elements of an Operational Definition for NCSL*

Name of Measure: NCSL

Used By: Estimators, engineers, and managers

Goal(s) Supported: Measure productivity, develop effort estimation models, track completion status, and monitor size growth

Questions(s) Answered: Reference a separate analysis report

Entity Measured: Source code for software modules (see Rules)

Attribute: Noncommented physical source lines

Scale: Absolute

Measurement Type: Direct

Collection and Reduction Rules:

Scope:

Apply the counting rules to the following types of source code:

Type of Code:

  Mission functions

  Support functions

---

[9] The COCOMO II software estimation model measures size in *logical* statements. See Figure 2.1 in [Boehm, 2000, page 16] and Table 2.53 in [Boehm, 2000, pages 77–81]. The COCOMO 1981 model, however, uses *physical* lines of code. This affects the calibration of the two COCOMO models.

Table 9-15 *Elements of an Operational Definition for NCSL (continued)*

Prototypes
Tooling
Origin:
New Code
Reused code (modified)
Reused code (unmodified)
Inserted code (e.g., $INCLUDE directive)
How Produced:
Manually
Converted using tools
Generated using ICASE tools

Count the lines in each source file as follows. Read each physical line in the set of source files. For each line assign a type. Add 1 to the count if the type is included.

Statement Type:
     Executable
         Computation (expressions, function and procedure calls)
         Control (IF, THEN, CASE, LOOP, EXIT)
         Data transfer and formatting
    Nonexecutable
         Data declarations
         Compiler directives
         Comments
            In header (prolog)
            On separate lines
            On lines with source code ("mixed" lines)
            Blank lines

Frequency of Collection:	When the programmer completes the module and submits it to the CM department (This is the UTC milestone.)
Collected By:	CM Specialist using the code count tool
Frequency of Reporting:	The total size of all submitted modules is reported on the first of each month
Reported By:	CM department

9.8.2 Using Size to Estimate Effort

Each of the activities in Figure 9-5 takes a different amount of effort to perform. How can you estimate the effort needed? Assuming that effort equals size divided by productivity, there are three possible approaches:

1. Adjust the size, keeping the productivity constant.
2. Adjust the productivity, keeping the size constant.
3. Adjust both size and productivity.

For new code, the size equals all of the code. For reused code, most estimators use Approach 1. (For conversion, some estimators use Approach 2.) The usual assumption is that the productivity value is the same for all types of code (new, copied, and modified).[10] They define an "equivalent size," which is a function of the actual size of the adapted code (the "adapted size") and other factors. This allows the sizes to be simply added, and a single productivity value to be used to compute effort.

In particular, the apparent and economic productivities are affected when the product contains some reused code. Norman Fenton and Shari Pfleeger provide a numeric example in Section 11.2 of [Fenton, 1997].

The following sections address each type of code identified in the SEI definition:

Type of Code	Section
Programmed (new)	9.9
Generated	9.9.5
Converted (translated)	9.10.2
Copied (unmodified)	9.10.4
Modified	9.10.3
Removed (deleted)	9.10.1

---

[10] A refinement is to subdivide the code into categories and use a different productivity for each category. For example, NASA's Software Engineering Laboratory subdivides modified code based on the amount of source lines modified. "Slightly modified" has fewer than 25% modified, and "extensively modified" has 25% or more modified. Copied lines ("reused verbatim") are also a distinct category.

9.9 Estimating New Code

The main challenge in sizing new software is to ensure that you have identified all the pieces of software that have to be built. This must be done at a detailed level. Figure 8-2 (the software iceberg) illustrated the problem. Overlooking components and functions will cause the software size to be too low, resulting in underestimation of the development effort, cost, and time. Chapter 8, "Estimating Software Size: The Basics," presented checklists based on roles in the operational concept, and a checklist based on the types of functions (mission, support, transition) and the timing of their execution (continuous, periodic, and on demand). You can also use the product (or software) architecture, defined in Section 7.6,[11] to systematically identify the components whose size you must estimate. This prevents multiple counting of functions and overlooking key functions. There is a more subtle benefit, however. A good architect can identify common functions that can be reused in many parts of the system, thus reducing the total amount of software and so the costs for development and testing.

Design and implementation considerations may affect the estimated product size. For example, designers may partition the product to isolate classified, proprietary, or sensitive data or algorithms, or uncertain or poorly understood requirements. This may require additional interface code or the use of temporary stubs. If the product is built and delivered in stages or increments, some previously delivered code may have to be modified in a later release ("breakage").

To make meaningful size estimates, engineers need a list of components, accompanied by short descriptions. A written description helps engineers form a common mental model of the product. See the box "The Narrative Architecture Description." The next section provides an example.

The Narrative Architecture Description

A narrative architecture description identifies the parts of the system, and briefly describes the nature and scope of each component or subsystem. (The narrative can include tables and diagrams as well as text.) The description of a component indicates the functions performed by that component, and any functions specifically excluded. These are functions that you might ordinarily expect to be performed by the component. For example, the description of a component responsible for managing all messages transmitted over the network might identify functions such as

---

[11] Briefly, the *product architecture* identifies components, defines which components will perform specific functions, and defines how the components will interact. It also identifies shared, purchased, and reused components.

transmitting, verifying, retransmitting, and archiving messages, and might also state that encryption will be performed by some other component. (Otherwise, the estimator might include lines of code for the encryption function.)

The narrative architecture description will not be very detailed or even correct at the beginning. It will get better with time. It is just important to start somewhere. Writing it down will stimulate a dialog between the participants (engineers and estimators), leading to refinement of the list of components, the descriptions of their nature and scope, and the estimated sizes. This will lead to a better understanding of the system by all participants and better estimates.

9.9.1 Example: NMCMS Architecture

Table 9-16 shows a high-level description of a Numerically Controlled Machine Monitoring System (NCMSS). This is at the level of a product vision, but does not mention any design or implementation constraints.

Table 9-16 *The Numerically Controlled Machine Monitoring System (NCMSS).*

Background
• Large factory with a bank of identical NC machines.
• Cutting tools wear out at varying rates.
• A repairman must manually replace worn cutting tools.
Purpose of System
• Use sensors to continuously monitor each machine.
• Report trend data on tool wear.
• Alert repairman if wear exceeds specified threshold.

Figure 9-6 shows the "physical architecture" for this product. The boxes represent physical components. The phrases under each box indicate the functional capabilities allocated to each component. (Most of these capabilities will be implemented using software modules that execute on processors inside of each physical component.)

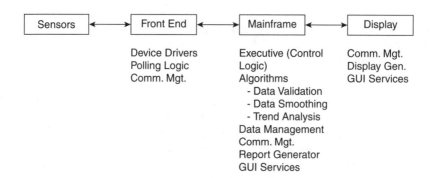

Figure 9-6 *NCMMS physical architecture*

Figure 9-7 shows the software architecture. This is the "functional view" of the same NCMMS product. This view will guide the construction of the product. Note that several software modules (e.g., Communications Management) operate in two physical components, but appear only once in the software architecture because the developers will build the code for both ends of the interface together. (In large systems, different teams or even different companies may implement the two ends of an interface. This will increase the development effort and integration risk.) The functions followed by "(?)" appear twice because the designers have not yet allocated the function to a particular subsystem. All such decisions must be made before the engineers can estimate the software size. The "tooling" component identifies any special development tools. Include these in the size if you will deliver them. Otherwise, include a level-of-effort task to build them.

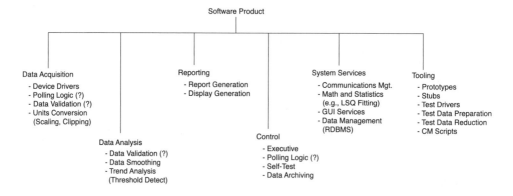

Figure 9-7 *NCMMS software architecture*

To estimate sizes, software developers need descriptions of the "nature and scope" of each component. Table 9-17 shows an example. This illustrates the information needed to prepare a meaningful size estimate. To prepare an effort estimate you need additional information such as staff experience, labor rates, and project constraints. See Note N48, "Microestimation Using COCOMO II."

Table 9-17 *Descriptions of NCMMS Components*

Data Acquisition
This component manages the data acquisition and signal conversion, converts the data to internal units and scales it, signals if bad values are received, stores the (good) data in files, and conducts status and health checking of the external equipment. One file is produced each day.
Data Analysis
This component periodically (i.e., once daily) reads the converted data from the file, and processes it by performing least squares fits to produce trend curves. (The parameters of these curves are used to compute if tool wear is out of tolerance or is predicted to go out of tolerance within the next 24 hours.)
Report Generation
This component reads specified daily data files and produces summary reports showing tool wear trend plots for each machine tool. A separate report is produced, which alerts the operator of all tools whose observed or predicted wear exceeds a specified threshold for the tool type.
Control
This component provides the overall control and timing for the other components. It handles initialization, sequencing of functions, and error recovery.
System Services
This component provides the common functions and services used by the other architectural components. These transfer, manage, and display data.
Tooling
This component provides emulators, stubs, drivers, and simulated data needed to test the system before installing it in the plant. It may include programs to reduce and analyze test data. It may also include scripts for compiling, linking, and executing test cases, and managing the various files of code, executables, and data.

9.9.2 Estimating Module Size

The best option is historical data for analogous modules. You must measure so that you can estimate! Some commercial sizing tools contain files of historical data for various types of components. Such data may help indicate the order of magnitude of a component's size. Because of potential problems with units of measure, different design and coding standards, and other factors, however, you should not depend on such data for accurate size estimates.

John Gaffney and Richard Werling describe empirical relations to estimate software size in SLOC using counts of "externals" suited for real-time command and control systems [Gaffney, 1991]. (This is another example of proxy-based estimation.) Section 7.6 in [Gaffney, 1995] briefly describes the approach. They state that four attributes (inputs, outputs, queries, and interfaces) are often identified early in the development cycle, and so are a good choice for early size estimation. Their equations are linear, of the form Size = A + B*C, where A and B are constants determined by fitting historical data, and C is the count of externals. You can choose other units of size and then fit coefficients as illustrated in Section 9.6.1.

If developers use Program Design Language (PDL) to express the detailed design of each module, and you have some measurements of the "expansion ratio" of lines of PDL into lines of source code in the finished product, you can use this to update the estimate of the total amount of code that will be written by multiplying the lines of PDL times the expansion ratio.

9.9.3 Using the Sizes of Prototypes

Prototypes are a special case of "historical data." People often assume that because they have a working prototype, most of the operational software is written. A typical prototype is designed to demonstrate the primary features of a product or to provide quantitative information about high-risk algorithms or performance drivers. The prototype does not implement many of the secondary functions needed to create a complete, working product. (Many of these functions are identified in the software iceberg figure.)

We once built a prototype tool and then a vendor paid us to "productize" it. Here are the size values:

20,000 statements	Prototype of key functions
120,000 statements	Product with all required functions

The size increased by a factor of six. In addition, the second project produced additional help files and user documentation, and also presented monthly status reviews. Having a working prototype does not mean that the product is "90% complete!"[12]

A more fundamental problem is that there are three types of code involved:

- Used in both prototype and product
- Used in prototype only
- Used in product only

Figure 9-8 illustrates their relation. The prototype models only the "core functions" of interest (e.g., primary mission functions or key algorithms). These "core functions" are also in the operational system. The prototype also contains code related to support the simulation. The complete product contains additional "secondary functions" and none of the simulation support code. Only the core functions represent size that is relevant to the final product. These differences make it difficult to directly relate the sizes of the prototype and product software. Also, if there are several prototypes having some overlap of functionality, simply adding the sizes of the prototypes will count a particular "core function" multiple times, and so will inflate the estimated size of the operational system. To avoid this, you need architecture descriptions for the prototypes. Even a simple diagram, such as Figure 9-8, will be a big help in clarifying the objects being sized.

9.9.4 Reverse Backfiring Function Points

The backfiring technique, described in Section 9.6.3, estimates the size of an existing application in unadjusted function points (UFPs) using the size in logical source statements (LSTMT) and a conversion constant. If you estimate the software size in UFP, you can apply the backfiring technique in reverse to provide an estimate of the size of a system in LSTMT. (Some people call this "forward firing." This is another example of proxy-based estimating.) Table 9-18 illustrates this for the three components shown on the left side of the table. The estimators have obtained the sizes in unadjusted functions points (specifically, UFP3s) shown in the second column. The third column shows the language to be used to implement the particular component. The fourth column gives the backfire value. The last column gives the estimated size (in LSTMT) of the chosen source language. The total is 30,200 LSTMT. Since backfire values have an error of ±15%, the error in the estimated size is ±26% (= SQRT(3)*0.15). The estimated size has a 68% chance of lying between 22,300 and 38,000 LSTMT.

---

[12] On the other hand, if you use modern development tools with integrated libraries of prebuilt components, an early working prototype may actually contain 80% of the final product functionality.

(Actually, the error is larger since the initial size estimates [in UFP3s] have errors as well.) Assuming, as most SLOC-based models do, that productivity is the same per LSTMT, and has a value of 2.5 LSTMT/phr (for some specified set of phases and activities), the estimated effort is 12,100 phr ± 3,100 phr.

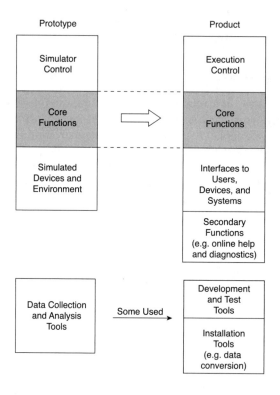

Figure 9-8 *Prototype versus product*

Table 9-18 *Reverse Backfire Example*

Software Component	Size (UFP3)	Programming Language	Backfire Value	Size (LSTMT)
Sensor Manager	100	C	128	12800
Data Analyzer	200	Ada 1995	71	14200
Report Generator	100	Visual Basic 3	32	3200
			Total =	30200

This technique is simple and quickly gives an approximate size that you can use to crosscheck software sizes that are estimated using other techniques. (For example, you can use the Dutch Method to quickly get the size in UFP.)

There are two important points to note when using reverse backfiring. First, the computed sizes are measured in logical statements and not physical source lines of code.[13] Second, the initial size estimates are measured in unadjusted function points (UFPs), not adjusted function points (AFPs). (Sizes estimated in this way are often used as inputs to parametric estimating models, which use various "cost driver" parameters to account for the characteristics of the application, the product, the process, and the project. These cost drivers are similar to the 14 general system characteristics used in function point counting. If you computed the estimated size using AFPs, and then used this value as input to a parametric model, then you would be in effect adjusting for the application characteristics twice.)

9.9.5 Generated Code

Some software development tools generate code to implement various design objects. Ideally, there is no effort associated with producing this code and so its size is not of interest. However, if the code is only a "skeleton" that must be filled in by a human programmer, you must estimate the size of the additional code to estimate the effort required. Because this code is produced from design objects maintained by the tool, you can use proxy-based estimation. (One possibility is some subset of the UML diagrams described in Section 9.2.)

9.10 Sizing Reused Source Code

Section 9.8.1 identified different ways to manipulate existing source code to incorporate it into a software product. This section addresses each alternative.

9.10.1 Converted Code

For converted code, the assumption is that all modifications can be done using an automated tool that translates the source code. Let TSize denote the amount of code to be translated. The COnstructive COst MOdel estimates the effort to perform the automated translation, E_{AT}, using

---

[13] If you want to convert to size in physical source lines of code, you should measure some actual application code produced by your organization, counting both logical statements and physical source lines of code. Then use the ratio of the two values to compute your conversion factor. Choose applications that have characteristics similar to those of the application being estimated. The characteristics include design and coding standards, and the nature of the application itself (relative amounts of data manipulation, numeric calculation, and complex decision logic).

$$E_{AT} = TSize / ATPROD$$

where ATPROD is some appropriate productivity value. TSize and ATPROD must use the same size measure. The effort used to estimate the value of ATPROD must include the same phases and activities to be performed during the planned conversion.

Automated translation, per se, is fast. This might lead you to expect large values of ATPROD (e.g., 1,000 SLOC/phr). You must consider the entire process, however. Engineers will expend effort to locate the code, verify that all the components are present, and then test the converted code. Usually, the automated translator tool encounters nonstandard constructs (vendor extensions) in the language and fails. Engineers must research and correct these problems. For example, if it takes 40 person-hours to perform these activities for 10,000 SLOC of code, plus 10 person-hours to actually run the translation program (10,000 SLOC/1,000 SLOC/phr), then ATPROD = 200 SLOC/phr, 5 times lower than the ideal value.

The speed of the translator tool does not usually determine the conversion effort. Instead, use the Linear Method to estimate the effort for all of the contributing activities:

1. Locate all the code (includes libraries and compile scripts).
2. Prepare code for use by the translator tool (load, convert format).
3. Run the translator tool.
4. Fix the translation problems (and rerun the translator tool).
5. Test the converted code.
6. Document metrics and suggested improvements.

9.10.2 Modified Code: The COCOMO 1981 Model

For modified code, you can precisely measure the actual size of the source code in your chosen size measure. (The following discussion uses "SLOC" to denote the chosen size measure.) Most estimators define an "equivalent size" that is a function of the actual size of the code (the "adapted size") and other factors, and assume that the productivity (in SLOC/phr) is the same for all types of code: new lines, (equivalent) modified lines, and deleted lines.

Many cost models use the following simple model described in Section 8.8 of [Boehm, 1981, p. 133ff.]. The model computes the equivalent number of new source lines of code (denoted by ESize) for a reused component whose actual (adapted) size is denoted by ASize:

ESize = ASize*AAF

where

$$AAF = 0.4*DM + 0.3*CM + 0.3*IM$$

AAF is called the adaptation adjustment factor and ranges from 0 to 1. (It may even exceed 1 in some cases. See below.)[14] It is the weighted sum of three parameters. DM is the fraction of the design that must be modified in order to adapt the component to meet the functional and interface requirements of the new system. CM is the fraction of code that must be modified in order to implement the new functions and interfaces. IM is the fraction of integration effort required to integrate the adapted software into the overall product, and to test the resulting product compared to the normal amount of integration effort for software of comparable size.[15] The weights are based on an assumed allocation of the total development effort to design, code, and integration and test. For the rationale, see page 137 in [Boehm, 1981].

This model is easy to use. For example, suppose that you have 10,000 SLOC of code to adapt, and that DM = 10%, CM = 30%, and IM = 50%. Using these values gives AAF = 0.4*0.1 + 0.3*0.3 + 0.3*0.5 = 0.28, and so ESIZE = 2,800 SLOC.

The challenge for estimators is determining reasonable values for DM, CM, and IM. This is difficult because there is seldom time to "look inside" the code to determine the scope of modifications required. (If you must buy the component, you might not even have the component yet.) Table 9-19 provides some guidance. The values increase going down the rows of the table, and so the equivalent size increases, as does the effort required to design, modify, and test the reused code relative to the effort to build new code.[16] If the changes are major, the values of the parameters may even exceed 100% percent. (In some cases, it is more expensive to modify code than to develop new code from scratch. See below.)

---

[14] The COCOMO II sizing model, described in [Boehm, 2000], defines AAF in "percent," and so divides the values in its AAF equation by 100. In this book, I differ from the COCOMO II convention for handling values expressed in percent. A value of 53% literally means 53 *per hundred* (i.e., 0.53). This means that the various factors of "100" do not appear in my version of the COCOMO II sizing equations shown in this chapter and in Notes N46, "The COCOMO II Sizing Model" and N47, "Macroestimation with COCOMO II."

[15] IM differs conceptually from DM and CM. DM and CM gauge the changes made to the code. IM is essentially a ratio of the two efforts (adapted and normal). This ratio is used to scale the size. The calculation assumes that size and effort will be *linearly* proportional.

[16] Although subjective, the adjectives *minor, small, moderate,* and *major* are ordinal scale ratings, and so the table at least enforces some structure and regularity on the values chosen for DM, CM, and IM. A little constraint is better than none at all.

Table 9-19 *Representative Values of Adaptation Parameters*

Type of Changes	DM	CM	IM
None	0	0	10–20
Minor interface changes only	10–20	10–20	20–40
Small number of interface and internal changes	20–30	20–40	40–80
Moderate number of interface and internal changes	30–50	40–60	80–90
Major changes (redesign and recode)	> 100	> 100	90–100

This simple model is approximate, but it provides a useful way to think about the problem. Although there are no hard rules, based on my experience I usually see

$$DM \leq CM \leq IM$$

The reason is that a large design modification implies a larger code modification. Similarly, a large code modification implies a larger amount of integration and testing. Thus, you should be suspicious of a set of values like this:

$DM = 60\%$

$CM = 30\%$

$IM = 10\%$

Safety critical software should always have a high value of IM. Many estimators always set IM = 100%. Boehm provides several good examples on pages 133-138 of [Boehm, 1981], one of which has DM > CM.

Barry Boehm and his co-workers extended the reuse model when developing COCOMO II, adding terms to AAF to account for the extra effort needed to understand the code, and to assess and assimilate it [Boehm, 2000, pp. 22–26]. See Note N46, "The COCOMO II Sizing Model." I use a simplified form of their model:

$$AAM = SU*UNFM + 0.4*DM + 0.3*CM + 0.3*IM$$

where

AAM   = Adaptation adjustment multiplier

SU   = Software understandability

UNFM   = Unfamiliarity with the code

The parameter SU ranges from 10% to 50% depending on the "understandability" of the code, defined using the criteria shown in Table 9-20.

Table 9-20 *Rating Scale for Software Understandability (SU)*

	Very Low	Low	Nominal	High	Very High
Structure	Very low cohesion, high coupling, spaghetti code.	Moderately-low cohesion, high coupling.	Reasonably well-structured; some weak areas.	High cohesion, low-coupling.	Strong modularity, information hiding in data/control structures.
Application Clarity	No match between program and application world-views.	Some correlation between program and application world-views.	Moderate correlation between program and application.	Good correlation between program and application.	Clear match between program and application world-views.
Self-Descriptiveness	Obscure code; documentation missing, obscure or obsolete.	Some code commentary and headers; some useful documentation.	Moderate level of code commentary, headers, and documentation.	Good code commentary and headers; useful documentation. Some weak areas.	Self-descriptive code; documentation up-to-date, well-organized, with design rationale.
SU Value (%)	50	40	30	20	10

*From Table 2.5, page 23 in [Boehm, 2000]

SU can never be less than 10%! (Reuse is never free.) In my simplified sizing model, SU includes the extra effort needed to determine if the reused module is appropriate for the application, which might be a few percent. (COCOMO II has a separate parameter for this.)[17]

The parameter UNFM ranges from 10% to 100%. Table 9-21 gives the criteria for assigning a value to UNFM. I believe that poorly structured code always requires some extra effort, and so I set the lower bound to 10%. (COCOMO II uses 0%.) The UNFM factor multiplies the SU factor, thus reducing the size (and the adaptation effort) if the programmer is familiar with the code. The value of UNFM will be high when the reused code is first transitioned into a development organization and it should decrease with each successive build as the programmers become increasingly familiar with it. The staff "learns" the code. (If there is staff turnover, however, you should increase the value of UNFM again to cover their learning curve!)[18]

Table 9-21 *Rating Scale for Programmer Unfamiliarity (UNFM)*

UNFM Increment (%)	Level of Unfamiliarity
10	Completely familiar
20	Mostly familiar
40	Somewhat familiar
60	Considerably familiar
80	Mostly unfamiliar
100	Completely unfamiliar

*From Table 2.7, page 24 in [Boehm, 2000].

---

[17] You could make the ratings less subjective by using tools to *measure* the code. Useful measures are the number of blank lines, the average comment density (comment lines divided by total physical lines), the distribution of module size, and the distribution of module complexity (e.g., Halstead's cyclomatic complexity). Chapter 25, "Determining Product Quality," gives an example.

[18] To make the UNFM rating less subjective, you could define it in terms of the months of experience the programmer has with the code.

The adaptation adjustment multiplier, AAM, only applies to the reused code that is adapted by human programmers, which is denoted by ASize ("adapted size"). The sizing model increases the total estimated size to account for the effort to handle requirements growth and volatility, applying the adjustment to both the new and adapted code. The model assumes that growth does not affect the adapted code. (Section 8.5.2 discusses the migration of reused code into new code.)

The simplified sizing model ignores converted code. The complete equations, in order of computation, are

$$AAF = 0.4*DM + 0.3*CM + 0.3*IM$$
$$AAM = AAF + SU*UNFM$$
$$ESize = ASize*AAM$$
$$DSize = NSize*(1 + G) + ASize$$
$$PSize = (NSize + ESize)*(1 + G)*(1 + V)$$

where the parameters are

Symbol	Description
AAF	Adaptation adjustment factor (0% to 100%)
AAM	Adaptation adjustment multiplier (0% to 100%)
ASize	Actual size of the existing code that is modified ("adapted")
CM	Percent code modified (0% to 100%)
DM	Percent design modified (0% to 100%)
DSize	Size of delivered code
ESize	Equivalent size of modified existing code (equivalent new lines)
G	Growth over duration of project (%)
IM	Percent of integration required for the adapted software (0% to 100%)
NSize	Size of newly developed code
PSize	Size of processed code (proportional to effort)
SU	Percentage of software understanding (10% to 50%)
UNFM	Programmer unfamiliarity with software (10% to 100%)
V	Volatility over duration of project (%)

The simplified software-sizing model has seven parameters, plus the size of the adapted code, ASize. You can measure ASize objectively. The seven "size drivers" (SU, UNFM, DM, CM, IM, G, and V) are all subjective estimates. By considering these seven parameters, the estimator gains a better understanding of the work needed to adapt the component. (There may also be some cancellation of errors in the estimates of the individual parameters.) The box "Example of Size Calculation" shows how to apply the simplified sizing model. You apply the sizing model to each separate component that will be incorporated into the final product. Figure 9-9 shows a spreadsheet that you can use.

Example of Size Calculation

Suppose that you have 10 KSLOC of code to adapt, and you have applied the model's criteria to obtain these values:

ASize	= 9 KSLOC
SU	= 25%
UNFM	= 80%
DM	= 20%
CM	= 30%
IM	= 50%
NSize	= 10 KSLOC
G	= 10%
V	= 3%

Use these values to compute the equivalent size:

$AAF = 0.4*0.20 + 0.3*0.30 + 0.3*0.50 = 0.32$

$AAM = AAF + SU*UNFM = 0.32 + 0.25*0.8 = 0.32 + 0.20 = 0.34$

$ESize = ASize*AAM = 9.0\ KSLOC*0.34 = 3.06\ KSLOC$

Now compute the delivered and processed sizes:

$DSize = NSize*(1 + G) = 10\ KSLOC*(1 + 0.1) = 11.0\ KSLOC$

$PSize = (NSize + ESize)*(1 + G)*(1 + V)$

$\qquad = (10.0\ KSLOC + 3.06\ KSLOC)(1 + 0.1)(1 + 0.03)$

$\qquad = (13.06\ KSLOC)*(1.133) = 14.8\ KSLOC$

	ASize	SU	UNFM	AA	DM	CM	IM	AAF	AAM	ESLOC	Justification
Project Name:							ESize =	2228			
Date Prepared:							ASize =	4000			
Prepared By:							AAM (avg) =	56%			
	ASize	SU	UNFM	AA	DM	CM	IM	AAF	AAM	ESLOC	Justification
Units:	SLOC	%	%	%	%	%	%	%		SLOC	
Component Name											
abc	1000	50%	20%	4%	10%	10%	10%	10%	16%	160	
def	500	10%	80%	2%	30%	30%	35%	32%	39%	193	
ghi	2500	20%	40%	8%	50%	60%	70%	59%	75%	1875	

Figure 9-9 *Sample spreadsheet for size estimation*

9.10.3 Unmodified Code

Many individuals naively assume that existing software can be reused without modifications (i.e., just copied and compiled with the rest of the code). This is a rare occurrence. Usually, developers must modify a software component to integrate it into a new environment. The types of modifications, listed by increasing cost and risk, are as follows:

- "As is" (plug compatible)
- Converted (translated)
- Configured (via parameters, setup tools, or editors)
- Tailor (minor modifications, bindings)
- Cut and paste (major modifications)
- Salvage the algorithms only

The value of AAM increases monotonically as you go down the list. When you review estimates, look for consistency between the AAM value and the type of modification assumed.

Very low values of AAM (or AAF) are unlikely for two reasons. First, the minimum value for SU*UNFM is 1% (= 0.1*0.2). Second, any reused code, even if unmodified, must be regression tested so the value of IM will never be zero. Assuming the minimum value of IM is 50%, this gives AAF = 15% (= 0.3*50), and the lower bound for AAM would be 16% "best case" values for the other parameters: DM = CM = 0.

If the code was designed from the start to be reusable ("multiple use"), the modifications will be easier and so require less effort. (The value of AAM will be smaller.) However, the original developers will expend more effort because they will add more features and/or documentation, and will probably test the code more thoroughly. Many authors place the extra cost at 30% to 40%. (The COCOMO II model does not increase the size of new code to account for this extra effort. Instead, it increases the effort using a reuse multiplier. This is equivalent to lowering the productivity.)

9.10.4 When Reuse Is *Not* Cheaper

A simple model investigates the relative size (effort) between reusing existing code and building totally new code [Stutzke, 1996a]. The model uses the original COCOMO II sizing model (i.e., AAM without the factor UNFM):

AAM = SU + AA + AAF

which omits the UNFM factor, and includes the parameter AA. Using this equation, plus other assumptions about nonlinear effects and additional effort to verify interfaces, gives the relative effort to adapt code as a function of the fraction of code modified, the relative cost of reuse:

RCR = SU + AA + f*(2 – f)

where f is the fraction of modified code, given by

f = AAF * ASize/(NSize + ASize)

and size, effort, and cost are assumed to be proportional.

Figure 9-10 shows a plot of this function. Breakeven occurs at a value of 1.0 on the vertical axis, where the cost of new code equals the cost of adapting the existing code. The upper curve corresponds to low-quality code that has SU = 50% and AA = 8%. The lower curve shows the best case for code that has high quality. This corresponds to SU = 10% and AA = 0%.

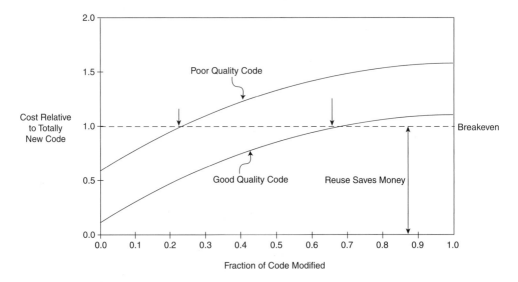

Figure 9-10 *Reusing code may* not *save money!*

This simple model yields two interesting results. First, if the code has extremely poor quality, the breakeven point occurs when approximately 24% of the code is modified. Even minor modifications of poor quality code quickly make reuse too costly. Second, even with the highest possible quality code, the breakeven point occurs at approximately 68%. This means that even if the code is "perfect," at some point it still becomes more cost-effective to start with a blank sheet of paper.[19]

Initial estimates often underestimate the value of AAF and overestimate the quality of the code. In addition, as work proceeds, the value of AAF usually increases and the perceived quality of the code decreases. This causes the point representing the original estimate to move up and to the right in the figure, pushing the project closer to the breakeven point. Assumptions about the amount of code that can be converted are also frequently overoptimistic. (Section 8.5.2 discusses the migration of code from "unmodified" to "modified" to "new" as the project proceeds.)

The lesson of Figure 9-10 is to be skeptical of designs that assume high levels of reuse. Otherwise, your project might end up like the one described in the box "A Tale of Overoptimistic Reuse." Of course, such skepticism only applies to cases where source code is being directly manipulated. For software development environments that support visual programming and provide tools to configure and integrate components, much higher levels of reuse are possible at reasonable costs.

A Tale of Overoptimistic Reuse

A project was to develop a scaled up version of a product for a new customer. The team assumed that 70% of the code could be reused from earlier versions of the product. As the project unfolded, however, it became clear that much of the old software could not be reused. At the end of the project, only 20% of the final delivered product consisted of reused code. (Of the original 70%, 50% had to be written as new, custom code.) This led to a large cost overrun.

---

[19] Reusing code is like renovating an old house. When you first purchase the house you do not know the state of the plumbing, the wiring, the floors, and so on. As you make repairs, you often encounter unpleasant surprises. First, the plumbing must be replaced. Then, the wiring needs to be replaced. Finally, you find termites in the floorboards and support beams, and so you must bulldoze the entire house and start over on the cleared ground. This analogy also applies to some software components.

> To estimate the impact, assume that the productivity for reused code is five times higher than the productivity for new code, P. (This is equivalent to assuming that AAM = 0.2.) If the total size of the system is S, the original effort was $(0.3 + 0.7/5)^* S/P$ or $0.44^*S/P$. The final effort, ignoring growth and volatility, was: $(0.8 + 0.2/5)^*S/P$ or $0.84^*S/P$, almost twice the original estimate. Growth and volatility will increase the final processed size even more.

9.10.5 Deciding to Reuse or Build Code

Is it cheaper to construct a product by modifying existing code and developing the remaining code from scratch, to build the entire product from scratch? You can use the simple reuse sizing model plus backfiring to evaluate the tradeoffs. Suppose that the product's estimated size is 100 KLSTMT of C code.[20] Suppose that your organization has Ada 95 code that performs some of the functions. Should your team develop all new C code, or reuse the Ada 95 code, and write the rest of the new code in Ada 95? Table 9-22 summarizes the calculations for three options. The 100 KLSTMT of C code represents 781 UFP3s (= 100,000/128). Assume that the amount of reused Ada 95 code is 25 KLSTMT and that the estimated value of AAM for the Ada 95 code is 0.6. The Ada 95 code represents 510 UFP3s (= 25,000/49), and the equivalent size (for estimating the effort) is 15 KLSTMT (= 0.6*25). The amount of new Ada 95 code needed to supply the remaining 271 UFP3 of functionality is 13.3 KLSTMT (= (781 − 510)*49). Reuse results in lower development costs because the engineers will write less code.

Consider the third option shown in the table. Use the Ada 95 library but write the new code in C. The additional new C code needed is 34.7 KLSTMT (= 271 UPF3*128 KLSTMT/UFP3). The total delivered size would then be 59.7 KLSTMT (= 25.0 + 34.7). Reusing some Ada 95 code still reduces the overall size. Using C increases the development effort, however (49.9 versus 28.3 KLSTMT of equivalent size). There is also more delivered code to maintain. Chapter 6, "Estimating Annual Maintenance Costs," explained that a programmer can only maintain a certain amount of code. Since there is more C code, more maintenance programmers will be needed. Using Ada 95 throughout gives lower development costs and lower maintenance staffing than using a mixture of Ada 95 libraries and new C code. (There are a lot of other cost factors to consider such as the availability of development tools and skilled programmers.)

---

[20] I use logical statements, LSTMT, for this example since the backfire values use logical statements.

Table 9-22 *All New C Code Versus New Plus Reused Ada 95 Code*

Option	Type of Code	Size for Effort (KLSTMT)	Delivered Size (KLSTMT)	Functionality Delivered (UFP3)
1	All New C	100.0	100.0	781
2	Modified Ada 95	15.0	25.0	510
	New Ada 95	13.3	13.3	271
	Totals:	28.3	38.3	781
3	Modified Ada 95	15.0	25.0	510
	New C	34.9	34.7	271
	Totals:	49.9	59.7	781

9.10.6 Deleted Code

Deleted code does not actually contribute to the delivered size of the final product, but deletion does consume effort. Someone must identify it and ensure that deleting causes no adverse effects. You can handle deleted code in one of two ways. Approach 1 computes the equivalent size of the code, and uses the productivity value for newly developed code. You can relate the activities to the COCOMO sizing model as follows. Developers must identify what code must be removed (SU, DM), actually remove the code (CM), retest the remaining code to ensure that the removal has not introduced errors (IM), and update the associated documentation (assumed to be included in CM). If the developers do not understand the code well, then UNFM is large. You need to select values, calculate AAM, and compute ESize for the deleted code.

Approach 2 assumes that the productivity to delete code is, say, 10 times the productivity to develop new code. This approach has the advantage that you can possibly measure the effort expended and so obtain historical data to determine the productivity. (Approach 1 involves three to five subjective parameters for each component and so it would be harder to collect objective calibration data.)

9.11 "Sizing" Commercial Off-the-Shelf Software Components

This section addresses the ways to estimate the "size" of COTS, and effort to select, configure, and integrate COTS components into the overall product. Developers do not receive any source code for commercial off-the-shelf (COTS) components. Thus, you cannot use code size to estimate the effort for COTS integration and testing. Because the developer has no access to the source code, you must choose some other size measure (proxy) that is proportional to effort. The box "COTS Sizing Parameters" identifies some size measures that one organization found useful.

COTS Sizing Parameters

Erik Stensrud describes size measures used to estimate the effort for COTS integration, specifically for the SAP product [Stensrud, 1998]. These include the following:

# of users (primarily drives the amount of training)

# of business units (a key driver of specification and configuration complexity)

# of countries per business unit (affects specification and configuration complexity)

# of plants (a driver of specification and configuration complexity)

# of sites per business unit (affects roll out effort)

# of SAP modules

# of interfaces (electronic documents, faxes, bar code readers, etc.)

# of conversions (importing operational data from legacy systems)

# of SAP enhancements (custom modules)

# of custom reports

# of third-party tools integrated

The sizing issue is deeper, however, because COTS integration involves multiple activities. The effort for each activity is driven by a different size measure. For example, the evaluation effort is proportional to the number of candidate components examined. Instead, you need to consider the activities of the process to identify "sizes" that affect the effort. (This is the same approach used for the software maintenance model described in Chapter 6.) The next section describes such a model.

9.12 The COCOTS Model

The COnstructive COTS integration cost model (COCOTS) estimates the effort ("cost") to integrate COTS software components [Boehm, 2000]. The COCOTS model identifies four specific activities:

1. *Assessment* examines a set of candidate COTS components, comparing their functionality and performance to the requirements of the overall product, and then selects a suitable component.

2. *Tailoring* configures the COTS product for use in a particular context. This involves setting options, initializing parameters, granting security privileges, and possibly specifying screen and report layouts. Tailoring excludes modifying or extending the product's functionality.

3. *Developing glue code* produces code to interface a COTS component to the rest of the system. Glue code transfers data between the COTS component and other parts of the system, and coordinates processing performed by the COTS component and other parts. Glue code also provides any needed functionality that is missing in the COTS component.

4. *Accommodating COTS changes* (volatility) includes replacing COTS components with updated versions, and reworking completed code in the rest of the system if needed.

The COCOTS model uses four submodels to estimate the effort for these activities. The *assessment submodel* assumes that there are two passes. "Initial filtering" rapidly eliminates products that are clearly unsuitable for the system's needs. "Final selection" evaluates the remaining products in detail and selects the best component based on some set of criteria. The effort to identify and select a component is proportional to the number of components analyzed. The effort is reduced if the engineers have substantial prior knowledge of one or more of the components. (Ideally, assessment occurs before the team commits to the project's cost and schedule, and so assessment costs are not part of the project estimate.) The *tailoring submodel* assumes that effort depends on the number of components to be tailored, and considers the type component the type and amount of tailoring activities that are done, and the degree of assistance (setup utilities) provided to help the integrator. The *glue code submodel* assumes that the estimator can identify the amount of glue code needed. This can be new code or, if the COTS component has been used previously, existing code that is modified. The effort is based on the estimated size, adjusted for volatility, and other factors. The *system volatility submodel* computes the effort to update versions of COTS components during development, including rework of "completed" code in the rest of the application due to updates of COTS components, the "usual" rework due to changes in the system's requirements. (The glue code submodel accounts for the rework of glue code.)

Table 9-23 shows the four size measures used in the COCOTS model, and the three volatility parameters that affect the effort for reworking code.

Table 9-23 *Size and Volatility Parameters for the COCOTS Model*

NIC	= number of initial candidates
NFC	= number of final candidates
NSC	= number of selected components
GSize	= size of the glue code (logical statements)
CREVOL	= rework of glue code due to requirements or COTS volatility (%)
SCREVOL	= rework of system code due to COTS changes and volatility (%)
REVL	= rework of system code independent of the COTS effects (%)

COCOTS has limitations for early estimation. Early in a project, the engineers can usually prepare a "short list" of candidate COTS components, and can probably indicate which ones merit detailed analysis. This provides the information needed by the Assessment submodel. The parameter values of the other three submodels depend strongly on the characteristics of the particular COTS product(s) selected. Since selection does not occur until partway through the product design phase, it is harder to obtain accurate early estimates of the input parameters for these three submodels. The COCOTS developers suggest using rules of thumb based on historical data from past projects [Boehm, 2000, p. 246]. The box "Sizing Glue Code" also provides additional information.

Sizing Glue Code

"Glue code" connects a COTS component to the rest of a software product. (Other terms for glue code are *bindings*, *wrappers*, and *glueware*.) Glue code performs three functions:

1. Transfer data between the COTS component and other parts of the system (custom code or other COTS components).

2. Coordinate and control data transfers and processing performed by the COTS component and the other parts.

3. Provide additional functionality that is missing in the COTS component.

The "additional functionality" compensates for deficiencies in the COTS component itself. If this deficiency is known beforehand, there is a potential problem of double counting: The team may define additional modules to provide the missing functionality, and include size estimates for these additional modules, or the team may include the functionality in the glue code. The functions (and associated size) cannot appear in both places.

Some estimators treat glue code as if it were new code, just adding its size to the total size. Other estimators believe that the productivity values for new code and glue code are different [Boehm, 2000, p. 250]. One reason is that the structure and design of glue code is often highly constrained by the design of the component itself, making it more difficult to develop.[21] This means that you may want to keep the size estimates for these two types of code separate, and use two different productivity values.

If a component was integrated previously, some glue code may already exist and can be reused. If so, treat it like other reused code by defining a size, GSize, and an adaptation adjustment multiplier, AAM_G.

If the developers discover deficiencies in the COTS component late in a project they have two choices: (1) discard the component and locate a more suitable component, or (2) create additional glue code to provide the necessary functionality. This "surprise" may cause an increase in the size of the custom code, the glue code, or both. For additional discussion, see Section 5.4.9 of [Boehm, 2000].

9.13 Recommended Reading

Bob Hughes describes several measures of software size in Chapter 6 of [Hughes, 2000]. For additional information on using use cases for sizing, see [Schneider, 2001], and [Jalote, 2002]. Kirsten Ribu finds that use case points work well for small to medium business applications, but are not suitable for real-time applications [Ribu, 2001]. Bente Anda et al. report estimation accuracy for three projects and lessons learned in [Anda, 2001]. Bente Anda compares effort estimates based on use case points with expert estimates [Anda, 2002]. Suresh Nageswaran reports using use case points to estimate testing effort [Nageswaran, 2001]. Thomas Fetcke, Alain Abran, and Tho-Hau Nguyen discuss the mapping of use cases into function points [Fetcke, 1998]. Said Labyad

---

[21] The COCOTS model defines a set of "glue code cost drivers" that adjust the productivity to account for various factors. See Table 5.31 in [Boehm, 2000, p. 252].

and colleagues describe an algorithm that estimates size in function points using elements from UML's use case diagram (actors, use cases, and the relations between use cases) [Labyad, 1999]. Also see [Stutzke, 1998] and [Stutzke, 1999]. Valéry Bévo and his colleagues describe an initial attempt to map UML descriptions to full function points [Bévo, 1999]. John Smith describes using use cases to estimate size in SLOC, and so development effort [Smith, 1999].

William Roetzheim mentions several possible size measures for estimating effort for Internet development [Roetzheim, 2000]. These include use case points, Internet points, and class method points. His article also discusses differences between traditional and Internet development, and identifies several process models ("software life cycle templates").

Capers Jones provides an excellent summary of functional measurement, and explains various types of function points and their history in Chapter 2 of [Jones, 1997]. Chapter 2 described a warehouse inventory management system. Thomas Fetcke applies functional size measurement to a warehouse management application [Fetcke, 1999]. His study is noteworthy because he applies five different functional size measurement methods to the same problem. The methods are: IFPUG function point analysis, releases 4.0 and 4.1, Mark II function point analysis, and the full function point approach, versions 1.0 and 2.0. (See note N10, "Extensions to Function Points.") These methods share common abstractions of software functionality, but differ in the details of their definitions and procedures. Fetcke's case study shows the core abstractions common to the methods, and highlights the differences in their respective measurement processes.

David Garmus and David Herron describe how to apply function point counting to web-based applications, graphical user interface (GUI)-intensive applications, and object-oriented applications. For details, see Chapters 12, 13, and 14 of [Garmus, 2001]. Garmus and Herron's book contains an extensive bibliography [Garmus, 2001]. They also mention several websites. The software engineering archives for the USENET newsgroup, maintained at Queen's University (Kingston, Canada) has an extensive bibliography on function points: http://www.cs.queensu.ca/Software-Engineering/funcpoints.html. The Software Engineering Management Research Laboratory at the University of Quebec at Montreal provides information about functional size measurement: http://www.lrgl.uqam.ca/functionpoints.jsp.

International bodies continue to improve and extend the counting rules, and standardize functional size measures. See note N11, "Functional Size Standards." The International Function Point Users Group (IFPUG) publishes a manual for counting function points and also conducts certification exams. For details, consult the IFPUG website at http://www.ifpug.org.

The International Software Benchmarking Standards Group (ISBSG, pronounced "ice bag"), is a nonprofit organization based in Australia devoted to benchmarking. ISBSG maintains a repository of measurement data on software products and projects. All project data accepted into the repository must contain functional size measures, and is validated before acceptance. For each completed project there are 30 data values (5 elements times 3 complexity levels, plus 14 GSCs, plus the final size in function points). The data is available on disk directly from http://www.isbsg.org.au. Release 6 contains data from almost 800 projects. (The cost is several hundred dollars.) The recently concluded projects on the disk use newer development environments (C, C++, Java, Visual Basic, Oracle, etc.).

Vinh Ho and Alain Abran describe automated counting of function points and provide a literature review [Ho, 1999]. Note N12, "Using Function Points to Manage Scope Creep," describes an interesting use of functional size measurement.

The work of Shyam Chidamber and Chris Kemerer is the basis for many proposed object-oriented size measures [Chidamber, 1994]. Clark Archer and Michael Stinson define a taxonomy for object-oriented software measures, and provide an annotated bibliography [Archer, 1995]. Bob Hughes describes how to measure object-oriented software in Chapter 5 of [Hughes, 2000].

Bob Park describes an operational definition for a "line of code" [Park, 1992]. IEEE Standard 1045, "Software Productivity Metrics," defines various size measures for gauging productivity, including how to handle reused code [IEEE Std 1045, 1992]. Barry Boehm et al describe the COCOMO II sizing model in Chapter 2 of [Boehm, 2000]. Norman Fenton and Shari Pfleeger discuss software sizing in Chapter 7 of [Fenton, 1997]. In Section 7.3, they discuss sizing reused code for estimating development effort. In Section 11.2, they discuss the effect of reusing code on productivity. (The actual productivity is based on the new lines developed while the apparent productivity is based on the total lines delivered.)

Randall Jensen describes a model of effective size that is similar to the Adaptation Adjustment Factor used in COCOMO [Jensen, 1997]. He extends the basic equation by providing ways to estimate values DM, CM, and IM (which he calls F_{des}, F_{imp}, and F_{test}, respectively). He discusses ways to estimate values of the three factors and states that there is a lower bound to all three parameters. (Some of his model parameters echo the SU and AA parameters in the COCOMO II sizing model.) In effect, his model states that the equivalent size can never be less than the number of lines of existing code that are modified, and may be significantly larger. He observes that reusable components with clean interfaces and functionality are black boxes, and contribute nothing to the effective size. Looking inside the black box, however, increases the effective size. The amount of the increase depends on the characteristics of the internal code and its supporting documentation.

Section 5.4 of [Boehm, 2000] describes the COCOTS model, which is still under development. For the latest information on the COCOTS model, visit the USC website: http://sunset.usc.edu/COCOMO/research/COCOTS/index.html. Note N13, "COCOMO's REVL Parameter and Incremental Development," explains how to handle successive increments that have different amounts of growth and volatility.

9.14 Summary

There is no single, universal measure of software size. Some definitions of software size use information available in the early phases of a project, while others use information available only in later design phases. Estimating later increases estimation accuracy. (This is the funnel curve in Figure 1-3.)

Use cases are emerging as a proxy for developing information systems (but not real-time systems). A standard, validated definition of use case points, analogous to the one for function points, is needed. No consensus exists yet on the proxies to estimate size and effort for web applications.

Function point counting is another example of proxy-based estimation. The proxies are inputs, outputs, queries, internal logical files, and external interface files. Function point sizing is independent of implementation language and can be used early in the development process. The same measure of size is used throughout the development process. Function point analysis distinguishes the "value" of the system from the "size" that drives the development effort.

Functional size measurement is widely accepted and several versions exist. These include function points, feature points, and full function points. Even though they must be counted manually, these seem to represent a reasonable compromise between early availability, acceptable accuracy, and the cost of estimation. The ISO/IEC 14143 standard, described in note N11, defines criteria to evaluate functional size measurement (FSM) methods. These criteria provide useful guidance for anyone who wants to define software size measures.

There is no standard size measure based on objects. Researchers have defined object-oriented size measures based on proxies such as classes, methods, and depth of inheritance. One issue is whether or not to count objects from the solution domain. For scaling schemes, an important question is: do different analysis methods identify more application objects than others? If so, the value of the expansion factor must depend on the method used. Another issue is how to account for reused objects in the size measure.

Source lines of code (SLOC) are easily measured, but must be carefully defined. There are no clear advantages to counting logical lines versus physical lines. Choose a definition that is appropriate for your needs, and then use this definition consistently when measuring your software. Use an automated counting tool to ensure consistency and accuracy, and reduce measurement costs. (Free tools for several languages are available at http://sunset.usc.edu/.) After your organization has accumulated a reasonable amount of consistent data, you can use it to help estimate the size of future systems. You may want to collect software size in more than one unit of measure to allow comparative analysis.

Reusing code is not free. The "equivalent size" for reused code depends on several subjective factors. Tools such as GUI builders and visual programming tools may make measures such as function points and SLOC obsolete. COTS integration involves several activities, each with a characteristic size measure.

Chapters 12, "Top-Down Estimating and Allocation," and 13, "Parametric Models," explain how to use the estimated software size to estimate the effort for specific project tasks.

Chapter 10

Production Processes (Project Life Cycles)

A project is a collection of resources assembled to achieve a specific objective within specified cost and time constraints. To help plan and manage a project, a project life cycle partitions and organizes project activities into a sequence of phases. The activities use resources, including labor, materials, equipment, tools, and facilities. There are many project life cycle models, each having different implications for estimation. This chapter describes agile life cycles suited for small projects, and plan-driven life cycles suited for large projects with well-defined requirements. The chapter also explains how to extend the basic software life cycles to handle system engineering, hardware development and production, and operations and support. You will use this knowledge to define a list of tasks or a work breakdown structure that you will use to estimate and schedule resources for projects.

10.1 Elements of a Project Life Cycle Model

A *project life cycle model* (or simply a *project life cycle*) is a high-level description of activities to "transform" requirements into a working product and to provide associated services. The description of a life cycle identifies phases, milestones, work products, activities, and the time phasing of the activities. The early phases gather and analyze information about user needs, product requirements, and alternative designs. Later phases design, build, and test the product. These engineering activities usually overlap to some degree, and the relative amount of effort expended on each activity varies during the project life cycle. Support activities, such as management, occur throughout a project.

Figure 10-1 shows a hypothetical project life cycle consisting of a single iteration containing the following typical activities:

- Managing (planning, tracking, and controlling)
- Analyzing (identifying and understanding the requirements)
- Designing (defining the product)
- Coding (constructing the product's components)
- Testing (integrating, verifying, validating)

There are many possible ways of arranging these activities. Some life cycles are iterative, performing certain activities multiple times. The vertical axis shows the fraction of effort expended on the various activities. Time increases toward the right.

To facilitate planning and tracking, the production process is usually viewed as a series of distinct phases. The phases appear across the top of Figure 10-1. Phases may include multiple activities. In addition, activities are usually not confined to a single phase. For example, requirements analysis may extend over multiple phases. An initial "Requirements Definition" phase might write a product specification, and later phases might update this specification based on new information. Thus, the project life cycle must describe what portions of each activity are performed in each phase.

Each phase ends with a milestone, which constitutes a "control gate" to review and approve work products and progress. (The approved work products establish the "baseline" used by later activities. Note the implied assumption of a sequence of transformations.) The triangles at the bottom of the figure indicate the milestones. The abbreviations for the milestones are as follows:

SOP: Start of project (project authorized and receives resources)

SRR: Software requirements review (product requirements baselined)

PDR: Product design review (product architecture and test strategy completed)

UTC: Unit test complete (all code completely written)

IOC: Initial operational capability (product delivered)

Note N14, "The COCOMO Waterfall Model and Work Breakdown Structure," provides a sample life cycle description and illustrates the detail needed for a precise definition.

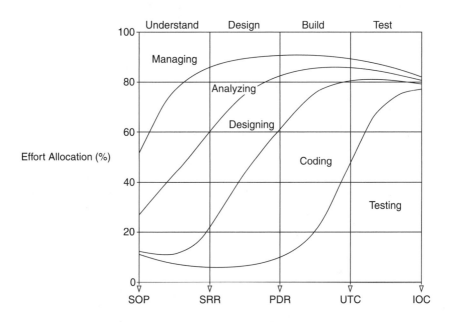

Figure 10-1 *Effort allocation for software development (single iteration)*

10.2 The Spectrum of Software Life Cycles

Various software development life cycles use the basic activities just described to design, build, and test products, but choose particular activities and iteration sequences based on customer needs, cost or schedule constraints, business objectives, anticipated volatility, and risks. You can loosely categorize project life cycles based on how the stakeholders define the product's requirements:

- *Agile*. The customer and developer negotiate requirements throughout the project based on user needs, business value, and implementation cost.
- *Flexible*. The customer defines basic requirements for the next release, and then negotiates the details with the developer based on available resources.

- *Disciplined.* The customer specifies firm, detailed requirements, often tied to constraints arising from physical devices.

There is no sharp distinction between these three categories. You can see the implications for planning, however. Agile life cycles plan in a series of iterations throughout the project. Flexible life cycles plan in terms of a major release but adjust the content of the release to fit the available money and time. Disciplined life cycles prepare detailed plans at the start of the project, and may allow minor revisions later.

Table 10-1 lists several project life cycle models ("life cycles"), ordered from light to heavy. Light methods use little documentation and use informal reviews. Heavy methods require detailed documentation and use formal reviews. This section discusses each in turn, emphasizing the estimating implications.

10.2.1 Agile Project Life Cycles

The old notions that specifications will be correct, consistent, concise, and stable are passé. Agile life cycles produce a working product quickly, before anything changes (requirements, technology, tools, or the external environment). Each "build" only takes 2 to 10 weeks, depending on the particular method. Users prioritize requirements based on business value, and so implement only the most valuables ones ("design to cost" or "design to schedule"). Agile developers design the test cases before they design the code. This quickly reveals if requirements are poorly stated, inconsistent, or untestable. This clarifies the requirements early in the development process before expending large amounts of effort. (The user agrees to work alongside the developers to provide rapid feedback on requirements.) Agile methods produce little formal documentation. Instead they capture user requirements in working code by using development tools to select, configure, and integrate pre-existing components.[1] Capturing requirements in executable code provides three benefits. First, the developers and the users can directly perceive during execution if the specified requirements, embodied in the complex object they have constructed, are complete and consistent. Second, users, viewing the execution of the working code (model), can immediately perceive the implications of their requirements. Third, at any point in the development process, the customer has a working version of the product (although with possibly limited capabilities). Planning is done, iteratively. See the box "Agile Planning and Estimation." Agile life cycle models are descended from Barry Boehm's spiral model, described in the box "The Spiral Model."

---

[1] Such tools make agile development possible. Modern tools greatly increase developer productivity and so decrease development time. Today, teams of a few people can produce the same functionality in a few months that 30 years ago required hundreds of people working for several years.

Table 10-1 *Project Life Cycles*

Life Cycle Model	Characteristics	Well Suited For	Examples	Comments
Agile (value-driven)	A craft performed by a small team of experts. Evolves the product rapidly through a series of releases. The team decides the best way to handle current tasks ("self-organizing"). Tasks "emerge" during the project.	Software only. Operates on COTS platforms. Includes in-house products and commercial products.	Adaptive Software Development, Crystal, Feature-Driven Deployment, SCRUM, eXtreme Programming (XP), Lean Development, Dynamic Systems Development Method	The eXtreme Programming (XP) method is fairly rigorous. For example, it requires that test cases be defined before or during coding, and that programmers work in pairs.
Flexible (goal-driven)	Defines phases of conception, elaboration, construction, and transition. Defines a set of required work products. All work products are produced simultaneously, and accumulate detail during successive phases.	Software only. Operates on COTS platforms. Primarily, commercial software applications for sale, supported by the developer.	Rational unified process (RUP), Model-Based (system) Architecting and Software Engineering (MBASE), Microsoft Solutions Framework (MSF)	RUP has been used successfully to develop software-intensive systems [Royce, 1998]. MSF is very similar to RUP, naming its phases envisioning, planning, developing, and stabilizing.
Waterfall	Systematic transformation of requirements to design a finished product (software or hardware). No overlap of phases, and no iteration of phases. Complete documentation of each phase to verify traceability and correctness. The work products of a phase are baselined to provide a stable basis for the next phase.	Hardware and software, especially complex systems developed by large teams; often multiple organizations working together.		The original model for software development. Mainly of historical interest.
Disciplined (plan-driven)	Use a defined process that is planned in advance and then executed. Iterates some process stages to accommodate changes and to deliver products incrementally. Complete documentation of each phase to verify traceability and correctness. As the project proceeds, work products from earlier phases or iterations may be revised and expanded, plus new work products may be produced. The work products of a phase are rebaselined to provide a stable basis for the next phase.	Hardware and software, especially complex systems developed by large teams; often multiple organizations working together.	Staged, Incremental, Evolutionary	Handle varying degrees of change in requirements and technology over the course of a project.
Spiral	Develops products using a set of iterations, choosing the activities for an iteration based on perceived risks. Prepares a plan for each iteration.	Generating the other models.	Basis for RUP/MBASE	

Agile Planning and Estimation

Users or other stakeholders create "stories" describing business activities that the system must support. The stories identify capabilities that the system must provide. The end user also assigns a business value to each capability. The developers then identify the functions and data structures needed to implement each capability. This allows the customer to prioritize requirements based on business value and development cost (or on return on investment).

In eXtreme Programming the project team performs planning at multiple times and at different levels of detail:

Timescale	Activities Performed
• Monthly	Release planning, identify iterations (high-level build content), release to users
• Weekly	Iteration planning (detailed build content), daily tasks, release to customer representative
• Daily	Standup team meeting, pair programming, release to development team (shared libraries, nightly build)
• Hourly	Design, code, test, refactor, regression test

The SCRUM method is probably the next most popular agile method after eXtreme Programming. SCRUM uses a form of time boxing, dividing development into 30-day periods called *sprints*. Each sprint begins with a short planning phase, during which a limited number of stakeholders plan the next release of the system. This provides a set of requirements that remains stable for 30 days, allowing the team to develop and test a new version of the software that meets the requirements. The cycle repeats for subsequent sprints. Requirements are gathered in a series of sprints, and incorporate increased knowledge of the end user (who observes the working model of the system) and the developers (who better understand the necessary data structures and functions needed to implement the business functions).

The Spiral Model

The Spiral Model uses an iterative approach to develop increasingly detailed descriptions of the product [Boehm, 1988]. At the end of each cycle, all stakeholders review the results and choose the engineering activities for the next cycle based on the results, stakeholder perceptions, the availability of new technology, financial considerations, and perceived risks. Then they approve the plan for the next cycle and commit resources to carry out the plan. No operational product is produced until some initial cycles are completed.

You can view each cycle as a mini-project that successively reduces the remaining risks. After the developers have resolved all of the risks, they can finish the remainder of the project using one of the other life cycle models, such as the Waterfall Model. The project team can choose any project life cycle model for a particular cycle. The Spiral Model provides a way to choose the best sequence of project life cycle models for a particular project [Boehm, 1989, page 34, LH bottom].

The Win-Win Spiral Model (WWSM) specifies how to identify the objectives, constraints, and alternatives at the start of each iteration [Boehm, 1994]. The Win-Win Spiral Model explicitly emphasizes continuous collaboration among the various stakeholders [Boehm, 1998]. The Win-Win Spiral Model adds activities to the original Spiral Model to identify and involve the stakeholders for the next iteration. Barry Boehm and Wilfred Hansen describe six "essential elements" needed to apply the Win-Win Spiral Model successfully [Boehm, 2001a]. For more details see [Boehm, 2000b], [Boehm, 2001b], and [Boehm, 2002]. (The MBASE/RUP model, described later, is based on the Win-Win Spiral Model.)

The Spiral Model has no fixed number of phases so there is no way to estimate the project's total cost and schedule in advance. The stakeholders plan and estimate at the start of each cycle. Boehm et al. explain how to use the Spiral Model to support three types of estimation constraints [Boehm, 2002]:

CAIV   Cost as independent variable

SAIV   Schedule as independent variable

SCQAIV   Schedule-cost-quality as independent
            variable

10.2.2 Flexible Project Life Cycles

Three project life cycle models are based on the Spiral Model, but limit the number of iterations. They structure the iterations to provide milestones to give a basis for planning and tracking. The phases are loosely mapped to successive cycles of a Spiral Model.

The *MBASE/RUP* Model is a fusion of two very similar models. The *Rational Unified Process* (RUP) Model integrates early work done by Ivar Jacobson, Grady Booch, and James Rumbaugh [Jacobson, 1999]. Barry Boehm and his colleagues at the University of Southern California (USC) developed the *Model-Based (System) Architecting and Software Engineering* (MBASE) Model [Boehm, 1999a] and [Boehm, 1999b]. MBASE extends the Win-Win Spiral Model [Boehm, 1994]. USC and Rational Software collaborated to ensure the compatibility of the two process models [Boehm, 2000a, page 302]. RUP adopted MBASE's process anchors [Boehm, 1996]. MBASE adopted RUP's phase names.

The MBASE/RUP Model focuses on developing a software product. Development occurs in four sequential phases, each ending with a well-defined milestone. (Various types of iteration can occur within each phase.) Table 10-2 shows the phases and milestones for the MBASE/RUP Model. (I have added the "solicitation" phase. During this phase, a customer sends out a request for proposal or request for tender.) The inception phase achieves concurrence among the various stakeholders on the project objectives, identifies a feasible architecture, identifies risks, estimates the cost and schedule for the entire development project, and estimates the operating costs. (These estimates are used to prepare a business case.) The elaboration phase defines the final architecture, and mitigates many significant risks. (There is a working implementation of the architecture at the end of this phase.) The construction phase defines, develops, and integrates the remaining components needed to provide the required features, and thoroughly tests the integrated product. The transition phase performs activities needed to deploy the product to the users. This phase begins when a "usable subset" of the system is available. Product development continues during this phase to provide alpha and beta releases. The transition phase concludes when all features identified in the product vision have been successfully implemented, tested, and documented. At this point, the team may repeat the cycle (inception through transition) to develop the next version of the product. Alternatively, the developers may deliver a technical data package (TDP) to a customer or to a third party who will be responsible for the operation, maintenance, and enhancement of the system.

Table 10-2 *MBASE/RUP Phases and Milestones*

Phase	Terminating Milestone	Abbrev.	Terminating Conditions
Solicitation	Inception readiness review	IRR	Statement of need documented. Stakeholders ready to proceed.
Inception	Life cycle objectives	LCO	Stakeholders agree on the concept of operations, requirements, and scope of the IOC version.
Elaboration	Life cycle architecture	LCA	Stakeholders agree on life cycle architecture.
Construction	Initial operational capability	IOC	Product passes FAT or is released for beta testing.
Transition	Product release review (similar to FOC)	PRR	System activated at key sites. Personnel fully qualified to operate the system. Maintenance agreement in place.

The MBASE/RUP Model expects the system's operational concept, requirements, architecture, prototypes, product life cycle plan and, later, the product itself, to co-evolve as the phases unfold. The key documents accumulate detail in successive phases, and are revised as needed to reflect improved understanding. The MBASE/RUP Model explicitly maintains the coupling between these representations of the product so that all evolve in harmony. For additional details, see [Boehm, 2000b].

Interestingly, it is not until the life cycle architecture (LCA) milestone that the developer has sufficient information to commit to a firm fixed price bid [Royce, 1998, Section 5.3, page 77]. Many projects building large, unprecedented software-intensive systems experience cost and schedule overruns. (Recall the Standish report mentioned in Chapter 1, "Introduction.") *A common cause of overruns is committing too soon.* Many contracts require the software developer to commit to a binding offer when the stakeholders' level of knowledge corresponds to the life cycle objectives (LCO) milestone for the system, which occurs well before the inception readiness review (IRR) milestone for the software portion of the system.

The *Microsoft Solution Framework* (MSF) Model also focuses on developing software products for sale and distribution to customers. Scott Wilson, Bruce Maples, and Tim Landgrave provide a detailed description of the current version in [Wilson, 1999].

The MSF Model combines milestone-based planning with the iterations of the Spiral Model. The spiral has four cycles (called "phases"). Table 10-3 shows the phases, milestones, and products. The four milestones are externally visible and are considered freeze points. The last column of the table shows the corresponding phase of the MBASE/RUP Model.

Table 10-3 *The Microsoft Solution Framework Process*

Phase	*Terminating Milestone*	*Work Products Completed*	*Corresponding MBASE/RUP Phase*
Envisioning	Vision approved	Business needs, product vision, project scope and goals, risks	Inception
Planning	Project plan approved	Architecture, functional specification, project plan (build content and schedule), updated risks	Elaboration
Developing	Scope complete	Working code, updated functional specification ("as built"), test cases, updated schedule and risks	Construction
Stabilizing	Release	Final code, user documents, training materials	Transition

The developing phase of the MSF Model has two noteworthy features with regard to estimation:

- Each release is implemented in three successive builds.
- The estimated schedule for each build includes buffer time.

The team implements each release of the product in three distinct steps or builds. The first build contains the most important features, ones essential for product success. The second build has useful, highly desirable features. The third build has features that are "nice to have" if time permits. If resources run out, the third build is not implemented.

Each build sequence consists of development and unit testing, integration testing, and "buffer time." Buffer time provides extra resources (effort and schedule) to handle unanticipated events [Cusumano, 1995, p. 200]. The amount of buffer time depends on the product type. Application products have 20% to 30% of the estimated schedule. Operating systems have 50%.

10.2.3 Plan-Driven Project Life Cycles

The plan-driven project life cycle models are all derived from the Waterfall Model. These models assume that all of the specified requirements must be implemented. (Tacitly, they assume that every requirement has equal value for the end user.) In addition, they assume that

- The product requirements are sufficiently defined and understood at the start to permit project planning.
- The product requirements are stable.
- A suitable product architecture can be identified early.
- The platform, COTS components, methods, and tools are stable.
- Each milestone "freezes" a product (specification, design, etc.).
- There is no overlap of activities.[2]

These assumptions allow all builds to be identified and planned at the start of the project. The builds and the project cost and schedule are thus "predictable." Planning only occurs once, at the start of the project. These life cycle models expend large amounts of effort early in the project to define the requirements completely and correctly, and to define a product architecture that meets those requirements. Then they document this information in detail, and so they are called "heavy methods." The project duration is typically a year or more, although some of the individual iterations (stages, increments) have durations of three to six calendar months. Due to the large effort spent preparing plans and design documents, the cost of changing requirements becomes increasingly expensive as the project proceeds.

The *Waterfall Model* is the original software development life cycle model. It is mainly of historical interest because it spawned other models (described next). The Waterfall Model executes the basic activities shown in Table 10-4. (The unshaded entries are the engineering activities. The shaded activities at the end are continuing support activities.) The Waterfall Model is also called the "Big Bang Model" because all of the parts are integrated at the same time. This is

---

[2] For most projects, the activities actually overlap to some degree. For example, Steve McConnell describes the Overlapped Waterfall Model, which he calls the Sashimi Model [McConnell, 1996]. Chapter 12 discusses how to allocate effort and duration when activities overlap, or extend over multiple phases.

risky since major problems do not surface until integration and test. Another disadvantage is that large systems take years to progress through the various phases, causing end users to wait for the system, and increasing the amount of change in requirements and technology that the project team must confront.[3]

Table 10-4 *Software Development*

Activity	Description
Requirements analysis	Elicits, validates, and records the functional and performance requirements of the product. Records any constraints on the product's design and implementation.
Product (architectural) design	Defines the product architecture and assigns application-specific names to the components, producing the "top-level design."
Detailed design	Identifies algorithms, data representations, and logic to control processing and manage data (storage, retrieval, input, and output), and assigns these to modules to be implemented. (Modules are packages of functions, data, or both.)
Code and unit test (combined)	Expresses the module design in a compilable language, reviews the code to remove defects, and verifies the module's functions, accuracy, behavior, and ability to handle abnormal input values.
Integration test (functional test)	Assembles the modules into an executable program, and executes the program to verify functions and interfaces. Integration Testing is performed by an independent tester.
Dry-run test	Debugs the acceptance test procedures that will be used to perform factory acceptance testing (FAT). DRT ends with the test readiness review (TRR) milestone.)
Acceptance test	Verifies that the total product meets all of the customer-specified requirements.[4] FAT is done at the developer's facilities and is witnessed by the customer. Following the successful completion of FAT, the team installs the product at the user site(s).

---

[3] Projects are becoming shorter so that they can finish before changes overwhelm the team. This suggests that the maximum duration of a feasible project roughly equals the lifetime of a generation of technology.

Activity	Description
Configuration management	Identifies and controls work products such as documentation, software, test data, and operational data. Identifies the configuration of the product at discrete points in time, and systematically controls changes to this configuration to maintain the integrity of the overall system, as well as traceability between versions throughout the product's entire life cycle.
Quality assurance	Independently checks to ensure that all products conform to their specifications, and to verify that the members of the project team correctly perform the defined, approved production process. Logs discrepancies and tracks each one to closure. Quality assurance is independent of the project manager, and has the authority to elevate unresolved discrepancies to senior management, ensuring that any unresolved problems are addressed.
Project management	Defines and plans the project, obtains necessary resources, establishes the development organization, directs the participants to execute the approved project plan, monitors progress, and resolves problems.

The Staged Development Model produces a series of "engineering builds" that are not released to the customer. The project team completes requirements analysis and product design. During the product design phase, the project team defines the content of each build that they will produce, choosing sets of features that represent significant project milestones in terms of required capabilities or resolution of major risks. (For example, an early engineering build might contain the architectural services needed by the applications modules, which will be developed in later builds.) These builds are approved at the product design review and provide a means to gauge subsequent progress. To produce each build, the project team cyclically executes a series of threads (detailed design, coding, unit testing, and integration testing). Note that if the engineering build is demonstrated to a customer (a "demo"), this usually elicits additional requirements, and the project transitions to an evolutionary development life cycle (described next).

---

[4] Factory acceptance testing is usually called formal qualification testing in U.S. Department of Defense publications. A better name is first article testing because this emphasizes that this test only validates the design. For software, the first article is the product so there is no distinction.

The *Incremental Delivery Model* is essentially identical to the Staged Development Model except that a series of releases are delivered to the customer during the project. Each increment provides some usable functionality and provides tangible evidence of progress. The customer must identify the sets of capabilities needed at specific times. (Steve McConnell refers to incremental delivery as staged delivery. Some authors refer to it as phased delivery.) The builds must be carefully defined. If the architecture is not sound or the build content is not well chosen, then previously delivered code may require expensive rework. (This is called "breakage.") If the deliveries give rise to new requirements, incremental delivery changes into evolutionary development.

TIP: Staged development differs from incremental delivery because delivery requires additional resources. Delivery may incur shipping and installation costs and, more importantly, the team will have to expend time and effort providing user support. (The phone will ring.) Include user support costs in your estimates if you deliver any product, even a prototype!

The *Evolutionary Development* Model produces a series of builds, like the life cycle models described earlier, but all of the requirements are not known in enough detail to be able to plan the entire series of builds in advance. (The team usually develops the most important or well-understood features of the system first.) During evolutionary development, the developers determine the requirements for subsequent builds based on the users' feedback at the end of each cycle (either from a demo or from usage of the latest installed version). The developers may also receive updated requirements from the customer, other engineers, or analysts. Iteration stops when the project team and the customer agree that the product is "good enough," or when some prespecified cost or time limits are reached. Evolutionary Development assumes that the product architecture can accommodate all of the needed changes. (That is, none of the changes break the architecture.) Evolutionary development is similar to agile development, except it assumes that changes occur more slowly, typically over years. In contrast, agile development assumes that changes occur continuously.

Estimators should distinguish *evolutionary demonstration* (demo) from *evolutionary delivery* since delivering a build requires additional resources, the same as incremental delivery. (Steve McConnell refers to evolutionary demo as evolutionary prototyping. Another name is the Rapid Prototyping Life Cycle Model.)

10.3 Choosing an Appropriate Project Life Cycle

At the start of a project, planners must select a project life cycle model whose characteristics fit the needs of the particular job. The SEI CMMI requires planners to choose an "appropriate life cycle model" (CMMI, Project Planning Process Area, Activity 5: "A software life cycle with predefined stages of manageable size is identified or defined." This is a Level 2 requirement in the CMMI's staged representation.)

Figure 10-2 summarizes the characteristics of five project life cycles described previously and their applicability to particular situations. (MBASE/RUP and MSF are essentially forms of evolutionary development.) Generally, increasing the project scope and the product complexity drives the choice toward the right side of this figure. The Waterfall Model is good for known, stable requirements. At the other extreme, evolutionary elaboration (using demonstrations or actual deliveries) is good if there are uncertain requirements or unproven technology. If funding is constrained, a product may be developed or evolved in increments. The builds (releases) are sized to match the funding cycle ("design to cost"). Schedule constraints are another reason for partitioning the product ("design to schedule"). Delivering any product to users will increase project costs because users require support.

The choice of project life cycle affects the estimated effort and time. For example, I distinguish staged development from incremental delivery because the latter implies some costs associated with user support. (The builds in staged development are not delivered to users.) Also note that different parts of a project may use different project life cycles.

The plan-driven project life cycles are appropriate for systems that have firm requirements based on physical constraints (e.g., aerodynamics, orbital mechanics, process control). These life cycles are also applicable for organizations that develop a series of similar products (a product line) that have stable requirements and are based on stable technologies. In this case, the products and production processes are well understood and predictable. Problems arise when the system has a great deal of human interaction that is inherently hard to standardize (e.g., man-in-the-loop, GUI). If you must use a plan-driven life cycle, document your interpretations of the requirements in your proposal, estimating assumptions, and contract terms and conditions. If the project involves poorly understood requirements, tools, or technology, then a better approach is to choose one of the project life cycles that evolve software thorough a series of releases. The ultimate form of evolutionary development is agile methods.

Increasing Project Complexity and Scope ⟶

NAME	Waterfall	Staged Development	Incremental Deliveries	Evolutionary Elaboration*	Agile Development**
CHARACTERISTICS	Known, Stable Requirements	Developer Specifies Internal Builds (to reduce risks, etc.)	End User Specifies Deliveries	Builder and End User Work Together Periodically	Builder and End User Work Together Continuously
APPLICABILITY	Adequate Funds and Time	Deferred Requirements	Sequenced Capabilities	Uncertain Requirements and/or Unproven Technology	Uncertain Requirements and/or Unproven Technology

INCREASING USER PARTICIPATION ⟶

* This is used for software maintenance.
** Joint application development (JAD).

Figure 10-2 *Comparison of project life cycles*

Agile life cycles are suited for products and systems where the rules and constraints are artificial (and so easily changed). Examples are business and financial systems that must implement rules and regulations driven by market needs, competitive pressures, or regulatory agencies. Agile methods require skilled developers and a knowledgeable customer who will work with the developers on a daily basis. Do not use agile development if the team size is more than 50 people, if the product performs safety-critical functions, or if the contract has a fixed scope.

The Microsoft Solutions Framework (MSF) life cycle is focused on delivering a working product by a specific date. Delivery is achieved on schedule, even if some features are not implemented.

10.4 Extending the Basic Development Life Cycle Models

Software development life cycles ignore some activities that are important for producing systems. At the start of a project, system engineers devise the operational concept and allocate requirements to hardware, software, and people. At a high level of abstraction, all products, hardware, software, software-intensive systems, and even courseware are defined, designed, constructed, and deployed in a similar manner. This section explicitly describes differences that are related to estimation. Once a product (or first article) has been built and accepted, copies must be made and delivered to customers. Developing "high-integrity" systems involves additional activities as well. This section discusses these activities to provide a basis for estimating resources. Pick the activities that make sense for your project. (Chapter 20, "Crafting a WBS," provides several work breakdown structures to address different types of projects.)

10.4.1 System Engineering

System engineering and software engineering have been combined in the integrated capability maturity model, CMMI-SE/SW. This section describes system engineering and provides a way to estimate the amount of labor that should be expended on system engineering.

System engineering addresses specifying, designing, constructing, testing, validating, installing, and maintaining systems. (Many authors use the phrase systems engineering.) System engineers are responsible for looking at the system as a whole to ensure that it meets the operational needs to the user in a cost-effective manner. The system engineer is responsible for the following:

- Operational concept
- System requirements (functions and overall performance)
- Decomposing the system into subsystems (system architecture)
- Overseeing design, construction, and testing of the subsystems
- The acceptance test (test and evaluation master plan)
- Installation and deployment
- Maintenance and logistics support
- Plan production and deployment (concurrent engineering)
- Develop user training (instructional system development)

How much system engineering effort is adequate? Figure 10-3 shows a plot is based on unpublished NASA data from Werner Gruhl.[5] This data from NASA seems to indicate two things:

- If a complicated project expends less than 5% of the total effort on system engineering, the cost overrun will exceed 60%.
- Expending more than 10% or so provides little additional benefit.

This chart illustrates how even very simple data helps to set a range for the "adequate resources" for system engineering. Here the range is 5% to 15% of the core effort (i.e., the total effort for nonrecurring engineering).

---

[5] The data in the figure is based on data from three memos by Gruhl (Nov 84, Mar 85, Jun 88) in the NASA Marshall Space Flight Center Redstar Library. No single memo has all of the projects shown in the figure, however. Two references that reproduce most of the data are [Hooks, 1994] and [NASA, 1995].

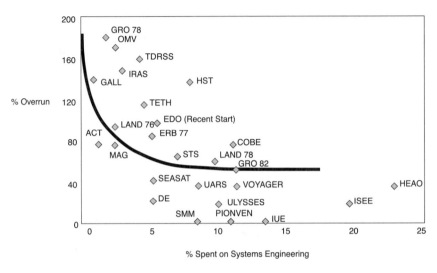

*Source: Werner M. Gruhl, Chief Cost & Economics Analysis Branch, NASA Headquarters

Figure 10-3 *How much system engineering is needed?*

Gruhl's data is widely dispersed, indicating that other factors play a role. Figure 10-4 shows some factors you might want to consider to adjust this amount up or down. (These factors are also potential sources of risk.) To gauge the impact of the item on system engineering effort, each item in the table has four attributes. Number is only relevant for items 1, 2, 3, 7, and 8. Complexity reflects some sort of rating (e.g., Very Low to Very High). For software-intensive systems, Complexity reflects the degree of coupling between internal parts, and with external entities in terms of data transfer and the timing of coordinated activities. The number of near-simultaneous events is also a consideration. If the system must operate near the limits of available technology (materials, processor speed, effective algorithms), this usually increases system complexity. For example, for software, you could use the COCOMO II complexity cost driver, CPLX. For stakeholders, complexity indicates their degree of cohesion and consensus. For deliverables, complexity refers to the formality of the process (amount of documentation and oversight). Understanding is "precedentedness," plus COCOMO's SU and UNFM parameters (part of the sizing model described in Chapter 9, "Estimating Software Size: The Details"). Basically, the first one (of anything) is harder to design and build. Stability refers to the amount of change in the preceding attributes, primarily the number. It is requirements volatility plus growth. The box "Cost Drivers for Systems" gives additional factors to consider.

Drivers	Number	Complexity	Understanding	Stability
1. System Functional Requirements				
2. System Performance and Service Requirements (TPMs)				
3. System External and Internal Interfaces				
4. System Architecture and Platforms Including Security Requirements				
5. Technology Availability and Maturity				
6. System Integration and Test				
7. Stakeholders				
8. Deliverables				
Legend: Number = Estimated/Actual Number Stability, Complexity and Understanding = Low, Medium, High Indicate whether project is cost reimbursable ☐ or fixed price ☐				

Figure 10-4 *System engineering cost drivers*

Cost Drivers for Systems

If you are planning to build a large system, the following system characteristics will increase development, integration, and test costs:

- "Space-based" system (redundancy, fault handling)

- Safety-critical system (usually manned, but may control explosives, high power, heavy machinery, etc.)

- Mission-critical system (key to the organization's survival)

- Highly secure system (encryption equipment, extra user authentication and activity logging, facility accreditation, cleared personnel)

- Operational system not available (need separate test system that mirrors the real system)

Interfaces, item 3 in Figure 10-4, are a big source of problems and risks. The system engineer begins to lose control wherever the system touches the "outside world," (i.e., other systems, human users, or both). No external entity is under control of the development team. In particular, interfaces change their behavior independently of the project team. As Eberhard Rechtin says, "The greatest dangers and risks are at the interfaces" (from a talk given at USC in 1994).[6]

10.4.2 Developing Hardware and Using COTS Components

To reduce costs and provide useful functionality sooner, developers may decide to buy some functionality instead of building it. How does this affect process models, and particularly estimation?

Figure 10-5 shows activities added to purchase commercial off-the-shelf (COTS) hardware and software, and to develop hardware. The detailed design activity applies to all components. The upper horizontal line buys COTS components. Configure means to set parameters or properties in a software product, or to adjust mechanical or electrical properties in a hardware product. (For example, switch a power supply from 110V AC to 240V AC.) You can buy and configure both COTS hardware and COTS software. The vertical line below detailed design applies to custom hardware components. Fabricate means to construct a hardware item or assembly from approved drawings. The developer or a subcontractor may fabricate an item. Assemble means to bolt hardware components together, connect cables, and update parts lists and inventory records. Every

---

[6] He also said that all of the big mistakes are made in the first two days. These are the "obvious" assumptions that turn out to be incorrect.

hardware item must be inspected for conformance to the drawings, and to ensure that it has no manufacturing defects such as bad solder joints or broken wires. This need to inspect every (identical) hardware item requires extra resources. Inspection may be done before assembly, after assembly, or both. Using COTS components actually requires some additional activities that are not shown in the figure. See the box "Capability-Driven Development."

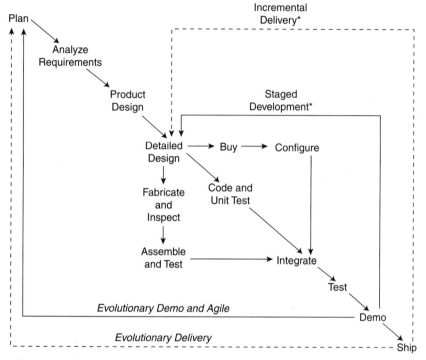

* The content of all builds are defined in the first pass

Figure 10-5 *The basic activities extended for hardware and COTS components*

Capability-Driven Development

In capability-driven development, the developers utilize existing commercial off-the-shelf (COTS) components to implement some set of useful features quickly and inexpensively.[7] Initially, the list of product requirements (or features) is flexible. After developers choose a particular suite of COTS products, however, the major requirements and the architecture become fixed.

Capability-driven development is actually driven by some high-level requirements. The team must define the product vision (application domain, user needs, general scope, and top-level capabilities required) before they can identify the relevant COTS components, evaluate the relative merits of candidate components, and choose the best component. Because COTS software components are sold as executable code, the developers can only configure the COTS components. (They may also write "glue code" to integrate the various components of the system.) The other activity that consumes resources is coping with the new releases that arrive from the vendors ("COTS volatility"). (Section 9.11 describes the life cycle model used by the Constructive COTS (COCOTS) estimation model.)

10.4.3 Building High-Integrity Systems

"High-integrity" systems and products must meet one or more requirements such as reliability, availability, safety, security, and information assurance. Examples of such systems are aircraft, military weapons, control systems for industrial plants, and e-commerce websites.

There are dozens of standards for processes used to build various types of high-integrity systems. See note N15, "Standards for Developing High-Integrity Systems." Such standards require additional activities that you must estimate. Figure 10-6 illustrates the process activities used to produce safety critical software, and is based on IEEE Standard 1228. The three shaded rows represent the "normal" life cycle activities described in Section 10.1. The unshaded rows in the figure represent additional activities explicitly mentioned in the standard. For example, engineers must analyze potential hazards that could cause the system to fail, identify conditions that could cause failures to occur, and the actions that can be taken by the system or by the human operators to restore the system to safe operation. As is typical of process standards for high-

---

[7] Other names for capability-driven development are COTS-based development, component-based development, and COTS integration.

integrity products, hazard (safety, threat) analysis focuses on the total system: hardware, software, user, and external influences (other systems, environment, and hostile threats). This analysis might be called a HAZard and OPerability (HAZOP) study or a Failure Modes, Effects, and Criticality Analysis (FMECA).

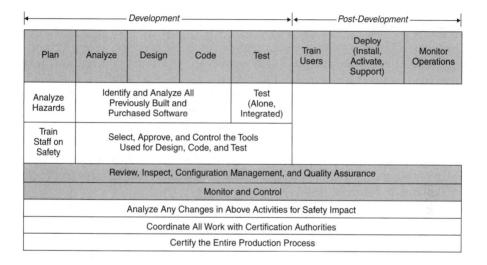

Figure 10-6 *Activities for safety-critical software development*

Engineers must also analyze previously built code and purchased software components to determine the compliance of the code with its design documentation, and also how the failure of the item could impact other parts of the system. The team must also test this software to ensure that it operates correctly, first in isolation, and then integrated with the rest of the system. The developers and testers must produce additional artifacts (e.g., traceability tables and test logs) that are used to certify the products and the process used. Most standards of this type require very detailed traceability between requirements, design, software modules, and tests.

All of the tools used to design, build, and test software must be approved for use. These include tools for requirements traceability, Computer-Aided Software Engineering (CASE) tools, compilers, linkers, and various test support tools. Upgrades to these tools must be carefully controlled as well.

Individuals responsible for the safety-related aspects of the process may have to be formally certified or licensed. One example is a Designated Engineering Representative (DER) who acts as a representative of the United States Federal Aviation Administration in reviewing and approving DO-178B processes and artifacts for avionics software. Some types of products must be tested and/or certified by an independent organization. (Security products are one example.)

The "normal" engineering activities shown in the shaded rows may also require more effort to perform. To explicitly address safety concerns may require more stringent analysis methods or additional analyses (e.g., a HAZOP study). Tighter configuration management of work products and tools is required. (Similar activities and reviews are done for maintenance, but are not shown in the figure.) Project team members require special training in the safety-related aspects of their particular work responsibilities.

The first step in estimating development resources for high-integrity products is to examine the relevant standard(s) to identify the additional artifacts and activities. Then, define tasks for each one. Next, estimate the resources that will be needed, especially people having special skills or certification, and unusual tools, equipment, and facilities. The costs for such resources will be higher than "normal" resources. Some organizations report that projects to develop high-integrity products cost 4 to 10 times more than projects that build "normal integrity" products. The schedule will also lengthen since there are more activities, reviews, and approvals required. Longer schedules will increase fixed costs for facilities and support staff.

10.4.4 Additional Testing and "Test Hooks"

Projects that build different types of software-intensive systems often perform the tests shown in Table 10-5. (Note N16, "Types of Testing," defines these.) These tests require resources and coordination with the customer or outside test facilities. Estimators should ask which tests are planned before preparing an estimate.

Table 10-5 *Types of Tests for Various Products*

Commercial Products
• Functional test
• Alpha test
• Beta test
• Performance test
• Regression tests
Large, Special-Purpose Systems
• Interoperability test
• "Dry run" test
• Formal qualification test

Factory acceptance test

- Reliability growth testing ("burn in")
- Stress test (maximum workload)
- Site acceptance test (installed system)
- Comparative tests (verify processing accuracy)
- Regression tests

Embedded Systems

- Hardware/software integration test
- Endurance test (burn-in)
- Stress test (maximum workload)
- First article test
- Field test
- Development test and evaluation
- Operational test and evaluation
- Comparative tests (verify processing accuracy)
- Regression tests

For large projects, engineers define the test strategy for a project concurrently with the product's architecture and top-level design. The team should identify the types of test cases early (by the time the product architecture is chosen, the product design review).[8] Test cases can be tied to operating modes, use cases, or scenarios. The number and complexity of test cases affect testing effort. (The type and source of test data should be determined as well since it may be hard to obtain or to generate.) The test strategy should also identify any test tools that will be needed. These include tools to prepare, inject, collect, and analyze test data, and extra features built in to the product to make it easier to test ("test hooks"). Test tools may also include stubs and drivers that simulate portions of the software product that are not yet available.

After the engineers decide how testing will be done, the estimator then determines the resources required. Figure 10-7 helps you identify additional software that may be needed. The collection of elements shown by white boxes is called the test harness, and provides the execution environment to test the software component(s) shown in the shaded boxes. The test harness provides a controlled environment, and makes it easy to rerun tests, reducing test effort and promoting regression testing (which increases product quality).

---

[8] For COTS-based systems and agile projects, the architecture is chosen when you pick the platform and development tool set. The test strategy emerges only after the team identifies operational scenarios, user stories, or use cases. For custom (unprecedented) systems, the team must invent the architecture. The RUP/MBASE and plan-driven life cycles do this.

Test data can be a significant cost for some systems. Real and simulated data have different associated costs. To record real data you must buy or build tools, set up equipment, collect the data, and possibly reformat it. You may also have travel costs and other expenses. (Collecting data from an operational site may be a long lead item. Plan accordingly.) Simulations can generate data for situations that rarely occur, that cannot be reproduced using the current equipment, or that would be too expensive or too dangerous to reproduce. (Core meltdown in a nuclear reactor is best simulated.) You must design, develop, test, and validate the simulation software. (Validation means that the model faithfully represents the relevant behavior of the simulated object to the degree of fidelity required. Stakeholders often disagree on what is "realistic" and "good enough.")

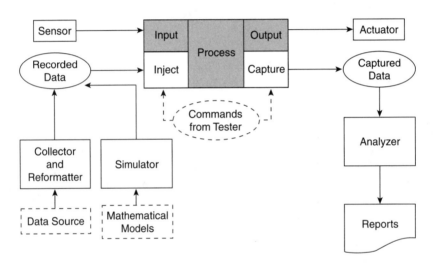

Figure 10-7 *Tools to support system testing*

Engineers must compare the additional costs of the analysis tools, simulators, and test harnesses with the reduction in the testing costs. Estimators can help to calculate the amount of code added, and the various costs to help choose the best test approach. (On one large system, we sold the data injection and capture capability to the customer as a way to test the system and to train new operators.)

10.4.5 Prototyping

Prototyping supports other activities in the project life cycle by providing information about design options, component compatibility, product performance, and risks. The box "Estimating Prototyping" provides guidance. Some developers hope to reduce development costs by reusing or "productizing" a prototype. Section 9.9.3 explained why this is usually a bad idea.

Estimating Prototyping

To estimate the effort to build and evaluate a particular prototype, you should first identify specific questions. The type of questions varies by project phase:

Project phase	Typical prototyping activities
Requirements analysis	Assess feasibility
Product design	Choose the best architecture, algorithm, or data structure
Detailed design	Tune algorithms for optimum performance

For each question, describe an "experiment" designed to answer the question. Then estimate the number of labor hours required to perform the experiment. Do not forget to include costs for equipment, supplies, travel, and any other direct costs. If a prototype is large and expensive, you can treat it as a small project.

10.5 Production and Delivery Activities

Development is nonrecurring engineering (NRE) to produce an approved first article. At the end of development, the customer formally accepts the first article. For commercial products, this is the "gold master" disk that will be copied. For large, custom systems, the customer approves the technical data package (TDP) that describes the first article. The technical data package is the "blueprint" to create copies of the product. (See the box "The Technical Data Package [TDP].") If the system is one of a kind, then the first article is the product and no copies are needed. (This also applies to any updated version of the system. The system is updated in place.) Otherwise, copies must be produced and delivered to users. During production, the developer (or another firm) produces copies of the product or system using the approved TDP.

The Technical Data Package (TDP)

The technical data package, also called the "reprocurement package," provides all the information needed to manufacture, test, install, and use copies of a product, as well as all information needed to repair and enhance the product. This information is usually a set of documents such as specifications, design documents, interface definitions, engineering drawings, software source code, component libraries, test procedures, user manuals, and training materials. The technical data package may also include descriptions of tooling and manufacturing processes. For software, tooling includes scripts to compile and link code. For hardware, tooling includes dies and assembly fixtures. Manufacturing processes include procedures to compile, link, and test software, and hardware fabrication processes such as a heat-treatment procedure and component assembly sequences.

Depending on customer desires and the type of product, the production and delivery activities will be performed in different ways. Estimators need to understand these differences because they affect costs. This section examines three cases:

- Unique product, developer maintained
- Unique product, owner maintained
- Commercial product, developer maintained

10.5.1 Unique Product, Developer Maintained

Figure 10-8 shows a unique product that is maintained by the original developers. The product is a single, complex system such as a large in-house application for a commercial firm that may be installed at multiple sites. The top left of the figure shows the original development, which concludes with a factory acceptance test performed in the development facility ("factory"). The technical data package (TDP) defining the initial product baseline is placed under configuration control. The developers update the TDP during maintenance and enhancement of the system, shown at the lower left in the figure. The developers install all versions of the system, and perform a site acceptance test at each site. In this example, the users only operate the system, and are assumed to require little user support, indicated by the dashed box at the right center of the figure. (If they do need support, you must estimate the resources needed.) The developer performs all of the activities in the unshaded part of the figure.

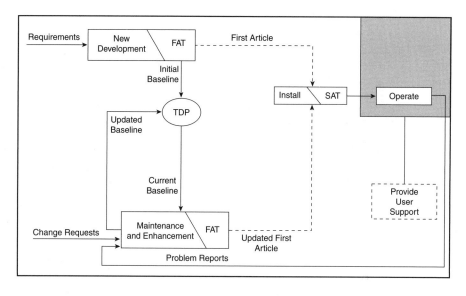

Figure 10-8 *Delivery of a unique, developer-maintained system*

10.5.2 Unique Product, Owner Maintained

Figure 10-9 shows a unique product that is maintained by the owner of the product, again assumed to be a single, complex system. An example is a large software-intensive system that is custom built and then delivered to a government organization. The top left of the figure shows the original development, which concludes with a Factory Acceptance Test. The technical data package (TDP) is transitioned (delivered) to the owner and is placed under configuration control. The TDP is updated by the owner's in-house programmers during maintenance and enhancement of the system, shown at the lower left in the figure. The developers install the original system, and perform a site acceptance test. (There may be multiple sites.) The owner's programmers install and test all subsequent versions of the system. The owner's users operate the system. The in-house users are assumed to require user support, indicated by the solid box at the right center of the figure. Figure 10-9 is similar to Figure 10-8, but the shaded area is quite different. The owner must now pay for more of the necessary activities. The developer performs only the activities in the upper part of the figure.

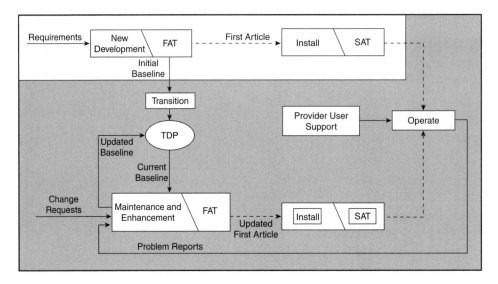

Figure 10-9 *Delivery of a unique, owner-maintained system*

10.5.3 Commercial Product, Developer Maintained

Figure 10-10 shows a commercial product that is developed, maintained, and sold by the developer. The product is a mass-market "shrink-wrapped" product such as a word processing application. The figure shows some new activities. During production, the developer (or another firm) produces copies of the product or system using the approved technical data package or the "gold master" disk. Making identical copies of a software product usually consumes a negligible amount of resources. You just duplicate the software, data (help files, configuration data), and documents by copying them onto magnetic or optical media. You will also usually make hardcopies of certain documents. Making and distributing thousands of copies of a product can be expensive, however. For example, commercial, mass-market "shrink-wrapped" products often have colorful, expensive packaging. Section 10.5.4 discusses estimating for hardware manufacture.

The commercial vendor must also establish user support, which is performed by a separate customer service (or technical support) department. The transition activity transfers the technology (hopefully all documented in the TDP) to the manufacturing and user support departments. When transition, production, and establish user support are completed, the vendor can distribute the product and provide user support. A sales department distributes the copies of the product. The vendor pays for all the activities shown in the unshaded part of the figure.

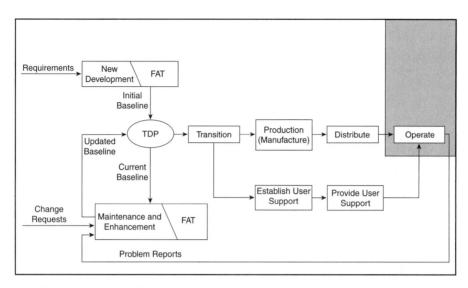

Figure 10-10 *Delivery of a commercial, developer-maintained product*

The preceding three figures illustrate how a picture of a process provides a framework for understanding, communicating, and estimating. These figures are another example of a key diagram for a project. They also raise some questions. For example, the diagrams show problem reports going directly from users to the maintainers. Shouldn't they go via the user support department? Also, who is allowed to submit change requests? (In commercial firms, it is usually the marketing department. For software-intensive systems, it is usually the buyer.)

Note N17, "A Closer Look at Delivery and Transition," provides additional information to help you estimate these activities.

10.5.4 Estimating Hardware Production and Maintenance

The simple diagrams described in the previous section also apply to hardware development and manufacture. There are some slight changes to the activity definitions, however.

Software	**Hardware**
Production	Manufacture
User support	Preventive maintenance
Maintenance and enhancement	Repair and upgrade

Hardware products require significant effort and resources to produce additional copies. Factory workers use the approved design of the first article and a proven production (manufacturing) process. Engineers may have to design and build special tooling and facilities to support high production rates or to lower production costs. For example, the metal panels of the first article may have been made by hand. For high-volume production, tool and die makers must design a set of dies to form a flat sheet of metal into the desired shape. (Trying to form a complex shape in one step causes the metal to tear. The set of dies forms the sheet in a series of gradual steps. This illustrates some of subtleties of the estimating costs for hardware production.) Many manufacturers address "producibility" and logistics support as an integral part of the original product design. (This is called concurrent engineering.) Defining manufacturing processes and the associated tooling is a unique feature of hardware production and requires additional resources.

Hardware production costs also depend on the costs of raw materials, the degree of automation, the skill needed by the workers (and so their labor rate), and the learning curves for production workers (increase of productivity over time). Large production runs make it possible to purchase materials in bulk at discounted prices. However, the costs of storing large numbers of units for a long time may outweigh the savings of the bulk purchases. For hardware, there may also be multiple levels of repair, each with associated costs. Field repair replaces a failed unit (line replaceable unit). Depot repair actually fixes the failed unit. Factory repair handles difficult problems. Major upgrades are usually performed at the factory as well. Because the original manufacturer does the work in the factory, this implies a combination of Figures 10-8 and 10-9.

10.6 Recommended Reading

Many authors provide overviews of software development life cycles. I recommend [McConnell, 1996] for classical models. Chapter 3 of [STSC, 1995] describes development activities and life cycles for large military systems. Alistair Cockburn provides the best overview of agile methods [Cockburn, 2002]. Ken Schwaber and Mike Beedle describe the SCRUM method in [Schwaber, 2002]. Mary and Tom Poppendieck describe "lean development" in [Poppendieck, 2003]. Barry Boehm and Richard Turner contrast agile and disciplined (plan-driven) methods in [Boehm, 2004].

Kent Beck and Martin Fowler describe how to plan eXtreme Programming (XP), one of the agile process models, in [Beck, 2001]. They cover planning, estimating, and tracking.

For a detailed comparison of the MBASE/RUP and Waterfall process models, see Appendix A in [Boehm, 2000a]. Marc Rettig and Gary Simons define an iterative planning approach that is similar to Boehm's Spiral Process Model [Rettig, 1993] called PADRE (Plan, Approve, Do, Review and revise, and Evaluate).[9] Their approach provides a way to schedule small projects using evolutionary process models (including agile methods).

Steve McConnell's Table 7-1 in [McConnell, 1996] lists possible criteria that you can use to select the project life cycle that is most appropriate for a particular project. Figure 4.3 in [Boehm, 1989] gives a decision table to help select the best project life cycle for a particular situation. He also provides examples.

Walker Royce discusses planning and managing of RUP/MBASE projects in [Royce, 1998]. Appendix D in his book describes the use of MBASE/RUP concepts to build a large, software-intensive system called the Command Center Processing and Display System Replacement (CCPDS-R).

Many plan-driven models can also be used to develop hardware or entire systems. For more on the costs of production and construction see [Stewart, 1995], especially Chapters 10 through 12.

10.7 Summary

Project life cycles provide a basis to decompose a project so that you can plan, estimate, track, and manage it. Any project life cycle model must define the following:

- Activities (and their products)
- Phase endpoints (milestones)
- Phase(s) during which the activity is performed

This chapter described several software development life cycles. Iteration plays a significant role in most software development life cycles. This chapter also described processes for testing, production, and distribution of hardware and software products. Many factors influence the choice of the project life cycle model. Estimators need to know the activities of the chosen project life cycle because each consumes resources, which must be included in the project estimates.

The next chapter shows how to construct a work breakdown structure (WBS) based on the product architecture and the project life cycle, and use it to estimate and schedule a project. Chapter 20 covers work breakdown structures for large projects.

---

[9] They note the similarity to the Plan-Do-Check-Act cycle used in total quality management.

Chapter 11

Bottom-Up Estimating and Scheduling

In the Bottom-Up Method, estimators start with a detailed list of project tasks and separately estimate the resources (effort, duration, materials, and consumables) needed to perform each task (or a group of related tasks). Then they add the results together to produce the total for the entire project. Planners arrange the tasks in a logical network to explicitly handle constraints on task sequencing, the available resources, the total cost, and total time. (The ability to handle such constraints distinguishes the Bottom-Up Method from the Linear Method described in Chapter 3, "A Basic Estimating Process: The Linear Method.")

This chapter shows how to define a work breakdown structure by partitioning project work in various ways. It also explains how to diagram task dependencies using a task network. This chapter also describes how a group of individuals can interactively develop such a network. Such task networks can also be used to track progress during a project. (See Chapter 16, "Collecting Data: Basics," Chapter 21, "Earned Value Measurement," and Chapter 22, "Collecting Data: Details.")

11.1 Summary of the Process

Figure 11-1 summarizes the Bottom-Up Method. It distinguishes planning, estimating, and scheduling, but these distinctions are only approximate. (For example, scheduling estimates task duration when assigning resources to tasks.) Table 11-1 shows the steps of the method. The following sections of this chapter address these steps in more detail. The information in Steps 1, 3, and 5 may come from the detailed definition of your project life cycle model (the production process). You can use any of the techniques described in Chapter 3 to estimate the resources (effort, cost) for individual tasks. Adding these estimates gives the totals for the project. You compute either the task durations or the required amount of resources given the effort required for the task. You can adjust size, productivity, number of staff, staff availability, or the work schedule (calendar) to "tune" the resource loaded network (RLN) to accommodate schedule, staffing, or cost constraints. The Bottom-Up Method has some potential disadvantages, described in the box "Disadvantages of the Bottom-Up Method."

Table 11-1 *Steps of the Bottom-Up Method*

---

1. Define project tasks (the WBS based on architecture and life cycle).

2. Estimate resources required for each task.

3. Identify milestones by type:

   a. Customer directed

   b. Process related

   c. Management directed

4. Assign dates to each milestone (based on master schedule).

5. Construct and verify the task network (task dependencies).

6. Assign resources to tasks.

7. Estimate task duration (see text).

8. Compute the critical path, near-critical paths, and evaluate reasonableness.

9. Compare calculated dates with required dates in the master schedule.

10. Adjust the task network to achieve required dates:

   a. Reduce the critical path if possible (repeat Steps 2, 6, 7, 8).

   b. If not feasible to achieve imposed milestones, renegotiate them with customer.

11. Evaluate risks (amount of float and number of near-critical paths).

12. Tune the network (optional):

   a. Level the resources to the extent possible using the available total float.

   b. Balance the task durations to the extent possible.

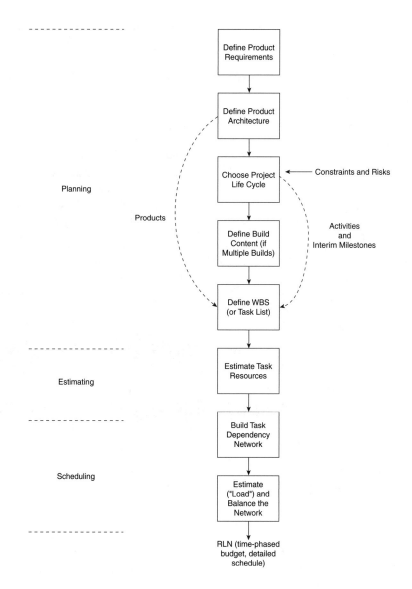

Figure 11-1: *The Bottom-Up Method*

Disadvantages of the Bottom-Up Method

The development team may expend a significant amount of effort to prepare a bottom-up estimate. Another potential danger is multiple counting of some activities, overlapping activities, and inflated estimates. Some activities can be included multiple times. For example, reviewing cost estimates for a very large proposal, we found that three different groups had included efforts to write the system test plan: the system engineers, the software engineers, and the logisticians. This problem arose because the work breakdown structure tasks assigned to the various groups were not clear and unambiguous. One way to detect such multiple counting is to conduct thorough reviews of course. The best way is to prepare precise work package descriptions.

Another potential problem with the Bottom-Up Method is inflated estimates. I once worked on a proposal with a large aerospace contractor who used a bottom-up estimating technique. Each of the functional organizations tended to overestimate the resources that they would require to perform the project. When the individual estimates were added up, the initial estimate for the total cost of the project was more than $10 million. Part of the problem was overlap in task responsibilities due to ambiguities in the WBS dictionary. Another cause was Parkinson's Law. After the WBS tasks were clarified, and the "padding" was removed, the final estimate came in at approximately one-half of the initial estimate.

11.2 The Work Breakdown Structure

For small projects, a list of tasks is adequate for planning, estimating, and tracking. Moderate to large projects have more tasks, so it is best to organize them to provide a basis for budgeting the project, authorizing work, allocating funds, and collecting data needed to track task status. Chapter 7, "Preparing to Estimate (Precursors to Estimation)," described several ways to partition the product. Chapter 10, "Production Processes (Project Life Cycles)," described project life cycles that partition the production process into phases and activities. You use the work breakdown structure to organize these pieces to aid estimating, scheduling, and tracking a project.

A *work breakdown structure* (WBS) is a hierarchical decomposition of project elements that is used to plan, manage, and analyze the work performed on a project. Elements can be physical products (hardware, software, data), services (installation, user training), or project activities (e.g., requirements definition and project management). The shaded box defines some important terms related to WBSs.

WBS Terminology

Work breakdown structure (WBS): A product-oriented or service-oriented hierarchical decomposition of project elements used to plan, manage, and analyze the work performed by a project.

WBS element: The individual elements of a WBS. These may be tangible items (hardware, software, or data) or may be engineering services or support activities.

Work package: A task at the lowest level of a WBS. It has clearly defined criteria for completion (deliverables, completion date), and estimated resources. See *cost element*. Often called a task because most low-level elements represent activities needed to buy and build product components.

Cost element: A type of cost identified for estimating, collecting, and reporting costs. Examples are effort (labor), materials, overhead, travel, and other direct costs (ODCs).

WBS dictionary: A detailed description of all the work packages in a WBS. These descriptions identify work that is included in the work package, work that is excluded, and relationships with other tasks.

11.2.1 Structure

You can organize a WBS as a product hierarchy, an activity hierarchy, or a hybrid. A product hierarchy partitions a large system or product into subsystems, assemblies, and components. This reflects the product architecture but does not show level of effort (LOE) tasks such as project management and testing. An activity hierarchy decomposes the project in terms of the production process (project life cycle). Essentially you expand "Build Product X" into lower-level activities, eventually reaching tasks small enough to be assigned to individuals or small teams. This does not give direct visibility of the status of product components. To overcome the limitations of each type, most WBSs are hybrid. The official U.S. government view is that WBS elements can *only* be products and "common support elements." For a commercial product, the top level of the WBS might correspond to phases (inception, elaboration, construction, and transition) with specific products identified as lower levels for each phase. (The "Recommended Reading" section cites several examples.)

The WBS elements are numbered to show their hierarchical relationship. (The numbering does *not* imply any particular time order. Scheduling defines the time sequencing and precedence of the tasks. See Section 11.4.) As an example, Table 11-2 shows a work breakdown structure for a small project that produces a product that contains hardware and software. The top level, Level 0, is usually not shown. The Level 1 tasks are numbered 1, 2, 3, and so on. Second-level tasks are numbered 1.1, 1.2, 1.3, 2.1, 2.2, and so on. A task with the identifier 2.3.1.6.3 is at the fifth level.

High-level work breakdown structure elements represent major deliverable items and services specified by the customer. To plan and estimate projects, however, engineers decompose a hardware subsystem into assemblies, and the assemblies into individual components. Lower-level WBS elements also identify specific activities (tasks) needed to build, fabricate, and inspect a component. Similarly, for software components, the architecture identifies major subsystems needed to meet the product requirements. Software engineers identify lower-level components (such as modules, or classes), and finally the tasks.

Table 11-2 *Schematic View of a WBS*

1. System
1.1 Hardware subsystem
1.1.1 Hardware assembly
1.1.1.1 Component
1.1.1.1.1 Design
1.1.1.1.2 Fabricate
1.1.1.1.3 Inspect
1.1.1.1.4 Assemble
1.2 Software subsystem
1.2.1 Software component
1.2.1.1 Software module
1.2.1.1.1 Design
1.2.1.1.2 Code
1.2.1.1.3 Peer review
1.2.1.1.4 Unit test
1.3 Integrate and test subsystems
1.4 User manuals
2. User Training
2.1 Develop course materials
2.2 Teach course

3. Services
    3.1 Convert operational data
    3.2 Install the system at user's site

4. Project Management
    4.1 Supervision
    4.2 Project control
    4.3 Network and tool support
    4.4 Configuration management
    4.5 Quality assurance

This work breakdown structure also includes tasks for other engineering services and management. Network and tools support is shown under management, but other organizations might consider it part of engineering and production. This sample work breakdown structure has no tasks for support activities performed by departments such as contract management, purchasing, finance and accounting, and human resources. Most organizations pay for these out of overhead and so they are not included.

You could include engineering tasks such as tool development, test data generation, and preparing technical documents and test procedures at a lower level, or could put them at the second level. You may subdivide the hardware and software tasks if there are multiple components or subsystems. In addition, if the team plans to produce multiple builds (e.g., using staged development or incremental delivery), you will probably want to subdivide these as well. (Section 20.3 gives examples.) Finally, if you consider certain components to be risky, you would assign a separate WBS element to them to facilitate tracking.

11.2.2 Work Packages and the WBS Dictionary

For larger projects especially, each task should have a written description that includes the following:

- Products to be produced (or services to be delivered)
- Schedules
- Resources required
- Dependencies on preceding tasks
- Required inputs
- References to relevant documents

These descriptions (also called *work packages*) provide the detail needed by estimators, schedulers, workers, and supervisors. Each description is typically less than one page in length. References to relevant documents such as the customer's statement of work, specifications, blueprints, or process descriptions (standards and procedures) provide detail and keep the description succinct.

For a small project, the task or work package description can be very brief, as shown in Table 11-3. You should provide more detail for a large project, or if the system is safety critical. (See Section 20.1.)

Table 11-3 *A Brief Work Package Description*

Task Identifier: 2.7.4.2
Task Name: Code and Unit Test User Logon Screen
Inputs:
Product specification, Section 5.3 (interfaces)
Sketches provided by the designer
Project design and coding guidelines
Outputs:
Module source code (C++)
The sections of the user manual corresponding to this module
Suggested test cases
Records from the peer review
Activities:
Position the widgets onscreen. Code the action routines.
Assumptions and Constraints:
Goal: Response time for each command should be less than 10 milliseconds.
Risks:
None
Resources:
Labor:
Software Engineer   40–60 phr
Peer review (mixed grades) 10–20 phr

Each work package requires resources, which include effort, materials, consumables, and duration. Effort is often subdivided by skill level or labor category. Consumables include operating expenses and travel. Duration is the number of work-days allowed to accomplish the work. For each work package, someone on the project team estimates the amount of each resource type needed. These estimates are the basis for the project's budget and schedule.

11.3 Creating Your WBS

This section describes a process to create a WBS, various criteria that you can use to partition a WBS, and when to stop partitioning.

11.3.1 A Seven-Step Process

Richard Fairley and Richard Thayer describe work breakdown structures in [Fairley, 1997]. Their article gives a concise overview of process, product, and hybrid WBSs with examples of each type. They define a seven-step process to develop a WBS:

1. Determine the purpose of the WBS.
2. Identify the top of the WBS (project or product name).
3. Partition the WBS into major components.
4. Partition each major component.
5. Terminate partitioning based on a criterion (see text).
6. Describe each lowest-level WBS element.
7. Document the results.

Your purpose might be to determine the cost of a system, or to plan and manage a project. The top WBS element is the name of a project or the product to be built. They recommend partitioning each element into 7 ± 2 subelements. After you have partitioned the work, you must describe the lowest-level tasks or "work packages." Section 11.2.2 explained how to do this. Your team will use these descriptions to prepare estimates and schedule tasks. You should update the work package descriptions to incorporate changes during the project. (These are baselined, so reviews and approvals are required.)

To be useful for project tracking, you must tie the tasks to your organization's accounting using "control accounts" or "charge numbers." Section 16.5 describes this at a conceptual level. Chapter 22 describes the details related to collecting data for large projects.

11.3.2 Possible Partitioning Criteria

Partitioning decomposes the top-level WBS elements to identify all of the lowest-level tasks, the work packages. (Partitioning is also called "planning" in many texts.) You can decompose a WBS to any level of detail that makes sense. The objective is to decompose the overall job into tasks to facilitate budgeting, planning, and tracking. Pick your WBS elements based on how you intend to manage the project. You have to live with your choice throughout the project, so take the time to get it right. (Chapter 22 addresses this in detail.)

The decomposition depends on many factors, including the following:

- Purchaser's statement of work (contract WBS)
- Reporting requirements
- Product architecture
- Customer-specified incremental deliveries
- Project life cycle
- Number and location of work sites
- Organization (multiple departments, firms, subcontractors, and suppliers)
- Resource constraints
- Business objectives (contract line item number [CLIN] structure, payments, and cash flow)
- Desired visibility of task status
- Risks associated with any of the above elements

The customer may specify the high-level breakout (called the contract work breakdown structure) tied to deliverables, and the developer further decomposes this WBS to lower levels to create the project WBS, which details the production activities.[1] The purchaser may also specify detailed reporting requirements. Obviously, you must partition to the level of detail needed to support the specified tracking and reporting requirements. See Sections 15.5 and 22.3 for advice.

The product architecture influences the work breakdown structure partitioning. One consideration might be purchased versus custom-built components. Purchasers may specify incremental deliveries. Engineers may also decide that staged development is advantageous (basic data structures and architectural services first, followed by higher-level applications). It is best to deliver a new capability as a complete and separate component. In some cases, however, you may have to add functionality to a previously delivered component and then redeliver the component in the next release. Revising code produced in earlier builds ("breakage") increases development costs.

Choose the partitioning of the product and the work so that a single organization, department, or subcontractor is responsible for a single package. This ensures clear accountability. Be careful to allocate the work reasonably. See the box "Schizophrenic Allocation."

---

[1] There are really two kinds of "decomposition." The first is "complete," meaning that the entire "content" of an element is decomposed and allocated to subordinate lower-level elements (the children). This occurs in a WBS. Only the lowest-level elements have resources. The second is "partial," meaning that some "content" remains at the parent. This happens in requirements allocation. Some requirements apply to the parent, and others apply to the children.

Schizophrenic Allocation

I once worked on a large project to convert and rehost a large amount of existing code. The senior managers of the various firms (the prime contractor and several subcontractors) met to assign portions of the code to each firm. The managers had only a list of filenames and source file sizes to work with. The files were main programs, subroutines, and compilation scripts. The sizes were in source lines of code. The managers just picked names off the list at random, continuing until a given firm had accumulated some desired percentage of the total lines. (Lines are lines, right?) These assignments were then documented in the legal contracts. In some cases, the main program was assigned to one contractor, and all of the subroutines it used were assigned to another subcontractor. The managers did not want to change the contract (!), and so *both* teams had to write unnecessary code (test drivers or stubs, respectively) to do functional testing. Correctly partitioning the work would have made all of this extra effort unnecessary.

For nonlabor items (e.g., purchasing several computers), you might partition the work packages by subsystem, components, subdivided if needed by vendor. If items will be purchased over time (e.g., for different increments), you might group items by the date required to manage cash flow.

You might want to choose work packages or product versions that are small enough to be produced with the resources available (staffing, funding, or duration).[2] A typical example is projects that are funded on a fiscal-year or calendar-year basis. The stakeholders choose the build content (features implemented) based on what the project team can implement within the annual funding cycle. This produces a working version each year, helping to justify continued funding for the following year.

You may subdivide the WBS to view the status of key components or subsystems (e.g., architectural services, key functions, or capabilities), or to track high-risk tasks (technically challenging, inexperienced development team, or first-time supplier). To keep work synchronized, WBS tasks should *not* span major milestones.

---

[2] These three are related, of course. Chapter 12, "Top-Down Estimating and Allocation," describes some of these relations.

11.3.3 When to Stop Partitioning ("Optimal Size")

You can stop decomposing a task when all of the following are true:

- A single person (or team) can take responsibility for the task.
- You can estimate the resources needed to perform the task.
- You can schedule the task.
- The task is small enough to be completed in a "reasonable" time.
- The risk associated with the task is acceptable.
- The level of detail supports tracking and reporting requirements.

Assigning responsibility means that a person or team has the authority to direct all resources needed to complete the specified work within an acceptable time. Note that there is no rule requiring you to decompose tasks so that a *single individual* has sole responsibility! The second item means that the element has a well-defined scope with clear deliverables, and you understand how these will be produced. The third criterion means that you know the duration of the task and its predecessor tasks (the activities that must be completed before the task can be started). The project life cycle model often indicates many of the tasks and their precedence relationships. For additional tasks or new situations, the chief engineer and the project manager need to provide guidance to the estimators.

The time to complete a task depends on the resources required (the "task size") and the resources assigned to perform the task. A "reasonable" amount of time for visibility is one calendar-month. For example, if the task is assigned to a programming pair, the task should represent approximately two person-months of effort. A person-month is approximately 160 person-hours, so the task size should be approximately 300 person-hours. As a general guideline, Fairley and Thayer state that sizes between 40 and 160 person-hours are good for assigning work to individuals. To define tasks for *teams* of two to three people, I like to use a value of 300 to 400 person-hours.[3] Smaller task sizes should be the exception, *not the rule*. What is a reasonable number of work packages for a project? At $100K/pyr, a $1M contract (all labor) has 10 pyr or about 20,000 phr. If the average task size is 200 phr, the WBS should have approximately 100 work packages.

A risky task might be a poorly understood activity, or may be assigned to a development team that is far away and whose capabilities are not well known.

---

[3] If a task lasts more than two weeks, you should have some way to track progress. See the discussion of "inchstones" in Chapter 17, "Tracking Status." Rettig and Simons also describe a similar concept in [Rettig, 1993]. Chapter 22 also discusses how the "resolution" of the WBS affects project tracking.

For example, do not define a single 12 calendar-month task to build and test a key subsystem or component. Instead, define a series of tasks, such as document the design, fabricate the component, and test the component. Each task should ideally produce a well-defined product so that there is an *objective basis* to determine when the task is completed. For example, the task produces a document that must pass a peer review. A document is done and approved, or it is not. This is not always possible, however, for level of effort (LOE) tasks. Examples are support tasks such as configuration management. (Even if a task is LOE, you can (and should) still describe it! Remember the example of "training the users" in Chapter 4, "Measurement and Estimation.")

One way to choose the task size is to ask, "How much can I afford to lose?" Five person-years of effort amount to $500K to $600K. If there is a 50% probability that the team will not complete the work, the expected loss is $250K to $300K. If other tasks depend on the timely completion of this particular task and they are delayed, the project will incur more losses. Breaking the task into 12 tasks, each lasting 1 calendar-month decreases the loss that can occur before you detect it to $21K to $25K.

The sixth reason to stop partitioning is that the level of detail supports purchaser-mandated tracking and reporting requirements. Chapter 20, "Crafting a WBS," discusses this for large U.S. government contracts.

11.3.4 Summary Tasks

It is not always possible to completely decompose the work breakdown structure at the start of a project, however, due to limited resources or lack of knowledge. Thus, descriptions of higher-level tasks may also be included as "placeholders" until the lower-level tasks can be identified. (This is also used when allocating and authorizing budgets. See the box "Rolling Wave Planning.")

Rolling Wave Planning

Generally, it is not worthwhile to plan future tasks in great detail because something will always change. (*Plan* here means to place the tasks in the network and connect them up.) Instead, you should identify many low-level tasks and estimate the resources for each in detail to get a good estimate, but then you aggregate the estimates into larger tasks for budgeting purposes when the project starts. You show each aggregate as a *single* task on the network (a "summary task") and in the project budget. As the time approaches to start these tasks, you use the latest information to update their estimated resources and durations. Then you enter the detailed tasks with their updated values in the network to obtain a more accurate plan. This is called *rolling wave planning*.

11.4 Scheduling

Scheduling links the project tasks into a meaningful picture (a task network) that is related to some set of specified milestones, and then assigns resources (personnel) to each task to achieve specified milestone dates. (This is true for both plan-driven and agile project life cycles.)

11.4.1 Basic Concepts

Table 11-4 shows key terms to describe scheduling. A *task* is an activity that occurs over time (e.g., work that must be accomplished to produce some part of the product). A *milestone* is an event that happens at a specific moment in time. Milestones link events that occur during the production process to the project schedule. *Relationships* are logical or temporal constraints between the start and/or finish of one task or milestone (a predecessor) and the start and/or finish of another task or milestone (a successor). (A milestone may have multiple predecessors and successors.) For example, a certain task cannot start until hardware arrives from a vendor. (The arrival is an external event.) A *task network diagram* depicts the relationships between the tasks and milestones in a graphical way to help humans visualize the dependencies between project elements. A *resource loaded network* (RLN) is a task network with resources assigned to each task. The most important resource is usually people. (Project schedulers often mean "people" when they say "resource.") You either assign available resources and calculate the task's duration, or you specify the desired duration and calculate the resources needed. (This is an iterative process. See below.)

Table 11-4 *Project Scheduling Terminology*

Term	Description
Tasks	Activities with their required resources (effort, duration); the lowest-level WBS elements.
Milestones	Events of particular significance (zero duration).
Relationships	Logical or temporal constraints between the start and finish dates of tasks or milestones.
Task network diagram	A graphic depiction of the logical and temporal relationships between tasks and milestones.
Resource loaded network	A task network diagram where resources are assigned to the tasks.
Critical path	The sequence of tasks in a task network that has the longest duration. This path determines the earliest possible project completion date.

Task network diagrams and resource loaded networks use the following symbols:

Activity   □
Milestone   ▽ or ⬭
Constraint   →
Critical path   ➔

Figure 11-2 shows an example of a simple task network for a software development project. The project has three contract milestones: Start, Product Design Review, and Contract Complete. The light lines with arrowheads indicate the constraints between the tasks; the arrowheads show the direction of the dependency. The task touched by the arrowhead cannot start until the preceding task is completed. The darkened lines with arrowheads indicate the *critical path*, which is the sequence of tasks in a task network that has the longest duration. This path determines the earliest possible project completion date. Any delays in a task that lies on the critical path *will* delay the project.[4] The start date for each task is shown above the box representing the task. The task duration (work-days) is shown below the box. (Automated scheduling tools allow users to select and position various values above and below the task boxes.)

A good task network should have one start milestone from which all tasks emanate and one finish milestone into which all tasks culminate. This task network assumes that the project starts with an approved software specification. The figure also shows one intermediate milestone, Product Design Review. This is an example of a "control gate." *Clusters of tasks converge at control gate milestones.* The purpose of a control gate milestone is to ensure that successor tasks do not start until all the products of the preceding tasks are reviewed and approved. You can place additional milestones at key points in the network to facilitate tracking progress. See the box "Reviewing Task Networks."

The diagram in the figure only shows finish-to-start relationships. Other relations are sometimes used. See the box "Types of Precedence Relations." Two tasks may also have a time delay imposed between them, which is called a lag or slack. For example, you might use a lag to account for shipping delays. A lag placed on a finish-to-start relationship forces a delay in the start of the successor. Negative lags are also possible.

---

4 This is true only if the path has no float, which is a "time reserve" provided by planners to reduce the risk of a schedule slip. When delays consume all of the float, however, the completion date will slip.

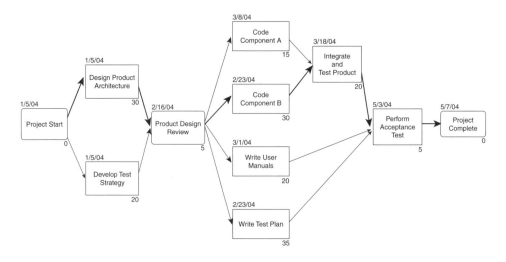

Figure 11-2 *Network for a software development project*

Reviewing Task Networks

Just looking at the pattern of tasks in a task network gives some indication of the quality of the plan. A good task network has groups of tasks making a diamond shape. Several tasks fan out from a milestone. These tasks may have some number of successor tasks but eventually the tasks come together at another milestone, giving a characteristic "diamond shape" between the milestones. Poorly structured task networks often have long "stovepipes" composed of sequential tasks. Sometimes these stovepipes do not even connect to other milestones. This means that the product of that particular stovepipe is not used by other tasks. You should ask why the work product is being created at all.

Types of Precedence Relations

Tasks can have various types of relationships. Sequential tasks are performed one after the other. Concurrent or parallel tasks are performed at the same time, or may possibly overlap for a portion of their time. Sometimes, certain activities cannot happen until some other activity has either started or completed. For example, a programmer must code a module before someone can test it. Tasks may also have constraints such as an earliest possible start date or a latest possible finish date. Other tasks are independent, providing the opportunity to perform them in parallel. Planners often exploit this independence to compress the overall project schedule.

Dependency constraints are described in terms of predecessors, successors, and lags. Any task or milestone without a predecessor is a *start*. Any task or milestone without a successor is a *finish*. Four types of relationships can exist between two tasks:

Finish-to-start	Predecessor must finish before the successor can start.
Start-to-start	Predecessor must start before the successor can start.
Finish-to-finish	The predecessor must finish before the successor can finish.
Start-to-finish	Predecessor must start before the successor can finish.

Finish-to-start relationships are used most often, followed by start-to-start, and then by finish-to-finish.

Float is the amount of time that a task can be delayed without impacting other tasks in the network. Float is typically defined as the latest required start date for a task, minus the earliest possible start date for that task. If a task cannot start later than its latest required start date, it *will* delay the start of dependent (successor) other tasks downstream and may cause a delay in the project. (If the task is on the critical path, then if it is delayed it will lengthen the project completion date.) *Free float* is the amount of time that a task can be delayed without delaying any subsequent tasks. *Total float* is the amount of time that a task can be delayed without delaying project completion.

TIP: Some planners use lags rather than float boxes and then adjust the lag as the project proceeds to account for the amount of float that is either consumed or restored. A lag indicates that some undocumented event or activity must occur before the successor task can be started. It is generally better to eliminate lags and explicitly show the appropriate milestones or activities. For example, perhaps the task cannot start until a customer approves a work product.

Some estimators and planners develop schedules using Gantt (or bar) charts. See the box "Gantt Charts."

Gantt Charts

Developed by Henry L. Gantt in 1917, Gantt charts are a two-dimensional layout with time increasing from left to right, and tasks ordered by their start time from top to bottom. Each task is represented by a horizontal bar extending from the task's start time to its stop time. The bars are shaded to show actual completion status of tasks.

There are a number of serious disadvantages with using Gantt charts. First, a classical Gantt chart does not *explicitly* depict the dependencies between the various tasks. Clearly identified dependencies are especially important for tasks that are assigned to different organizations or to multiple subcontractors. (Some tools, such as Microsoft Project, provide a linked Gantt chart to overcome this limitation.) Second, classical Gantt charts provide no quantitative picture of the conflict between time and resources for tasks that are compressed between fixed milestones. Third, they have no way of showing which tasks have the greatest effect on the project's finish date. (Some versions do indicate the critical path.) They also have little ability to show the effects and costs of mandated schedule compression. For these reasons, I recommend the use of resource loaded networks or at least task network diagrams.

The starting point for scheduling is the task list (or work breakdown structure) and a master schedule that is usually provided by the customer. The master schedule is a top-level view of time relationships between tasks, task durations, and milestones such as project start, project completion, and formal reviews, demonstrations, or deliveries.

The milestones in the customer's master schedule are typically at too high a level to permit timely tracking of the project. You can add *interim milestones* to help manage the work, and detect and resolve problems sooner. The team identifies interim milestones based on a particular development process. For agile methods, these might correspond to major iterations, each culminating with the delivery of a release. For plan-driven models, these might be the product design review (PDR), unit test complete (UTC), and initial operating capability (IOC). (In many cases the customer specifies high-level milestones and in effect imposes a particular project life cycle.) Steve McConnell discusses the use of "miniature milestones" for project tracking and control in Chapter 27 of [McConnell, 1996].

Scheduling is done in five steps, which are iterated as follows:

1. Identify major project milestones (the master schedule).
2. Identify the project's tasks (the WBS).
3. Determine task dependencies (build the task network).
4. Estimate the resources (load the task network).
5. Adjust (tune) the network to meet the imposed schedule (if possible).

Figure 11-3 illustrates the basic sequence of steps. First, identify the major milestones (the event plus the date that it must occur). These usually come from a master schedule provided by the customer. See the tip "Including External Events." Based on the product architecture, project life cycle, and other factors, define the project's work breakdown structure. Next, construct the task network based on the constraints between tasks. Then assign durations and resources to each task in the network. This is called *loading the network* and it allows you to calculate the critical path. Then adjust the network to accommodate required dates and resource availabilities.

Including External Events: You should include key "external events" in your task network. For example, if your project depends on receipt of customer-furnished items or regulatory approvals, indicate these as events that must occur before one of your tasks can start. This clearly identifies customer responsibilities for project success, and provides a way for the project manager to monitor the associated risks. (The project manager does not control external agents. Instead, the project manager must rely on legal or political means to compel these agents to meet their commitments [Block, 1983].)

Depending on the size and duration of the project, the perceived degree of risk, and customer desires, planners may develop an intermediate and possibly even a detailed schedule. The milestones in the master schedule correlate with the corresponding milestones in the next lower schedule, which serve as "main milestones" to anchor the additional milestones of the more detailed schedule. For each level of schedule, planners assign the due dates for specific milestones.

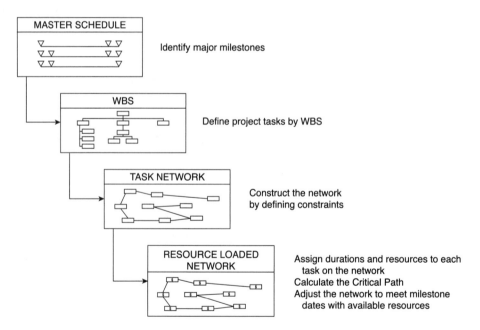

Figure 11-3 *Basic scheduling sequence*

11.4.2 Assigning Resources to the Tasks

The next step is to assign resources to each task in the network. A *resource* can be a machine or facility (e.g., a crane or a test facility), but is usually an individual or a small team. Estimating identifies the types and amounts of resources needed for each task. To determine a task's duration, you must know the task's effort, the "resource" assigned to perform the task, and the availability of that "resource" for the time period of interest. A *resource calendar* shows the availability of the "resource" on each calendar day. A typical worker is available eight hours per day on Monday through Friday. The resource calendar defines which calendar-days are work-days, and also the hours that will be worked.[5] This allows planners to specifically account for holidays, plant shutdowns, and weekends that will or will not be worked, and multiple shifts. Scheduling tools allow planners to define multiple resource calendars, allowing great flexibility when assigning resources.

11.4.3 Using Parametric Models

Various parametric models estimate project effort and schedule and account for the diseconomy of scale that is not handled by the Linear Model described previously. These models allocate the total effort and schedule to project phases and activities using tables, thus generating resource estimates for large numbers of individual tasks that are part of the task network associated with the project's chosen life cycle. (Chapter 12, discusses these tables.) Many of the automated tools that support parametric models export machine-readable files that can be directly read by various project-planning tools. For such exported data to be useful, however, the product architecture and the process model (phases and activities of the project life cycle) must match those that will be used for the project. In other words, the exported data must be compatible with the task network being developed.

11.4.4 Scheduling Algorithm

After you have created the task network, you determine when each task should start. To do this, you need an estimate of the duration of each task. If you know the effort for task and you have assigned some number of individuals to work on that task and know their effort delivery rate, then you can estimate the duration. (Scheduling is actually iterative so these values are only a starting point.

---

[5] Note the two different measures of time. *Schedule* measures calendar time (calendar-days). *Duration* measures the days when people perform project tasks (in work-days). Ignoring holidays, five work-days equals seven calendar-days.

You adjust the amount of resources applied, or possibly re-estimate the amount of resources required, to change the task duration to achieve your planning objectives. This is why automated tools are advisable.)

The scheduling process is iterative for three reasons. First, if the estimated size, effort, or duration for a task is revised, this will cause changes to the schedule. Second, there is often contention for critical resources such as people or facilities. (Contention for key resources generally lengthens the schedule.) Third, during the planning process, engineers, estimators, and schedulers may discover additional constraints. These constraints can be specific dates (milestones, task start, and task finish) or they may be new dependencies between tasks.

There are two ways to estimate the task duration. The basic constraint equation is assumed to be linear because each task is a small amount of work:

$$TE = TDUR*R*FTE$$

where:

TE	=	Total effort for the task	[phr]
TDUR	=	Task duration	[work-days]
R	=	Individual effort delivery rate	[phr/(person* work-day)]
FTE	=	Number of people assigned to the task	[persons]

Typically, either the duration is fixed (to meet some imposed milestone date) or the available resources are fixed (due to availability). If the duration is fixed, you apply enough resources to deliver the effort needed: $FTE = TE/(R*TDUR)$. If the resources are fixed, compute $TDUR = TE/(R*FTE)$. Of course, you can vary both TDUR and FTE if desired, subject to the constraint equation.[6] In practice, you will do this in an iterative way. The usual goal is to "level the resources" across tasks to prevent rapid fluctuations in the number of project staff. Resource leveling smoothes out the peaks and valleys. (Fluctuations in staffing are undesirable because hiring, transferring, and terminating employees is expensive. Keeping the staff stable and performing useful work reduces wasted effort. To shift resources off of a task without delaying the project, there must be some slack in the schedule (i.e., there is float). You can trade resources for duration, reducing the resources until the float in the particular path is reduced to zero.

---

6 Section 12.1 also describes a simple way to calculate the effects of overtime and average availability on the overall project duration. This approach is useful for "quick and dirty" estimates for large projects, and is adequate for small projects, including agile projects.

TIP 1: Contention for key resources will increase the project duration.

TIP 2: Unplanned outages, illnesses, or temporary assignment of resources to other tasks during a project will increase the project duration.

For each iteration, after you have an initial duration for each task, you analyze the network in two passes. The *forward pass* calculates the earliest dates when tasks *can* start and finish based on the assumed durations and the task linkages. The *backward pass* calculates the latest dates when tasks *must* start and finish based on the assumed durations and the task linkages.

The forward pass begins with the project's starting milestone. You progress through the network toward the right, and calculate the earliest dates that each task can start and finish. (By convention, you position tasks in a network so that time increases toward the right.) The *forward pass rule*: The earliest start date for a task (or milestone) is the *latest* of the earliest finish dates for all tasks (paths) that flow into that task. (The early start date of a task is equal to the early finish date of its *latest* predecessor.) The earliest finish date equals the earliest start date plus the duration of the task.

The backward pass begins with the final milestone for the project and works backward toward the starting milestone. You set the latest finish date for the project to the (just calculated) earliest finish date for the ending milestone. (You assume that you want to complete the project as early as possible.) The *backward pass rule*: The latest finish date for an event is the *latest* of the latest start dates for all tasks that flow out of that task (or milestone). (The latest finish date of a task is equal to the early start date of its *earliest* successor.) The latest start date for that task is its latest finish date minus its duration.

In mathematical notation, the scheduling rules are as follows:

$$ES = \text{Maximum(EF of predecessors)}$$
$$EF = \text{ES + Task duration}$$
$$LF = \text{Minimum(LS of successors)}$$
$$LS = \text{LF – Task duration}$$
$$TS = \text{LS – ES = LF – EF}$$
$$FS = \text{Minimum(ES of successors) – EF}$$

where

ES	=	Earliest start for the task
EF	=	Earliest finish for the task
LS	=	Latest start for the task
LF	=	Latest finish for the task
TS	=	Total slack (total float)
FS	=	Free slack (free float)

Total slack (float) is the largest delay in a task that will not affect the project completion date. Free slack (float) is the largest delay in a task the will not affect any subsequent tasks.

11.4.5 Critical Path Analysis

You determine the critical path by analyzing the total float of all activities in the network. This is a complicated process if there are many paths, and this is why automated tools are essential. (See the box "Scheduling Tools.") A delay in any task on the critical path will delay the completion of the project unless a schedule reserve ("float") is inserted in the critical path. You should also consider tasks that are on "near-critical paths" because these tasks impact the project completion date if they are delayed or any float in these paths is consumed.

Scheduling Tools

Large task networks with hundreds or even thousands of tasks cannot be maintained and analyzed manually. Various project-scheduling tools exist for this purpose. Examples are Microsoft Project, Scitor's Project Scheduler, Welcom's Open Plan, and Primavera Systems' Primavera. These tools enable the users to show detailed information about each task on the task diagram. Users can choose to display the task's start date, end date, duration, and number of days of float, and can display this information inside, above, or below the box representing the task. For example, the task might appear like this:

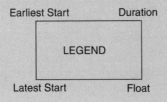

These tools also support analyses of uncertainties in the estimated quantities such as the effort and completion date. Most support the PERT technique. (Indeed, PERT was originally invented to support project scheduling.) Some scheduling tools perform Monte Carlo simulations using user-specified probability distributions, and so can help quantify the uncertainty in project milestone dates, resource consumption, and so forth.

When selecting a scheduling tool, check that it distinguishes between *effort* and *duration*. The tool should allow you to enter effort explicitly and to either specify the resource level (the number of people assigned) or the duration. The tool can then compute the third quantity using an equation such as this:

Effort = Duration*Number of people*8 phr/(person*work-day)

Planners often discover that the critical path is too long. Table 11-5 shows some actions that you can perform to reduce the critical path. The first two items in the table result from assuming dependencies in the network that do not really exist. You can move such tasks out of the critical path so they can be performed concurrently with the critical tasks (assuming you have adequate resources to do so). You can also sometimes overlap sequential tasks. This involves using the start-to-start, lags, and other types of constraint relations. The remaining actions shown in the table involve shortening tasks that cannot be removed from the critical path. Generally speaking, you can only shorten the tasks that your organization controls. The main way to shorten tasks is to decrease their scope, and so reduce the amount of effort that they require. For software modules this usually means reducing the size of the module, either by devising a simpler design, or by reducing the amount of new code that must be built. (You can reuse existing code or buy functionality in the form of commercial off-the-shelf [COTS] products.) You can also increase the effort delivery rate of the staff by having the staff work overtime, assigning more staff to work on the task, or improving their productivity using new tools, or some combination of these actions.

Table 11-5 *Ways to Shorten the Critical Path*

Eliminate tasks on the critical path.
Unlink sequential tasks that are not really dependent.
Overlap sequential tasks.
Shorten the duration of tasks on the critical path.
Shorten the longest tasks.
Shorten early tasks.
Shorten tasks that cost the least to speed up.

During a project, the critical path may change as a result of when tasks are actually completed. You must repeat critical path analysis during the project, just like estimation. (In both cases, you should use actual measured data for completed tasks, and updated estimates for the tasks to be performed.) Automated project planning tools allow you to analyze "what-if" scenarios during the course of the project to anticipate problems.

11.5 Building the Network: Cards on the Wall Method

Generally, it is a good idea to have more than one person plan a project, identify the tasks, and define the task network. This section describes an informal, interactive process to develop a list of tasks and their dependency relationships. The Cards on the Wall Method is a team planning approach that appeared in the mid-1970s.[7] The process appears deceptively simple, yet it helps a team develop a comprehensive project plan in the form of an integrated task network.

---

[7] The Cards on the Wall Method is a form of brainstorming applied to project scheduling and appeared in the 1970s. Early proponents were the Canadian Pacific Real Estate Division (now Marathon) in Montreal (presented at a Project Management Institute conference in 1975) and the Center for Systems Management (Hal Mooz in the late 1970s). The precursor is the Crawford Slip Method, first proposed by C. C. Crawford in 1925 [Crawford, 1983]. The project schedulers were apparently unaware of Crawford's work.

11.5.1 Steps of the Method

Table 11-6 lists the steps of the team planning process.

Table 11-6 *Steps of the Team Planning Process*

Sequential Steps
• Make a list of tasks.
• Record task data on the task card.
• Build the milestone spine.
• Group the tasks in related clusters.
• Connect the cards with yarn to show task sequencing and dependencies.
• Identify lag relationships, if any.
Ongoing Activities
• Upgrade task descriptions.
• Document assumptions.
• Identify and document risks.

First, make a list of tasks. This is usually based on the work breakdown structure, which in turn is based on the product requirements, the product design, and the production process (project life cycle). You can also use checklists based on past projects or brainstorm to help identify the project's tasks. The second step is to record the task data on a card. Figure 11-4 shows a card for tasks (activities). The OBS ID identifies the entity (e.g., a person, team, department, or subcontractor) that will supply the resource. (This is optional. You can add this after the network becomes stable. This may cause some changes in the network, of course, due to contention.) The Inputs and Outputs are products such as documents, modules, assemblies, and data. Any "special" or key resources are identified. The identifiers (WBS ID) of the predecessor and successor tasks are not shown, but you can add them if desired. (In my opinion, the yarn suffices. When the network is done, you enter it into a tool and it handles all of these linkages.) You can print these forms on paper and use tape or thumbtacks. Even simpler, just use large Post-It notes. (The 3×5-inch size works well.)

TIP 1: Use a broad pen with dark ink so that you can read the text from several feet away.

TIP 2: Have someone capture task details *during* the process. (Use a laptop computer.)

Task Name:		
WBS ID:	Effort: _____ phr	
OBS ID:	Workers: _____ people	
Required Start Date:	Required End Date:	

Inputs	Activities	Outputs
1.	1.	1.
2.	2.	2.
3.	3.	3.
4.	4.	4.
5.	5.	5.

Special Resources (Skills, Eqpt., Facilities):

Prepared By:	Date Prepared:

Figure 11-4 *Sample task description form*

Next, the team uses the master schedule to identify the top-level project milestones. They record these on yellow Post-It notes and stick them on the wall to create a "spine" of major milestones. This provides a basis to organize the other tasks when the team puts them on the wall. (Use a different color or shape for the milestones.) Next, place the cards on the wall from left to right to show their time sequence. This is best done in two steps. First, cluster the cards for tasks that are performed about the same time. Second, connect the cards with yarn to show their sequencing and dependencies. (To give a neater layout, you can reduce the number of lines that cross by moving some cards.) Then refine the sequencing and verify that the necessary constraints are satisfied. (Initially, you only show finish-to-start dependencies. Later, you can introduce some overlapping of tasks to compress the overall time.) Placing the cards on the wall, connected by yarn, allows all participants to see and participate in the ordering process and also allows the task ordering to be easily and rapidly changed.

In practice, the best way to accomplish the process is in two well-defined steps. The first step consists of brainstorming and listing all the tasks on the cards. This includes providing estimates for the resources, and so forth. The second step is to take the tasks that have been identified and to place these cards on the wall as described in the preceding paragraph. Throughout both steps, the team updates task descriptions, captures assumptions, and records any risks that are identified. Note: Only later do you capture the results using a scheduling tool such as Microsoft Project.

Have the engineers estimate their own tasks if at all possible. This forces them to think about what must be done. However, their estimates will be inaccurate if they are unfamiliar with the application domain and product architecture. In this case, have several engineers estimate as a team. Use group techniques (brainstorming, Delphi) to promote synergy. The facilitator can suggest analogies, provide historical data, and perform simple feasibility calculations. For example, ask the engineers how long it took them to code a similar module.

11.5.2 Assigning People to Tasks

After the team has agreed on the task network, they assign specific individuals to perform the tasks. Ideally, you only assign a single person to a particular task. However, you can also assign multiple individuals to one task. You can also define "work groups" consisting of two or more people (e.g., a programming pair) and then assign the work groups to tasks.

If the team has less than a dozen or so members or work groups, you can use small, colored tags or Post-It notes to denote individual assignments. (The 1.5×2-inch Post-It notes cut in half work well.) Assign a unique color to each individual or work group. The facilitator guides the team members (or the small teams) to "sign up" for tasks. When they commit to perform a task, the facilitator places the appropriately colored tag on the card. The team can easily see who has responsibility for tasks, and can quickly see if one individual or work group is overloaded. This visibility produces an interesting result. For a well-jelled team, someone will usually volunteer to perform some of the tasks assigned to the overloaded individual. The team thus balances their workload. This is simple, fast, cheap, and it works!

The team can also update status during their regular team meetings because the diagram is on the wall. You can also mark each completed task by drawing an X or pasting a large green dot on the card. (Office supply stores sell these.) At the end of the iteration, you clear the cards and yarn off the wall, except for any uncompleted tasks, and the team plans the next cycle, adding new tasks to accomplish the objectives of the next increment.

11.5.3 Applying Cards on the Wall

The Cards on the Wall Method enables a team to gain an initial understanding of a large, complicated project very quickly. The team can then elaborate the task network by subdividing and adding tasks. See the box "Applying Cards on the Wall to Very Large Projects." The final task network provides the basis for estimating costs, authorizing work, and tracking progress.

Projects using agile methods are much smaller and do not need the same level of formal planning and tracking as large projects. Nevertheless, such projects can use the Cards on the Wall Method to plan a single iteration. See the box "Applying Cards on the Wall to Agile Projects." Similarly, projects using iterative life cycles such as the Rational Unified Process and the Microsoft Solutions Framework can use Cards on the Wall to plan their iterations.

Applying Cards on the Wall to Very Large Projects

Cards on the Wall works best when the team size is a dozen or so people. You can handle larger groups (up to 50 or so) by applying Cards on the Wall in two steps. First, assign individuals to subgroups, tasking each to address a specific part of the project (e.g., to develop the software, the hardware, or the user training materials). Alternatively, you might subdivide the software into user interfaces, data management, and various application functions. Each subgroup develops their task network. Second, everyone then meets and integrates their networks into a single network. (Assign the teams to work in different sections of the wall in one room. Alternatively, you need to provide a way for each group to carry their task network into the same room.)

Applying Cards on the Wall to Agile Projects

For each iteration or "sprint," the project team has a short planning session (no more than four hours or so) to identify the tasks needed to complete the next iteration and the dependencies between these tasks. The cards and yarn remain on the wall, providing a visible roadmap for the project team. (Post the task network in the room where the team has its daily or weekly meetings.)

The Cards on the Wall process is similar to using "user stories" to plan agile projects. However, Kent Beck and Martin Fowler state that the stories are highly independent, and so task networks are not needed [Beck, 2001, page 64]. The larger the project team, however, the more you will want to plan and coordinate their work. You will have to make your own decision.

The benefits associated with the six-step method include the following:

- The team gains a better understanding of the work to be done by sharing their knowledge and experience.
- The planners obtain a more accurate estimate of the project's scope.
- The team produces a documented list of tasks, assumptions, and dependencies.
- The process fosters joint ownership of the project.

TIP: Schedule the difficult tasks early if possible. These are usually the most expensive and risky tasks in the project. It is better to start working on them early so that if any difficulties arise you will have more time to resolve the problems.

11.6 Recommended Reading

Section 20.2 describes a generic WBS for large projects. Section 20.3 provides additional guidance and examples for partitioning large projects. You might want to look at Section 20.4 for ways to improve the work breakdown structure to address standard processes, CMMI measurement requirements, and rework. Section 22.4 discusses practical constraints.

Barry Boehm discusses work breakdown structures for software development in Section 4.7 of [Boehm, 1981]. See the notes "The COCOMO Waterfall Model" and the "COCOMO Work Breakdown Structure."

John Goodpasture provides succinct discussions of work breakdown structures and scheduling, with emphasis on quantitative analysis techniques [Goodpasture, 2004]. Robert Wysocki and Rudd McGary cover project management for information technology projects in [Wysocki, 2003]. They cover defining the work breakdown structure (Chapter 4); estimating resources, durations, and costs (Chapter 5); constructing the task network diagram (Chapter 6); and applying and leveling resources (Chapter 7). Chapter 8 discusses joint project planning. Their book includes a CD-ROM with examples tied to Microsoft Project, and a trial version of Microsoft Project.

Hal Mooz and his colleagues describe the Cards on the Wall Method in [Mooz, 2003, pages 113–114] and [Forsberg, 2000, pages 176–183].

11.7 Summary

The Bottom-Up Method consists of planning, estimating, and scheduling. Planning identifies a list of project tasks and describes each task. For large projects, planning produces the project's work breakdown structure (WBS), which is a hierarchical partitioning of the work, and whose lowest level is a set of work packages that you can estimate separately. To identify work packages, you must consider the contractual requirements to deliver specified items, the firms and organizations that will be responsible for producing these items, the product architecture, delivery schedules, and phases of the project life cycle. Subdivide work packages that require large amounts of effort, that represent an especially risky activity, that must be assigned to a different organization, or that represent large costs (such as purchasing significant amounts of hardware). The WBS dictionary contains the descriptions of all work packages.

Estimating calculates the amount of resources needed by each work package. These resources include effort, materials, consumables, and duration. Effort is often subdivided by skill level or labor category. Consumables include operating expenses and travel. Duration is the number of work-days allowed to accomplish the work. The estimates for the work packages are the basis for the project's budget and schedule.

The scheduling process sets dates and identifies the amount of resources required to achieve those dates as follows. Scheduling integrates the work packages into logical time sequence, taking dependencies and constraints into account to create a task network. A "good" network should start with a single milestone and end with a single milestone. Paths should fan out from a milestone, and then converge toward the next milestone. Scheduling then assigns resources to tasks in the network, and so calculates how long each task will take. For most projects, the key resource is labor. (It could, however, be a critical piece of equipment or a facility.) Summing the task durations along a path gives the total estimated time to complete that path. Resource calendars convert work-days into calendar-days. The critical path has the longest total duration, and determines the earliest possible completion date for the project. Planners then adjust task definitions, dependencies, estimates, and assigned resources to achieve milestones in the customer's master schedule.

The task network provides an integrated view of how the project (the production process) will unfold. Because each WBS element in the task network has resources associated with it, it is a resource loaded network (RLN). The resource loaded network constitutes a detailed plan for the project. It is a time-phased budget for the project, which is a key input for cash-flow calculations. The RLN is also a detailed schedule because it shows the timing of all WBS tasks. The resource loaded network is also the basis for critical path analysis. The scheduling process

- Defines when project events are supposed to occur.
- Provides a way to validate milestones specified by the customer.
- Identifies possible contention for resources.
- Promotes efficient use of resources.

During the project, the manager must obtain and apply the needed resources to make the planned activities occur on schedule. The resource loaded network is the basis for tracking progress using earned value measurement, described in Chapter 21, and provides a tool to analyze alternative ways to correct problems that arise.

Having a team prepare task lists, estimates, and networks helps to surface omissions and conflicts, and so provides more accurate estimates of project effort, cost, and time. Team network building improves the quality of the project plan and encourages participants to commit to the final plan.

The Bottom-Up Method provides a way to adjust estimates to accommodate project constraints on cost, schedule, and staffing level. Bottom-up estimation requires more effort than top-down estimation (described in the next chapter) because there are many separate tasks to be estimated. A benefit, however, is that the total effort and schedule values tend to be more stable because of compensating errors. The Bottom-Up Method can provide arbitrary levels of detail, but can consume more time and effort. The next chapter describes a less-costly technique called the Top-Down Method. The Top-Down Method proves useful for initial estimates of project scope and provides a way to check estimates made using other techniques.

Chapter 12

Top-Down Estimating and Allocation

The Top-Down Method is useful for quickly estimating the total resources required for some object (typically a project), and allocating this total to lower-level objects (such as project activities or subsystems). This gives initial estimates for each of the various activities or subsystems. These estimates may be sufficient for early planning. You can also use these estimates to crosscheck estimates prepared using other methods, such as the Bottom-Up Method described in Chapter 11, "Bottom-Up Estimating and Scheduling."

You can use the Top-Down Method to estimate effort, cost, and schedule (or duration) for project tasks. You can also use it to estimate the project's average staffing level and staffing profile (staffing as a function of time). The Top-Down Method estimates the total project effort by dividing the total estimated size by the productivity. (Chapter 13, "Parametric Models," describes more sophisticated parametric estimation models.)

This chapter describes simple relations between effort, duration, and the number and availability of people working on the project. You can use these relations to quickly estimate the project schedule, and to make simple tradeoffs. For example, you can estimate the amount of schedule reduction that is achievable by adding staff to a project.

This chapter also shows how to allocate the total effort and total duration to a project's activities and phases. You can use the allocation technique for any type of project (software, hardware, system development) or life cycle. As long as you have some way to estimate the total effort and total schedule, you can allocate these totals. (Parametric models also use the allocation technique described here. You can apply the allocation technique independently of parametric models, however, which is why I describe it in this chapter.) Finally, this chapter provides some examples, a budget with multiple labor grades, and some tips.

Section 12.1 reviews the estimation of total effort using size and productivity. It also explains the difference between duration and schedule, and how to convert one to the other. It shows a simple way to estimate the development schedule given the total effort for a project, which is good for quick estimates, and is also useful to check schedules developed using other techniques. Then it uses the development effort and development schedule (or duration) to estimate the average number of full-time people that must be assigned to the project. You can use this information to estimate costs for office space, desktop computers, and other facilities (e.g., parking). Section 12.2 discusses average availability, which affects schedule estimates. Section 12.3 discusses schedule compression, a common requirement for many projects, and briefly mentions Brooks's law. Section 12.4 shows how to allocate effort and schedule using the Rayleigh curve and allocation tables. Section 12.5 provides some examples, including a simple budget. Section 12.6 gives recommended reading. Section 12.7 is a summary.

12.1 Relating Effort, Duration, and Staffing

Let EDEV denote the total effort for all tasks performed by a project team between the start and end of a development project (or between two specified life cycle milestones). EDEV can include the effort for only the engineering activities, or for engineering plus support activities. (Typical support activities are configuration management, quality assurance, and project management.) You can choose either option. Note: You must define the "project team" consistently with your choice (engineers only, or all project staff, respectively). The following discussion and examples assume that EDEV is the total effort for all required project tasks, and that the project staff includes all individuals who work on these tasks.

Assume that you have estimated EDEV. If the production process is labor intensive, the total effort is approximately given by

EDEV = Size/Productivity

where EDEV is the total effort, size is the amount of product to be produced or developed, and the productivity is defined appropriately. Section 4.2 described the definitions of and the relations between size, productivity, and effort. Chapters 8, "Estimating Software Size: The Basics," and 9, "Estimating Software Size: The Details," described how to measure and estimate size in function points and in source lines of code. You can measure the productivity using historical data (as discussed in Chapter 2, "Planning a Warehouse Inventory System"). You can adjust the historical values for productivity, size, or even the effort using techniques described in Section 5.4. You can also use parametric models, described in Chapter 13, which essentially calculate an average productivity based on multiple factors.

Time is the interval measured between defined project or life cycle milestones, for example, the difference between the start date and the completion date. There are two measures of time. Development time, denoted by TDEV, is the total time elapsed to build a product, and is measured in calendar-days.[1] Duration, denoted by TDUR, is the number of days when the project staff delivers effort to perform project tasks. Duration is measured in work-days. (I use hyphens to indicate the unit of measure, to prevent confusion with the English word *workday*.[2]) It is important to distinguish these two measures. Duration is always less than development time because

$$\text{Calendar-days} = \text{work-days} + \text{weekend-days} + \text{holidays}$$
$$+ \text{average vacation days} + \text{downtime}$$

The terms in this equation are self-explanatory except for downtime. Downtime arises due to plant shutdowns, unplanned outages, or work stoppages directed by the customer (e.g., due to lack of available funding). The precise relation between work-days and calendar-days depends upon the number of holidays and vacation days in the period of interest, whether the staff works weekends or not, and the amount of downtime. To provide an approximate conversion factor for examples that follow, assume that the project staff will work five days per week and will receive approximately 10 days of holidays and 10 days of vacation plus sick leave per year. This means that they will only work 48 out of 52 weeks each calendar year. Here is the calculation of the factor to convert calendar-days (CD) to work-days (WD) showing the units explicitly:

$$\text{CD2WD} = (5 \text{ work-days}/\text{work-week})(48 \text{ work-weeks}/\text{cyr})$$
$$(1 \text{ cyr}/365 \text{ calendar-days})$$
$$= 0.66 \text{ work-days}/\text{calendar-days}$$

---

[1] Project planners refer to it as "elapsed time" to avoid confusion with the schedule, which is a time-phased linkage of tasks. Most estimation books unfortunately use the word "schedule" to denote both.

[2] Time and effort are often stated in ":hours" or "days." To avoid possible confusion and errors, I use hyphens in units of measure for effort (person-hours, person-days, person-months), duration (work-days, contact-hours), and development time (calendar-days). For other quantities, industry standard units do not use hyphens. Examples include function points (FP), Source Lines Of Code (SLOC), and use case points (UCP).

Note that the units cancel out correctly. (You should compute your own conversion constant based on your organization's holiday schedules and the average measured amounts of sick leave and vacation.) The factor to convert work-days to calendar-days is WD2CD = 1/CD2WD ≈ 1.5 calendar-days/work-days.

The number of work-days per calendar-month, still assuming only 48 work-weeks per calendar-year, is

$$
\begin{aligned}
\text{WDperCM} &= (365 \text{ calendar-days}/12 \text{ calendar-months}) \\
&\quad *\text{CD2WD} \\
&= (30.4 \text{ calendar-days}/\text{calendar-month})* \\
&\quad (0.66 \text{ work-days}/\text{calendar-month}) \\
&= 20.1 \text{ work-days}/\text{calendar-month}
\end{aligned}
$$

There are only about 20 work-days per calendar-month so a single full-time person can only deliver 160 person-hours/calendar-month.[3] If the project is to last 12 calendar-months, the team will have about 240 work-days, assuming that they are assigned full-time to the project. Contrast this to the "theoretical maximum" of 173 phr/calendar-month which is based on 52 work-weeks per calendar-year (173 = 8*5*52/12). Factoring in holidays, and an average amount of vacation and sick days, reduces the available person-hours by about 8%. This is a significant difference. On some projects, the staff may work seven days per calendar week in crisis situations. (The end of this section shows an easy way to handle part-time and overtime work. Section 12.3 shows how to handle additional "nonproductive" effort expended when more people are assigned to a project.)

Explicitly distinguishing duration from development time provides a simple way to compute the effects of nonstandard work schedules and the effect of overtime.[4] The key equation is

FTE = Effort/Duration

where

FTE = The number of full-time equivalent workers (the "staffing level")
Effort = The estimated amount of labor needed to perform the project's
       tasks

---

[3] The abbreviation for person-hours is phr.

[4] Chapter 11 mentioned the resource calendars in project planning tools that allow planners to define detailed work schedules for individual resources. These provide very fine-grained control over the mapping from work-days to calendar-days.

Duration = The time that workers actually work on project tasks (work-days)[5]

Many cost models measure effort in person-months (PM) or staff-months (SM) and development time in calendar-months (CM). For example, COCOMO II [Boehm, 2000] gives the equation

FTE = EDEV/TDEV

where TDEV is the development time. If EDEV = 24 PM and TDEV = 12 CM, then FTE = 2 people. This expression obscures the difference between duration and development time, and the effects of overtime.

I have found the following formulation better for analyzing cost and time tradeoffs. Define the *individual effort delivery rate, R,* as the average number of person-hours of effort delivered by one worker working one work-day. Most cost models assume that R is 8 phr/work-day, but R really depends on the average availability, AA, of the person. AA is less than 1 if the person works part-time. AA is greater than 1 if the person works overtime. So R = AA*8 phr/work-day. The theoretical maximum for AA is 3 (corresponding to 24 hours per work-day). A practical limit is probably no more that 2, which might correspond to a short, intense project lasting only a few months. The improved formulation is

FTE = EDEV/(R*TDUR)

where

FTE	= Number of full-time equivalent workers [persons or people]
EDEV	= Effort [phr]
TDUR	= Duration [work-days]
R	= Individual effort delivery rate [phr/(person*work-day)]
	= AA*8 phr/(person*work-day)

and AA is the average availability for the entire team, which is dimensionless.

Suppose that you estimate that a project requires 10,000 phr of effort. You decide that the staff will work 10% overtime, so AA = 1.1. The desired schedule is 9 calendar-months. Assuming 20 work-days/calendar-month gives TDUR = 180 work-days available. You compute:

---

[5] The definition of "project tasks" is important. Some estimators only include the core "productive activities" and ignore attending meetings and training. For example, the Personal Software Process only estimates "time (effort) on task" and assumes a low effort delivery rate such as 15 task-hours per calendar-week. This shows why precise definitions are critical for estimation.

$$FTE = \frac{10{,}000 \text{ phrs}}{1.1 * 8 \text{ phrs} / (\text{person} * \text{work-day}) * 180 \text{ work-days}} = 6.3 \text{ people}$$

Observe how the units cancel out. Alternately, suppose that you only have five people who will all work 10% overtime. What is the duration and the schedule?

TDUR = EDEV/(R*FTE) = 10,000/(1.1*8*5) = 227 work-days

Using the previous conversion value for work-days to calendar-days gives TDEV = TDUR/CD2WD = 227/0.66 = 344 calendar-days or about 11.3 CM. You can also express the model in terms of TDEV using TDUR = TDEV*CD2WD:

$$FTE = \frac{EDEV * CD2WD}{8 * AA * TDEV} = \frac{EDEV}{8 * AA * WD2CD * TDEV}$$

where WD2CD = 1/CD2WD. The "8" appears because you must convert work-days to person-hours. (The units for all of the quantities are as defined above.)

This simple model shows all the factors that affect the relationship of effort, time, and staff level. The model is useful for rough estimates of the total development time. You can also use it to explore ways to reduce the development time ("compress the schedule").

12.2 Planned Versus Actual Availability

There is an overlap between AA and WD2CD. The origin is the choice of the basic time unit. I use work-days for TDUR. Thus, AA affects the phr delivered per work-day. WD2CD is based, in part, on the number of work-days per calendar-week. If the team goes to a seven day work week, then you would adjust WD2CD. On the other hand, if you choose your time unit to be calendar-months, everything is included in AA. Assuming that a full-time person works 2080 person-hours per calendar-year gives 173.3 person-hours per calendar-month.[6] Then "173.3*AA" gives the total number of person-hours delivered per calendar-month. (The average availability can be above 100% if the employees work overtime.) This is another example of the importance of understanding the definitions of estimated (and measured) quantities and their units of measure.

Planners assume that each employee will deliver some average number of hours per month. Call this the *planned average individual delivery rate, P*. This defines the person-hours in a person-month for estimating labor costs. In the real world, employees may take no vacation, sick days, or holidays during a

---

6 This value is too optimistic because it ignores sick leave, vacation, and holidays. A more realistic value is 150 to 160 person-hours per calendar-month. The exact value depends on the organization's policies.

particular month or may work overtime, and so will deliver more than the planned number of labor hours. On the other hand, if employees work on "nonproject" activities, they deliver less than the planned number of hours. Nonproject activities include the following:

- Demonstrating prototypes or products to support marketing
- Supporting old projects (advice, maintenance)
- Taking training (technical, administrative)
- Writing proposals

These two competing effects influence the *actual average individual effort delivery rate, R,* and so affect the task completion time.

Figure 12-1 illustrates how the value of R varies with the project's headcount, FTE. The plot uses P = 156 phr/(person*calendar-month) and OT = 0.15. The lower curve shows the effects of sharing personnel among projects, and asymptotically approaches P for large projects. The upper curve shows the effects of overtime, and asymptotically approaches P *(1 + OT), which equals 179.4 phr/(person*calendar-month) for this example.[7]

Most parametric estimating models address large projects, where all employees are assigned full-time to the project and take the average number of vacation days, sick days, and holidays as expected. Thus, these models assume that R = P. If the staff works continuously (no vacations) or works overtime, then R can exceed P. If employees expend effort supporting other projects, however, R will be less than P. This is often the case for small projects.

This discussion suggests a simple way to quickly estimate a realistic development time for a project:

TDEV = EDEV/(FTE*R)

where EDEV is the total required effort in person-hours and R is the average individual effort delivery rate in person-hours per calendar-month. You should determine the value of R based on historical data for your organization. In real life, R always seems to be less than P.[8] I have found that 140 phr/(person* calendar-month) works well if the workers are dedicated to the project "full time."

---

[7] There is another effect to consider. Each time a person switches to a different project, the person expends some effort to become "resynchronized" with the current status of the project. Repeated switching increases the total effort expended to complete the project tasks. You might model this effect by multiplying the project's effort by a function such as $f(N) = [a+(1 - a)/N]$ where N is the average number of projects that a person works on, and $0 \le a \le 1$. If a = 1, there is no penalty. If a = 0, the penalty is large. For teams working on several small projects, you might use such a function to increase the estimated effort and so increase your estimation accuracy.

[8] R exceeds P if the team works overtime. By setting R' = P*(1 + OT) or, more pessimistically, R' = R *(1 + OT), you can use this equation to estimate the reduced development time.

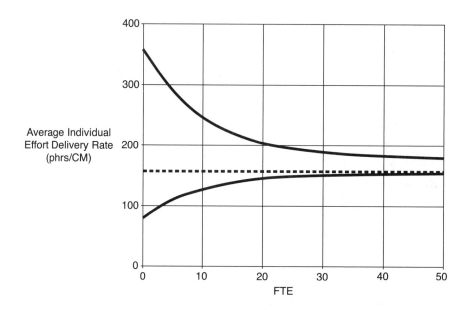

Figure 12-1: *Effort delivery rate vs. full-time equivalent staff*

Some authors refer to the decrease in delivered hours using the term "staff availability." Capers Jones gives two values. For normal projects, he has a value of 185 working-days/calendar-year (= 123 phr/(person*calendar-month)). For critical schedule-driven projects, he has a value of 197 work-days/calendar-year (= 131 phr/(person*calendar-month)). He also discusses other sources of delay that consume a worker's time such as slack time between tasks and worker training. For details, see [Jones, 1991, pages 213–214].

Other organizations just compute the development time (TDEV) assuming a full 156 phr/calendar-month, but then add a "pad" to the schedule. For example, Microsoft routinely inserts a "buffer time" of 20% to 30% in its schedules. [Cusamano, 1995, pages 204-206]. NASA's Software Engineering Laboratory recommends a value of 10% [NASA, 1993, page 7-5]. They do not add effort to increase the cost, however, assuming that the direct charged staff will be able to work productively on other project tasks. This may overlook increased indirect costs, however. The reason is that project support personnel typically charge continuously, and so adding buffer time will increase the indirect costs.

Comparing P and R

Some of my students ask about the discrepancy between the size of the person-month, P, and the effort delivery rate, R. If the purchaser pays for a person-month that contains 156 phr but each person only delivers 140 phr per calendar-month, aren't we somehow cheating the buyer? The answer is no, because the two quantities measure different things. A person-month is used to compute the billing rate for a person working "full time" for a calendar-month, and provides enough money to pay for 174 phr, of which, say, 156 phr are direct charge, and the remaining 18 phr are expended on allowed overhead or fringe activities (such as vacation, sick leave, and holidays). (These activities are part of the costs included in the indirect rates negotiated with the buyer. See Chapter 15, "Calculating Cost and Price: The Basics.") The effort delivery rate, R, represents only the rate at which workers actually spend the money directly working on the project.

An example makes this distinction clear. Suppose that you estimate that a task needs 1,000 phr of effort and that you plan to assign 1.5 full-time equivalent people to do the work. Assume that one person-month, fully loaded, costs $10K. Using the values in the preceding paragraph, the estimated effort, schedule, and cost are as follows:

Effort   = 1,000 phr/(156 phr/[person-month]) = 6.41 PM
Schedule = 1,000 phr/(1.5 people*140 phr/(person*calendar-month))
          = 4.8 CM
Cost   = ($10K)*(6.41 person-month) = $64.1K

12.3 Schedule Compression

You can estimate the total development time by rearranging the simple model:

$$TDEV = TDUR * WD2CD = \frac{EDEV * WD2CD}{8 * AA * FTE} = \frac{WD2CD * (Size / Productivity)}{8 * AA * FTE}$$

In the last expression, I have replaced the estimated effort, EDEV, by the size divided by the productivity. (You can use any of the size measures described in Chapter 9.)

You can use this simple equation to crudely estimate various options to reduce the development time.[9] For example, to reduce TDEV you can have the staff work more days, represented by increasing the value of WD2CD. You can also decrease the size of the software, either by decreasing the amount of functionality that you must build, or by purchasing prebuilt components instead of building custom code from scratch. You can also increase productivity by purchasing suitable tools or hiring more capable, experienced workers. You can increase the average availability of the staff by having the staff work overtime.[10] You can add more people to the project by increasing the value of FTE. Adding people to a project in an attempt to accelerate schedule is not a simple Linear Model, however. See the box "Brooks's Law." The box "Other Alternatives to Reduce Development Time" suggests additional options.

Brooks's Law

Adding staff to a project increases the total effort delivery rate for the team, but also increases the project's total effort since the new staff must be hired and trained. Training is often done by existing members (the "mentors") of the project team. During the "assimilation period," the mentors are unable to deliver their full quota of useful work to the project. Also, the new people are expending effort learning instead of producing. There is thus the possibility that the net useful effort provided to the project will be decreased by adding staff.

The view commonly held by many managers was stated in 1974 by Fred Brooks: "Adding manpower to a late software project makes it later" [Brooks, 1974]. Under certain conditions, however, you can add staff to a late project to meet a specified product delivery date (or even to accelerate the delivery date). For details, see [Stutzke, 1994], which is included on the book's CD-ROM. The mathematical model of Brooks's Law provides a quantitative way to investigate options to compress or recover

---

[9] This equation is adequate for small projects. For very large projects, the effort and time are not directly proportional because workers must expend more effort to communicate and coordinate their activities, decreasing their average productivity. Parametric estimation models have equations that quantify the nonlinear relation between effort and time. A typical model is $E = A*S^B$ where $A > 0$ and $B > 1$. Because B is greater than 1, the average effort per unit size (the production coefficient) increases with the size and so productivity decreases.

[10] There are limits to the amount of overtime that people can work. After three or four months of overtime, the staff becomes exhausted and their productivity decreases. Tarek Abdel-Hamid and Stuart Madnick discuss this effect in Section 7.5.2 of [Abdel-Hamid, 1991], and provide several references to the literature.

schedule. You can use it separately or in combination with other alternatives to devise an optimum plan for any particular project.

Note that Brooks's Law deals with project effort and duration. The impact on project costs depends on whether the mentoring and learning are charged to the customer, or are paid out of corporate profits.

Other Alternatives to Reduce Development Time

There are two ways to reduce development time:

- Deliver more effort to the project tasks
- Reduce scope of the project tasks (and so the amount of effort required)

Specific actions you can perform include the following:

- Pay the current staff to work overtime
- Add more staff (working single shifts or multiple shifts)
- Replace custom code with commercial off-the-shelf components
- Reduce product functionality
- Move low-priority functions to later releases (if there are any)
- Reduce the scope and formality of deliverable documents
- Defer noncritical deliverables such as documentation
- Reduce rework by finding errors in code and documents sooner
- Automate repetitive activities
- Simplify administrative paperwork

Most of the actions listed are self-explanatory. Paying the current staff to work overtime is good for short surges, assuming that the workers are salaried, and are paid at "straight time." (You are just expending the budgeted effort faster and incurring no extra costs above the original estimates.) Multishift operations may be possible during the later implementation activities of a well-planned project [Stutzke, 1993]. (Some multinational firms accomplish this by having distributed development spread across multiple time zones.) You will typically use some combination of the preceding options.

12.4 Allocating Effort and Time

The first half of this chapter explained how to estimate the total effort and total schedule (or duration) for a software project utilizing the total size and an assumed value for the productivity. For detailed planning and tracking, you must distribute the effort and schedule to the activities and phases of the project life cycle, which are described in Chapter 10, "Production Processes (Project Life Cycles)." This section discusses how the expenditure of effort and duration are related. Then it explains how to use simple tables to allocate effort and time to phases and activities that are tied to the work breakdown structure, described in Chapter 11, "Bottom-Up Estimating and Scheduling."

The expenditure of effort (effort delivery) varies with time on most projects. Every project has a beginning and an end. Most large software development projects typically start with a small number of people and gradually add people to do the detailed design, programming, and testing. The number of people often decreases slightly toward the end of the project. This means that the expenditure of effort increases after the project starts, rises to a peak, and then (usually) decreases as the project concludes.

The shape of the project staffing curve also affects other direct costs because the number of staff drives facilities costs and the number of computers. In addition, because computer resources are consumed more heavily in compiling, linking, and executing test cases later in the project, the amount of computer processing increases as illustrated in Figure 12-2. If the staff lacks adequate computer resources, this will decrease their productivity. Usage increases sooner if the software developers use front-end computer-aided software engineering (CASE) tools. You need to be aware of this phenomenon so that you can plan to provide more resources during the later stages of a project. You might decide to include purchase additional equipment or go to double shift operation. (Double shifts often occur if the team must use a single testbed having unique or expensive equipment. In this case, you cannot buy additional equipment.)

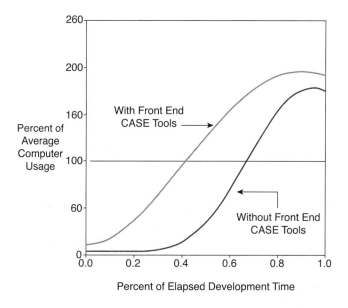

Figure 12-2 *SEE/STE usages versus time*

12.4.1 Distribution Functions

You can use mathematical functions to model project staffing versus time. These functions have some important constraints. The top half of Figure 12-3 shows the number of staff, identified as full-time equivalent staff (FTE), as a function of time. FTE(t) is the staffing profile.[11] The team's total effort delivery rate equals FTE(t)*R where R is the average individual effort delivery rate described in Section 12.1. (The value of R depends on the units of measure for the various quantities, and the average availability, which encompasses overtime.) The integral of the staffing profile versus duration must equal the total effort expended by the project team, EDEV. The equation is

$$\text{Area} = R * \int_{0}^{\text{TDUR}} \text{FTE(t)dt} = \text{EDEV}$$

---

[11] Boehm refers to FTE as full-time software personnel (FSP). Other authors call it the "staffing level" or "average headcount."

This integral will only give an accurate result if the time is duration (work-days).[12] This equation represents a normalization constraint for any effort distribution function. The other important result, shown in Figure 12-3, is that the cumulative effort increases in an S-shaped curve. This shape is a common feature of all projects. (Such a shape results when integrating any function that rises to a peak and then decreases to zero again.)

There are a number of possible staffing profiles. Figure 12-4 shows two. The left half of the figure shows the case of constant staffing. This means that the staffing function FTE(t) is constant with respect to time, giving the rectangular distribution shown. The integral of this function is the straight line shown in the bottom left of the figure. If the constant staffing level is N people, and the average effort delivery rate for a person is R, then the cumulative value at any time t is simply $N*R*t$. The right half of Figure 12-4 shows a popular staffing profile called the Rayleigh curve, discussed in the next section. The staff starts at zero, rises to a peak, and then decreases, and the integral is S-shaped. Some organizations approximate the shape of the Rayleigh curve with a trapezoidal distribution. Others use a parabolic shape. The functions are chosen because they represent historical experience of the organization.

12.4.2 The Norden/Rayleigh Model

Peter Norden was one of the first people to study project staffing patterns [Norden, 1958], [Norden, 1970], and [Norden, 1977]. Norden asserted that many projects' staffing profiles resembled a Rayleigh curve (originally studied in the late 1800s by Lord John Rayleigh, an English physicist). Lawrence Putnam was the first to apply Norden's staffing model to the software development projects [Putnam, 1978]. Putnam's work is the basis of the Software LIfe-cycle Model (SLIM).

The Rayleigh curve has some convenient properties, summarized in the box "Properties of the Rayleigh Curve," and so it is used in various estimation models. The Rayleigh curve is not a "universal law" of project behavior, however.

---

[12] Using calendar time corresponds to assuming that the staff delivers work on weekends as well, giving an area that is larger than the total effort on the project.

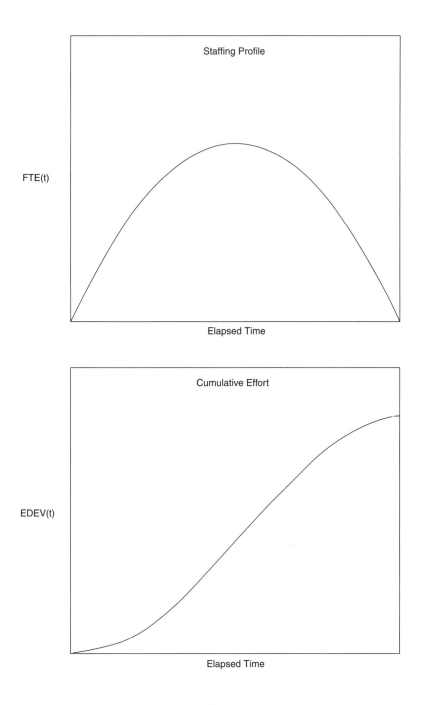

Figure 12-3 *Staffing profile and cumulative effort versus duration*

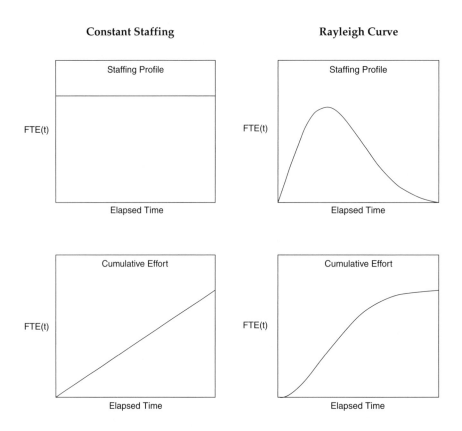

Figure 12-4 *Constant and Rayleigh staffing models*

For project estimation, the Rayleigh curve is assumed to represent the number of Full-Time Equivalent people working on the project (the "staffing level") as a function of time. The usual form is

$$\text{Staffing Level} = \text{FTE(t)} = \frac{dy}{dt} = \frac{Kt}{t_d^2} \exp\left[\frac{-t^2}{\left[2t_d^2\right]}\right]$$

Staffing peaks when the first derivative of FTE(t) equals zero. This occurs when t = td. The Rayleigh curve is integrable in closed form:

$$E(t) = \int_0^t FTE(t)dt = K * \left(1 - \exp(-a * t^2)\right) = K\left(1 - \exp\left[\frac{-t^2}{(2t_d^2)}\right]\right)$$

where E(t) equals the total (cumulative) effort expended by the staff from time 0 to time t. For the integral to be valid, time must be duration, not calendar time. K has physical significance. As time goes to infinity, K represents the total effort expended over the lifetime of the product.

Properties of the Rayleigh Curve

The mathematical form of the Rayleigh curve is

FTE(t) = 2*K*a*t*exp(-a*t²)

Some important properties are as follows:

- It is determined by one scale parameter, K, and one shape parameter, a.
- Its value is zero at t = 0.
- Its value peaks when t = 1/SQRT(2*a).
- It has an inflection point at t = SQRT(3/(2*a)).
- It exhibits an exponential decay for large values of t.
- It can be integrated in closed form.

Most estimation models set the value of t_d to the project's development time (which should be TDUR, not TDEV, to ensure proper normalization). This time corresponds to the initial release of the product (i.e., the initial operational capability [IOC] milestone). Because t_d is chosen to equal TDUR, the value of the cumulative effort at t = t_d equals the total effort expended on the project (i.e., the development effort). Substituting t_d in the equation for cumulative effort gives

Development effort = E(t_d) = K*(1 - e^{-0.5}) = 0.393*K = EDEV

Thus, K = 2.54*EDEV. K is interpreted as the total life cycle effort for developing and maintaining the product. (This result is often cited to explain that 60% of the life cycle effort for a software product is spent in maintenance.)

The slope of the staffing function, dFTE/dt, represents the rate at which people are added or removed from the project. (This quantity is also called the "manpower buildup" rate.) The slope is given by

$$\frac{dFTE}{dt} = 2*K*a*(1-2*a*t^2)*exp(-a*t^2)$$

For t = 0, the slope is 2*K*a. The slope gradually decreases, reaching zero when the Rayleigh curve reaches its peak at t = 1/SQRT(2*a). Then the slope becomes increasingly negative past the peak. The slope reaches its maximum negative value at an inflection point, which occurs at t = SQRT(3/(2*a)). Thereafter, the slope decreases asymptotically toward zero.

12.4.3 The Modified Rayleigh Curve

Barry Boehm argues that the Rayleigh curve is unrealistic because no project ever starts with zero workers. He shows a modified Rayleigh curve in Equation (5-4) of [Boehm, 1981, page 69]. Specifically, he only uses the portion of the Rayleigh curve from 0.3 td and 1.7 td to represent the full development time, TDUR. His staffing function is:

$$FTE(t) = MM * \left(\frac{0.15*TDUR + 0.7*t}{0.25*(TDUR)^2} \right) exp \left(\frac{-(0.15*TDUR + 0.7*t)^2}{0.5*(TDUR)^2} \right)$$

where MM is the total development effort (in person-months). The units are correct because MM/TDUR equals FTE. The dimensionless Rayleigh function just multiplies FTE. The normalization of his equation is not correct, however. If the limits are defined as $(1-k)*t_d$ to $(1+k)*t_d$, the area under the curve is

$$Area = \frac{2*\sinh\ k}{k} * exp\left[\frac{-(1+k^2)}{2} \right]$$

To obtain the correct normalization, divide Boehm's Equation (5-4) by this area. For his Equation (5-4), k = 0.7 and the area is 1.029.

Figure 12-5 compares the pure Rayleigh function and a modified Rayleigh function. Time is measured as the percent of total development time (duration). The vertical axis, staffing level, is measured as the percentage of the average staffing level. This figure also depicts a simple approximation to the shape of the modified Rayleigh curve using the four rectangles shown. (This approximation assumes a Waterfall Model.) The widths of the rectangles are determined by the phase durations defined for the life cycle model. The height of each rectangle is chosen so that the area of the rectangle equals the area under that portion of the curve between the start and time of the phase(s) shown. This approximation is the basis for defining simple tables that can be used to allocate the total effort and total schedule for a project. The next section describes these tables.

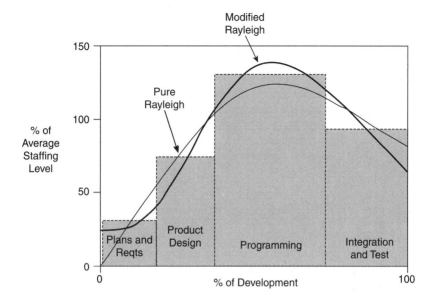

Figure 12-5 *Staffing level versus time*

12.4.4 Allocation Tables

Allocation tables are another way to distribute effort and time between the activities and phases of a project's life cycle model (and so provide estimated values for the corresponding WBS elements). Table 12-1 shows the distribution of effort by development phase. The phases belong to the COCOMO Waterfall Model, which is described in note N14, "The COCOMO Waterfall Model and Work Breakdown Structure." There are three sets of values, corresponding to the exponent of the model's nominal effort equation (Effort = A*Size^E). Essentially, higher values reflect increasing project size, product complexity, and process formality. The allocation percentages vary based on the total size of the product, indicated by the column headings. (The size is measured in thousands of source lines of code, KLOC, defined as logical statements. See Section 9.8.) As explained in Chapter 13, the COCOMO model estimates the "core" engineering effort after the product specification is complete (which allows the size to be estimated). The effort estimated by COCOMO excludes the effort for the Plans and Requirements phase. This is why the values for this phase are indented to the right in Table 12-1.

Table 12-1 *Effort Allocation by Phase*

Exponent	Phase	Size				
		Small 2 KSLOC	Intermediate 8 KSLOC	Medium 32 KSLOC	Large 128 KSLOC	Very Large 512 KSLOC
1.05	Plans and requirements (%)	6	6	6	6	
	Product design	16	16	16	16	
	Programming	68	65	62	59	
	Detailed design	26	25	24	23	
	Code and unit test	42	40	38	36	
	Integration and test	16	19	22	25	
1.12	Plans and requirements (%)	7	7	7	7	7
	Product design	17	17	17	17	17
	Programming	64	61	58	55	52
	Detailed design	27	26	25	24	23
	Code and unit test	37	35	33	31	29
	Integration and test	19	22	25	28	31
1.20	Plans and requirements (%)	8	8	8	8	8
	Product design	18	18	18	18	18
	Programming	60	57	54	51	48
	Detailed design	28	27	26	25	24
	Code and unit test	32	30	28	26	24
	Integration and test	22	25	28	31	34

Table 12-2 shows the distribution of schedule for the same phases and for the same three exponent values. The values also vary based on the size of the product being developed. The schedule associated with the Plans and Requirements phase is also not included in the schedule estimated by the model and so the corresponding values are also shown indented to the right. Note that the Programming phase is not subdivided into Detailed Design and Code and Unit Test in this table. If you need separate time values for each phase, the usual approach is to split the published value equally between these two phases. For example, for a size of 128 KSLOC and an exponent of 1.2, the programming value for Schedule is 36%. You would assign 18% to Detailed Design, and 18% to Code and Unit Test.

A simple example shows how to use such tables. Suppose that you have a large-size project (128 KSLOC) for which the estimated effort and schedule are 1,216 person-months and 24 calendar-months, respectively. To calculate the effort and duration for each phase using the tables, choose the set of values based on the model's exponent, and the product's size. Then multiply the estimated effort by the effort percentages, and multiply the estimated schedule by the schedule percentages. Table 12-3 shows the calculated values assuming that the exponent is 1.20. Note that the resources for the Plans and Requirements phase have to be added to the "core" engineering effort. Thus, in Table 12-3 the total effort adds up to 108% of the estimated value, and the total time adds up to 136% of the estimated time. (This is an example of why it is important to understand the definitions and assumptions used by a parametric model.) Compute the average staffing level for each phase by dividing the effort for that phase by the duration for that phase. (The units work because COCOMO uses units of person-months and calendar-months.)

Table 12-2 *Schedule Allocation by Phase*

Exponent	Phase	Size				
		Small 2 KSLOC	Intermediate 8 KSLOC	Medium 32 KSLOC	Large 128 KSLOC	Very Large 512 KSLOC
1.05	Plans and requirements (%)	10	11	12	13	
	Product design	19	19	19	19	
	Programming	63	59	55	51	
	Integration and test	18	22	26	30	
1.12	Plans and requirements (%)	16	18	20	22	24
	Product design	24	25	26	27	28
	Programming	56	52	48	44	40
	Integration and test	20	23	26	29	32
1.20	Plans and requirements (%)	24	28	32	36	40
	Product design	30	32	34	36	38
	Programming	48	44	40	36	32
	Integration and test	22	24	26	28	30

Table 12-3: *Allocation Example*

Phase	%	Effort	%	Time	FTE	Cum. Time	Norm. Cum
P&R	8	97	36	8.6	11.3	36	26
PD	18	219	36	8.6	25.5	72	53
DD	25	304	18	4.3	70.7	90	66
CUT	26	316	18	4.3	73.5	108	79
I&T	31	377	28	6.7	56.3	136	100
Totals	108	1,313	136	32.5		442	

Figure 12-6 plots the number of full-time equivalent staff for each phase. The table has reproduced the approximation to the modified Rayleigh curve illustrated in Figure 12-5, showing that tables are equivalent to distribution functions. You can easily implement such tables in spreadsheet models to automate the estimation process.

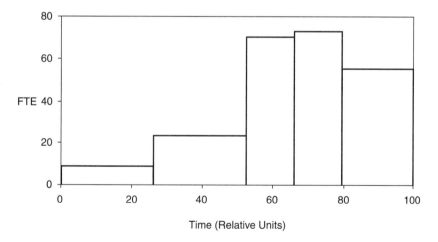

Figure 12-6 *FTE versus time*

Just as you allocate the total effort and total time to the development phases for a project life cycle, you can use tables to allocate the total effort to activities. This is sometimes desirable because the activities typically span the phase endpoints. (The next section gives an example.) You can use similar tables for other project life cycle models. Appendix A in [Boehm, 2000] has tables for the MBASE/RUP Model.

The cells in the allocation tables tie directly to tasks in the COCOMO work breakdown structure (described in note N14) so you can easily link the allocation tables to the metrics you collect. This supports future calibration and refinement of your estimating relations. In addition, you can easily adapt allocation tables to new life cycles. (See Section 12.4.6.)

Some organizations use a different approach. Specifically, they estimate the effort for each phase using a separate productivity value for each phase. This may seem odd at first because phases such as Requirements Analysis and Product Design produce no code. Thus, saying that there is a known software size during these phases is somewhat artificial. However, remember that you are just estimating the effort and schedule for the project at the start of the project based on your estimate of the total product size. Table 12-4 shows these two different approaches. The top half shows the calculation to estimate the bulk effort and then allocate it by activity. In the table, the estimate assumes a productivity of two source lines of code per person-hour and a size of 100 source lines of code. The bottom half of Table 12-4 shows the use of separate productivities to estimate the effort for each activity. The productivities shown will generate exactly the same estimated effort values that are shown in the top half of the figure. For example, for requirements analysis, dividing 100 SLOC by 20 SLOC per person-hour gives an effort of 5 person-hours.

Table 12-4 *Two Ways to Estimate Effort for Activities*

1. Estimate the bulk effort and then allocate by activity:
MM = Size/P where P = 2 SLOC/phr and S = 100 SLOC

MM_{RA}	= MM*0.10	= (50 phr)(0.10)	= 5.0 phr
MM_{PD}	= MM*0.25	= (50 phr)(0.25)	= 12.5 phr
MM_{PROG}	= MM*0.35	= (50 phr)(0.35)	= 17.5 phr
$MM_{I\&T}$	= MM*0.30	= (50 phr)(0.30)	= 15.0 phr

2. Use separate productivities to estimate each activity:

MM_{RA}	= Size/P_{RA}	where	P_{RA} = 20 SLOC/phr
MM_{PD}	= Size/P_{PD}	where	P_{PD} = 8 SLOC/phr
MM_{PROG}	= Size/P_{PROG}	where	P_{PROG} = 5.71 SLOC/phr
$MM_{I\&T}$	= Size/$P_{I\&T}$	where	$P_{I\&T}$ = 6.67 SLOC/phr

12.4.5 Activities Spanning Phases

On real projects, the various activities actually spread across to multiple phases. This is illustrated in Figure 12-7, which is based on Figure 1-1, page 1–3 in [NASA, 1990]. Some design starts before requirements analysis is completed, for example. In addition, discoveries that occur later in the detailed design phase or the coding phase can cause some revisions to the requirements.

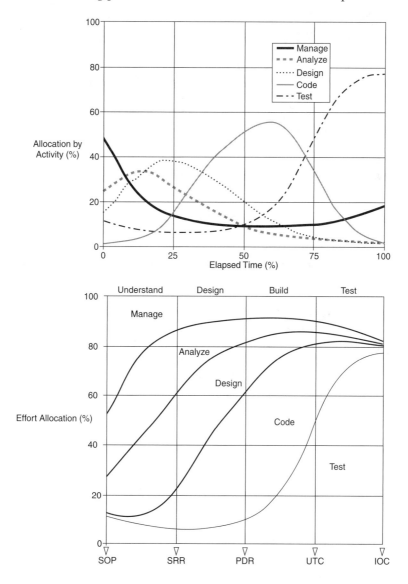

Figure 12-7 *Activities spread across phases*

Tables provide a way to handle such situations. Table 12-5 shows values from Table A.10 in [Boehm, 2000] for E = 1.12 and Size = 128 KSLOC. This table lists the activities down the left column. The remaining columns show the percentage of effort expended by the development team on that activity during each phase of the project. The row at the top of the table shows the overall phase percentages. These are the same amounts that were previously shown in Tables 12-1 and 12-2, the allocation of effort and schedule by phase. Table 12-5 breaks out the effort distribution to another level of detail. For example, during the Plans and Requirements phase, 45% of the effort is expended performing requirements analysis. During the Product Design phase, 12.5% of the effort is expended performing additional requirements analysis. During the Programming phase, 4% of the effort is expended on requirements analysis. The waterfall nature is illustrated by the large values on the diagonal in the table. Most of the requirements analysis activity is done during the Plans and Requirements phase. Most of the product design activity is done during the Product Design phase. Most of the programming is done during the Programming phase. The support activities shown in the bottom half of the table, of course, are more uniformly distributed across all phases of the project life cycle.

I have actually modified Barry Boehm's original table by splitting the effort for configuration management and quality assurance to reflect the modern view of quality assurance being an independent activity. You may wish to modify the percentages for configuration management and quality assurance for other reasons. For example, distributed development of systems often requires more effort for configuration management because there are multiple platforms located at multiple sites. For maintenance projects, configuration management usually requires a greater portion of the total engineering effort because there is a large amount of existing information (code, data, and documents) that must be placed under configuration control at the very start of the project. (A new development project starts with little information and the amount grows as the project progresses.) Based on data from our maintenance projects, configuration management consumes approximately 5% of total effort.

Table 12-5 *Allocation of Effort to Activities by Phase**

	Phases				Cumulative
Overall Phase Percentage	Plans & Requirements	Product Design	Programming	Integration and Test	
	7	17	55	28	
Activity Percentage					
Requirements Analysis	45.0	12.5	4.0	2.5	5.0
Product Design	17.5	41.0	8.0	5.0	13.0
Programming	5.5	13.5	56.5	39.0	44.5
Test Planning	4.0	6.0	5.5	3.0	5.0
Verification & validation	7.5	7.5	8.5	28.5	13.5
Project Office	12.5	10.0	6.0	7.0	7.0
CM	1.5	1.5	3.5	4.0	3.0
QA	1.5	1.0	3.0	4.0	3.0
Manuals	5.0	7.0	5.0	7.0	6.0
	100.0	100.0	100.0	100.0	100.0

*From Table A.10 in [Boehm, 2000] using E = 1.12 and Size = 128 KSLOC. Also see Tables 7-1, 7-2, and 7-3 in [Boehm, 1981].

Chapter 7, "Preparing to Estimate (Precursors of Estimation)," discussed how the product architecture defines the major components of the system to be developed. You can use the relative sizes of these components to further sub-divide the allocated resources for the process activities (analyze, design, code, and test) for individual product components. (Chapter 13 shows how to do this.)

12.4.6 Handling New Production Processes

Even though the allocation tables in the preceding section are based on a Water-fall Model, the basic concept is still sound. You can construct similar tables for other software development models. Just use different names for the phases and activities, and different percentages. (For agile methods, the table's values will be more uniform.)

As technology continues to evolve, teams will use new production processes. Chapter 10 described the modern processes used by Microsoft Corporation and Rational Corporation. Figure 12-8 illustrates the shift of effort to earlier activities in these newer processes. The top half depicts the "whale curve" of the tradi-tional Waterfall Model. The bottom half shows a hypothetical future life cycle where tools generate new code, and link it with existing library components. Table 12-6 shows the corresponding allocation table for effort and duration by phase. (You could also allocate effort by activity.) Such a table provides a simple structure to collect data and devise new estimating models for future processes.

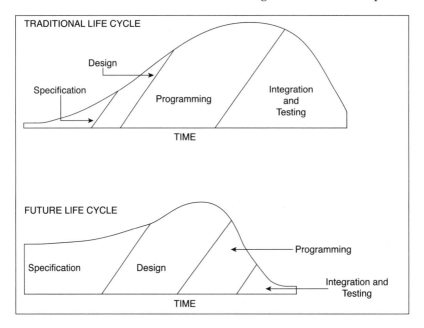

Figure 12-8 *Effort allocation for two project life cycles*

Table 12-6 *Allocation by Phase**

Phase	Effort	Duration
Specification		
Design		
Programming		
Integration And Testing		

*Assumes nonoverlapping phases.

12.5 Some Examples

This section shows how to use the allocation tables for effort and time to prepare simple estimates.

12.5.1 Constant Staffing

Many small projects uses constant staffing. The number of personnel is the same for every phase, i, giving the constraint:

$$\frac{EDEV_i}{TDEV_i} = \frac{Total\ Effort}{Total\ Duration} = \frac{EDEV_{TOTAL}}{TDEV_{TOTAL}}$$

and so

$$\frac{TDEV_i}{TDEV_{TOTAL}} = \frac{EDEV_i}{EDEV_{TOTAL}} = e_i$$

where the effort allocation table (Table 12-1 or its equivalent) gives the values for e_i. Given $TDEV_{total}$, you can then compute the $TDEV_i$, and so determine when the end of each phase should occur. (You do not use the schedule allocation table.)

As an example, assume that you have estimated that the project will take 36 person-months of engineering effort and 9 calendar-months. The average staffing level is 4 full-time equivalent people. Assume these effort allocation percentages for the phases of a Waterfall Model

Phase	PD	DD	CUT	I&T	TOTAL
%	30	30	15	25	100

These give

Quantity	PD	DD	CUT	I&T	TOTAL
EDEV$_i$	10.8	10.8	5.4	9.0	36.0
TDEV$_i$	2.7	2.7	1.4	2.2	9.0

Figure 12-9 shows a plot of these results, plus two refinements. First, I have added effort at the end for Formal Acceptance Test. Second, I have shown constant levels of support for project management, configuration management, and quality assurance. (These have been lumped together at the bottom to give one full-time equivalent person in the figure.) The key point is that support activities continue throughout the entire project.

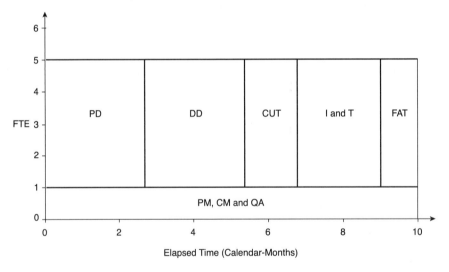

Figure 12-9 *Allocation for constant staff*

12.5.2 Stepwise Staff Increase

As a second example, suppose that you are using a Waterfall Model and you want to increase the staff on a project in two distinct steps. You decide to double the engineering staff just before product design review and again just before critical design review. Using Table 12-2, the schedule distribution of the phases for a size of 128 KSLOC and an exponent of 1.12 gives

Phase	COCOMO Schedule Allocation (%)	Renormalized (%)
RA + PD	22 + 27	40
DD	24	20
CUT + IT	20 + 29	40

where the right column shows renormalized values to 100%. Compute the initial staffing level, S, using the constraint on total effort:

$$EDEV = \left(\frac{EDEV}{TDUR}\right)[S * 0.4 * TDUR + 2 * S * 0.2 * TDUR + 4 * S * 0.4 * TDUR]$$

$$= EDEV * S * [0.4 + 0.4 + 1.6] \Rightarrow S = \frac{1}{2.4} = 0.42 \text{ persons}$$

12.5.3 Simple Budget with Labor Mix

For projects that are competitively bid, the average labor cost is often a concern. To reduce the average, firms use a mix of workers having different capabilities and different salaries. For example, engineering hours might be split like this:

Labor Grade	Allocation	Comments
Senior	20%	Heavier concentration at start of project
Mid-Level	40%	Relatively constant throughout project
Junior	40%	Does not start work until after PDR

The rationale for this particular assignment is that the senior experienced people are used at the beginning to carefully plan the project, design the product, and define the production process. They are assisted in this by the mid-level personnel. After the product design is well defined and the process is well established, the project brings on less-skilled (and cheaper) workers who can then elaborate the design using the architecture and programming guidelines that have been defined. This allows them to work with less supervision on simpler, well-defined tasks. Each organization has its own guidelines for assigning labor grades, which may vary based on project type, win strategy, or other factors. Consult your senior management or pricing staff for specific guidance. See the box "Reviewing Cost Estimates."

Reviewing Cost Estimates

In large procurements, the technical, management, and cost proposals are prepared as separate volumes. Often, different individuals write these volumes, although the proposal manager and other senior personnel are involved with parts of all three. Reviewers should look for consistency between the assumed levels of staff skill and experience used by the engineers to estimate the required labor, and the labor grades used to determine the labor costs in the cost proposal. If the engineers base their estimated effort on having senior personnel, this assumption cannot be met if the cost proposal has assigned a labor rate to the personnel that is so low that it will be impossible to hire individuals with the necessary skill and experience.

Figure 12-10 shows a sample project budget with four labor grades ("positions") calculated using a spreadsheet. The column on the right shows the costs computed for each person. The lower half of the figure shows the loading for fringe, overhead, administrative services, and fee to build up the total budget. (Chapter 15 describes rates and loading.) No risk reserve is included for this particular project. This is usually adequate for small projects. A refinement is to subdivide the effort for each person by phase and/or activity (analysis, design, etc.) using one of the methods described earlier. This decomposition produces values for specific time-phased tasks, and provides a basis to monitor expected progress.

Position	Task Hours by Accounting Period (4 Weeks)								Total	Rate ($/phr)	Cost
	1	2	3	4	5	6	7	8			
Project Manager	160	152	150	150	150	152	152	160	1226	$ 45.00	$ 55,170.00
Lead Developer	160	160	160	160	160	150	150	160	1260	$ 35.00	$ 44,100.00
Developers	40	80	160	300	360	360	300	250	1850	$ 25.00	$ 46,250.00
Testers	0	40	80	160	240	320	320	320	1480	$ 25.00	$ 37,000.00
				Costs							$182,520.00
Labor				$ 182,520.00							
		Applied To									
	Rate										
Fringe	40%	$ 182,520.00	$ 73,008.00								
Overhead	50%	$ 182,520.00	$ 91,260.00								
Subtotal			$ 164,268.00								
Admin. Services	5%	$ 164,268.00	$ 8,213.40								
Subtotal			$ 172,481.40								
Fee	10%	$ 172,481.40	$ 17,248.14								
Total Budget			$ 189,729.54								

Figure 12-10 *Sample project budget*

12.6 Recommended Reading

Pankaj Jalote gives five steps for top-down estimation in Section 4.2.2 of [Jalote, 2002]:

1. Estimate the total size.
2. Determine the productivity value.
3. Compute effort as size divided by productivity.
4. Distribute the effort to phases.
5. Refine the estimates to account for project-specific factors.

He also provides an example where the size is measured in use case points.

12.7 Summary

In top-down estimation, you first estimate the total effort and time for the entire project, and then allocate these values to phases and activities. (This is the inverse of bottom-up estimation, which divides the work into pieces, and then estimates each piece separately.) The first part of this chapter explained how size, effort, and time are related, and described simple ways to estimate the effects of overtime on project effort and time.

Top-down estimation thus requires estimates of the total size (amount of product to be developed), and of the productivity (using historical data and adjusting for project-specific factors). Typically, the estimated effort equals size divided by productivity, defined in some compatible set of units. This is simple but neglects the "diseconomy of scale," the decrease in productivity as the number of staff working on a project increase. Parametric models account for such effects, and also quantitatively represent the effects of various cost drivers on the average productivity. Chapter 13 describes parametric models. You can use such models to obtain better estimates for the total effort and schedule for a software project. (Chapter 25, "Determining Product Quality," describes parametric models for estimating product quality.)

The latter half of this chapter described how to allocate the total estimated effort and time to project phases and activities. Distribution functions are one option, but tables provide more flexibility. (Most computerized parametric models use tables.) Tables are easy to use and update, and are usually accurate enough for most estimates. Top-down estimation is useful for initial estimates of project scope, and also provides a way to check estimates made using other techniques. You can also use top-down estimation to estimate a subset of a project's WBS tasks. Figure 12-11 summarizes the Top-Down Method. The box "Comparing the Top-Down and Bottom-Up Methods" contrasts the two methods.

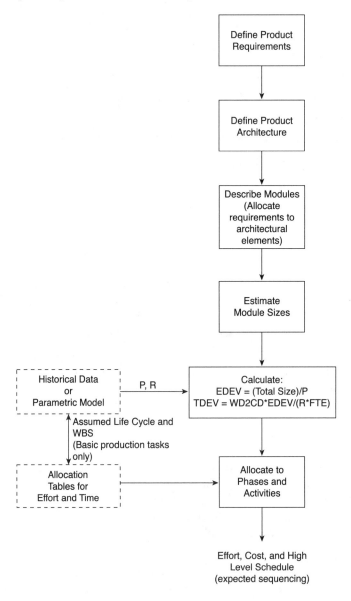

Figure 12-11 *The Top-Down Method*

Comparing the Top-Down and Bottom-Up Methods

The Top-Down Method estimates the total effort and total time for a project, and then uses tables to allocate these totals to individual activities and phases of the project life cycle. These activities only represent a subset of all the project's tasks. You must estimate any additional tasks separately! Parametric models, described in the next chapter, are one way to implement the Top-Down Method.

In contrast, the Bottom-Up Method first identifies all tasks needed to accomplish the project based on the product's architecture, the chosen production process (project life cycle), customer constraints, and perceived risks. (Often, planners choose the project life cycle based on customer constraints and risks.) Then engineers and estimators estimate the resources required to perform each task. These resources include labor, materials, and consumables. Summing the estimates for each task provides the totals for the entire project. Planners assign people ("resources") to each task and calculate its duration. Linking the tasks in a precedence network reveals the critical path, which determines the project's duration.

You often use both methods to estimate different portions of a particular project. The Top-Down Method is useful to obtain initial estimates for the major portion of the project and also provides a way to check estimates made using other techniques. The Bottom-Up Method provides a more detailed estimate, but consumes more time and effort than the Top-Down Method. The Bottom-Up Method can provide arbitrary levels of detail, and it addresses all of the tasks needed to construct a detailed project schedule.

Pankaj Jalote describes the steps of each method in Section 4.2 of [Jalote, 2002].

Chapter 13

Parametric Models

This chapter describes the essential features of parametric models. It provides examples that show their utility for handling constraints and analyzing trade-offs. It identifies popular models. It briefly discusses calibration. (Chapter 27, "Ranking and Selecting Items," provides a deeper discussion.) It concludes with advice on how to obtain good values for the input parameter from people who are not expert estimators.

13.1 Types of Parametric Models

Parametric models use algorithms and user-specified values for various parameters to produce estimates of quantities. An algorithm is a set of steps to compute some value. These steps often use mathematical functions, values selected or interpolated from values in tables, and a set of specific rules for combining the resulting numeric values.

There are three types of parametric models. *Theoretical models* are based on theories of how humans perform the programming process and postulated mathematical laws that govern this process. (Sometimes the theories are simply heuristics that seem plausible to the researcher.) *Statistical models* use functions (linear or nonlinear) derived from regression fits to historical data collected from many projects. (Statistical techniques such as a cluster analysis can be used to choose the "best" functional form to fit a particular set of data.) Regression models received heavy emphasis during the 1970s and are still useful today. *Composite models* combine both theory and regression fits for certain coefficients. Most models in use today are composite models. The composite approach is necessary because no one has enough historical project data to perform a regression fit to a model with dozens of parameters.

13.2 Core Effort and Schedule

Figure 13-1 shows the typical structure of a parametric model that estimates development effort and time. Inputs include the estimated size of the product and various parameters that represent characteristics of the product, the platform, the process, the personnel, and the overall project. John Gaffney calls these "holistic models" because they use the estimated size of the product to estimate the development effort and schedule as a whole without considering in detail the individual activities that compose the development process [Gaffney, 1995, p. 145]. Each model builder chooses a set of parameters that he or she thinks significantly influence the estimated quantity and chooses the form of the model. (There are constraints on the functional form. See the box "Acceptable Functions.") The model itself consists of various equations and tables. For estimating development effort, the model in effect computes an "average productivity" based on various characteristics (product, process, personnel, and project), and then computes development effort as size divided by productivity. Development time is usually computed as some function of the development effort, possibly adjusted by additional factors such as the amount of schedule compression. (For new development, the total development time for large projects typically scales as the cube root of the total effort. For small rapid application development projects, the total development time scales as the square root of the effort. For very small, constant staffing projects, the total time is proportional to the effort.)

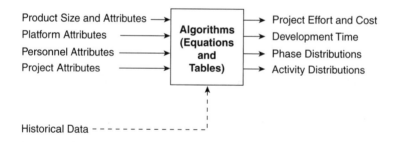

Note: Attributes also include any constraints on the item.

Figure 13-1 *Elements of a typical parametric model*

Acceptable Functions

Horst Zuse describes constraints on the acceptable form for any prediction model in his comprehensive book [Zuse, 1997]. His Section 8.9 presents five theorems for prediction models. (These were previously presented by Peter Bollmann-Sdorra and Horst Zuse in [Bollmann, 1993].) These theorems deal with the need for a ratio scale for the input and output measures, the desire to have a strictly monotonic function, and other desired properties. The final result of these theorems is that the functional form

$$V(p) = A*S(p)^B$$

with A > 0 and B > 0 is the only possible prediction model if the external variable, V, and the size measure, S, are to be ratio scales.[1] (The argument p designates the particular program being estimated.) Nearly all software estimation models use functions of this type. (Zuse examines function points in his Section 9.6. He examines the COnstructive COst MOdel, COCOMO, in his Section 9.7, with additional comments in Section 8.8.)

The output of the model consists of the project effort (cost), project time (schedule), and the distribution of the effort and schedule by phase and by activity. The model's equations estimate the total development effort and time for the "core" activities. Most parametric models uses tables to allocate the core development effort and time to phases, and to activities within a phase. Similarly, values for other phases are usually computed as percentages of the core values, although some models use separate functions.

Software size is the primary independent variable affecting software development effort. Many parametric estimating models for software development effort measure size in source lines of code (logical or physical, depending on the model). Other parametric models measure size in function points or some other proxy. Some parametric models use both SLOC and function points, using backfire values to convert to a common measure.

---

[1] Appendix B, "Measurement Theory and Statistics," describes the five measurement scales: nominal, ordinal, interval, ratio, and absolute. A ratio scale preserves certain relations between entities (ordering, relative sizes of the intervals between them), has a zero value, and has a linear scale of units. Applying the usual arithmetic operations to the measured values yields the expected results. (One example is scaling by a multiplicative constant.) These properties make ratio scale measurements useful for estimation.

13.3 A Simple Parametric Model

To illustrate the characteristics and use of parametric models, consider the following simple estimation model for the total development effort and development time:

Effort = $A*Size^B$ = $2.94*Size^{1.1}$

Time = $C*Effort^D$ = $3.67*Effort^{0.32}$

where Effort is in person-months, Size is measured in KSLOC, and Time is in calendar-months. (The size measure, SLOC, depends on how the model is defined and calibrated. The particular choice is irrelevant for the following examples.) For these equations to be meaningful, however, additional definitions are needed. The Time value represents the calendar time between two specific milestones, which correspond to the start and end of the "core development phases" addressed by the model. (Loosely, these are the start and end of the project.) The Effort value includes the effort for all direct charge activities performed between the two specific milestones. This is the "core effort" for the project. (The core is defined by the particular phases and activities specified.) Similarly, Time is the "core time." The values of the coefficients A, B, C, and D are determined by calibration. For this model, assume that one person-month equals 152 person-hours.

Suppose that the total size of the product to be developed is 25 KSLOC. The two equations give

Effort = $2.94*(25)^{1.1}$ = 101.4 PM = 15,400 phr

Time = $3.67*(101.4)^{0.32}$ = 16.1 CM

The average staff level is the number of full-time equivalent people (FTE) working on the project:

FTE = Effort/Time = 101.4/16.1 = 6.3 (full-time) people

This equation works out nicely because of the choice of units for Effort and Time. One person-month is one person working for one calendar-month. If Effort were measured in person-hours, however, then you would have to adjust for the average individual effort delivery rate. The general equation is

$$FTE = \frac{\text{Total Effort}}{\text{(Effort delivered per person per time)} * \text{Time}}$$

and the units cancel correctly:

phr/([phr/(person*CM)]*CM) = persons

The average productivity is

Productivity = 25 KSLOC/15,400 phr = 1.62 SLOC/phr

This simple model illustrates many features of more sophisticated parametric models. The first thing to note is that the exponent, B, in the effort equation is greater than one. This means that the average productivity of the staff decreases for larger projects. This is called the diseconomy of scale. To see this, use the same equations to calculate the average productivity for a project that develops 250 KSLOC of software:

Effort = $2.94*(250)^{1.1}$ = 1,277 PM = 194,100 phr

Time = $3.67*(1277^{0.32})$ = 36.2 CM

FTE = 1277/36.2 = 35.3 people

Productivity = 250,000/(1277*152) = 1.29 SLOC/phr

The productivity is approximately 20% less. The diseconomy of scale is usually attributed to the increased overhead for communication among the people working on the project. If every person on the project must communicate with every other person on the project, the number of potential communication paths for a project with N people is $N*(N-1)/2$. This increases proportionally to N squared. Many authors discuss this effect. For example, see Sections 11.5 and 11.6 in [Boehm, 1981].

It is crucial to understand exactly which life cycle phases and activities are included in the estimated core development effort and time. Otherwise, the numbers produced by a parametric estimation model are meaningless. Figure 13-2 illustrates the situation. The central area of the figure enclosed with heavy lines depicts the usual set of core activities that are performed between the software requirements review (SRR)[2] and the formal acceptance test (FAT) milestones. The core activities include the engineering activities of product design, programming (detailed design, coding, and unit testing), integration, and product testing. The core activities also include the supporting activities of configuration management, quality assurance, and project management. (The figure also shows other milestones described in Section 10.1.)

Figure 13-2 also shows activities and phases that are excluded from the core activities. Project planning and requirements definition (P&R) provide the firm product specification needed to estimate the product's size. Thus, the modelers assume that core activities begin after the Requirements Definition phase has been completed. Trade studies and prototyping occur early in the project to

---

[2] Many U.S. government documents refer to the *software* requirements review (SRR) milestone as the software *specification* review (SSR) and use SRR to mean *system* requirements review, which this figure shows as the system specification review, SSR.

support requirements analysis and product design decisions. Independent validation and verification of the work may begin early and continue until product acceptance. Deployment occurs after the product is fully tested.

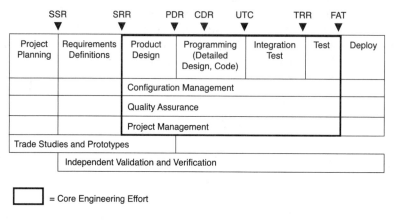

Figure 13-2 *Scope of a typical parametric model*

13.4 Adding Missing Phases and Activities

You can include additional effort and time for the missing activities in several ways. One approach is to simply add increments to the core effort and time. You can express these increments as absolute amounts or as percentages of the core effort and time. You determine the amounts or percentages from historical data or from an ancillary parametric model that considers the characteristics of the product, process, and project. (The ancillary model might use a table indexed by the characteristics, or some mathematical function of the characteristics.)

As an example, suppose that you wish to compute the additional effort and time needed to cover a Plans and Requirements Analysis (P&R) phase at the start of the project, and a Hardware and Software Integration and Testing (HW/SW IT) phase that follows the completion of software acceptance testing. Assume that you have determined the following percentage values from your organization's historical data:

Phase	Effort Added	Time Added
P&R	8%	15%
HW/SW IT	15%	20%

Applying these percentages to the values for the 25 KSLOC example described earlier, compute the total effort and schedule as follows:

Source	Effort (PM)	Time (CM)
Core value	101.4	16.1
P&R	8.1	2.4
HW/SW IT	15.2	3.2
Totals	124.7	21.7

Note that this model does not use the increased effort in the schedule equation because the additional activities are performed outside of the core region.

You can use these results to estimate the approximate cost for the project. Suppose that your organization's loaded labor cost is $10K/PM. The total estimated cost is then approximately $1.25M. The cost per line is approximately $50/SLOC (= $1,247 K/25 KSLOC). The average productivity is 1.32 SLOC/phr (= 25,000/[124.7*152]). The productivity for the earlier example with the same size (25 KSLOC) was 1.62 SLOC/phr. The apparent productivity has decreased by 18% (= (1.32 – 1.62)/1.62). This is another example of how the productivity value depends on which phases and activities are included in the effort.

There are other ways to estimate the effort and schedule associated with additional phases and activities. The SLIM and PRICE S Models use separate functions to estimate the quantities for different phases. If you do not have a model's tables or functions to calculate the increments, you can define WBS tasks for the additional activities, and then use the Linear Method or Expert Judgment to estimate the effort. You can calculate the required time to perform each activity by assuming a constant staffing level or some other staffing model. You can also construct a task precedence network to develop a more complete picture of the overall project.

13.5 Adjusting for Different Characteristics

Various factors influence the productivity of a project team. Many parametric models use the following approach. The model first estimates the nominal effort for the project using the total size. The nominal effort is just the core effort described earlier. The model then adjusts the nominal effort to account for productivity increases and decreases due to various factors.

Table 13-1 shows factors typically considered by parametric software cost estimation models. The models' parameters represent characteristics of the software product, target computer platform, development process and tools, personnel, and the overall project. Most models have over two dozen parameters.

Table 13-1 *Productivity Factors Found in Parametric Models*

Product
• Quality of the requirements (completeness, consistency, stability)
• Capability and stability of target computer platform
• Quality of existing code
• Maturity of COTS components and products used
• Sensitive data or algorithms (classified, proprietary, personal privacy)
• Safety or mission-critical functions (robust design, failsafe logic)
Process
• Restrictions on handling sensitive information (security classification, privacy laws)
• The level of formality (required documents and reviews)
• The types of testing required
• The capability and maturity of the development platform and tools
• Differences between the development and target platforms
• The process maturity level
Project
• Schedule pressure
• Incremental funding
• Quality of the staff (knowledge and skills)
• Staff experience (problem domain, technology, methods, and tools)
• The number and stability of organizations involved (customer, developer, supplier)
• The location and quality of physical facilities
• Experience working as a team

Parametric models typically quantify these factors using a Likert scale. (See the box "Likert Scales.") The models convert these qualitative judgments into numeric values that multiply the "nominal" development effort or time. The following paragraphs give an example of a Likert scale. The adjusted development effort is the product of the nominal effort and all of the effort multipliers:

$$\text{Adjusted Effort} = \text{Nominal Effort} * \prod_{i=1}^{N} \text{EM}_i$$

where EM_i denotes the effort multiplier for the ith cost driver. The adjusted effort is then used in the schedule equation:

$$\text{Time} = C * (\text{Adjusted Effort})^D$$

You adjust time similarly to account for schedule compression or expansion. (Note, however, that the time adjustments and the effort adjustments are coupled.)

Likert Scales

Rensis Likert defined a subjective (ordinal) scale for use in psychology [Likert, 1932]. Many parametric estimation models use Likert scales to measure qualitative characteristics. You enumerate a set of ranked levels such as very low, low, nominal, high, and very high, and extra high (VL, LO, NM, HI, VH, and EH) and define the characteristics of each value. For example, the COnstructive COst MOdel (COCOMO) rates "module complexity" based on the amount of computation, data transfer, and the number of logical decisions. Then it uses a lookup table to map the rating to an effort multiplier.

The two keys to using a Likert scale are as follows:

1. Provide precise, objective definitions of each rating. (Example: Assign a LO rating if years of experience are ≥ 3 years and < 6 years.)

2. Calibrate the corresponding numeric values using historical data. (This validates the mapping from the ordinal scale to the ratio scale.)

Fenton and Pfleeger identify six subjective rating schemes useful for software properties in Figure 2.2 of [Fenton, 1997]. Most of these are variations of a Likert scale using ratings of preference, importance, and frequency of occurrence. Forced ranking presents a set of n alternatives and asks the person to order them from best (1) to worst (n). (See the discussion in Chapter 27.) Their example of the ordinal scale asks how often software fails (hourly, daily, weekly, etc.). Thus, although the ratings appear Likert-like, they really represent an interval scale. Their comparative scale is similar to a qualitative ratio scale. The person compares two alternatives, indicating how much better or worse alternative 1 is than alternative 2.

The models assign a numeric value to a qualitative rating of the characteristic, and then use the value to calculate ratio scale quantities. (You could also map to an interval scale, but then you can only use addition and subtraction operations.)

The convention used in the COnstructive COst MOdel is that the nominal rating of a parameter ("cost driver") always has a multiplier value of 1.0. The nominal effort represents a case where all of the parameters have "average" values. Each effort multiplier adjusts the nominal value up or down. The amount is based on the estimator's rating of that particular parameter. (This ability to scale hinges on having a ratio scale.)

For example, to quantify the impact of staff turnover, the COCOMO II.2000 model uses the rating scale for "personnel continuity" shown in Table 13-2. The qualitative ratings range from very low (VL) to very high (VH). The second line in the table shows the criteria used to determine which rating to select. For example, if the team's average turnover rate is 24%/calendar-year, then the estimator would rate personnel continuity (PCON) as low (LO). The model uses this rating to select the corresponding numeric value from the values shown in the third line. For a low rating this value is 1.12, and it will increase the development effort by 12%. For the project estimated earlier (with size 25 KSLOC), if personnel continuity is low, the core effort will increase to 113.6 person-months (= 1.12*101.4). The corresponding development time will be 16.7 CM, approximately 3.7% longer than the 16.1 CM computed earlier.

Table 13-2 *A Simple Likert Rating Scale for Personnel Continuity*

Rating	VL	LO	NM	HI	VH
Turnover rate (%/year)	48	24	12	6	3
Effort multiplier	1.29	1.12	1.00	0.90	0.81

Similar rating schemes are used for other cost drivers. Not all rating scales are so simple, however. Some models allow users to refine the adjustments for a particular cost driver by interpolating between adjacent values in the rating table.

The adjustments described here apply multipliers to the total effort. This is called *macroestimation*. Note N47, "Macroestimation with COCOMO II," describes the COCOMO II Post-Architecture macroestimation model, and provides a complete end-to-end example showing how to use it. (Chapter 3 in [Boehm, 2000] also has several examples.) Note N14, "The COCOMO Waterfall Model and Work Breakdown Structure," precisely defines the phases and activities that are included in the estimated development effort and time. The COCOMO WBS is notable for its completeness, and it provides a good example of the detail needed to define work packages.

Because the parts of a software product have different characteristics, however, they should have different cost driver ratings. A technique called *microestimation* allows an estimator to assign different multiplier values to various parts of the product. Note N48, "Microestimation with COCOMO II," describes a complete microestimation model based on the COCOMO II Post-Architecture model. Note N49, "Designing the CLEF2PA Spreadsheet," explains how to implement the microestimation model.

Once you calculate the adjusted development effort and time using either macroestimation or microestimation, you allocate these totals to phases and activities of the model's assumed project life cycle. (Section 13.4 described allocation tables used for top-down estimation. The COCOMO II Model uses these same tables.) Similarly, when estimating the effort and schedule for additional phases and activities using percentages, you apply the percentages to the adjusted effort and schedule, not to the nominal effort and schedule.

13.6 Handling Size, Cost, and Schedule Constraints

You can use parametric models to estimate situations involving constraints on and trade-offs between size, effort, cost, and schedule (development time). The following subsections provide examples. To keep the calculations uncomplicated, the examples use the simple parametric model described previously. In practice, you can use any parametric model.

The simple parametric model represents requirements-driven development. Developers expend whatever amounts of effort and time are necessary to produce a product that meets a fixed set of requirements. (In a parametric model, the set of requirements is represented by the size of the product.)

Project planners and estimators often face multiple conflicting goals for product capability (functions and performance), project cost, project schedule, and sometimes product quality. (Table 7-5 in Section 7.7 illustrates the relative priorities of these four goals for different types of project.) Parametric models provide a very convenient and rapid way to quickly assess the impact of such conflicting goals. To illustrate this, use the same simple model defined earlier:

Effort = $A*S^B$ = 2.94*Size$^{1.1}$

Time = $C*Effort^D$ = 3.67*Effort$^{0.32}$

Loaded labor cost = $10K/PM

1 PM = 152 phr

Example 1: Given $120,000 for labor (loaded), how much software can you produce? First, calculate the available effort, and then invert the parametric model to estimate the size of the software:

Effort = $120K/($10K/PM) = 12 PM

Size = $(Effort/A)^{(1/B)}$ = $(4.08)^{0.909}$ = 3.6 KSLOC

This shows that you can produce about 3.6 KSLOC for $120,000. You can thus run parametric models "in reverse" to help the engineers design to cost. (This is also referred to as "cost as an independent variable" or CAIV, pronounced "cave.")

You can use this estimated size for a rough feasibility check. For example, suppose that the estimated size of the application is roughly 5.3 KSLOC. This means that the developers probably cannot build the system for $120,000. The team should either try to reduce the functionality (size), or obtain more money, or both.

Example 2: Given 12 calendar-months, how much money can the team productively spend, and how much software can they can produce? To answer this question, first invert the time (schedule) equation so you can compute the effort. Then apply the loaded labor rate to convert this to dollars. Also calculate the size in the same way as Example 1. Here are the calculations:

Effort = $(Time/C)^{(1/D)}$ = $(12/3.67)^{(1/0.32)}$ = $(3.26)^{3.12}$ = 40.4 PM

Loaded labor cost = (40.4 PM)*($10K/PM) = $405K

Size = $(Effort/A)^{(1/B)}$ = $(40.5/2.94)^{0.909}$ = 10.9 KSLOC

FTE = Effort/Time = 40.4/12 = 3.4 people

The model predicts that the developers can produce approximately 11 KSLOC in 12 calendar-months for a cost of approximately $400,000.

The preceding example estimated only the total labor cost. Any project must also include costs for materials, travel, and consumables. It must also earn a certain amount of profit. The next example shows how to handle this case.

Example 3: Start with the target price, and successively deduct the profit and the additional costs, finally obtaining the amount of money available for direct labor. Assume some values as follows:

Total price	$400K
Less 10% profit	–$40K
Less materials	–$18K
Less travel	–$5K
Less travel and consumables	–$5K
Available for development	$332K

Using $10K/PM gives 33.2 PM of available effort. Using the same equations as Example 1 gives

$$\text{Size} = (\text{Effort}/A)^{(1/B)} = (33.2/2.92)^{0.909} = 9.1 \text{ KSLOC}$$

Using this value in the other equations gives a schedule of 11.3 CM and an average staff of 2.9 people. The size is less than the 11 KSLOC in Example 2 because not all of the $400K will be spent on labor.

13.7 Evaluating a Hardware/Software Trade

System designers and estimators often have the option of buying more capable hardware to reduce the development effort. The hardware can be the target platform, or can be the software engineering environment (SEE) or the software test environment (STE). You can use a parametric model to evaluate such trades.

Suppose that you want to decide if you should invest in integrated computer-aided software engineering (ICASE) tools. You need to compute the development costs with and without the productivity enhancing tools, and factor in the costs of tools and training. To illustrate this, use the example from Section 13.3 as the baseline case. Then adjust the nominal value to account for development with and without tools as follows.

First, document your estimating assumptions. Assume that the tools cost $5,000 per seat. This price includes five days of training by the vendor in your facility. The estimate shows that the project will require approximately six full-time people so the tools will cost $30,000 if each developer receives a tool. The development staff must also expend the 30 person-days (= 6*5) or approximately 1.5 person-months of labor to attend the vendor training. (There are no travel costs for the students because training takes place in your facility. Assuming that the vendor will pay for the travel costs of the instructor.) For this example, ignore the costs for tool installation and any initial loss of staff productivity (learning curve).

To account for the change in productivity caused by using a tool, use the COCOMO II cost driver TOOL, which has the rating scale shown in Table 13-3. Assume that the project has only primitive tools (TOOL is rated very low) gives an adjusted effort of

Effort (poor tools) = (101.4)*(1.17) = 118.6 PM

Assuming instead that the new ICASE tools are strong, mature, and moderately integrated (TOOL is rated high), giving an adjusted effort of

Effort (good tools) = (101.4)*(0.90) = 91.3 PM

The use of the ICASE tools reduces the development effort by 27.3 PM.

Table 13-3 *COCOMO II Tool Cost Driver**

TOOL Descriptors	*Edit, code, debug*	*Simple, front-end, back-end CASE, little integration*	*Basic life-cycle tools, moderately integrated*	*Strong, mature life cycle tools, moderately integrated*	*Strong, mature, proactive life cycle tools, well integrated with processes, methods, reuse*
Rating Levels	Very Low	Low	Nominal	High	Very High
Effort Multipliers	1.17	1.09	1.00	0.90	0.78

*Based on Table 2.32, Page 50, in [Boehm, 2000]. Used with permission.

Table 13-4 compares the two options, assuming a loaded labor cost of $10K/PM. The total estimated cost without the ICASE tools is $1,186K. The total cost with the tools is $958K. This cost includes $913K for development labor, $30K to purchase the tools, and $15K for the staff to take the tool training. The net savings is $228K. The total investment is $45K (= $30K + $15K). The return on investment (ROI) is approximately 5. These numbers show that purchasing the tools is a good investment. For more examples of using estimates to prepare a business case, see [Reifer, 2002a].

Table 13-4 *Comparison of Project Costs With and Without ICASE Tools*

Quantity	No Tool	With Tool
Effort (PM)	118.6	91.3
Labor costs ($K)*	1,186	913
Tool costs	0	30
Staff training costs	0	15
Total costs	1,186	958

*Using $10K/PM.

13.8 Calibrating Parametric Models

You can improve the prediction accuracy of parametric models by determining values of model coefficients using historical data, a process called "calibration." This improvement extends to estimates made throughout the course of a project, as illustrated in Figure 13-3.

Every parametric model needs to be calibrated to your particular development environment. The typical accuracy of parametric cost estimation models is ± 20% of the actual effort 70% of the time. See the box "Measuring Estimation Accuracy." The measured accuracy is based on data from completed projects so the size is known exactly. Estimates for future projects will have larger errors because of errors in the estimated size. (You can use the law of propagation of errors, described in note N06, "Propagation of Errors," to estimate the expected accuracy.)

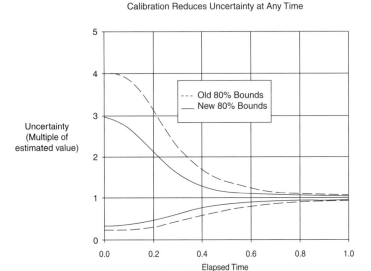

Figure 13-3 *Calibration improves estimation accuracy*

Measuring Estimation Accuracy

To measure the accuracy of an estimation model you need a set of paired values. Each pair consists of the estimated value, E, and the actual (true) value, A. The residual error, R, equals the difference between the two values:

$$R = A - E$$

An error of a particular size is more serious for a small quantity than for a large quantity. In addition, residuals can be positive and negative, so simply adding them may cancel out large errors, giving a false indication of accuracy. To overcome these problems, estimators use the magnitude of the relative error, MRE:

$$MRE_i = \left| \frac{A_i - E_i}{A_i} \right|$$

where i denotes the particular data pair. The mean magnitude of the relative error, MMRE is defined as

$$MMRE = \frac{1}{n} \sum_{i=1}^{n} MRE_1$$

where n is the number of samples.

Conte, Dunsmore, and Shen first defined the MMRE measure [Conte, 1986]. They also used MRE to define another measure called the prediction level, PRED.[3] For a set of n estimates, let k denote the number of estimates for which MRE is less than or equal to some value q. Define:

PRED(q) = k/n

For example, PRED(0.25) = 0.75 means that the model estimated the quantity within ±25% of actuals 75% of the time. Conte, Dunsmore, and Shen consider a "good" estimating model to have MMRE ≤ 0.25 and PRED(0.25) ≥ 0.75.

Appendix C, "Measures of Estimation Accuracy," describes some accuracy measures, including the estimation quality factor, which measures estimation accuracy over time.

13.8.1 Model Validation and Calibration

Defining and validating a general-purpose estimation model is a complex and difficult process. Model developers use historical data obtained from completed projects to determine the functional form of a model and the values of its coefficients. The data used should represent a range of projects performed by many organizations so that the model represents "industry average" behavior. This requires large amounts of consistent, accurate historical data.

The users of a particular model assume that it represents realistic behavior. They accept the basic form of the underlying model but may calibrate some of the model's coefficients using local data to increase estimation accuracy for their organization. There are two possible reasons for doing this. First, the original calibration data may not accurately represent current industry norms. Second, the organization may want to adjust for its local definitions of the following:

- Process activities, phases, and milestones
- Measures for software size, development effort, and time
- Person-hours per person-month
- Average availability
- Allocations of effort and schedule to project phases and activities

---

[3] They also defined three other measures: the coefficient of multiple determination (R2), the mean squared error (MSE), and the relative root mean squared error (RMS). The latter two are defined for regression models only. Most studies of estimation accuracy only use MMRE and PRED.

Concerning local calibration, Dan Ligett, the developer of the COSTAR tool, says, "As long as you're consistently wrong, you're not wrong!" Martin Shepperd observes that calibration makes the implicit assumption that the organization uses a repeatable development process [Shepperd, 1995]. (This is Level 2 in the SEI's staged CMMI model.)

Table 13-5 lists the steps in the calibration process. These steps show that measurement and estimation are closely intertwined. Standard measures provide reliable data to calibrate the estimation model. The data analysis and fitting process identifies new measures. In addition, Step 8 may also alter the form of the model itself (e.g., by revising, removing, and adding parameters).

In practice, you cannot perform the steps in the order shown. Otherwise, months or years will elapse before you have any data to analyze. To get started, you have to use whatever data you can get for initial calibration. (This is why measurement and analysis is a Level 2 process area in the staged CMMI model.) Analysis of this data typically reveals ways to improve the definitions of the measures and the collection process, leading to changes. The development process may also be changed, which alters the performance of the process. (Chapter 26, "Measuring and Estimating Process Performance," describes measures of process stability and control.) This causes the calibration process to begin anew. You should perform calibration periodically in any case.

Table 13-5 *Steps in the Calibration Process*

1. Choose the model to be calibrated (the functional form)
2. Define standardized measures
3. Buy or build tools to count, collect, and report data
4. Set up your cost accounting system to capture effort data
5. Train the staff to collect accurate data
6. Collect data from projects that are similar to future projects
7. Validate the collected data for correctness and consistency
8. Use the validated data to fit the model's coefficients
9. Evaluate the validity and accuracy of the resulting calibrated model
10. Document the data sources, methods, results, and supporting rationale
11. Revise and update data collection procedures as needed

13.8.2 Tips for Performing Calibration

To calibrate, you need consistent and correct data. For cost models, you need data from using similar processes, and that use the same measurement definitions. Suppose that you receive the data for five projects shown in Table 13-6. The project names suggest that there is a mixture of project types. The wide variation in their apparent productivity (from 100 to 2,500 SLOC/PM) confirms this. In addition, it is unclear if the projects use the same units of measure. (Recall the definition of productivity from Chapter 2, "Planning a Warehouse Inventory System.") All projects must use the same definitions.[4]

Table 13-6 *Sample Set of Calibration Data*

Project Name	Total Effort (PM)	Delivered Code (KSLOC)	Apparent Productivity (SLOC/PM)
F-15 Trainer	1,000	150	105
F4-J Trainer	1,200	200	167
Inventory Control System	60	60	1,000
Personnel Records System	1,000	75	57
Yacht Hull Model	4	10	2500

Table 13-7 summarizes the questions you should ask about the data for each project in your sample. You also need the answers so you can relate the measured values to the parametric model's units of measure and assumptions.

Table 13-7 *Key Questions for Productivity Data*

What items are being counted? (new reused, prototypes, tooling, breakage)
What are the units of size? (blank lines, comments, physical or logical lines)
What activities and phases are covered? (support activities? initial planning?)
How formal is the process? (reviews, documentation)
How skilled is the staff?
How many person-hours per person-month? (days off, paid overtime, uncompensated overtime)

---

[4] Similar requirements apply to data used to calibrate any type of parametric model.

Even if you have consistent data, there are other potential calibration problems caused by the following:

- Incorrect data
- Outliers
- Inadequate amount of data
- Possible correlation of the data values in a given set
- Inadequate coverage of the entire dynamic range

The following paragraphs suggest ways to avoid these problems.

Incorrect values may be hard to detect. For example, someone might have recorded transposed digits, writing 68 when they meant to write 86. Having another person manually verify or re-enter data values will detect some incorrect data. Automated data collection tools can make some checks when data is entered. For example, a person's weekly effort (in person-hours) must be in the interval [0, 130]. Similarly, labor hours reported on a holiday are suspect.

Some projects experience anomalous conditions and so produce values ("outliers") that differ greatly from those of "normal" projects. Extreme outliers may exert excessive influence on the computed coefficients. To identify and remove outliers, you can compute the sample mean, μ, and standard deviation, σ, and then discard all points lying outside the interval $[\mu - 2*\sigma, \mu + 2*\sigma\,]$. The Central Limit Theorem, mentioned in Section 5.5, says that the errors are normally distributed, so choosing 2σ limits only discards about 5% of the population.[5] Discarding outliers decreases the sample size however. Small sample sizes make the values of fitted coefficients less reliable. One approach is to use increasingly tighter thresholds to reject outliers, giving several subsets of decreasing size. Then compare the coefficients produced by fitting each set of points to gauge the variability due to the sample size.

There is an unavoidable conflict between the amount of calibration data and its relevance. Before you can collect data on a large number of projects, software technology and development methods evolve, making the older data less representative of future projects. (The data for all projects must use consistent units of measures, of course.) You can simplify the model so that it has fewer parameters and so is easier to calibrate.

---

[5] For a good discussion of this point, see Appendix B.2 in [Florac, 1999, pages 227-231].

Even if you have many data points the sample may not cover the entire "prediction volume" of the model. In practice, the data points from projects tend to cluster together. As one example, organizations tend to produce software products with similar characteristics using a standard process. (A product line is the archetypal case.) The level of detail, accuracy, and amount of data also varies based on process maturity. Organizations operating at SEI CMMI Levels 4 and 5 collect significant amounts of accurate data. Organizations operating at Level 1 collect little data, and it is usually of low quality. Thus, the sample may contain few data points from Level 1 organizations and many from Level 4 and 5 different organizations.

Finally, the measured attributes may be highly correlated with one another. This occurs if two model parameters represent the same effect. Statisticians call this "collinearity." Model builders use various tests to identify groups of highly correlated variables. Barry Boehm describes a variance inflation factor in Section 4.4.2 of [Boehm, 2000]. Sam Kachigan describes Factor Analysis in Chapter 15 of [Kachigan, 1986]. Then they reformulate the model, retaining only one variable from each group.

13.8.3 Bootstrapping

The various fitting techniques require multiple data points, the more the better. You can use "bootstrapping" techniques to assess a model's accuracy using a limited amount of calibration data. Bootstrapping samples with replacement form a set of data points to create multiple samples for evaluation. The basic process is as follows:

1. Select a subset of the available data points and fit the model's coefficients.

2. Evaluate the model's accuracy by using it to predict the values of the remaining data points.

3. Repeat the process by selecting a different set of data points.

4. Compute the accuracy by combining the accuracy values of the subsets.

You can easily automate this process using computers. There are several variants of the bootstrapping technique and related resampling techniques. Examples include the jackknife, the delta method, and cross validation. Michael Chernick discusses bootstrapping in [Chernick, 1999]. His book is an excellent reference on this topic, and includes an extensive bibliography.

13.8.4 Example: Calibrating the Proportionality Coefficient

This section describes two simple approaches that you can use to quickly calibrate parametric models. Even if you have only a single data point, you can calibrate the proportionality constant in your model, provided that you make certain assumptions. Suppose that your effort estimation model has the same functional form as COCOMO:

$$EDEV = EAF*A*S^B$$

where EDEV is the effort, EAF is the effort adjustment factor, A is the proportionality constant to be fitted, S is the size, and B is the exponent. To use this approach, you must assume a value for the exponent, B. Suppose that you select the value 1.10 for the exponent value. (This is the COCOMO II value with all scale factors rated Nominal.)[6] You must also assume that the COCOMO II effort multipliers, which are based on industry experience on hundreds of projects, apply to your local environment. This means that the effort adjustment factor, EAF, computed using the COCOMO values and ratings assigned for the completed project, is correct.

Given these assumptions, suppose that you have the following data for a completed project:

S = 40 KSLOC
EDEV = 30,000 phr
EAF = 1.17

The apparent productivity is

P = S/EDEV = 40,000/30,000 = 1.33 SLOC/phr

Express A in terms of the known parameters and solve:

$$A = \frac{EDEV}{EAF*S^B} = \frac{30,000}{1.17*(40^{1.10})} = 443 \text{ phr / KSLOC}^{1.1}$$

---

[6] The assumed value of B could just be 1, giving a Linear Model. There is actually little data that confirms that the exponent is greater than 1. Rajiv Banker and Chris Kemerer analyzed seven data sets to determine the form of the effort estimation equation. They found only one data set where the exponential value was different from 1 in a statistically significant sense [Banker, 1989].

The units of A are somewhat strange but are correct nevertheless. This calibration adjusts the model for the local definitions of size and effort that were used on the completed project. It also adjusts the average productivity (based on the single completed project). You can use this calibrated model provided that your future projects are "similar" and use the same definitions for size, effort phases, and so forth.

If you have multiple projects, you can obtain a better estimate for the proportionality constant, A, using the same procedure used for single point calibration, but now averaging the results using a spreadsheet. Again, assume that the underlying model (cost drivers and scale factors) are correct. To illustrate this approach, use the data from Table 4.17 [Boehm, 2000]. Assume that B = 0.91. For each completed project, compute the exponent using

$$EXP_i = 0.91 + SSF_i$$

where SSF_i denotes the sum of the five exponent contributions based on the ratings of the corresponding scale factors (the "sum of the scale factors"). Then compute the value of A needed to make the model's value exactly equal the actual value:

$$A_i = \frac{PM_i}{PEM_i * (KSLOC_i)^{EXP_i}} = \frac{PM_i}{FCN_i}$$

where the quantities use the notation in Boehm's Table 4.17. (PEM_i is the product of the effort multipliers. PM_i is the actual effort in person-months. FCN_i denotes the values of the denominator.) Table 13-8 shows the results. The average for A is 2.6280. This agrees within 0.4% the value of 2.6188 determined using a regression tool, as described on page 177 of [Boehm, 2000].

Table 13-8 *Simple COCOMO Calibration*

Project	PM(i)	KSLOC(i)	Prod EM(i)	Sum SF(i)	Effort(i)	Exp(i)	FCN(i)	A(i)
1	1854.55	134.47	1.89	29.28	2014.04	1.2028	686.7085	2.7006
2	258.51	132.00	0.49	16.72	278.777	1.0772	94.2928	2.7416
3	201.00	44.03	1.06	22.48	227.996	1.1348	77.7377	2.5856
4	58.87	3.57	5.05	18.19	59.5668	1.0919	20.2651	2.9050
5	9661.02	380.80	3.05	26.77	9819.961	1.1777	3338.7709	2.8936
6	7021.28	980.00	0.92	25.21	8092.762	1.1621	2753.5416	2.5499
7	91.67	11.19	2.45	23.50	114.2832	1.1450	38.8954	2.3568
8	689.66	61.56	2.38	26.48	886.2177	1.1748	301.0544	2.2908

13.9 Parametric Models for Hardware Costs

Parametric estimation models originated in the 1930s to estimate costs for producing airplanes. See the box "The Origins of Parametric Estimation." Hardware cost estimation models address activities such as the following:

- Nonrecurring engineering
- Production
- Deployment
- Servicing and preventative maintenance
- Repairs
- Modification and upgrade

Nonrecurring engineering is analogous to the new development of software, and so it is difficult to estimate. Typical parameters used in hardware estimation models are weight, physical size (height, length, square feet), power consumption, required reliability or availability, and planned service life.

The Origins of Parametric Estimation

Theodore P. Wright developed equations ("learning curves") to predict the cost of airplanes over long production runs [Wright, 1936]. In 1950, the Rand Corporation established a cost analysis department, which produced many reports for the next two decades. In particular, David Novick and others at Rand developed Cost Estimating Relationships (CERs). In the 1970s, Frank Freiman of RCA developed the Programmed Review of Information for Costing and Evaluation (PRICE) estimation model. This was the first model to view hardware development and production costs as a process describable by logical relationships of several key variables (parameters). Freiman defined algorithmic models of these relationships. He ran the models backward to calibrate them using historical data, and then ran them forward to predict the cost of future projects. Descendents of the original PRICE model are still in use. Joseph Hamaker describes the history of NASA cost estimating in [Hoban, 1994].

Production models estimate costs for manufacturing thousands of identical units. During production, productivity typically improves so most models to estimate hardware production include "learning curves." See note N18, "Learning Curves."

Models for hardware development and production usually estimate costs directly, not effort. The reason is that hardware development includes many nonlabor costs. Because of inflation, the cost is measured in monetary units indexed by (calendar) year. For example, a model to estimate the cost of developing a scientific instrument for a spacecraft is [Warfield, 1998]

$$\text{Cost} = 2.59*(\text{Mass}^{0.57})*(\text{Life}^{0.44})*(0.36^{\text{COPY}})*(0.70^{\text{UNIV}})$$

where

Cost	=	Total costs for design, development, test, and evaluation, plus the first flight unit (millions of 1998 U.S. dollars)
Mass	=	Mass of flight unit (kilograms)
Life	=	Planned mission life (years)
COPY	=	1 if copying a previously built instrument or 0 if new ("precedentedness")
UNIV	=	1 if built by a university or 0 if built by a contractor

This model estimates a cost of $19.6M 1998 U.S. dollars for a new instrument that has a mass of 10 kilograms and a mission life of 5 years, and that is built by a contractor. (The last two factors are really just two-valued effort multipliers. NO corresponds to 1.0. YES corresponds to 0.36 and 0.70 for COPY and UNIV, respectively.)

The costs of developing and producing hardware increase if the product

- Uses unproven or immature technology.
- Is safety critical (manned versus unmanned vehicles).
- Must operate unattended for long periods (spacecraft).
- Has tight resource constraints (low power, low weight).

For example, the cost per kilogram increases as engineers attempt to miniaturize components to reduce weight.

Deployment can usually be handled using the Linear Model described in Chapter 3, "A Basic Estimating Process: The Linear Method." Servicing and repair costs depend on the number of deployed units, the assumed operating conditions, and failure rates for various types of components. For hardware, parts wear out at a known rate so there are good models to estimate failure rates. A good reference is [Pecht, 1995].

There are families of integrated parametric models to estimate software development, hardware design, hardware production, and other processes. Examples include the COCOMO, PRICE, and SEER families of tools. See the CD-ROM for a list of vendors.

13.10 Selecting an Automated Estimation Tool

Automated tools that implement many estimation models are available. (Sometimes the model and the tool are the same object.) An automated tool reduces the effort needed to calculate values, ensures that the calculations are correct and repeatable, and makes it easy to update estimates based on new information.

Before you buy a commercial estimating tool, you should decide if the tool makes business sense. A good approach is to define your needs. How large are your projects? How often will you be making estimates? Will you have to update the estimates frequently? Have past estimates been inaccurate and, if so, why? Examine some of your past estimates to answer these questions. Also, obtain information from tool vendors and ask for the names of some of their users. Contact these users. Ask them how they are using the tool in their organization and their perception of the tool's strengths and weaknesses. To help define your needs, also consider prototyping your estimation method by building custom tools using the techniques and tools in this book. Then you can decide when and where a commercial automated tool can help.

Table 13-9 lists criteria to consider when selecting an estimation tool (or any other tool). The tool should allow customization to handle recurring situations (project, product, and process characteristics). As a minimum, you should be able to set default values for common situations. (Some tools call these "knowledge bases.") If possible, get a tool that allows you to add cost drivers to the underlying estimation model(s). The tool must provide the means to exchange data with spreadsheets and project scheduling tools so you can integrate these tools, making it easy to revise and update estimates. Most estimating and project management tools in use today are implemented as PC-based applications and use the Microsoft Windows operating system.

Table 13-9 *Criteria for Choosing an Estimation Tool*

Relevance
• Target application domain (MIS, real-time, etc.)
• Project life cycles (phases and activities covered)
Capabilities
• Accept desired size measure(s)
• Handle new, modified, and converted code
• Calculate all desired quantities
• Provide useful reports and graphs (level of detail, formats)
• Support sensitivity analysis
• Set default values for parameters
• Extend the model (add cost drivers)
• Calibrate the model's coefficients
• Update estimates during the course of a project
• Export data to other tools
• Import data from other tools
• Manage data for estimates and actuals
Implementation
• Computing platform (nearly all tools are PC based)
• Speed of computation
• Resource requirements (disk space, processor speed)
• Product maturity
• Calibration data used
Usability
• Number of input parameters
• Online help
• User documentation (level of detail, accuracy, readability)
• User training (level of detail, length of course, availability)
• User support (help desk, consulting services)
Costs
• Tool (purchase, annual license, upgrades)
• User training and support
• Initial setup
• Operating costs (metrics collection, analysis, and calibration)

Tools that provide more capabilities and features take a longer time to learn than simpler tools. Online help, user documentation, and training will help you use the tool correctly and efficiently. Public domain ("freeware") estimating tools often lack documentation, training, and support. Tools that implement COCOMO are a partial exception because COCOMO is extensively documented, and training is available in colleges, as well as from some commercial vendors. Most vendors provide training and some consultation as part of their license costs. You must cover your expenses to attend training, however. Tool license and support costs can be substantial, especially for small organizations that only prepare two or three estimates per year. You must also expend effort to become familiar with the tool (learning curve). Do not forget operating costs for data collection, analysis, and periodic model calibration.

Tools allow users to ignore the details of the model's calculations. However, the estimated values will only be accurate if the user understands the model's definitions and assumptions. Ignorance leads to a false sense of security. One disadvantage associated with estimating tools is the potential for misuse due to ignorance or the desire to manipulate the results. *If used correctly, however, tools force the estimator to confront many questions about the characteristics of the product, process, and project.* (You must understand these to set realistic values for the various parameters and cost drivers.) Paul Rook used to say, "Don't let a tool do your thinking for you!" Watts Humphrey says, "A fool with a tool is still a fool, but faster." These are wise words.

13.11 Helping Nonestimators Provide Good Parameter Values

This section provides detailed advice for using parametric cost estimation models so that you can obtain accurate, consistent results with a minimum of effort. (The advice presented in this section also applies to using other types of parametric models.) This section assumes that you have carefully selected a model that applies to your domain and that estimates the quantities you need.

Parametric estimation models can produce inaccurate results for the reasons listed in Table 13-10. Design and construction are the responsibility of the model builder (who may be you, of course). Assuming that the model is well constructed and validated, you must use it correctly.

Table 13-10 *Sources of Errors in Parametric Estimates*

Design and construction
• Loose definitions of the model's inputs and outputs (parameters)
• Incompatible definitions
• Approximations in the model's functions
• Based on nonrepresentative or obsolete historical data
• Implementation errors in the model's functions or look-up tables
Usage
• Not calibrated for local conditions, or calibrated using bad or obsolete data
• Misunderstanding the definitions of the model's inputs and outputs
• Supplying incorrect values for the model's inputs
• Supplying unrealistic values of the model's parameters

A key part of using any parametric model is to make it easy for these "nonestimators" to provide accurate values for the input parameters. Engineers and subject matter experts provide values for many of the input parameters of a parametric model, but often do not have the time or interest to understand details of the parametric model. They may supply inaccurate values due to ignorance, optimism, pessimism, lack of time, or political pressure. Table 13-11 shows possible actions to overcome these problems so that you can collect good inputs for your chosen model. The following paragraphs explain each action. Many of the actions for using a parametric estimation model also apply to estimating processes in general. (Note N19, "Actions to Obtain Accurate Estimates," provides a generalized version of Table 13-11. Also see Chapter 21 in [Boehm, 1981].)

Table 13-11 *Steps to Use a Parametric Estimation Model*

1. Tailor the model to your local environment:
a. Understand the model (scope, definitions, and assumptions).
b. Simplify the model (optional).
c. Collect consistent historical data.
d. Calibrate the model.
e. Assess accuracy (MMRE, PRED).

2. Partition the product to simplify estimation:

    a. Group components with similar characteristics.

    b. Set values for the "global parameters." (See text.)

3. Prepare to collect component sizes and characteristics:

    a. Provide descriptions of all the components.

    b. Provide a printed form or spreadsheet to capture values and rationale.

    c. Provide relevant historical data (if available).

    d. Write simple instructions to guide the participants.

    e. Train the participants (definitions, assumptions, and instructions).

4. Collect the data:

    a. Provide assistance and feedback.

    b. Collect the completed forms and spreadsheets.

5. Evaluate the data and iterate as needed:

    a. Analyze consistency.

    b. Analyze sensitivity.

    c. Identify key cost drivers.

13.11.1 Tailor the Model to Your Needs

This step is not mandatory, but you may want to consider it. You must first understand the parametric model's assumptions, the types of software included in the size, the phases and activities included in the development process, and the definitions used for size, effort, and time. In particular, this includes the definitions of the model's parameters such as cost drivers and scale factors. (This is the sixth "precursor to estimation.")

You can simplify the model by reducing the number of parameters (size, scale factors, and cost drivers). This provides two benefits. First, it reduces the amount of data needed to calibrate the model. Second, it eases the burden on nonestimators who are unfamiliar with the definitions of model parameters. Simplifying the model reduces confusion, decreases the estimation effort, and may even increase the accuracy of the values supplied. Use consistent historical data from completed projects to calibrate your simplified model.

13.11.2 Partitioning the Components

Microestimation allows you to apply different cost driver ratings to the various components of the system. This enables you to apply the "high-impact" cost drivers to only a portion of the total product, reducing the effect on the total effort and schedule. (Ideally, the designers should consider such impacts when they define the product architecture.) This section gives some suggestions.

The project team partitions the product based on functionality, multiple increments, and the computer platform(s), process, personnel, and assignment of components to specific groups or subcontractors. *The actual partitioning of the product (its architecture) may differ from the partitioning used for estimation.* Your goal is to reduce the size and complexity of the estimating problem, and so obtain accurate results with less effort. You need enough decomposition to capture the characteristics that affect the estimates without producing so many components that assigning values to the sets of cost drivers becomes overwhelming. (Automated tools reduce this effort, but recall that most of the effort is spent in the analysis, not the calculation.)

You might aggregate the system's components based on the similarity of their cost driver attributes: product, platform, process, and personnel. For example, you may be able to group all components requiring high reliability into one "subsystem." If you are planning to assign components to groups of developers having different capabilities, you might group the components based on work assignments (i.e., on work packages). Grouping similar components works for any type of parametric model.

Some parameters apply globally to the project, product, or process. You can determine these quickly, before involving the nonestimators. Interview the manager and lead engineer to learn the characteristics of the product, process, people, and project and then use this information to set the model's global parameters. Then engineers only have to estimate values for the remaining ones. Table 13-12 shows the parameters for the COCOMO II Post-Architecture model arranged in three groups. The project parameters apply to all components. (I split SITE into two parameters.) The Mixed parameters apply to the project team for a small project, and to individual components for a large project. The Component parameters, including size, apply to individual components. (I replaced REVL with GROW and VOLA.)

Table 13-12 *Scope of COCOMO II Parameters*

Project		
Type	*Symbol*	*Name*
Scale	FLEX	Development Flexibility
Scale	RESL	Architecture/Risk Resolution
Scale	TEAM	Team Cohesion
Scale	PMAT	Process Maturity
Scale	PREC	Precedentedness
Cost	DOCU	Documentation Match to Life Cycle Needs
Cost	SITE (1)	Multisite Development (collocation)
Cost	SITE (2)	Multisite Development (communication)
Cost	SCED	Required Development Schedule
Cost	PCON	Personnel Continuity
Cost	TOOL	Use of Software Tools
Mixed (Project or Component)		
Type	*Symbol*	*Name*
Cost	RELY	Required Software Reliability
Cost	DATA	Database Size
Cost	CPLX	Product Complexity
Cost	TIME	Execution Time Constraint
Cost	STOR	Main Storage Constraint
Cost	PVOL	Platform Volatility
Cost	ACAP	Analyst Capability
Cost	PCAP	Programmer Capability
Cost	APEX	Application Experience
Cost	PLEX	Platform Experience
Cost	LTEX	Language and Tool Experience

(*continues*)

Table 13-12 *Scope of COCOMO II Parameters (continued)*

Component		
Type	**Symbol**	**Name**
Cost	RUSE	Developed for Reusability
Size	NSize	New Source Lines of Code
Size	RSize	Reused (modified) Lines of Code
Size	TSize	Translated Lines of Code
Size	ASize	Adapted Source Lines of Code
Size	SU	Software Understandability (%)
Size	UNFM	Unfamiliarity with Adapted Software (%)
Size	AA	Assess and Assimilate Adapted Software (%)
Size	CM	Code Modified (%)
Size	DM	Design Modified (%)
Size	IM	Integrate and Retest Adapted Software (%)
Size	GROW	Growth During Project (%)
Size	VOLA	Volatility During Project (%)

For real systems, the various components are all not tightly coupled, nor are they totally independent of one another. The degree of coupling lies somewhere between these two extremes. Similarly, the degree of coupling between WBS tasks also impacts the uncertainty in the estimate. One cost model, SEER-SEM, addresses task coupling by producing two estimates, one where the modules are totally uncorrelated, and another where the modules are totally correlated (tightly coupled). The estimator then chooses a value between the two estimates. See the box "Effect of Task Coupling on Cost Variance."

Effect of Task Coupling on Cost Variance[7]

Consider a set of n tasks (work breakdown structure elements) with cost, C_i, mean cost, μ_i, and variance, σ_i^2. Basic statistics gives

$$C = \text{Total Cost} = \sum_{i=1}^{n} C_i$$

$$\text{Mean of Total Cost} = \sum_{i=1}^{n} \mu_i$$

$$\text{VTC} = \text{Variance of Total Cost} = \sum_{i=1}^{n} \sigma_i^2 + 2\sum_{i=1}^{n-1}\sum_{j=i+1}^{n} \rho_{ij}\sigma_i\sigma_j$$

For the best case, all of the tasks are not coupled, and so $\rho_{ij} = 0$ for all i and j. For the worst case, all tasks are strongly coupled, and so $\rho_{ij} = 1$ for all i and j. For this case,

$$\text{VTC} = \left(\sum_{i=1}^{n} \sigma_i^2\right)^2 \gg \sum_{i=1}^{n} \sigma_i^2$$

Because some correlation is likely, the Variance of the Total Cost will surely be larger than the sum of the individual cost variances.

To gauge the dependence, assume that all tasks have the same variance, σ^2, and correlation, ρ. Then

$$\text{VTC} = \sum_{i=1}^{n}\sigma^2 + 2\rho\sum_{i=1}^{n-1}\sum_{j=i+1}^{n-1}\sigma^2 = n*\sigma^2 + n*(n-1)*\rho*\sigma^2$$

$$= n*\sigma^2*\left[1+(n-1)*\rho\right]$$

You can choose a value for ρ, and can then calculate the worst case over or under estimation of the variance. The fractional overestimation of the total cost standard deviation is

$$\frac{n\sigma - \sqrt{n}\sigma\sqrt{1+(n-1)\rho}}{\sqrt{n}\sigma\sqrt{1+(n-1)\rho}} = \sqrt{\frac{n}{1+(n-1)\rho}} - 1$$

The fractional underestimation of the total cost standard deviation is

$$\frac{\sqrt{n}\sigma\sqrt{1+(n-1)\rho} - \sqrt{n}\sigma}{\sqrt{n}\sigma\sqrt{1+(n-1)\rho}} = 1 - \sqrt{\frac{1}{1+(n-1)\rho}} - 1$$

---

[7] This example is based on a tutorial presented by Stephen A. Book [Book, 1998].

Sometimes the pieces are sufficiently well partitioned that you can estimate them separately and then add the results. This gives four "independent" projects instead of one large project. To permit this, however, certain conditions must be met. See note N20, "Partitioning to Reduce the Diseconomy of Scale." Do not forget to include effort and time for tasks to integrate and test the software as a complete system!

13.11.3 Prepare to Collect Component Sizes and Characteristics

Written component descriptions, standard forms, and training help reduce the variation in parameter values provided by different estimators. Use a high-level architectural description to clarify the nature and scope of components so that developers can provide values for component sizes and characteristics. Section 9.9 provides a simple description of the NCMMS system. (The system designers should already be producing such high-level descriptions so this should not require additional effort!)

Prepare a simple printed form or, better, a spreadsheet, to collect values for the individual components. Only list the component names and the subset of cost drivers that they need to estimate. Also provide a way to capture the supporting rationale for each value. You can use a template to record this information. Table 13-13 shows an example for COCOMO II. You often have to prepare estimates for several different interpretations of the product size and characteristics. The "estimate description" describes the conditions of the estimate, possibly by referencing a plan or a list of assumptions. The "justification" gives concise supporting rationale, or may reference other documents or numbered notes if more detail is needed. The participants can also provide supplemental data (such as restated assumptions, modified descriptions of components, and new sources of historical data). For example, the participants can identify missing tasks, products, or phases (e.g., field tests or product deployment). Typically, you will refine the descriptions of the software components, clarifying the functions, and interfaces, and characteristics. This leads to better estimates in future rounds. (This is analogous to the refinement of task descriptions that occurs in the Cards-On-The-Wall Method described in Section 11.5.)

Clarify unfamiliar terms or subjective parameter definitions. This helps individuals estimate consistently and in accordance with the model's assumptions.

TIP 1: The Likert scale definitions used in parametric models are subjective. You can improve the consistency of estimates by your organization by extending the definitions. For example, instead of "somewhat familiar with the code," you define this as "have 6 to 9 months' experience working with the component or subsystem."

Table 13-13 *Template to Justify COCOMO II Cost Driver Values*

COCOMO II Post-Architecture Cost Drivers and Scale Factors				
Project Identifier:				
Date Prepared:				
Estimate Description:				
Prepared By:				
	Cost Drivers	**Symbol**	**Rating**	**Justification**
Product	Required software reliability	RELY		
	Data base	DATA		
	Product complexity	CPLX		
	Required reusability	RUSE		
	Documentation match to L.C. needs	DOCU		
Platform	Execution time constraint	TIME		
	Main storage constraint	STOR		
	Platform volatility	PVOL		
Personnel	Analyst capability	ACAP		
	Programmer capability	PCAP		
	Applications experience	APEX		
	Platform experience	PLEX		
	Language and tool experience	LTEX		
	Personnel continuity	PCON		
Project	Use of software tools	TOOL		
	Multisite development	SITE		
	Required development schedule	SCED		
	Scale Factors			
	Precedentedness	PREC		
	Development flexibility	FLEX		
	Architecture and risk resolution	RESL		
	Team cohesion	TEAM		
	Process maturity	PMAT		

TIP 2: Put the definitions in another tab in the same worksheet so that they are easily accessible when the person is filling out the values. This reduces frustration, and increases the accuracy of the data provided. You can also provide pull-down lists and descriptive information for each item using Excel's Data Validation feature.

TIP 3: Provide simple validity checks in all spreadsheets. The best time to detect invalid values is when they are entered. For example, module sizes can never be negative. Percentages must lie between 0 and 100. Cost driver ratings must lie in a specified range.

Prepare the component descriptions, definitions, printed forms, spreadsheets, and a list of data to be provided. Also provide instructions, e.g., actions tied to a due date. ("Submit your estimates for Round 1 by close of business on June 23, 2005.") You might need a more detailed plan for a large project involving many individuals who must provide estimates. Train the participants on definitions, assumptions, forms, spreadsheets, and procedures. This should only take an hour or so. Finally, provide any relevant quantitative historical data to engineers and estimators to help them set (or check for) realistic parameter values.

13.11.4 Collect the Estimates

Collect the completed forms and spreadsheets. Check them for obvious problems (empty fields, illegible values), and contact the author promptly to correct any problems. Answer any questions promptly. If the question affects others, distribute a memo or email giving the answer. For example, you might need to clarify the rules for counting code and assigning ratings for certain cost drivers.

Track the receipt of data using a log sheet to identify overdue items. Assemble all information from the estimates (input forms, worksheets, outputs, log sheets, and other documents). This is the "Estimating Notebook" and establishes the baseline for the estimate. This is all the information you need to reconstruct or revise the estimate six months later! (No matter how careful you are, something always seems to be missing! Although not widely known, Murphy was originally an estimator.)

13.11.5 Evaluate the Data and Iterate

The last step is to evaluate and analyze the results. Some estimation tools identify parameter settings that seem to be incompatible (i.e., "input anomalies"). For example, it is unlikely that the complexity will be low if the product size is 900 KSLOC and the product is unprecedented. Similarly, it is not a good idea to assign personnel with low capability and experience to work on such a project. Expert COCOMO, described in Section 5.7 of [Boehm, 2000], performs such consistency checks. The SEER-SEM model displays suspect parameter settings in yellow or red on the screen. Such aids help estimators to set realistic values. Inconsistencies between skill levels and labor rates are often hard to detect, however, because engineers (or estimators) set the skill levels, while managers or financial people set the labor rates. Independent reviews help to detect such problems.

You should also compare the values calculated by the parametric model to past experience on similar projects, and to values estimated using other methods such as the Bottom-Up Method. Experts are good reviewers at this point.

TIP: The capability and experience of the people on a large team are average. A project with 100 developers should not have very high ratings, or probably even high ratings for personnel capability. (You can assign some very good people to difficult components if you use microestimation.)

Whatever parametric model you use, you will want to

- Identify the factors that have greatest influence on the estimated value
- Quantify the amount of uncertainty in the estimated value

If you know the model's equations, you can easily identify the key factors. (You can calculate analytic partial derivatives.) If not, you can vary the input parameters and observe the variation in the output value. (These just are numeric partial derivatives.)

To estimate the range of uncertainty in the estimated effort, you can vary input parameters. For example, you could make three runs:

- Average values for size, cost drivers, and scale factors
- Smallest size and "best case" cost drivers and scale factors
- Largest size and "worst case" cost drivers and scale factors

The "best case" has the lowest effort adjustment factor (EAF), and the "worst case" has the highest EAF. (High ratings of some cost drivers lower the effort, while for other cost drivers high values increase the effort. Thus, the "best case" will have some cost drivers rated as low as possible, while the others are rated as high as possible, and conversely for the "worst case.") Scale factors in COCOMO II are uniform; that is, low values increase the exponent and high values decrease it. For a given size, low values of the scale factor increase the estimated effort. Run 2 is the lower bound, and Run 3 is the upper bound.

Another approach is to choose probability distributions for the size and EAF, and to use a bivariate probability distribution. Paul Garvey describes this technique for cost and schedule tradeoffs in Chapter 7 of [Garvey, 2000].

The best approach is to model the uncertainty of all of the model's input values and coefficients, and use Monte Carlo techniques to "roll up" the uncertainties due to all of these sources. (Chapter 24, "Determining Product Performance," describes Monte Carlo techniques for estimating computer performance.) Tools such as Crystal Ball support this.

Based on this analysis, you can iterate the process to refine the estimate. For example, you might *tune the parameter values to obtain estimates that are closer to*

desired values, but only if these changes are based on corresponding changes to charac-
teristics of the product, process, and project! This is usually an iterative process.
(Refer to the "Reducing the Price" feedback loop shown in Figure 15-5.)

13.11.6 Resisting Political Pressure

Another cause of estimating inaccuracy is political pressure. Because parametric models have dozens of parameters, users can produce any desired value by adjusting the settings. (Just the cost drivers of COCOMO II have a dynamic range of 2032. This means that the user can adjust the nominal effort estimate by a factor of 2000.) The temptation is to choose values to get the desired result, without regard to whether or not the values reflect reality. The box "Using Incremental Approval" suggests a way to prevent this.

Using Incremental Approval

Ray Kile proposed obtaining incremental approval of the parameters of the sizing model and the estimation model [Kile, 1991]. Using an average labor rate gives the costs. (You may add estimated costs for any activities, phases, materials, and supplies not covered by the parametric model.) To do this, the team prepares the following documents (which may only be a few pages or just a spreadsheet):

- Design description (architecture, major components, global characteristics)

- Module sizes and characteristics

- Process descriptions (build plan, methods, tools)

- Project environment (personnel, schedule constraints)

Each document is reviewed and approved in sequence. Then you use the approved inputs and the parametric model to calculate the development effort and time. You then calculate the cost using an average labor rate. (You may add estimated costs for any activities, phases, materials, and supplies not covered by the parametric model.)

When presented with the results, managers usually state that the cost is too high or the schedule is too long. The answer from the engineers is "These estimates were based on the characteristics of the product, process, and project that you previously approved. The values that we have estimated are based on these approved values. What characteristics would you like us to change to reduce the effort or schedule?" This approach forces management to take responsibility for the results of the estimate. It also prevents arbitrarily setting the parameter values to achieve some desired result.

13.12 Recommended Reading

The best documented parametric model is Barry Boehm's COonstructive COst MOdel (COCOMO). Barry Boehm describes COCOMO 1981 in [Boehm, 1981]. Boehm et al describe COCOMO II.2000 in [Boehm, 2000]. Section 5.1 in [Boehm, 2000] describes the Application Composition model. Chapter 2 in [Boehm, 2000] describes the Early Design and Post-Architecture models, including units of measure. COCOMO II accepts size estimated in logical statements or Unadjusted Function Points. Appendix A in [Boehm, 2000] defines assumptions, milestones, and phase/activity distributions. Table 2.54 in [Boehm, 2000, page 82] gives a side-by-side comparison of COCOMO 1981, Ada COCOMO, and the COCOMO II Early Design and Post-Architecture models. Table 13.5 in [Fenton, 1997, page 442] gives a side-by-side comparison of COCOMO 1981, and all three COCOMO II models. For the latest information on all COCOMO models, see the team's website at http://www.sunset.usc.edu/COCOMOII/suite.html.

Another venerable model is Larry Putnam's Software LIfecycle Model (SLIM). Lawrence Putnam, Sr., and Ware Myers describe the SLIM model in [Putnam, 1992]. Reprints of the original papers are in [Putnam, 1980].

There are other forms of parametric models for estimating software development effort and time. Lionel Briand and Isabella Wieczorek give an excellent summary of these in Section 3 of [Briand, 2001]. The Joint industry/Government Parametric Estimating Handbook, sponsored by the U.S. Department of Defense, provides guidance on developing and evaluating cost estimating relationships [ISPA, 1999], and also identifies commercial parametric models for hardware and software estimation [ISPA, 1999]. For more on the history of software estimation see my article "Software Estimation: An Overview" which appears in [Reifer, 2002b].

Norman Fenton and Shari Pfleeger discuss calibration [Fenton, 1997, page 449]. Barry Boehm describes the steps in Section 29.9 of [Boehm, 1981]. Chapter 4 in [Boehm, 2000] describes the challenges of calibrating COCOMO II. Bob Hughes provides a nice example of how to build a model to estimate software development in Chapter 8 of [Hughes, 2000].

The manual edited by Stewart, Wyskida, and Johannes describes parametric models for hardware estimation, learning curves, and cost estimates for manufacturing and concurrent engineering [Stewart, 1995]. Some good references for estimating spacecraft costs are [Wertz, 1999], [Wertz, 1996], and [Boden, 1996].

NASA's Johnson Space Center provides the NASA Cost Estimating Handbook at http://www.jsc.nasa.gov/bu2/NCEH/index.htm. This site also provides access to a wide range of cost models.

Parametric estimation models help investigate tradeoffs between functionality (size) cost (effort), and schedule (time). (Some models address a fourth variable, product quality. For more information, see [Boehm, 2002].) Examples include cost reductions from reusing code, training skilled, expensive people for less-skilled, inexpensive people, and the impact on development cost and time of schedule compression, platform time and storage constraints, and product reliability requirements. Section 2.6 in [Boehm, 2000] provides several examples. Also see Sections 8.3 and 8.4 in [Boehm, 1981].

13.13 Summary

A parametric model is a "crystal ball" that predicts average values for similar situations. Parametric models use algorithms to compute values of quantities (the dependent variables) based on values of several parameters (independent variables). Model builders define quantitative relations between the independent and dependent variables using empirical data, theories, statistical techniques, and heuristics. Parametric models promote completeness and consistency because the estimator must supply values for a set of parameters, which (hopefully) forces the estimator to carefully consider all the factors that affect the estimated quantity.

This chapter focused on parametric models that estimate software development effort and time for the phases and activities of the model's assumed process model (project life cycle). You estimate or measure the values of parameters based on the characteristics of the product, project, and process. Parametric models are most useful early in a project to

- Scope the needed resources.
- Determine project feasibility.
- Evaluate alternatives.
- Quantify risk impacts and mitigation costs.
- Investigate sensitivities to errors in the parameter values.

You can also use parametric models to support negotiations. If the customer has limited resources and is willing to discard less important product requirements, you can use parametric models to explore ways to build to cost (cost as an independent variable, CAIV) or build to schedule (schedule as an independent Variable, SAIV).

The COnstructive COst MOdel (COCOMO) estimates total development effort and schedule (time), and allocates these to the phases and activities of a life cycle model. COCOMO has 22 parameters, 17 cost drivers and 5 scale factors, which characterize the product, process, people, and project. The scale factors apply to the project as a whole, as do some of the cost drivers. Other cost drivers apply to components of the software product. (The COCOMO sizing model applies to components, and has 10 additional parameters.) Macroestimation applies one set of parameter ratings to the entire estimate. Microestimation uses different cost driver ratings for each software component.

All commercial parametric models that estimate software development effort and time have features similar to COCOMO. The devil is in the details, however, because models may differ regarding the following:

- Underlying assumptions
- Definitions of the process model (phases, milestones, activities)
- Definitions of sizes (new, built for reuse, modified)
- Factors included in the model's functional form (cost drivers, scale factors)

Such differences make it extremely difficult to compare "equivalent" values estimated by different parametric models. (See the discussion of the Rosetta Stone in Section 4.3.2 of [Boehm, 2000].)

Whichever parametric estimation model you choose, you can obtain more accurate predictions by

- Understanding model assumptions and parameter definitions
- Calibrating using historical data
- Providing "realistic" input parameters

Model underlying assumptions and definitions include phases, milestones, activities, sizes, and cost drivers. Models calibrated to industry data produce estimates accurate within 20% of the final actual values. If your future projects will be similar to your past projects, then calibrating a model with your own historical data may achieve accuracies within 5%. You must ensure that the historical data is correct and that the definitions of the measured values are consistent with the model's definitions. To produce accurate estimates, the values of the model's parameters (size, cost drivers, scale factors, etc.) must realistically reflect the characteristics of the customer, product, process, and project. (These are the first four "precursors to estimation.") Realistic parameter values reflect your best understanding of the anticipated or planned characteristics of the product, process, project, and personnel. You should expect to expend most of your effort to understanding the problem and assigning realistic input values. Whatever assumptions you make to prepare the estimate, the project will not achieve the predicted values unless (1) your estimating assumptions remain valid, and (2) the team follows the plan.

"Nonestimators" must estimate certain parameters. For example, software developers typically provide estimates for module sizes and product characteristics. To obtain accurate estimates with less effort, you need to limit the number of parameters that the nonestimators must estimate, and also provide a structured process to collect correct, consistent values. A process also helps prevent political pressures from decoupling the parameter values from reality.

No single parametric estimation model estimates all of the resources needed for a project. You must use other techniques, models, and tools to estimate the effort for other tasks (such as user training) and other costs (such as materials and supplies). Section 18.4 provides specific guidance.

Chapter 14

Estimating Risk Reserves

Every project has risks due to unknowns (e.g., requirements, external interfaces, platform performance, commercial off-the-shelf [COTS] characteristics, and personnel skills) and unanticipated changes (in the same), and estimation errors. This section describes how to identify risks, estimate their impact and mitigation costs, estimate a reasonable risk reserve, and integrate risk-related tasks into the project plans, budget, and schedule. Setting a "reasonable" reserve is important. A large reserve may cause the project's price to be non-competitive. A small reserve may be inadequate to handle the problems that will inevitably occur. This chapter describes a method to estimate an "optimal" reserve for a list of identified risks.

Section 14.1 defines concepts and terminology. Section 14.2 describes a high-level process. Section 14.3 contains checklists to identify risks and possible mitigation actions. Section 14.4 shows how to quantify the characteristics of risks and to estimate the resources needed to avoid or mitigate these risks. Section 14.4 also describes a spreadsheet to document your risk analyses and decisions regarding risk mitigation. Section 14.5 shows how to use the values in the spreadsheet to determine a reasonable risk reserve. Section 14.6 addresses planning, including how to decide which risks to prevent immediately, and which ones you monitor and mitigate later if it becomes necessary. Section 14.7 briefly mentions the need to track risks and monitor mitigation tasks. (Chapters 18, "Updating Estimates," and 19, "Consolidating and Applying Your Knowledge," address these activities in more detail.) Section 14.8 mentions two other ways to analyze project risks. Section 14.9 gives recommended reading.

14.1 Concepts

A dictionary definition of risk is "the possibility of loss or injury." A risk is an undesirable event that, if it occurs, could jeopardize project success.[1] A risk has three characteristics:

1. Its occurrence is uncertain.
2. If it occurs, negative consequences result.
3. Alternative actions can influence items 1 and 2.

There are four categories of risk:

- Technical
- Cost
- Schedule
- Business

Technical risks are directly associated with the product's functionality, performance, and quality. Engineers must initially estimate these characteristics, and these estimates can be a source of technical risk. Cost and schedule risks apply to the project. Software project effort (or cost) increases primarily due to size growth or volatility. Because software functions and behavior are so hard to describe, this risk is common to nearly all software projects. In some cases, the increase is due to lower-than-expected productivity. Contention for resources can cause schedule delays, which in turn increase costs as people either wait or try to "work around" the problem. From a cost accounting viewpoint, changes in rates (such as taxes, inflation, employee medical plan, and foreign currency conversion) can affect project costs. Even if the project delivers an acceptable product, it may do so too late, and so incur financial penalties. The product may even be acceptable to the customer, but may not receive necessary licenses or certifications from regulatory agencies. Business risk affects the entire enterprise. One example is if product failure causes extensive damage or loss of life. If consumers dislike a product, the seller may not recoup the costs of development, production, marketing, and distribution.

---

[1] Opportunities are the opposite of risks. Opportunities are events that, if they occur, will help the project.

There are two responses for identified risks:

- *Accept*—Ignore totally, after careful analysis
- *Mitigate*—Act to transfer, reduce, or eliminate consequences

Table 14-1 describes possible mitigation actions.[2] Each action requires resources. You estimate these resources using the same techniques used for estimating other resources, costs, and schedules.

You can execute mitigation actions immediately, or you can wait. You perform preventive actions at a scheduled time. You only perform contingent actions when a trigger event occurs. Contingent actions are predefined actions that the project team will take if an identified risk event occurs. Contingency reserves are provisions held by the project sponsor for possible changes in project scope or quality that can be used to mitigate cost and/or schedule risk.

Table 14-1 *Possible Mitigation Strategies*

Transfer
• Negotiate contract terms and conditions (delimit responsibility, limit liability)
• Provide a written, limited warranty
• Purchase insurance to cover losses
Reduce probability of occurrence
• Analyze and understand the causes (studies, simulations)
• Prototype high-risk areas
• Choose a better design (high reliability, fail-safe, excess capacity)
Reduce consequences
• Provide a backup and restore capability
• Provide a backup system (failover)
• Purchase insurance to cover residual loss
• Establish a reserve (to cover the losses)

---

[2] Some authors refer to risk mitigation as "risk avoidance." Other authors, however, use "avoid" to mean "eliminate totally." "Eliminate" is the preferred term. See Chapters 29–32 in [DeMarco, 2001].

Based on identification, analysis, and estimation of risks, planners add money to the budget (cost reserve) and slack time (float) to the schedule (schedule reserve).[3] No project can afford to mitigate all of the identified risks. Thus, choosing the amount of the risk reserve involves technical, managerial, legal, and financial considerations. The project manager holds the risk reserves, releasing them during the project as specific events occur.

14.2 The Risk Management Process

Table 14-2 gives a nine-step process to address risks. Section 14.3 addresses Steps 1 and 4. Section 14.4 addresses Steps 2, 3, 5, and 6. (Steps 2, 5, and 6 use the estimating techniques described in other chapters.) Section 14.5 addresses Step 7. Section 14.6 covers Step 8. Section 14.7 briefly addresses Step 8. Section 14.8 mentions two other ways to address Steps 1 through 6.

Table 14-2 *A Risk Management Process*

1. Identify risks.   • What could go wrong?
2. Estimate the probability of failure, and cost to correct.   • How likely is it that this risk will occur?   • How much will it cost to correct it if it does occur?
3. Calculate the impact.   • Impact = Probability of failure times cost to correct.
4. Define possible actions to mitigate each risk.   • Options are ignore, transfer, prevent, and reduce.   • Write as "if-then" statements.
5. Estimate resources needed for each mitigation action.   • Estimate the cost of each action.   • Estimate the schedule impact of each action.   • Estimate probability of failure and costs incurred assuming the proposed mitigation actions have been done. Multiply these to get the residual impact.   • Calculate the risk reduction leverage (RRL) for each action.

---

[3] The management reserve (or contingency reserve) is a portion of the project's budget set aside to cover expenses for unanticipated or uncertain events.

6. Choose the best mitigation approach for each risk.

7. Set the risk reserve.
 	
   • Calculate the risk rank.
 	
   • Rank the risks by decreasing RRL.
 	
   • Plot cumulative cost to mitigate versus risk rank.

8. Plan for risk management.
 	
   • Integrate preventive and tracking tasks into project plan and budget.
 	
   • Establish reserves for contingent tasks (budget).
 	
   • Assign responsibilities for tasks (mitigate, tracking).

9. Perform risk management.
 	
   • Track identified risks and update priorities, etc.
 	
   • Assess progress of the resolution tasks.
 	
   • Continue to identify new risks.
 	
   • Update plans and status.
 	
   • Communicate the status regularly.

Both the developer and the customer should actively participate in the risk management process. Figure 14-1 illustrates this, and is based on the SEI team risk management approach. Both customers and developers identify risks for the project, and then work together to produce a prioritized list of risks that need to be addressed. The risks requiring attention are assigned to either the customer or to the developer based on who can control the risk. For example, only the customer can control the delivery of customer-furnished items. Customers, developers, and suppliers (such as subcontractors and vendors) manage risks and opportunities cooperatively and continuously. Risk management is a continuing process.

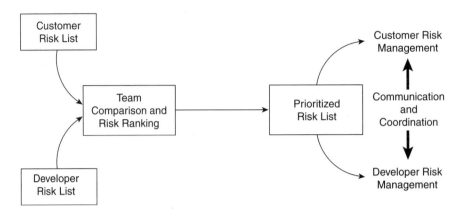

Figure 14-1 *Team risk management*

14.3 Identifying Risks and Mitigation Actions

A good way to identify risks is to use checklists based on past experience. (You can also "brainstorm" to identify new sources of risk.) Checklists provide a structured approach to identify risks in a wide number of areas. This section provides two lists to help you get started. Not all areas are applicable for a given product type or system. Just choose the areas that are relevant for your needs. (You can improve your risk identification process by adding items to the checklist.)

Table 14-3 lists sources of potential risks for developers of software-intensive systems, grouped by area, and is phrased as a question.[4] If the answer is yes, this indicates a potential risk.

Table 14-3 *Developer-Specific Risks*

Application Type
• Unprecedented?
• Uses or controls sensitive data? (classified, financial, medical, personal)
• Performs safety or mission-critical functions?
• Must outside agencies approve, license, or certify the product?

---

[4] There are other possible ways to organize the risks. For example, the Software Engineering Institute publishes a report that identifies a taxonomy of software risks [Carr, 1993].

Product Requirements

- All functions or external interfaces not yet identified?
- Are requirements (functions, external interfaces, and performance) poorly defined, conflicting, or unstable?
- Large number of functions or external interfaces?
- Significant complexity?
- Guaranteed minimum response time? (hard real-time)
- Reliability, fault tolerance, availability, maintainability requirements?
- Must the product operate in harsh conditions? (temperature, humidity, shock, vibration, electrical power range, and stability)
- Must the system resist active threats? (hackers, jamming, physical attacks)
- Does the system have failsafe or safe shutdown requirements?
- Critical components or modules? (performance driver, new algorithm, single point of failure)
- Are the underlying mathematical and physical models defined, validated, and accepted? (assumptions, test data, conflicting opinions)
- Must the product comply with designated standards? (IEEE, ANSI, ISO, military, etc.)
- Are statutory requirements or regulations applicable?
- Is the user inexperienced with the product's technology?
- Is the user foreign? (different language and/or culture)

Product Feasibility, Design, and Implementation

- Technology new, immature, or barely adequate?
- Constrained hardware?
- Is resource usage poorly understood? (processor, memory, data transfer)
- Use COTS or reusable components? (software or hardware)
- Will the project upgrade or modify existing software or hardware? (especially if multiple copies exist in different locations)
- Are any software licenses or patent rights required?
- Is the chosen technology so old that it will soon be obsolete?
- Must you design and fabricate custom hardware components? (especially if they have challenging performance or environmental requirements)

Product Installation

- Need to maintain operability during test and cutover? (fallback, dual operations)
- Is the facility new or greatly modified? (building, plant, equipment)
- Is the site primitive? (power, water, communications, work space)
- Is the site in a remote location?
- Is the site in a foreign country?
- Are there seasonal restrictions on shipping or outside work?

(continues)

Table 14-3 *Developer-Specific Risks (continued)*

Process
• Appropriate for the application domain and solution technology?
• Very formal? (excessive documentation, long review cycles)
• Poorly defined or low maturity level?
Project Staff
• New application domain and/or platform for team?
• Team inexperienced with the chosen technology?
• Methods and/or tools new to team?
• Team inexperienced in software production? (programming in the large)
• Team inexperienced with the chosen process? (reviews, documentation)
• Many new members on team?
• Staff untrained in methods, tools, technology, or process?
• New working environment for team? (language, culture, locale)
• Is the project dependent on one or more individuals with critical skills?
• Is the project staffed with fewer than four people?
• Personnel shared between multiple projects?
• High turnover likely?
Project Plan (applies to large projects only)
• Are many tasks undefined or loosely defined? (work packages lack detail)
• Does the task network have many interdependent tasks?
• Does the task network have many long "stovepipe" task sequences?
• Does the schedule have little or no slack time?
• Are some resource estimates very uncertain? (lack comparable historical data or calibrated estimating models)
• Are key costs poorly understood or not predictable? (no binding quote or bid, escalation)
Project Resources and Organization
• Strong dependence on Customer Furnished Items?
• New, unproven supplier(s)? (vendor, subcontractor)
• Financially unstable supplier(s)?
• Are the participants geographically dispersed? (developers, managers, suppliers)
• Are multiple organizations involved? (partitioning of work, interface control)
• Are the development and test facilities geographically dispersed?
• Is it difficult to obtain needed resources (people, tools, computers, facilities)
• Are special security clearances or skill certifications required?

Business (legal and financial)

- Severe contract penalties for product failure? (warranties, liquidated damages, consequential damages)
- Are there legal restrictions? (local laws, export licenses)
- Does the developer assume significant risks? (firm fixed-price contract)
- Is the project incrementally funded? (cash flow, erosion of sponsorship)
- Do incremental payments depend on "customer satisfaction?"
- Are payments made in a foreign currency? (exchange rate fluctuations, foreign taxes)
- Is the project controversial or politically sensitive? (adverse publicity)

Customer

- Are the end users not directly involved in specification and testing?
- Must outside agencies approve, license, or certify the product?
- Are there many stakeholders? (committees, competing organizations)
- Are the stakeholders geographically dispersed?
- Are elected officials involved?
- Is a foreign government involved? (different laws, language or culture, politics, instability)
- Do the stakeholders have unrealistic expectations?
- Are the stakeholders unfamiliar with formal development processes? (only applies to custom system development)
- Must any stakeholder supply information, data, software, or equipment?
- How many stakeholders must approve the product?

The risks shown in Table 14-3 are from the developer's or seller's perspective. Buyers are interested in many of these same risks but also have some additional concerns of their own. These risks are mainly associated with operating large, complex systems such as a bank or command and control system. Table 14-4 identifies customer-specific risks. In a team risk management environment, you need to consider these as well.

Table 14-4 *Buyer-Specific Risks*

Maintaining Operability During Cutover
• 24×7×52 operations?
• 24×7×52 Corruption of operational data?
• Loss or degradation of essential functions?
Loss of Business
• 24×7×52 Miss market window?
• Customers receive poor service or response?
Supportability
• Relies on COTS or "boutique" components?
• Requires highly skilled operators and maintainers?
Unprofitability
• Consumes considerable computing resources?
• Low availability?
• Vendor controls license and support costs?
• Requires highly paid personnel?
Liability (to customers)
• Corruption or loss of data?
• Consequential damages?
• Loss of reputation?

If the new system cannot maintain operations, then the user must "fall back" to the old system. This may not be easy. For example, master data files and tables may be in different formats. The box "Fallback: A Sad Story" describes one case where this was necessary. The designers (and customers) should decide if a fallback or "graceful recovery" capability is needed. If so, to mitigate cutover risk, they must devise an approach to "recover gracefully." For example, developers may build tools to convert data in master files back to the old formats, and test these tools to ensure that they work correctly. They may also need to build special cables, switch boxes, and so forth. to route data between the old and the new systems. You must define, estimate, and schedule the tasks to do these things.

Fallback: A Sad Story

A satellite control center used a data processing system to track the location and status of many satellites. The developers installed a new version of the system with improved algorithms. Unfortunately, subtle imperfections in these algorithms led to very small errors in the computed positions of the satellites. These errors were not apparent at first. After 30 days, however, the errors had accumulated enough that they were noticeable. At this point, the operators of the system decided to reactivate the old version of the system. The problem was that the developers had provided no tools to convert the data from the new file format back into the old file format. (In actuality, this was not a simple format conversion problem. It involved the inversion of extremely complicated mathematical equations.) In the end, the operators had to reinstall the old system with the database that was 30 days old, and then use recorded telemetry and radar data for the last 30 days, processing a day at a time, until the database was up-to-date. This took several frantic days to accomplish.

If the buyer operates the system to provide a service to external users, the buyer may lose business if the system cannot operate, or operates in a degraded mode. (An example is an e-commerce business that depends on a website.) The buyer may also lose business if the users find the new system too cumbersome to use and so switch to a competitor's system. (The inability to continue operating during cutover can also cause loss of business.) Late delivery can cause the seller to miss a market window, leading to loss of business. (This is an important risk for shrink-wrapped software, which the developer sells directly to consumers.) The buyer should also work with the developer to ensure that a robust system with the necessary features, performance, and quality is delivered on schedule. (Joint application development is a good mitigation approach.)

One potential supportability risk is that the vendor may discontinue commercial off-the-shelf parts, or the vendor may go out of business entirely. (This is one reason that long-lived systems tend to contain less COTS components.) You may not be able to locate people with the skills needed to maintain the product. This is particularly difficult in systems that have a very long life. Computer architectures, programming languages, and development tools all become obsolete. (It is not easy these days to find a programmer who knows JOVIAL or the assembly language for a Z-80 chip.) For more information on supportability risk see Chapter 4 in [USAF, 1988]. To mitigate this risk, you can provide training courses for the maintenance staff, and pay large salaries. A more practical approach is to periodically renovate the system, migrating it to new COTS versions. This fits well with the normal process of maintenance and enhance-ment. Eventually, of course, the architecture itself becomes obsolete and the system must be replaced.

The risk of unprofitability essentially arises from various other risks including excessive resource usage, poor system reliability or availability, higher than anticipated labor costs to operate and support the system, and system obsoles-cence before the investment has been recouped. The occurrence of these risks affects operating costs, revenues, and profitability. Steve Tockey discusses such analyses [Tockey, 2005]. Don Reifer also addresses such analyses in [Reifer, 2001]. Financial liabilities can also affect profitability. These often arise due to safety or security requirements. Robert Charette discusses safety and security risks, as well as other business risks, in [Charette, 1990].

You can also use checklists to identify possible mitigation actions. Table 14-5 gives an example for critical software components. The left column is the "if" condition. The right column is the "then" action.

Table 14-5 *Mitigation Actions for Critical Software Modules*

Potential Problem	*Mitigation Action(s)*
The module interfaces with hardware that is being developed concurrently with the software	Implement the module early so that it may be tested with the hardware during development. Simulate or emulate the hardware to verify under-standing of interfaces and behavior.
The module has a software interface with an external organization	Make early assignment of technical interface responsibility.
The development of other modules depends upon the availability of the module being evaluated	Implement the module early.
Algorithms to implement the module are poorly understood and/or untested	Begin algorithm development and/or testing early. Some prototyping is advisable.
The candidate algorithm for implementation of the module contains a structure that requires looping or searching	Investigate the execution timing of the algorithm. Prototype if appropriate.
There are accuracy or numeric convergence considerations in the use of the candidate algorithm	Investigate the numeric performance of the module. Prototype if appropriate.

Potential Problem	Mitigation Action(s)
The module has memory requirements that are large relative to the available memory	Investigate memory usage and hardware growth potential.
The module makes heavy demands on I/O (disk, ports, channels) and/or processing resources	Investigate resource usage and hardware growth potential.
The module has stringent constraints on response time	Investigate the execution timing of the module. Prototype if appropriate.

Table 14-6 shows another approach: a matrix that relates potential risks to mitigation actions. This matrix addresses types of requirements-related risks. The matrix shows that some actions apply to multiple risk types.

14.4 Analyzing and Prioritizing Risks: Risk Impact

You cannot afford to eliminate all risks, however. You must decide which risks to address, and how to choose the "best" amount of risk reserve.

14.4.1 Estimating Risk Impact

Two quantities help analyze risks. The first is the risk's impact:[5]

Impact = (cost of occurrence)*(probability of occurrence)

You estimate the costs using the same techniques that you used for estimating other resources, costs, and schedules.

Sorting risks based on the impact before mitigation, I_B, identifies the risks that should be mitigated. Engineers and managers must then define a mitigation approach for each risk and estimate the cost of the mitigation, C_M, as well as the reduced impact after mitigation, I_A. (A project may incur no costs if the firm has a Legal department that inserts terms and conditions in contracts or writes limited warranties.)

To be cost effective, a mitigation option must satisfy

$$I_A + C_M < I_B$$

---

[5] Some authors call this the risk exposure.

Table 14-6 *Mitigation Actions for Requirement Risks*

Potential Risks	Possible Mitigation Actions									
	Elicitation			Validate			Control		Communicate	
	Subject Matter Experts	Study Similar Systems or Products	Visit the Customer's Site	Joint Application Development	Feasibility Study	Prototyping or Simulation	Formal Analysis Models	Document the Requirements	Control the Document	Communicate (e.g., Project Glossary)	Negotiate Responsibility, Authority, and Cutoff Dates (Contract Ts and Cs)
Omissions	X	X	X	X			X			X	
Validity	X	X		X	X	X	X			X	
Changes								X	X	X	X
Binding Approval								X			X

where

I_A = Impact after mitigation

I_B = Impact before mitigation

C_M = Cost of mitigation

To help prioritize which options to implement, you can sort the options based on the second quantity, the risk reduction leverage:

$$RRL = (I_B - I_A)/C_M$$

Insurance is a special type of mitigation. The policy has a face value, C_F, which covers some or all of the cost of occurrence before mitigation, C_B. The cost of occurrence after mitigation is performed, C_A, equals the cost of occurrence before, C_B, minus the face value of the insurance, C_F, less any deductible amount, C_D. Thus

$$C_A = C_B - (C_F - C_D)$$

Purchasing insurance does not affect the probability of occurrence, and so $P_A = P_B$. The cost of purchasing the insurance is C_i. The impacts and RRL are as follows:

$$I_B = P_B*C_B$$
$$I_A = P_B*[C_B - (C_F - C_D)]$$
$$RRL = (I_B - I_A)/C_I = P_B*(C_F - C_D)/C_I$$

If the face value of the insurance, C_F, is less than C_B, then RRL is lower than for the case where $C_F = C_B$.

14.4.2 Tabulating the Risks

To analyze the set of identified risks and their associated mitigation actions, you can tabulate the information for each risk in a spreadsheet. Then you can apply criteria to rank the risks based on their risk reduction leverage and other criteria. This provides a way to determine the amount of reserve, and to determine which mitigation tasks should be scheduled and performed immediately instead of being postponed.

Figure 14-2 shows the risk analysis spreadsheet that records the results of your initial analysis. The spreadsheet has 14 columns. The following paragraphs describe the contents of each column. All costs and impacts are measured in your choice of monetary units.

The spreadsheet contains the project name and date prepared at the top. The remainder of the spreadsheet has six regions.

Project:													
Date Prepared:													

A	B	C	D	E	F	G	H	I	J	K	L	M	N
Description			Before Mitigation			Mitigation		After Mitigation			Analysis		
ID	Owner	Title	Probability	Cost ($K)	Impact ($K)	Action	Cost ($K)	Probability	Cost ($K)	Impact ($K)	Impact Red. ($K)	RRL	Notes
1		A	0.4	45.0	18.0	A-1	10.0	0.05	10.0	0.5	17.5	1.75	
2		B	0.5	75.0	37.5	B-1	75.0	0.00	0.0	0.0	37.5	0.50	
3		C	0.3	25.0	7.5	C-1	2.0	0.00	0.0	0.0	7.5	3.75	
4		D	0.2	100.0	15.0	D-1	15.0	0.00	0.0	0.0	15.0	1.00	
5		E	1.0	150.0	150.0	E-1	5.0	0.00	0.0	0.0	150.0	30.00	
6		F	0.3	375.0	112.5	F-1	100.0	0.15	200.0	30.0	82.5	0.83	
7		G	0.1	1000.0	100.0	G-1	150.0	0.01	900.0	9.0	91.0	0.61	
8		H	0.2	1125.0	225.0	H-1	90.0	0.05	100.0	5.0	220.0	2.44	
9		I	0.4	500.0	200.0	I-1	30.0	0.10	500.0	50.0	150.0	5.00	
10		J	0.4	1500.0	600.0	J-1	100.0	0.15	500.0	75.0	525.0	5.25	

Figure 14-2 *Risk analysis spreadsheet*

	Purpose	*Columns*
1	Description	A–C
2	Before Mitigation	D–F
3	Mitigation Action	G–H
4	After Mitigation	I–K
5	Analysis	L–M
6	Notes	N

Columns A through C describe the risk. (In addition, column N may reference numbered notes that provide additional description. The notes are text that is recorded in a separate document, allowing descriptions to be of arbitrary length.) Column A contains some unique identifier to aid in tracking the risk. (You can add extra columns if desired to indicate the type of risk to aid in tracking. Possible types might be software risks (SW), hardware risks (HW), etc.) Column B identifies the owner of the risk. Some person (or department) must have responsibility for the risk. This person has the knowledge and expertise to estimate the quantities, and supervises (or performs) the mitigation actions. Column C contains a short phrase describing the risk. (The column shown in the table is narrowed for publication purposes. The descriptions are represented here as single letters: A, B, C, etc.) If you need additional detail, provide notes in column N.

Columns D, E, and F describe the risk prior to performing any mitigation actions. Column D is the estimated probability of occurrence. Column E records the cost to correct the damage if the risk occurs, here measured in thousands of dollars. Column F shows the impact, computed as the product of the values in columns D and E. The impact is also measured in thousands of dollars. If needed, you can describe detailed calculations in a separate document and cite it in column N.

Column G identifies the action to be performed to mitigate the risk. As in column C, column G is narrowed and the actions are merely "described" as A-1, and so forth. For a real project, you may need to refer to a numbered note that provides additional details. (Essentially, you should provide a short work package that describes what action is to be done, when it will be completed, the resources needed, etc.) Column H shows the additional cost needed to perform the mitigation action, measured in thousands of dollars to maintain consistency with the other monetary quantities. (I assume that the person who performs the mitigation action is the owner identified in column B. If not, add a column to hold this information.)

Columns I, J, and K estimate the expected impact that will be incurred assuming that the mitigation action has been performed and that the identified risk still occurs. (This is called the residual impact.) For example, the mitigation action may not completely eliminate the probability that the risk will occur. Also, it may not totally reduce the associated cost of occurrence to zero. If needed, describe the details of the calculations in a separate document and cite it in column N.

Columns L and M contain calculated values that help to analyze the cost savings and return on investment. Column L gives the reduction in the expected loss (the impact), and equals the difference of the values in columns F and K. Column M gives the risk reduction leverage, which is the reduction in impact divided by the mitigation cost in column H. RRL uses the "expected loss" (i.e., the impact, instead of the estimated costs shown in columns E and J). The "worst case" loss is obtained by subtracting columns E and J.

14.4.3 Populating the Spreadsheet

During initial project planning, you use this spreadsheet to record data about potential risks. Members of the project team identify risks using various checklists plus past experience. Another good way to identify risks is to compare assumptions and estimated values with historical data from similar projects. This will identify overly optimistic assumptions or inconsistencies.

Next, identify possible actions to mitigate each risk. (You will document mitigation actions in the project plan or possibly in a separate risk management plan.)

A common way to assign probabilities is to use a Likert rating scale, mapped to probability values. For example, see [USAF, 1988], [Charette, 1989], and [Garvey, 2000].

To estimate the costs of occurrence and mitigation, you can use the techniques described in [Boehm, 1981] and [Stutzke, 2003]. To estimate the cost associated with the occurrence of a particular risk, you may want to first estimate the impacts of technical problems or schedule slips, and then convert these into costs. (You can use parametric models to do this.) For each risk, estimate the cost before and the cost after any mitigation actions have been done.

The cost of occurrence consists of tangible costs that will be incurred if the particular risk event occurs. You can also include intangible costs (such as loss of market share or customer goodwill) in the cost of occurrence. Such costs are difficult to estimate, however, and so it may not be appropriate to include them in the estimated amount for a hard reserve. Barry Boehm discusses some of these costs in the form of tangible benefits and intangible benefits in Section 31.7 of [Boehm, 1981]. From the standpoint of risk analysis, the occurrence of an adverse event causes the loss of benefits, which are represented by a cost.

The analysis documented in the spreadsheet assumes that risks are independent. In some cases, risks may be linked. Coupling occurs when mitigating one risk increases the impact of another risk. For example, purchasing software components instead of building them from scratch reduces the new development risk, but increases the risk associated with COTS volatility. Compounding occurs when a single risk source causes multiple occurrences of a bad consequence. One example might be the dependence upon and ICASE tool that is unproven, lacks needed features, and has inadequate reliability. Failure of the ICASE tool could impact various other tasks on the project, as well as other risks associated with software development. For additional discussion, see [Stutzke, 2002].

14.5 Calculating the Risk Reserve

Based on identification, analysis, and estimation of risks, you must add money to the budget (cost reserve) and slack time (float) to the schedule (schedule reserve). The risk reserve provides the resources needed to pay for the total "expected cost" of all the identified risks that have not been "prevented." (The "expected cost" of a risk is either the impact before mitigation, or the impact after mitigation plus the cost of mitigation.) The reserve must also cover the costs to perform the contingent mitigation actions. The project budget must include the costs to perform the preventive mitigation actions.

The spreadsheet described in the preceding section identifies all known risks and the expected financial impact if each occurs, before and after mitigation. The most conservative risk reserve covers the total costs of mitigation and occurrence after mitigation. Not all risks should be mitigated, however. Each mitigation task has a benefit, indicated by RRL. If RRL > 1 then the mitigation task "buys" a greater reduction in the expected loss (impact) than it costs to perform. If RRL < 1, the task is not a bargain.

You want to select the set of mitigation tasks that gives the most benefit. A reasonable solution is to order the mitigation tasks by decreasing RRL. Choosing tasks from this ordered list, select the tasks with the highest payoff first. Then move down the list, computing the cumulative decrease in impact and cumulative increase in mitigation cost as successive tasks are selected. To determine the value of the risk reserve, sum the cost of mitigating the risks with RRL > 1, the impact of these risks after mitigation, and the impact of all other risks before mitigation. This sum is the predicted total cost:

$$PTC = \sum_{RRL>1} I_A + \sum_{RRL\leq1} I_B + \sum_{RRL>1} C_M$$

Stop selecting tasks when the predicted total cost reaches a minimum. This is the amount of the risk reserve. So, the strategy is to mitigate risks for which RRL > 1, and accept the risks for which RRL < 1.

As an example, Figure 14-3 shows a set of risks ordered by decreasing RRL. Risk ID 4 (Title "D") has RRL = 1. (This risk is number 7 in the list.) Figure 14-4 shows a plot of the Predicted Total Cost as a function of the number of risks mitigated. (The calculated cost assumes that the risks are selected in order of decreasing RRL value.) The minimum predicted total cost occurs at $635.5K. (For this particular set of data, the total is identical for mitigating either the first six or the first seven risks because RRL = 1 for the seventh risk, Risk ID 4.) The predicted total cost increases after the seventh risk because RRL < 1 thereafter. It is more cost-effective to let the risk occur and pay the damages than to perform the mitigation task.

Project:																
Date Prepared:																
A	B	C	D	E	F	G	H	I	J	K	L	M	N			
Description			Before Mitigation			Mitigation		After Mitigation			Analysis		Rank	Cumul	Impact	Predicted
ID	Owner	Title	Probability	Cost ($K)	Impact ($K)	Action	Cost ($K)	Probability	Cost ($K)	Impact ($K)	Impact Red. ($K)	RRL	(RRL)	Mitig.	Remaining	Total Cost
													0	0.00	1465.50	1465.50
5		E	1.0	150.0	150.0	E-1	5.0	0.00	0.0	0.0	150.0	30.00	1	5.00	1315.5	1320.50
10		J	0.4	1500.0	600.0	J-1	100.0	0.15	500.0	75.0	525.0	5.25	2	105.00	790.5	895.50
9		I	0.4	500.0	200.0	I-1	30.0	0.10	500.0	50.0	150.0	5.00	3	135.00	640.5	775.50
3		C	0.3	25.0	7.5	C-1	2.0	0.00	0.0	0.0	7.5	3.75	4	137.00	633.0	770.00
8		H	0.2	1125.0	225.0	H-1	90.0	0.05	100.0	5.0	220.0	2.44	5	227.00	413.0	640.00
1		A	0.4	45.0	18.0	A-1	10.0	0.05	10.0	0.5	17.5	1.75	6	237.00	395.5	632.50
4		D	0.2	100.0	15.0	D-1	15.0	0.00	0.0	0.0	15.0	1.00	7	252.00	380.5	632.50
6		F	0.3	375.0	112.5	F-1	100.0	0.15	200.0	30.0	82.5	0.83	8	352.00	298.0	650.00
7		G	0.1	1000.0	100.0	G-1	150.0	0.01	900.0	9.0	91.0	0.61	9	502.00	207.0	709.00
2		B	0.5	75.0	37.5	B-1	75.0	0.00	0.0	0.0	37.5	0.50	10	577.00	169.5	746.50

Figure 14-3 *Risks ordered by decreasing RRL*

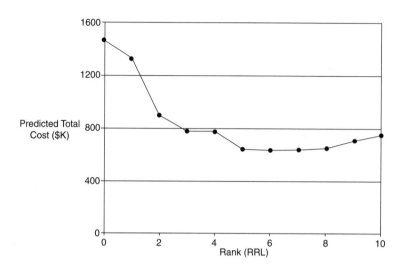

Figure 14-4 *Predicted total cost versus number of risks mitigated*

If you decide to mitigate the first seven risks, the remaining impact is $380.5K. (Of this amount, $250K is the impact for the risks that are accepted, the last three in the ordered list). The estimated mitigation costs are $252.0K. Based on this data, the expected costs to the project due to the identified risks will be $632.5K. This is the risk reserve. (This is a large portion of the assumed $3M project budget. The values chosen for the example are not realistic.)

14.6 Planning: Deciding to Defer Mitigation Tasks

You can still potentially do better, however. Some of the risks may never occur. If you delay performing some of the mitigation tasks, then the potential risk may "expire" and so will cost the project nothing. Here are two examples. First, if there is a "freeze date" on requirements, then there is no cost associated with requirements volatility risk after that date. Second, suppose there is a reserve for bad parts (scrap) produced during machining. Once all of the parts have been machined and passed inspection, the probability of having more bad parts becomes zero and the unused portion of the reserve can be released.

You need criteria to decide whether to execute or delay a mitigation task. (These tasks are called Preventive and Contingent, respectively.) The impact of some risks may increase the later you decide to mitigate them. Some risks may never occur. The recommended approach is twofold. First, select a set of risks to Prevent. Second, track the remaining Contingent risks and execute them "when appropriate." You can use various ranking techniques, described in Chapter 27, "Ranking and Selecting Items," to partition the set of risks. (These include the nominal group technique, multivoting, and the analytic hierarchy process.) Boehm mentions a betting analogy, adjective calibration (Likert ratings), and group consensus techniques such as the Delphi technique [Boehm, 1989, page 132].

To ensure consistency and reduce effort, however, it is best to use rules that you can automate in the risk analysis spreadsheet. This restricts the possible parameters to impact, mitigation cost, RRL, and probabilities. A good criterion is to perform a preventive mitigation task if either of two conditions is true:

1. Impact (before) $\geq$ 5% of total project cost.
2. RRL $\geq$ 2.

Condition 1 says that the expected loss (the impact) is a significant fraction of the project's total costs. The value of 5% is based on the assumption that the accuracy of the cost estimates is ±10% or so. (Recall that parametric cost models have an accuracy of ±20% or so.)

Condition 2 says that performing the mitigation action is definitely a winning bet. Strictly speaking, mitigation is cost effective as long as the amount of impact reduction exceeds the mitigation cost (i.e., RRL $\geq$ 1). The threshold of 2 is conservative because there are uncertainties in the estimates of costs and probabilities of occurrence.

There is another possible condition. If the cost of performing the mitigation task is smaller than the cost of continuing to track it, then you should perform the mitigation task to eliminate the risk. This assumes that the mitigation task completely eliminates the risk so that no further tracking is needed. In addition, the cost of tracking a risk is likely to be very small compared to the cost of a typical mitigation task. To keep the number of rules small, I decided to discard this criterion.

As an example, assume that the risks in Figure 14-4 apply to a project with a total cost of $3M. The rules are to prevent the risk if

Impact(before) $\geq$ $150K

or

RRL $\geq$ 2

Figure 14-5 shows these rules applied to the risks. Specifically, the spreadsheet adds columns O–S. Columns O–P correspond to the two rules. If the condition is met, a *P* appears in column O or P. Column Q sums the number of rules that have fired. For example, Risk ID 10 meets both conditions. (The parameters for the rules are in a separate worksheet named Rules.) Column S records the mitigation cost for each P task, with the sum in row 3, column S. This is the total budget for the preventive tasks. Only two tasks are deferred, 1 and 4, amounting to $25K in mitigation costs.

																		Total
Project:																		**Budget**
Date Prepared:																		227
A	**B**	**C**	**D**	**E**	**F**	**G**	**H**	**I**	**J**	**K**	**L**	**M**	**N**	**O**	**P**	**Q**	**R**	**S**
Description			Before Mitigation			Mitigation		After Mitigation			Analysis					Sum		Prevent
ID	Owner	Title	Probability	Cost ($K)	Impact ($K)	Action	Cost ($K)	Probability	Cost ($K)	Impact ($K)	Impact Red. ($K)	RRL	Notes	1	2	CP	Disp.	Cost
5	E		1.0	150.0	150.0	E-1	5.0	0.00	0.0	0.0	150.0	30.00			P	1	P	5
10	J		0.4	1500.0	600.0	J-1	100.0	0.15	500.0	75.0	525.0	5.25		P	P	2	P	100
9	I		0.4	500.0	200.0	I-1	30.0	0.10	500.0	50.0	150.0	5.00			P	1	P	30
3	C		0.3	25.0	7.5	C-1	2.0	0.00	0.0	0.0	7.5	3.75			P	1	P	2
8	H		0.2	1125.0	225.0	H-1	90.0	0.05	100.0	5.0	220.0	2.44			P	1	P	90
1	A		0.4	45.0	18.0	A-1	10.0	0.05	10.0	0.5	17.5	1.75				0	C	0	*
4	D		0.2	100.0	15.0	D-1	15.0	0.00	0.0	0.0	15.0	1.00				0	C	0	*
6	F		0.3	375.0	112.5	F-1	100.0	0.15	200.0	30.0	82.5	0.83				0	A	0
7	G		0.1	1000.0	100.0	G-1	150.0	0.01	900.0	9.0	91.0	0.61				0	A	0
2	B		0.5	75.0	37.5	B-1	75.0	0.00	0.0	0.0	37.5	0.50				0	A	0

Figure 14-5 *Categorization of mitigation actions*

Although simple, these rules illustrate the basic approach. You can use other prioritization schemes to select which mitigation tasks to defer if desired.

Table 14-7 summarizes the components of the reserve computed in the preceding sections. Risks 6, 7, and 2 are accepted. Risks 5, 10, 9, 3, and 8 will be executed immediately (preventive). The total cost to perform these tasks is $227K. Risks 1 and 4 are deferred (Contingent). The mitigation cost for these totals $25K. The remaining impact following mitigation (all preventive and contingent tasks) totals $130.5K. This is the amount that will have to be paid to cover the expected losses even though the mitigation actions have all been performed.

Table 14-7 *Summary of Estimated Costs*

Type	Amount	Category	Meaning
R	$250.0K	Accepted	Sum of IB for all nonmitigated tasks
P	$227.0K	Preventive	Sum of mitigation costs for tasks to be executed
R	$ 25.0K	Contingent	Sum of mitigation costs for deferred tasks
R	$130.5K	Remaining Impact	Sum of IA for all mitigated tasks (preventive and contingent)

These components will be identified in the project's budget. The "reserve for risk" consists of items 1, 3, and 4, and totals $405.5K. The remaining $227.0K (item 2) is allocated to specific preventive tasks in the project plan. The team executes these with the normal tasks in the project plan. (They are included in the budget and the schedule.) A portion of the plan describes the Contingent mitigation actions using "if, then" statements. For example, if a critical path slips more than one calendar month then you might request that additional engineers be assigned to the project. Thus, you defer executing these tasks until the impact (which is the expected loss) becomes larger than the mitigation cost, or other trigger events occur.

In some cases you may include a schedule reserve as well. Steve McConnell provides a good discussion in [McConnell, 1996]. If so, you will insert appropriate float amounts in the project schedule.

14.7 Tracking and Updating

Changes will inevitably occur during the course of the project. You must regularly track the status of all risks, and update the probability of occurrence, and the cost of occurrence as needed during the course of the project. In addition, you need to track any ongoing (active) mitigation tasks. You should track preventive tasks as part of the project's normal management process. (Chapter 18 covers project tracking, and Chapter 19 explains how to update estimates, which include risk indicators, probabilities, costs, and status.)

14.8 Other Approaches

This section mentions two other approaches for estimating the potential impacts of a set of risks.

14.8.1 The Risk Matrix Method

The "Risk Matrix" Method and supporting tool was developed by the MITRE Corporation. Paul Garvey and Zachary Lansdowne describe the method in [Garvey, 2000]. They describe a set of criteria for rating the severity of the risk ("impact category") and the probability of occurrence for a risk. They then provide mapping to combine the severity and the probability to give a risk rating. (This rating is equivalent to the impact discussed in this paper and in [Boehm, 1989].) Of particular interest, they rank the risks using a technique from voting theory, called Borda voting [Borda, 1781]. The Borda Method ranks the risks from the most to the least critical, on the basis of multiple evaluation criteria. They chose the Borda Method because it produces fewer ties in the rankings, and it does not require additional subjective assessments (beyond the two original values, the original cost of occurrence and the probability of occurrence). They also discuss using this information for a sensitivity analysis. For details, see their paper.

14.8.2 Cumulative Cost Risk

John Gaffney and his colleagues describe a simple method to estimate the cost risk for a program in [Gaffney, 1995]. They compute project cost (actually, effort) as the product of the software size and the average unit cost of production. The size is in SLOC. The cost to produce a line of software is in person-months per SLOC). (This is just the inverse of the productivity.) The estimators define a discrete probability distribution function for the size, and another for the unit cost of production. They convolve these two distributions to obtain the probability associated with a particular development "cost" (i.e., effort, which equals the size times the unit production cost). This produces pairs of values consisting of a probability of occurrence and an estimated project cost. Rank ordering these based on the cost of occurrence allows them to determine the cumulative probability as a function of project cost (effort). They define the risk as the difference between the cumulative probability and 1.0. For example, if a project cost of $1 million is associated with the cumulative probability of 80%, the risk is 20%. For details see Section 8.10 in [Gaffney, 1995].

14.9 Recommended Reading

Several good references deal with risk and uncertainty. A good reference on software risks is [Boehm, 1989]. Chapters 19 and 20 in [Boehm, 1981] cover risk analysis and statistical decision theory. (These two chapters are also reprinted in [Boehm, 1989].) For more information on the SEI Team Risk Management approach, see: http://www.sei.cmu.edu/programs/sepm/risk/team.risk.overview.html. The SEI site also has a good bibliography: http://www.sei.cmu.edu/programs/sepm/risk/risk.faq.html.

J. D. Hwang and H. M. Kodani describe a method for risk analysis that compares impacts before and after mitigation [Hwang, 1973]. The "Total Risk Assessing Cost Estimate" (TRACE) method extends their method [Cockerham, 1979]. John Edgar summarizes the TRACE method in [Edgar, 1982]. In particular, his Figure 4 shows a tabular layout that can be implemented in a spreadsheet. For details on the method described in this chapter, see [Stutzke, 2002].

Various industry standards provide guidance for documenting your risk management process. The best reference is the ISO Standard on risk management for software life cycle processes [ISO/IEC 16085, 2004], which is the same as IEEE Std 1540-2001. IEEE Standard 1058:1998 for Software Project Management Plans states that the risk management part of the plan should (1) identify and assess the risks associated with the project, and (2) describe the mechanisms to track risks and implement contingency plans.

14.10 Summary

A risk is an uncertain condition or event that, if it occurs, could negatively affect the project's cost and schedule, or the products it produces. Risks have a probability of occurrence and an associated cost of occurrence. The product of the probability of occurrence and the cost of occurrence is called the impact. (Some authors call this quantity the risk exposure.)

Project planners, assisted by engineers, managers, and other experts, identify risks that could jeopardize project success. Typical categories of risk are contract, technical, product size and complexity, personnel acquisition and retention, and customer acceptance [IEEE 1058, 1998]. These individuals also identify possible mitigation actions that can be performed to reduce the impact of each identified risk. Checklists are useful to identify risks and possible mitigation actions such as the following:

- Transfer the risk (use terms and conditions, buy insurance)
- Reduce the probability of occurrence (understand and eliminate causes)
- Reduce the consequences of occurrence (limit damage, buy insurance)

Contract terms and conditions are essentially free. Other mitigation actions require resources. In some cases, the producer may purchase insurance to cover the losses if the risk occurs. In others, engineers may create a more robust design.

You must carefully choose the size of the risk reserve. If the value is too small, the project will lack the necessary funds to perform the mitigation actions or to cover the costs associated with the damage caused by failures. If the amount is too large, the customer may find the total price to be too high. Many organizations require that the reserve be quantitatively justified. This is called a hard reserve. ("Management reserve" refers to money. In some cases, you may also include a schedule reserve. Chapter 11, "Bottom-Up Estimating and Scheduling," discusses "float.")

You must also decide how to expend the reserves. For risks that have a very low probability of occurrence, it makes sense to wait to see if the situation develops before expending funds to perform mitigation actions. For risks having a high probability of occurrence, it makes sense to take mitigation actions. You must plan and schedule the mitigation actions with the other project tasks. This chapter described a method to estimate an "optimal" reserve for a list of identified risks and a spreadsheet that implements the method.

Chapter 15

Calculating
Cost and Price:
The Basics

Ultimately, money buys the resources needed to produce the products and to deliver the services desired by the customer. Whether you are an estimator, an engineer, a manager, or a buyer, you need to understand the relations between resources, cost, and price so that you can do the following:

- Calculate the cost for a project
- Evaluate costs for proposed projects
- Prepare budgets and track expenditures
- Analyze historical cost and productivity data

Both sellers and buyers need to understand how project costs (and bid prices if relevant) are determined. Buyers internal to the developing organization need to evaluate costs compared to expected savings or other benefits. Buyers who are external to the developing organization often need to evaluate prices from multiple bidders. Bidders must understand how to set a price that is high enough to allow them to make a profit and yet is low enough to be competitive with other bidders. You need some knowledge of cost accounting to prepare budgets and plans for your projects. If you are a manager in a large firm, knowledge of basic accounting terminology will help you to communicate with business and financial staff. You need to understand the types of costs and how they are loaded to correctly interpret and compare historical cost data from different projects.

This chapter defines the types of costs that you will encounter in any project. These include direct costs for the engineering and testing activities, and indirect costs needed for support activities such as configuration management, quality assurance, program management, and facilities. It describes how costs are computed and evaluated based on business considerations such as cash flow, opportunity costs, and total ownership cost. This chapter also briefly explains how prices for products are set. (Chapter 23, "Calculating Cost and Bid Price," explains this process for large government and commercial contracts.) Since the first estimate is usually too high, this chapter explains how you can reduce the cost (or price) in a disciplined way.

Four quantities are important for any project that delivers products and services to external buyers:[1]

- *Resources.* Labor, materials, and consumables used to build the product and provide services.
- *Cost.* Expenses incurred to obtain the labor and materials.
- *Price.* Revenue received from the sale of the product.
- *Profit.* Negotiated selling price (or sales revenue) minus the actual cost.

The estimated resources are labor (effort), the materials to be purchased, the items (and their size, scope, etc.) to be provided by subcontractors, and consumable items (usually called other direct costs or ODCs).[2] Costing converts resource estimates to costs.

15.1 Direct and Indirect Costs

A direct cost can be traced to specific production activities. Examples of direct costs are labor (engineers) consultants, materials, ODCs, and user manuals. Indirect costs apply to activities of a general, continuing nature that are not directly traceable to specific production activities. Examples are the activities of the Personnel department, Legal department, and Training department.

---

[1] Price and profit are not relevant for projects internal to the developing organization. Instead, other quantities are of interest. Two examples are the return on investment and breakeven time. See [Reifer, 2001].

[2] Another resource that affects costs is project duration. See Chapter 12, "Top-Down Estimating and Allocation."

Some costs may be treated as direct or indirect based on customer directives and the organization's accounting conventions. Table 15-1 illustrates typical labor and nonlabor costs, and typical conventions for direct and indirect costs. (These conventions vary widely from organization to organization.)

Table 15-1: *Typical Cost Categories with Examples*

	Labor	Nonlabor
Direct	Engineers Project managers Supervisors	Materials Subcontracts Other direct cost (including any special equipment) Travel
Direct or indirect (based on directives and accounting rules)	Configuration management specialists Quality-assurance specialists Clerks Network and computer support technicians	Facilities Furniture Standard office equipment (phone, copier) Office automation (computers, staff training, network, email)
Indirect	General administrative departments (Personnel, Legal, Accounting, Facility Operations) Corporate officers and directors	Insurance Taxes Interest Depreciation

15.2 Calculating Direct Costs

The labor cost is usually based on an employee's labor grade (reflecting skill and experience). Each labor grade has an associated labor rate. For example, a senior engineer with some number of years of experience might be assigned a labor rate of X dollars per hour. Multiplying the estimated effort for that labor grade by its associated labor rate gives the estimated labor cost. Summing the amounts for all labor grades gives the total labor cost. A firm may use the actual labor rates for each employee, or an average of those employees who are being bid for the particular job. Larger firms use a standardized rate structure.

TIP: Many firms perform work in foreign countries because labor rates are lower. However, productivity may be lower as well. Newly industrialized countries often increase their productivity rapidly, but evidence seems to indicate that wages also arise as well [Krugman, 2003].

Nonlabor costs include the costs for materials, subcontracts, and other direct costs. For each item listed on the bill of materials, you compute the cost by multiplying the number of items by the vendor's catalog price. (There may be quantity discounts and rebates involved.)

You can calculate the costs of subcontracted items in various ways. (A statement of work defines the subcontracted work.) If you have chosen a subcontractor, use the actual cost negotiated with that subcontractor. If the work has not yet been negotiated, use the cost estimated by your engineers and business department.

Other direct costs are based on the size or amount of the item, and rates obtained from historical data, catalogs, vendor quotes, or other sources. Travel costs are based on per diem rates, published air fares, vendor quotes, and historical data.

Cost analysts and purchasing agents deal with many costs, taxes, and fees, many of which are unknown to resource estimators (planners and engineers).[3] Purchasing agents handle quantity discounts, shipping, storage, and insurance. Finance specialists handle taxes, interest, depreciation, and amortization. There are additional direct costs that arise when a firm does business involving suppliers or customers located in other countries. See the box "Costs for Multinational Operations."

Costs for Multinational Operations

Consider the following items if you are estimating costs involving operations, deliveries, or suppliers located in other countries:

- Shipping costs
  Overseas transportation (ship, air)
  Charges to load and unload freight
  Port storage and handling fees
  Local transportation costs
  Storage for inventory (if applicable)
  Import and export licenses
  Export insurance
  Customs brokerage fees

- Foreign taxes
  Payroll
  Business
  Value added tax

---

[3] The converse is also true. Project estimation requires multiple individuals with complementary knowledge and skills.

- Cost arising from fluctuations in exchange rates
  Transaction exposure
  Operating exposure
  Translation exposure

Long-distance shipping involves more activities, fees, and costs than domestic shipping. Taxes very widely by country. In many European countries, firms must pay a value added tax on all items purchased from subcontractors and suppliers. Foreign taxes may or may not be deductible when calculating a firm's domestic taxes. For a good discussion with examples, see [Moffett, 2003, pages 553-555]. Financial analysis of multinational firms is complicated because the different operating units keep their accounts in different currencies. When doing business overseas, you must determine what currency you will be paid in and when the payments will be received. Unpredictable changes in foreign-exchange rates can affect cash flow, taxes, and financial reporting. For more information see [Moffett, 2003, page 170].

To build some products, the supplier may ship unfinished goods or components, which are then assembled by the receiving firm. Setting the "best" costs (amounts paid) for goods, services, and technology (processes, patents, copyrights, and trademarks) transferred between multinational subsidiaries or suppliers involves taxes, cash flow, tariffs, quotas, and managerial incentives. Moffett, Stonehill, and Eiteman describe three methods to determine transfer prices [Moffett, 2003, pages 485–489]. Also see [Eiteman, 2001, pages 530–539].

15.3 Calculating Indirect Costs

Estimators typically calculate indirect costs by multiplying the estimated direct costs by various rates. This is called "loading" the (base) costs. You need to understand how loading is done so you can analyze and interpret historical cost data. (Section 15.5 provides sample calculations.) The most commonly used rates are as follows:

- Fringe (salary-related taxes, insurance, and benefits)
- Overhead (facilities, equipment, tools)
- Escalation (inflation)

Fringe refers to salary-related costs such as income tax withholding, medical insurance, life insurance, and other federal or state imposed taxes related to salary.

Overhead refers to the costs associated with the work environment such as facilities and computer equipment. These are costs that cannot be directly attributed to project-specific activities. (Travel expenses, ODCs, materials, and subcontracts may be treated as totally separate cost components because they can be directly attributed to project activities. Conventions vary for different industries, however.) Projects that have employees working in different facilities may have a different overhead rate for each facility. A typical example is when some employees work in the firm's office and others work in the customer's facilities. Since the customer provides office space, furniture, and telephones, the "customer site" overhead rate is less than the "firm site" overhead rate. For many commercial firms, overhead includes the cost associated with various support departments such as Legal, Contracts, Security, and Personnel.

Escalation refers to the estimated future increase in base labor rates due to inflation, and may apply to cost increases for other nonlabor items as well. (Negative rates are sometimes used for computer components whose unit price is expected to decrease over the product's life cycle.) Escalation is usually a concern only for projects that last longer than one year. Government rate forecasts are one source of inflation rates.

All of these rates represent legitimate costs of activities needed to deliver products and services. (Note: Some companies combine these rates or use different names.) It is merely an accounting convenience whether these costs are considered to be direct or indirect. Also, the particular activities whose cost is represented by these rates may vary between organizations. For example, quality assurance and configuration management activities may be included as direct charges by one firm but might be billed as an indirect (overhead) charge by another firm. Such differences can make simplistic comparisons of historical data treacherous. See the box: "Confusing Direct and Indirect." For U.S. government contracts, auditors annually review and negotiate each firm's proprietary set of "disclosed rates" and loading rules. Ask your financial and accounting personnel for the particular loading rules to use.

Confusing Direct and Indirect

You use historical data to calculate productivity:

Productivity = Size/Effort

Suppose that you receive a productivity value from a project where configuration management and quality assurance were charged as indirect labor, but you assume they were charged as direct. This means that the historical effort was

$$\text{Effort}_H = \text{Effort}_{ENG} \qquad \text{(the "core" effort)}$$

But you assume that the effort was

$$\text{Effort}_A = (1 + f_{CM} + f_{QA}) * \text{Effort}_{ENG}$$

Thus, the ratio of the assumed and the historical productivities is

$$P_A/P_H = 1/(1 + f_{CM} + f_{QA})$$

Assuming CM and QA are each 5% of the total effort, your estimated effort will be 9% low. This is another example of why the definitions of measured quantities are critical for accurate estimation and analysis.

Rates can vary widely so I can only give typical ranges for the various rates. Fringe rates depend on rules and regulations set by federal and state governments, and on the particular firm's accounting rules. The fringe rate can vary from 10% to 40% or so. The overhead rate depends upon which costs are considered to be "usual" in the course of conducting daily business and which cannot be clearly allocated to project-specific activities such as materials, subcontracts, or other direct costs (ODCs). Overhead rates vary widely with values for service organizations as low as 5% up to 150%. If the organization has capital-intensive manufacturing facilities, the overhead rate may be 300% or so. Causes of the wide variation in rates are the decision to bill certain support personnel as direct or indirect, and the need to maintain facilities to manufacture and test hardware. Escalation ranges from 1% to 10% for the United States. Some countries have much larger escalation values. Section 15.5 describes a set of simple rules with typical values for the rates to show you how the calculations are done.

15.4 Profit and the "Fee Rate"

Profit equals the revenues from the sale of products and services, minus the costs of providing these items. Setting the price is a business decision that is based on many factors. For example, managers may decide to sell a product at no profit to increase sales in a new market. Usually, however, the price includes some profit since otherwise the firm will soon go out of business.

Many firms perform internal projects where profit is not an issue. Consider a firm that develops and sells products such as shrink-wrap software. In this case, the "fee rate" is the percentage profit from the sale of the products (sales revenues minus the development costs).[4] These projects may have high profit but also entail the high risk. The seller invests internal funds to design and test a (hopefully) marketable product, and then to produce many copies of the product for sale. If no consumers purchase the product, then the seller has lost the costs of development, production, and distribution. If thousands of consumers purchase the product, however, then the profit can be large.

For Government and commercial development contracts, bidders estimate the profit using a stated fee rate that is negotiated with the customer. For commercial contracts, the fee rate might range from 15% to 40%, because some overhead expenses are not considered billable, either directly or indirectly. (Commercial purchasers only want to pay for technical staff, not management and administrative staff.) The competitive market also affects the fee rate.

15.5 Calculating the Loaded Cost

This section shows how the rates described in Section 15.3 are applied to each type of cost described in Section 15.4 to compute the loaded costs. These computations depend on specific loading rules of your organization. Developers of commercial shrink-wrap products compute price differently. (See Section 15.9.) In-house developers only care about cost. Nevertheless, the basic approach to calculate a loaded cost is still relevant for both, even though their rules may be slightly different.

The basic equation is

$$
\begin{aligned}
\text{Total burdened cost} \ = \ & \text{Burdened labor costs} \\
& + \ \text{Materials costs} \\
& + \ \text{Subcontract costs} \\
& + \ \text{Other direct costs}
\end{aligned}
$$

---

[4] Determining profit is more complicated since sales often continue over several years, and development and sales may be in different departments, making it hard to measure the values.

I have used the term *burdened cost* in these equations. (Some organizations use *loaded cost* to mean the same thing.)

For this example assume the following set of estimated costs:

Direct labor (DL)	=	$50,000.00
Materials	=	$20,000.00
Subcontracts	=	$10,000.00
Other Direct Costs (ODCs)	=	$ 5,000.00

Also assume the following rates:

Fringe (FR)	=	40%
Facilities-Related Overhead (OH)	=	50%

Recall that fringe is just salary-related overhead. Using these assumed costs and rates, calculate the burdened labor costs:

Burdened labor cost	=	DL*(1 + FR + OH)
	=	$50,000*(1 + 0.4 + 0.5)
	=	$50,000*(1.9) = $95,000

The burdened cost for labor is almost twice the amount of the direct labor paid to the employee because of the fringe and overhead costs. I show this example to my students because many engineers naively assume in quoting budgetary values to a customer that the labor cost will be what they themselves are paid. Actually, for the company to meet its financial obligations, the appropriate multiplier is closer to a factor of two or more as shown here. The total project cost is

Total cost = $95,000 + $20,000 + $10,000 + $5,000 = $130,000

15.6 Management Reserves

Most projects encounter unexpected (unknown unknowns) or unpredictable (known unknowns) problems. A *management reserve* is an amount included in the project's budget to handle such problems. When problems occur, you use the management reserve to purchase the resources needed to deal with the problem. (Managers also may establish a *schedule reserve*, which is time set aside in the project's task network in the form of slack or float.) To set a reasonable reserve amount, you can identify specific technical, cost, and schedule risks. Then you decide ways to avoid or mitigate the most important risks, and estimate the expected costs to do this. Chapter 14, "Estimating Risk Reserves," describes techniques to estimate monetary amounts to address specific risks.

Each organization has its own rules regarding how to calculate management reserves and who controls the disbursement of the funds. Managers must decide when to disburse funds from the management reserve, and how to account for these funds when determining a project's financial status. These topics are beyond the scope of this book. Quentin Fleming and Joel Koppelman discuss these aspects of management reserves [Fleming, 2000].

Other factors may affect the feasibility of bidding a project, offering a product for sale, or undertaking an internal project. These include interest costs, opportunity costs, the selling price for products, and total ownership costs. The next four sections discuss these.

15.7 Cash Flow and Interest Costs

For firms selling products and services, cash flow is important. Cash flow equals income minus expenses for some specified time period. Positive values mean that the business is accumulating cash. For many types of products, cash flow is often a problem because the developer must expend substantial resources before the product is delivered to the customer. The developer must borrow money from banks or investors to pay production costs. Borrowing from outside lenders incurs interest costs, which increases the total cost of production. Sometimes, projects borrow from internal sources of funds. If the production costs are high, this can have a severe impact on the organization's overall finances. It certainly represents opportunity cost that should be considered. (Section 15.8 explains opportunity costs.) In such cases, predicting the cash flow for the project becomes important.

Contributors to cash flow include the following:

- Income
  - Revenue from selling goods and services
  - Money from financing (loans, investors)
- Expenses
  - Cost of goods and services sold
  - Expenditures to develop and market new products
  - Payments of loan interest and principal
  - Payments of dividends to investors

Figure 15-1 shows a plot of cash flow versus time for a hypothetical project. The x-axis is defined in arbitrary units from 0 to 1 representing the total life of the product. In this figure, development starts at time 0 and is completed at approximately 30% of the product's life. The y-axis shows cash flow expressed in units such as dollars expended per calendar-month. During the development phase the cash flow is negative. Sale of the product begins at the 30% point. Thereafter, the cash flow becomes positive and rises to a peak at approximately 60% of the total life time, decaying to zero at the end of the useful life of the product. The revenue steadily increases after the product is introduced to the market, then reaches its maximum sales volume, and finally decreases as the product is replaced by another product or the market becomes saturated. The breakeven point occurs when the total development costs (including interest, depreciation, and taxes) equal the revenues gained from the sale of the product (less taxes on the revenues). In the figure, this means that the area below the curve equals the area above the curve up to the time at which breakeven occurs. This occurs at an elapsed time of approximately 45% in the figure.

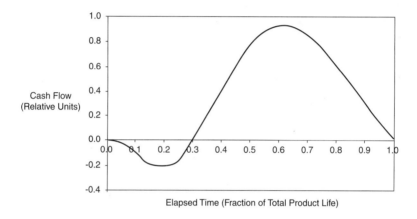

Figure 15-1 *Cash flow versus time*

For software especially, there is a trade-off between the time to market versus the quality of the product. Usually, software quality increases with time since more testing can be done. Many firms, however, find it necessary to deploy a product with known defects to meet a market window. They do this to obtain revenues needed to obtain favorable cash flow, or to capture market share. They must balance the costs of deploying a better product later, against the costs for handling an increased number of customer problems (help desk calls, distribution of patches, loss of goodwill).

Recall that a resource loaded network is a task network where each task has resources assigned to it. The resource loaded network captures the overall project plan (cost and schedule). In particular, it is a time-phased budget for the project, which is a key input for cash flow calculations. Steve Tockey describes types of cash flow in Chapter 3 of [Tockey, 2005].

15.8 Opportunity Cost

Firms that sell products sometimes evaluate proposed projects based on opportunity cost. Opportunity costs are also useful to evaluate internal projects. Opportunity cost is the highest revenue or rate of return that an alternative use of funds could provide. You must estimate the costs and benefits (revenues, cost savings) for multiple alternatives, ranking them to identify the best alternative.

The following example shows how to use opportunity costs to evaluate the merits of a project. Suppose that a company has $25,000 to invest. They have a number of possible actions as shown in Table 15-2. They can develop zero, one, or two products, placing the remaining cash in a savings account to accrue interest. Table 15-2 shows assumed values for the cost and revenue for each of the six possible actions, giving the rate of return shown in the last column.[5]

Table 15-2 *Cost and Revenue for Six Actions*

Action #	Basic Costs	Abbrev.	Cost	Revenues (discounted)	Rate of Return
1	Develop Product A	DPA	$10.0	$25.00	105%
2	Develop Product B	DPB	$15.0	$45.00	200%
3	Place A's cash in a savings account	SCA	$10.0	$0.50	5%
4	Place B's cash in a savings account	SCB	$15.0	$0.75	5%
5	Place A & B's cash in a savings account	SCAB	$25.0	$1.25	5%
6	Place no cash in a savings account	SNO	$0.0	$0.00	5%

---

[5] The revenue stream (sales or cost savings) will not start until the project is completed and the product begins operation. Thus, you should use discounted present value to assess the current worth of the future revenue stream. Many books on financial analysis describe this technique. A good reference is Chapter 8 of [Tockey, 2005]. Also see Chapter 14 in [Boehm, 1981].

Table 15-3 shows four alternatives, consisting of different choices of compatible actions. (Compatible here means that the total cost of the actions cannot exceed the $25,000 available.) For example, Alternative 1 is to develop product A and place the remaining money (equal to the cost of developing product B) in the savings account. The total cost for all alternatives, by assumption, is always $25,000. The table shows the total revenue for an alternative, which equals the sum of the revenues for the actions performed for that particular alternative. The next column shows the rate of return calculated for each alternative. The last column shows the rate of return for the next best alternative. For example, Alternative 4 gives the highest rate of return, 180%. If the firm decides for some reason that this alternative is too risky, they might want to choose the next best alternative, which is Alternative 2, giving a return of 82%. The loss associated with making this decision in terms of the rate of return is 98%.

15.9 Determining the Selling Price for a Product[6]

For some commercial products, the price quoted to the customer is determined based on markup, on a margin applied to the direct costs, or possibly on some desired rate of return on the amount of resources invested in production. For some products, the price might be based on the cost of equivalent competing products, the desire to achieve a certain market share, the desire to maintain a specific level of cash flow (current revenue), or to achieve a target profit. (Economists also mention other types of market-based pricing schemes. These include market skimming, promotional pricing, and demand-differential pricing.) The price of some products is set based on the value to the buyer in terms of net cost savings. The prices for some products and services may be set by law or regulation. For contracted work, the (bid) price is based on the actual cost of production. Chapter 23 discusses this case.

Even if the price of a product is not based on actual production costs, cost estimates are still of interest. Estimated costs, even if crude, support many important business decisions. Cost estimates can determine the lowest possible (breakeven) price. Estimates also provide insight into the major contributors to the production costs, thereby identifying ways to reduce costs and so increase profits. Two useful books dealing with such decisions are [Reifer, 2002] and [Tockey, 2005].

---

[6] Actually, you never actually buy a commercial "shrink-wrapped" software product. Instead, you purchase a *license* to use it under terms specified by the seller.

Table 15-3: *Cost, Revenue, and Return for Four Alternatives*

Alt. #	Options	Actions Chosen						Total Cost	Total Revenues	Rate of Return	Next Best Return
		DPA	DPB	SCA	SCB	SCAB	SNO				
1	DPA + SCB	X			X			$25.00	$25.75	3.0%–95%	3.0%–95%
2	DPB + SCA		X	X				$25.00	$45.50	82.0%	3%
3	CAB					X		$25.00	$1.25	-95.0%	
4	DPA + DPB + SNO	X	X				X	$25.00	$70.00	180.0%	82%

15.10 Evaluating the Total Ownership Cost

The purchaser of a product must consider more costs than the developer. The purchaser is really interested in the trade-off between development (purchase) costs versus the operating and maintenance costs for the product.[7] The *total ownership cost* is the sum of the purchase, operating, and maintenance costs for the life of the product. For shrink-wrapped software, the operating and maintenance costs are typically low. For long-lived military or commercial systems that are operated for 10 or 20 years, however, the costs of operation and maintenance are quite significant. (To estimate operating and maintenance costs, you first need to define the operational and product maintenance concepts. Then choose the relevant labor and nonlabor components from those identified in Section 15.1. For an example, see the model to estimate software maintenance costs described in Chapter 6, "Estimating Annual Maintenance Costs.")

Figure 15-2 illustrates how the total life cycle cost (LCC) is allocated for two types of product. The x-axis shows time expressed as a fraction of the total life of the system or product. (The total life time includes the initial development time plus the operational life.) The point marked IOC indicates the initial operational capability of the product (i.e., the point at which the product is first provided to the user and operational use begins). In this example, IOC occurs at 10% of the total life time. The y-axis shows the cumulative fraction of the system's total life cycle cost (LCC). The figure shows two curves. The upper curve shows the behavior for a product that is not updated after it is placed into service. Examples are automobiles, aircraft, and consumer electronics. For example, a DVD player might be developed in six months and have a total life of five years. The majority of the cost (90%) is spent producing the initial version of the product. Very little is spent thereafter on maintenance. The lower curve shows the behavior for a product such as a long-lived, mission critical system. Such systems would typically be found in a financial institution or a military installation. Such a system might take two years to develop, and have a total life of 10 to 20 years. Only 30% of the total life cycle cost is expended to develop the initial version of the product. Thereafter, the product undergoes a significant amount of maintenance. Maintenance primarily consists of adding enhancements to accommodate changes in the external environment such as business rules and regulations. (Chapter 6 describes how to estimate maintenance costs.) The curve for a typical shrink-wrapped product such as an office automation application would lie somewhere between the two curves shown in the figure.

---

[7] The purchaser might also use return on investment or opportunity costs when evaluating a product or service.

Estimators, as well as the designers, sellers, and purchasers of custom systems, need to be aware that design decisions can have a substantial impact on the overall operating and maintenance costs of a system. (These decisions should be described in the product's life cycle operational concept.) For example, the developers might design a "bare bones" system suitable for skilled (and expensive) users. If the operator of the system wants to reduce labor costs, however, then it may be better to invest additional money to develop a system that has more automated functions and so is easier to operate by less skilled users. (Another way to interpret Figure 15-2 is that it shows the effects of such design decisions on the total life cycle cost.)

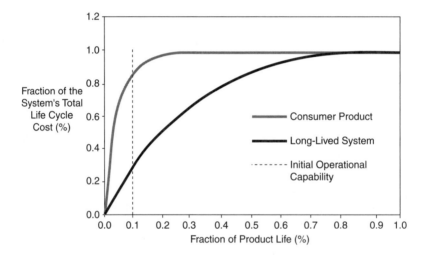

Figure 15-2 *Life cycle cost allocations for two products*

Poor product quality increases the product's repair costs. For the purchaser (user), this increases operating costs. For the seller (developer), this increases support and warranty costs. Figure 15-3 shows the trade-off between various costs and testing time. Testing longer increases testing costs (open circles), but reduces the number of defects in the delivered product. This reduces the lifetime repair costs (solid circles), whether paid by the operator of the system or the vendor who sold the system. (The operator of a system may incur additional rework costs to recover corrupted data or repeat production runs.) The dashed line shows another cost that increases with time, beginning at time 0.4, due to lost revenues (for commercial developers) or savings from more efficient operations (for an in-house system). The top curve shows the sum of these three costs. The minimum of the curve represents the optimum testing time.

The shape and relative height of the cost curves determine where the minimum lies for a particular project. For a safety-critical system, failure causes great financial losses, and so the minimum shifts to the right. For a commercial application, such as a videogame targeted for the Christmas buying season, the minimum shifts toward the left. If the only costs are repairs and testing, the optimum point shifts to the right, as shown in Figure 15-4. If the developer incurs no repair costs, the optimum amount of testing is zero!

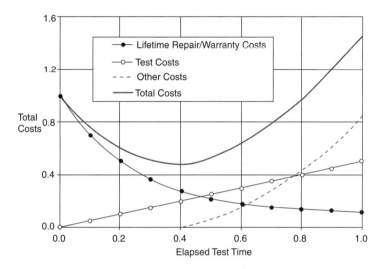

Figure 15-3 *Total costs versus elapsed test time*

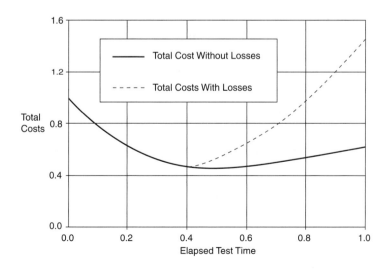

Figure 15-4 *Including other losses reduces the optimum test time*

15.11 Evaluating a Product or Project

Table 15-4 summarizes the activities to evaluate a commercial product or internal project, grouped in four sequential steps. The last column shows the participants (roles) for each activity. (Appendix A, "Roles and Responsibilities for Estimation," defines the responsibilities of each role.) Resource estimates ultimately drive the estimated costs, which in turn drive the price. Thus, it is important to obtain good resource estimates. Resources include money, people, time, tools, equipment, and facilities. The resources needed by a project depend on characteristics of the product and process, and the organization and individuals that do the work. Usually, the engineers themselves prepare the resource estimates for a project. These may include system engineers, software engineers, and hardware engineers. Some firms, however, have trained estimators who specialize in preparing resource estimates. In commercial organizations, the project manager and/or business manager helps prepare resource estimates and convert these estimates to costs. No Terms and Conditions are considered since the "customer" is the development organization itself. For commercial products, however, lawyers will write the end user license agreement (EULA) prior to product release. This contains various terms and conditions related to usage and warranties.

Table 15-4 *Project Evaluation Process for Commercial and Internal Developers*

Step	Activities	Participants
1. Specify project	Define product requirements or features	Product manager or internal customer (user)
	Define project constraints (cost, time)	Product, project, and business managers
2. Estimate resources	Identify items to be delivered	Product manager and project manager
	Identify all items to be produced	Engineers
	Identify tasks to produce the items and mitigate risks	Engineers
	Estimate effort, time, materials, supplies, and travel	Resource estimators*
	Analyze cost/schedule and supply historical data	Project manager and business manager

Step	Activities	Participants
3. Compute estimated costs	Compute costs of materials	Purchasing agent
	Compute costs of sub-contracts (if any)	Business manager
	Compute costs of supplies and travel	Business manager
	Compute labor costs (use base labor rates and loading rates)	Business manager
4. Evaluate business value	Calculate total project cost	Project manager
	Choose the selling price and estimate revenue stream	Product manager, assisted by Marketing
	Compute return on investment and opportunity cost	Business and project managers

*With assistance from system, software, and hardware engineers.

Evaluating a product or project involves many other considerations. For example, it may be hard to obtain the necessary resources. The most important resource is money because it buys the other resources. That said, it may be difficult to obtain talented people with the required skills. Time may also be an important resource in some cases (e.g., if the product is part of an interplanetary spacecraft that must be launched by a specific date). Such resource constraints may affect project feasibility and risk.

The business and legal aspects of a project can have important impacts on project cost, schedule, and risks. Laws and regulations may constrain the design, construction, and operation of the product. Some products cannot be constructed using certain materials, such as asbestos. The product or system may need to be licensed in order to sell it. Three examples are commercial aircraft, nuclear power plants, control systems, and implantable medical devices such as pacemakers. Contract terms and conditions, product warranties, or commercial law may also subject the developer to financial penalties.

Most firms have to worry about making a profit when they develop a product or system. Organizations such as governmental agencies do not. Cash flow is a concern for many businesses. Cash flow is a concept in finance, and basically equals the amount of cash received from sales revenues or payments minus the amount of cash paid for operating expenses during a defined period of time. (There may be adjustments for depreciation and amortization.) If expenses exceed revenues, the firm must borrow money to meet its obligation, incurring interest charges. For some commercial products (e.g., computer games), timing product releases to hit "market windows" affects cash flow, and so this constraint must be considered when planning and estimating the project. See "Recommended Reading" for books that address business case analysis and investment decisions.

For firms contracting with the U.S. federal government, the type of contract affects the financial risk associated with performing a contract. (Section 23.2 discusses these contract types.) In addition, U.S. federal government contracts pay on the basis of individually priced contract line items. Because of cash flow considerations, the contract line item structure may influence how a firm plans and schedules project tasks. (See Section 20.1.)

15.12 Reducing the Cost or Price

Organizations are usually interested in reducing the cost of the project, the selling price of the product, or the bid price. This usually leads to iteration between the management, engineers, estimators, and cost analysts. This section describes a disciplined process for reducing the project cost (and the bid price if relevant).

Figure 15-5 shows a series of feedback loops that indicate possible actions to reduce the project cost and the bid price. The shading in this particular chart shows the individuals who participate in each of the steps. Proceeding from the upper-left corner of the figure, the engineers first define the requirements for the product, either by analyzing a product feature list or a customer-supplied specification. Next, they describe a feasible product that will meet these requirements. Then they define the production process, which includes the project life cycle, methods, and tools. Next, they define the project in terms of staff skills, facilities, and organizational and business structures (e.g., contract type). They then identify and evaluate risks, and identify activities needed to either avoid or mitigate the effects of the risks. Next, they estimate the resources needed to perform the production activities and address the risks. (Chapter 14 discusses estimation of risk reserves.) Once these resources have been identified, "costing analysts" compute the associated costs, including those for risk mitigation. Adding up the values gives the total estimated project cost.

For commercial products or internal projects, the project, product, and business managers evaluate the project cost using return on investment, opportunity cost, or some other criterion. (These require estimates of expected revenues or reductions in operating costs.) If the project meets the desired business objectives, the managers approve and fund the project.

For external bids, management sets the appropriate fee value based on their confidence in the accuracy of the various estimates, their independent assessment of the risks involved, and business objectives. (Management also influences the values for the other rates, and the amount of risk reserve.) The lower portion of the figure shows other management decisions. If the computed price meets the organization's business objectives, the firm will submit the bid.

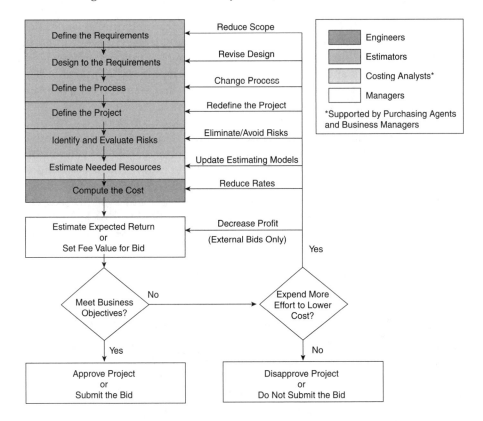

Figure 15-5 *Possible ways to reduce project cost or bid price*

If the project or product cost does not meet the business objectives, then managers must decide whether or not to lower the cost (or bid price) by expending more time and money to reduce the estimated costs. (This may also reduce the uncertainty in the estimated values.) If the managers decide not to do this, then the firm will not undertake the project, develop and sell the product, or bid the project. If the managers do decide to invest more resources, there are a number of possible actions that can be taken at each step in the process that was used to build up the total computed price. These are summarized by the various feedback loops shown in the figure. The following paragraphs describe each loop, proceeding down the center of the chart.

The team can *reduce the scope of the product or project by reducing functionality or eliminating deliverable items such as documents*. The team negotiates these changes with the customer. Direct negotiation may not be possible for competitive bids based on a written specification, however.

If you cannot negotiate project scope directly, you can interpret the specification to delimit the scope of the project more precisely using contract terms and conditions, pricing assumptions, or examples in your proposal. Contract terms and conditions ("Ts and Cs") can document estimating assumptions and so communicate them to the buyer. They are also a means to limit risks. For example, if the customer must furnish component X by a certain date, you might state: "Our proposed schedule is based on receipt of component X not later than <some date>." Some contract Terms and Conditions protect the buyer (contractor), while others protect the seller (subcontractor), or the vendor (of a product). Always have competent legal counsel review any clauses you choose to use prior to negotiating the final contract. Section 2.3 described some terms and conditions for the warehouse inventory management system. See Note N21, "Overview of Contracts," for additional information. Pricing assumptions are part of the documented basis of estimate (BOE) required for U.S. government bids.

You can also provide explicit statements or examples in your proposal to define your interpretation of the requirements, the size and level of detail of documents, the number of items delivered, delivery dates, and assumptions about users' prior knowledge and capabilities. Recall the estimate to "train the users."

The second possible action is to *revise the design of the product*. The developers might choose a new architecture for the product, or decide to provide certain functionality by purchasing commercial off-the-shelf (COTS) components or by reusing existing software. The team could *change the production process*. For example, the team might decide to reallocate effort between development, peer reviews, and testing. They might decide to build custom tooling to increase productivity. To reduce the learning curve of the team, a project could provide training in the production process, methods, and tools.

The team may *redefine the project* by hiring more qualified individuals, training existing individuals, and optimizing the use of staff via choice of labor mix and staffing profile. For example, you could assign highly skilled and expensive individuals to the most difficult parts of the product, and assign less expensive and less skilled individuals to produce the simpler parts of the product. You could design the staffing profile to allow the team to start small and grow larger once tasks have been defined in more detail.

The team may investigate ways to *eliminate risks or reduce their impacts.* Chapter 14 described ways to totally eliminate risks or mitigate their effects.

Updating estimating models may reduce the estimated amount of resources needed for a project. By this, I refer to using additional, valid historical data to recalibrate cost estimating relations and parametric models. In some cases, you may readjust the model's input parameters, but only based on documented changes in the characteristics of the product, project, and process. (Chapter 13, "Parametric Models," describes calibration and the proper use of parametric models.) You may also include a "learning curve" model that calculates the increase in productivity as the staff learns during the project. See note N18, "Learning Curves."

You may be able to reduce the rates for the project (e.g., by reducing employee fringe benefits). (This could lead to increased employee turnover, however, and could increase the estimated costs for relocation, employee orientation, training, and lost work.) You can reduce facilities-related overhead by using facilities provided by the customer, or by establishing facilities that are totally dedicated to the specific project and that cost less than your standard facilities. (These facilities options are only associated with U.S. government contracts.) For external bids, management may decide to reduce the fee rate for the project, remembering that fee rate should always realistically reflect the amount of risk associated with the project.[8] For products, management may reduce the selling price to increase sales volume or market penetration.

After the project team has completed these activities, you can compute the revised cost (and price). The cycle either terminates or can begin again, depending on the resources available and the stamina of the team. The key point is that *all participants interact in an iterative process to produce the final cost (or price).*

The cost estimation process shown in Figure 15-3 provides a basis for rational negotiation between all the parties involved to reduce the project's cost. Generally, you reduce the cost by taking something away. You can reduce functionality or deliverables. You can ask the purchaser to assume more of the perceived risks. You may also revise your estimated costs based on additional information. (For example, a vendor may reduce published prices.) These actions reduce the cost (and bid price, if relevant) because the cost is based on a documented set of requirements, product designs, process assumptions, and historical productivity data. *To change the output, you must change one or more of the parameters in the sequence of calculations. This process also establishes a known,*

---

[8] There is no fee for in-house projects. Instead, the internal customers may decide that the additional cost, while over their previously specified target value, is justified, and does not invalidate the supporting business case.

well-understood reference point for the cost.[9] The estimation process provides documentation to justify for the cost. Section 3.6 describes this documentation, and contains a box "Basis of Estimate (BOE)."

You might argue that if a product's price is based on the prices of competing products or market expectations, then the process shown in Figure 15-3 is not needed. However, business managers still need a good cost estimate for a project to determine expected profits or the return on investment. (Anyone can sell a product that costs $1,000 to make for $100, but they will not stay in business long.)

You can actually estimate more than one cost for a particular project. Andrew Sage and James Armstrong distinguish three types of cost [Sage, 2000, pages 498–499]:

- *Could cost.* Lowest reasonable cost to deliver an operational system with only essential features assuming no significant obstacles or surprises
- *Should cost.* Most likely cost to deliver an operationally ready system
- *Would cost.* Highest estimated cost to deliver an operational system if significant difficulties arise

These loosely correspond to least possible, most likely, and highest possible estimates used in the PERT technique.

15.13 The Need for Multiple Models

No single estimation model estimates all of the resources needed for a project. Parametric estimation models allocate software development effort and time to phases and activities of the project life cycle, which comprise some of the tasks in the project's work breakdown structure. You must use other techniques, models, and tools to estimate the remaining tasks. For example, you might use a separate model to estimate the effort for training users, and another to estimate the effort for data conversion. (I call such collections of models a "federated model." COCOTS, described in Section 5.4 in [Boehm, 2000], is an example of a federated model.) You need multiple models because the equations to estimate effort use different size parameters (software size, number of sites, number of students, number of residual defects, and number of change requests). Similarly, for the resource dimension you must use different size measures to estimate other resources (materials, supplies, travel).

---

[9] You can use a similar cyclic process to estimate product quality and performance parameters. See Chapters 14 and 15.

A problem with using a federated model is that coupling usually exists between some inputs and outputs of its constituent models. For example, a "facilities cost model" may use the software development time to estimate the rental costs (equal to the monthly rental rate times the length of the schedule). If so, there is a coupling between the facilities costs and the software size, since the software size determines the project's effort and schedule (ignoring effects of resource contention).

Identifying and tracking such dependencies becomes very difficult for large projects because there are hundreds or thousands of cost elements, and different individuals or departments often estimate the costs for various parts of the job independently. This can hide dependencies between the parts or assumptions that may contribute to increases in the total cost or schedule. In some cases, tasks representing large costs may even become lost. To avoid such problems you can build an integrated cost model by linking spreadsheets for the software size and level of effort tasks to other cost estimating tools, and to planning tools that maintain the project's integrated task network. This is usually not too difficult since most tools provide links to spreadsheets.

Such an integrated cost model provides several advantages. Just building the model may help you uncover missing or overlapping tasks. You can use the integrated model to rapidly and accurately assess the impacts of proposed changes during a proposal, or to support negotiations with a customer. If you are negotiating an internal project, you can include the customers (buyer, end users, operator) in this iterative process to help them understand the cost impacts of their requests.

If your organization performs many similar projects, it pays to build such an integrated cost model because you can reuse it. For custom system development, you must build a new integrated cost model for each project since the cost elements (product, processes, and work breakdown structure) are different. You might be able, however, to define a set of standard tasks and cost elements tied to sections of a standard work breakdown structure template. (Chapter 20, "Crafting a WBS," describes a "generic" work breakdown structure.) Then you can use these as "piece parts" to construct a model for a particular project.

15.14 Recommended Reading

For guidance on estimating labor, materials, and other costs see [Ostwald, 2003], [Stewart, 1995], and [Stewart, 1991]. Two good books dealing with estimating costs for multinational enterprises are [Moffett, 2003] and [Krugman, 2003]. Three excellent books that discuss business case analysis are [Reifer, 2002], [Tuckey, 2005], and [Denne, 2004].

Don Reifer provides several examples of business case analyses in [Reifer, 2002]. Steve Tockey provides an in-depth coverage of ways to analyze return on investment [Tockey, 2005]. Parts Two and Three of Tockey's book address for-profit business decisions, while Part Four addresses decisions for government and nonprofit organizations. Mark Denne and Jane Cleland-Huang describe a method to identify "minimum marketable features" for software products and optimize return on investment [Denne, 2004].

There are not many references for commercial software contracting and law. Stephen Fishman covers intellectual property from both developer and buyer perspectives without legal jargon [Fishman, 2004]. He covers contemporary topics such as web content and domain names. The book has a CD-ROM over two dozen forms in RTF format that you can use. Kenneth Humphreys and Lloyd English, although dated, provide useful information if you can find a copy [Humphreys, 1993].

Good references on handling contracting, purchasing, and procurement are [Oyer, 2000], [Stanberry, 2001], and [Worthington, 1998].

Professional societies provide books, journals, and training. These include the National Contract Management Association at http://www.ncmshq.org, and the International Association of Contract and Commercial Managers at http://www.iaccm.com. A good online source to purchase documents relating to federal contracting is http://www.mgmtconcepts.com.

15.15 Summary

Table 15-4 showed the process to calculate costs as four sequential steps, and identified the participants. The resource estimators (assisted by engineers et al.) typically deal with quantities that are directly charged to the contract. Direct costs are directly related to production activities. Direct costs include labor, materials, subcontracts, and "other direct costs" (supplies, facilities, and travel). Indirect costs are not directly related to production, and are estimated using rates for fringe, overhead, and inflation.

Many individuals work as a team to identify and quantify needed resources, calculate costs, and set the price for a project. Engineers estimate effort and duration for tasks, list items to be purchased, and identify needed supplies. Purchasing agents determine costs for material and supplies. Business managers negotiate subcontract costs. "Cost analysts" use approved labor rates to calculate labor costs. Managers consider risk and financial objectives, including profit (costs versus price or revenues), cash flow (costs versus payments), and return on investment (profit versus assets used). Arriving at the final estimates involves an iterative dialog among all participants. This chapter described a process (shown in Figure 15-3) that establishes a known, well-understood reference point for the cost and provides guidance to help the participants reduce the estimated cost. The documentation and data produced by the various steps of the process provide a detailed justification for that price. (A similar iterative process can be used to estimate product performance and set feasible target values for product performance.)

Part 3

Closing the Feedback Loop

Chapter 16

Collecting Data: Basics

You need to collect measurement data for

- Tracking quantities that characterize projects, products, and processes.
- Updating estimates.
- Calibrating, updating, or building estimation models.

Chapter 4, "Measurement and Estimation," discussed measurement and the need to limit the data collected. This chapter discusses practical aspects of implementing a measurement process. It provides tips, plus forms and spreadsheets that you can use to implement your measurement process.

16.1 Why Should You Even Collect Historical Data?

The project that is finally completed is not the project that you initially planned and estimated. In addition, software technology, methods, and tools change at a rapid rate. Because historical data represents past experience (quantitatively or perhaps only qualitatively), why should you collect and analyze it? These are at least two good reasons. First, *historical data provides a point of departure to estimate totally new but similar or analogous situations.* (Section 5.6 describes analogy-based estimation.) For example, historical data may only tell you how much change to expect. But even this information is useful. Second, *historical data can set some bounds on feasibility.* For example, suppose that a new project team uses a productivity of 5 SLOC/phr to estimate the effort for a new project. If you know that no other project in the organization has ever exceeded 2 SLOC/phr, you need to question their assumed productivity value.

16.2 Collecting Data

Table 16-1 gives recommendations for collecting data.

Table 16-1 *Recommendations for Collecting Data*

Collect data at the level at which it is generated within the process.
Validate data at the time it is entered or captured to detect errors.
Collect both planned (estimated) and actual data values.
Collect any updates to estimates and planned values.
Collect data over time if possible (time history).
Collect data at an appropriate frequency.
Analyze raw data promptly to detect problems with the collection process.
Question unusual trends and inconsistencies in the data.
Report results in a timely manner.
Perform independent analysis to learn and then share your findings.
Periodically assess the utility of your metrics.

TIP 1: Define and use standard identifiers for projects, products (and their many versions), and processes (especially if they are tailored in some way). Without standard identifiers it is very difficult to identify related data. Designate a single department or person to assign identifiers for all projects.[1]

TIP 2: Provide tools so that individuals can validate (and easily correct) data as they collect it.

TIP 3: Provide prompt, useful feedback to the individuals who supply data. For example, your data collection tool can generate plots and summary statistics.

---

[1] Establish policies to ensure that *every* project gets an identifier. One approach is to tie the existence of the identifier to the release of funds or to opening charge numbers. This ensures that all projects get into the organization's tracking system.

> **TIP 4:** Use the data you collect. Periodically analyze the data from all products, projects, and processes to observe similarities and trends. For example, why are some projects more productive than others?

The frequency of measurement increases as the amount of deviation increases and as "key decision points" approach. Table 16-2 illustrates how often you might measure project cost and schedule. A "low slack path" has little unused time compared to the critical path. Low slack paths are "near critical." If a task on a low slack path is delayed, it can become the critical path for the project.

Table 16-2 *Measurement Frequency*

Cost Statusing	Time Until Next Decision Point			Schedule Statusing
	1 Month	3 Months	1 Year	
Actuals exceed ± 10% of plan	Daily	Weekly	Biweekly	On critical path
Actuals between ± 5% to 10% of plan	Weekly	Biweekly	Monthly	Low slack path
Actuals within ± 5% of plan	Biweekly	Monthly	Monthly	High slack path*

* Repeated task slippages requre more attention, or they will become the critical path.

16.3 Data Collection Templates

Templates and forms can help you implement a cost effective and useful metrics program to support estimating and tracking. They provide several important advantages:

- They structure the collection process, ensuring that you collect complete and consistent data for every project.
- They are inexpensive to implement.
- Standardization reduces the amount of training needed.
- They provide a basis to define a database schema once you decide to automate your data collection and analysis.

Chapter 4 discussed the importance of collecting data to track progress, update estimates, calibrate and refine estimating models, and improve processes. A typical approach is to define five forms to do this:

- Project profile form
- Project initial estimates form
- Project updated estimates form

- Project final actuals form[2]
- Project closeout form

These forms are time oriented. You would fill out the first two forms at the start of the project, the third form (if needed) during the project, and the last two at the end of the project.

If you just want to improve the estimating process, you can simplify data collection and analysis by defining a different set of forms. Because you want to compare "like" data, it makes sense to organize the forms so that a single form contains the initial and updated estimates, and the final actual value for some particular type of object. (Automated data collection tools will only display the portions the user needs to see at any particular time. This includes any data previously recorded, plus empty fields that the user will fill in.) The improved forms are as follows:

- Project profile form
- Product size form
- Product critical resources form
- Product quality form
- Process performance form
- Project effort summary form
- Project schedule form
- Project closeout form

There are now eight forms. Most are only a single page. (The CD-ROM has copies of these eight forms.) Also, I have simplified the forms so that they collect only the minimum essential metrics required for a project. These are adequate for small projects. Larger projects can provide more detail as discussed next.

I have listed these forms previously in the order that you would fill them out. You first define the job, the product, and the process (the precursors of estimation). Then estimate the product size and, if necessary, any critical computer resources. Also estimate product quality and process performance. (Because both of these relate to defects, I put both on the same form.)

Given this information, you can estimate effort and schedule using the methods, techniques, and models described in this book. The staffing level, total effort, and total schedule are related of course. Total effort is essentially constant, given some set of product features and required quality. You can vary the staff level or the schedule. (This ignores the nonlinear effects that increase the effort in order to compress the schedule.)

---

[2] The word *actuals* is a contraction of the phrase *actual values*, just as *estimates* are *estimated values*.

All forms have certain features in common. The upper-right corner of every form has the project identifier. Assigning unique project identifiers is critical to associate data collected during the course of a project! Each form has a "Planned" and "Final Actual" column. You can also add one or more "Updated" columns between these (e.g., by adding columns to a spreadsheet). The estimator only fills out one column at a time (and so each column of values includes a date). Each form has a "Notes" column on the right to record assumptions, rationale, references, anomalies, etc. Use check boxes when possible to predefine standard categories. This makes it easy to extract data from the database for all objects having similar characteristics.

The following paragraphs describe the details of each form and provide some implementation guidance. Be sure to update the appropriate forms if project characteristics or estimated values change during the project.

16.3.1 The Project Profile Form

The project profile form contains information you need to partition project data into categories for analysis. This information consists of attributes of the project, its products, and its processes, plus business-related factors such as the contract type. It also records any unusual or nonstandard characteristics of the product, project, or processes.

Figure 16-1 shows a sample project profile form. This form has values for a project to develop a system to monitor the tools in a bank of numerically controlled machine tools in the XYZ Corporation's factory. (The values entered for this particular project are shown in italics.) I call this project the Numerically Controlled Machine Monitoring Systems (NCMMS). The form has five sections. The top section records standard information to uniquely identify the project. The second section of the project profile form records important product characteristics. This form has the application domain, impact of failure, amount of usage, and architecture. You could add other product characteristics such as the target platform and programming language(s) used. The third section describes the production process. In this example, the project profile form simply lists the possible life cycles (described in Chapter 10, "Production Processes [Project Life Cycles]"). You might also identify methods and tools. The fourth section captures the characteristics of the project and the development team. The form shown in the table includes the number of organizations involved and the development team's familiarity with the application domain, the product architecture and technology, and the methods and tools used in the process. The fifth section indicates any constraints that may influence the product, process, and project. This form shows four—two that apply to the product and two that apply to the project. The form asks that these be rank ordered from 1 to 4, with 1 being the most important.

PROJECT PROFILE

> **Project ID:** *2002-017*
> **Prepared By:** *Sally Smith*
> **Date:** *15 August 2002*

Project Title: *Numerically Controlled Machine Monitoring System (NCMMS)*

PRODUCT

Domain:
☐ Banking   ☒ Factory Control   ☐ Embedded

Impact if Fails:
☐ None   ☐ Inconvenience   ☒ Serious   ☐ Catastrophic

Usage:
☐ Occasionally   ☐ Daily   ☒ Continuous (24x7x365)

Architecture:
☐ Desktop   ☒ Mainframe   ☐ Client/Server

PROCESS

Lifecycle:
☐ Waterfall   ☒ Staged   ☐ Incremental   ☐ Evolutionary   ☐ Agile

PROJECT

#Organizations Involved = 4 *(XYZ Contracts, Engineering, and Production Departments, plus our firm.)*

Familiarity of Development
Team with Domains:
☐ None   ☒ Somewhat   ☐ Very

CONSTRAINTS (Rank Order: 1 most important)

1	3	2	4
Product Functions/Features	Product Quality	Project Cost	Project Schedule

COMMENTS:
This is similar to other SCADA systems we have built. We are unfamiliar with the NCM's sensors that detect tool wear. We will need a consultant to provide mathematical models of tool wear dynamics.

Figure 16-1 *Project profile form*

This form uses check boxes to predefine standard categories. This makes it easy to extract data from your database for all items having certain characteristics. Of course, if you fail to identify a particular characteristic, it will not be collected. In practice, you will iterate your forms several times. Robert Grady and Deborah Caswell show three successive versions of their form to collect project data in [Grady, 1987].

You might want to add other items to analyze your business. One is the type of products produced (hardware, software, operational databases, studies, and user training). Another is project scope in terms of total effort (phr), total time (calendar-months), and the average number of full-time equivalent personnel assigned to the project. You might also be interested in the total value of the contract, possibly subdivided into labor and materials costs.[3]

The particular attributes that you choose to collect depend on how you plan to divide the data for analysis. The number of data "bins" scales as the product of the number of values of each characteristic. For example, if you define two types of product and six possible life cycles, you have 12 bins. Picking too many characteristics gives so many bins that it will take a long time to collect enough sample points in each bin to give good statistics. Thus, you must balance your desire for detail against the realities of collecting adequate amounts of data.

16.3.2 Product Size Form

Figure 16-2 shows a form to record the product size for software, documents, data files, or other categories of interest (hardware assemblies, etc.). Under each category you may list one or more items. For example, for software these could be subsystems, online and offline components, etc. For small projects, you only need to record the software size for the total system, using whatever size measure you choose. Enter the name of the language or development environment in the "HOL" column because it may affect productivity. Your project may write software in multiple languages, or you may use multiple size measure for different types of components (e.g., web points and function points). If so, provide separate size values for the components written in each language. For each software item record the source language, the units of measure, and the size. You should distinguish new, modified, and unmodified code. (The latter two are types of reused code. Unmodified code is used "as is.") This helps to gauge the amount of reuse, and to adjust productivity values. The Updated and Final Actuals parts of the form have the same three columns. (The Updated part is not shown in the figure.) You handle documents and data files similarly, except that the HOL column is not needed. (For documents you might, however, want to indicate if the document is a formal deliverable or an internal document.) The figure includes the uncertainty in the estimated values, either as a mean and standard deviation (10.7 ± 2.1) or a range (40–50). Provide notes to indicate the source of the values, assumptions, and supporting rationale.

---

[3] Always tie any monetary values to a calendar year so that you can adjust historical data for inflation. For a four-year project starting in year 2004, suppose that the estimates are all in "year 2004 dollars." The actual costs are measured in dollars for the years 2004, 2005, 2006, and 2007. Cost analysts adjust the values for each year to obtain a "normalized" cost in "Year X dollars," where X is some reference year. (Similarly, they can adjust the estimated "Year 2004" values using assumed values for future cost inflation.) "Year X dollars" is a more precise unit of measure for cost than "dollars." The distinction is often ignored, however.

	Project:	Sample										
	Author:	R.Jones										
	Last Revised:	12-Jan-05										

Size				Planned 12-Sep-04			Final Actual			Notes
Type	Object	Language	Units	New	Modified	Unmodified	New	Modified	Unmodified	
Software										
	Server Side	C	KSLOC	10.7 ± 2.1	7.6 ± 1.1	12.3 ± 1.4				See Design Concept, Version 2.1.
	Client Side	Java	KSLOC	4.1 ± 0.6	2.2 ± 0.3	3.4 ± 0.4				
Documents										
	User Manual	N/A	Pages	40-50	50					Proposal stated150 pages each.
	Design Description	N/A	Pages	80-90	10					Proposal has a Table of Contents for each.
Data Files										
	Internal Files	N/A	ILF	6-8	2	2				
	External Files	N/A	BF	2-3	0	4				

Figure 16-2 *Product size form*

16.3.3 Product Critical Resources Form

Figure 16-3 shows a form to record the product's critical computer resources (if any). This form gives the name of the quantity, the units of measure, and the "Type" of bound. If the required performance value is an upper or lower bound, indicate this in the "Type" column with "U" or "L," respectively. (If the allowed values are a range, provide the values on two lines.) This form has an additional column, "Required Value," which is specified by the customer. (This may be an allocated amount based on some decomposition of the customer-specified total amount.) The "Planned Value" is what the engineers estimate that the design will provide. (This is their design target.) The "Final Actual Value" is measured for the completed product. You may include additional columns for "Updated Values," which represent changes to the "Planned Values." (If the "Required Value" changes, indicate this in the "Notes" column and create a new entry on the form for the same quantity. You might want to number the entries in the form to facilitate cross-referencing.) The minimum data for each critical resource is the required, planned, and final actual values. (The chief engineer or lead developer identifies the critical resources when the team is defining the approach for the project because these impact product design, cost, and schedule.)

Project:	Sample					
Author:	R.Jones					
Last Revised:	12-Jan-05					
Name	**Units**	**Type of Limit**	**Required Value**	**Planned Value**	**Final Actual Value**	**Notes**
			12-Jul-04	12-Jan-05		
Response Time	Seconds	U	1.0 (95% level)	0.8 (95% level)		Test Case 12.
Video Data Storage	GB	U	300.00	200.00		2000 MPEG Clips at 0.1GB each
Clip Transfer Rate	Clips/Sec	U	0.05	0.10		0.1GB Clips, XYZ Protocol, 100MHz Fiber

Figure 16-3 *Product critical resource utilization form*

Figure 16-4 shows a log to track the values of a critical resource over time. Engineers use this form during the project to detect potential problems. You do not need it for the project closeout report, but I include it here for completeness. Each line records one value. The "Type" column indicates whether the value is required, planned, estimated, or measured. (Use R, P, E, or M.) Use the "Notes" column to provide additional details on the method, tools, and source data used. For example, you might indicate that the value was derived from other measurements (indirectly measured) or estimated using a simulation model.

Project:	Sample		Resource Name:	Response Time
Author:	R.Jones		Units of Measure:	Seconds
Last Revised:	12-Jan-05			

Date	Type	Value	Notes
22-Jan-04	R	1.00	Specification, Version 1.1, page 36
14-Apr-04	P	0.80	Target 95% for 100 users and the "Normal" Scenario
4-Jun-04	E	0.6 ± 0.3	Queueing Network Model
16-Aug-04	E	0.67 ± 0.14	Monte Carlo Simulation
2-Oct-04	M	0.53 ± 0.11	Lab Prototype (Without Background Tasks)
12-Jan-05	M	0.72 ± 0.09	First Benchmark with Actual Software

Figure 16-4 *Critical resource tracking log*

16.3.4 Product Quality and Process Performance Form

Figure 16-5 shows a form to track CMMI Level 4 data at a highly aggregated level. The top part of the form records product quality for software and for documents. The bottom part of the form gauges process performance. The project team agrees on "planned" values based on the organization's process capability baseline. The "Final Actual" values (mean and standard deviation) are based on data collected during the project. The values shown are merely intended to be representative for code and detailed design documents. If you produce other types of products, you will need to add additional metrics. For example, if you produce hardware assemblies, you might track how many assemblies fail the final inspection.

The metrics product quality are normalized in terms of defects per size unit (KSLOC or pages) so you can easily compare values between projects.[4] The sizes used are Added plus Modified. My rationale is that the defects arise in any part of the product that the engineers create or change. Sometimes software received from another supplier contains defects. You need to distinguish these "inherited defects" because your process did not introduce these. (You can gauge the supplier's process performance by measuring the number of inherited defects per unit of product delivered; e.g., defects/KSLOC.)

				Planned	Final Actual	Notes
				13-Sep-04	12-Jan-05	
Type	Quanity	Units	Notes			
Product Quality						
	Defect Density	Defects/KSLOC	1	15.0	12.7 ± 3.1	
	Defect Density	Defects/Page	1	0.50	0.46 ± 0.15	
Peer Review Process Performance						
	Time Ratio	None		3.0	2.7 ± 0.7	
	Scan Rate	SLOC/phr	1, 2	100	107 ± 22	
	Scan Rate	Pages	1, 2	5.0	6.0 ± 1.6	
	Detection Cost		3	0.40	0.37 ± 0.06	
	Detection Cost		3	0.30	0.28 ± 0.08	

Project: Sample
Author: R.Jones
Last Revised: 12-Jan-05

Last Line

Notes Regarding Definitions	
1	Size equals added plus modified
2	The effort is for preparation only
3	The effort is for preparation plus the review meeting

Figure 16-5 *Product quality and process performance form*

You will need many data points to compute meaningful statistics. Many organizations measure the performance of their peer review process. The following are three useful measures:

- Scan rate
- Time ratio
- Detection cost

---

[4] You can replace SLOC with your preferred software size measure.

The *scan rate* measures, on average, how fast that a single reviewer reads the code or the document during preparation. The measures shown in the form are SLOC/phr and pages/phr. As before, size is defined as Added plus Modified. This is adequate for documents. (A precise size measure suitable for predicting effort is difficult to define. See the box "Measuring Size for Modified Work Products.") For code, however, reviewers may need to scan all of it due to the interactions between modules. The true amount scanned thus lies somewhere between (Add plus Modified) and Total Size. My advice is to record both values, analyze the data, and decide which works best for you. (Or you can devise some way of computing an "equivalent size.") The effort includes only the preparation (reading) effort, not the meeting time. For example, if the average preparation time per reviewer is 4 phr and the size of the code module is 500 SLOC, the scan rate is 125 SLOC/phr. This measure is useful to detect if the reviewers are skimming rapidly through the document instead of reading it carefully. High scan rates result in finding fewer defects. Steven Quigley describes a nice analysis in [Quigley, 1996].

Measuring Size for Modified Work Products

Defining a size measure for new documents must account for different font sizes and pagination, and for the fact that some pages (text, figures, and tables) require more work than others. Defining a good size measure is even more difficult for modified documents. Nominally, a peer reviewer only examines the pages added, changed, and deleted. Just summing the number of pages of each type may not reflect the actual amount of work done by the reviewer, however, because the reviewer may need to read unmodified pages in the document to obtain contextual information, or to crosscheck information for consistency. Thus, a size that is larger than the sum of the modified pages would be appropriate in estimating the required effort. Similar problems exist for reviewing modified code modules.

Another issue arises when modifying existing code in a maintenance environment. Usually, programmers modify both code and its associated documents to add a feature or to repair a bug. To check for completeness and consistency, and to reduce review costs, reviewers must examine the code and documents together. However, code and documents have different measures. To my knowledge, there is no good definition of a common size measure for the amount of "product" reviewed in such cases. There is also the issue of mixing code defects and document defects. This makes it hard to measure peer review performance in a maintenance environment.

The *time ratio* is the average preparation effort per person, divided by the average review meeting effort per person. For example, if four people spend 4 phr each studying a draft document, and then spend 1 phr each in the review meeting to consolidate comments, then TR = 4.0 (= 4/1). This measure tells whether the reviewers are preparing adequately. (I like to see TR > 2 or so.)

Detection cost is the total effort for all reviewers (preparation plus review meeting) divided by the number of defects found.[5] An ineffective or inefficient process will have high values. (Alternately, the product may be of very high quality. To decide which, you must do more analysis. Some organizations have found that they can eliminate peer reviews of some work products because they add no value.

You can refine the product quality and process performance measures by subdividing the defects based on their type, severity, and the activities that injected and detected them. (Chapter 6, "Estimating Annual Maintenance Costs," referenced the orthogonal defect classification scheme.) In the Waterfall Process Model, the activities imply the phase or time when the defect was detected and injected. This helps to understand how defects are created and which detection activities are most effective. Some studies have shown that peer reviews are good at detecting certain types of defects, while testing is better for other types of defects. Two references are [Kelly, 1992] and [Porter, 1995]. For example, perspective-based reading is good for reviewing requirements. See [Basili, 1996] and [Shull, 2000].

You must collect data from individual peer reviews to provide the summary data shown in the product quality and process performance form. Because the moderator and scribe record different data, it is helpful to use two separate forms for peer reviews. The scribe fills out the peer review defect log shown in Figure 16-6. The top of the form provides identifying information. (The Scribe uses multiple pages if needed during a single peer review.) The producing activity indicates the phase of the project life cycle that detects the defect. The bulk of the form consists of a table with multiple columns. Each row records the number and location of the defect and a brief description. To help analyze product quality and process performance, you need to record defect severity, defect type, and the injecting activity (the activity that created the defect). Table 16-3 illustrates some possible definitions for these three columns. Each item has a single letter abbreviation to facilitate rapid entry in the form. Our group does not count trivial editorial changes. We just provide them to the author as "redlines" on copies of the review material. We also distinguish defects caused by "external activities" because our process did not inject them. These "inherited defects" could be errors in a work product that were previously undetected by the originator, and are just now being discovered by our process, or they could

---

[5] Some organizations use yield, defined as defects discovered per person-hour.

be errors in work product being reviewed that were caused by mistakes in other (external) work products that the Author referenced. You can define categories suited to your organization and processes.

#	Location of Defect	Description	Severity	Type	Injecting Activity	Date Corrected	Verified (Initials)

(Peer Review Defect Log — Project ID:, Prepared By:, Date:, Page of; (Use multiple pages if necessary. Attach editorial corrections as redlined pages.); Name of Work Product:; Producing Activity:)

Figure 16-6 *Peer review defect log*

Table 16-3 *Defect Classification Codes*

Severity
C (Critical): A major problem. An essential function is inoperable or cannot pass acceptance test. Also includes errors affecting product safety or regulatory compliance.
S (Significant): A minor problem. Any other error that the team agrees should be fixed. (Excludes editorial corrections.)
Type
M (Missing): Specified feature or capability not present or only partially satisfied.
W (Wrong): Author attempted to provide the feature or capability but failed.
E (Extra): The feature or capability is not required, i.e., it is not traceable to a customer requirement or process standard.

(continues)

Injecting Activity
A (Analyze): Requirements definition (operational concept, specification).
D (Design): Product architecture, top level design, drawings, diagrams, PDL, etc.).
C (Construction): Writing code or documents.
E (External): Another organization caused the defect. (Applies only to documents or code received [inherited] from a vendor, prime contractor subcontractor, or customer.)

Figure 16-6 has two additional columns on the right of the heavy vertical line. The author records the date that he/she corrected each defect in the "Date Corrected" column. Then the peer review moderator verifies each correction and initials the "Verified" column.

> **TIP:** Print this form as a double-sided sheet with the defect log on the front, and the definitions of the defect classifications on the back. This ensures that the users always have the definitions readily available.

The moderator fills out the peer review summary form shown in Figure 16-7. The top part contains the same identifying information shown on the Peer Review Defect Log. The Moderator captures information about the product and the process. (Re-reviews are a possible symptom of inadequate preparation, sloppy work, or volatility in upstream work products.) You capture the product size so you can calculate the defect densities on the product quality and process performance form. The moderator records the names of all participants, their role, and the effort they spent preparing for the review. Record the effort in person-hours and person-minutes. (We found that recording effort to the nearest half-hour caused instability in calculated values. You need effort to at least five person-minutes resolution.) The readiness checklist indicates whether the review should proceed. If not, the moderator reschedules the review. If everyone is ready, the team reviews the product and the scribe records the results on the peer review defect log.

Peer Review Defect Log

Project ID: [ ]
Prepared By: [ ]

(Use multiple pages if necessary.
Attach corrections as redlines.)

Date: [ ]
Page [ ]
of [ ]

Name of Work Product: [ ]

Work Product Type:	Document/Drawing
Work Product Size:	567 pages
Producing Activity:	Analysis
Is this a Re-review?	N

Totals:		2	12.5	3.0
Participant	Role	Prep Time [XX.X phrs]	Mtg Time [XX.X phrs]	
Mary Smith	A	0.5	1.0	
John Brown	SR	6.3	1.0	
George White	M	5.7	1.0	

Readiness Checklist:

Was the work product adequate? [Y]
Are all reviewers prepared? [Y]

. . . .
. . . .

Peer Review Results

Total Defects = [7]

Severity

Critical (major) [4]   7
Significant (minor) [3]

Type

Missing [1]   [6]
Wrong [2]
Extra [2]
Retractor [1]

Injecting Activity (root cause):

Analysis [5]   [6]
Design [1]
Construction [ ]
External (inherited) [ ]

Outcome:
Passed with Some Defects [Pass]

Time Ratio = [4.17]
Scan Rate = [22.7] Pages per phr

Figure 16-7 *Peer review summary*

At the conclusion of the peer review, the moderator records the time spent in
the meeting, and records totals obtained from the columns of the peer review

defect log in the Results area. (The total number of defects found should equal the sum of the defects of each category: severity, type, and injecting activity.) Then, the moderator determines the outcome of the review.[6]

Following the peer review meeting, the author corrects all defects identified on the defect log. Then the moderator verifies all the corrections and records the author's total correction effort. (You use it to measure the amount of rework.)

16.3.5 Project Effort Summary Form

Figure 16-8 shows a project effort summary form suitable for small projects. I have reduced this to the smallest possible number of activities that is useful to distinguish. The first part of the form covers planning, supervision, and coordination. I separated project team meetings from customer meetings (such as formal reviews). For projects using Integrated product teams or joint application development, customers often attend these meetings. If so, the team records their effort under "team meeting," not "customer meeting." Some small projects have no formal customer reviews. They often provide "customer support," so this is recorded under "customer meetings." (Some customers require a lot of support, in addition to the project-related work.)

Project:	Sample			
Author:	R.Jones			
Last Revised:	12-Jan-05			
Totals:	3430	4108	4116	
Activity	**Planned** 15-Jun-04	**Updated** 18-Aug-04	**Final Actual** 12-Jan-05	**Notes**
Planning, Supervision, Coordination, and Team Meetings	600	720	687	
Customer Meetings and Support	120	160	134	
Product Design and Development	1800	2000	1973	
Peer Reviews (Prepare, Conduct, Correct)	80	120	112	
Product Testing	600	900	1043	
Product Fielding	60	60	38	Simply Mail Disks
SEE/STE Operations	100	100	89	
Staff Training	70	48	40	

Figure 16-8 *Project effort summary form*

---

[6] More mature organizations also calculate the scan rate, preparation rate, and defect density for the review. If any calculated value is outside the organization's corresponding control limits, the moderator records the reason on the form.

The next part of the project effort summary form records the effort for product design and development. For small projects these activities are lumped into a single entry. (For larger projects, you should subdivide this into analyze, design, code, fabricate, etc.) Note that the effort excludes the effort for testing and peer reviews, which are recorded separately in the next two lines of the form. The reason is that these latter two activities remove defects, while the other activities add defects (hopefully not intentionally). Distinguishing these allows you to crudely gauge how the relative effort expended on production versus verification (reviews and testing) affects product quality and process performance. Separating peer reviews and testing also ties to the cost of quality concept (defect prevention versus defect removal).

TIP: To simplify daily time recording, we have the engineers charge all of their engineering and peer review effort to the "Product Design and Development" activity. Use the peer review summary sheets, shown in Figure 16-6, to collect the effort for preparation, review meeting, and correction. At the end of the project, add up the total effort spent on peer reviews and subtract this amount from the total engineering effort reported. This gives the total project effort expended on engineering without the peer reviews that are shown on the project effort summary form in Figure 16-8.

The effort for configuration management and quality assurance are not shown in this particular form because they are assumed to be indirect support activities in this organization.

The bottom portion of the project effort summary form captures effort for product fielding or distribution. This is optional. For some products, a separate organization does the distribution. If you are to do it, you may want to subdivide "product fielding" into activities such as installation, user training, and operational data conversion. If product fielding is a major undertaking, you may even decide to plan, track, and manage it as a separate project.

TIP: Define the work breakdown structures (WBSs) for larger projects so that the low-level activities map cleanly into the same high-level categories used in the project effort summary form. This allows you to easily obtain the effort for categories shown in the project effort form (or whatever top-level categories your organization chooses) by just summing the effort for tasks of the large project.[7]

---

[7] If the hierarchical partitioning is not clean, you will have to *allocate* the measured effort for some WBS tasks to the high-level activities. This inevitably involves some estimation, and so introduces errors in the measured effort data for the high-level categories.

This allows you to compare data from large and small projects, without requiring the small projects to have a complex work breakdown structure. To do this, you must plan your data collection and analysis in advance! You must consider stakeholder needs, and then define a general-purpose WBS and a suitable charge number scheme. (Chapter 22, "Collecting Data: Details," describes the use of charge numbers.)

The numbers shown in Figure 16-8 are for a project that involved approximately three people for six months. The initial core effort was 3,000 person-hours, which equals the sum of the effort for project management, requirements analysis, product design, product development, and testing. (The other activities were either estimated as a percentage of this core value, or were estimated separately.) Including these additional activities, the estimated effort for the project was 3,430 person-hours. The team updated the estimate two months later because features were added, increasing the total estimated effort by almost 20%, to 4,108 person-hours. At completion, the team had expended 4,116 person-hours, slightly above the revised estimate.

You could improve the project effort summary form by subdividing the engineering effort into requirements definition, product design, and implementation. This would give a more equal partitioning of the effort. Assuming that these three activities are equally divided, each would represent about 17% of the "product design and development" effort. This is comparable to the effort for project management and for testing. The next section describes a form to do this.

16.3.6 Effort Collection Worksheet

Figure 16-9 shows a worksheet to collect the effort for tasks of a small software development project. A project administrator normally fills out the identifying information in the first four rows in the upper-right corner,[8] and then distributes copies to members of the project team. Each person only fills out entries on the row(s) corresponding to his or her role(s). (Some people may perform more than one role.) Column A lists the roles. Columns B through J indicate activities, with columns B, C through F, and G loosely corresponding to time-phased activities of the project life cycle. (You may update plans during the project, however.) People may perform the activities in columns H, I, and J at any time during a project. Note: The total hours that a person enters for each week need not exactly equal 40 because a person may work on other projects, perform administrative activities, or take vacation, holidays, or sick leave.

---

[8] The fourth row, WBD ID, is optional. You would use it if you want to collect effort for distinct tasks of the work breakdown structure.

	A	B	C	D	E	F	G	H	I	J
1								**PROJECT:**		
2								**WEEK ENDING:**		
3								**NAME:**		
4								**TASK ID:**		
5				**Weekly Effort Worksheet**						
6										
7		Project Planning	Product Development				Deploy Product	Attend Meetings	Provide Customer Support	Take Training
8	Role		Analyze Reqmts	Design Product	Construct Product	Test Product				
9	SW Developer									
10	SW Tester									
11	HW Technician									
12	Network Admin.									
13	CM Specialist									
14	QA Specialist									
15	Manager									
16	Metrics Analyst									
17				*Last Line*						
18										
19										
20		Notes (Optional)								
21										
22										
23										
24										
25										

Figure 16-9 *Weekly effort collection worksheet*

Unlike the other roles, the engineers and testers (rows 9 and 10) have more cells (in columns C through F). Typically, engineers and testers expend approximately 80% of the total project effort. The other members of the project team expend the remaining 20%. Thus, it makes sense to subdivide the product development activities for engineers and testers as shown. This partitioning provides "bins" containing similar amounts of effort. This reduces the total number of cells (tasks or activities), and yet provides reasonable resolution for tracking and analysis.

Testers should reinterpret the engineering activities as follows:

Engineering	*Testing*
Analyze requirements	Review requirements for testability
Design product	Define the test strategy and main test cases
Construct product	Identify remaining test cases, write test procedures and scripts
Test product	Conduct the tests (possibly various types)

For larger projects, you might also subdivide by the type of testing (e.g., functional, stress, and acceptance). (Engineers mainly perform repairs during the Test Product phase, but they may also help with testing.)

16.3.7 Project Schedule Form

Figure 16-10 shows the project schedule form with a suggested minimum set of milestones. The project cannot (or should not) start until the team has tailored the organization's defined process. This means choosing the project's process model, methods, and tools. You usually do this as part of preparing the offer or proposal. When the team receives funding, work begins. The next important activity is to either create or update the project plan(s) and get it (them) approved. The next milestone is product(s) accepted by the customer. If there are multiple products, or multiple versions or releases of a product, provide a date for each on a separate line. The last milestone is the acceptance of the project closeout report by the organization's process group (or metrics group). The key point is that an independent third party reviews the closeout report against an organizational standard and approves it for completeness.

TIP: To encourage the project manager to submit the closeout report, establish a policy that the Finance department will not close the project's accounts and post the profit until the Process Improvement department sends notification that it has accepted the project's closeout report.

The milestones shown are the bare minimum. Larger projects should insert additional milestones. You need to link the main milestones on the project's master schedule to those on the "minimum essential" schedule (Figure 16-10) so you can compare large and small projects.

Project:	Sample
Author:	R.Jones
Last Revised:	12-Jan-05

Milestone	Planned	Actual	Notes
Tailored process approved	17-Nov-04	20-Nov-04	
Begin work (project kickoff)	10-Jan-05	15-Jan-04	Funding arrived late.
Project plan(s) approved (See Note)	1-Feb-05	15-Feb-04	
Design(s) approved (See Note)	15-Apr-05	1-May-04	Revised requirements delayed design.
Implemention completed (See Note)	30-Aug-04	15-Sep-04	COTS compatability problems slowed development.
Funtional Test(s) complete (See Note)	1-Oct-04	12-Dec-04	Added test cases for exceptional scanarios.
Acceptance Test(s) complete (See Note)	15-Nov-04	9-Jan-05	Year end holidays delayed testing.
Project Closeout Report Accepted	1-Dec-04	12-Jan-05	

Last Line

Note
If there are multiple plans and/or work products, then identify them separately and supply a date for each one.

Figure 16-10 *Project schedule form*

16.3.8 Project Closeout Form

The project closeout form captures the lessons learned from a project. This information helps improve your processes, and also helps to interpret the data collected using the other forms. Figure 16-11 shows an example. Basically, I view this form as a way to indicate the content of a short report, not as a specific form to fill out.

Here are some practical hints to collect the information needed for the project closeout report:

- Hold a closeout meeting.
- Capture lessons during the project.
- Implement good ideas immediately.

```
┌─────────────────────────────────────────────────────────────────────────────┐
│                                                                               │
│  Project Closeout Report                    Project ID: _____     │
│                                                                               │
│  (Attach additional pages as appropriate)   Prepared By: _____     │
│                                                                               │
│                                             Date: _____     │
│                                                                               │
│          1.  What worked well?                                                │
│                                                                               │
│          2.  What failed or worked poorly?                                    │
│                                                                               │
│          3.  Which of these problems will other projects likely encounter in  │
│              the future?                                                      │
│                                                                               │
│          4.  What would you do differently next time?                         │
│                                                                               │
│          5.  What modules, custom tools, or techniques have a high potential  │
│              for reuse?                                                        │
│                                                                               │
│          6.  What changes do you recommend to the organization's standard     │
│              process?                                                         │
│                                                                               │
└─────────────────────────────────────────────────────────────────────────────┘
```

Figure 16-11 *Project closeout form*

At or near the end of the project, assemble the project team for a two-hour closeout meeting to identify the key lessons. Use the questions on the project closeout form and the list of topic areas above as a guide. Then the project manager writes up the results as a short report or just several briefing charts. This should only take three to four hours. Do not delay! After the project is closed out, the staff will quickly disappear to other projects, taking their valuable lessons learned with them!

Use "ought to have been done" (OTHBD) memos to collect lessons during the project. As events happen and ideas occur during a project, write a note and file it. Also have members of the project team send in OTHBD ideas. A good way to do this is to establish an e-mail account called "Lessons" so that people can submit ideas and suggestions. Read through the messages at the closeout meeting and use the information to assemble the closeout report. (Sometimes the closeout meeting is called a project postmortem. This name has negative connotations, so I don't use it.)

Depending on the size of the project, you may want to conduct meetings during the project to discuss and analyze problems, and to implement changes to the process. More mature organizations review the messages periodically during the project to identify opportunities for improvement. (The team software process calls these "launches" for successive phases. Agile methods also do this). If the team identifies problems that can be quickly corrected, do so immediately. Rapid resolution is part of risk management. If the organization's process must be changed, coordinate the changes with the process owner.

16.4 Automating Data Collection and Analysis

Automated tools increase data accuracy, reduce effort, and promote standard-ization and consistency. Using a tool to count objects is more accurate and cheaper than having a person count the objects by hand. Many software mea-surement tools are available. Some software development tools also produce measurements of design objects. Most organizations collect effort data using a time reporting or cost accounting system. (See the next section.) Unfortunately, not all measures can be automated. Function Point counting, described in Chapter 9, "Estimating Software Size: The Details," is a specific example. If automation is not possible, use detailed procedures and counting rules to obtain the measurement or count. You need operational definitions in either case.

Automation reduces effort and costs to collect and analyze data, to plot results, and to disseminate information. It also makes possible more detailed and sophisticated analyses than can be done by hand. (You can reduce costs, ana-lyze more data, or some combination thereof.) Automation helps standardize the measurement process, ensuring consistency and repeatability.

You can use spreadsheets to quickly analyze data, try out new estimating rela-tions, and store data for model calibration. Spreadsheets provide many func-tions for mathematics, statistics, and data management, and also a variety of graphs and plots. (Note N49, "Designing the CLEF2PA Spreadsheet," provides more information on using Microsoft Excel for analysis and plotting.)

You can store and manage the data you collect using database applications such as Microsoft Access and SQL Server. Use project scheduling tools such as Microsoft Project and Scitor's Project Scheduler to measure project schedules and task completion status. The book's CD-ROM and associated website pro-vide references to additional tools (vendors, tool descriptions, and websites).

Robert Grady and Deborah Caswell observe that initially you will not have a lot of data. Thus, a few paper forms and a spreadsheet tool suffice to get you started! Grady and Caswell explain how they started small, and then improved their measurement process [Grady, 1987].

16.5 Collecting Effort and Cost Data

Cost and effort are usually the hardest measurements to collect. The work breakdown structure provides a basis for budgeting the project, authorizing work, allocating funds, and collecting data needed to track task status. You must link each task to the agent who is responsible for performing the work.

Figure 16-12 illustrates this concept. The hybrid work breakdown structure is shown across the top of the figure, decomposed into levels down to individual tasks. The *organizational breakdown structure (OBS)* similarly decomposes the project into organization levels: firms, departments, and engineering teams. The organizational breakdown structure is shown down the left side. The lowest levels comprise a matrix: Columns are tasks and rows are agents that perform tasks. A *control account* links the lowest level (terminal) tasks of the WBS (the work packages) to specific agents (the lowest-level organizational units) by linking a WBS identifier and an OBS identifier. In the figure, the task "Build Analog Handler" divides into two work packages, which are mapped to two organizational units: Software Development and Test. Each work package has a separate control account. This allows you to trace any overruns to a particular organizational unit. (Identifying the source of an overrun is difficult if your project has hundreds of tasks.) Every control account is assigned to a person, the control account manager, who monitors and controls the activities, cost, and schedule for the work package.

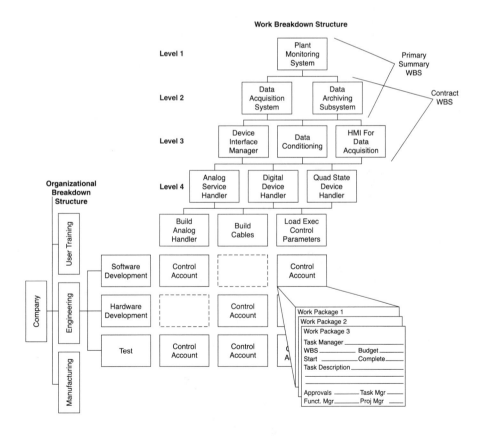

Figure 16-12 *Linking tasks to performers*

Control accounts are an abstract concept. Within your organization you implement control accounts using charge numbers in a cost accounting or job cost system. Workers in an organization charge labor hours, travel, materials, and other expenses to accounts identified by charge numbers. Ideally, you should define a regular rule to map WBS elements to charge numbers, giving consistency and traceability.[9] This can be challenging if multiple organizations are involved because each has its own accounting system. If you have a subcontractor on your team, you must collect their costs through your company's accounts payable system. (You might also have to make arrangements to collect additional data from their accounting system.) If you must provide cost accounting data to customers, or if your firm is a subcontractor to another firm, then you do this via your accounts receivable (invoicing) system.

Constraints on the format of available charge numbers may restrict the possible ways that you can map work packages to charge numbers. Ask your organization's accountants or project control experts for help when defining work breakdown structures and charge numbers. (Chapter 22 provides more details.)

What will measurement cost? Typical measurement costs for an organization are 0.5%–1.0% of the organization's total labor expenditure. If the organization has 100 full-time employees, measurement should require about one full-time person. For a larger organization, the percentage decreases. For example, an organization with 1,000 people might only need 2 or 3 full-time people to handle the metrics. Use automation where possible to reduce measurement costs. Chapter 22 discusses the challenges for very large projects, where tracking can consume several percent of the total project costs in extreme cases.

16.6 Recommended Reading

Robert Grady and Deborah Caswell provide useful checklists and guidance on implementing a practical metrics program [Grady, 1987]. Robert Grady also has a later book on the subject [Grady, 1992].

The Practical Software Measurement handbook defined by the U.S. Department of Defense is a good source of information. PSM is based on actual experience, and so provides a good source of proven techniques and tools. The best reference on Practical Software Measurement is the book by John McGarry et al. [McGarry, 2002]. In particular, Appendix A in [McGarry, 2002] provides precise definitions for many quantities of interest. Chapter 3 in [McGarry, 2002]

---

[9] Project planners may also define summary charge numbers to hold the totals for subordinate work packages. This facilitates "rolling up" the values for tracking and reporting.

has an excellent discussion of choosing measures. You can find additional information and examples related to software measurement at the Practical Software Measurement website: http://www.psmsc.com. The site also provides some tools.

William Florac and Anita Carleton identify possible measures, and discuss selecting, collecting, and analyzing metrics in [Florac, 1999]. The Software Engineering Institute has published several reports on software measurement, which are available on the Institute's website.

16.7 Summary

Table 16-4 summarizes the keys for successful measurement. Measurements are important to determine how a project is proceeding and to collect historical data needed to estimate future projects. This data can also help the organization improve its processes. Precise, consistent definitions are essential for all quantities that you measure and estimate. Standard definitions make meaningful communication possible. The definition of a measure must cover assumptions, scope, units of measure, and the conditions of measurement. The conditions are important to ensure that different people will obtain the same measured value for a quantity (within the error inherent in the particular measurement technique). Many organizations use "operational definitions" that focus on how the measurement is actually collected. If you know how the value was collected, then you know what the measured value means. Operational definitions also ensure consistency and repeatability because they contain the rules for collecting and reducing the data values.

Table 16-4 *Summary of Key Concepts*

1. Use Goals to Drive Your Measurement Requirements
• Many people need measurement data.
• You cannot afford to measure everything (cost/benefit).
• Do not collect data that you do not use (write-only database).
• Start small. (Use a few measures that you understand well.)
• The quantities that you measure will change over time.
• Adapt to meet specific project, product, and process needs.

(continues)

Table 16-4: *Summary of Key Concepts (continued)*

2. Define Each Measure Precisely
• Use scales and units correctly.
• Use operational definitions.
3. Plan for Accurate, Efficient Collection
• Use automated tools where possible.
• Provide data collection templates.
• Seamlessly integrate measurement into your processes.
• Validate raw data promptly.
• Verify that collection is occurring correctly.
4. Implement Carefully
• Analyze data in a timely manner.
• Protect individual privacy (aggregate data, report averages).
• Provide useful results to the data providers.
• Plan ahead. (Without planning nothing will happen.)

You must balance the benefit gained from measurements against the costs of obtaining the measurements. Templates and forms can help you implement a cost effective and useful metrics program to support estimating and tracking. Forms and procedures structure the collection process, ensuring that complete and consistent data is collected for every project. Paper forms are simple to start with. After you have stabilized the content and layout of the form, you can implement an electronic version. You can use a laptop computer to record information during meetings and peer reviews. Automation also promotes consistency, reduces collection costs, and increases accuracy by detecting errors when data is entered.

Analysis converts data into useful information. Charts and plots present information to decision makers. The next chapter describes some useful plots, and explains how to analyze data to extract useful information.

Chapter 17

Tracking Status

Tracking uses collected data to determine project status and performance trends. (Tracking also monitors the product's key technical performance measures and process performance. See Part 5, "Estimating Products and Processes.)" Analysis converts the data into useful information. The easiest way is to plot data in various ways. "A picture is worth a thousand words." You can fit trendlines to plots of time series data to predict (estimate) future values. You can use histograms to discern the distribution of samples in a population. You can also use various statistical techniques. Microsoft Excel is a powerful tool for analyzing data and presenting information. This chapter focuses on it.

Section 17.1 shows an example, and how to interpret the project's status. Section 17.2 covers the tracking process to establish the context for the types of information needed. Section 17.2 explains useful plots that you can generate using Excel. Section 17.3 discusses how to prepare "good" charts. Section 17.4 shows how to track with error bars. Section 17.5 covers trendlines and correlation. Section 17.6 covers (briefly) regression fitting. Section 17.7 discusses "perceptual" measurements. Section 17.8 lists recommended reading. Section 17.9 summarizes the key points.

17.1 Assessing Status

Table 17-1 summarizes the four basic steps of status checking. First, determine whether anything has changed. Consider the scope of the project, the product's requirements, and the estimating assumptions. Second, compare your planned value and the corresponding observed value for each quantity of interest for the product, project, and process. The expected values are the ones in the project's baselines. You obtain these values by estimating when planning the project. If you revise the project's baselines, use the revised values. (Chapter 18, "Updating Estimates," discusses updating estimates and revising baselines.) You obtain the observed values either by direct measurement, indirect measurement, or by updating estimates (e.g., based on new information or data). Third, compare the computed differences with the threshold criteria established for the corresponding quantity to determine if the difference is significant. Also check for adverse trends. Trend analysis gives early warning that the project is heading for trouble. The sooner you detect this, the more time you will have to take corrective action.

Table 17-1 *Status Checking Activities*

1. Compare Inputs with Previous Values   • Assumptions changed or violated?   • New item(s) identified?   • Counts of a particular item different?   • Size or amount of an item changed (increased)?   • Productivity values different (lower)?   • Other parameter values changed?
2. Compare Planned (Estimated) and Actual Values For   • Product size, performance, and quality   • Project effort, cost, and schedule   • Process performance
3. Decide Whether the Differences or Changes Are Significant   • Difference exceeds predefined decision threshold?   • Adverse trends?
4. Take Actions as Appropriate   • Determine causes   • Redirect the staff   • Revise estimates and plans (Chapter 19)   • Obtain better measurements   • Revise threshold values

The fourth step shown in Table 17-1 is to decide what to do if the difference exceeds the threshold. Determining the cause(s) of the differences usually involves various members of the project team. Based on the results, the project manager may redirect the team members, or even decide to replan or reprogram the project. In some cases, the manager must negotiate changes in scope with the customer or resort to legal remedies to constrain or compel the customer or third parties that are causing problems.

Managers may also request better measurements because the observed values are suspect. It is possible, although infrequent, to change the threshold value. You only do this based on renegotiated requirements or scope, or approved reallocations of budgeted resources (money, time, computer capacity).

The types of quantities that you track depend on the particular products and services that you will deliver, the processes that you will use, and the type of project. For example, because effort is proportional to software size, and because effort dominates software development costs, tracking size provides insight into project cost. (Chapter 21, "Earned Value Measurement," explains how to use earned value to define project cost and schedule variances measured in monetary units. You can use these variances to diagnose the general state of a large project.) If product performance is important, you might track some technical performance measure such as the average time to process a transaction. Risk management identifies some of the quantities you must track, identifies mitigations, and sets thresholds to trigger these actions.

17.2 Tracking Test Status

You can use a simple spreadsheet to track the status of testing and identify bottlenecks in the testing process. For example, you can detect if some individuals on the project team are overloaded. To do this, count and plot the number of validated unique software trouble reports (VUSTRs) versus time for three categories: Found, Fixed, and Retested. For simplicity, I will refer to VUSTRs as "bugs" in the remainder of this section. Testing discovers and reports bugs, the number found. Programmers analyze and correct the reported problems, the number fixed. Testers retest the fixes, the number retested. (Sometimes the fixes are bad, leading to rejection of the fix, or to the creation of a new bug. I ignore bad fixes for this example.)

A refinement is to classify the bugs by severity and track each category separately. Possible categories include the following:

- *Critical*. Failure impedes testing (cannot run certain other test cases).
- *Important*. Test case fails, but this does not impede other testing.

- *Cosmetic.* The software functions as expected, but produces minor anomalies (e.g., screens and reports show correct values but the formatting is incorrect).

All of these affect product acceptance, of course. For functional testing, you might further subdivide bugs based on whether or not they affect acceptance. For simplicity, the following example only considers one type of bug.

Table 17-2 shows sample data for each week that testing is occurring. The four columns at the left record the direct measurements: date plus the numbers of bugs that have been found by the testers, fixed by the developers, and retested by the testers. The other columns contain values calculated using the measurements. The center columns show the cumulative totals not fixed and not retested. The three columns at the right show the find (detection) rate, fix rate, and (re)test rate, measured in bugs (VUSTRs) per week.

Table 17-2 *Sample Test Data*

Week Ending	Found	Fixed	Retested	Not Fixed	Not Retested	Find Rate	Fix Rate	Test Rate
11-Jan-02	2	0	0	2	0	0	0	0
18-Jan-02	3	1	0	2	1	1	1	0
25-Jan-02	4	2	1	2	1	1	1	1
01-Feb-02	6	3	1	3	2	2	1	0
08-Feb-02	7	5	1	2	4	1	2	0
15-Feb-02	10	7	1	3	6	3	2	0
22-Feb-02	12	9	2	3	7	2	2	1
01-Mar-02	16	12	3	4	9	4	3	1
08-Mar-02	22	15	3	7	12	6	3	0
15-Mar-02	26	19	4	7	15	4	4	1
22-Mar-02	30	22	6	8	16	4	3	2
29-Mar-02	35	25	7	10	18	5	3	1
05-Apr-02	39	30	8	9	22	4	5	1
12-Apr-02	44	36	11	8	25	5	6	3
19-Apr-02	48	41	15	7	26	4	5	4
26-Apr-02	52	44	17	8	27	4	3	2
03-May-02	57	50	20	7	30	5	6	3

Week Ending	Found	Fixed	Retested	Not Fixed	Not Retested	Find Rate	Fix Rate	Test Rate
10-May-02	63	54	24	9	30	6	4	4
17-May-02	67	59	28	8	31	4	5	4
24-May-02	72	65	31	7	34	5	6	3
31-May-02	76	69	35	7	34	4	4	4
07-Jun-02	79	73	39	6	34	3	4	4
14-Jun-02	81	76	44	5	32	2	3	5
21-Jun-02	82	78	47	4	31	1	2	3
28-Jun-02	82	79	52	3	27	0	1	5
05-Jul-02	83	80	56	3	24	1	1	4
12-Jul-02	83	81	61	2	20	0	1	5
19-Jul-02	83	82	65	1	17	0	1	4

Figure 17-1 plots the cumulative values from the table as a function of time. (I set the dates to start and end on a Friday, and to give precisely six weeks between major gridlines using Excel's axis Scale option.) The top curve (marked with the open circles) shows the cumulative number of bugs found. The center curve (marked with solid circles) shows the number of bugs fixed by the developers. The bottom curve (marked with solid squares) shows the cumulative number of fixed bugs that have been retested by the test team.

Figure 17-1 shows a number of things. First, the curve showing the cumulative number of bugs found is roughly S-shaped. The number of bugs found per week is small initially, then rises to a peak, and finally decreases as all bugs have been discovered.[1] Second, the programmers respond rapidly to the reported problems and correct them quickly, as indicated by the closeness of the found and fixed curves. (Perhaps they have finished writing all of the required code, and so are available to fix problems.) By the end of the period shown (July 19, 2002), they have corrected essentially every bug that has been identified. The testers, however, are unable to retest the fixes rapidly enough to keep up with the programmers. The divergence of the fixed and retested curves indicates this lag. (Perhaps the testers are behind because each fix requires a

---

[1] The product may still contain bugs. The current set of test cases is just incapable of exposing them. A set of test cases only explores a portion of the code. Once all of the test cases have been run and the bugs corrected, the number of new bugs discovered finally decreases to zero. The particular set of test cases can provide no additional information.

large amount of regression testing and associated analysis.) This tells the project manager to assign more people to do testing. (Usually, the manager assigns some programmers to work as testers. They cannot test their own code, of course.) Around April 4, 2002 the rate of retesting increases due to the addition of people, and the testers are making steady progress in the latter half of the time period shown. (This plot will also show if the programmers are not fixing problems fast enough to keep the testers busy. This could happen if the problems require major redesign of the software, for example.)

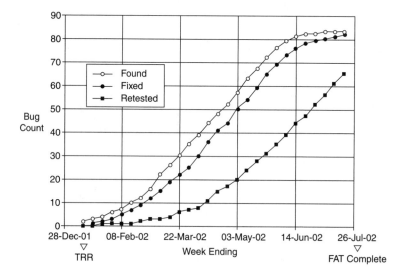

Figure 17-1 *Cumulative bugs versus time*

Figure 17-2 confirms the interpretation of Figure 17-1. It shows the total number of items that are not yet fixed, and not yet retested. The developers' backlog (open circles) increases at first but then remains constant at 8–10 bugs. It decreases at the end of the interval because no more new bugs are being found and the developers are fixing the ones already reported. The testers' backlog (solid circles) also increases, indicating that the testers are not able to keep up (or possibly that the bugs found later require more retesting). What is interesting in this chart is that the manager saw the decrease in the number of bugs to be fixed, and realized that fewer programmers were needed for repair work. The manager shifted these employees onto the test team, allowing the rate of retesting to increase. This is why the number of fixed, not tested, bugs starts to decrease rapidly at the right side of the figure. Tracking the number of bugs fixed and the number of fixes retested allows you to see where the bottleneck is. Are the developers not fixing the bugs fast enough? Are the testers not retesting the fixes fast enough? (You can refine this basic approach by tracking bugs by type, severity, etc.)

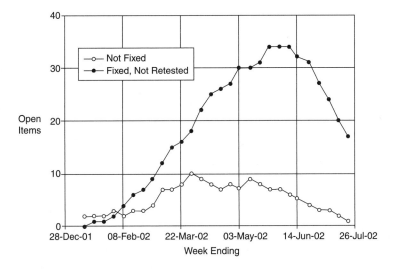

Figure 17-2 *Backlog versus time*

Figure 17-3 provides more insight into the testing process. This figure plots the number of bugs per week that are found, fixed, and retested (indicated by the black, gray, and dashed lines, respectively.) There is a large amount of fluctuation in the rates from week to week. To convey useful information, I suppress the data points themselves, and show only a six-point moving average trendline for each of the three data sets. The number of bugs found rapidly increases early in the test process, then levels out for a while, and then finally decays toward zero. The reason for this behavior is that early in the test process there are certain bugs that "crash" the system, making it impossible for the testers to execute large portions of the code. Until these bugs are corrected, the testers cannot detect the remaining defects. The number of bugs found per week typically levels out because there is a limit to how fast the test team can execute test cases and document the defects. (The testing staff is saturated.) Finally, after the testers have sampled the "entire" operational envelope of the software, essentially all of the defects have been found. ("Entire" may not be all of the envelope. It depends on how thoroughly the set of test cases covers the software's functions, modes, and decision paths.) This is why the defect discovery rate (the number of defects found) declines toward zero.

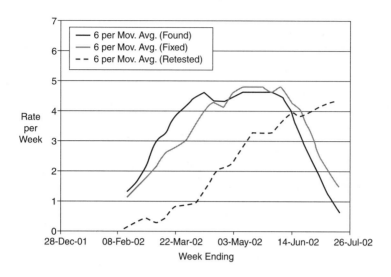

Figure 17-3 *Moving averages of rates with markers suppressed*

There is an inevitable time lag in fixing the bugs that have been found because the developers must receive the trouble reports and analyze the problem before they can fix the problem. The gray line in Figure 17-3 shows the number of fixed bugs. These delays cause the peak of the fixed curve to be displaced to the right relative to the peak of the Found curve. The fixed curve also has a flat top. This suggests that the developers make repairs at an increasing rate until the central portion of the curve, at which time they become saturated at 4–5 bugs per week. Eventually, the number of bugs being reported decreases and the developers have corrected the identified bugs. At this point, the backlog of uncorrected bugs and the repair rate both decrease.

There is also an inevitable time lag in testing the repaired code because the testers cannot begin testing until the fixes have been completed and turned over to the test team. These delays cause the retested curve (shown by the dashed line) to be displaced even more to the right. The rate increases steadily. No saturation is apparent in the data shown. This may be because the manager assigned additional people to the test team. (Charts do not give you all the answers. They do help you discern interesting behavior that leads to further investigation.)

The simple plot shown in Figure 17-3 indicates whether the "test, fix, and retest" process is converging. (Assuming that no more bugs will be found, simple extrapolation of the cumulative number of bugs retested shown in the figure gives approximately three calendar-weeks to complete the retesting.

This is approximately August 9, 2002.) The weekly plots of backlogs and rates help the manager assign workers in a more optimal way.

For tracking purposes, it would be helpful to have curves showing the predicted number of defects found, fixed, and retested versus time. These curves depend on several parameters. To predict these curves you need a way to estimate the total number of defects in the product, the productivity (defects per person-hour) or the "production rate" (defects per time unit) for finding, fixing, and retesting, and some way to determine the shape of the basic curves. This is not an easy task. (See the discussion of defect discovery curves and Reliability Growth Models in Chapter 25, "Determining Product Quality.") You may have different curves for each type of defect as well.

17.3 Tracking Size and Productivity

Figure 17-4 shows a simple spreadsheet to track size, effort, and productivity versus time (quarterly in this example). The primary project activities being performed in the four quarters correspond to enhance, repair, perfect, and enhance, respectively. The base size increases over time. (The Net Increase row shows the growth for each quarter.) The reported effort (in person-hours) is collected from the employees' time cards. The production coefficient is based on the total work done, divided by the reported hours. (The Total Work row is the sum of the function points added, changed, and deleted. The "volatility" corresponds to the Change row.) The values in this example remain fairly stable. You can plot such data to determine process capability and stability. I also recommend making a second plot using the actual hours worked, including uncompensated overtime. (This is often unreported so you may have to devise a way to collect it.) This will give a more accurate value for the production coefficient. You can also observe whether the amount of overtime is unusually high.

You must present information so that stakeholders can quickly and correctly understand it. Preceding chapters have shown various types of plots. Note N22, "Types of Plots," provides a summary. This section provides specific guidance on producing good charts. For example, the use of color and labeling is important. Appendix E, "Excel for Estimators," explains how to prepare plots in Excel. (Excel calls plots "charts." This is useful to know when you query the Help Wizard.) Although Excel provides many useful features, you should avoid certain defaults and features. Table 17-3 gives specific recommendations.

		Q1	Q2	Q3	Q4	Q5
Size (FP)	*Base Size*	1000	1025	1045	1045	1060
	Add	30	20	10	20	
	Change	10	40	20	20	
	Delete	5	0	10	5	
	Total Work	45	60	40	45	
	Net Increase	25	20	0	15	
Reported						
Effort	*For Period*	490	575	410	460	
(phrs)	*Cumulative*	490	1065	1475	1935	
Production						
Coefficient						
(phrs/FP)						
	For Period	10.89	9.58	10.25	10.22	
	Cumulative	10.89	10.14	10.17	10.18	

Figure 17-4 *Project data: reported hours*

Table 17-3 *Recommendations for Good Charts*

Label Everything
• Title, axes, and lines.
• Put filename, worksheet, date, and time in the header (on every sheet).
• Define unfamiliar acronyms in a text box.
Make All Text and Lines Legible
• Choose a point size large enough to be read.
• Avoid vertical text.
Use Only Black and White
• Avoid light pastel colors.
• Avoid red and green colors.
Reduce the "Ink to Paper" Ratio
• Remove the default gray background.
• Avoid fancy fill effects.
• Remove gridlines that are not needed.

When you have dozens of spreadsheets, plots, and charts, you need a way to identify what the purpose of each one is, and which is the most current version. Figure 17-5 shows an example of a "good" chart prepared using Excel. It has a title, and labels on each axis (which show the units of measure). The label for the vertical axis is rotated so you can read it without turning the page. (This is not a firm rule, but is generally a good idea.) Each of the three lines is labeled and lines connect the data points to help the eye see the trends. The page heading shows the filename, worksheet, date, and time.

Use a large point size if you must project the chart in a large room. If you must copy or fax the chart, the following can cause problems: small type, light pastel colors, and colored or shaded backgrounds. For example, charts with Excel's default gray background often appear darker when copied, obscuring the data points and the lines. Do not rely on color to make your point. Some colors (especially pale ones) do not project, copy, or fax well. In addition, some individuals are color blind, and cannot distinguish some colors. Do not use fancy fill effects for the background (gradient shading, textures, patterns, and pictures). Remove unnecessary gridlines to keep the chart uncluttered. You can also include text boxes on a chart to define unfamiliar acronyms or provide other information. See Appendix E.

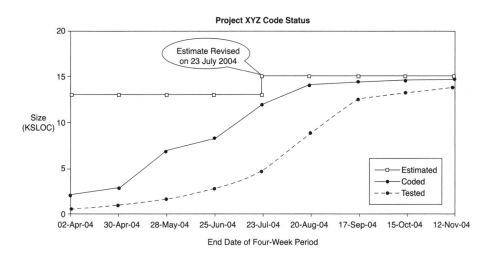

Figure 17-5 *Example of a good chart*

17.4 Tracking Size with Error Bars

Excel enables you to add error bars to a data series. If you can estimate the error in a measured value, you can plot error bars on charts. This helps you see if a particular data point lies "too far away from" a fitted line.

Suppose that you plot the total size of a software product (in whatever size units you desire) and the amount of code completed. The difference in these two quantities is the amount of code that the programmers must still write. (This indicates the development effort.) Early in a project, the size is all estimated. As the project proceeds, some code is completed and so its size becomes known. The remaining amount is still estimated, however. Using statistics, the standard deviation of a count (size in this case) is approximately the square root of the number. Table 17-4 shows the data. Figure 17-6 plots the total size, and the delivered size, with error bars. The error bars are plus and minus one standard deviation in this plot. (Appendix E explains how to add error bars.) As expected, the uncertainty in the size decreases as the end of the project approaches. (Note that some growth in the estimated amount occurs over time. There are ways to use historical data to estimate the amount of growth expected versus time. See Chapter 8, "Estimating Software Size: The Basics.")

Table 17-4 *Size Versus Time*

Elapsed Time	Completed Size	Estimated Size	Total Error In Size	Estimated Size
0.00	0	100	100	10.0
0.15	0	105	105	10.2
0.30	3	112	110	10.6
0.40	8	112	120	10.6
0.50	12	110	122	10.5
0.60	70	55	125	7.4
0.70	100	25	125	5.0
0.75	120	5	125	2.2
0.80	123	3	126	1.7
0.90	125	1	126	1.0
1.00	126	0	126	0.0

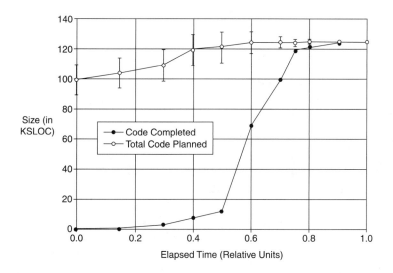

Figure 17-6 *Size Versus time*

17.5 Trendlines

You often measure (or estimate) the characteristics of an object over time. You plot these measured data points versus time using a scatter plot or a run chart to observe the trend or direction of the data values. Excel allows you to add trendlines to visualize and quantitatively describe the trend. (Appendix E explains how to create trendlines.) Microsoft Excel offers a choice of functions for trendlines: linear, logarithmic, polynomial, exponential, power, and a moving average. A regression algorithm adjusts the coefficients of the chosen function to produce the "best" fit to the set of data points. There are several ways to define what "best" means. The one most often used is the least squares criterion: Minimize the sum of the squares of the differences between each measured point and the value predicted by the fitted function. You can choose the type of function based on the following:

- Some assumed model (e.g., $y = ax^b$)
- Preferred shape or asymptotic behavior (e.g., exponential decay)
- The pattern of the plotted data points
- The highest r^2 value among several fitted functions (See text.)

The measured values contain errors so the best fit is never perfect. One way to gauge the quality of a fit is the coefficient of determination, denoted by r^2, where r is the Pearson product-moment correlation coefficient.[2] The value of r^2 indicates the percentage of variation of the independent variable accounted for by the fitted function. Opinions differ, but a "good" fit has $r^2 > 0.8$ or so. (Excel provides other statistical measures. Appendix E describes Excel's built-in functions to calculate population statistics.)

Figure 17-7 shows a plot with a trendline chosen to be a third order polynomial with a zero intercept. The fit is reasonably good because $r^2 = 0.72$, indicating that the fitted polynomial accounts for 72% of the variation observed in the data points. The curve is also extrapolated backward 15 units to show that the fitted curve goes through the origin. Figure 17-8 shows a third order polynomial fitted to the same data except that the Y value of the point at $X = 100$ has been changed from 9.21 to 5.61. The fitted curve is quite different. A single bad data point has distorted the curve and the fit is worse ($r^2 = 0.60$). The next section gives another example.

You can extrapolate ("forecast") the fitted curve forward, backward, or both for some specified distance along the x-axis, and so predict future values, which is a way of estimating.

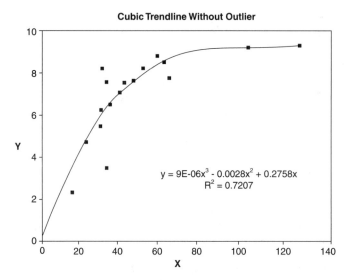

Figure 17-7 *Plot of data with no outlier*

---

[2] Excel refers to r^2 as R^2 or R-squared in charts and menus. Statisticians use a capital R to refer to the correlation coefficient for multiple independent variables.

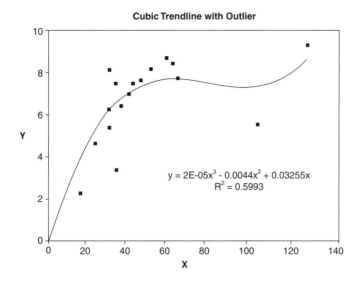

Figure 17-8 *Plot of data with one outlier*

17.6 Regression Fitting

Estimators are often interested in the functional dependence of one quantity on one or more independent variables. For example, the function could be an estimating model. Errors in the measured values often mask this dependence. Mathematicians and statisticians have devised various clever ways to select and fit functions to measured data. Regression techniques calculate the coefficients of some (assumed or specified) function to produce the "best" fit to a set of measured data points. (See note N23, "Fitting Data That Contains Errors.")

Excel and other commercial tools provide many ways to fit data and analyze the goodness of fit. One technique is analysis of variance (ANOVA). Refer to the books referenced at the end of this chapter for more information.

There is a trade-off between responsiveness and stability in all fitting schemes. Averaging data over several samples gives more stability, but cannot quickly detect changes in the underlying trend. Figures 17-9 and 17-10 show an example. The first figure has 10 data points, with the point at X = 7 being an obvious outlier, and shows three trendlines fitted to the data: linear, two-point moving average, and four-point moving average. Note how the outlier distorts both of the moving average trends. The four-period moving average is disturbed less, however. Figure 17-10 shows linear and two-point moving average trendlines with the outlier at X = 7 removed. The moving average follows this "well-behaved" data reasonably faithfully. So, if you could remove extreme outliers, using a two-point moving average would give a good response. You can remove most outliers by computing the sample mean μ and standard deviation σ, and then discarding all points lying outside the interval [μ − 2*σ, μ + 2*σ].

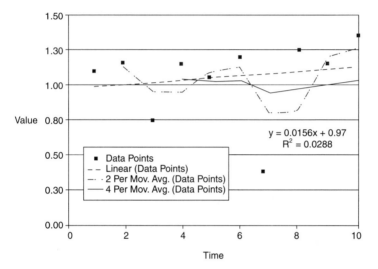

Figure 17-9 *Fitting noisy data with outliers*

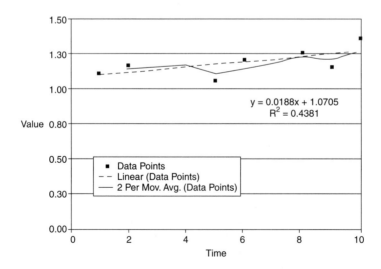

Figure 17-10 *Noisy data without outliers*

The trade-off between responsiveness and stability affects statistical process control. The problem is essentially how to distinguish the signal from the noise. (This is related to hypothesis testing in statistics, which categorizes errors as Type 1 [false rejection] and Type 2 [false acceptance].) Statistical process control defines various rules to make the best possible decision. One example is counting the number of successive points on the same side of the average line. For more details, see Section 6.2 in the excellent book by William Florac and Anita Carleton [Florac, 1999]. Florac and Carleton also provide many examples relating to software processes.

17.7 Other Ways to Detect Trouble

Not all status indications are based on measurements. Managers should use both "measurable" and "perceptual" data, as illustrated in Table 17-5. Any unexpected (unplanned) event can jeopardize project success. For example, if a piece of test equipment fails, testing cannot proceed until it is repaired. I frequently observe this progression: Technical problems arise, leading to a schedule slip. The schedule slip increases costs (due to the burn rate). The customer and management become unhappy. This says that product performance measures give the earliest warning on complex projects. The second best indicator is schedule. The third best indicator is cost (or effort).

You can measure volatility by the number of times that requirements or documents are revised. (The documents have to be under configuration control to detect changes, of course.) Some revisions are inevitable because requirements and interface definitions are imprecise and so subject to interpretation. The thing to watch for is revisions that occur late in a project. At this point, tasks may be behind schedule and resources are increasingly scarce. For large projects, the revisions are sometimes just reinterpretations that result in the "migration" of requirements, functions, and databases from one subsystem to another. (The flow is usually from the prime contractor's subsystems to the subcontractor's subsystems.)

Table 17-5 *Warning Signs*

Measurable
• Increasing size
• Slipping schedule
• Actual costs exceed planned costs
• Technical difficulties (problem reports, action items)
• Volatility in requirements, interface definitions, etc.
Perceptual
• Errors reappear
• Excessive need for overtime
• Customer dissatisfaction
• Staff morale low
• High staff turnover

Perceptual information can also be important. For example, bugs do not stay fixed. This can occur for two reasons. First, poor configuration control may allow later changes to overwrite a previous fix. Second, the same bug may appear in multiple places, perhaps because programmers copied and customized pieces of code as they rush to deliver working code by some deadline. (This action also increases the software size!) CMMI Level 5 organizations typically look for patterns of similar code when an error is detected, and then fix all occurrences.

Workers may ask to stagger their work schedule. For example, you might hear, "I will come in at noon and work until 9:00 p.m. because the turnaround is better." The underlying cause might be contention for resources, distracting noise in an open office environment, telephone calls, or meetings. Frequent meetings are a common management response to crises. ("We'll keep having these meetings until we discover why no one is getting any work done.")

Don't underestimate the value of informal communication. You can learn a lot just by walking around. Look for cartoons and signs indicating frustration on doors and bulletin boards. Sense the morale in the team's break room or coffee area. Come in occasionally on nights and weekends, especially if the project is in "crunch mode."

17.8 Recommended Reading

The *Practical Software Measurement Guidebook* [Bailey, 1966] provides good advice and examples for tracking software projects. Chapter 3 of Part 1 discusses collecting, analyzing, and reporting data. Part 5 provides several excellent case studies for software projects showing the use of multiple plots to diagnose problems. The authors have distilled this into a book [McGarry, 2002].

There are many books dealing with tracking and process improvement. I recommend [Florac, 1999]. The Six-Sigma Method is another approach to process improvement. George Eckes provides an overview in [Eckes, 2003]. Benchmarking is another tracking technique that supports process improvement. Two references are [Jones, 1997] and [McNair, 1995].

Press et al. discuss regression fitting in Chapter 15 of [Press, 1992].

Tom DeMarco and Tim Lister describe the productivity losses due to open work areas and public intercom systems [DeMarco, 1999].

17.9 Summary

You must track status during a project because estimates and plans are not perfect, things change, and unexpected events occur. During a project, regularly collect data and track status at appropriate intervals. The frequency depends on the project's size, health, and the degree of interest expressed by the project's stakeholders.

Tracking primarily uses measurements (although estimation does play some part in the process). Perception is also useful. Project tracking has four steps:

1. Track status against plan.
2. Update estimate (using new information).
3. Redefine the project (requirements, design, process).
4. Update estimate (using the redefined project).

Normally, you perform only the first two steps. The next chapter explains how to update estimates.

Chapter 18

Updating Estimates

Inaccurate initial information and inevitable changes mean that you must update estimates during the project. Figure 18-1 shows the same "two loop" diagram shown in Chapter 1, "Introduction." This chapter describes the actions that occur in the inner feedback loop (loop 1) during the project. To update estimates, you will use the techniques and methods described in Parts 1 and 2 to estimate product size and performance, project effort, cost, and schedule, product quality goals, and process performance goals. This chapter focuses on when to prepare updated estimates, and how to select different methods to exploit the additional information available.

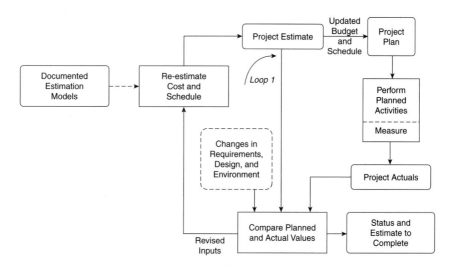

Figure 18-1 *Updating estimates during a project*

18.1 Reasons to Update Estimates

You will usually have to update or revise estimates during a project (or proposal) for one or more of the reasons listed in Table 18-1. The first seven items address significant deviations from the plan, unplanned events, or new requirements. The last two items allow you to take advantage of new information. Figure 18-2 illustrates how you use new information to reduce the uncertainty in your estimates. During a project, more accurate estimates help you control the project's processes, products, and resources better. During a proposal, updated estimates help you produce a more accurate basis for the bid price.

Table 18-1 *Reasons to Update Estimates*

Observed performance differs from plan
Known risks become problems
New problems arise
New risks identified
Revised requirements (new, changed)
Altered scope, ground rules, and assumptions
Change in planned resources (availability, capability)
Improved understanding of the product (size, performance)
Improved understanding of the process (productivity, costs)

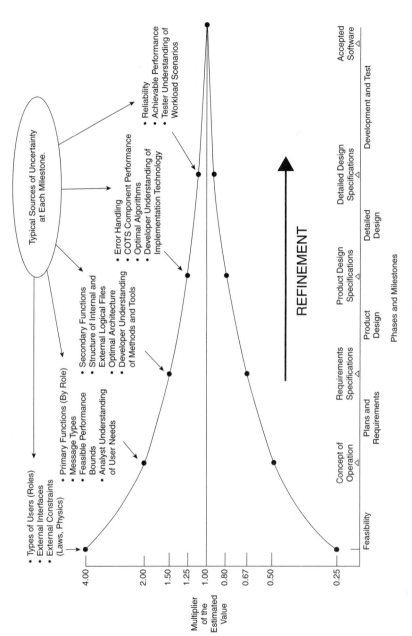

Figure 18-2 *Refinement reduces uncertainty*

18.2 The Basic Process

You may have to prepare more that one estimate for a particular quantity. Generally, you will perform one or more of the following four activities:

- Track status against the plan (the baselines)
- Update estimates (using new information)
- Redefine the project (requirements, design, process)
- Update the estimate (using the redefined plan)

You always continue to track the status (since something else might change, plus you want to see if the corrective actions have had any effect). If there are unacceptable variances, or if you receive new information, then you update your estimates using the new information. These updated predictions may indicate that the project cannot achieve its goals (product performance or quality, project cost or schedule, process efficiency, or some combination thereof). If so, and if the deviations cannot be corrected within the scope of the existing plan, then the team must devise a new approach. (This is the reprogramming situation.) In this case, the team must examine the old and new requirements, the product design, the production process, the project characteristics, and possibly even the estimating methods. The team revisits the precursors of estimation. In essence, the team follows the steps previously described in Section 15.12 to reduce the price. The team can then prepare the new estimate, budgets, schedules, and plans. This may require some iteration. Be sure to compare your updated estimates with your old estimates and try to understand any major differences. This helps catch blunders and provides insight useful for future estimates.

18.3 When to Prepare Updated Estimates

You should update your estimates

- Iteratively during project conception or proposal preparation.
- At project kickoff.
- At each major milestone (formal review).
- When the purchaser requests a change in scope.
- When unexpected or significant events occur.
- Monthly, if the necessary data is available.

During project conception, a team is learning at a rapid rate so there is always a lot of new information. (This is especially true for large proposals that have a time limit.) To take advantage of this, update your estimates of the project cost, product performance, etc. Project kickoff is also a good time to update estimates. Sometimes negotiations change deliverables, schedules, constraints, etc. In addition, the prudent project team will prepare estimates to ensure that the proposal made feasible, achievable promises. (Proposal teams often take a bit of "artistic license," perhaps more so if they know that they will not have to work on the project.) The milestone reviews defined in the project's life cycle are a good opportunity for all stakeholders to confirm that they still have the same product vision and project goals. (Perceptions can diverge, especially if original players are replaced, and if new stakeholders enter the scene.) See the box "Periodic Replanning." Estimates are important because they are the basis for project plans, budgets, and schedules. Estimates of product performance may be important as well. Purchasers may request a change in scope, which leads to reprogramming as described earlier. Unexpected events are deviations from the plan (the expected baselines). Significant events are anything that might affect the project or product. For example, a vendor may cease to offer a particular commercial off-the-shelf (COTS) component that is a key part of the product's architecture.

Periodic Replanning

Replanning is built in to some of the project life cycles described in Chapter 10, "Production Processes (Project Life Cycles)." Agile development processes replan at the end of every iteration, which may occur as often as every week or two. Evolutionary and spiral development processes plan at larger intervals, usually tied to the completion of a build or the end of a cycle. Long-duration projects may replan even more often, possibly every three to six months. In the team software process, the team does a "relaunch" to revise and update the plans at the end of each phase. Reasons to replan include the following:

1. Accommodate changes requested by stakeholders and approved by the project manager.

2. Exploit new information from the reviews at the end of each phase or cycle.

3. Prepare detailed plans for upcoming activities. ("Rolling-wave" planning reduces effort spent revising overly detailed plans by postponing the detailed planning of future tasks until they are imminent.)

18.4 Preparing Updated Estimates

Preparing updated estimates is essentially the same as preparing initial estimates. You can use any of the methods and techniques described in Parts 1 and 2. There are three primary differences to consider. First, you have a better understanding of the application and solution domains. Second, you should also have new information and even some actual data on product size, team productivity, and actual costs. This means that you can substitute actual measured values for some quantities that you had to estimate initially. For example, you may have actual salaries instead of estimates. You might know the increases in airfares, shipping charges, and cost of living adjustments. You might also know that personnel with different labor grades (and hence different salaries) are performing some tasks. (The grades may be higher or lower, depending if the task is more or less difficult than originally envisioned.) Also, productivity may be higher or lower than you originally estimated. For hardware production, the learning curve may have been too optimistic. You also know if certain risks have occurred or can no longer occur. There may also be some new risks.

You can choose different estimating techniques and methods to take advantage of this additional information. The next section explains how to select appropriate estimation methods. Then prepare your updated estimates, document them, and obtain an independent review. There are several good reasons to document the entire estimate. First, this records the values and assumptions used to establish the baseline used for bidding, setting performance criteria for products, gauging risks, etc. Second, it permits others to review the baseline and the associated assumptions. Third, it communicates the baseline to other stakeholders, including people who will become involved in the future. These baselines are the basis for product design, project plans, and so forth. Thus, new engineers and managers who join a project will need to know this information. Fourth, good documentation (e.g., estimating assumptions) can protect the development team. Tables 3-5 and 3-6 provide guidance on what to record.

If there are major changes in the estimates or project scope, senior managers and customers will want to approve the new estimates. This may lead to iteration similar to that used to reduce the project cost or the bid price.

18.4.1 Choosing an Estimating Technique

No single technique, model, or method estimates every quantity of interest. Table 18-2 shows possible estimating methods by resource type and project phase. The left column lists various types of quantities. The next column identifies techniques that you could use when bidding a new project. Vendor quotes are provided for materials, subcontracts, and some services. In some cases, these are based on catalog prices, possibly with quantity discounts. Standard rates are often used for labor and are similar to catalog prices. The designers and estimators must of course specify the number of items to be purchased and the amount of labor required. You can use techniques such as Delphi and PERT to improve the estimates of the various counts and amounts.

Table 18-2: *Use of Different Estimating Methods*

Time Type of Item	Bid	Execution (Early Stages)	Execution (Late Stages)
Life cycle tasks	Parametric model, historical data, analogy, Delphi, PERT	Scaling based on life cycle phase allocations, expert Delphi, PERT	Earned value, trend extrapolation
Other project tasks	Linear, historical data, analogy, Delphi, PERT	Expert judgment, learning curves, actual productivity	Earned value, trend extrapolation
Materials	Linear, vendor quotes, Delphi, PERT	Revised quotes, actual invoices	Actual invoices
Support costs	Standard rates, historical data, analogy, Delphi	Provisional rates, projections, actual costs	Provisional rates, actual costs

The two rightmost columns of the table show additional techniques such as scaling, trend analysis, learning curves, and projections (extrapolations) that can be used after a project is underway and you begin to collect actual data. Learning curves are commonly used when estimating costs for a "production run" that produces many identical items. A good example is the manufacture of automobiles. The effort required to fabricate and assemble a vehicle decreases over time as the workers learn how to do their tasks more efficiently. Cost analysts analyze data and construct various functions ("learning curves"), and then use these functions to predict the decreases for similar manufacturing processes. In some cases, engineers can improve the design of the item as well as reduce the nonlabor resources needed to manufacture the product. Boh, Slaughter, and Espinosa examine learning curves for software development [Boh, 2003].

Figure 18-3 illustrates how the usage of different estimating techniques changes during a project. Very early, experts can gauge the approximate size and scope of a project. Analogies to similar previous projects are better, especially if you use a standard process or build similar items as part of a product line. The best analogies use quantitative techniques. (Chapter 5, "Estimating Techniques," mentioned ways to adjust historical data to account for small differences.) The Top-Down Method described in Chapter 12, "Top-Down Estimating and Allocation," lies between analogies and parametric models, and is not shown in the figure. Parametric models are useful early to analyze alternatives and prepare initial estimates. They are also useful during a project to evaluate changes requested by customers or the impact of problems. The Bottom-Up Method provides the most detailed and accurate estimates. The level of detail depends on the size of the job and customer desires. Once the project starts, you begin to obtain actual data on progress, effort expended, and costs. You may also have information on requirements growth and volatility, and software size growth. You can use this information to prepare updated estimates using parametric models or the Bottom-Up Method. You can also extrapolate trends to forecast the total cost and schedule at project completion. (Chapter 21, "Earned Value Measurement," describes the earned value technique, which provides a way to estimate a project's completion cost and dates.)

Use the guidance in Table 18-3 to choose the appropriate techniques, models, or methods. Section 13.10 provides advice for selecting automated estimating tools.

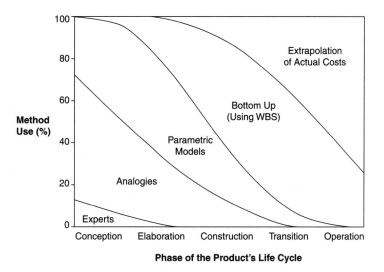

Figure 18-3 *Use of estimating techniques versus time*

Table 18-3 *Considerations in Selecting a Method*

Capabilities
• Does it estimate the quantities you want?
• Does it provide acceptable accuracy?
• Will others accept the results?
• Does it use validated historical data? (calibration, analogies)
Practicality
• Is it appropriate for the overall scope and complexity of the project? (level of detail, traceability)
• Can you estimate the necessary input parameters?
• Will it provide results soon enough?
• Can you afford to use it? (license costs, estimating effort)

18.4.2 Applying the Chosen Techniques

After you have chosen appropriate techniques, models, methods, and tools, how should you use them to prepare a particular estimate? You should use more than one technique, model, or method to estimate each particular quantity or set of related quantities because each estimating technique and model has strengths and weaknesses in terms of accuracy (biases and uncertainty), objectivity versus subjectivity of inputs, and cost of use. Two different models will never give exactly the same value. Some differences may arise from different assumptions about the core phases and activities, and the units of measure. (Some may arise from incorrect arithmetic calculations but I assume that you will have someone check your calculations! Rough order of magnitude calculations and dimensional analysis are also useful techniques.)

When should you stop iterating? There are two considerations. First, iterate your estimates until you understand all of the significant differences. This helps you understand the problem and the factors that affect the estimated values. Continue iterating until you reduce the differences to an acceptable level. The definition of "acceptable agreement" depends on the purpose of the estimate, the maturity of the information used to prepare the estimate (i.e., the funnel curve in Figure 1-3), and the amount of risk the sponsor (who pays for the resources) is willing to accept. For most development projects my rule of thumb is 10% to 20%. The remaining differences reflect the uncertainty inherent in the estimate. Report the estimated values and the uncertainties in these values to stakeholders and decision makers.

18.5 Preparing an Estimate to Complete

During the course of a project, the project manager, and usually the customer, will want to know the estimate at completion (EAC). (Other terms are the *latest revised estimate*, LRE, and *final indicated cost*, FIC.) The EAC equals the actual (known) cost of what is done plus the estimated cost of what is left to do:

EAC = ACWP + ETC

where ACWP is the actual cost of work performed and ETC is the estimate to complete. Note that ACWP includes the actual direct costs plus accruals. (Accountants use accruals to collect funds to pay for services, etc. that will be billed at a later date. For example, a computer service center may only submit charges quarterly.) The ACWP represents "sunk" costs. The money has been spent. The ETC includes estimated costs for all authorized work remaining plus any commitments. (Commitments are items or services that the organization has legally committed to buy by placing purchase orders, but have not yet been received, and so have not yet been billed to the organization.)

You will also need to update the project schedule. This might be as simple as shifting the start and completion dates for some tasks. If some events fail to occur as originally scheduled, however, you may need to revise the task network, adding tasks and changing task dependencies. For example, if a supplier fails to deliver a key component, you might add a task to build a temporary substitute. You might also shift the order of downstream tasks that depend on the component, postponing them and scheduling other tasks to be performed earlier than originally planned.

A formal estimate to complete is a complete bottom-up estimate that uses your detailed understanding of the project, actual data collected to date, and the latest information. You also prepare an updated schedule. Large projects typically update their resource Loaded Network, which integrates cost and time.

That said, the next two subsections show some quick and dirty ways to estimate the cost to complete a project. You should only use these to check the estimate made using the Bottom-Up Method! They are also useful for evaluating potential outcomes and tradeoffs. For small, informal projects, however, the techniques described next may be all you need.

18.5.1 Using Simple Scaling

If you know the allocation of effort and duration by phase for your project life cycle, you can use this data to prepare a simple estimate to complete. Table 18-4 shows sample data for a small project. The table has three parts. The top part shows the allocation tables for effort and schedule by phase. The values are based on the organization's historical data. The percentages by phase are normalized to 100%. The center part of the table shows the project's plan. The total effort is 2,000 phr. The schedule is 12 calendar-months, giving a duration of approximately 240 work-days. Applying the allocation percentages to these totals gives the "plan" values shown in the center part of the table. The bottom part of the table shows the actuals to date. For this example, the values are for the product design review (PDR) or life cycle architecture (LCA) milestone. What is the prognosis for this project?

Table 18-4 *Data for a Small Project*

Historical Data (% allocation)

	Units	Phase					
		RA	PD	DD	CUT	SWIT	Total
Effort	%	7	17	24	26	26	100
Schedule	%	17	27	17	17	21	100

Project Plan (EDEV = 2000 phrs, TDEV = 12 CM, TDUR ≈ 240 w-days)

	Units	Phase					
		RA	PD	DD	CUT	SWIT	Total
Effort	Phrs	140	340	480	520	520	2000
Schedule	CM	2.0	3.2	2.0	2.0	2.8	12.0
Duration	W-days	41	65	41	41	50	240

Observed Data (through PDR or LCA)

	Units	Phase					
		RA	PD	DD	CUT	SWIT	Total
Effort	Phrs	165	400				
Schedule	CM	2.5	4.0				

Table 18-5 shows the estimate at completion computed using a simple scaling approach. For effort, the plan and actual values are 480 and 565 phr, respectively. The amount of "work" accomplished as of PDR (or LCA) is 24% of the total. (This equals 7% for RA and 17% for PD as shown in Table 18-4.) If you assume that the remaining work will suffer the same amount of overrun as the previous work, you can (ratio) scale the estimated total, EDEV, to obtain a new effort estimate of 2,354 phr (= 2000*[565/480]), an overrun of 18%. Similarly, the plan and actual values are 5.2 and 6.5 calendar-months, respectively. The calculation for schedule gives 15.0 calendar-months (= 12.0*[6.5/5.2]), an overrun of 25%.

Table 18-5 *Estimate at Completion for a Small Project*

	Effort (phr)	*Schedule (CM)*
Plan	480	5.2
Actual	565	6.5
"Work" accomplished at PDR	24%	44%
Estimate at completion	2,354	15.0

There is another way to compute this:

$$\text{Expected Total Effort} = \frac{\text{Cumulative Actual Effort}}{\text{Cumulative Fractional Effort}}$$

In this case, based on the historical data, 24% of the project has been completed for 565 phr, giving an estimated total effort of 2,354 phr (= 565/0.24). (This identical result is not surprising since the same 24% was used to prepare the "plan" values used in Table 18-4.) The expected remaining effort (the estimate to complete) is 1,789 phr. You can compute this value using the percentages as 2,354*(1.0 – 0.24), or as the estimated total minus the actual value (2,354 – 565).

You can make similar estimates for schedule provided that your tasks are independent (i.e., no contention for resources). If the tasks are also sequential, you can estimate the remaining milestone dates as well. You can build a simple spreadsheet to track sequential tasks, provided that your task linkages are correct and your staffing profile matches the one used to generate the allocation table.

Even if the project does not have well-defined phases or the phases overlap, you can still use the scaling approach to estimate the effort needed to complete. (The values in Table 18-4 must then represent activity allocations instead of phase allocations.) The simple scaling method can thus be used for projects employing agile methods. For small projects, staffing is usually constant, so you can still estimate the final completion time as well use the techniques described in this section or Sections 12.1 and 12.3.

18.5.2 Using Earned Value Measurement

You can use earned value measurement, described in Chapter 21, to calculate the estimate at completion. (Section 21.6 explains how to do this, and the conditions affecting the accuracy of the estimate.) Of particular interest for large projects, you can use earned value techniques to update the estimate at completion monthly, provided that the necessary status and cost data is available. This is easy to do if you use an automated project tracking system that is linked to your cost accounting system.

Earned value measurement depends on the project's plan, represented by a time-phased budget. Because the plan values are a crucial part of the estimation calculations, revising the plan is done carefully and deliberatively. Project planners distinguish four levels of revision, described in the box "Revising the Project Plan."

Revising the Project Plan

Revisions to the project plan can range from very minor to major. Project planners usually distinguish four levels:

- Redirection
- Internal replanning
- External replanning
- Reprogramming

Redirection might be as simple as asking an expert to advise someone who is having problems on a task. There is no need to modify the plan. The funds for this assistance would come from a level-of-effort task identified in the original project plan.

If the problem is more serious, the team will have to alter the project plan. The project team initiates internal replanning to compensate for technical, cost, or schedule problems that have made the original plan unrealistic. The project goals are still achievable within the cost and schedule parameters of the original contract. The customer initiates external replanning to change the work, perhaps because priorities have changed or requirements have been clarified. In either case, these changes are small enough that the project needs little or no additional resources. The scope of the project is essentially the same; only the details are altered. The manager pays for these activities using funds from the management reserve.

If the project scope has increased significantly or productivity is lower than originally estimated, then additional resources are needed The project team, the customer, and senior management agree on the changes and who will pay for the extra work. The team then replans and re-estimates all uncompleted tasks plus the new tasks. This is called reprogramming. Reprogramming actually creates a new (different) project.

You will have to prepare updated estimates when replanning or reprogramming. Also note that you are changing one or more of the baselines that are used for performance measurement. Thus, the project's earlier performance metrics become irrelevant for the new project.

18.6 Recommended Reading

Parts 1 and 2 of this book describe techniques you can use to prepare updated estimates. Chapter 21 describes earned value measurement, which provides a way to calculate an independent estimate at completion (IEAC).

18.7 Summary

You can prepare more accurate estimates by using new information obtained as a project unfolds. (Remember Barry Boehm's funnel chart.) The estimate to complete (ETC) equals the estimated costs for uncompleted work plus committed amounts. The actual cost of work performed (ACWP) equals the actual costs to date plus accrued amounts. The estimate at completion (EAC) is the total expected project cost, and equals ACWP plus ETC. Your EAC should be an independent estimate based on the latest information. To prepare an estimate to complete, you should do a full bottom-up estimate, following the same steps used to prepare the initial estimate, adjusting for scope changes, work completed, and observed productivity. You use multiple methods, choosing from ones described in preceding chapters. (These may not be the same methods you used to make the initial estimates.) The precursors of estimation still apply! To check your bottom-up EAC, you can use earned value techniques to independently estimate the likely completion cost.

You can estimate the new completion date for the project in various ways. One is to calculate the duration using the remaining effort and the assumed staffing profile (or just the average staffing level), and convert the duration to calendar-days. You can also use schedule allocation tables as explained in Section 18.5.1. Earned value techniques provide the most accurate schedule estimate. (See Chapter 21.)

Chapter 19

Consolidating and Applying Your Knowledge

The first three parts of this book covered a wide spectrum of topics related to estimation and measurement for projects that develop software-intensive products and systems. (Parts 4, "Handling Large Projects," and 5, "Estimating Products and Processes," cover topics of special interest for some readers.)

This chapter concludes Part 3, "Closing the Feedback Loop," by surveying what you have learned, and then addressing how you can apply your new knowledge and techniques to your particular needs. Section 19.1 recaps the key estimation and measurement concepts covered in this book (including Parts 4 and 5). Section 19.2 covers implementing estimation and measurement. Section 19.3 discusses defining an estimation process. Section 19.4 offers suggestions to help you establish your own integrated estimating process. Section 19.5 identifies recommended sources of information to help you get started. Section 19.6 discusses the need to adapt to new technologies and development processes. Section 19.7 gives recommended reading. Section 19.8 is a brief summary.

19.1 Review of Estimation and Measurement

The greatest challenge for estimators is deciding where to start when faced with a blank sheet of paper. Estimators need to identify project products and services, and the activities to design, build, test, and deliver them. Key diagrams can help you understand an unfamiliar product or system quickly, and to identify all the items that you must estimate. The operational concept, product architecture, and project life cycle model (process model) all provide a basis to "divide and conquer" the estimating problem.

Bottom-up estimates use a project task list, bill of materials, and a work breakdown structure to identify items, which are independently estimated using appropriate methods and techniques. Scheduling links tasks to create a network and applies resources to obtain a time-phased budget. The critical path is the longest path through the network and determines the project's earliest possible completion time.

Top-down estimates use the total product size, based on product features or architectural components, and productivity, based on historical data for similar projects to calculate development effort and time. Parametric estimating models essentially determine an average productivity based on parameters that characterize the product, process, and project, including the "diseconomy of scale," the productivity decrease for large projects due to the increased effort to plan and coordinate activities. Parametric software estimation models calculate effort, time, and cost for the activities of a particular software development life cycle, but do not cover other project tasks and related costs.

Bottom-up and top-down estimation use multiple cost-estimation models because costs depend on different size measures. An integrated cost model links individual models to account for coupling between the models' parameters. For example, the estimated development time affects the lease costs for development facilities. You must understand direct and indirect costs, and the types of loading rates to calculate costs, to correctly interpret historical cost and productivity data.

Every project has risks, which are uncertain events that can affect project success. Risk reserves provide resources to cope with risks. You use the estimation techniques described in the book to estimate various costs and probabilities associated with risk occurrence and mitigation.

All estimates are uncertain, so you need to (1) state the uncertainty in your values, and (2) collect measurements to update estimates during a project. (Another reason to update is to accommodate the inevitable changes and surprises that occur.) You need to collect measurements during a project to detect changes and to provide better information to prepare the updated estimates. You can also use the measurement data to develop and calibrate estimating models or even develop your own models. (Part 1, "The Essentials," showed a process with two feedback loops to accomplish these actions.)

Precise definitions of measured quantities are essential to interpret the meaning of estimated values. There are many measures of size, some suited to estimate development effort, and others to estimate computer resource usage, and product performance. The key example is the definition of productivity used to estimate development effort, which involves the "size" of the product and the productivity associated with a particular process and project environment.

For a summary, see note N24, "Estimation and Measurement Context." Note N25, "Degrees of Estimation Difficulty," summarizes the quantities for products, projects, and processes, and rates their relative degree of difficulty.

19.2 Implementing Estimation and Measurement

Estimators usually rely on engineers and subject matter experts to provide resource estimates and parameter values for estimating models. Your estimating process should make it easy for these "nonestimators" to provide accurate values. Table 13-11 showed possible actions to collect good inputs from nonestimators for parametric models. Note N19, "Actions to Obtain Accurate Estimates" is a generalization of that table, and identifies steps you can take to obtain accurate estimates using any method, not just parametric models.

Table 19-1 provides advice for implementing any estimation technique, model, or method. Be sure you understand the definition of measures for historical data. For updated estimates, the project is underway so you can have future performers prepare estimates for their area of responsibility. Help the participants by providing techniques, models, tools, etc. in checklists, forms, templates, and spreadsheets to *capture information in a standardized way*. This ensures completeness (no omissions) and consistency. Capture supplemental information using numbered notes. Spreadsheets increase legibility, prevent computational errors, and reduce preparation time and effort. Be sure to validate the calculations in the spreadsheets!

Table 19-1 *Implementation Advice*

Use many sources of information.
• Use historical data.
• Use information available at each stage.
• Have future performers prepare the estimates.
• Use independent reviews.
Structure the estimation process.
• Capture information in a standardized way (forms, checklists).
• Use quantitative relations where possible.
• Use tools (validated spreadsheets).
Assist the participants.
• Reduce the information requested (aggregate related items).
• Provide descriptions of items and definitions of parameters.
• Provide documented instructions.
• Train the participants as appropriate.
• Answer questions and provide clarifications.
Check submitted data for errors and inconsistencies.

19.3 Defining an Estimation Process

Estimators must identify types of resources needed and their amounts. (This often involves estimating product and process characteristics as well.) A process helps users choose and apply appropriate techniques, models, methods, and tools. The process also defines the roles and responsibilities of the participants.

Your estimating process must specify how to prepare and document an estimate. Documentation includes the following:

- Purpose of the estimate (scope, level of detail, and accuracy desired)
- Conditions on the estimate (effort and time available)
- Constraints (resources available to prepare the estimate)
- Assumptions (about the product, process [project life cycle], and project)
- Models and methods used
- Sources of data (historical data, textbooks, reports)

- Input parameters (for all models and methods used)
- Calculated output values (including the uncertainty in the values)
- Potential risks and unknowns
- Key factors and sensitivities

This documentation provides a baseline that you can review, update, and consult later as historical data in the future. Even if technology, processes, and tools change, historical data provides at least a point of departure, a known reference point to some, hopefully similar, situation or product.

You document a process so that

- Workers can apply it consistently.
- You can teach it to others.
- Experts can review it for completeness and consistency.
- You have a baseline that you can improve.

A *process model* is a formal description of a process, and typically consists of the following:

- *Policies*. High-level guidance on organizational goals and areas of responsibility
- *Standard*. A description of an artifact (any tangible item produced by a process, including measurement data)
- *Procedure*. A set of steps to produce artifacts; may cite techniques, methods, and aids
- *Agent*. A person or department that performs activities
- *Role*. An agent responsible for specific classes of activities
- *Aid*. A form, template, or tool
- *Architecture*. A framework to organize the other elements

The formality and level of detail of a process description depend on the organization's goals, size, product types, development processes, customer requirements, and perceived risks.

Many process descriptions are procedurally oriented. For estimation, however, the *information* contained in the work products is of particular importance. The data collection forms described in Chapter 17, "Tracking Status," are examples, as are the book's various spreadsheets. (Paper forms are static. However, implementing forms using spreadsheets makes them "active," so they become simple tools.)

You can never take someone else's defined process and use it "out of the box."
You must define a process that fits the types of projects that your organization
performs, your organizational structure, and your business needs. This book
provides a "toolbox" of methods, techniques, and tools, along with an understanding of how and when to use them. You can use the material in this book
and on the CD-ROM to assemble your own defined process. See Section 19.5.

19.4 Establishing an Integrated Estimation Process

Table 19-2 shows six steps to establish and sustain an integrated estimating
process that is repeatable, dependable, and affordable.

Table 19-2 *Steps to Establish an Effective Estimation Process*

1. Choose "Significant" Organizational Goals • Have business value • Fit product line and type of business • Establish policies and priorities
2. Assign Responsibility • Group or department • Milestone schedule • Funding and support
3. Measure and Analyze • Choose metrics relevant to your goals • Examine available data • Define each metric (operational definition) • Establish a collecting and reporting process
4. Define the Process • Select appropriate estimation techniques and methods • Document the techniques and methods (standards, procedures) • Automate where possible (spreadsheets, tools) • Calibrate (using available data) • Describe the overall process (who, what, when)
5. Transition the Process • Establish a central data repository • Training • Mentoring • Pilot projects

> **6. Sustain the Process**
> - Assess benefit (accuracy, timeliness) versus costs (preparation, update, reviews, archiving data)
> - Monitor industry (techniques, tools, trends)
> - Refine and improve the process and tools

Senior management performs the first two steps in the table. Senior management must sponsor and support any organizational change, including process improvement. Management must set organizational goals for measurement and estimation that are tied to business objectives, and fit the organization's business environment, products, and project types. Management establishes policies that embody these goals. Senior management must also assign responsibility for defining, operating, and improving the process of an organizational unit or department. Many organizations have a designated group that is responsible for process definition and improvement. Management needs to establish and work with the designated group to define meaningful milestones and a schedule. Without a schedule, nothing happens. Management must also provide sustained funding and support. Many managers focus only on the money and forget about the support. Any type of process improvement requires political support to make key individuals available and to overcome resistance. Support also includes maintaining a continuing interest in the activities of the group and monitoring progress on a regular basis. See the box "How Management Can Help."

How Management Can Help

Managers can encourage improved estimation by doing the following:

- Demanding more accurate, well-documented estimates
- Supporting data collection and analysis
- Using these estimates and measured data when tracking project progress
- Tracking estimation accuracy
- Funding process definition and update, tools, and training
- Providing tools and training
- Providing support (motivating, enforcing compliance)

The designated process group performs the last four steps in Table 19-2. Assuming that you are a member of this group, your first task (Step 3 in the table) is to identify the measurements you need using the goal-question-metric model. Tie your goals to specific business needs (e.g., estimating, tracking, controlling, process efficiency, and customer satisfaction). These goals can relate to the product, project, or process. Focusing on goals helps determine what you must measure and why. Here is an example:

Goal. Reduce our production costs.

Questions. What is our productivity before and after process change X?

Measurements. Conditions (X or not X), product size, and resources expended.

Collecting and analyzing the measurements enables you to answer the questions, and so decide if the change achieved the desired goal. Start small, collecting measurements for only a few quantities. After you understand these, then add others.

After you have identified candidate metrics, define standard measures for all quantities of interest, and an *integrated* approach for collecting, storing, and analyzing all measurements. Standardize data collection by defining forms and templates. Automate data collection, analysis, and display where possible. Your support organizations (configuration management, quality assurance, finance, and accounting) can typically collect, analyze, and report many useful measurements.

You should also analyze data that is already available to determine whether it will meet some of your needs. Initially, you will have very little data, so establishing a metrics database is not a major undertaking. You can use spreadsheets and later migrate to a relational database. (Some of the needed data depends on what sort of estimating technique you choose, and so Step 3 and Step 4 are coupled to some degree.)

TIP 1: Start small. (Collecting reliable data on a regular basis is harder than you think!)

TIP 2: Use existing accounting and project tracking systems to collect data when possible.

TIP 3: Build on what you already have (forms, checklists, and spreadsheets).

TIP 4: Examine processes used by other organizations. (See Section 19.5.)

In Step 4, you define the process. You must select appropriate techniques to estimate the quantities of interest, such as the following:

Project: Effort, schedule, costs (labor, materials, ODCs, travel)

Product: Size, technical performance, quality

Process: Productivity, effectiveness, efficiency, rework

(You may also need different techniques for different points in time.) Then describe each technique and provide any associated forms, spreadsheets, or tools. The best way to encourage the use of estimating technique and to promote consistency is to automate as many of the calculations as possible. By far, the most common tool is a spreadsheet. Most individuals are familiar with spreadsheets, and it is simple to develop custom estimating models based on your own data. If you have usable data from Step 3, use it to develop simple cost estimating relations, and to calibrate commercial estimating models if you decide to purchase them.

Tools automate estimating, measuring, and tracking, reducing costs and increasing accuracy and consistency. Tools include the following:

- Parametric estimating models
- Accounting systems to collect resource expenditures
- Project planning and control tools
- Measurement tools for code, documents, and performance
- Spreadsheets for data analysis

Parametric estimating models are useful early in a project. As a project proceeds, however, you can use actual measurements and accounting data to prepare estimates that are more accurate. (You may still use parametric estimating models to evaluate planning options quickly.) Project planning and control tools manipulate plans (networks of tasks), record actual accounting and status data, and compute status (e.g., earned value). Special tools measure code, documents, and system performance. Spreadsheets provide a good way to integrate data from different tools, and to analyze and display information. Tools must support *your* process. Choose tools that can easily exchange data.

Step 5 transitions the process into actual use. You may perform pilot studies with selected projects to validate the process. You may develop the overall process in increments, and deploy each increment in succession. (This is like incremental delivery.) Training and mentoring are important for success.

In Step 5, you also train all participants in the process. This training should describe the responsibilities of each role, and motivate individuals by explaining how the process will simplify their work and enable them to perform better. *All engineers need training in resource estimation techniques* because resource estimates drive project cost and schedule. Train tool users to ensure correct, effective use of the tools. Training is especially important for estimating models to ensure proper calibration and correct setting of input parameters.

You must also provide mentoring to project managers and other individuals who need help with estimation and measurement. Some organizations establish a separate department that is responsible for performing certain estimation and measurement activities. Some organizations maintain a small group of individuals who are skilled in using certain parametric estimation models and are available to support projects as needed. (This is a good approach because these tools are typically complex and require substantial end user training and experience to produce reliable results. The same individuals can be responsible for collecting data and calibrating the tool.)

Step 6 sustains the integrated estimation process. You can use measurements to improve your estimating methods, models, tools, and processes. The process group and senior management periodically assess the benefits and performance of the estimating techniques, and compare it to the costs incurred. Potential benefits include the following:

- Increased accuracy
- Fewer cost overruns
- Fewer schedule overruns
- Reduced time to prepare estimates (analogous to cycle time for software development)

Costs include the following:

- Preparation, update, and review of estimates
- Training individuals in the use of the process, techniques, and tools
- Training staff, collecting, analyzing, and storing historical data
- Monitoring industry trends to identify new techniques and tools
- Updating the process documents and tools to improve the process

19.5 Useful Resources

This book's CD-ROM has templates, spreadsheets, supplemental notes, and Excel tips. These tips give step-by-step instructions on how to calculate, analyze, and plot information using Microsoft Excel. The CD-ROM also contains the references used in preparing this book, cross-indexed by chapter and topic area. You can search this bibliography using a browser. The book's website, http://sw-estimation.com, supplements the book by providing updated information and links to relevant websites, including professional organizations and tool vendors.

Many organizations have "process guides" that consist of the defined process itself, plus implementation guidance and other aids. A typical process guide includes the following:

- The defined process (policies, standards, procedures, roles, flows)
- Supplemental information (e.g., acronyms, glossary)
- Guidelines for process tailoring and usage
- Templates and tools
- Training materials (course/role map, course charts, and tests)
- Examples (sample documents, design guidelines)
- Historical measurement data (analysis results, process baselines)
- Sources of additional information (e.g., books and web links)

Some authors refer to this collection as "organizational process assets" that are stored in the organization's process asset library (PAL).

Many organizations record their processes in electronic form so that users can easily locate and understand the information. Several publicly accessible websites provide fully defined processes, many based on the criteria in the SEI's CMMI. (For a list, see the book's CD-ROM.) These examples show how other organizations have defined processes that meet their particular needs. These process guides are a valuable source of ideas and documents that you can adapt to fit the needs of your organization. In addition, you can use the spreadsheets on the CD-ROM that accompanies this book. The CD-ROM also identifies professional organizations, estimation and measurement conferences, and additional websites.

19.6 Addressing New Technologies and Processes

Technology and development processes continue to evolve. Engineers now build some software products from suites of reusable components conforming to a predefined architecture, configuring and assembling them using integrated development environments. To exploit these capabilities, new development processes have emerged. Examples include component-based development, capability-driven development, and agile methods. In some cases, these technologies and processes can yield high productivities. It is a challenge, however, to identify which factors affect productivity, and to quantify their influence. Developing estimation models for software is especially difficult because no valid theoretical models exist for software development processes. Estimators must use judgment and intuition to define heuristic models, and then validate them by analyzing actual project data. The box "Tackling Unprecedented Situations" suggests an approach.

Tackling Unprecedented Situations

Use the following steps to measure and estimate projects that use new technologies, methods, or tools:

1. Study and understand the new technologies, methods, and tools.

2. Identify the process's time-sequenced activities and work products.

3. Collect and analyze historical data to quantify the process.

4. Collect measurements and analyze them to verify hypotheses and relations.

5. Abstract the process into clearly defined components (tasks, phases).

6. Use your data to define estimating models for the components.

7. Validate your models using available data.

8. Use your new models to estimate new products, processes, and projects.

9. Collect and use new data to calibrate and refine your estimation models.

Even a simple model based on your own data can be surprisingly accurate.

Usually, adopting new technology decreases estimation accuracy, as illustrated in Figure 19-1. As you gain experience and measurements, however, you can apply this knowledge to update your integrated estimating process, and so increase your accuracy.[1]

---

[1] Figure 6.1 in [Boehm, 2000, page 292] is similar, but shows that the asymptotic estimation accuracy increases with each new generation of technology. I am more pessimistic, and show the estimating accuracy approaching the same asymptotic value.

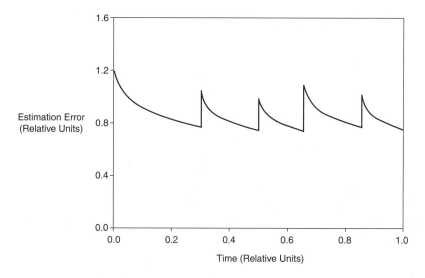

Figure 19-1 *Adopting new technology decreases estimation accuracy*

19.7 Recommended Reading

Barry Boehm describes a seven-step estimation process in Chapter 21 of [Boehm, 1981]. Robert Grady and Deborah Caswell describe a simple estimation process in [Grady, 1987]. They show how their data collection forms evolved as they learned, improving their process. Robert Grady addresses software metrics and process improvement in [Grady, 1992]. David Peeters and George Dewey discuss sources of estimating bias in [Peeters, 2000]. Albert Lederer and Jayesh Prasad give nine management guidelines for better cost estimating in [Lederer, 1992].

Most books on software engineering and process improvement also have chapters on estimating. Two good references are [Pressman, 2004] and [Sommerville, 2000].

Catherine Tilton and Konstantinos Triantis discuss improving system engineering cost estimation in [Tilton, 1994]. Phillip Ostwald and Timothy McLaren cover estimating for hardware and system development [Ostwald, 2004]. Also see [Stewart, 1995].

19.8 Summary

A disciplined and repeatable estimation process will increase the consistency and accuracy of your estimates. A process model defines

Why	Policies
What	Standards
How	Procedures
Who	Roles
When	Architecture

The (process) architecture is a framework that organizes and standardizes the other elements. It defines the sequencing and synchronization of activities and the flow of information.

You can define an estimation process for your organization using the checklists, techniques, procedures, implementation tips, and spreadsheets described in this book. The formality and level of detail of your process will depend on your organization's goals, size, product types, development processes, customer requirements, and perceived risks. You can also use the knowledge, techniques, and tools described in this book to tackle new estimating situations in the future.

Estimation is more than clever techniques, parametric models, and tools. The precursors of estimation provide the information that you need to prepare an estimate, including the following:

- Customer needs and operational environment
- Products and services to be delivered
- Production process to be used
- Project goals and constraints
- Estimate purpose and constraints
- An understanding of applicable estimating techniques and tools

You must have all of this information *before* you can prepare estimates for projects, products, and processes. The first four items help identify and organize the items to estimate. The fifth item determines how detailed your estimate must be. The last item means that you know how to use the techniques and tools correctly, and understand their assumptions, limitations, and inherent accuracy.

Large, custom development projects present their own unique challenges. Part 4 provides advice on devising an appropriate work breakdown structure, and explains earned value measurement, which is a way to measure project status. It also discusses how to use cost accounting systems to collect project effort and cost data.

Part 5 addresses the estimation and measurement of software-intensive product performance, computer resource usage, product quality (defects), and process performance. It defines the relevant quantities and units of measure, describes the challenges, and explains techniques to estimate and measure these quantities. Part 5 also describes ranking and selection techniques that you can use to analyze alternatives and make decisions.

Part 4

Handling Large Projects

Chapter 20

Crafting a WBS

Planning produces the project's work breakdown structure (WBS), which is a hierarchical organization of project elements. A good work breakdown structure is important because it is the basis for estimating, scheduling, costing, tracking, and controlling a project.

This chapter provides guidance on constructing a "good" work breakdown structure for large projects, plus examples showing alternate decompositions. Section 20.1 describes additional concepts. Sections 20.2 and 20.3 describe two work breakdown structures, one for software development, and one for general projects, which provide a starting point for a wide range of projects. Section 20.3 gives examples for projects with multiple builds and multiple firms. Section 20.4 provides implementation guidance. You may have to add some activities or eliminate activities based on the needs of your project.

20.1 The Work Breakdown Structure: Additional Concepts

Section 11.2 described basic concepts for work breakdown structures. The shaded box repeats the definitions of important terms related to work breakdown structures from Chapter 11, "Bottom-Up Estimating and Scheduling." A WBS can be organized as a product hierarchy, an activity hierarchy, or a hybrid. The WBS elements are numbered to show their hierarchical relationship. The ordering of the WBS elements does not imply any particular time order. (Scheduling defines the time sequencing and precedence of the tasks. See Chapter 11.

WBS Terminology

Work breakdown structure (WBS): A product-oriented or service-oriented hierarchical decomposition of project elements used to plan, manage, and analyze the work performed by a project.

WBS element: The individual elements of a WBS. Also called a task because most low-level elements represent activities needed to buy and build product components. Tasks may produce hardware, software, data, or may deliver services and perform support activities.

Work package: A task at the lowest level of a WBS. It has clearly defined criteria for completion (deliverables, completion date), and estimated resources. See cost element.

Cost element: A type of cost identified for estimating, collecting, and reporting costs. Examples are effort (labor), materials, overhead, travel, and other direct costs.

WBS dictionary: A detailed description of all the work packages in a WBS. These descriptions identify work that is included in the work package, work that is excluded, and relationships with other tasks.

Each WBS work package should have a written description. Table 20-1 shows the contents of a narrative description for a task to build an actuator for a package conveyor to be used in the XYZ warehouse. These descriptions (also called task descriptions) provide the detail needed by estimators, schedulers, workers, and supervisors. Each description is typically less than one page in length. References to relevant documents such as the customer's Statement Of Work, specifications, blueprints, or process descriptions (standards and procedures) provide detail and keep the description succinct. Smaller projects can use less detail by omitting some items. Some organizations also include the predecessor task(s) in the task description and the successor task(s), but modern project scheduling tools can track this information more accurately and with less effort. (The inputs and outputs also imply predecessor and successor tasks, respectively.) The resources include labor, materials, subcontracts, supplies (other direct costs), and travel, as appropriate for the particular task.

The work package description contains more detail for a large project, or if the system is safety critical. For U.S. government contracts, the contract line item number (CLIN) indicates the "deliverable" to which this item belongs. The developer is only paid when a CLIN is completed and accepted by the government. To optimize cash flow, planners often consider the contract's contract line item number (CLIN) structure when they partition the work to create the work breakdown structure. If tasks are not coupled, the manager has the option of selecting which tasks to do next to manage cash flow during the project. (This also applies if the firm receives progress payments for completing certain tasks.)

Table 20-1 *Sample Detailed Work Package Description*

Task Identifier: 2.7.4.2			
Task Name: Design the Controller for Package Conveyor Revision History: (optional)			
	Date 17May04	Made By R. Jones	Approved By F. Smith

CLIN: 00014
Inputs:
     System Specification, paragraphs 3.4.1 and 3.4.6.
     Interface Control Document, paragraph 2.4.7.
     SOW Task: 8.4.6
Outputs:
     Drawing package (hardware components)
     Module Design Description (software: functions, modes, timing, critical behavior)
     Charts for Product Design Review
Activities:
     Build data model. Build State Transition Diagram. Conduct Peer Review.
Assumptions and Constraints:
     Must be completed 15 work-days prior to PDR.
     Safety Engineer must approve the design. (Must participate in Peer Review.)
     All work will be done in our Huntsville facility.
Risks:
     This device is safety critical because it carries heavy boxes at high speed.
     The interface to the master warehouse control program is not yet defined.
Resources:
     Labor:
          Senior Mechanical Engineer   100 – 125 phrs
          Software Engineer   40 – 60 phrs
          Peer Review (mixed grades)   30 – 40 phrs
     Materials:
          None
     Tools:
          Computer with ICASE tool
     Travel:
          None
     ODCs:
          Computer Service Center
     Consultants:
          None

20.2 A Generic WBS (HW, SW, Data, Services)

This section describes a "generic" WBS useful for estimating projects to build and test the "first article," produce copies, and deliver copies to users. It is based on the work breakdown structure described in [MIL-HDBK-881B, 1998], and summarized in the box "MIL-HDBK-881B." I have combined and renumbered various elements, and have added a top-level WBS element called "Services."[1] You can use the generic WBS to design, build, produce, and deliver complex, software-intensive systems, hardware products, and consumer (shrink-wrapped) products. This WBS omits continuing user support, operations, and maintenance. (Chapter 10, "Production Processes (Project Life Cycles)," discussed these activities.) It does, however, cover preparations for user support, plus some interim support. Also, the production and delivery activities in the WBS can apply to any repaired or enhanced versions produced during operation and maintenance of the product.

Overview of MIL-HDBK-881B

The U.S. government has been purchasing complex, unprecedented systems for decades. MIL-HDBK-881B defines several WBSs to support the acquisition of large systems containing both software and hardware. It focuses on the nonrecurring engineering of the product (designing and testing the first article), and preparations for producing, delivering, and installing copies of the product. (MID-HDBK-881B assumes that copies of the system will be procured under a separate contract.) Its WBS elements cover everything needed to do this: the technical data package (see Section 10.5) and industrial facilities used for manufacture, storage, maintenance, or repair. If the system is "one-of-a-kind" (i.e., the first article is the product that is installed at the operational site), MIL-HDBK-881B also identifies tasks for delivery, interim support, and site testing.

MIL-HDBK-881B focuses on the government's procurement needs. For large procurements, the government provides a WBS to three or four levels. These top-level WBS elements are deliverable end items or prime mission equipment identified by the customer. The lower levels identify specific activities needed to produce these items such as analyze requirements and design the product. The contractor defines these lower levels based on the process model(s) to be used. The contractor considers use on the product architecture, the process model, and the contract structure, (e.g., contract line item numbers), cash flow, and tasks assigned to subcontractors (if any). The only requirement is that the contractor's detailed

---

[1] MIL-HDBK-881B states that WBS elements can only be products.

WBS can produce totals for the higher level, customer-specified WBS elements. (The values in your lower-level WBS elements must "roll up" into the proper categories.) The contractor uses these lower levels to plan, estimate, and track the work.

MIL-HDBK-881B provides appendices showing WBSs for seven types of product (aircraft, ships, data processing systems, etc.). Government program managers use these to identify work packages when procuring major systems. Another appendix identifies elements that are common to all seven types: program management; systems engineering; integration, assembly, and test; system testing; common support equipment; spare parts; facilities; installation and site activation; and user training. If you build large systems, MIL-HDBK-881B is a source of useful ideas.

Table 20-2 shows the generic WBS. No single project will probably need all of the elements shown. Just consider it a checklist to help you identify products and activities. To help you tailor the WBS, the following paragraphs describe selected elements of the WBS. (Chapters 7, "Preparing to Estimate (Precursors of Estimation," and 10 have already described some of the items listed.) You can put some items in different places. The discussion explains the options, and provides suggestions for selecting an option.

Table 20-2 *The Generic WBS*

1.0	**Products**
1.1	Software
1.1.1	Custom Applications Software
1.1.2	COTS Middleware
1.1.3	System Software
1.1.4	Computing Platform (or put under 1.2.1)
1.1.5	Software Integration and Test
1.2	Hardware
1.2.1	COTS Items
1.2.2	Fabricated Items
1.2.3	Hardware Integration and Test
1.3	System Databases
1.3.1	System Configuration Files
1.3.2	Diagnostic Data
1.3.3	Operational Data

(continues)

Table 20-2 *The Generic WBS (continued)*

1.4	System Integration, Assembly, and Test
1.4.1	System Test Plan
1.4.2	System Test Procedures
1.4.3	Generate/Collect System Test Data
1.4.4	Perform System Test
1.5	Product Documents
1.5.1	User Manuals
1.5.2	Engineering Documents
1.6	Support Equipment
1.6.1	Common Support Equipment
1.6.2	Peculiar Support Equipment
2.0	*Services*
2.1	Technical Interchange Meetings
2.2	Data Collection and Validation
2.3	Interoperability Testing (with other systems)
2.4	Field Testing of Prototypes
3.0	*Project Management*
3.1	Task and Staff Management
3.2	Contract Management
3.3	Supplier Management
3.4	Project Control (includes metrics collection)
3.5	Configuration Management
3.6	Quality Assurance
3.7	Administrative Support
3.8	Office and Lab Facilities
3.9	Computer and Network Operations
3.10	Staff Training
3.11	Process Improvement and Mentoring
4.0	*System Engineering*
4.1	Requirements Analysis
4.2	Architectural Design
4.3	Feasibility Studies & Prototypes
5.0	*System Test and Evaluation*
5.1	System Acceptance Testing (first article)
5.1.1	Acceptance Test Plan
5.1.2	Acceptance Test Procedures

5.1.3	Acceptance Test Dry Run
5.1.4	Factory Acceptance Test (FAT)
5.2	Development Test and Evaluation (See text.)
5.3	Operational Test and Evaluation (See text.)
5.4	System Test Environment
5.4.1	Test Bed
5.4.2	Test Tools
5.4.3	Test Data
6.0	**Deliverable Documents**
6.1	Product Documents
6.1.1	User Manual
6.1.2	Operator Manual
6.1.3	Programmer Manual
6.1.4	Installation Manual
6.1.5	User Training Course
6.1.6	Operator Training Course
6.2	Engineering Documents (See text.)
6.3	Management Documents (See text.)
6.4	Process Data (metrics, other records)
6.5	Customer Data ("Depository")
6.6	Data Management
7.0	**Production**
7.1	Production Management
7.2	Manufacturing Facilities
7.3	Manufacturing (Build, Assemble, Test Copies)
7.4	Inventory Management
7.5	Quality Control
8.0	**Transition**
8.1	Product Support Plan
8.2	Support Facilities
8.3	Support Equipment (acquire and install)
8.4	Custom Installation Tools and Scripts
8.5	Support Staff (hire and train)
8.6	Interim User Support
8.7	Initial Spare Parts

(continues)

Table 20-2 *The Generic WBS (continued)*

9.0	*Delivery*
9.1	Distribution
9.1.1	Marketing and Advertising
9.1.2	Sales and Returns
9.1.3	Product Packing and Shipping
9.1.4	User Support
9.1.5	User Training (See text.)
9.2	Deployment
9.2.1	Product Packing and Shipping
9.2.2	Site Preparation (See text.)
9.2.3	Installation and Testing
9.2.4	Converted Operational Data
9.2.5	User Training (See text.)
9.2.6	Site Acceptance Test (See text.)
9.2.7	Contractor Technical Support
10.0	*User Training*
10.1	Facilities
10.2	Equipment
10.3	Courseware Development
10.4	Simulated Data
10.5	Course Delivery

20.2.1 Products

The platform goes under WBS element 1.1.4 if the product uses commercial off-the-shelf (COTS) hardware such as computers, peripherals, sensors, and actuators. The platform goes under WBS element 1.2.1 if the computing platform is being custom built (avionics, for example). In the latter case, the software engineers will still need some type of SEE/STE. Do not forget to include the costs!

WBS element 1.2.2, Fabricated Items, includes custom-designed parts and assemblies. Do not forget that software-intensive systems need cabling, cabinets, mounting fixtures, and so forth. Put them into WBS element 1.1.4.

WBS element 1.2 covers hardware components. You need to further subdivide these by subsystem as appropriate. Also, hardware development is broken into nonrecurring engineering and recurring engineering (production).

For nonrecurring engineering (development), your bill of materials must include items for the following:

- All units to be delivered (including spare parts and "mod kits")
- Development prototypes
- Expendable units (destructive testing)
- Custom tools and fixtures for testing and possibly production

MIL-STD-881B assumes the project (nonrecurring engineering) produces a technical data package, described in Section 10.5. A separate contract then procures copies of the item. The box "Estimating Hardware Production Costs" provides some guidance. Also see note N18, "Learning Curves."

Estimating Hardware Production Costs

You must estimate the effort to perform the following activities:

- Purchase and inspect items
- Fabricate and inspect items
- Assemble and inspect subsystems
- Test completed units
- Ship (and possibly install) units

The effort to fabricate and assemble one unit usually decreases as workers learn and production tooling is improved. Workers must inspect every assembly and unit produced. (This is quality control.) Packing and shipping may be complicated due to a harsh environment (deck of a ship) or customs regulations. You may also need to build, assemble, and test production jigs, fixtures, and tooling. The bill of materials for production is based on a parts list, which is part of the TDP, and the number of units to be produced.

There are many kinds of machine-readable data for a software-intensive system. (MIL-HDBK-881B overlooks this item entirely.) WBS element 1.3, System Databases, provides the data needed to configure and diagnose the system. (Diagnosis is done by the operators on a regular basis.) WBS elements 1.4.3 and 5.4.3 generate or collect data that is used for testing. WBS element 9.2.4 converts or loads operational data. WBS element 10.4 provides the data used for operator training. (This might be a recording of site data, simulated data for special scenarios, etc.)

WBS element 1.4 covers the engineering activities needed to combine the hardware and software components, and to test the functionality of the system or product. The system engineer supervises these activities.

WBS element 1.5, Product Documents, includes both user-oriented documents and engineering documents. You could also put these into WBS element 6.0. (This is the MIL-HDBK-881B approach.) See the discussion in Section 20.2.6.

20.2.2 Services

WBS element 2.0, Services, is added. There are few services during nonrecurring engineering. (MIL-HDBK-881B doesn't even include this item. It focuses on "tangible" products.) For commercial firms, however, the entire "product" may only be services. An example is "provide user training and support." You could put some of these into WBS elements 7.0 and 8.0, too.)

20.2.3 Project Management

WBS element 3.0, Project Management, handles cost, schedule, suppliers, and resources (people, facilities, and equipment). There are no WBS elements for items such as labor, materials, travel, and office supplies. These are included as "cost elements" under a work package. If the costs cannot be specifically allocated to a particular activity, they are handled as indirect or overhead costs. Activities such as clerical support, finance, and accounting are in this category. (See Chapter 15, "Calculating Costs and Price: The Basics.")

WBS Element 3.0 also includes configuration management and quality assurance support. You can also place these under WBS elements 1.1 (Software) and 1.2 (Hardware), or as separate second-level WBS elements 1.6 and 1.7.

Finally, WBS element 3.3, Supplier Management, should be split if two departments do the work (e.g., a Subcontracts Management department and a Purchasing department). (Section 20.3.2 discusses splitting these by firm.)

20.2.4 System Engineering

System Engineering, WBS element 4.0, manages the entire solution. This includes the product requirements, the top-level architecture and design, testing, and so forth. (See Section 10.4 for details.)

20.2.5 Product Testing

System Test and Evaluation, WBS element 5.0, covers tests of the completely integrated product. This activity is the responsibility for the system engineers, but is usually assigned to a separate WBS element. Acceptance testing is performed in the developer's facility and is witnessed by the customer (or whoever has the authority to legally accept the product). This WBS element includes preparing test reports. Any rework is included in engineering tasks under WBS element 1.0.

This WBS element shows the formal system acceptance test, development test and evaluation, and operational test and evaluation. MIL-HDBK-881B puts all of this testing in a single "Test and Evaluation" WBS element because they are the responsibility of the system engineers. Depending on your project, however, you may include any of the system-level tests described in note N16, "Types of Testing." For a single system, development test and evaluation (DT&E) is the same as site acceptance test (SAT). For multiple sites, however, every site needs a site acceptance test, so I would then place these tests under WBS element 9.2, Deployment. This helps identify all the necessary resources. Because dual operations are also done at the site, you would place them under WBS element 9.2 as well.

WBS element 5.4, System Test Environment, is identified separately from the development environment used in WBS element 1.0 if it is large, complex, or unique. For example, the "test bed" contains a computing platform, equipment, and software to perform system-level tests. It may include emulators for site equipment, mockups to check clearances and accessibility, etc. Obtaining adequate amounts of valid, realistic test data can require significant resources. The data may represent a typical workload, special cases, heavy workloads for stress tests, etc. The test team must generate or collect this data. This may require special tools and custom software such as simulators.

20.2.6 Documents

WBS element 6.0, Deliverable Documents, is called "Data" in MIL-HDBK-881B.[2] Documents include the following:

- Engineering data (TDP)
- Technical publications (users)
- Management data (plans, costs, schedules)
- Process data (standards, procedures, metrics)
- Customer data ("depository")
- Data management

---

[2] In the DoD vernacular, "data" refers to *documents*, not computer data. For example, a contract data requirements list (CDRL) identifies deliverable documents.

The engineering activities produce the engineering data and technical publications. There are two types of product documents, each serving a different purpose, although they contain much of the same information. Engineers design and build the system using the architectural decomposition, and their engineering documents ("data") reflect this structure.[3] After the system is built and integrated, however, the users and maintainers want to see the "whole thing." They do not need to see information organized by the hierarchical decomposition (the "construction scaffolding") but instead by subsystem, combining hardware and software. This is the purpose of the "technical manuals" called out in MIL-HDBK-881B. The technical publications intended for users are often prepared as part of the transition phase (MBASE/RUP) and stabilize phase (MSF). This is addressed under WBS element 6.1.

Some projects may include the engineering documents in the software, hardware, and system engineering elements (1.0, 4.0). Similarly, plans for management, CM, QA, and so forth. may be included in WBS element 3.0. Technical publications such as user manuals would remain under WBS element 6.0. If you decide to do this, you can raise the product documents up one level in WBS element 6.0.

The management activities produce the management data. Because some reports are deliverables, however, you would identify them in WBS element 6.3. This prevents overlooking them.

Process documents are not explicitly identified in MIL-HDBK-881B (but are considered to be part of project plans). Process documents include policies, standards, procedures, and metrics. Most of these are produced by the organization, and are just reused by the project. Tailoring of the organization's standard process is usually part of planning, and so would go in WBS element 3.0. Other possible places are WBS element 4.0 (System Engineering) and 1.0 (Software).

Metrics are collected and analyzed in most of the WBS elements, with analysis and reporting centralized in WBS element 6.4. WBS element 3.4, Project Control, may perform this function in some organizations.

MIL-HDBK-881B also describes a "data depository" containing the master copies of designated official government documents. The government approves all changes to these documents. The contractor acts as a custodian for the government, operating the "depository" (facility) to maintain these documents at the latest approved revision level. These master documents may be delivered at the end of the project.

---

[3] The hierarchy for defense systems is system, subsystem, configuration item, component (or assembly), and unit (module or part).

WBS elements 6.1.5 and 6.1.6 deal with developing training materials for users and operators. (These materials may include real and simulated data to produce realistic situations.) You could also place these work packages in WBS element 10.0, or possibly under WBS element 8.0. (WBS element 10.0 is good if your organization has a separate training department.) See Section 20.2.11.

20.2.7 Production

WBS element 7.2, Manufacturing Facilities, establishes facilities for the production, warehousing, inventory management, and repair of products. You may acquire, convert, or modernize facilities to do this. WBS element 7.3, (Manufacturing, Build, Assemble, and Test Copies), may require a very complicated manufacturing process. If so, you will need to prepare a separate WBS in such cases.

20.2.8 Transition

WBS element 8.0, Transition, plans how the product will be supported, establishes the support capability, and provides interim support while the support capability is being established. The support facilities and staff can be part of the developer's or the customer's organization. Support capabilities include operating a "help desk," providing "technical support," and performing product maintenance (called depot maintenance for military systems). You may have to acquire, build, or modify facilities, provide equipment, and train the support staff (which may include installers or "field engineers" who travel to customer sites). The developer's engineers provide user support until the customer support capability is ready. You may also have to provide initial spare parts.

Transition activities are also called logistics planning, product rollout, and preparation for fielding. These activities are performed during the "Transition" phase of MBASE/RUP, and the "Stabilize" phase of the MSF process model. The COCOMO 1981 WBS, described in note N14, "The COCOMO Waterfall Model and Work Breakdown Structure," calls it "implementation." COCOMO II now calls it "transition."

20.2.9 User Support

User support, customer support, or technical support is covered in several WBS elements. Transition, WBS element 8.0, prepares the support team (either part of the developer's organization or the buyer's organization). For complicated systems with only a few copies, the users are engineers. The developer's engineers (who actually developed and built the system) provide technical support as needed. They may also travel to the sites to install the product so there is no need to train separate installers. (Some organizations include these services as part of the product warranty.) WBS element 8.6, Interim User Support, covers support and assistance provided by the developer's engineers until the customer support capability is ready. (They may provide this support from their home office or may have to travel to the site.)

20.2.10 Delivery

Distribution, WBS element 9.1, handles the sale of standard products to consumers. A good example is selling shrink-wrapped software applications.

Deployment, WBS element 9.2, may have to be replicated for every site. You may also have to subdivide some of the tasks if a single site has several systems that must be installed, or upgraded. WBS element 9.2.2, Site Preparation, can refer to acquiring, constructing, or modifying a facility, a ship, a vehicle, or an aircraft.

If fielding is a major effort (in terms of cost or time), you may choose to treat it as a totally separate project. If so, your WBS would have groups of appropriate tasks for each site where the product is to be installed. For example, you might define the pair of tasks "Prepare to visit site X" and "Install product at site X." (The first task encompasses WBS elements 9.2.1 and possibly 9.2.4. The second task encompasses WBS elements 9.2.2, 9.2.3, 9.2.6, and possibly 9.2.5.) This facilitates scheduling and tracking the deployment activities, and makes it possible to assign specific sites to a particular installation team.

20.2.11 User Training

WBS element 10.0, User Training, covers the case where a separate department is responsible for user training. Developing formal training courses can itself be a process. There are actually many similarities between developing courseware and software. For example, "piloting" the beta version of a course is analogous to testing a software product. For a description of the U.S. Air Force Instructional System Development Process, see [AFM 36-2334, 1993] and [AFH 36-2335, 1993].

For deployed products, the engineers or installers may train the users at each site. (See WBS element 9.2.5.) For distributed products, the vendor may establish a training facility or offer courses at various locations. (See WBS element 9.1.5.)

20.2.12 Support Equipment

MIL-HDBK-881B defines *support equipment* as deliverable items (physical components) and associated software that are needed to support and maintain the system while the system is not directly engaged in performing its mission. Examples include equipment for system test, measurement, and handling.

Common support equipment refers to any items currently in the inventory for the support of other systems. Examples are voltmeters and code analyzers. *Peculiar support equipment* refers to any support equipment that is not common support equipment. An example is a code analyzer for a programming language that is not used by any other product in the organization.

Identify the type, number, and costs for all support equipment. You should determine if additional copies of the common items will be needed for the new system. The unstated assumption in MIL-HDBK-881B seems to be that all support equipment is COTS, and so it can be purchased. If peculiar support equipment must be designed and tested, however, add appropriate work packages under WBS element 1.0, and estimate the needed resources (labor, materials, etc.).

20.2.13 Additional Tasks

The basic WBS shown in Table 20-2 identifies possible "core" tasks that a project may perform. Your project team may add tasks that are needed for a particular project, or may subdivide tasks to provide increased visibility, accommodate incremental development, or assign work to multiple organizations. (Section 20.3 mentions examples of WBSs to handle these situations.) Different parts of a product can also be built with different process models, and so you can combine WBS tasks from multiple process models into a single integrated WBS.

Most of the tasks are performed sequentially, except for the project management tasks, which always execute concurrently with the engineering tasks. Projects using incremental, phased, or evolutionary development will have more tasks that must be performed in a particular sequence.

Projects that develop interactive, multimedia products need additional WBS elements. See the box.

WBS Elements for Interactive, Multimedia

For multimedia products, websites, and games, a project expends most of its effort developing content ("operational data"). The software developers build software to format and display data, and to support user interaction and navigation. (They may also build tools to help the "content developers.") You will need to add WBS tasks for data collection, formatting, and updating. Data includes drawings, audio clips, animation sequences, video clips, world models (e.g., terrain), and behavioral rules. You may even need sets, costumes, and actors. The process of planning a motion picture is a good place to start. Shawn Presson describes the similarities and differences between software development and multimedia production in [Presson, 2002]. Also see [Baumgarten, 1995] and [Daniels, 1998].

Man-in-the-loop trainers for pilots and real-time plant monitoring and control systems are also highly interelative, like games, but their mathematical models must have fidelity (i.e., obey the laws of physics, and faithfully represent the behavior of the system being modeled). For the estimator, this means additional tasks to gather and validate information, develop and validate the models, and validate performance with experts (pilots, operators) and with historical data (especially anomalous events). This table contrasts their characteristics.

	Guaranteed Response	Safety Critical	High Reliability and Availability	Fidelity Accuracy	Pushes Existing Technology
Plant monitoring	X	X	X	X	—
Flight trainer	X	X?	X?	X	—
Game	—	—	—	—	X

20.2.14 Additional Level of Effort Tasks

You may also want to include some of the following as level of effort (LOE) tasks in your WBS:

- Answering customer questions
- Analyzing and negotiating proposed changes
- Reviewing estimates, plans, designs, code, documents, and so forth
- Interviewing job applicants
- Taking training (technical, administrative)

Although some of these are funded indirectly, you may still want to identify and estimate the resources needed.

The two-level WBS shown in Table 20-2 is not adequate to plan and estimate a project. For example, you will need to decompose WBS element 1.0 to show the production activities. For software development, you can use the COCOMO WBS described in note N14 as guidance. Hardware development is similar, because it is nonrecurring engineering. Production engineering designs the hardware manufacturing process. In concurrent engineering, hardware (first article) development and production engineering are performed concurrently. This ensures that the product is designed to reduce the cost of making many copies. (Reproduction costs are usually negligible for software.) This is also called "designing for manufacturability." For information on hardware production, building construction, and concurrent engineering, see Chapters 10-12 in [Stewart, 1995]. The preceding subsections described some third-level decompositions, which are shown in Table 20-2.

20.3 Examples of Alternate Partitioning

Section 11.3 discussed criteria for partitioning a project's WBS. This section provides some examples based on the generic WBS defined in Section 20.2.

Suppose that your organization must build a system consisting of two software components that will operate on a common platform. Component A might be mission software that executes continuously (or every business day). Component B might be support software that executes occasionally (or periodically).

Table 20-3 shows a possible WBS. To keep the example simple, this WBS assumes that the platform consists entirely of commercial off-the-shelf components. Products and services can be deliverable or nondeliverable, but no nondeliverable items are shown. In addition, the dashed lines indicate omitted elements that are common to both partitionings.

Table 20-3 *WBS for Typical Software System (Product Elements)*

1.0	**Products**
1.1	Application Software
1.1.1	Component A
1.1.2	Component B
1.1.3	Common Software Components
1.1.4	Integration, Assembly, and Test
1.2	Platform
1.2.1	Processor
1.2.2	Peripheral Devices
1.2.3	Network Devices
1.2.4	Operating System
1.2.5	Middleware
1.3	Integrate and Test System

(continues)

Table 20-3 *WBS for Typical Software System (Product Elements)*
           (continued)

The Common Software Components, WBS element 1.1.3, includes shared data and services. These might be a custom operating system, a data management system (or a master database schema), GUI services, and so forth. The Peripheral Devices, WBS element 1.2.2, include human-machine interface (HMI) equipment, sensors, and actuators. HMI equipment includes keyboards, mice, joysticks, displays, sound cards, speakers, tape drives, and disk drives. (Software device drivers are usually included with the hardware as well.) The Operating System, WBS element 1.2.4, manages the platform's computing resources, and is platform-specific. Network Devices, WBS element 1.2.3, are the hardware and device drivers for the LAN, WAN, and wireless. Middleware typically includes the relational database management system, network communications software, and browsers. (For some systems, the device drivers and the network management software are part of the operating system.) For systems with custom hardware, you will need additional WBS elements. Integration and testing of the platform (hardware) and the application software is performed in WBS element 1.3, Integrate and Test System.

This is a product-based breakout. To plan and manage the work, you must identify the activities actually needed to design, build, and test these products. You will thus add another level to show these, giving a fourth-level WBS. The lowest-level WBS elements typically map to multiple instances of the activities in the project's chosen life cycle model. (For small projects, these activities may be aggregated.) The WBS quickly becomes complex for large projects involving multiple builds and multiple development organizations. The following extensions of the initial example illustrate this.

20.3.1 Two Builds

Suppose that you decide to produce the system using two builds. Assume that the platform is completely established and configured during the production of Build 1. You might choose the WBS levels to be

First = Products

Second = Component type

Third = Build

Fourth = Component

Table 20-4 shows how the Products portion of the WBS would look. The notation "Component A (Build 1)" denotes the portion of Component A that is implemented in Build 1. (This is the "build content" of Build 1.) Later builds add functionality, and may cause breakage.

Table 20-4 *WBS for Two Builds (One Developer)*

1.0	***Products***
1.1	Application Software
1.1.1	Build 1 Software
1.1.1.1	Component A (Build 1)
1.1.1.2	Component B (Build 1)
1.1.1.3	Common Components
1.1.1.4	Integrate and Test Build 1
1.1.2	Build 2 Software
1.1.2.1	Component A (Build 2)
1.1.2.2	Component B (Build 2)
1.1.2.3	Common Components
1.1.2.4	Integrate and Test Build 2
1.2	Platform
1.2.1	Processors
1.2.2	Peripheral Devices
1.2.3	Network Devices
1.2.4	Operating System Software
1.2.5	Middleware

20.3.2 Two Subsystems Built by Two Organizations

As another example, suppose that you have to build a system consisting of two loosely coupled subsystems that operate on different nodes, and that each subsystem will be built by a different organization. Assume that Organization 1 will also build the common components, and will integrate and test the system. Each subsystem has two components (A and B, and C and D, respectively). Assume that the complete platform is established during Build 1. One way to break out the WBS is using these levels:

First = Products
Second = Subsystem
Third = Build
Fourth = Component

Table 20-5 shows how the Products portion of the WBS would look.

Table 20-5 *WBS for Two Builds (Two Developers)*

1.0	**Products**
1.1	Subsystem 1 (Organization 1)
1.1.1	Build 1 Software
1.1.1.1	Component A (Build 1)
1.1.1.2	Component B (Build 1)
1.1.1.3	Common Components (Build 1)
1.1.2	Build 2 Software
1.1.2.1	Component A (Build 2)
1.1.2.2	Component B (Build 2)
- - - -	
1.1.3	Subsystem 1 Platform-Unique Items
1.1.3.1	Subsystem 1 Processors
- - - -	
1.2	Subsystem 2 (Organization 2)
1.2.1	Build 1 Software
1.2.1.1	Component C (Build 1)
- - - -	
1.2.2	Build 2 Software
1.2.2.2	Component C (Build 2)
- - - -	
1.2.3	Subsystem 2 Platform-Unique Items

(continues)

1.2.3.1	Subsystem 1 Processors
- - - -	
1.3	Common Components (Organization 1)
1.3.1	Common Software Components
1.3.1.1	User Interface
1.3.1.2	Data Transfer Between Nodes
1.3.1.3	Other Services
1.3.2	Common Platform Items
1.3.2.1	Processors
- - - -	
1.4	System Integration and Testing (Organization 1)
1.4.1	Integrate and Test Build 1
1.4.2	Integrate and Test Build 2
- - - -	

Alternatively, you could group all of the tasks together by build:

First = Products

Second = Build

Third = Subsystem

Fourth = Component

As before, the platform is established during Build 1 and nothing is added to it in later builds. Table 20-6 shows how the Products portion of the WBS would look.

Table 20-6 *Alternate WBS for Two Builds (Two Developers)*

1.0	**Products**
1.1	System (Build 1)
1.1.1	Subsystem 1
1.1.1.1	Component A (Build 1)
1.1.1.2	Component B (Build 1)
1.1.1.3	Common Components (Build 1)
1.1.1.4	Integration and Test Subsystem 1 (Build 1)
1.1.2	Subsystem 2
1.1.2.1	Component C (Build 1)
1.1.2.2	Component D (Build 1)

(continues)

Table 20-6 *Alternate WBS for Two Builds (Two Developers) (continued)*

1.1.2.3	Common Components (Build 1)
1.1.2.4	Integrate and Test Subsystem 2 (Build 1)
1.1.3	Common Components (Build 1)
1.1.4	Integrate and Test System (Build 1)
1.1.5	Platform
1.1.5.1	Processors
1.1.5.2	Peripheral Devices
1.1.5.3	Network Devices
1.1.5.4	Operating System Software
1.1.5.5	Middleware
1.2	System (Build 2)
1.2.1	Subsystem 1
1.2.1.1	Component A (Build 2)
- - - -	
1.2.2	Subsystem 2
1.2.2.1	Component C (Build 2)
- - - -	
1.2.3	Common Components (Build 2)
1.2.4	Integrate and Test System (Build 2)

Which WBS is best? The choice depends on many factors. Section 20.2 described some factors that you should consider. The next section provides additional guidance. Also consult the experts in your organization for help.

20.4 Customizing Your WBS

The generic WBS generally follows the guidance in MIL-HDBK-881B. This section provides suggestions to improve the structure.

20.4.1 Numbering Scheme

If your organization does many similar projects, and if you are allowed to choose the WBS numbering scheme, you can place the WBS elements for common activities first, so that they are always the same number. For example, WBS element 1.0 might be Project Management and WBS element 2.0 might be Systems Engineering. The WBS elements for Products and Services would be near the end. (You would split these into multiple WBS elements on larger systems.) *Consistency reduces planning effort, and provides a standard structure for collecting metrics on the common activities done by all projects.*

If you use a tool (e.g., a parametric model) to estimate certain WBS elements, decompose your WBS to fit the tool's WBS. For example, if you use the COCOMO cost estimation model (described in Chapter 13, "Parametric Models"), you should try to align portions of your WBS with the structure described in note N14. This makes it much easier to transfer estimates between tools. (Chapter 12, "Top-Down Estimating and Allocation," discuss allocation of effort and duration to WBS tasks.)

20.4.2 Handling CMMI Metrics Requirements

The SEI's CMMI requires "adequate resources" for activities such as quality assurance and configuration management. To show this, the WBS needs an element for each specified activity that can be used for estimating, budgeting, and tracking. Defining a large number of work packages, however, consumes time and money, not just for the initial planning and estimating, but also for collecting and analyzing the data. In addition, tracking many work packages requires many charge numbers, stressing the organization's cost accounting system.

Because it is not cost-effective to estimate and track many small tasks, you can aggregate all peer reviews into a single WBS task. The project schedule will show individual peer reviews where appropriate, but the WBS will only show a single WBS task. (This violates the standard scheduling convention of a 1:1 relation between scheduled tasks and WBS elements. But, for small projects, this is an appropriate simplification. You have to know when to break the rules.)

To meet CMMI requirements, you must subdivide the effort for specific functional areas, such as configuration management (CM) and quality assurance (QA). There are two ways you could enter this in a WBS. First, you could subdivide the tasks to an additional level such as .1 for engineering, .2 for testing, .3 for configuration management, and .4 for quality assurance. For example, for the second-level task 3.4, Detailed Design, you could define third-level tasks 3.4.1, 3.4.2, 3.4.3, and 3.4.4. However, subdividing each engineering activity in this way creates many small tasks because configuration management and quality assurance are usually a small fraction of the engineering and test effort. The second, and better, approach is to add two second-level WBS elements, such as 3.11 "CM for Build X," and 3.12 "QA for Build X."

20.4.3 Tracking Rework

If your project can define reasonable milestones, you can measure rework, and so gauge the efficiency of the process. Suppose that task 4.2 represents the effort to prepare an architecture description document, and that this document is approved at the life cycle architecture (LCA) milestone. Any effort expended after this point represents "rework," either due to customer-directed changes or to an ineffective design process. You can track this "rework" in various ways. You could record effort for each work product or activity, and then manually calculate the amounts recorded before and after the LCA milestone. This is tedious. A better approach is to split the WBS element into 4.2.1 for "Work" and 4.2.2 for "Rework," with two different charge numbers. This simple approach can provide useful insight. Nonrecurring engineering has a lot of rework. Philip Crosby says that 50% of software development effort is spent in rework. A possible refinement is to collect rework effort due to external causes and internal causes (related to your engineering process).

TIP: Be sure to close the "Work" charge number once the relevant milestone is completed. This prevents workers from posting any more charges to the account.

TIP: If a problem arises due to the customer's action or inaction, immediately open a new charge number to capture the costs incurred resolving the problem. This provides data to negotiate compensation for the unanticipated costs. (This is called *cost isolation.*)

20.5 Recommended Reading

Richard Fairley and Richard Thayer explain how to describe a work package, and provide a case study for a project to develop an Automated Teller Machine [Fairley, 1997]. Shari Lawrence Pfleeger describes a WBS for building a house on page 78 of [Pfleeger, 1998].

Barry Boehm describes WBSs for software development in Section 4.7 of [Boehm, 1981]. His discussion is particularly interesting because he shows how the structure of the WBS changes over the life of a project.

Barry Boehm et al. describe the WBSs used by the COCOMO II parametric model. See Tables A.8 and A.9 in [Boehm, 2000, pp. 315–319]. Walker Royce gives a detailed description of the WBS in Table A.8 in Chapter 10 of [Royce, 1998, p. 139 ff.]. Their default WBS splits by Activity at the first level, and by phase at the second level. The seven activities are management, environment and configuration management, requirements, design, implementation, assessments, and deployment. The four phases are inception, elaboration, construction, and transition. This gives 28 (= 4*7) work packages. Walker Royce also provides a detailed discussion of iterative program planning in Chapter 10 of [Royce, 1998, p. 139 ff.].

A standard reference for large, software intensive systems is the U.S., Department of Defense Handbook for Work Breakdown Structures [MIL-HDBK-881B, 1998]. This document includes seven appendices that suggest WBSs for specific types of systems, and another appendix that identifies common elements applicable to all seven types. If you build large systems, it is a useful reference. Chapter 2 of MIL-STD-881B shows how a WBS evolves during a procurement and gives an example. It stresses the role of system engineers in the evolution process. Section 3.2.1 addresses software and software-intensive systems, and provides guidelines for placing software components into appropriate WBS elements at various levels. Section 2.2.5 identifies pitfalls in constructing a WBS. (These are from the DOD's perspective, but are informative nonetheless.)

The Project Management Institute (PMI) publishes a guide for work breakdown structures [PMI, 2001]. This guide elaborates on information contained in the PMI's Guide to the Project Management Body Of Knowledge (PMBOK Guide) [PMI, 2000]. (The PMBOK is available in several languages. There is also an extension specifically addressing government projects.)

Rettig and Simons define an iterative planning approach that is similar to Boehm's Spiral Process Model [Rettig, 1993]. Their approach provides a way to schedule small projects using evolutionary process models (including agile methods). They call their approach PADRE (Plan, Approve, Do, Review and revise, and Evaluate).[4] They address planning at three levels: project, stage, and module. Each level uses the PADRE steps. They essentially break a big project into several stages (iterations). Each stage produces a build (which may or may not be delivered). Within an iteration, programmers plan how to develop and test individual modules. Rettig and Simons emphasize team consensus. Plans and products that are prepared by a few people are reviewed and approved by the rest of the team. Their Figure 4 shows a simple way to track progress. (This is the same as the "inchstone" concept described in Chapter 19, "Consolidating and Applying Your Knowledge.")

---

[4] They note the similarity to the Plan-Do-Check-Act cycle used in Total Quality Management. They think that PADRE better expresses the development cycle used by small teams.

20.6 Summary

A work breakdown structure (WBS) is a hierarchically organized set of elements representing products, services, and support activities for a particular project. The WBS integrates the views of the product and process, establishes the basis for planning, estimating, scheduling, negotiating, budgeting, authorizing, tracking, and control.

The WBS decomposition depends on many factors, including customer directives and how the developer plans to perform and manage the work. This chapter described a generic WBS for large projects (based on MIL-HDBK-881B). Section 20.1 provides guidance on describing WBS elements. Later sections provided guidance on partitioning, and for tailoring the general-purpose WBS.

Chapter 21

Earned Value Measurement

Earned value measurement (EVM) is a way to track the status of projects having hundreds or even thousands of tasks. Earned value measurement was originally developed to provide a way to track and control government programs that developed complicated systems having many components and suppliers. (You can also use earned value measurement for smaller projects. In either case, automated tools are essential.) Earned value measurement uses the project cost and schedule baselines described in Chapter 19, "Consolidating and Applying Your Knowledge," and provides a way to distinguish cost problems from schedule (time) problems. You can also use earned value measurement to predict when a project will finally finish and to estimate the cost at completion.

21.1 Concepts

The only common measures for project tasks are cost and schedule. The project plan contains a time-phased budget. Figure 21-1 shows the total estimated and actual costs versus time. The Budget line is the planned expenditure. The Actual Cost line shows the reported costs to date. The problem with this chart is that you cannot tell whether the project is ahead of schedule or is overrun in cost. There is no way to measure the amount of "progress" that the team has made. Tracking the cost alone does not reveal the project's true status.

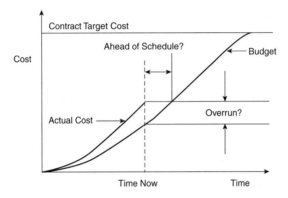

Figure 21-1 *Budget and actuals versus time*

Earned value measurement uses the project's cost and schedule baselines. The cost baseline is the allocated budget for the project tasks. (The allocated budget equals the project's total authorized budget minus any management reserves.) The schedule baseline identifies project milestones and their planned dates of accomplishment. For larger projects, the Resource Loaded Network (RLN) captures the integrated project schedule and ties the schedule and cost baselines together. The Resource Loaded Network enables users to track progress in an integrated manner to support earned value measurement.

Earned value measurement defines the following quantities:

TC	= target cost	
BAC	= budget at completion	
MR	= management reserve	= TC – BAC
ACWP	= actual cost of work performed	
BCWP	= budgeted cost for work performed	
BCWS	= budgeted cost for work scheduled	
EAC	= estimate at completion	
ETC	= estimate to complete	= EAC – ACWP

Note that all of these quantities have the same units: dollars. (Because software development projects are labor intensive, you can measure these quantities in person-hours if desired. This approximation gives a good indicator of project status, and avoids the need to interface with your organization's accounting system.)

Figure 21-2 shows these quantities overlaid on the plot of Figure 21-1. BCWP is called the earned value.

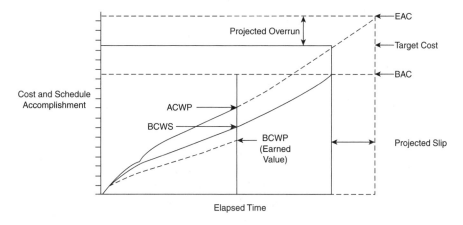

Figure 21-2 *Earned value quantities applied to time-phased cost data*

Every task in a Resource Loaded Network has a cost, a start time, and a completion time. These are planned values. At any specified time, you can sum the cost of all tasks that should have been completed to get BCWS. The earned value, BCWP, is the sum of the planned (budgeted) cost for only those tasks that have been completed at the specified time. You obtain the actual costs expended for the completed tasks and any tasks that have been started but not yet completed from the organization's cost accounting system. You sum these costs to obtain ACWP. (There are some fine points about assigning credit for partially completed tasks. See the box "Crediting Task Completion.")

Crediting Task Completion

The most conservative approach for assigning completion credit to a task is to add 100% of the task's estimated (budgeted) value to BCWP only when the task is totally completed. (This is called 0/100 crediting.) Long-duration tasks present a problem, however, because the team working on a task will incur costs each accounting period (increasing ACWP), yet the task will not receive any completion credit (BCWP) until it is finally completed. This gives a false indication of a cost overrun. There are two ways to address this problem: partial crediting and partitioning tasks to fit the accounting cycle.

Partial crediting assigns some completion credit, say 25%, when a task starts, and assigns the remaining amount, 75%, when the task completes. (This is called 25/75 crediting.) Most organizations use either 50/50 or 25/75 crediting. If you can define meaningful interim milestones (sometimes called inchpebbles), you can assign the credit in several smaller steps. (Section 21.4 explains interim milestones.) You need not use the same crediting scheme for all project tasks.

Sizing tasks to fit the accounting cycle means that no task can extend longer than one accounting period. For a labor task, one person working full time for a two-week accounting period delivers 80 person-hours, and so no labor task can exceed 80 person-hours. There is no need to define a separate task for each worker, however. A reasonable time between task completions is one calendar month or so. If a three-person team works on a task for 4 calendar weeks, the maximum task effort is 480 person-hours (= 3 × 4 × 40). Even though the task spans multiple accounting periods, you can use interim milestones to estimate the task completion status. (Note that you are estimating instead of measuring. This is less accurate but cheaper.)

Instead of using well-defined interim milestones, some organizations allow engineers to estimate the percentage of task completion. This is unreliable, however, because software developers tend to be optimists. Quite often, modules quickly reach 90% complete, and then remain at that level for the remainder of the project.

For other ways to assign completion credit, see Chapter 8 in [Fleming, 2000].

Earned value measurement defines cost and schedule variances:

CV   = Cost Variance   = BCWP – ACWP
SV   = Schedule Variance   = BCWP – BCWS

Both variances are measured in dollars. You can use the schedule variance [dollars] to estimate the amount of schedule slip [calendar months], as explained in Section 21.3.[1] You can also express the variances as percentages:

CV% = 100*CV/BCWP
SV% = 100*SV/BCWS

---

[1] Strictly speaking, the schedule variance, SV, as defined here is the "planned accomplishment variance" for all tasks in the Resource Loaded Network. A true schedule variance would be based only on data for the tasks on the critical path.

You can use these variances to see if a project has a cost overrun, a schedule overrun, or both. Section 21.5 gives an example.

Earned value measurement defines normalized performance indices so that you can compare values for different times on a project or values for projects of different sizes. Two of the indices are as follows:

CPI = cost performance index   = BCWP/ACWP

SPI = schedule performance index   = BCWP/BCWS

CPI and SPI essentially indicate the "efficiency" or "capability" of the project's processes. Some authors use CPI_e rather than CPI to emphasize the efficiency aspect. Others use CPI_p for "performance." (Note: Some authors define CPI_p = ACWP/BCWP, which is the reciprocal of CPI_e.) CPI (CPI_e) measures the amount of "value" that the project produces per unit of money expended. If CPI is less than 1, it is costing more to perform the work than was estimated in the project plan (represented by the Resource Loaded Network). Similarly, if SPI is less than 1, the project is producing less "value" than was originally scheduled. For example, if CPI = 0.9, the process produces $0.90 of product value for every $1.00 expended. If SPI = 0.9, the process completed the product, but it took 11% (= 1.0/0.9) longer than planned to do it. You can compute CPI and SPI using values from one accounting period, or using a moving average based on values from the last N accounting periods, or using cumulative values to date. The latter choice is better to track trends. (Section 21.2 shows how to use plots of CPI and SPI over time to diagnose a troubled project.) The variances and the indices are equivalent. The relations are as follows:

CPI = 1 + CV/ACWP

SPI = 1 + SV/BCWS

Another index is the To Complete Performance Index, TCPI, defined as follows:

TCPI = $(BAC - BCWP_{cum})/(EAC - ACWP_{cum})$

TCPI equals the remaining budget for uncompleted work, divided by the estimated cost of performing the remaining work. Note that TCPI uses the cumulative values of the quantities BCWP and ACWP. TCPI represents the projected (extrapolated) value earned for every dollar expended in the future. As for CPI and SPI, a value less than 1 indicates performance is less than planned.

Another measure is the percent complete, PC, defined by

PC = percent complete = $100*BCWP_{cum}/BAC$

PC equals the work completed, divided by the budget at completion, BAC, which may or may not include the management reserve.[2]

21.2 Assessing Overall Project Status

Tracking cost and earned value can disclose the failure of a project to follow its plan (for whatever reason). The preceding section defined project cost and schedule variances measured in monetary units. Negative values indicate over cost or behind schedule. You can use these variances to diagnose the general state of a large project. (You can also apply them to portions of a large project (e.g., portions assigned to particular organizations or subcontractors.) There are four possible situations, shown in the four quadrants of Figure 21-3. For example, if SV > 0 and CV < 0, then the project is ahead of schedule and over cost.

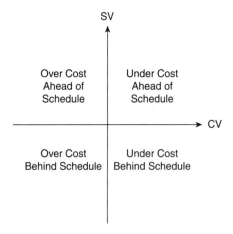

Figure 21-3 *CV and SV show project status*

The preceding section also defined the indices CPI and SPI. Tracking CPI and SPI versus time exposes trends, giving early warning of potential problems. Figure 21-4 shows a plot of CPI and SPI versus time for a project. This project is ahead of schedule. It is also over budget. (Possibly this project was staffed with expensive, senior people who were very productive. This allowed them to complete work sooner than scheduled, but their labor costs were higher than

---

[2] Some organizations may or may not include undistributed budgets and authorized, unpriced work, or may use an over-target baseline. For details, see [Fleming, 2000].

planned.) The cost overrun is decreasing, as shown by the CPI moving back up toward 1.0. (Possibly some of the senior people have been replaced by less-experienced and less-expensive people.) The schedule and cost seem to be stabilizing, with TPI ≈ 1.04 and CPI ≈ 0.93. It appears that the project will finish approximately 4% ahead of schedule and 8% over budget (= 1/0.93).

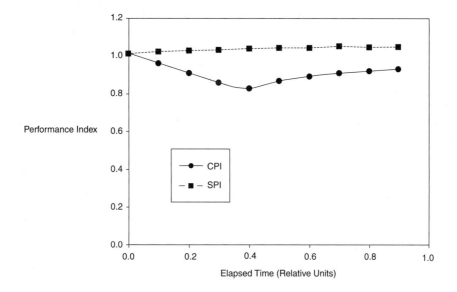

Figure 21-4 *CPI and SPI versus time*

21.3 Converting Schedule Variance to Time

The schedule variance, SV, is measured in dollars (or some other monetary unit).[3] You can estimate the time delay by converting SV into (calendar) time units using either budget or earned value data. The basic equation is as follows:

$$\Delta T = SV_{cum}/CR$$

---

[3] Person-hours is often used for labor tasks.

where CR denotes the completion rate measured in dollars per calendar month. CR can be based on BCWS or BCWP.[4] For either choice, you can use either the value for the current accounting period or an average based on the total to date (cumulative value). The cumulative value is the better choice. Let TDEV be the total schedule, measured in calendar months. The average for a cumulative quantity is Q_{cum}/TDEV. The quantity Q_{period} represents the value for a particular accounting period. Most organizations use monthly accounting periods. These are not of equal size, however. Another approach is to divide the year into 13 four-week accounting periods. (This makes it difficult to prepare quarterly financial reports, however!) In either case, you will have to adjust for any special situations such as a two-week plant shutdown during Christmas/New Year holidays.

To illustrate the proper units conversion, compute averages assuming 13 four-week accounting periods. The length of an accounting period, in calendar months, is as follows:

TPER = 12 calendar months/13 periods = 0.923 calendar months/period

The adjusted completion rate for the period is as follows:

CR = Q_{period}[dollars/period]/TPER[calendar months/period]

= 1.08*Q_{period} [dollars/calendar month]

As an example, suppose that a project is behind schedule (SV < 0) and has these values:

TDEV	= 10 calendar months
TPER	= 0.923 calendar months
SV_{cum}	= −$100
$BCWS_{cum}$	= $950
$BCWS_{period}$	= $90
$BCWP_{cum}$	= $850
$BCWP_{period}$	= $80

---

[4] Choosing BCWS will give a higher value of CR, and so a lower value of ΔT. The reason is that BCWS represents the *planned* progress, whereas BCWP represents the *actual* progress. If a project is behind schedule, SV = BCWP − BCWS < 0, and so choosing BCWP gives a lower value of CR, and a higher value of ΔT.

You can compute the time schedule variance (ΔT) from the dollar schedule variance (SV) four ways:

- Based on budget:

$$\Delta T = SV_{cum}/(BCWS_{cum}/TDEV)$$
$$= -\$100/(\$950/10 \text{ calendar months})$$
$$= -1.053 \text{ calendar months}$$

$$\Delta T = SV_{cum}/(BCWS_{period}/TPER)$$
$$= -\$100/(\$90/0.923 \text{ calendar months})$$
$$= -1.026 \text{ calendar months}$$

- Based on earned value:

$$\Delta T = SV_{cum}/(BWCP_{cum}/TDEV)$$
$$= -\$100/(\$850/10 \text{ calendar months})$$
$$= -1.176 \text{ calendar months}$$

$$\Delta T = SV_{cum}/(BCWP_{period}/TPER)$$
$$= -\$100/(\$80/0.923 \text{ calendar months})$$
$$= -1.154 \text{ calendar months}$$

The negative values indicate a "behind-schedule" status.

21.4 Interim Milestones

Many software modules progress through the same set of sequential activities. If you used a "brute-force" approach, you would have a task (box) on the RLN for each activity (detailed design, code, unit test) for each module. If you have 700 modules, each with an average size of 100 source lines, this is only 70,000 source lines (equivalent to several hundred function points) of software, but you would have 2,100 tasks! To reduce your project control costs, you exploit this regularity of software development tasks. You represent each sequence of activities by a single box, and then track earned value for the box using interim milestones or inchpebbles. Based on historical data, you define the percentage of effort for each activity with respect to the total effort for the entire sequence (which is represented by the single task that appears on the RLN). For example, you might decide that the three activities (detailed design, code, unit test) are each 33% of the total. The total effort for the module, Em, is size/productivity (where the productivity is based only on the three activities of interest). If you have completed detailed design, then BCWP = 0.33*E_m. If f_m represents the % complete (based on inchpebbles completed), then for a task representing M modules:

$$BCWP = \sum_{m=1}^{M} f_m E_m$$

You can easily automate this calculation using a spreadsheet.

The allocation tables described in Chapter 12, "Top-Down Estimating and Allocation," are one source of the weights, f_m.[5] As an example, consider the Coding and Unit Testing (CUT) of a module. For the COCOMO model, Coding and Unit Testing consumes approximately 20% of the total effort for a project. You can allocate the total Coding and Unit Testing effort to each module (or group of modules) based on their relative sizes. For example, assume that the project's total effort for Coding and Unit Testing is 1,000 phrs, and the total size of the modules is 5 KSLOC. The allocated effort for a module of size 600 SLOC is 120 phrs (= 1000*0.6/5.0). Table 21-1 identifies a set of subactivities for Coding and Unit Testing, and shows the amount of the total Coding and Unit Testing effort allocated to each subactivity. These amounts can be based on historical data, Delphi estimates, and so on. You can define the subactivities to fit the phases or activities of your particular process model. Two examples are defining operational scenarios and test cases.

Table 21-1 *Inchpebbles for the CUT Activity*

Subactivity	Allocated Effort (%)
Clean compile	35
Code peer review done	15
Corrections approved	10
All units executed	20
All test results approved	10
Code and PDF accepted by CM	10
Total	100

---

[5] Another source is the original estimated effort of the related activities, normalized by their sum. For software modules, however, the effort for each of the activities is usually *not* independently estimated. Instead, you use top-down estimation plus the allocation tables to estimate the effort for the activities. (See Chapter 12.) Using the allocation tables reduces the labor expended on estimating multiple activities for each of the many modules.

Continuing the example, suppose that the module has completed the code peer review, the programmer has made all of the corrections, and the moderator has reviewed and approved the corrections. This module receives a completion credit of 60% (= 35 + 15 + 10). The earned value is 72 phrs (= 0.6*120 phrs).

There are three key conditions to use interim milestones successfully. First, choose subactivities that have objective, verifiable completion criteria. (They are interim milestones.) Do not allow a programmer to simply estimate that his or task is "90% complete." Second, use the same value for all modules. Third, do not change the values in mid-project. (Yes, I once saw a manager try this in an attempt to increase his earned value. What happened to him was not pretty.)

21.5 Earned Value Example

Figure 21-5 shows a simple RLN with five tasks scheduled to occur over three accounting periods. Time increases toward the right in the figure. The figure has four horizontal sections. The top section shows the Resource Loaded Network. The second section shows the milestones (triangles). Completed milestones are shown as black triangles. The third section shows the values of the five earned value quantities (BCWS, BCWP, ACWP, CV, and SV) for the current accounting period. The fourth section of the table shows the cumulative values of these same quantities, plus CPI and SPI.

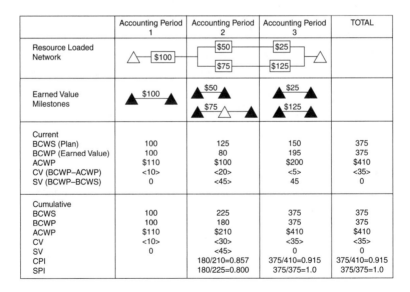

	Accounting Period 1	Accounting Period 2	Accounting Period 3	TOTAL
Resource Loaded Network	$100	$50 / $75	$25 / $125	
Earned Value Milestones	$100	$50 / $75	$25 / $125	
Current				
BCWS (Plan)	100	125	150	375
BCWP (Earned Value)	100	80	195	375
ACWP	$110	$100	$200	$410
CV (BCWP–ACWP)	<10>	<20>	<5>	<35>
SV (BCWP–BCWS)	0	<45>	45	0
Cumulative				
BCWS	100	225	375	375
BCWP	100	180	375	375
ACWP	$110	$210	$410	$410
CV	<10>	<30>	<35>	<35>
SV	0	<45>	0	0
CPI		180/210=0.857	375/410=0.915	375/410=0.915
SPI		180/225=0.800	375/375=1.0	375/375=1.0

Figure 21-5 *Earned value for a simple network*

The calculations are straightforward. BCWS and BCWP are based on the tasks started and completed in the accounting period. The $75 task was scheduled to complete in accounting period 2, but did not actually finish until accounting period 3. To keep the numeric values simple, I chose 40/60 crediting.[6] For accounting period 2, BCWP equals $50 plus (0.40*$75) or $80. Because this task completes in accounting period 3, the BCWP there is $195 (= $25 + $125 + 0.60*$75). The organization's accounting system gives the values for ACWP. CV and SV are computed as shown, with negative values shown in angle brackets. The project shows cost overruns in each accounting period. It falls behind schedule in accounting period 2 but then recovers to finish on schedule as planned at the end of accounting period 3. At the end of accounting period 3, the project is still over budget. The final cost overrun is $35. (The next section explains how to use the earned value quantities to sanity check the estimate at completion for this project.)

21.6 Prediction Completion Costs

You can also use earned value data to compute the estimate at completion (EAC). Part of the true power of earned value measurement is its ability to estimate the completion costs for a project based on the earned value performance to date. This is called the "Independent Estimate At Completion" and is denoted by I_{EAC}. The basic concept is to add some multiple of the work remaining to be done to the actual costs to date:

$$I_{EAC} = ACWP + PF*(BAC - BCWP)$$

where PF is a "performance factor" based on observed trends, technical risk, or other factors. The choice of the performance factor is subjective. Three common choices result in these formulas:

$$EAC_{low} = ACWP + (BAC - BCWP)$$
$$EAC_{mid} = ACWP + (BAC - ACWP)/CPI_e = BAC/CPI_e$$
$$EAC_{high} = ACWP + (BAC - BCWP)/(CPI_e*SPI)$$

where CPI_e is defined as BCWP/ACWP. The low and high values add an estimate of the remaining cost to the actual cost that has been incurred to date. EAC_{low} assumes that the project will complete all remaining work as planned; there will be no future cost or schedule performance problems. This results in a low estimate. The EAC_{high} value adjusts for the observed historical performance of the project by expanding the cost by the CPI and SPI values. EAC_{mid}

---

[6] The "standard" choices are 0/100, 25/75, and 50/50. You can also use interim milestones to define a multistep allocation scheme.

just inflates the remaining work to be done by the "cost inefficiency," CPI_e. For details, refer to [Fleming, 2000], [Bent, 1996], and [Humphreys, 1993].

Some authors refer to the estimate to complete (ETC). Thus, EAC = ACWP + ETC. The ETC value includes any commitments, the total cost of items ordered but not yet paid for. Be aware, however, that project controllers typically use ETC to refer to a full, bottom-up estimate based on current data. The "real" ETC is thus an updated project estimate. The "estimated" ETC is based on the earned value measurements and corresponds to the term PF*(BAC-BCWP) in the equation for I_{EAC} previously.

To illustrate these equations, use the values for the 40/60 crediting example shown in Table 21-5 at the end of period 2. The (cumulative) values are as follows:

BAC	= 375
BCWP	= 180
ACWP	= 210
CPI	= 0.857
SPI	= 0.800

Using these values in the preceding equations gives the following:

EAC_{low} = 210 + (375 – 180) = 210 + 195 = 405
EAC_{mid} = 375/0.857 = 438
EAC_{high} = 210 + (375 – 180)/(0.857*0.800) = 210 + 284 = 494

The final value shown in Table 21-5 is 410.

The To Complete Performance Index (TCPI) indicates the required Cost Performance Index (CPI) needed to finish all remaining planned work using the remaining budget:

TCPI = (BAC – BCWP)/(BAC – ACWP)

If the value of TCPI is larger than the cumulative CPI, the project will have to work more efficiently than it has to date. Due to project inertia, large improvements are unlikely. If the TCPI is much larger than CPI, completing the work within the budget is unlikely. Using the values for the preceding example gives the following:

TCPI = (BAC – BCWP)/(BAC – ACWP)
= (375 – 180)/(375 – 210) = 195/165 = 1.182

The cumulative value of CPI is 0.857. It is very unlikely that this project can avoid a cost overrun.

The EAC values computed using earned values measurements are accurate for very large projects. Large projects do have a lot of inertia, and in such cases earned value techniques are effective. Quentin Fleming describes the cancellation of the Navy's A-12 program based on earned value estimates [Fleming, 1992]. These estimates assume that "things will proceed as they have in the past" (e.g., the team's productivity will remain the same), and also that the plan for the future activities will be as good as the plan was for the past activities (no front or back loading).

The accuracy of the EAC value depends on the quality and stability of the cost and schedule baseline! If the team makes major changes to the plan (represented by the project's Resource Loaded Network), you must discard the old plan and its associated performance data. You lose the "estimating baseline" and cannot use earned value techniques to calculate a new Estimate At Completion until the project accumulates performance data for the new plan.

21.7 Recommended Reading

One of the best references for earned value measurement is [Fleming, 2000]. [Bent, 1996] is also good. John Goodpasture provides a succinct discussion of earned value with several examples in Chapter 6 of [Goodpasture, 2004]. Mark Christensen and Richard Thayer discuss project performance monitoring, including the limitations of performance indices in Section 12.5 of [Christensen, 2001].

Several good articles deal with earned value measurement in *CrossTalk, the Journal of Defense Software Engineering*, which are available via the Web. Quentin Fleming and Joel Koppelman provide two overviews of earned value project management in [Fleming, 1998] and [Fleming, 1999]. Walt Lipke has several interesting articles with practical advice. He describes several ways of calculating the Independent Estimate At Completion in [Lipke, 2004]. He uses earned value techniques to estimate the probability of successful project completion in [Lipke, 2003]. Lipke explains how to adjust staff level and the amount of overtime to recover either cost or schedule in [Lipke, 2000]. He also explains how to determine whether the planned course of action is achieveable. Finally, Lipke discusses the relation between statistical process control and earned value in [Lipke, 2000].

The American National Standards Institute (ANSI) publishes a standard for earned value management systems, ANSI 748-1998. The Project Management Institute publishes a "Practice Standard for Earned Value Management," as well as other related standards. See http://www.pmi.org. Some of the PMI terminology differs from that in ANSI 748 (e.g., "earned accomplishment" rather than "earned value").

21.8 Summary

Earned value measurement tracks progress with respect to a plan (represented as a time-phased budget) and is especially important for large projects having hundreds or thousands of tasks. Earned value measurement compares the amount of progress (BCWP), which is based on the initial estimated cost for the tasks, to the costs incurred (ACWP), and to the amount of work that you had planned to complete (BCWS) by a given time. Earned value techniques can identify cost and schedule problems. A task is over budget if ACWP > BCWP. A task is late if BCWS > BCWP.

Modern project control tools enable managers to track projects with hundreds of tasks, obtain an overall picture of the project's status, and estimate the cost and time needed to complete all planned work. Managers can also identify which tasks are causing problems by "drilling down" to lower-level WBS tasks to isolate specific causes. (This requires careful partitioning of the WBS and assignment of control accounts. If you do not split the work assigned to separate organizational units, you cannot "see" which one is over budget.)

To prepare an estimate to complete (ETC), you should do a full bottom-up estimate, following the same steps used to prepare the initial estimate, adjusting for scope changes, work completed, and observed productivity. Your ETC should be an independent estimate based on the latest information. The estimate at completion (EAC) equals the actual costs ("actuals") to date, plus the ETC. You can estimate EAC values using earned value techniques to check your bottom-up EAC.

Chapter 22

Collecting Data: Details

This chapter describes the challenges of collecting accurate effort and cost data for large projects. To obtain data at a reasonable cost, you must carefully plan to collect only the data you need and to automate its collection. Typically, your organization's management information system (MIS) collects cost and effort data, and may collect additional data as well. (Another term is *cost collection system*.) However, limitations of these systems affect the timeliness and accuracy of the data. This chapter explains the problems and identifies some solutions. Sections 22.4, 22.5, and 22.6 deal with special topics of interest to only a few organizations. Most readers will want to skip them.

22.1 Project Tracking Systems

Tracking collects and analyzes detailed data at frequent intervals to provide the information needed to control a project as it proceeds. Tracking uses measurements of product size, performance, and quality; project effort, cost, and schedule; and process effectiveness and efficiency. A few additional quantities are only of interest for tracking: personnel availability and workload, budgets, and trends. Effort is the most difficult quantity to collect accurately. Cost is the second hardest. Some of the reasons for this arise because of the differences between systems designed for project tracking, and ones designed for time reporting and cost accounting. (See Section 22.2.)

To track the progress of a project, you must collect data during the course of the project subject to the constraints discussed earlier (accuracy, timeliness, etc.). Figure 22-1 shows the flow of data into and out of a conceptual project tracking system (PTS).[1] The project plans provides the cost and schedule baselines (milestones, resource loaded network, budgets). The organization's effort and cost reporting systems, described in Section 22.2, provide effort and cost data. (Employees report *effort* on their *time*cards so the effort reporting system is often called the time reporting system.) Status information comes from the workers themselves, augmented by data from the process (completed milestones, items placed under configuration control, etc.). The project tracking system combines this information to produce an integrated picture of the project's cost and schedule status.[2] The key point is that *a project tracking system needs to collect more data than is usually provided by an organization's time reporting and cost accounting systems.*

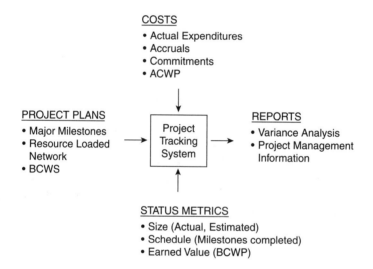

COSTS
- Actual Expenditures
- Accruals
- Commitments
- ACWP

PROJECT PLANS
- Major Milestones
- Resource Loaded
  Network
- BCWS

Project Tracking System

REPORTS
- Variance Analysis
- Project Management
  Information

STATUS METRICS
- Size (Actual, Estimated)
- Schedule (Milestones completed)
- Earned Value (BCWP)

Figure 22-1 *Sources of data for project tracking*

Sometimes the project tracking system is semi-automated (usually using linked spreadsheets). On larger projects, integrated, automated systems may be purchased or built. (In my experience, customized systems are usually built since

---

[1] Section 21.1 defines the quantities BCWS, ACWP, and BCWP shown in the figure. These quantities are used in earned value measurement.

[2] Technical baselines are tracked analogously. Just delete the item "Costs" in the upper part of the figure.

every customer wants to receive different cost and performance data, and because projects building different types of products cannot use the same process or set of metrics.)

22.2 Time Reporting and Cost Accounting Systems

Failure to understand some of the basics of accounting systems can mislead estimators, managers, and customers about the true status of a project. The following may not be of interest to some engineers or managers (who should already know it). If so, skip over it.

Many stakeholders need effort and cost data. The management information system (MIS) measures effort and costs, which are an essential part of project tracking. Every organization has a "finance and accounting department" that operates the organization's management information system. The management information system actually consists of several distinct but coupled subsystems, and is used to manage the organization's business and finances. The organization's "time" reporting system collects effort data, specifically the labor hours expended by individuals to perform various activities and tasks. The effort data is provided to the organization's cost accounting system. The cost accounting system provides data needed for accounts payable (which includes payroll), accounts receivable (billing and invoicing), and finance (borrowing and managing money). The general ledger system maintains the organizations' financial accounts (e.g., assets, liabilities, and cash flow). The management information system produces reports each accounting period for these departments. (The accounting period is usually one calendar-month.) Section 22.4 explains some limitations of accounting systems.

Planners, estimators, and managers are also interested in effort and costs for individual, low-level activities, but split in ways that are different than those used by accountants and business managers. Project managers deal with work breakdown structure tasks that are tied to the project's schedule and task precedence network. Thus, the project tracking system and management information system are often separate.

22.3 Defining "Good" Charge Numbers

A cost accounting system uses a set of charge numbers designed to support cost tracking and financial analysis. Accountants want charge numbers that distinguish cost types, and tie to the organization's general ledger accounts. Contract managers want charge numbers that support mandated reports. For example, government procurement agencies often need to relate cost data to the sources and types of funding. Project managers want earned value (defined in Chapter 21, "Earned Value Measurement"). To aggregate the raw accounting data to produce the particular "view" needed by each stakeholder, the accounting system must provide a set of charge numbers that subdivides the data in multiple ways.

The key to using cost accounting data for project tracking is how well the charge numbers used for cost accounting map to the project-specific work breakdown structure.[3] (In some firms, charge numbers and WBS identifiers are one and the same.)

Defining a good set of charge numbers is especially important for large projects. Too few charge numbers provide insufficient cost information for analyzing problems, understanding the causes of variances, and building new estimation models. On the other hand, too many charge numbers can create confusion, especially if the task descriptions are vague or ambiguous about the activities covered by each task. If presented with several similar tasks, workers will record their labor hours based on their interpretation and judgment. Such problems lead to "noise" in the effort data. You are not collecting what you think you are.

TIP: To increase the accuracy of reported effort, limit the number of charge numbers that workers can use at any given time. This reduces possible confusion. To enforce this, have your accountants open and close charge numbers as a project proceeds. (*Open* means to allow charges to be posted to the account number.)

Large projects must track at a more detailed level than small projects because you typically track at a resolution that is consistent with the amount of resources (effort, money, or time) that you can afford to lose. You want to detect and correct problems before a substantial portion of the resource has been wasted. (This is analogous to the tradeoff between the cost [frequency] of backing up project data and the cost of losing the productive effort of the staff if a disk crashes.) Because work packages are the basis of tracking, reducing the amount of potential loss means that there is a maximum size for work packages, and so a large project will need to identify and track more work packages than a small project. In addition, large projects usually involve multiple firms. Thus, large projects can have literally tens of thousands charge numbers. (I know of one that had more than 14,000 active charge numbers.)

---

[3] Control accounts link the tasks of the work breakdown structure to the entities of the organizational breakdown structure (i.e., the project's organization chart) that perform the tasks. A control account has one or more charge numbers.

For cost accounting, like estimating, you get what you pay for. Project planners (and the people who measure and estimate) strive to balance the level of detail and the cost of collection. Having many small tasks provides more detailed information and so increases management visibility. This detail helps to control the project and develop cost estimating relations. There is a practical lower limit on the task size, however, because defining and tracking each individual task costs money. (The next section provides an example.) You need to identify goals and objectives and then use these to identify the tasks and activities of the production process for which you need to collect detailed data. (The Weekly Effort Collection worksheet, described in Section 16.3, provides an example.)

TIP 1: Define an adequate charge number scheme before the projects starts because you will use the scheme for the duration of the project. (A technique, called rolling-wave planning, defers detailed planning of some tasks until later in the project. You can set aside "blocks" of charge numbers for the tasks to be identified later.)

TIP 2: Do not open all the charge numbers at the start of the project. Open them just before you need them. Close them when the task is finished.

TIP 3: Unexpected changes in project scope are not included in the project's planned work. Such changes are especially dangerous for firm fixed price projects. When you detect potential scope changes, immediately open new charge numbers to "isolate" the costs arising from the change.

Defining a "good" set of charge numbers is an art. In most large organizations, project controllers work with managers and financial analysts to define a set of charge numbers for a project. (Ideally, estimators, engineers, and process improvement specialists participate as well.) A carefully designed set of charge numbers is necessary but not sufficient, however, as the next section explains.

22.4 Limitations of Accounting Systems

Accounting systems have practical limitations:

- Achievable resolution
- Time delays
- Approximate support costs

Resolution: The accuracy of the cost data collected depends on how finely the accountants (and project controllers and managers) subdivide the tasks and cost elements, and on the clarity and disjointedness of the work package definitions. If the tasks are "large" (thousands of person-hours each), each encompasses many little activities.[4] If you make the tasks small, a few person-hours, the overhead generated by the direct labor will not cover the costs of collecting and reporting the highly detailed data. Automated time reporting systems help reduce the costs, but there is ultimately a limit. To see the trade between visibility and cost, consider a task with only eight person-hours of effort. For a typical large project, the amount of administrative overhead allocated to define and track tasks is seldom more than 5% of the direct labor. (Very large projects involving hundreds of individuals and dozens of firms may expend as much as 8% on tracking costs and status.) This overhead must pay an accountant to open a charge number, enter the budgeted amount, and close the charge number. (Most organizations have an automated interface between their cost accounting system and their project tracking system so accountants do not have to enter the actual effort expended from employee timecards.) Assuming a 5% loading rate for task tracking, an 8 person-hour task generates only 0.4 person-hours (about 24 person-minutes) for the accountant to establish and track the task so such a small task cannot cover the costs of tracking. In contrast, an 80 person-hour task provides 240 person-minutes or approximately 4 person-hours per task, which is adequate to cover the tracking costs.

Time delays: Managers must receive information in time to make use of it. Any accounting system has built-in delays. Most accounting systems only produce reports by accounting period, which is typically one month long. Accountants record costs during the period, but managers only receive reports at the end of the accounting period. This means that posted costs are always a little late.

There is also a subtle source of inaccuracy due to delays in the business process itself. These arise because of the difference between committed and actual costs. As an example, suppose that the project must purchase a $100,000 computer. The project budget includes the necessary funds, and the accounting system tracks costs against this budget. The organization commits to buy the

---

[4] It is also hard to determine status. See Chapter 21 on earned value and interim milestones ("inchpebbles").

computer by issuing a purchase order. The vendor builds and ships the computer, which may arrive months later. The vendor does not send an Invoice for the costs until the computer is shipped. The organization's Accounts Payable department then pays the invoice, and the management information system shows that the available funds are reduced by $100,000. If the project manager depends on the management information system data to determine the available funds, there is a possibility of spending money that is already committed, leading to a cost overrun.

A good project tracking system tracks commitments, and reconciles commitments against actual invoices. When the purchase order is issued, the tracking system records a commitment against the project's costs. The amount of the commitment is the estimated cost of the computer, including taxes, shipping, and insurance. When the invoice finally arrives, the project controller must reconcile the committed amount (estimated cost) against the actual cost because they are seldom identical. (For example, the purchase order has estimated shipping charges, whereas the invoice has the actual shipping charges.) Reconciliation replaces the committed amount with the actual amount.

Approximate support costs: Classical accounting allocates the costs of indirect and support activities in various ways. One source of costs is facilities-related overhead and administrative support. One way to allocate these costs is to multiply the direct costs of production by rates reflecting the indirect costs. Many organizations establish a separate department (sometimes called a "service center") to provide services and support. Some type of accounting entity is established to isolate and collect the associated costs. (This is called an indirect cost pool.) At the end of an accounting period, the total costs incurred to operate the service center are allocated to the various projects in the organization. For example, the costs might be allocated based on the number of personnel assigned, the labor hours charged, or the amount of floor space occupied.[5] (This also leads to time delays. See above.)

Another source of inaccuracy and delay in reported (measured) costs for services is the need to use provisional (estimated) rates. The actual costs and resource usage are not known until the end of the averaging period (usually one quarter or one fiscal year). Until then, cost accountants use "booking rates" to accrue costs. At the end of the period, they post adjustments to the accrued costs. Until then, the reported cost data is only as good as the estimated service center rates. The same problems arise with estimated costs for taxes, medical claims, and shipping, as well as for the actual number of sick days and vacation days used. At the end of the project, the final actual values are known. (This is not necessarily true because accounting errors may have occurred and gone undetected. I used to think that accounting was exact...I think of the Red

---

[5] Activity-based costing tries to allocate overhead and support costs based on actual usage. This gives more precise information, but may increase accounting costs. See Section 22.5.

Queen in Lewis Carroll's *Alice in Wonderland* who said: "When I use a word [number] it means exactly whatever I want it to mean." This is true of all measures, of course. Cost is just another quantity that happens to be measured in monetary units.)

22.5 Activity-Based Costing

Activity-based costing (ABC) is a method of detailed cost accounting. (Here, *costing* denotes cost accounting, not the conversion of resource amounts to costs.) Like traditional cost accounting, activity-based costing provides information used to calculate unit production costs, determine profit margins, set prices, measure the performance of production processes, and estimate future costs. Activity-based costing was developed to analyze the continuous manufacturing of products from a product line (a set of similar or related products). The classic example is the production of many identical hardware units in a factory.

Classical accounting allocates the costs of support activities to the various projects or departments in the organization. This allocation is sometimes approximate. ABC distinguishes between resource usage and resource spending [Cooper, 1992]. Activity-based costing assigns costs to individual products ("cost objects") based on the resources actually consumed by the production and support processes. The total cost of a product is the sum of the costs of all the activities required to design, produce, deploy, maintain, and decommission the product.

An activity-based costing accounting system relates three quantities: resources, activities, and "cost objects." Resources can be labor, materials, and other direct costs. Activities accomplish steps of the production or service delivery process. Cost objects can be products, services, customers, or distribution channels. Resources, activities, and cost objects can all be hierarchically decomposed.

In a typical activity-based costing model, a matrix ties consumed resources to specific, low-level production activities. (Each cost object has a separate matrix.) The columns of this matrix identify all activities that are performed to produce and deliver the cost object. The rows identify the resources consumed by each particular activity each time that the activity is performed. The cells at the intersections of the rows and columns have a cost account (or charge number). The challenge in using activity-based costing is to choose the correct level of detail. You must balance the benefits (e.g., cost savings achieved through better understanding) and the costs of collecting the data. See the "Recommended Reading" section for references on implementing activity-based costing.

22.6 Tracking Heterogeneous Project Teams

Heterogeneous project teams (HPTs) use resources (people, facilities, etc.) from multiple organizations to develop various types of products, including software and systems.[6] Collecting the cost, effort, and task status data needed to obtain an integrated view of the project status is challenging because each organization has its own accounting system.[7]

Figure 22-2 illustrates a project managed by a "lead" government organization for a project office, which is the purchaser.

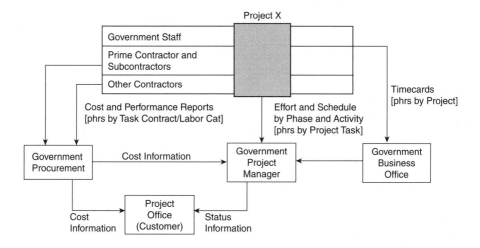

Figure 22-2 *Data flow for integrated product teams*

This project involves individuals from the lead government organization, a prime contractor with subcontractors, and other contractors. Each organization has its own accounting system for labor and costs. Government employees usually report the effort they expend on project tasks to the lead government organization's business office using biweekly time cards. Employees of each of the various contractors (and their associated subcontractors) report their effort

---

[6] A related concept is integrated project teams (IPTs), which include the customer as well as the developers. For example, agile methods often require close, continued customer participation in all phases of the development process. Integrated project teams present the same challenges for collecting effort and cost data as heterogeneous project teams.

[7] This also presents challenges for defining a standardized production process and standard metrics, as well as for collecting the measurements.

via biweekly time cards (which may not be synchronized with the government's biweekly intervals) to their company. Each contractor's accounting department reports effort, cost, and schedule information to the government procurement office. This information is reported by contract task, often decomposed into labor categories. The government procurement organization provides this information to the lead government organization's project manager, who assesses overall program status information from the government employees and the contractors, plus effort and schedule information obtained directly from the project. The project manager reports this data to the customer, the project office. (The government procurement organization also provides cost information to the project office.)

The problem illustrated by the figure is that effort and cost are reported based on organization type, illustrated by horizontal layers shown in the figure, whereas a project slices vertically through the three horizontal layers. You need to measure the effort and schedule for a project in terms of its phases and activities to track project progress, to prepare estimates, and to improve processes. This means that you need a way to collect data in the vertical slice. One solution is to collect effort data by having every employee fill out a special "Weekly Effort Collection worksheet," like the one described in Section 16.3. For additional details, see [Stutzke, 2001].

22.7 Tracking IDIQ Contracts

The U.S. Federal Acquisition Regulations define indefinite delivery, indefinite quantity (IDIQ) contracts, which specify a set of rates and rules to negotiate and award a series of "task orders" or "delivery orders," which are not defined until some time after the contract is signed.[8] Estimation and tracking are important for these contracts to avoid cost overruns and loss of profit. The next two paragraphs describe the challenges.

For indefinite delivery, indefinite quantity contracts, the contractor must track and report effort and costs for each separate delivery order. The costs may be divided by cost type (labor, materials, travel, and other direct costs). Labor is usually further subdivided into labor categories. The project manager must not overrun the funds provided for each cost type, and possibly the funds provided for each individual labor category. (Depending on the contract, funds may or may not be transferred between cost types, or between labor categories.) The funding is often received in increments and must be used within a

---

[8] These are typically time and materials or cost plus contracts. Section 23.2 defines the types of U.S. government contracts.

specified "period of performance." The funds often come from different (customer) sources, which must also be tracked as well. These tracking and reporting requirements add more complexity to the tracking. (Billing is also complicated because accountants must apportion the costs to multiple sources of funding, usually to the funding increment that will expire first.)

Task managers estimate the resources needed, assign labor categories, and forecast personnel availability and workload. They usually prepare a time-phased budget. Then they track the work and expenditures to ensure that the available funding is not exceeded (within cost type, labor category, or both). Failure to do so can result in cost overruns. Often they must also ensure that the estimated number of labor hours for each individual labor category is not exceeded. Also, for some contracts, failure to meet the effort and cost targets in the original budget can result in loss of profit. Accurate estimation and careful tracking are essential.

22.8 Recommended Reading

Harold Kerzner has written several books on project management, and covers planning, scheduling, and tracking. See [Kerzner, 2003]. Margaret Worthington and Louis Goldsman cover cost accounting standards, and control and management systems [Worthington, 1998]. Kenneth Humphreys and Lloyd English provide a good overview of cost estimating and accounting [Humphreys, 1993]. Darrell Oyer describes pricing and cost accounting for government contractors [Oyer, 2000].

Robin Cooper and Robert Kaplan give an overview of activity-based costing in [Cooper, 1992]. Gary Cokins provides an introduction to activity-based costing [Cokins, 2002], with more detailed information in [Cokins, 1996]. Tom Pryor explains how to use activity-based management for continuous improvement [Pryor, 2000].

The U.S. Navy provides information at http://www.acq-ref.navy.mil/wcp/abc2.html. The Activity-Based Costing Benchmarking Association (ABCBA) conducts benchmarking studies and provides a means for organizations using activity-based costing to share information. Their website is http://www.abcbenchmarking.com.

22.9 Summary

Project tracking uses measurements of task status and cost collected over time. Time reporting systems collect expended effort from employee timecards. Cost accounting systems collect and track many kinds of costs. (They also calculate labor costs using the effort data supplied by the time reporting system.) Project tracking systems compare effort and cost data to the project's plan (specifically, its time-phased budget). Task size and accounting costs limit the achievable resolution of cost data. A good charge number scheme balances the need for details against the cost of collecting the data. Effort and cost data may have errors and biases, however. Employees can be confused by unclear task descriptions or by having too many tasks to choose from. Reported cost data may be inaccurate due to delays in receiving data on commitments, and allocation of costs without regard for actual resource usage. Examples are indirect costs collected by department, and then allocated to projects based on headcount, floor space occupied, or some other criterion. Such rules may not allocate the costs "reasonably," leading to inaccuracies in the indirect costs. Activity-based costing (ABC) can track the true costs for each activity, but at some point, the cost of managing all the necessary charge numbers becomes prohibitive.

You should update estimates during a project by using new information obtained from tracking and measurement. Chapter 18, "Updating Estimates," discusses how to update estimates. Section 21.5 explains how to prepare estimates using earned value measurements.

Chapter 23

Calculating Costs and Bid Price

Large projects, as used here, develop custom systems for government or commercial customers. This chapter provides information to help you prepare plans, budgets, and bids for large projects.

23.1 Review of Direct and Indirect Costs

Chapter 15, "Calculating Costs and Price: The Basics," explained the relations between resources, cost, and price. It explained direct costs for the engineering and testing activities, and as indirect costs needed for support activities such as configuration management, quality assurance, program management, and facilities. It also described ways to calculate project cost and set the price for products and bids. It also explained how to reduce costs if the first estimate is too high. Finally, it described cash flow, opportunity cost, and total ownership cost.

Table 23-1, reproduced from Section 15.1, illustrates typical labor and nonlabor costs, and typical examples of direct and indirect costs. Some costs may be treated as direct or indirect based on customer directives and the organization's accounting conventions, which vary from organization to organization. A "direct" cost can be traced to specific production activities. An "indirect" cost is of a general, continuing nature and so is not directly traceable to specific production activities.

Table 23-1 *Typical Cost Categories with Examples*

	Labor	*Nonlabor*
Direct	Engineers Project managers Supervisors	Materials Other direct cost (including any special equipment) Travel
Direct or indirect (based on directives and accounting rules)	Configuration management specialists Quality-assurance specialists Clerks Network and computer support technicians	Facilities Furniture Standard office equipment (phone, copier) Office automation (computers, staff training, network, email)
Indirect	General administrative departments (personnel, legal, accounting, facility operations) Corporate officers and directors	Insurance Taxes Interest Depreciation

23.2 Rate Types for U.S. Government Contracts

For large U.S. government contracts, "costing analysts" multiply direct costs by various rates to obtain the total cost. For U.S. government contracts, five rates are typically used to "load" the (base) costs. A sixth rate, fee, is applied to the loaded cost to compute the profit. The total price equals the loaded cost plus the (estimated) profit. The six rates are as follows:

- Fringe (salary-related taxes, insurance, and benefits)
- Overhead (facilities, equipment, tools)
- Materials and subcontracts surcharge (handling costs)
- General and administrative (corporate infrastructure)
- Escalation (inflation)
- Fee (proposed profit)

Fringe, overhead, and escalation are the same rates described in Section 15.3.

The materials and subcontracts (M&S) surcharge is essentially a tax applied to the dollar value of all items that are purchased as materials or via subcontracts. This tax provides the funds needed to pay the purchasing agents and subcontract administrators who handle the necessary paperwork.

General and administrative (G&A) costs cover corporate infrastructure, which includes corporate officers, and various departments such as legal, contracts, security, and personnel. (These costs are included in the overhead or gross margin rates for commercial bids.)

All of these rates represent legitimate costs of activities needed to deliver products and services. These rates are proprietary and vary from one organization to another due to the decision to bill support personnel as direct or indirect, and the need to maintain manufacturing and test facilities. These rates are usually defined on a company-wide basis, although different subsidiaries of a company may negotiate their own set of rates. For U.S. government contracts, auditors annually review and negotiate each firm's set of "disclosed rates" and loading rules. (Each company's disclosure statement defines their rules for U.S. government contracts.)

Firms bidding custom systems to government and commercial buyers compute the price quoted to the purchaser using a fee rate, expressed in percent. The bid price equals the total estimated cost times (1 + Fee rate).[1] The fee rate depends on the particular project, and is a function of the perceived risk borne by the seller, the organization's financial objectives, competitive pressures, and the promise of follow-on business. Commercial development contracts typically have high fee rates because some overhead expenses are not considered billable, either directly or indirectly. The fee rate for commercial contracts typically ranges from 15% to 40%.

For U.S. government contracts, the fee rate is influenced by the contract type. See the box "Types of U.S. Government Contracts." Note that the actual profit may not equal the estimated profit (equal to the total estimated cost times the fee rate) for reasons described later.

---

[1] Some bids only apply the fee rate to certain costs, not to the total cost. For example, buying catalog items is not risky, and so there may be no fee applied to materials.

Types of U.S. Government Contracts

Different contract types affect the amount of risk borne by the seller of the product. Part 16 of the U.S. Government Federal Acquisition Regulations defines several types of contracts. For full details, see the FAR website at http://farsite.hill.af.mil, or the U.S. government Acquisition Net, which is at http://www.acqnet.gov/far/current/html/FARMTOC.html. The following paragraphs summarize the characteristics of these and some other types of contracts.

The least risky type of project is internal research and development (IRAD). This is any type of project that is performed for the organization itself and so has no fee or profit associated with it. IRAD projects may develop new technology and products (hence the name), but may develop software, equipment, or systems to be used by other departments of the organization. Projects to develop shrink-wrapped products sold to outsiders are discussed later in this section.

For a time and materials (T&M) contract, the seller is paid at a fixed rate for every hour billed directly to the contract. These rates are built up by loading an average cost with the various rates, and compared with the expected actual rates to determine the expected profit. (The expected actual rate is the estimated average labor rate when the work is actually performed some time in the future.) Then these rates are negotiated with the purchaser.

For a cost plus fixed-fee (CPFF) contract, the seller provides a budgetary estimate at the start of the work, but is actually reimbursed for the actual costs incurred until the budget amount (the contract ceiling) is reached. The seller receives profit as a lump sum, which is computed as the fixed fee times the original budgeted cost. The initial budgetary estimate is usually based upon some assumed number of labor hours times the expected actual labor rate.

A variation of the CPFF contract is the cost plus fixed-fee level of effort contract (CPFF LOE). Under this type of contract, the seller submits a budgetary estimate. The seller bills the actual cost of the work performed until the budget value is met. The fee for this type of contract, however, is calculated on a per-labor-hour basis. That is, the total amount of fee available is computed as a fixed fee times the original budgeted cost. This computed total fee is then divided by the number of budgeted hours in the original estimate to obtain a fee amount per labor hour. The seller receives a fee only for the number of hours that are expended. In a cost plus fixed-fee level of effort contract, the seller is unable to recoup the entire fee unless the employee's labor rate exactly matches the labor rate used to prepare the initial budgetary estimate. The reason is that both a cost cap and an hours cap apply. If the employee's rate is higher than the estimated rate, the cost cap will be reached before all of the budget hours have been expended, reducing the fee. If the employee's labor rate is lower than the negotiated rate, the employee will deliver more hours than were originally budgeted but the fee pool will be exhausted when the budgeted number of hours, the hours cap, has been reached. There will be no additional fee paid on the additional hours worked.[2]

A cost plus incentive fee (CPIF) contract awards fees to a seller based upon meeting a predefined target cost value. (The "incentive" has nothing to do with meeting specified schedule dates, or with achieving technical performance measures for the product itself.) Cost plus award fee (CPAF) is also a cost reimbursable contract. In this case, however, the seller is awarded a variable amount of fee based upon the purchaser's assessment of the quality of the work performed. The assessment is based on criteria chosen by the purchaser, although the seller may suggest criteria. Typically, the seller is awarded a small base fee, say 2%, and receives the remainder of the fee, say 8%, based on the evaluation. The total fee that can be actually awarded would thus range from 2% to 10% for this particular example. The seller thus has an incentive to perform well, where *well* is defined by the award criteria.

Firm fixed-price (FFP) contracts are the most risky for the seller, but can also potentially provide the highest profit. In firm fixed-price contracts, the seller agrees to deliver a specified product to the satisfaction of the purchaser for a fixed price by a specified date. Under U.S. commercial law, the seller must continue to expend resources until the buyer agrees to accept the product. (Another description of firm fixed-price contracts is "bet your company.") There is substantial risk for sellers when using a firm fixed-price contract to develop unprecedented products, especially software, because it is difficult to describe their characteristics in enough detail to precisely estimate costs. In addition, the external environment, and possibly even the technology being used, usually changes during the project.

---

[2] There are many different calculations for Level Of Effort contracts. Generally, the customer requires the seller to deliver a certain number of labor hours, and specifies a monetary penalty if the seller fails to deliver that number of hours.

Table 23-2 illustrates the approximate range of fee values in percent for the contract types just described. The fee percentage is very low for contracts governed by the U.S. government Federal Acquisition Regulations, which specify a maximum fee value of 10% for contracts delivering services and a maximum fee value of 15% for contracts that perform "research and development."[3] Fee percentages vary more widely for commercial development projects, and for firms that sell shrink-wrapped products.

How can government contractors stay in business with such low fee values? The answer is based on the rules used to calculate the charges that the government agrees to pay. Under the Federal Acquisition Regulations, most of the costs for management and administration are included in loading factors and are paid by the purchaser, allowing the firm to survive with a small fee. Commercial purchasers, on the other hand, typically only pay for technical work, not management or administrative support. To cover these costs, the producers must charge a higher fee rate (or may include some of the expenses in the gross margin, described later). The money to run the organization must come from somewhere. The only difference is the particular rules that are used to estimate and account for the various costs. (Section 23.4 provides numeric examples.)

Table 23-2 *Fee Range (%) and Total Amount Paid*

Project or Contract Type	Defined in U.S. Federal Acquisition Regulations	Approximate Fee Range (%)		Total Amount Paid by Buyer
		Low	High	
Internal development project (e.g., IT)		0	0	Total actual costs.
Independent research and development	X	0	0	Total actual costs (funded by a percentage of corporate profits approved by the government).
Time and materials	X	4	6	Labor hours worked times a fixed, loaded hourly rate (for each labor category).
Cost plus fixed fee	X	7	8	Actual costs times (1 + fee), where fee is a negotiated constant value.

(continues)

---

[3] The fee rate determines the Profit Before Tax for a government contractor. Under the FAR, interest is not an allowable expense, and is paid out of profit, as are taxes (and some other expenses). Profit After Tax equals Profit Before Tax *minus* interest and taxes. Profit After Tax is typically *half* of the Profit Before Taxes.

Cost plus incentive fee	X	8	10	Actual costs times (1 + fee), where fee is based on the project's actual cost and schedule performance compared to the project's plan.
Cost plus award fee	X	8	12	Actual costs times (1 + fee), where fee is based on periodic government ratings of contractor performance based on stated criteria.
Firm fixed price	X	12	18	Estimated costs times (1 + fee); fixed amount the government will pay for the product.
Large commercial system		15	35	Total direct costs times (1 + gross margin); Section 23.4.2 defines gross margin.
Product for mass market		0	150	Product's unit price times number of units sold (less any discounts).

The "rates" discussed previously are bid and actual rates. Firms doing work on U.S. government cost reimbursable contracts also use billing and booking rates. These complicate financial and earned value calculations. See the box "Rates for Cost-Reimbursable Government Contracts" for a brief explanation.

Rates for Cost-Reimbursable Government Contracts

There are four types of rates for cost-reimbursable government contracts:

Bid rate — Rates used to compute the estimated cost and price of a task. These rates are mutually agreed to by the buyer and seller. Specifically, a company's bid rates are based on government-audited financial data ("historical actual data") for completed projects.

Actual rate — Rates used to pay a provider for resources expended in performing a task. (These also include loading the actual direct costs to cover support costs [actual indirect costs] using rates such as fringe, M&S surcharge, and G&A.)

Billing rate	Rates used to compute the amount actually charged to the buyer. These may not equal the bid rate due to delays in billing, crossing fiscal year boundaries, and so forth. These are typically the rates in effect at the time the developer prepares the invoice. (Each government contract specifies the various rate values and when they become effective.)
Booking rate	Rates used during the course of a year to record estimated actual indirect costs to a project. Booking rates can be applied to direct labor, material, and other direct costs (ODCs).

Billing rates account for time variation in the rates. Booking rates accrue estimated indirect costs during the firm's fiscal year, and so provide a more accurate picture of the financial status of the project and the organization. (Accountants replace the estimated indirect costs by actual indirect costs when they close the general ledger accounts at the end of the firm's fiscal year.)

23.3 Financial Risks of U.S. Government Contracts

Figure 23-1 illustrates the dangers of a firm fixed-price contract. The x-axis shows cost, and the y-axis shows profit. The maximum profit occurs if the company can do the job for zero cost. The company makes zero profit if the actual cost of performing the job equals the bid price. If the actual project cost exceeds the bid price, profit becomes negative. There is no limit to how high the project costs can go, and so the firm can lose an unlimited amount of money.

Another significant risk when performing U.S. government contracts is termination for default ("T for D"). Table 23-3 provides an example. The top half of the table summarizes the costs. Assume that the value of the original contract was $35 million, and that the original supplier has expended $22 million up to the time that the contract was terminated. The U.S. government will conduct a formal procurement to select a new supplier. Assume that the new supplier is awarded a replacement contract for $48 million. In addition, the government charges the original supplier for the administrative costs of this reprocurement, $2 million, and termination costs to close out the contract with the original supplier, an additional $1 million.

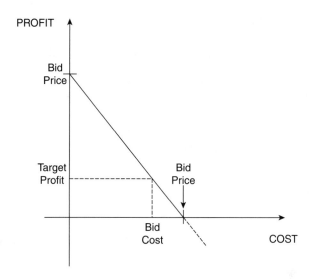

Figure 23-1 *Profit versus cost for a firm fixed-price contract*

Table 23-3 *The Impact of Termination for Default*

Summary of Costs	
Contract value for original supplier	$35M
Contract expenditures to date	$22M
Contract value with new supplier	$48M
Government administrative costs of reprocurement	$ 2M
Government's termination cost for original supplier	$ 1M
Profit Impact to Original Supplier	
Unrecovered costs to date	$22M
Contract value cost differential	$13M
Government administrative costs of reprocurement	$ 2M
Government's termination costs for original supplier	$ 1M
Total profit impact	$38M

The bottom half of the table shows the profit impact to the original supplier. The supplier loses all unrecovered costs to date, $22 million, and must pay the difference in the values of the two contracts ($48 million – $35 million), amounting to $13 million. In addition, the original supplier must pay the government's cost for reprocurement and termination. This amounts to $38 million, which the original supplier pays out of its profits. To see the tremendous impact on the company, assume that the average profit before tax is 8% for the supplier. To recoup $38 million of profit, the firm must perform and complete contracts having a total value of $475 million (= $38 million/0.08).

23.4 Calculating a Bid Price

This section shows how to apply the rates to each type of cost to compute the loaded costs and the bid price. These computations depend on the type of customer and the specific loading rules of the bidding organization. This section provides two examples: (1) a U.S. federal government bid, and (2) a U.S. commercial bid.[4]

23.4.1 U.S. Government Bid

The two basic equations for a U.S. government contract are as follows:

Total burdened cost =   Burdened labor costs

+ Burdened M&S costs

+ Burdened ODCs

Bid price   =   (Total burdened cost) * (1 + Fee)

I have used the term *burdened cost* in these equations. Some organizations use *loaded cost* to mean the same thing. If you are involved in computing costs and price, ask the Contracts and Finance departments in your organization what terminology and definitions they use.

For this example, assume the following set of estimated costs:

Direct labor (DL)	=	$25,000.00
Materials and subcontracts (M&S)	=	$ 2,000.00
Other direct costs (ODCs)	=	$ 5,000.00

---

[4] I was unable to obtain similar examples for other countries. I would like to add such examples in a later edition.

Also assume the following rates:

Fringe (FR)	=	40%
Facilities-related overhead (OH)	=	50%
General and administrative (G&A)	=	5%
Materials and subcontracts surcharge (M&S Rate)	=	7%
ODC handling surcharge (ODC Rate)	=	4%
Fee	=	10%

Recall that fringe is just salary-related overhead.

Using these assumed costs and rates, calculate the burdened costs using the following assumed loading rules:

Burdened labor cost	=	DL(1 + FR + OH)*(1 + G&A)
	=	$25,000(1 + 0.4 + 0.5)*(1 + .05)
	=	$25,000*(1.995) = $49,875
Burdened M&S costs	=	M&S[1 + M&S_RATE*(1 + G&A)]
	=	$2,000[1 + .07*(1 + .05)]
	=	$2,000*[1.0735] = $2,147
Burdened ODCs	=	ODCs*(1 + ODC_Rate) = $5,000*(1 + .04)
	=	$5,200
Total burdened cost	=	$49,875 + $2,147 + $5,200 = $57,222
Bid price	=	$57,222*(1 + .10) = $62,944.20

The burdened cost for labor in this example is almost twice the amount of the direct labor paid to the employee. The reason is the fringe and overhead costs. I show this example to my students because many engineers naively assume in quoting budgetary values to a customer that the labor cost will be what they themselves are paid. Actually, for the company to meet its financial obligations, the appropriate multiplier is closer to a factor of two or more as shown here.

The burdening of the M&S costs is done in an interesting way. One typical approach to compute the amount of money for handling the materials and subcontracts is to multiply the total amount of materials and subcontracts purchased by the M&S rate. The general and administrative (G&A) rate in this case is applied only to that handling fee, not to the total amount of materials and subcontracts purchased. (This method of loading the costs is not standard for all contracts. Your Contracts department can provide the rules for your particular contract or organization.)

For this example, the other direct costs are simply burdened with the ODC rate. No G&A rate is applied. The $200 covers the costs of ordering, receiving, storing, and distributing consumable items. The total burdened cost in this particular example amounts to approximately $57,000. Applying the 10% fee gives a bid price of approximately $63,000.

23.4.2 U. S. Commercial Bid

The cost and price for U.S. commercial bids are computed using a gross margin rate. A typical calculation uses the following equations:

TDC	= Total direct costs	= Labor (loaded with fringe)
		+ Materials
		+ Subcontracts
		+ ODCs
GM	= Gross margin (%)	= OH + G&A + Fee
Bid price	= TDC*(1 + GM)	

Another firm's set of rules might put the fringe rate into the gross margin. If a firm does both government and commercial work, the firm must use the cost accounting rules and rates disclosed to the government that were described earlier. (A firm must perform cost accounting consistently for all of its projects.)

Using the same values for the costs and rates that were used in the preceding example, the calculations for the commercial bid are as follows:

Labor = ($25,000.00)*(1.40) = $35,000.00

Materials and subcontracts = $2,000.00

Other direct costs = $5,000.00

TDC = $35,000.00 + $2,000.00 + $5,000.00 = $42,000.00

Gross margin (GM) = OH + G&A + Fee = 0.50 + 0.05 + 0.10 = 0.65

Bid price = TDC*(1 + GM) - $42,000.00*1.65 = $69,300.00

The total direct costs (TDC) for this project amount to $42,000. The gross margin percentage totals 65%. The computed bid price is slightly more than $69,000. Even though this example uses the same costs and rates as the preceding example, the commercial price is higher by approximately $6,000 even though no M&S surcharge was applied to the materials and subcontracts costs. The reason is that the overhead charges for the facilities are applied to both the materials and subcontracts costs and to the ODCs.

There is nothing dishonest in the fact that the commercial bid price happens to be higher than the government bid price in this example. The bid price (or the selling price) is based on the actual cost of production. The bid prices are simply computed using whatever set of rules that the buyer and seller mutually agree upon. Different industries and countries have their own particular conventions.

23.5 Management Reserves

Government and commercial contracts allow the bid price to a management reserve, an amount of money set aside to handle unexpected problems. (Managers also may establish a schedule reserve, which is time set aside in the project's task network in the form of slack or float.) Because the reserve is part of the price, the customer usually requests justification for the estimated amount. A management reserve can be hard or soft. A *hard reserve* is an estimate based on identified technical, cost, and schedule risks; your risk reserve will be called hard reserves. A *soft reserve* is calculated as a percentage of the total estimated costs (direct and indirect) for the project and so lack a detailed basis of estimate. During negotiations, soft reserves are less defendable than hard reserves. Each organization has its own rules regarding management reserves. Quentin Fleming and Joel Koppelman discuss management reserves [Fleming, 2000].

23.6 Cash Flow and Interest Costs

For large projects, cash flow is often a problem because the developer must expend substantial resources before the product is delivered to the customer. The developer must borrow to pay production costs. Borrowing from outside lenders incurs interest costs, which are not allowable costs under U.S. government contracts. (Interest is paid out of the firm's profits.) On the other hand, if the project borrows from internal sources of funds, large production costs could impact the organization's overall finances. These funds also represent an opportunity cost that should be considered. (Sections 15.7 and 15.8 describe cash flow and opportunity cost.)

23.7 Setting a Bid Price

Firms developing large custom ("bespoke") systems for external customers either engage in competitive bidding with other firms, or must provide a detailed justification of their price. In this case, the customer issues a Request For Proposal (U.S.) or a Request For Tender (Europe). This contains a scope of work identifying the deliverable products and services, and any constraints (e.g., cost, time, and statutory).

Table 23-4 shows the activities for this case grouped into four sequential steps. Many people are involved in these activities. Resource estimates ultimately drive the estimated costs, which in turn drive the price. Thus, it is important to obtain good resource estimates. Usually, the engineers themselves prepare the resource estimates for a project. These may include system engineers, software engineers, and hardware engineers. Some firms, however, have trained estimators who specialize in preparing resource estimates. In small organizations, the project manager and/or business manager helps prepare resource estimates and convert these estimates to costs. In large organizations, project controllers may assist in preparing resource estimates. (A project controller is a person who is responsible for the detailed planning, cost and schedule tracking, and analysis of cost and schedule variances for large projects. Project controllers have access to historical data for many completed projects, which is useful to prepare future estimates.)

Purchasing agents, subcontract managers, and costing analysts convert the estimates for various types of resources into estimated costs. A contract manager also participates in the costing process, providing advice on contractual and legal rules and regulations, and interpreting specific clauses of the contract.

After the costs have been computed, the proposal manager, senior corporate executives, and the proposed project manager decide how much profit is appropriate for the project and set the price for the project. The profit amount is based on the seller's perceived degree of risk, the contract type, and competitive pressures.

Table 23-4: *Pricing Process Used by Large Development Contractors*

Step	Activities	Participants
1. Specify project	Define formal scope of work (tasks, services, products, constraints)	External customer (purchaser, user)
	Write product specification (high level)	External customer (user, operator)
2. Estimate resources	Identify items to be delivered	Contracts manager
	Identify all items to be produced	Engineers
	Identify tasks to produce the items and mitigate risks	Engineers
	Estimate effort, time, materials, supplies, and travel	Resource estimators*
	Analyze cost/schedule and supply historical data	Project controller
3. Compute estimated costs	Compute costs of materials	Purchasing agent
	Compute costs of subcontracts (if any)	Subcontract manager/administrator
	Compute costs of consumables and travel	Costing analyst, assisted by purchasing agent
	Obtain approved base labor rates and apply loading rates	Business manager
	Prepare terms and conditions	Business manager
4. Set bid price	Calculate the selling price	Proposal/project manager
	Decide whether the fee rate is consistent with the perceived risks	Contracts, proposal, and senior managers
	Negotiate the selling price with the customer	Proposal/project manager, and senior managers
	Compute return on investment	Senior and business managers

*With assistance from system, software, and hardware engineers.

23.8 Reducing the Price

Organizations are usually interested in reducing the bid price or the purchase price of the system. Figure 23-2 shows a series of feedback loops that indicate possible actions to reduce the project cost and the bid price. (Section 15.12 described these actions.) For external bids, management sets the appropriate fee value based on their confidence in the accuracy of the various estimates, their independent assessment of the risks involved, and business objectives.

(Management also influences the values for the other rates, and the amount of risk reserve.) If the computed price meets the organization's business objectives, the firm will submit the bid. See the box "Making the Bid Decision."

The lower portion of the figure shows other management decisions. If the bid price does not meet the business objectives, the managers may decide not to bid the project, or to invest more resources to reduce the estimated costs. If so, the possible actions are summarized by the various feedback loops shown in the figure. (Chapter 15 described each loop, proceeding down the center of the chart.) For the large projects addressed in this chapter, the bidder can also adjust the fee rate based on the (Government) contract type, the perceived risks, and competitive posture.

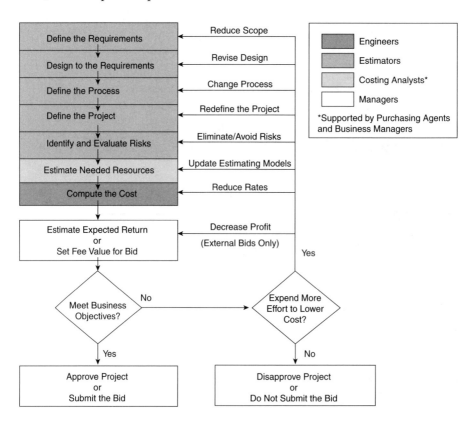

Figure 23-2 *Possible ways to reduce the bid price*

Making the Bid Decision

Making the bid decision is not easy because many quantities are estimated. The quantities are as follows:

$$C = \text{Total project cost}$$

$$F = \text{Fee rate}$$

$$B = \text{Cost of preparing the bid}$$

$$P = \text{Profit} = F^*C$$

$$P_{win} = \text{Probability of winning the bid}$$

The cost includes writing the proposal itself, and for commercial bids, understanding the customer's requirements and devising a feasible solution (architecture, project life cycle), and possibly even some marketing.

The profit depends on the accuracy of the estimated total project cost, and the assumption that the project will earn the expected fee percentage. For firm fixed-price contracts, any cost overruns are borne by the developer, and are paid out of the profit (or, when that runs out, other corporate funds). Variable-fee contracts (cost plus incentive fee or award fee) may also not receive the assumed fee rate.

If there are N bidders, a conservative estimate is $P_{win} = 1/N$.

As an example, choose these values:

$$C = \$10,000,000$$

$$F = 12\%$$

$$B = \$100,000$$

$$P = F^*C = \$1,200,000$$

$$N = 5$$

$$P_{win} = 1/5 = 0.2$$

The expected return on investment is this:

$$\text{ROI} = \frac{\text{Gain} - \text{Bid Cost}}{\text{Bid Cost}} = \frac{P_{win} * P - B}{B}$$

$$= \frac{(0.2)(\$1.2\text{M}) - \$0.1\text{M}}{\$0.1\text{M}} = 1.4 = 140\%$$

23.9 Recommended Reading

Scott Stanberry provides a good introduction to U.S. government contracting in [Stanberry, 2001], including procurement procedures. In particular, Part V of his book describes the types of government contracts in detail. Worthington and Goldsman cover important concepts, including defective pricing, cost accounting standards, and control and management systems [Worthington, 1998]. A good guide for pricing and cost accounting for government contractors is [Oyer, 2000]. John Goodpasture provides numerical examples for fixed-price, cost plus, and time and material contracts in Chapter 9 of [Goodpasture, 2004]. Note N26, "U.S. Government and Commercial Contracts," provides additional information. Also see note N21, "Overview of Contracts."

Unfortunately, there is little structure and consistency to commercial contracts. There are not many references for commercial software contracting and law. Stephen Fishman covers intellectual property from both developer and buyer perspectives without legal jargon [Fishman, 2004]. He covers contemporary topics such as web content and domain names. The book has a CD-ROM with over two dozen forms in RTF format that you can use. Kenneth Humphreys and Lloyd English, although dated, provide useful information if you can find a copy [Humphreys, 1993].

Professional societies provide books, journals, and training. These include the National Contract Management Association at http://www.ncmshq.org, and the International Association of Contract and Commercial Managers at http://www.iaccm.com. A good online source to purchase documents related to federal contracting is http://www.mgmtconcepts.com.

23.10 Summary

Many individuals participate in estimating resources, calculating costs, and setting the price for a government or commercial bid. The estimating process is more formal than for smaller commercial or internal projects. Many individuals with specialized skills participate, including purchasing agents, subcontract managers/administrators, financial analysts, legal advisors, and cost analysts. Cost analysts apply the approved ("disclosed") rates for fringe, overhead, materials and subcontracts, surcharges, general and administrative expenses, and fees. For some contracts, they also use approved labor rates to calculate labor costs. The bid price is based on a documented set of requirements, product designs, process assumptions, and historical productivity data. The documentation and data produced by the various steps of the process provide a detailed justification for the price. Arriving at the final bid price involves an iterative dialogue among all these participants. Then the bidder negotiates the selling price with the customer. (This usually involves additional iterations.)

Part 5

Estimating Products and Processes

Chapter 24

Determining Product Performance

Estimators often support the analysis of trade-offs between performance, cost, and schedule for system development, upgrade, and capacity planning. This chapter identifies possible performance measures, and describes ways to estimate and measure product performance. This chapter also describes a process to engineer the performance of software-intensive systems, and explains the role of estimation and measurement in this process. Performance engineering is a discipline in itself. This chapter only gives an overview, and provides references to books on the topic.

24.1 Types of Product Performance

Performance affects the acceptability and the utility of a product, development costs and risks, and operating costs for the deployed system. Performance is especially important for systems that perform life-critical or safety-critical functions (e.g., medical devices), perform indispensable business functions (e.g., an e-commerce site), and have strict timing requirements (e.g., missile control). Product capacity and performance can also significantly impact development costs and risks. Figure 24-1 shows the "shoehorn effect": Software development effort greatly increases when the system is being designed to use most of the available capacity of some computing resource such as processor cycles, memory, disk storage, or channel capacity. Resource usage is not a concern for many applications, however, because computer hardware

633

has become relatively inexpensive. Software developers can simply specify a target computer platform that provides a certain minimum set of capabilities such as processor speed, amount of main memory, and disk capacity.

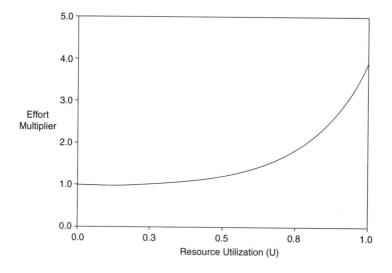

Figure 24-1 *The "shoehorn effect"*

Table 24-1 shows typical performance measures for software-intensive systems ranked in rough order of precedence. If a system produces inaccurate results, the other performance measures do not matter. Similarly, if it cannot provide the results (or service) when the user needs them, resource consumption does not matter. (Many real-time systems respond to a specific event or complete some function within a specified time interval. For example, the avionics to control a supersonic aircraft must send steering commands to flight control surfaces dozens of times per second.)

Users and operators of a system are most interested in the performance of the system as a whole. For interactive systems, performance measures include response time and throughput as seen by the user. System performance arises from the capacity and performance of its components, as Figure 24-2 illustrates. Thus, estimating product performance ultimately requires estimating the usage of various resources such as processors, memory, networks, and peripherals. Depending on the application and user needs, the usage of certain resources is critical. Critical resources are ones that affect system performance (such as user-perceived response time) or because they affect development cost and schedule. The computer resource may be in the host development environment or the target environment. Estimators and planners must identify, measure, estimate, and track these "critical resources." See the box "Technical Performance Measures."

Table 24-1 *Typical TPMs for Computer Systems*

Accuracy
• Correctness (corresponds to real world)
• Adequate precision (resolution)
Dependability
• Reliability
• Availability
• Probability of failure on demand
Speed
• Response time (GUI)
• Execution time (per function, transaction, etc.)
• Data transfer rates
Resource Consumption
• CPU usage
• Storage (memory, disk)
• Transmission channel usage (I/O, LAN)
• Peripherals

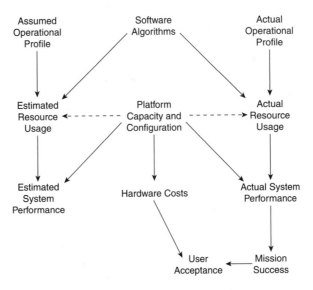

Figure 24-2 *Resource usage versus product performance*

Technical Performance Measures

A *technical performance measure (TPM)* is any system (or product) parameter that impacts system acceptance or project success. A technical performance measure has four important characteristics:

1. It must have a clear definition (units of measure and the conditions of measurement).

2. It has a known "good" target value (specified by the customer or derived from engineering analyses).

3. Its value can be estimated early in a project and can be objectively measured (possibly indirectly) later.

4. Its target value is usually difficult to achieve.

The target value is the "planned" value used for tracking. The measured value is the "actual" value used for tracking. There is always risk associated with the Technical Performance Measure. If possible, only commit to performance measures associated with the pieces of the system that you control. If the product has critical Technical Performance Measures, then identify these as risks, establish risk reserves, and track and mitigate the risks.

Even if all stakeholders agree on the choice and definition of performance measures, other factors affect the estimated or measured values. These factors include the expected workload and the operating modes of the system. A potential estimation risk is that the operational workload may differ from the workload assumed by the designers and agreed to by the stakeholders. (The same problem arises when testing the software to identify defects. See Section 25.4.) You must also specify the conditions with each performance parameter. These include the system configuration, the external environment, and the workload. Quantitative performance objectives without such associated conditions are meaningless.

24.2 Estimating and Measuring Software Performance

Designers need to do the following:

- Determine feasibility and scalability
- Estimate the needed capacity of equipment

- Predict saturation points
- Identify bottlenecks

Table 24-2 shows the types of questions that occur at different phases of the project life cycle related to performance estimation and measurement. Section 24.7 describes the performance engineering process. Also see the "Recommended Reading" section at the end of this chapter.

Table 24-2 *Performance Questions by Project Phase*

Requirements Analysis
• How will the system be used (operational concept, usage scenarios)?
• What are the quantitative performance goals for each scenario?
• What are the critical performance parameters?
• Are there performance constraints (e.g., specified reserve capacity)?
Product Design (Architectural Design)
• Can the performance requirements be achieved (feasibility)?
• What are the performance characteristics of proposed alternative designs?
• What amount of computer resources are needed to provide the performance?
• What are the critical computer resources?
• What is the uncertainty in the estimates (range, upper/lower bound)?
Implementation and Construction
• Have any design changes occurred that will affect previous predictions?
• Can we now estimate the product performance more accurately?
Integration Testing and Acceptance Testing
• Are the quantitative performance objectives met?
• Are the performance constraints met (required reserve capacity)?
Operations and Maintenance
• What is the impact of a proposed modification on system performance?
• How much capacity will be needed to support expected increased usage?

To measure a system's performance, you must carefully design the measurement "experiment," and control the conditions during the measurement (system configuration and workloads). One problem with measuring software-intensive systems is the "uncertainty principle": Inserting code to collect performance data affects the product's performance because the inserted code consumes resources when it executes. Some measurement activities are part of the usual development activities (analysis, design, code, and test). Others involve extra effort and special equipment.

You use analysis and simulation when it is too dangerous, costly, or impractical to measure an existing system, or when the system does not yet exist. Table 24-3 lists some options. Always remember that any analytic model or simulation may produce inaccurate results due to omission of important effects, approximations, mathematical errors, and coding errors. Simulation is more expensive than mathematical analysis, however, because the simulator's code must represent the system under study, any missing components, external objects that interact with the system, and the "physics" of the environment. This increases development costs.

Table 24-3 *Ways to Estimate Performance*

Analysis
• Order of magnitude calculations (scaling)
• Analytic models (spreadsheets)
• Queueing network models
Simulation
• Commercial network models
• Vendor's benchmarking models
• Hybrid models (queueing model results plus custom code)
• Custom-built models (very flexible, any desired fidelity)

It is often difficult to relate the estimated or measured performance of the low-level components to overall system performance. Table 24-4 summarizes challenges to measuring and estimating the performance of software-intensive systems. Essentially, these systems are complex, interactive, and adaptive.

Table 24-4 *Estimation and Measurement Challenges*

Platform Characteristics
• Multiple processors
• Memory caching
• Configurable COTS components (e.g., buffer size)
• "Hidden" factors (operating system's scheduler)
• Internal workload (other concurrent processes)
External Environment and Workload
• Number of users
• External stimuli (probabilistic events, multiple scenarios)

Algorithms

- Use of loops, iteration, searches, or sorts
- Suitability for assumed workload (scalability)
- Choice of parameters (e.g., convergence criteria)
- Not known or poorly understood

Relating Component Behavior to System Behavior

- Complex (and possibly unknown) interactions of components
- Many states and modes (dynamic load balancing, fault tolerance)

24.3 Performance Measurement

Measurement plays an important role in product performance estimation. You need data to define and validate system performance models, as well as models of the system's workload. What should you measure? Table 24-5 shows five types of measurement data, and relates these types to six uses in system performance estimation.[1] Examining the left column first, measurements help understand the system. Measurements of existing systems provides insight if you are developing a similar system. (This is also true for an existing system that you are planning to modify.) Measurements of similar systems, as well as controlled experiments, provide information on workload and resource usage. Later in a project, as software components and subsystems become available, you can measure them and use the measured values to replace your initial estimates of input parameters. This improves the model predictions since the input values are more accurate. You may also use the information to refine the models. Measurements provide data to verify the correct implementation of performance prediction models, and to demonstrate that the model reflects reality (i.e., validate the model). When the system is completed and operating, you use measurement data to monitor and tune system performance, and to evaluate proposed improvements. Thus, the performance models built during development have value during the operational phase. (These models also serve as a starting point for future projects or for future iterations of product development, closing the loop.)

---

1 This table is based on and extends Figure 8-1 in [Smith, 2002].

Table 24-5 *Data Used for Software Performance Engineering*

		Types of Performance Data			
	Workload	Operational Data	Execution Properties	Processing Overhead	Computer System Usage
Possible Uses	Functions, Rates, Patterns	Record Sizes and Access (Type, Frequency, Pattern)	Path Frequency, Resource Usage (Type, Number of Requests, Average Time)	Device Services Used (CPU, Disk, Network)	Response Time and Throughout by Scenario, Busy Time, Queue Lengths
Understand the System	Yes	Yes	Yes	Yes	Some
Specify and Develop Models	Some	Some	Yes	Yes	Some
Update and Refine Models	Yes	Yes	Yes	Yes	Yes
Verify and Validate Models	Yes	Yes	Yes	Yes	Yes
Monitor System Performance	Some	Some	Some	Yes	Yes
Evaluate Proposed Improvements	Yes	Yes	Yes	Yes	Yes

The table shows five types of measurement data, and relates each type to the uses just described. Workload data indicates the pattern of requests, the rate of arrival, and any patterns, such as heavy processing at certain times. The type and amount of data stored and processed are important. Measure the size of tables and frequency of access, plus any patterns such as groups of records that are usually accessed together. Execution properties characterize the behavior of "key functional threads" in terms of their execution frequency and the types and amounts of resources used. Processing overhead ties resource requests to actual service demands for specific devices. Computer system usage addresses overall performance, as well as internal details such as device utilization and queue lengths. (The operating system can usually provide this data.)

TIP: Perform sensitivity studies early to identify areas that have a large effect on performance. Use this knowledge to identify what additional data you should collect, and to construct models that are more precise.

Table 24-6 identifies types of computer resources and possible units of measure for each type. The particular quantities of interest depend on the type of system or product. You will need to define the meanings of *record* and *transaction* for your particular application. (You may have different performance requirements for specific types of records or transactions.) Most of the quantities shown in the table refer to the dynamic behavior of the system (e.g., it performs certain actions within a desired time interval or at a specified rate). Examples are computations and data transmission. Some performance requirements, however, refer to static properties of the system (e.g., memory capacity).

Table 24-6 *Types of Computer Resources*

Computer Resource	Units of Measure
CPU usage	Instructions/second, floating-point operations per second (FLOP/s or flops), percent of available capacity
Main memory usage	Bytes, percent of available capacity
Disk storage usage	Bytes, percent of available capacity, total records
Data transfer rate for disks, buses, channels, ports, networks, and peripherals	Bytes/second, records/second, transactions/second
Peripheral processing rate	Pages/minute for printers

The following sections describe ways to estimate the performance of software-intensive systems.

24.4 Rough Order of Magnitude Calculations

You can use rough order of magnitude (ROM) calculations to estimate the resources used by various processing threads to identify the activities that consume the most resources. This helps you estimate the total resources used and identify which activity requires more detailed analysis.

Consider a warehouse billing application. Customers order items during the month and receive a statement monthly statement. Suppose that you want to look at disk usage when preparing the monthly statements. (For most commercial applications, the time spent reading and writing data outweighs time spent performing calculations.) Define the following parameters:

NC = number of customers = 1,000

NO = number of orders per customer per month = 5

NI = number of items per order = 20

To generate a statement, the program will have to read each customer record, read the orders placed by that customer, and then look up the catalog price of every item on each order. The activities and the number of disk accesses are as follows:

Retrieve customer data	NC	10^3
Retrieve customer's orders	NC*NO10^3*5 = 5*10^3	
Look up catalog prices	NC*NO*NI	10^3*5*20 = 10^5
Write customers invoice	NC	10^3

Looking up the catalog prices clearly consumes the most disk resources.[2]

Compute-intensive programs often involve deeply nested loops, iteration, and evaluating large numbers of possible states or configurations. Applications of this type include analysis of large amounts of data, detailed simulations of physical processes, and processing data from real-time sensors. You can estimate their execution time by analyzing the calculations to determine the number of instructions executed, and using the time to execute one instruction.

This very simple example illustrates the concept. The next section shows how to extend order of magnitude calculations to multiple computer resources by using a resource usage matrix. Order of magnitude calculations and resource usage matrices are sometimes called scoping models. You can use them to estimate the amount of resources needed. The estimated values serve as targets for the system designers, who either can purchase additional hardware to provide the needed capacity, or can consider different processing algorithms that trade the use of one resource for another. (The typical trade involves processor time and the use of main memory.) You can also use scoping models to allocate portions of the available resource to specific processing activities. Note N27, "Performance Model for a Credit Card Billing System," develops detailed quantitative models to evaluate two different design options. It shows how you can use these models to determine the operational conditions where a particular design performs better.

24.5 The Resource Usage Matrix

You can construct a simple system execution model by ignoring contention and using a resource usage matrix, which relates software resource requirements to the amount of service that each requires from specific computing devices. (Smith and Williams call this an "overhead matrix." See Table 15-1 in [Smith, 2002].) Table 24-7 shows an example. The top gives the execution time for each "computer resource unit" in milliseconds. The bottom gives the amount of computer resources used for each type of software work unit. You can use this matrix to create a linear software execution model that estimates the computer resource usage. Figure 24-3 shows an example. The top part shows the estimates for each use case in a scenario. The bottom part of the spreadsheet uses the values in the preceding table to compute the time for each type of computer resource, using the estimated amount of each software resource and the estimated workload (represented by the number of executions of each use case).

---

[2] Calculations of computer performance and system reliability often involve very large or very small numbers. You can use scientific notation to represent such numbers. See Note N50, "Scientific Notation."

Table 24-7 *A Resource Usage Matrix for Execution Time*

Computer Resources				
Device	CPU	Disk	Delay	LAN
Service units	Kops	Access	Visits	Messages
Time per unit (msec)	0.010	15.0	750.0	10.0
Software Work Units				
Standard calculation	1			
Database accesses	70	5		
Messages	25			5
Delays			1	

Project:	Credit Card System			
Design Version:	1.0-A			
Scenario:	Posting and Invoicing			

Use Case	# of Executions in Scenario	Estimated Software Work Units Used		
		Calculations	Data Base Accesses	Messages	Delays
Post Daily Transactions	10000	20	6	1	2
Prepare Monthly Statements	500	55	15	1	5

Use Case	Estimated Time Used (secs)				Total Time (secs)
	CPU	Disk	Delay	LAN	
Post Daily Transactions	378	6000	10000	1500	17878
Prepare Monthly Statements	52	750	500	188	1489

Figure 24-3 *A combined software and computer resource estimation model*

24.6 Modeling Web-Based Systems

You can build a more detailed resource usage model. This section describes a performance model tied to the states of a system.

In a web-based system, each user communicates with a web server, which typically makes many short accesses to a data server. Figure 24-4 illustrates a simple website. To gauge the performance of a website, you measure the number of visits to the site and the numbers of pages served. To predict revenue, you could measure how often customers submit an order per site visit and the average price of an order. Table 24-8 lists some possible performance measures for a website. Typically these are expressed as rates; i.e., the number of users, hits, or dollars measured during a specified period of time. Another reference is [Treese, 1998].

Figure 24-4 *A simple website*

Table 24-8 *Possible Metrics for a website*

Hits	Number of pages (HTML file plus any embedded image files) provided by the Web server
Page views	Number of individual pages served
Unique visitors	Number of different users who visit the Web site (home page)
Click-throughs	Number of users who click an online ad to obtain more information
Revenue throughput	Monetary value of sales completed
Potential revenue loss	Monetary value of items in a customer's shopping cart that are not sold because the customer leaves the site

To obtain a deeper understanding of the user interactions, you can identify states and the functions performed in each state. Table 24-9 gives these for a simple e-commerce website.[3] You could add other functions (e.g., to check the status of a previous order or download products [data, software]). You can measure how many times a user invokes each function per visit.

---

[3] This example is a simplification of one in [Menascé, 2000], and is used with permission. Menascé and Almeida provide a good list of e-business functions in Table 2.2 of [Menascé, 2000, page 54].

Table 24-9 *States and Functions for a Simple E-Commerce website*

Entry	The system is waiting for a customer to access the home page.
Home	The customer attaches to the home page using a browser.
Search	The customer searches for a product.
Login	The customer enters identifying information.
Register	The customer supplies information to create an account.
Select	The customer selects a link returned by the search function.
Add to cart	The customer selects an item to purchase.
Pay	The customer provides shipping and payment information.
Exit	The customer leaves the site.

To describe user behavior, you can build a customer behavior model graph (CBMG), as explained in Section 2.3 of [Menascé, 2000]. Figure 24-5 shows a customer behavior model graph for the simple e-commerce website. The nodes of the customer behavior model graph, represented by squares, represent the different states (activities) of a customer during a visit to the site. For example, the customer could be searching for product information. Arrows between the states indicate the allowed transitions. To produce a true state diagram you must add an Exit state (the customer leaves the site). Except for the Entry state, all states can transition to the Exit state, and so the Exit state is usually omitted to improve readability. (The L-shaped arrows show the exit paths.)

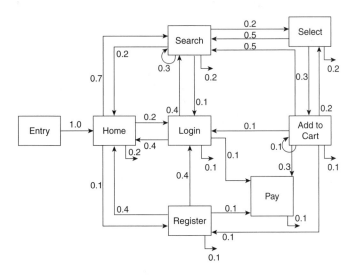

Figure 24-5 *Customer behavior model graph*

The customer behavior model graph is a static picture of the possible navigation paths that a customer can use to traverse the site, as viewed from the server side. To provide a dynamic view, you need to indicate the probability that each particular allowed path will be traversed. (This is one way of describing a scenario.) The figure shows the probabilities beside each line in the customer behavior model graph. The possible paths and transition probabilities are for illustration only. A real e-commerce Web site will have additional paths and different probabilities. The box "Building a Customer Behavior Model Graph" provides tips.

Building a Customer Behavior Model Graph

Building a customer behavior model graph requires four steps:

1. Determine the functions provided to the users of the site.

2. Refine the set of functions based on their resource consumption.

3. Map the functions to states (may assign multiple functions to a state).

4. Determine transitions between the states.

Step 2 refines the functions to identify the ones that require significantly more processing or utilize particular types of resources. For example, downloading a large document or an audio track might consume significant amounts of bandwidth and so be of particular interest.

If there are many states and transitions, the diagram becomes rather messy. A better approach is to use a transition matrix. If there are n states, the matrix is $n \times n$, and each cell contains the probability of transition from state i to state j, p_{ij}. Figure 24-6 shows the transition matrix for the customer behavior model graph shown previously. The rows are the FROM states, and the columns are the TO states. The cells are the transition probabilities. The transition probabilities are in the range C9:K17. For example, cell E14 is the transition from Select to Search, which is 0.5.

The customer behavior model graph and the associated transition matrix are a way to describe the workload for a website (or any other interactive computer system). You can use it for capacity planning. As a simple example, if you have the transition matrix, you can solve to find the number of visits to each state relative to the entry state, which is called the "visit ratio." You can then analyze the functions in each state to identify the processor usage for the web and data servers. (You could refine this analysis by identifying subfunctions in each state, and by considering additional resources such as multiple disks, network traffic, and the like.) Multiplying the visit ratio by the resources used in that state gives the usage per customer visit. Knowing the number of customer visits per hour enables you to compute the processor usage on the two servers.

Transition Matrix for a Simple E-Commerce Web Site

			$A$9	$A$10	$A$11	$A$12	$A$13	$A$14	$A$15	$A$16	$A$17
Average Session Length =	7.21										
Buy to Visit Ratio =	17.1%										
		SOLUTIONS CELL	$A$9	$A$10	$A$11	$A$12	$A$13	$A$14	$A$15	$A$16	$A$17
Visit		RESIDUALS	1.000	0.000	0.000	0.000	0.000	0.000	0.000	0.000	0.000
Ratios		From % To	Entry	Home	Search	Login	Register	Select	Add to Cart	Pay	Exit
1.000		Entry	0.00	1.00	0.00	0.00	0.00	0.00	0.00	0.00	0.00
2.035		Home	0.00	0.00	0.70	0.20	0.10	0.00	0.00	0.00	0.00
3.071		Search	0.00	0.20	0.30	0.10	0.00	0.20	0.00	0.00	0.20
0.826		Login	0.00	0.40	0.40	0.00	0.00	0.00	0.00	0.10	0.10
0.225		Register	0.00	0.40	0.00	0.40	0.00	0.00	0.00	0.10	0.20
0.658		Select	0.00	0.00	0.50	0.00	0.10	0.00	0.30	0.00	0.10
0.219		Add to Cart	0.00	0.00	0.30	0.10	0.10	0.20	0.10	0.30	0.10
0.171		Pay	0.00	0.00	0.00	0.00	0.00	0.00	0.00	0.00	1.00
1.000		Exit	0.00	0.00	0.00	0.00	0.00	0.00	0.00	0.00	0.00

Figure 24-6 *Transition matrix based on the CBMG in Figure 24-5*

Menascé and Alemeida describe how to use Excel to determine the relative time in each state from the transition matrix (CBMG) (the Customer Behavior Model Graph) in [Menascé, 2000]. Let **P** denote the transition matrix, and **v** denote the vector of states (visit ratios). When the system is in equilibrium, the following matrix equation is true:

Pv = v

This is a set of linear equations, which you can rewrite as follows:

Pv – Iv = 0

where **I** is the identity matrix. For one single row, the equation is

$$\sum_{j=1}^{m} P_{ij} * v_j - v_i = 0$$

where index i denotes the FROM state, and j denotes the TO state. Spreadsheet Visit Ratios Stutzke.XLS on the CD-ROM uses Excel's Solver to solve this set of linear equations for the matrix. (In the spreadsheet, i is the row and j is the column.) The visit ratios are in column A, rows 9-17 in Figure 24-6. The figure also shows the "buy to visit" ratio, which is the number of visits to Pay, divided by the number of entries to the site (which equals 1). (This model assumes that no customers decide to cancel their order after they are in the Pay state. If they did, the number of "pays" must be reduced by the number of "cancellations.")

Figure 24-7 shows a linear model to estimate the processor time for the web and data servers. The states and visit ratios are from the preceding figure. For each function, the worksheet shows the estimated count and processor time (in milliseconds) for the Web server and the data server. The product of the visit ratio, count, and time per action (or query) gives the average CPU time per customer visit for each server. For this example, the values are 52.9 and 157.3 milliseconds, respectively. Assuming an average of 25,000 visits per hour gives these values:

	Web Server	Data Server
Time (seconds)	1323.0	3931.9
Utilization	37%	109%

The utilization is the usage (in seconds) divided by 3,600 seconds per hour, the interval of measurement for the workload. This simple estimate indicates that the data server will be overloaded. This example illustrates the basic concept. You can also use this technique for other types of applications. See [Zaiane, 1998].

State	Visits	Web Server			Data Server		
		# of Actions	Action Time (ms)	Total per Visit (ms)	# of Queries	Query Time (ms)	Total per Visit (ms)
Entry	1.000	1	1.00	1.00	0	0.00	0.00
Home	2.035	1	0.50	1.02	0	0.00	0.00
Search	3.071	8	1.50	36.85	16	0.80	39.31
Login	0.826	2	0.60	0.99	6	0.80	3.97
Register	0.225	12	1.00	2.71	24	1.20	6.49
Select	0.658	20	0.70	9.21	200	0.80	105.29
Add to Cart	0.219	3	0.60	0.39	2	0.80	0.35
Pay	0.171	4	0.80	0.55	8	1.00	1.37
Exit	1.000	1	0.20	0.20	1	0.50	0.50
			Web Server =	52.92		Data Server =	157.28

Figure 24-7 *Using visit ratios to estimate processor time*

Daniel Menascé and Virgilio Almeida discuss capacity planning in detail in [Menascé, 2000]. Their Chapter 3 explains a client/server interaction diagram, which quantitatively describes the interactions and performance for each business function. Their Chapter 10 discusses modeling the contention for software servers, and contains several good examples. They address surges in customer demand in Chapter 12. Chapter 13 presents several business-to-consumer case studies that illustrate the quantitative methods described in their book. One example considers a hypothetical electronic retailer. One examines the performance and cost implications of downloading digital products. Menascé and Almeida explain how to use the performance estimates to make business decisions. On page 384, they discuss the relationship between site traffic and sales revenue. From this, they derive performance metrics (throughput and average response time) for the system that must support the e-commerce website. They stress the need to understand customer behavior, and to consider traffic bursts that may occur during certain times of the day or year. One example is increased buying during December in preparation for Christmas. Chapter 14 of their book discusses business-to-business processes, as opposed to business-to-consumer processes.

24.7 Queueing Models

The preceding sections described order of magnitude calculations and analytic models to estimate the performance and resource utilization for a system. These techniques use average values for system parameters such as execution time, message size, the number of loop traversals, and workload parameters such as the number of transactions and their arrival rate. In a real system, the values of these quantities vary over time. If you know how the arrival and service times vary, you can use queueing theory to obtain more accurate estimates of various performance parameters.

This section describes queues, some examples of their uses, the types of problems that have been solved, and areas that are not amenable to this approach. It mentions some approximations that you can use to asymptotically bound system performance and to identify bottlenecks.

24.7.1 Basic Concepts

Queues form because a service provider is unable to immediately service all customers that arrive.[4] The three basic elements of a queue are customers, a waiting line, and servers.[5] A service center contains the waiting line and one or more servers. Figure 24-8 shows these elements and defines basic notation. The letter m (machines) denotes the total number of servers installed in the service center. Customers (small vertical rectangles) arrive at the service center (box with solid lines) at a rate λ. Each server (circle) serves (or processes) one customer at a time. If all servers are busy, the customer joins the waiting line (located in the gray shaded area). When a server finishes, it immediately selects a new customer from the waiting line based on a service policy, queue discipline, or scheduling algorithm. Customers depart the service center at a rate μ. The letters beneath the box representing the service center are counts and times. The queue length, denoted by the letter Q, is the total number of customers in the service center, and includes the customers who are waiting for service and the customers who are receiving service. The letter L denotes the number of customers who are waiting in line to be served. If $L > 0$, the number of customers being served, c, equals the number of servers m. In general, $0 \le c \le m$.

WARNING: The terminology and notation used in the literature are not standardized. Most authors use *queue* to refer to the entire service center. Some authors, however, use *queue* to denote only the waiting line, and so use the letter Q to denote the number of customers who are waiting, and the letter N to denote all customers in the service center. Be careful when reading equations in journal articles and books.

---

[4] In England, a *queue* is a line of people. Most authors retain the English spelling of the word *queueing*, which is the only English word with five vowels in a row.

[5] Synonyms for *customer* are request, job, task, transaction, message, packet, and workload. Synonyms for *server* are processor, device, channel, circuit, machine, and resource. Authors use the term that best fits the context. The service centers are shared resources such as processors, main memory, disks, and communications channels. Some authors refer to service centers as resources.

Customers: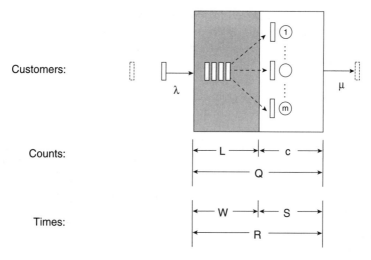

Counts:

Times:

Figure 24-8 *Terms to describe queues*

The service policy addresses two principal questions. First, which request should be selected next? Second, if the customer being serviced is not the one that you would now choose (because of a change in the system's state or processing priorities), should you allow the job being serviced to finish or should you preempt it? There are many possible service policies, depending on the answers to these two questions. (The selection may also consider the type [class] of customer and the customer's priority.) Table 24-10, adapted from [Sauer, 1981, page 20ff], lists some common ones. Note N28, "Service Policies for Queues," defines these service policies. Most queueing models assume FCFS. A communications channel is FCFS. A stack is LCFS.

Table 24-10 *Common Service Policies for Queues*

Abbreviation	Name
FCFS	First come, first served (or first in, first out; FIFO)
LCFS	Last come, first served (or last in, last out; LIFO)
LCFSPR	Last come, first served with preemptive resume
RR	Round robin (time slices, cyclic selection)
PS	Processor sharing
SPT	Shortest processing time
EDF	Earliest deadline first
SIRO	Select in random order
IS	Infinite servers
FISH	First in, still here

At the highest level of abstraction, the "customer" may be the user and the "service center" may be the entire system. Within a system, a job usually receives service from a series of "service centers." Table 24-11 shows three queues in the warehouse order system, and identifies the major components of each queue. You can connect queues into networks to describe the sequence of processing that occurs in a computer. Before addressing configurations of queues, however, consider a single queue.

Table 24-11 *Some Queues in a Warehouse Order System*

Customer	Server	Example	Action Performed
Data read/write (data + action)	Disk storage unit	Product description	Read/write data to disk
Message (destination + data)	Communications network	Customer order (product identifier + quantity)	Transmit order to warehouse
Transaction	Processor	Filled order	Calculate shipping cost and taxes (operation + data)

24.7.2 Operational Laws for Single Queues

Jeffery Buzen and Peter Denning developed "fundamental laws" that describe the average behavior of all queues [Buzen, 1976] and [Denning, 1978]. These are also called "operational laws" because many of the quantities can be directly measured. Many books on queueing theory derive these laws. The material in this section generally follows the notation presented in the paper by Peter Denning and Jeffery Buzen [Denning, 1978]. Edward Lazowska and his co-authors also use the same notation [Lazowska, 1984]. Some authors use slightly different notation [Jain, 1991, page 567] and [Gunther, 2000, page 84].

The operational laws assume that the system is operating in a steady state, and so describe "average behavior." The operational laws make no assumptions about the distribution of interarrival times or service times, and so provide a powerful tool to quantitatively describe the behavior of queues. You can use these laws for estimation, and to deduce performance parameters from measured data.

Because the number of customers in the system cannot become infinite, the arrival rate must be less than the service rate:

Stability condition: $\lambda < m\mu$

Conservation of customers: $Q = L + c$

Total time: $R = W + S$

Because the counts and times are all independent random variables, the mean values satisfy

$$\langle R \rangle = \langle L \rangle + \langle c \rangle$$

and

$$\langle R \rangle = \langle W \rangle + \langle S \rangle$$

where $\langle X \rangle$ denotes the mean value of the quantity X. If the service rate of each server is independent of the number waiting in line (L), then

$$Var(Q) = Var(L) + Var(c)$$

and

$$Var(R) = Var(W) + Var(S)$$

where Var denotes the variance of the quantity.

Table 24-12 summarizes the operational laws. Table 24-13 lists all the symbols used in the operational laws. The table shows the units of measure because *use of consistent units is the key to success when combining quantities from various queueing models.* As already mentioned, various authors use slightly different notation for the quantities in queueing models. This can lead to confusion when comparing results. (The problem is exacerbated because U and ρ are identical when m = 1.)

Table 24-12 *Operational Laws of Single Queues**

Utilization Law	$U_k = X_k {}^* S_k = X^* D_k$
Little's Law	$Q = X^* R$
Forced Flow Law	$X_k = V_k {}^* X$
Flow Balance Assumption	$A = C$ (and so $\lambda = X$)
General Response Time Law	$R = \sum\limits_{i=1}^{q} R_i * V_i$
Interactive Response Time Law	$R \geq N/X - Z$
Response Time Bound	$R \geq \max[D, N^* D_{max} - Z]$
Throughput Bound	$X \leq \min[1/D_{max}, N/(D + Z)]$

*For other representations, see Table 3.2 in [Lazowska, 1984] and Box 33.1 in [Jain, 1991]

Table 24-13 *Symbols Used in Queueing Models**

Symbol	Description	Units	Calculation
T	Length of observation interval	seconds	Measured
A_k	Number of observed arrivals	requests	Measured
C_k	Number of observed completions	completions	Measured
λ_k	Arrival rate	requests/second	A_k/T
X_k	Throughput	completions/ second	C_k/T
B_k	Busy time	seconds	Measured = U_k*T
U_k	Utilization	fraction (number)	B_k/T
S_k	Service requirement (time)	seconds/request	$\dfrac{B_k}{C_k} = \dfrac{U_k*T}{C_k}$
μ_k	Service rate	requests/second	$\mu_k = 1/S_k$
N	Number of requests in system	requests	Specified or calculated
R_k	Residence (response) time	seconds	
Z	Think time of terminal user	seconds	Measured
V_k	Number of visits	visits	$\dfrac{C_k}{C}$
D_k	Service demand	seconds/customer	$\dfrac{B_k}{C_k} = V_k*S_k = \dfrac{U_k*T}{C}$
Q_k	Number of requests in a queue		
L_k	Number of requests waiting		
c_k	Number of requests receiving service		
m_k	Number of servers		Specified
ρ_k	Server utilization (traffic intensity)		$\lambda_k/(m_k\mu_k)$

*Derived from [Denning, 1978] and Table 3.1 in [Lazowska, 1984]

The quantities in both tables represent average (or mean) values. The preceding discussion assumed that all customers have the same characteristics. These are called single-class models. Multiple-class models have multiple types of customers, each with its own workload intensity and service demand at each service center. Multiple-class models can be open or closed. (See Section 24.7.5.) For simplicity, many multiple class models assume that the scheduling algorithm is class independent. You can also apply the operational laws to estimate performance parameters for multiple-class models.

Service centers are distinguished by type: queue or delay (processing). Suppose that you observe a service center for a time interval. Define:

T = Duration of measurement interval

A = Number of arrivals in this time interval

C = Number of completions in the same interval

From these quantities, you can calculate

λ = Arrival rate = A/T

X = Throughput of the system = C/T

If the system consists of a single resource (server), you can measure B, the length of time that the resource was busy, and so can define two more quantities:

U = Utilization = B/T

S = Average service requirement (resources consumed/request) = B/C

Usually, the resource is time, so S is in seconds per request.

The Utilization Law states: $U = X*S$. If a disk drive processes 100 requests/second, and the service time is 2 milliseconds, the utilization is 0.2 (= 100*0.002) or 20%. Little's Law generalizes this result for the entire system [Little, 1961]:

$Q = X*R$

where

Q = Average number of requests in the system (the queue)

X = Throughput

R = Average time spent in the system by a request (response time)

Q includes the requests waiting and the requests being processed. R does not necessarily correspond to the apparent response time since some requests may be in the queue at the beginning and end of the measurement interval. Little's Law applies when no customers are lost due to buffer overflow (finite waiting line), balking (leaving instead of joining the waiting line), or reneging (leaving the line after waiting a while). Other forms are

$$Q = \lambda^*R$$
$$L = \lambda^*W$$

All quantities are time averages.

Little's Law is important for three reasons:

- It depends on very weak assumptions.
- If you know two of the three quantities in the equation, you can use Little's Law to compute the third one. (This is often useful to compute quantities that you cannot measure directly.)
- It plays an important role in evaluating queueing network models described in Section 24.7.5.

24.7.3 Using Little's Law: Examples

You can apply Little's Law at many levels in a computer system: to resources, to a resource plus its queue, to subsystems, or to the system as a whole. For example, consider a disk drive unit that queues requests. Assume that the disk drive unit services 100 requests/second, and that you measure the average number of requests in the unit (queue plus disk server) to be 10. Using Little's Law, the average time spent at the disk unit (which includes both waiting time and processing time) is $R = N/X$ or 0.1 second ($= 10/100$). Using the result from the Utilization Law example previously, the average time spent waiting in the queue is the residence time minus the service time, or 0.098 seconds ($= 0.1 - 0.002$). Thus, the requests spend most of their time waiting for the resource to become available. (This is common in most computer systems.) Because the utilization is 20%, on the average there are 0.2 requests receiving service. The average number of requests waiting is the difference between the total number of requests in the system and the number being serviced. For this example, the average number waiting is 9.8 ($= 10 - 0.2$).

Users are more interested in the response that they experience. Suppose that you have human users who enter data at terminals. The users are not constantly active. Instead, they enter data, observe a response from the system, spend time thinking what to do next, and then enter more data. You can use Little's Law to analyze this case. This situation is so common that it is called the Response Time Law: $R = N/X - Z$, where Z is the "think time." For example, suppose that a system has 100 users, the average think time is 10 seconds, and the system throughput is 5 interactions/second. The response time must be

$$R = N/X - Z = 100/5 - 10 = 20 - 10 = 10 \text{ seconds}$$

R is the average time perceived by each user. As N increases, so does R. The users perceive no delay ($R = 0$) until $N = Z^*X$. For the preceding example, this occurs when $N = 50$ ($= 10^*5$). Thus, the system has adequate capacity to give good service for up to 50 users. For more than 50 users, response time increases linearly with N.[6] Little's Law is just a special case of the Response Time Law obtained when $Z = 0$.

Because the system is assumed to be operating in a steady state, no backlogs can occur in any subsystem. All subsystems must do "comparable amounts" of work. Let the subscript k denote a specific resource. Quantities without the subscript refer to the entire system. Define the "visit count," V, to a particular resource, k, as $V_k = C_k/C$, where C denotes "completions" at the resource (C_k) or the system (C). Rewriting this as $C_k = V_k*C$, using $X_k = C_k/T$, and recalling $X = C/T$, gives the Forced Flow Law: $X_k = V_k*X$. Stated another way, $X_k/V_k = X$ where X is a constant for the system. The Forced-Flow Law states that the flows through all parts of a system must be proportional to one another.

You can combine Little's Law and the Forced Flow Law to estimate many quantities of interest. For example, consider an interactive system with these parameters:

50 terminals ($N = 50$)

20 seconds average think time ($Z = 20$)

20 visits to a specific disk per interaction ($V_{disk} = 20$)

40% utilization of that disk ($U_{disk} = 0.4$)

10 millisecond service requirement per visit to that disk ($S_{disk} = 0.01$)

You would like to compute the response time of the system using the Response Time Law, but you lack the throughput, X. You do know the visit count at one disk, however, so you can use the Utilization Law: $U_k = X_k*S_k$. You compute the following quantities:

Disk throughput: $X_{disk} = U_{disk}/S_{disk} = 0.4/0.01 = 40$ disk visits/second

System throughput: $X = X_{disk}/V_{disk} = 40/20 = 2$ interactions/second

Response time: $R = N/X - Z = 50/2 - 20 = 25 - 20 = 5$ seconds

Define the *service demand* at resource k as $D_k = V_k*S_k$. This is the number of seconds per interaction. For the above example, $D_{disk} = $ (20 visits/interaction)* (0.01 seconds/visit) = 0.2 seconds/interaction. So each interaction (user job) consumes 0.2 seconds of processing time at the disk. The usual convention is that D_k denotes the total service requirement for resource k. D without the subscript is the sum of the D_k values. (The reason for introducing the variable D_k is that it is usually easier to measure the value of D_k rather than the corresponding V_k and S_k.)

---

[6] Actually, the response time may increase faster than linearly due to contention for system resources. N reflects the number of jobs active in the processor and each active job consumes resources. As N increases, X may decrease due to resource contention, thus increasing R.

The Flow Balance Assumption states that the number of arrivals equals the number of completions; that is, $A = C$. This is another way of saying that the system is operating in a steady state and so the queues do not fill up. The consequence is that $\lambda = X$. Using the Flow Balance Assumption, the Forced Flow Law, and Little's Law enables you to compute utilization values for a system whose workload is described in terms of an arrival rate.

Little's Law applies to any device (queue) in a system (provided that the job flow is balanced for that queue). For the total system: $Q = X^*R$. Let Q_i denote the queue length for each device, i. Then

$$Q = Q_1 + Q_2 + \ldots + Q_q$$

where q is the number of devices (queues) in the system. Because $Q_i = X_i^*R_i$, this gives

$$X^*R = X_1^*R_1 + X_2^*R_2 + \ldots + X_q^*R_q$$

Dividing by X, and applying the Forced Flow Law gives

$$R = V_1^*R_1 + V_2^*R_2 + \ldots + V_q^*R_q$$

This is the General Response Time Law. It states that the total time a job spends at a queue (service center or device) equals the average time per visit, times the number of visits. It also states that the job's total time in the system (all service centers) equals the sum of the times for all of the service centers. (It is possible to show that this law holds even if the job flow is not balanced.)

Using the definition of demand, $D_i = X_i^*S_i$, and the Forced Flow Law, $X_i = X^*V_i$, in the Utilization Law gives

$$U_i = X_i^*S_i = X_i^*(D_i/V_i) = X^*D_i$$

Thus, the device utilization is proportional to the service demand: $U_i \propto D_i$. In a network containing multiple service centers, the service center with the highest total service demand limits the throughput of the system and is called the *bottleneck device*. Improving the performance of this service center will improve the throughput of the system. (This is analogous to locating tasks on the critical path in a resource loaded network to determine the fastest completion time for a project.) For this reason, locating the bottleneck device should be the first step in trying to improve system performance.

24.7.4 Queueing Theory

This section describes the main concepts of queueing theory and some key results. The intent is not to make you an expert, but rather to indicate the types of queueing models, the types of outputs they provide, and the types of input parameters that they use. The end of the chapter provides references to several good books on this topic.

A *queueing model* describes a service center (queue) in terms of the following:

- The probability distribution that describes the customer arrival times
- The probability distribution that describes the processing times
- The number of servers
- The method used to select the next customer to serve

Queueing theory analyzes a queueing model in a mathematically rigorous way to predict averages, variances, and probability distributions for performance measures, such as the following:

- *Residence time.* The average time spent at the service center by a customer, waiting plus servicing (i.e., the observed response time)
- *Waiting time.* The average time spent in the queue by a customer
- *Queue length.* The average number of customers waiting for service
- *Number of jobs.* The average number of customers at the service center, both waiting and receiving service
- *Throughput.* The rate at which customers pass through the service center
- *Utilization.* The proportion of time that the server is busy

Queueing models also compute many other quantities. See [Jain, 1991] for details.

There are mathematical models for different many kinds of queues. See the box "Kendall Notation." Not all configurations can be solved. Still, in many cases these models provide adequate accuracy to predict bounds on system performance. You can use the results for particular queueing models to predict product performance directly, as parts of a larger analysis, or even as components of a simulation model.

Kendall Notation

David George Kendall defined a concise notation to categorize single queues [Kendall, 1951]. All customers wait in a single queue, and a customer is selected for service whenever a server becomes available.[7] Six letters, separated by forward slashes, describe a queue: A/S/m/C/N/P. The symbols represent

A   The probability distribution that represents the times between arrivals; e.g., M, U, D, and G. (See text.)

---

[7] Kendall notation does not cover service centers having multiple parallel queues, such as the checkout counters at a grocery store. Gunther briefly discusses parallel queues on pages 42–44 and 57–60 of [Gunther, 2000].

S   The probability distribution that represents the times to service requests; e.g., M, U, D, and G. (See text.)

m   Number of servers ("machines") at the service center.

C   Maximum capacity of the service center. May be finite or infinite.

N   The number of customers. May be finite or infinite.

P   The type of service policy; e.g., FIFO, LIFO, RR, PS, et al.

Mathematicians have studied many types of distributions for the interarrival and service times. See Chapters 29 and 30 in [Jain, 1991] and pages 38–40 in [Gunther, 2000]. The exponential distribution is denoted by M, denoting Memoryless or Markov. (See below.) U denotes the uniform distribution. D denotes a deterministic pattern. General (G) means that the model's results are valid for all distributions, and so is especially desirable. (Some authors use GI for general distribution, independent events.) For data networks, S describes the length of the packet or message. (The service time is the link transmission time.) For voice networks, S describes the call duration. You can model a computer with multiple processors as a multiple server queue. The maximum capacity (C) includes customers waiting and being served. (Some authors call this the buffer size, which is misleading.) Table 24-10 shows some possible values for P.

When not needed (or clear from context), the last two or three symbols are omitted. The usual case is that C and N are infinite, and the service policy is FCFS (FIFO). The queue is then described using only the first three letters (A/S/M); e.g., M/M/1.

The simplest models assume that the arrival and processing times are random, and follow an exponential distribution, $\exp^{-m*t}$, where m is the rate and t is the time between successive events. The exponential distribution has some unique properties that facilitate calculations of special models called Markov processes. (See Note N29, "Markov Processes.") Even though event times in computer systems are not usually exponentially distributed, models based on this assumption often produce accurate results. Thus, they are often used for analysis. (You can also use combinations of exponential distributions to better approximate the actual behavior inside the computer.)

One of the simplest queueing models is the isolated single server with exponential distributions for arrival and processing and a FCFS scheduling algorithm. It is designated M/M/1 and has only two parameters, the arrival rate, λ, and the service rate, μ. (Steady-state operation requires that $\mu < \lambda$.) The M/M/1 model predicts the following:

$\rho = \lambda/\mu$ Utilization (per server)

$U = 1^*\lambda/\mu$ Service center utilization

$Q = \rho^2/(1 - \rho) = \lambda^2/[\mu(\mu - \lambda)]$ Mean queue length

$N = Q + U = \rho^2/(1 - \rho) + 1^*\rho$ Mean number in system

$\qquad\quad = \rho/(1 - \rho) = \lambda/(\mu - \lambda)$

$R = 1/(\mu - \lambda)$ Response time

The fourth expression for N has two terms. The first is the mean number of jobs waiting for service (Q in the line above). The second, U, is the mean number of jobs being processed. The expression for R is obtained from Little's Law: $N = \lambda^*R$.

Researchers continue to extend queueing theory. They have addressed finite buffer (waiting line) sizes and service rates that depend on the number of customers waiting. Another extension to queueing theory is the ability to handle multiple classes of customers that arrive at different rates, require different amounts of processing, and have different priorities. Two noteworthy developments related to the performance of modern digital systems are described in Notes N30, "Petri Nets," and N31, "Digital Networks and Self-Similar Traffic."

24.7.5 Queueing Networks

Many systems of interest consist of several queues. A job may receive service from multiple queues as it passes through the system, and may return to a particular server multiple times. (Two examples are multiple disk accesses and processing a job in a series of time slices. You can model most computing and communications systems as a network of interconnected queues.)

Queueing network models (QNMs) are sets of individual queues connected to construct a model that represents a computer system. *Open networks* receive customers from an external source and send processed customers to an external destination (sink). Figure 24-9 shows an open network. Open networks have a variable number of customers. One example is an online e-commerce website where customers place orders. *Closed networks* have a fixed population that moves between the queues. (Some authors call these *cyclic networks*.) Figure 24-10 shows a closed network. One example is the servicing of multiple tasks by an operating system scheduler. A set of *traffic equations* describes the flow of customers between the queues in a network. There are also *mixed queueing networks* that are open for some workloads and closed for others. For example, a computer system might support both batch jobs (open) and interactive users (closed). The word *class* refers to jobs that have the same service demands and arrival characteristics.

There are many types of queueing network models and techniques for solving them. Only certain types of networks can be solved. Good references are the books by Gunter Bolch and his co-authors [Bolch, 1998], Raj Jain [Jain, 1991], and Neil Gunther [Gunther, 2000].

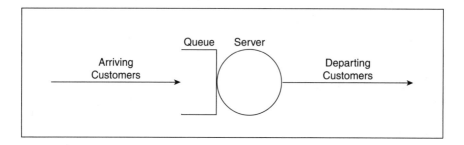

Figure 24-9 *Open model*

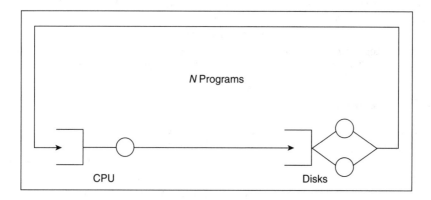

Figure 24-10 *Closed model*

Open network models are suitable for transaction processing systems where the arrival rate of the transactions does not depend on the loading of the servers. You can exactly solve the equations for open networks if you make certain assumptions. First, all servers must be either fixed capacity (single server whose service time is exponentially distributed) or a delay center (an infinite number of servers with exponentially distributed service times). Second, the response time for all fixed capacity service centers is

$$R_i = S_i^*(1 + Q_i)$$

This assumption is not testable operationally and so this is not an operational law. Using this assumption with the operational laws makes it possible, however, to calculate average values for the system performance parameters. Raj Jain discusses the solution of open queueing networks in Section 34.1 of [Jain, 1991] and provides a detailed example. These techniques can typically estimate device utilizations to within 10% and response times to within 30% of actual measured values. These accuracies are reasonable given the typical accuracy of the input data.

In a closed queueing network, all the service centers interact with one another, and so their states are interdependent. There are no closed form solutions for closed networks, but there are iterative methods to solve them provided that the network satisfies the BCMP criteria. (See Note N32, "BCMP Networks.") This makes it possible to evaluate performance measures for each service center independently, and then construct the performance of the network by combining the separate solutions. The original technique is called the *convolution algorithm* [Buzen, 1973]. Chapter 35 in [Jain, 1991] describes the convolution algorithm. Reiser and Lavenberg devised a simpler technique called *mean value analysis (MVA)* to determine average queue lengths and response times [Reiser, 1980]. (If you need distributions or variances of queue length and response times then you must use convolution.) One reference is Chapter 34 in [Jain, 1991]. Also see Note N33, "Mean Value Analysis."

Most of the analysis techniques use the average queue length at each service center to derive other performance measures such as the system response time and the system throughput. These techniques work because the system is assumed to be in a steady state and so the queue lengths fluctuate about average values that remain constant over time. Gunther discusses transient analysis in certain types of networks in Chapters 12 and 13 of [Gunther, 2000]. Gunther also discusses cases where the length of a queue can fluctuate between two stable values, with a region of instability in between. One of the stable values is an optimal queue length and the other one is significantly longer, degrading overall system performance.

24.7.6 Limitations of Queueing Models

Queueing models make many assumptions. Table 24-14 identifies situations where queueing models do not work well. (Jain discusses most of these items on pages 620–622. Gunther discusses them on pages 122–124, and on pages 289–290.)

Table 24-14 *Behavior That Challenges Queueing Models*

Blocking	Failure to release a resource because the queue for the next needed resource is full, causing the job to wait. (A service center cannot function because a downstream service center refuses to accept more customers.)
Bulk arrivals	Bursts of heavy traffic.
Contention resolution	Back off and retry algorithms used in communications protocols.
Fork/join primitives	Forking and joining processes violates the assumption of job independence.
Load dependent arrivals	Adaptive load balancing that feeds jobs to underutilized resources.
Mutual exclusion	Several jobs try to seize a particular resource. Similar to blocking.
Nonexponential service times	This violates an assumption of most QNMs.
Queueing defections	A customer refuses to wait (balks), leaves after waiting (reneges), or jumps from one queue to another (defects).
Response-dependent arrivals	Retransmitting unacknowledged messages, which increases arrivals at the receiving center.
Sharing finite resources	Similar to mutual exclusion.
Simultaneous resource possession	Jobs may hold multiple resources simultaneously. Similar to fork and join.
Think time	It is difficult to predict what users will do!
Transient analysis	The system is not in a steady state, violating an assumption of most queueing models. Similar to response-dependent arrivals.

Some of these areas have been successfully addressed using approximations. When a job holds more than one resource, usually one resource (the active resource) determines how long the other (passive) resources are held, and so determines the overall performance. This is analogous to the bottleneck analysis discussed earlier.

Execution times in computer systems usually do not have exponential distributions due to job characteristics, time slicing, and priority scheduling schemes. You can sometimes assume exponential distributions and obtain useful results. For example, if you assume that the task-switching overhead is negligible, you can use models for FCFS and processor sharing to bound the performance of a round-robin scheduler.

Aggregation is the most important type of approximation. *Aggregation* replaces a subnetwork by a single, composite queue whose service rate depends on the queue length. This composite queue mimics the behavior of the subnetwork in terms of its interactions with the rest of the network. For details and an example, see Section 36.2 in [Jain, 1991].

Approximations reduce computation time, and allow you to obtain estimates for many intractable system configurations, but they may introduce unknown amounts of error. Analytic models, even with approximations, cannot handle complex, time varying interactions and nonlinear variations in the service time as a function of workload. You must estimate such cases using simulation models.

The preceding subsections only covered the basics of queueing models and illustrated their use to analyze the performance of computer systems and networks. The "Recommended Reading" section at the end of this chapter cites several excellent books on this topic.

24.8 Simulation

Some systems are just too complex to use order of magnitude estimates, analytic models, or queueing network models. To estimate performance and resource usage for such systems, you must build and validate simulation models. This section describes the characteristics and uses of simulation to estimate system performance, some potential pitfalls, and advice to help you implement simulation models.

Simulation uses a computerized mathematical model (a simulation model or simulator) to study the behavior of a real or proposed system. The simulation model can be a spreadsheet, a commercial tool, a custom-built computer program, or some combination of these. Simulation addresses the following:

- Systems that do not yet exist or cannot be directly measured
- Situations that occur rarely or cannot be created
- Complex behavior that cannot be analyzed mathematically
- Interactions between components and subsystems
- Effects of random variation (stochastic phenomena)

Simulation allows you to estimate the performance of new systems without building them, or to study proposed changes to existing systems without disturbing them. You can use simulations to compare alternate designs, locate bottlenecks, and test changes before installing them in an existing system. A simulation model allows you to view internal variables that are not visible in the operational system. (The model must faithfully represent the system, of course.) A simulation model must emulate any missing pieces of the system under study, generate the workload, mimic interactions with external objects, and provide the "physics" for the environment (e.g., weather, physical forces, and kinematics). Because the simulator provides all of the "physics," you can "interfere with the physics" to cause failures to occur at specific locations and times, permitting you to study them. Some of these situations may occur rarely, be too dangerous, or be too expensive to study with the real system.

Simulation models can be deterministic or stochastic. A deterministic model (merely) implements known equations and algorithms and computes results. The necessary calculations are straightforward but lengthy. The simulation model just does the "number crunching." In some cases, the model may use analytic results from queueing theory to represent the behavior of lower-level subsystems, and then aggregate these results to obtain the performance of the overall system. (Neil Gunther describes this approach [Gunther, 2000].) Even if the equations are known, you may choose to use approximations to reduce the execution time of the simulation model.

Most systems, however, involve random phenomena or uncertainties, which you must describe using probability distributions. For such systems, you must use stochastic models, which combine deterministic equations with random values. (See the next paragraph.) In either case, the analyst specifies the system's configuration, behavior, modes, and workload, and then executes the model to predict how the system will perform under the specified conditions.

Monte Carlo simulation is a technique to calculate the output values for models that contain a combination of deterministic and probabilistic elements (e.g., functions, algorithms, interactions, behavior, and workload). Once built, an analyst uses the model to study situations of interest. Unlike deterministic models, however, the computer executes the model multiple times, each time using a new set of random values. The computer calculates and records the model's outputs for each set of inputs, providing a set of estimated values. The modeler uses statistical techniques to analyze the sample and calculate the desired performance measures. Figure 24-11 summarizes the steps of a Monte Carlo simulation.

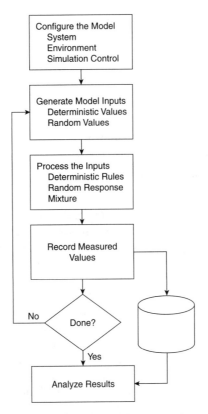

Figure 24-11 *Monte Carlo simulation*

Table 24-15 shows some common mistakes in simulation.[8] Any model is a tool for answering specific questions about a particular system. You must clearly understand the purpose of the simulation to determine what system components, external objects, and environmental effects are relevant to the model, and how much fidelity and accuracy are needed. These decisions affect the level of detail and so the cost of building and operating the simulator. (Modelers sometimes include more detail than necessary when they are not sure which effects are significant. This increases costs and may not increase accuracy. For a discussion, see Section 24.1 in [Jain, 1991].)

---

[8] Raj Jain provides more detailed checklists in Boxes 2.1, 2.2, and 24.1 [Jain, 1991].

Table 24-15 *Common Mistakes in Simulation*

• Purpose not clearly stated
• Inappropriate level of detail
• Invalid models (system, workload)
• Incorrect implementation (coding errors)
• Poor random number generators
• Inadequate sample size (run duration)
• Failure to account for transients
• Inadequate planning and resources

Invalid models of a system result from making incorrect assumptions about functions, interactions, and behavior, or making inappropriate approximations. If the model does not represent a particular phenomenon, it cannot account for its effect on system performance. Konstantin Kreyman and David Parnas discuss the difficulty of describing models of physical phenomena in adequate detail to build a computer model [Kreyman, 2002]. Always clearly state all of your assumptions. If you derive a mathematical formula, have someone independently check your derivation. (Minus signs and factors of two can be deadly.) Inaccurate models of the system's workload usually result from overlooking classes of users or making incorrect assumptions about the environment or operational scenarios. Note N34, "Trace-Based Simulation," describes one way to obtain a realistic workload. Also see Note N31.

You must also implement the (mathematical) model correctly in working code. This includes choosing good numerical algorithms and associated convergence criteria. (Press et al. is a good reference [Press, 1992].) Also see the box "Handling Time." You must also implement the algorithms correctly in code. You can apply standard software engineering techniques and processes. Carefully inspect and test components just as you would any other software.

TIP: If you modify a simulation model, always rerun some of the known test cases to verify that it still performs correctly.

Handling Time

Simulations differ from real-world programs because they must control the flow of time. Physical systems (vehicles, fluid flow, etc.) are described by differential equations, and so time usually flows continuously. For physical models, the simulator program maintains a time variable, incrementing it repetitively by a fixed amount. For systems handling discrete objects (transactions, messages), the simulator is usually event driven. Events are significant changes in the states of the system or the (simulated) external environment. Each event has a time of occurrence. The simulation program maintains a list of events ordered by time of occurrence. The program selects the event with the earliest time, sets the clock to this time, and performs the necessary actions. (These actions often generate additional events that are added to the event list.) Event-driven systems run faster than time-driven simulations if the events occur at widely spaced intervals. (For physical processes, "events" occur continuously.) See Note N35, "Example of Event-Driven Simulation."

There are various simulation languages and related tools. Some support discrete or event-driven simulations. These are well suited for modeling computer systems. Others handle continuous variables, and are good for modeling real-time or process control systems. Some tools support a mix of discrete and continuous simulation. The book's website lists tools and addresses for vendors.

Generating truly random numbers is not easy. The best choice is to use a proven function provided by experts. For more information on generating random numbers and testing the quality of random numbers, see Chapters 26, 27, 28, and 29 in [Jain, 1991] and Chapter 7 in [Press, 1992]. You can use the tests described to check your random number generators. Note N36, "Generating Random Numbers," describes how to generate random values for any distribution using a uniform random number generator.

A series of Monte Carlo runs generates a sample distribution of the model's outputs. The sample variance and the confidence intervals depend on the number of data points in the sample. To achieve your desired accuracy, you may need thousands of data points. Because simulation runs consume time and money, the tendency is to keep the runs short. You should choose the accuracy when you plan the experiment, and then calculate the required duration of the run.

Transient phenomena further increase the run time. When the simulation starts, a transient phase occurs before the system reaches a steady state. For example, if the system has several queues, the simulation may start with all of the queues empty. Thus, the system processes the first jobs that arrive immediately (no waiting in line), and so the average response time measured early in the run will be less than the value when the system is in its steady state and the queues are "loaded up." (To avoid this, you should run a simulation for some period before starting to collect data.)

24.8.1 Estimating Simulation Costs

Plan the building of a large simulator like any other software development project. You will need to recruit a staff with the necessary mix of skills (including subject matter experts), choose the target platform, select the programming language and development tools, and obtain adequate project resources (effort and time). Raj Jain provides a good discussion of this in Section 24.2 of [Jain, 1991].

Systems operate in an external environment. This includes the workload just described. It also includes objects (users, other systems) that interact with the simulated system, as well as environmental effects appropriate to the system (e.g., wind, temperature, and power surges). In addition, some parts of the system, such as sensors, actuators, peripherals, and subsystems, may not be available. The simulation model must represent all such objects and effects in order to evaluate the performance of the system.

These additional items affect the software size. Estimating the size of a simulator is subject to the iceberg shown in Figure 8-2. Figure 24-12 shows the main types of additional code. Checkpointing requires additional code, but is well worth the extra cost in some cases. See the box "Checkpointing."

Checkpointing

For extremely long simulations or calculations, you should protect your investment in execution time if the computer should fail. To do this, install extra code to periodically save "checkpoint data." This data enables you to restart the run from the last checkpoint if the computer should fail. The time between checkpoints is typically an hour or so. You must determine the best point in the calculation to snapshot the state of the program. You must also identify all variables to be saved. Be sure to test your checkpointing by comparing data from an interrupted run and a restarted run.

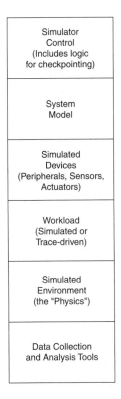

Figure 24-12 *Components of a simulator*

Another factor to consider is the number and duration of the simulation runs. The duration of a run depends on the time for transient effects to subside, and the acceptable level of confidence (variance). The sample variance scales inversely to the square root of the number of points in the sample. The number of runs depends on the number of system configurations, workload scenarios, and sensitivity studies. These depend on your particular project. Make a list of your planned experiments, and then count the number of simulation runs. You might find Part IV in [Jain, 1991] helpful.

24.9 Choosing a Technique

Table 24-16 summarizes the advantages and disadvantages of various techniques to estimate and measure the performance of software-intensive systems. Analytic models provide information on a limited number of performance measures, and are often restricted to fairly simple systems. The effort to formulate, solve, and validate an analytic model ranges from high to extra high, and may require great mathematical skill. Unrealistic assumptions and approximations may also be necessary. The effort to calculate values using an analytic model is usually low. In contrast, simulation models can represent any desired level of detail and can provide many different measures. They can handle steady state and transient response, as well as a wide range of conditions and system configurations. The effort to formulate a simulation model ranges from low to high. The effort to run the simulation model ranges from low to very high, depending on the complexity of the model. (Running the model means the time it takes to set up and configure the simulation, and to execute the simulation program.)

Table 24-16 *Comparison of Estimation and Measurement Options*

	Estimation		Measurement	
Characteristic	*Analytic Models*	*Simulation*	*Benchmark Runs*	*Smart Stubs*
Choice of performance measures	Limited	Many	Limited	Limited
Level of detail	Limited	Arbitrary	Varies	Varies
Accuracy (realism and fidelity)	Approximate	Good	Perfect	Good
Steady-state behavior	Yes	Yes	Yes	Yes
Transient response	Limited	Yes	Yes	Yes
Range of off-nominal conditions	Some	Wide	Limited	Some
Effort to develop and validate the model or tool	High to extra high	Low to high	Not applicable	Low
Effort to use the model or tool (set up, configure, calculate, measure)	Low	Low to very high	Nominal to very high	Nominal to very high

Measurements provide the most accurate and credible performance values, but the system must exist and be operating. Benchmark runs collect data under controlled conditions. It may not be possible to measure the actual system, however, due to cost, safety, or accessibility constraints. In addition, it may not be possible to measure particular quantities of interest, or to measure values under specific conditions, because the system's design does not allow the injection of data with known characteristics or the collection of certain types of data. The table also shows the use of smart stubs embedded within portions of the actual system, which mimic missing components and may capture some performance data.

To choose the "best" technique, you must consider the desired accuracy, costs, development time, and credibility of the technique. In a nutshell, you can:

- Use analytic models for quick, approximate results.
- Use simulation models to study a wide range of options (alternative configurations, workloads, unusual situations).
- Use measurement (benchmarking) to obtain the most accurate values for existing systems for a limited range of options.

24.10 Performance Engineering Process

Software performance engineering (SPE) is a systematic, quantitative process to construct software to meet specific performance objectives that begins early in the development life cycle and continues throughout the life of the system [Smith, 2002]. Early in a project, you use estimates to validate the feasibility of the design, and to help specify the target resources (capacity, speed) that will be needed by the software being developed. You can also use analytic models and simulations to identify potential bottlenecks in the system that limit performance. Later, you use them to validate your assumptions about system performance. Still later, you may use simulations or measurements to fine-tune algorithms to improve accuracy or reduce execution time.

Figure 24-13 summarizes the main activities of the iterative software performance engineering process.[9] As shown, it first assesses the degree of product performance risk related to determine the appropriate amount of effort for performance engineering.

Software performance engineering directly ties system performance requirements to end-user requirements via use cases. Not all use cases for a system are critical from a performance perspective. To reduce estimation and measurement costs, you must identify the "critical use cases" that influence system performance. (Some use cases may still be critical even though they rarely occur. Rapid recovery from component failures is a good example.) Each use case identifies one or more scenarios. Each scenario describes a sequence of actions to accomplish some business or mission function.

---

[9] This is an extension of Figure 2-1 in [Smith, 2002]. I restructured it to emphasize the basic process flow.

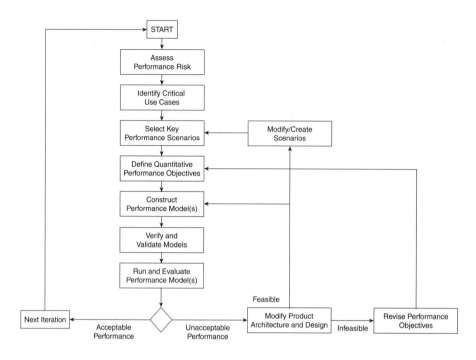

Figure 24-13 *The software performance engineering process*

Each performance scenario should have at least one quantitative performance objective that ties directly to system performance. You should establish these quantitative performance objectives early. Initially, these are the top-level system performance requirements. Once engineers have chosen the architecture and formulated the design of the system, you may be able to break the top-level performance objectives into lower-level performance requirements for specific subsystems and components. (Use the resource usage matrix described in Section 24.5. This is similar to the way you allocate effort and time for project tasks described in Chapter 12, "Top-Down Estimating and Allocation.")

This iterative process uses a range of techniques and performance estimation models. Measurements validate these models and help develop better models. During each iteration, software performance engineering constructs better performance models of the system, and verifies and validates them. (Verification tests to ensure that the model is built correctly. Validation confirms that the model represents reality.) Typically, you use simple models early and detailed models later, matching the level of detail of the model to your current knowledge of the system, environment, and workload. Table 24-17 shows how the focus of performance modeling shifts during a project and the applicable techniques. For example, early in the project, you build the simplest possible model that will identify problems with the proposed system architecture or design. The focus is on gross feasibility estimates. Because models rely on estimates of the various input parameters as well as various assumptions, it is a good idea to explore the effect of these uncertainties. You can use best and worst case estimates to do the following:

- Establish bounds on the expected performance
- Re-evaluate the risk of achieving the quantitative performance objectives
- Identify significant design parameters

If the system is operating in a steady state, you can estimate resource usage using order of magnitude calculations or simple analytic models. (These include the operational laws for queues.) If the usage of the various resources varies with time, and if the variations can be described in terms of probability distributions, you can use queueing network models to predict performance for certain well-defined cases. If the interactions are complex and time varying, they give rise to nonlinear effects as system workload increases. If so, you must use simulation models. See Note N37, "Types of Execution Models."

Table 24-17 *Models Used in SPE*

Model Type	Focus	Applicable Techniques
Simple	Gross feasibility	Rough order of magnitude, analytic model, simple queueing results
Best and worst case	Feasibility, bounds on the uncertainty	Rough order of magnitude, analytic model, queueing results, bottleneck analysis
Software execution	Identifies type and amount of resources needed	Analytic, simple queueing results, semi-analytic model
System execution	Maps software resources to service demands on actual computing devices; includes overhead and contention among tasks (scenarios)	Queueing networks, semi-analytic model, simulation model

For each iteration, use the verified and validated performance models to estimate the performance of the system. If the results show acceptable performance, the project can proceed. If the performance is unacceptable, however, there are a number of choices, as shown by the feedback loops in Figure 24-13. First, the engineers attempt to change the product's architecture and design in order to achieve the specified performance objectives. If this is feasible, the engineers proceed with the necessary changes, and the performance analysts (estimators) modify the performance models to reflect the revised design. (They may also have to modify the performance scenarios and create additional scenarios.) If it is not feasible to modify the product concept, the only alternative is to revise the performance objectives for the system. (The process resembles "Reducing the Cost or Price" described in Chapter 15, "Calculating Costs and Price: The Basics.")

24.11 Estimating Costs for Performance Engineering

The effort for performance engineering should depend on the amount of perceived performance risk. For a low-risk project, the performance engineering effort might be 1% of the engineering effort, whereas for a high-risk project with difficult performance requirements, it might be 10%. To estimate the required effort, you should separate performance engineering activities into two types: activities that are part of the usual development activities (analysis, design, code, and test), and other activities such as special studies and prototyping. Estimate the latter as separate level of effort tasks. Some of these activities can be viewed as risk avoidance. You would include the costs for these activities as part of the risk management costs. (Connie Smith likens the costs of software performance engineering to paying an insurance premium [Smith, 1990, page 531].)

You can use the techniques described in the preceding chapters to estimate the cost and schedule to develop new simulators or to modify existing simulators. There are three key points to keep in mind, however. First, simulators have a great deal of requirements volatility! Second, modifying or reusing existing simulation code may be more expensive than you might think. My experience is that for many domains the only reusable components are low-level components. If the architecture is not preserved, this drastically increases the adaptation adjustment factor (AAF) in the COCOMO reuse sizing model. Third, validation typically consumes substantial effort for simulator development. (Requirements definition effort is also high.) You can validate a simulation model (or any other model for that matter) if you either know the correct answer or you have actual performance data for certain cases. For example, you can see if the equations approach the correct asymptotic limit, or produce the correct answers for simple cases having a known solution. If the model predicts observable behavior, collect data for known conditions (benchmarks) and confirm that the model's predictions are correct.

TIP 1: Document complex models, and then peer review the documents. (Treat them like peer-reviewed articles in technical journals. Scientists accept this process.)

TIP 2: Model validation becomes difficult if the model's results do not agree with the interests or opinions of various stakeholders! Define your validation strategy early and get it approved.

Another potential problem related to model validation is choosing "realistic values" for the model's parameters. You can measure some parameters. For example, you might set up a loop to time the execution of, say, 10,000 executions of a key module. You can also use this approach to measure the performance of commercial off-the-shelf (COTS) components. For example, to measure the response of a commercial database management system, our team once defined tables of known size, and timed the operations of add, change (replace), and delete. We varied the size of the table and the sizes of the records being added, replaced, and deleted to profile the response time as a function of table size. We then fitted a curve to this data. If you can only estimate a range of likely values, you can execute the simulation multiple times with values chosen from the estimated range to determine sensitivity.

Getting stakeholders to agree on workloads and scenarios presents similar problems to validating simulation models. The workload describes the types and numbers of users, messages, transactions, and so forth. and their arrival rates (which may be specified in terms of probability distributions). Scenarios describe exogenous events that stimulate the system. Examples are operator selection of new modes or the failure of an external device.

Careful design can reduce the verification and validation effort. Engineers must first define how they will test the system and verify its performance during the Product Design phase. Then they can "design in" the test hooks to capture key data to support their test strategy. (Section 10.4.4 describes test hooks.) If these are included early, the cost is low. (Often the customer will find some of these capabilities useful for diagnostics during system operations. If so, they can be left in the delivered code.) The engineers and testers should also decide at this point how they plan to reduce and analyze the data captured since additional analysis tools may be needed. To estimate the resources, you can include instrumentation functions (data injection, collection, and reduction) in the size of the product and the test tooling, as appropriate. Executing the software to collect data and analysis of the collected data will also consume additional effort so include a level of effort task for this activity in the plan. (Tracking product performance measures is usually considered a risk mitigation task. See Chapter 14, "Estimating Risk Reserves.")

24.12 Recommended Reading

There is no standardized name for the performance estimation and measurement process. The following are some of the names in use:

- Software performance engineering (SPE) [Smith, 1990], [Smith, 2002]
- Capacity planning [Menascé, 1998]
- Computer systems performance analysis [Jain, 1991]
- Performance by design [Gunther, 2000]

Connie Smith and Lloyd Williams provide a practical, comprehensive guide to software performance engineering [Smith, 2002], which is a completely updated version of [Smith, 1990]. They define a nine-step process that is suited for modern, object-oriented systems, and explain how to extend the Unified Modeling Language to capture the information needed for performance analysis. They specifically address web applications, distributed systems, and embedded real-time systems. Their book provides practical advice without complex mathematics. Their Chapter 15 discusses the entire SPE process, and provides a list of process artifacts. If you want to start using SPE, this is a good place to start.

Daniel Menascé and Virgilio Almeida have co-authored several books dealing with capacity planning. (*Capacity planning* is a term primarily used for older, mainframe computing systems.) Their most recent book, *Scaling for E-Business*, addresses modern client/server applications and describes techniques to estimate the performance of e-business systems [Menascé, 2000]. They also describe the key features of queueing theory including the basic performance laws useful for estimators. They explain how to identify bottlenecks and analyze scalability. They provide free spreadsheets that implement the performance models described in their book.

Neil Gunther provides a more mathematical look at queueing theory [Gunther, 2000]. However, his philosophy is to use simple techniques that are fast and cheap. He argues that modern, fast-paced projects do not have the time or resources to conduct detailed studies. His book addresses a wide range of applications, including parallel computer architectures, multiprocessor systems, client/server applications, web servers, packet-switched networks, and circuit-switched networks. He provides a free package of C software routines called "pretty darned quick" (PDQ) that you can use to build computer models for estimating performance. For an overview of Gunther's performance by design, see http://members.aol.com/CoDynamo/Services.PBD.htm.

Raj Jain provides an excellent and very comprehensive book covering computer systems performance analysis. He provides exact solutions for many queueing problems, but the mathematics can be daunting. Of more importance to estimators, Jain discusses techniques for designing experiments, conducting measurements, simulating performance, and the algorithms used to solve various types of queueing networks. Part II of [Jain, 1991] describes measurement techniques and tools in some detail.

Thomas Robertazzi addresses specialized techniques such as stochastic Petri nets, discrete time queueing systems, and network traffic modeling. He also provides an excellent chapter on the numeric solution of models. Like Jain, his book requires a good knowledge of mathematics.

Bruce Powel Douglass discusses the estimation of performance bounds for embedded real-time systems that use various scheduling algorithms. This is a specialized topic and will be of interest to engineers who need to estimate the performance of operating systems and other high-speed digital devices. His book is also noteworthy because it addresses the use of object-oriented methods to design embedded systems. He specifically covers the use of Unified Modeling Language to express the design and performance characteristics of these systems. His early chapters provide a good overview of real-time systems and safety critical systems.

Killelea and Mui also address web-based systems [Killelea, 1998]. Neil Gunther mentions benchmarks for web servers in Chapter 9. Chapter 9 in [Jain, 1991] also addresses capacity planning and benchmarking. Also see Part 2 in [Gunther, 2000]. To search the World Wide Web, some good keywords to use are: computer performance engineering, capacity planning, load balancing, and job scheduling.

Note N38, "Estimating Performance for Specific Computer Architectures," describes analytic scaling models for the performance of multiple processor systems, and additional comments on web-based and real-time systems.

The website for this book provides references to various websites, some of which have entire textbooks on the subject that can be downloaded free, and other that provide tools and spreadsheets to analyze queueing systems. It also identifies tools that you can use. Many of these are also free.

24.13 Summary

Product performance includes accuracy and correctness. However, to most people, performance means the dynamic behavior of a system or its components with respect to specific functions or services. Examples are response time and throughput. Users and operators of a system are most interested in the performance of the system as a whole. Engineers and designers are often interested in the performance of low-level components. Ultimately, product performance addresses the usage of resources such as processors, memory, networks, and peripherals. Depending on the application and user needs, certain resources are critical for product acceptance and project success. Estimators and planners must identify, estimate, and track these "critical resources." A technical performance measure (TPM) is any performance parameter that impacts system acceptance or project success.

It is often difficult to relate the estimated or measured performance of the low-level components to overall system performance, however. System performance also depends on factors such as the expected workload and the system's operating modes. If the operational workload differs from the workload assumed by the designers, estimated and measured values will be wrong.

Measurements play an important role in performance estimation. Except for external hardware monitors, performance measurement in a computer involves inserting code to collect data. The inserted code consumes resources when it executes, and so measurement affects the product's performance. Engineers and estimators must decide how much distortion is introduced and how much can be tolerated. In addition, careful design of the performance measurement "experiment" is important. Be sure to control the conditions during the measurement (system configuration and workload).

Measurements can be expensive. Some measurement activities are part of the usual development activities (analysis, design, code, and test). Others involve extra effort and special equipment. You should estimate these as separate levels of effort tasks. Some of the measurement activities can be viewed as risk avoidance and so are funded as part of risk mitigation.

Measurements of system performance are only possible if the system exists. Even though a functioning product exists, however, it may still be too costly, dangerous, or impractical to measure it. In addition, some internal performance characteristics may not be directly measurable. For these situations, you must estimate performance.

If the system is operating in a steady state, you can estimate its performance using rough order of magnitude (ROM) calculations, simple analytic models (including spreadsheet models), or queueing models. The operational laws of queues quantitatively describe the average behavior of any queue. You can also use these laws to estimate quantities that you cannot directly measure. If the arrival (workload) and service time probability distributions are known (or assumed), queueing theory can calculate performance characteristics for many types of queues, expressing the results as simple formulas. Queueing network models combine various types of queues to represent an entire system. (In most cases, solving these models requires numerical techniques.) Even though queueing models are an idealized representation of the real system, their results are often accurate enough for initial design and determining upper and lower performance bounds. Queueing models cannot handle complicated situations like blocking/locking, forking/joining, simultaneous resource possession, and synchronization. If the interactions are extremely complex and time varying, or if the service time varies nonlinearly as a function of workload, then you must use simulation models.

Executable simulation models estimate performance by representing individual activities taking place within a system. You can construct simulation models using commercial tools or toolsets, custom code, or a mixture of these. You can also use the formulas from queueing models as part of a larger simulation model. Simulation is very flexible. You can use simulation models to analyze a new system without building it, proposed changes to an existing system, and transient phenomena. Simulation is more expensive than mathematical analysis. The simulator's code must represent the system under study, any missing components, external objects that interact with the system, and the "physics" of the environment. This increases development costs. A simulation model may produce inaccurate results due to omission of important effects, approximations, mathematical errors, and coding errors.

If product performance is important, you should start performance estimation early and continue throughout the project. ("The big mistakes are usually made in the first few days of the project!" says Eberhard Rechtin.) The product architecture has a large influence on the performance of a software-intensive system. Performance engineering is a process that starts as early as possible and continues throughout the life of the system. It uses a range of techniques and performance estimation models. Early in a project, you use simple analytic models and simulations to assess feasibility, investigate design trade-offs, identify performance bottlenecks, set threshold values, and estimate needed processing capacity and speed. Later, you use models and simulations to validate your assumptions about system performance. Still later, you may use simulations or measurements to fine-tune algorithms to improve accuracy or reduce execution time. As the project proceeds, you supplement your estimates with actual measurements. You also use measurements to validate the various models and to develop better models. Plan to improve your performance models as your project proceeds. Above all, estimating system performance requires a good understanding of the system.

Chapter 25

Determining Product Quality

Quality is an important characteristic of any product, especially software-intensive systems. Unfortunately, quality is in the eye of the beholder. This chapter explains the motivation for estimating and measuring the quality of software-intensive systems and products, identifies possible quality measures, and identifies challenges to estimating and measuring product quality. This chapter also surveys ways to estimate and measure software quality and describes some simple techniques. This chapter also explains the concepts of some advanced mathematical techniques, and provides references to books that treat these in detail.

25.1 Why Product Quality Is Important

There are many reasons to estimate and measure product quality. Product developers want to satisfy their customers so that they can remain in business. Whoever has the responsibility for supporting a delivered product is interested in quality because it affects sustainment costs. Customers must pay for operations and maintenance. Developers must pay for customer support and warranties. Managers and engineers measure quality so that they can control and improve their production processes, and so that they can allocate resources between development, reviews, and tests to obtain the maximum benefit. Quality measures reveal the causes of rework, and so help identify process areas needing improvement.

25.2 Defining Quality

Figure 25-1 shows nine different quality factors and their importance to two different stakeholders: users and developers.[1] Quality is in the eye of the beholder. Product quality may also include product performance parameters (speed, accuracy). Product quality may also be perceived in terms of intangible characteristics. See the box "Product Value."

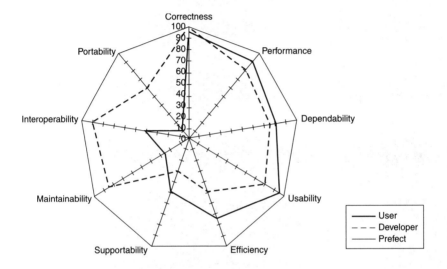

Figure 25-1 *Importance of quality factor by stakeholder*

Product Value

A product has business value; otherwise the customer would not buy it. In the simplest terms, the costs saved by using the product should exceed the costs of buying, building, operating, and maintaining the product. But there are intangible factors as well so it is difficult to measure business value. It depends on functionality, response time, dependability, and quality. These may give the buyer a market advantage, the ability to avoid or recover from failures, or the means to quickly adapt to new business

---

[1] Robert Charette provides a similar view in Chapter 3 of [Charette, 1990].

opportunities and rules. These are often hard to express in monetary terms. This is a challenge in preparing a business case or evaluating economic benefits. Some good references are [Reifer, 2002a], [Tockey, 2005], [Boehm, 1981], and a short article by Barry Boehm and Sunita Chulani in [Reifer, 2002b].

One of the quality attributes shown in Figure 25-1 is "dependability." Stakeholders might interpret this in terms of access security, operator safety, data integrity, or system reliability. Often they do not clearly state their interpretation in specifications. Consider one aspect of dependability: reliability. Reliability deals with the failure of a system to perform its functions over some time interval or at a particular time. The precise definition depends on the type of application. Three possible measures are [Sommerville, 1996, Figure 18.4]

MTTF   Mean time to failure

AVAIL   Availability

POFOD   Probability of failure on demand

The mean time to failure is an important measure if the system must operate without failure for a specified time interval. Availability is important for systems that operate continuously, such as a plant monitoring system or the central server for a network of automated teller machines. The Probability of failure on demand is important for systems that provide service intermittently such as an automated teller machine.

Table 25-1 shows possible definitions for *failure* and *time* used to measure reliability. The type of system determines the type of failure that is important. In fact, you may use different measures of software quality or reliability for different subsystems of the overall system.[2] Similarly, different time measures are appropriate for different types of systems. Calendar time is good for systems that operate continuously. For products that operate intermittently, such as aircraft avionics, you would measure time in terms of the actual processor execution time. For some systems, you measure "time" in terms of transactions (appropriate for automated teller machines) or hits (appropriate for an e-commerce website). Ian Sommerville provides a good discussion of these distinctions in Sections 18.1 and 18.2 of [Sommerville, 2004].

---

[2] It typically costs 50% more to develop a high-dependability software product than to develop a low-dependability product [Boehm, 2001]. You can reduce software development costs and schedules by carefully partitioning the system so that only certain sybsystems need high dependability.

Table 25-1 *Defining the Basic Quantities*

Failures
• Permanent or transient
• Recoverable or Nonrecoverable
• Corrupting or Noncorrupting
• Severity (amount of damage)
Time
• Calendar time (continuous: plant monitoring and control)
• Processor execution time (intermittent: avionics)
• Transactions (demand-driven: ATM, website)

Table 25-2 shows possible definitions for a *defect*. Terminology is not standard across the industry. Commonly used synonyms for a fault are *error* and *bug*. The definitions shown are based on IEEE Standard 610.12, Glossary of Software Engineering Terminology. The fault-tolerance discipline distinguishes between a human action (a mistake), its manifestation (a hardware or software fault), the result of the fault (a failure), and the amount by which the result is incorrect (the error). User documentation faults are excluded because they do not directly cause a program to fail. (They can indirectly cause failures, however, by misinforming users.) An omitted requirement is a fault, however. Testing and operational use disclose failures. Analysts locate the causal faults (root causes). Peer reviews, walkthroughs, and "desk checking" also locate faults during development. Problems may be due to a defect, a mistake, or may even be a desired capability or suggested enhancement. Distinguishing the true nature of a "problem" is important in analyzing operational reliability. For a way to do this, see the box "Orthogonal Defect Classification (ODC)."

Table 25-2 *Possible Definitions for Defect*

Fault	An error that could cause a program to fail; a potential failure; a flaw
Failure	A manifestation of a fault; an incorrect result
Defect	An observation of incorrect behavior caused by a failure or detection of a fault
Mistake	A human action that causes a failure or incorrect result (operator error, misuse, misunderstanding)
Problem	A user's report of a program's unexpected behavior (a "trouble report")

Orthogonal Defect Classification (ODC)

Orthogonal defect classification (ODC) uses defect data to locate problems in process phases and to evaluate product quality. Ram Chillarege invented ODC circa 1989 [Chillarege, 1992]. Engineers collect and analyze defects during software development, collecting information at two different times. When a tester finds a defect, she records the following:

Activity	The particular test phase (unit test, system test, etc.)
Trigger	The condition causing the fault or failure (workload, logic error)
Impact	The defect's effect on the user if it had not been found ("severity")

When the programmer completes the repair, he records the following:

Defect type	The type of correction(s) made
Defect qualifier	Omission, commission, or extra (extraneous)
Defect source	Source of the problem (when injected)
Defect age	Phase discovered (when detected)

An organization customizes the generic scheme to its local process by defining the Activities during its development process and the mapping to ODC triggers. (This makes it difficult to compare data from different organizations.) Several software companies use ODC, and research continues at universities. For more information see http://www.research.ibm.com/softeng/ODC/ODC.HTM, and http://www.chillarege.com/odc/index.html.

25.3 Determining Quality During a Project

Over the development life cycle, emphasis shifts from estimating quality values, to measuring quality values during testing, and finally to observing the quality during actual operations. Each activity has its own particular challenges and requires different techniques and tools. Figure 25-2 shows that the accuracy of software quality ("dependability") values increases over the course of a project. (This figure applies to both product performance and product quality.) During concept definition, stakeholders agree on goals for product quality and performance. During development, engineers define requirements in some detail and choose the architecture. Estimators use characteristics of the application, requirements, and design to estimate the quality or performance of the product. After the team has built the components and integrated them, testers can execute the product and observe actual failures. During testing, you use different techniques to measure quality (and performance) values.

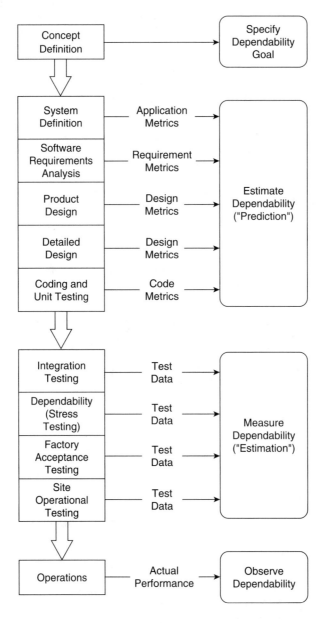

Figure 25-2 *Determining product dependability*

25.4 Estimating Defects During Design and Construction

Table 25-3 shows challenges for estimating the failures that will occur during future operational use. Understanding fault generation and detection requires knowledge of the product's architecture and design, and the processes and tools used to build and test the product. Another challenge is that the test cases comprising the "test profile" may not represent the actual operational profile. This means that some areas of code may never be tested. In addition, using failures observed during testing to predict operational reliability is also difficult. (See the discussion of reliability growth models later in this chapter.) Last, the product's requirements and design change during the course of a project, and so the estimator is thus trying to hit a moving target.

Table 25-3 *Estimating Challenges*

Understanding fault generation and detection
• Product requirements and architecture
• Process (methods, reviews, tests, tools)
Relating faults to operational failures
• Assumed operational profile
• Predicting the actions of users and abusers
The "product" evolves during development

Static estimation models estimate defects based on characteristics of the product, process, project, and personnel. They are parametric models. Static models are useful during early planning and development before you have any test data. Different types of models exist to calculate quantities such as the following:

- Number of defects in a specified time interval or development phase
- Number of defects normalized by size (defect density)
- Time between successive failures

Here, a *defect* can be a fault or a failure. Some models estimate faults. Others estimate failures. During development, the emphasis is on faults that can be detected using peer reviews or inspections. Most models estimate software defects, but models also exist to estimate defects in requirements and in documents. (See the discussion of COQUALMO.)

Productivity and defect density are two measures of process performance. Defect density is of particular interest because it relates to product quality.

Defect density depends on process characteristics, especially the amount of effort allocated to peer reviewing and testing. Managers need to know the amount of effort needed to achieve a desired quality level so they need ways to estimate defect density early in the project life cycle. Several models attempt to estimate defect density using one or more parameters. Additive models add the influence of several factors [Takahashi, 1985]. Multiplicative models multiply factors representing the influence of several factors. (Multiplicative models are the standard for estimating hardware failure rates.) Examples of multiplicative models are the RADC model [McCall, 1992] and COQUALMO [Boehm, 2000].

25.5 RADC Model

The Rome Air Development Center (RADC) model is probably the best documented static defect estimation model. (See the box "Origins of the RADC Model.")

Origins of the RADC Model

The Rome Air Development Center funded a project (September 1986 through December 1989) to help acquisition managers estimate and measure software reliability, and provide a quantitative basis to do the following:

- Choose test techniques

- Allocate test effort among types of testing or software components

- Determine cost trade-offs in testing

This project evaluated various testing and review techniques using code from two large, previously developed Air Force software systems. They used six different testing techniques for each code sample, and analyzed the test results determine the error detection capability of various testing techniques, the degree of test coverage achieved, and the effort expended. The project also measured reliability characteristics of the complete software systems. The goal was to define a method to predict software reliability based on characteristics of the software system (and to some extent on the development process), and to address ways to predict the reliability based on test results. The "RADC Software Reliability Prediction and Estimation Guidebook (SRPEG)," Volume II of [McCall, 1992], describes the complete defect estimation model.

The RADC model predicts defect density of the delivered software product in the phases of the development life cycle prior to testing. Like the COCOMO model, the RADC model has different versions depending on project phase. (COCOMO has application point, early development, and post-architecture versions.) Table 25-4 shows a summary of the different RADC models. The phases and corresponding milestones are across the top. The model begins with system definition ("predevelopment"), indicated here as system requirements analysis (SYS RA). This phase ends with a review similar to the life cycle objectives (LCO) milestone. Early software requirements analysis covers work done to prepare the System Segment Specification, approved at the system requirements review (SRR). The later milestones are the usual software development milestones. The left column indicates the level of detail, with typical document types indicated in the second column. (I have replaced the DoD-Std-2167A document names.) The rightmost column shows the model's various parameters. Row 3 shows the estimation equations for each phase of development. The model adds factors as more information becomes available. The cells in the center of the chart indicate worksheets (W/S) that the estimators use to determine the value of a particular parameter. The model has 11 worksheets, some with multiple versions (A through D). Each worksheet requires the estimators to specify several additional parameters which, when combined, produce the value for a particular model parameter. Obviously, the model is quite complicated to use and calibrate.

Table 25-4 *RADC Model Parameters by Project Phase**

	Phase:	SYS RA	SW RA (early)	SW RA (late)	PD	DD	CUT		
	Milestone:	~LCO	SRR	SSR	PDR	CDR	UTC	Sym	Parameter Name
	Estimation Equation:	A	A*D	A*D*S1 where S1 = SA*ST*SQ			A*D*S1*S2 where S2 = SL*SM*SX*SR		
Level	**Documents**								
System	Ops Concept System Spec	W/S 0						A	Application type
Project	Plan and process		W/S 1A W/S 1B					D	Development environment
Software	Specification			W/S 2A W/S 3A W/S 4A				SA	Anomaly management
								ST	Traceability
								SQ	Quality review
Subsystems	Architecture				W/S 2B W/S 3B W/S 4B			SA	Anomaly management
								ST	Traceability
								SQ	Quality review
Modules	Design					W/S 2C, 2D W/S 3C W/S 4C, 4D		SA	Anomaly management
								ST	Traceability
								SQ	Quality review
Modules	Code						W/S 8D W/S 9D W/S 10D	SL	Language type
								SM	Modularity
								SX	Complexity
Modules	Code						W/S 11D	SR	Standards review

*Adapted from Table TS100-3 in [McCall, 1992]. I have translated the military acronyms into general definitions.

"W/S xx" denotes a specific worksheet in the model.

The RADC model estimates the initial fault (defect) density, DD0, using 10 factors. Regrouping the factors with parentheses indicates the parameters that relate to the characteristics of the product and the process:

$$DD_0 = (A*SX*SL*SM*SU)*(D*SA*ST*SQ*SR)$$

and the total number of injected faults (defects), W_0, is

$$W_0 = DD_0*SS$$

The six product-related parameters are

A = Application type (real-time control, information management, etc.)

SX = Program complexity

SL = Language type (high order, assembly, etc.)

SS = Program size (delivered source instructions; SLOC without comments)

SM = Modularity

SU = Extent of reuse

The five process-related parameters, followed with relevant CMMI process areas, are as follows:

D = Development process, methods and tools, rated using COCOMO 1981's development modes: organic, semi-detached, and embedded

SA = Anomaly management (configuration management and causal analysis and resolution)

ST = Traceability (requirements management)

SQ = Using (document) reviews to remove defects (verification [peer reviews] and quality-assurance audits)

SR = Using (code) reviews to remove defects (one method of verification)

The RADC model instructs users to rate particular parameters at specific phases as data becomes available. You could, however, estimate all of these parameters early in a project. The RADC model also provides a means estimate failure rate, which is useful for some reliability predictions. See the box "Estimating the Failure Rate."

Estimating the Failure Rate

The RADC model also estimates the initial failure rate, at the cost of introducing three more parameters. The initial failure rate, λ_0 is

$$\lambda_0 = W_0{}^*K{}^*R/I$$

where

W_0 = Total number of injected faults

K = Fault exposure ratio

R = Average instruction execution rate of the computer

I = Number of object instructions executed excluding looping and branching

The fault exposure ratio represents the "detection efficiency" of the test or operational environment, and depends on the scenario, workload, and other factors. The RADC data give $1.4{}^*10^{-7} \leq K \leq 10.6{}^*10^{-7}$. The ratio R/I is the "linear execution frequency" and represents the number of times the program would be executed per unit time if the program had no loops or branches [Musa, 1987, p. 121]. It appears that the model assumes that an error will be detected the first time that a path is taken (if it is to be detected at all), and so the linear execution frequency is appropriate. The model estimates I by multiplying SS by an average expansion ratio, Q_x, which is typically 4 or so. (You could increase Q_x to account for looping and branching because the paths are executed with different data values, and so could expose more faults, but estimating the appropriate value will be difficult.) Using Q_x in the above equation gives

$$\lambda_0 = W_0{}^*K{}^*R/(SS{}^*Q_x) = DD_0{}^*K{}^*R/Q_x$$

This equation has 14 parameters, of which only R is known with certainty.

Due to its complexity, the RADC model is difficult to adapt and calibrate to a particular organization. As with other parametric models, you may be able to simplify the model. If your organization builds similar systems, using a particular programming language and tool set, you might be able to reduce the model to the five or less process-related parameters, and use historical data to fit the remaining coefficients. This is analogous to the COCOMO II calibration approach described in [Boehm, 2000]. Instead of the productivity range for each parameter, you can define a "defectability range."

25.6 COQUALMO

The COnstructive QUALity MOdel (COQUALMO) is simpler than the RADC model, and has the advantage of estimating three different types of defects. COQUALMO estimates defect density at delivery. It calculates the defects injected, DI_j, into each product type (requirements, design, and code) using a multiplicative model. It uses another multiplicative model to estimate the defect removal efficiency, f_j, for each artifact. Multiplying the defect removal efficiency by the defects injected for that artifact gives the remaining defects in that artifact, DR_j. The equations are

Injection Model:

$$DI_j = \text{Defects Injected} = A_j * QAF_j * S_j^B$$

where

j = Artifact type (requirements, design, code)

QAF_j = Quality adjustment factor (based on 21 parameters)

Removal Efficiency:

$$f_j = \text{Removal Factor} = C_j \prod_i \left(1 - DRF_{ij}\right)$$

where

j = Artifact type (requirements, design, code)

i = Removal technique (automated analysis, peer reviews, testing)

DRF_{ij} = Defect removal factor for technique i and artifact j

Remaining Defects:

$$DR_j = \text{Residual Defects} = DI_j * f_j$$

Table 25-5 shows the 21 parameters of the COQUALMO Defect Injection Model used to calculate the quality adjustment factor (QAF_j). These multiplicative drivers are divided into four categories (platform, product, personnel, and project) and are a subset of the 22 parameters of the COCOMO II software cost estimation model. The choice of using COCOMO II drivers makes it relatively straightforward to integrate COQUALMO with COCOMO II.

Table 25-5 *Parameters Used in COQUALMO's Defect Injection Model*

Category	Variable	Name
Platform	RELY	Required software reliability
	DATA	Database size (for *test* data)
	CPLX	Product complexity
	RUSE	Develop for later reuse (increases effort)
	DOCU	Appropriate level and amount of documentation
Product	TIME	Execution time constraint
	STOR	Main storage constraint
	PVOL	Platform volatility (replaces VIRT)
Personnel	ACAP	Analyst capability
	PCAP	Programmer capability
	PCON	Personnel continuity (handles turnover)
	APEX	Applications experience
	PLEX	Platform experience (OS, GUI, DBMS, middleware, etc.)
	LTEX	Language and tools experience (combines LEXP and MODP)
Project	TOOL	Use of software tools
	SITE	Multisite development (site collocation and communications support)
	SCED	Required development schedule (schedule constraint)
	PREC	Precedentedness
	RESL	Architecture/risk resolution
	TEAM	Team cohesion
	PMAT	Process maturity

You can investigate proposed changes to a process by changing parameters such as process maturity (PMAT), the amount of time spent on architecture definition and risk resolution (RESL), and the effect of automation (TOOL). Besides these, COQUALMO has three additional process-related parameters: automated analysis, peer reviews, and execution testing and tools, described in Table 5.35 of [Boehm, 2000]. For additional details, see Section 5.5 in [Boehm, 2000] or the website at http://sunset.usc.edu/research/coqualmo/index.html.

25.7 Measuring Defects During Testing

Collecting enough high-quality data is not easy for the reasons listed in Table 25-6. The testers' assumed operational profile may not match the actual operational profile. Testers may not encounter some faults, and may not see the failures caused by other faults.[3] Some faults lie in areas that are seldom executed (e.g., only at year-end close, once every leap year). Some faults are triggered by conditions that seldom occur. Example: an employee with more than 15 children (when the number of dependents is packed as a 4-bit field). Edward Adams of IBM analyzed data for nine well-tested, operational systems [Adams, 1984]. He found that only 9% of the errors were detected in the first 178 kilo-hours of operation, which is more than 20 years of continuous operation for a single system (e.g., a single testbed). (One year of continuous operation is 8.8 kilo-hours.) No developer can afford to test this long.

Table 25-6 *Testing Challenges*

Test Profile Differs from the Operational Profile
Detection is flawed (Type 1 and Type 2 errors).
• Test case (or peer review) fails to expose a real fault.
• Test case reports a defect when there is actually no fault.
Comprehensive Testing Is Seldom Possible
• Many combinations to cover (inputs, modes, internal states).
• Testing time is limited.
• Never trigger some faults (so never see resulting failure).
Every Change Gives a New "Product" to Sample
• Changes due to modification or repairs.
• Some repairs introduce new defects ("bad fixes").

Repairs change the product. Testing actually measures a series of different products, whose errors may have different probability distributions. If testers collect N failures for a version, they are attempting to fit the probability distribution function that describes failures for that particular version using N data points. Usually N is small, giving low confidence in the accuracy of the estimates of the model's coefficients. (See the discussion of reliability growth models later in this section.)

---

[3] Fault tolerant systems complicate detection because they handle failures and continue processing.

In addition, some repairs introduce new defects ("bad fixes"). Edward Adams found in his study that 15% of the fixes were incorrect. Some authors report cases where 25% of the fixes are bad. The next section describes a way to make the most of the defect data you can collect.

25.8 Estimating Software Reliability

Dynamic estimation models measure the quality of the product using observed failures. You can only use these models after the product is executing in a test environment. Estimators use these models to do the following:

- Gauge product quality (determine the value of the chosen quality measure)
- Decide when to stop testing (reach quality goal, confidence level, or both)
- Predict operational performance (expected reliability)
- Predict maintenance costs (expected repairs)

Figure 25-3 shows the typical behavior of defect discovery rate versus time for a project. Early, testers report few defects, usually because the software crashes repeatedly and it is impossible to execute large portions of the software. Once the developers correct these serious faults, testers find defects more rapidly. The higher defect discovery rate continues for some time. Once the testers have fully explored most of the code, however, they find fewer and fewer defects and the curve tails off as shown. You can think of testing as filtering out the errors having high rates of occurrence.

Dynamic estimation models attempt to exploit this behavior. The model builder assumes a shape (functional form) of the curve. The analyst fits data to determine the "best" values for the function's coefficients. (Analysts use various criteria to measure the goodness of fit. The goodness of fit indicates the quality of the estimate, and if the testers need to collect more data.) The analyst then extrapolates the fitted curve to predict the total number of defects in the product. In this figure, "time" is the cumulative number of defects, not time as you might expect. The point where the discovery rate curve crosses the horizontal axis is the total number of defects in the product.

Reliability growth models (RGMs) quantify the increase in reliability as testing discovers and removes faults in a software product. The goal is to obtain a more accurate prediction with the limited data available. Essentially, a reliability growth model "stretches" the available data by making assumptions about the product's defect density, and the failure, testing, and repair processes, and so derive the form of the underlying statistical distribution function.

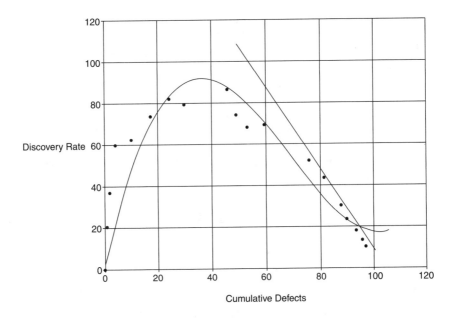

Figure 25-3 *Defect discovery data with trendlines*

Various combinations of assumptions give rise to literally hundreds of different reliability growth models. There is great variation in the accuracy of software reliability prediction models [Abdel-Ghaly, 1986]. Researchers find that

- No single model gives accurate results for all situations.
- The accuracy of a particular model varies from one data set to another.
- There is no way to identify *a priori* which particular model will provide the "best" predictions for a particular situation.

The industry best practice for using reliability growth models is to fit several different models and then pick the one that seems to perform the best for your situation. The basic steps are as follows:

1. Choose your "time" variable (monotonic).
2. Choose multiple models to predict failures versus "time" or "time" interval.
3. Collect failure data over "time."
4. Fit the models' coefficients to the data.
5. Predict using the model that has the "best" fit.
6. Continue measuring, fitting, and tracking.

Recalibration is a technique that quantifies the inaccuracies in a predictive model (i.e., a reliability growth model) based on early observations, and then uses this knowledge to adjust the model's predictions to increase the accuracy. The striking result is that recalibration provides better predictions, regardless of the form of the original prediction model. The recalibration technique works well in most situations. It also allows you to identify cases where this technique does not work. (For an overview, see the box "Recalibration.") Of course, just because a model has produced good predictions in the past does not guarantee that it will do so in the future. However, experience suggests that such reversals are rare. Thus, we assume that if method A has been producing better predictions than method B, then method A will probably continue to do so in the future.

Recalibration

Reliability predictions can be inaccurate in one of two ways:

1. Successive predictions for a given data set may vary widely (noise).

2. Predictions may consistently depart from the correct value (bias).

Detecting noise and bias is hard because you do not know the true reliability of the product. In addition, the observed reliability of a software product can change due to repairing defects or to uncertainty or problems with the prediction model. Recalibration addresses both noise and bias.

Noise

You must distinguish how well a particular model fits a given set of data and how well that model will actually predict future events. To measure the predictive accuracy of a model, you recursively compare the predictions of the model with the eventual outcomes. You take a set of experimental data, fit the predictive model to it, and then make a prediction of the next failure point. When that failure finally occurs, you compare the predicted time with the actual time of the occurrence and calculate the error. (You can compare other parameters as well.) By repeating the process of prediction and observation, you generate a sequence of values. (You can predict one step ahead, or you can predict several steps ahead.) You can generate such a sequence for each of several predictive models using the same set of data points. (Computer models are essential.)

You can use prequential likelihood ratios to compare the sets of predictions, and so select the prediction function that produces the "most accurate" predictions. The prequential likelihood ratio is a completely general technique for comparing the accuracy of different predictive models [Dawid, 1984]. Prequential likelihood ratios do not indicate, however, if the predictions are objectively accurate. You must use a second technique to determine the amount of bias.

Bias

Consider a model to estimate the interfailure time, t, which has the true cumulative distribution function F(t). The predictive model produces an estimate of the cumulative distribution function, $\hat{F}$(t). If $\hat{F}$ were perfect, then the two distributions would be identical.

The random variable $u_i = \hat{F}(t_i)$ gives the probability that the random variable, t, will be less than the time t_i. If you obtain a set of n measured values $\{t_i\}$, then you can use $\hat{F}$(t) to compute the set $\{u_i\}$. It can be shown that if the random variable t has the distribution $\hat{F}$(t), then the random variable u_i will be uniformly distributed over the interval [0, 1]. The times t_i increase monotonically, and so do the u_i. You can draw the expected cumulative distribution and compare the observed values with the expected shape for a perfect prediction model, namely a 45° line with a unit slope. For n data points, the cumulative probability increases by 1/n for each point. (The literature uses n to count the number of data points used to fit the coefficients of the prediction model, which is then used to predict the value of the latest point. Thus, the cumulative probability increases by 1/(n+1).) Plotting the cumulative probability versus the u_i gives a sample cumulative distribution. To do this, you sort the $\{u_i\}$ in ascending order, increment the cumulative value, and plot the points to obtain a stepped curve, called a u-plot:

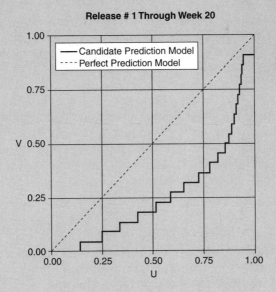

A sample u-plot

The u-plot determines if the predictions of a model are close to the true (observed) distribution. By observing how the predicted values vary from the line, you can determine the type of bias in the assumed distribution function (the predictive model). If the model's predictions are always above the 45° line, there are too many small u values and the model tends to underestimate the probability of failure; the model is too optimistic. On the other hand, if the model's predictions are usually below the line, the model is too pessimistic. (You measure the degree of deviation using the Kolmogorov distance, which is the maximum vertical distance between the two curves.) If you construct a correction function, G, by smoothing the cumulative distribution based on the sample data, then $G[\hat{F}(t_i)]$ gives more accurate predictions.

The basic procedure to produce a recalibrated prediction is this:

1. Check that the error in previous predictions is approximately stationary. Abdel-Ghaly, Chan, and Littlewood describe a plotting technique that detects nonstationarity [Abdel-Ghaly, 1986].

2. Construct the u-plot for predictions made before t_i. The u-plot gives precise information about the incorrect shape of the predictive model. Join these to form a polygon and smooth it to form the function G. (Sarah Brocklehurst uses a spline fit.)

3. Use the basic prediction system to make a raw prediction, $\hat{F}$, and recalibrate the raw prediction using $\hat{F}^* = G[\hat{F}]$.

4. Repeat the procedure at each stage.

For additional details, see [Brocklehurst, 1990] or the summary in Sections 10.4 and 10.5 of [Fenton, 1997]. Fenton and Pfleeger provide a numerical example in Section 10.5.

Even if you have identified the appropriate model, conditions may change during the course of gathering data. For example, programmers may repair the code. Teams using agile methods often refactor (restructure) the code. Such changes may invalidate the model's assumptions, or at least may change the "best fit" values of the model's coefficients.

The other problem with reliability growth models is that extrapolating a fitted curve is often dangerous. Figure 25-4 illustrates why. This plot shows a series of measured mean time between failure (MTBF) values versus the execution time, t, accumulated during testing or operation. The chart shows two models that fit the data equally well (using some appropriate statistical test). The two models have quite different asymptotic behavior, however, and so their predictions differ greatly. This is a common problem with reliability growth models.

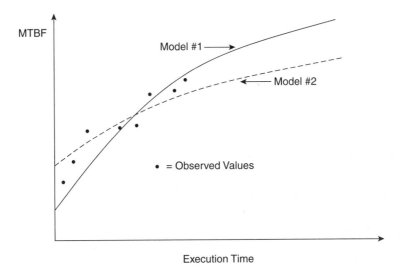

Figure 25-4 *Reliability growth models*

The software reliability growth approach is only practical in situations where you require relatively modest reliability levels. If you require ultrahigh reliability (above 10^{-6} or so), there is currently no way to determine this. Bev Littlewood states that the length of time needed for a reliability growth model to acquire the evidence that a particular target mean time to failure has been achieved will be many times that target value [Littlewood, 1993]. Worse, he says that this multiplier tends to become larger for higher target values. There is a law of diminishing returns operating in software reliability growth. This result seems to occur regardless of the model that you use and the nature of the reliability measure adopted. This effectively precludes the use of these techniques from providing evidence that a system has achieved ultrahigh reliability. There are limits to what you can estimate.

25.9 Error Trending

You can use a simple reliability growth model to estimate the total number of errors in a software product, the number of undetected errors remaining, and the amount of effort needed to discover some percentage of the remaining errors.

Several models predict the rate at which errors are found, $\lambda(t)$. Integrating $\lambda(t)$ with respect to time gives the cumulative number of errors, $N(t)$. One such model is the Weibull function:

$$\lambda(t) = (p/t)*[(t/t_{max})^p]*\exp[-(t/t_{max})^p]$$

$$N(t) = K*(1 - \exp[-(t/t_{max})^p])$$

where t is the cumulative test time or test effort, p is the shape parameter, t_{max} is the scale parameter, and K is the total number of estimated errors. With $p = 1$, the function is an exponential and with $p = 2$, the function is the Rayleigh curve. For more information about the Weibull model, see [Kan, 2003, page 189].

An *error trend* is a plot showing the cumulative number of reported errors (y-axis) as a function of the amount of testing performed (x-axis). Figure 25-5 shows an error trend from [Fodeh, 1999]. Fodeh uses test effort, expressed in test-days, to measure elapsed time. (One test-day equals the effort of one tester working for one day, i.e., eight person-hours.) The dots in the graph represent the reported errors, while the curve is the Weibull function that best fits the points. The fitted value of K is the predicted number of total errors in the product. Subtracting the number of errors found so far gives the number of remaining errors (assuming that repairs inject no new errors).

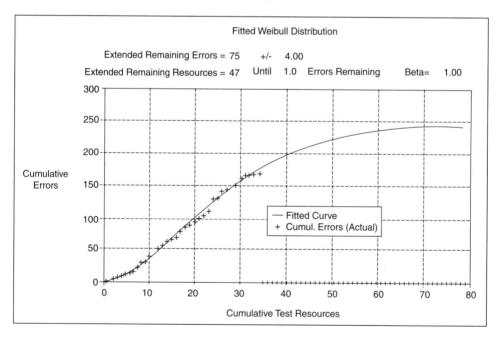

Figure 25-5 *Fitted Weibull distribution*

This S-shaped curve is typical of many software reliability growth models, and correlates with experience on typical software projects. At the start of integration testing, the error discovery rate is low because testing samples only small portions of the functionality due to "crashers." The error discovery rate increases as the "crasher" errors are found and corrected, allowing the tests to probe more of the code. Eventually, the error discovery rate starts to decrease because it becomes harder to find new errors. Ultimately, the curve flattens indicating that the software is ready for release. Finding further errors at this stage require huge test effort [Adams, 1984].

John Fodeh implemented a Microsoft Excel spreadsheet, and used the Solver function to adjust the parameters K, t_{max}, and p of the Weibull function to minimize the sum of the squared residuals (i.e., a least squares fit), with the constraint that the total number of errors, K, is greater than the number of errors already found. The spreadsheet uses the fitted parameters to draw the best-fit line running through the plotted data. (The book's CD-ROM has a modified version of his spreadsheet.) For further information about the model, see [Fodeh, 1999].

Niels Svendsen describes the use of the model [Svendsen, 1998]. Each day testers record the number of errors detected and the number of person-hours expended. Then they recalculate the trend. By monitoring the S-curve, they decide when to stop testing. They also predict the number of errors remaining, and the number of test-days needed to reach a specified number of remaining errors (i.e., desired quality level or defect density). Svendsen says that you can obtain good predictions if you use data from the later stages of system testing, obtained after the system has become stable. He also observes that even though the initial predicted values are not highly accurate, "almost any estimate is better than none." Error trending at least shows that there are "a lot" of errors left and not just "a few" errors left. They observe fluctuations in the total number of estimated defects when

- Testing of new regions of code begins.
- The type of tests changes.
- Developers add new features (new builds).

Svendsen describes a case where, midway through a test phase, the estimates of the total number of errors drastically increased because the testers started testing new areas of the code. As a result, Svendsen explains that his firm now selects an initial set of test cases to obtain broad coverage of the overall product. This gives a better estimate of the product's quality early in the test phase.

25.10 Measuring Defects Using Capture/Recapture

Error trending provides one way to measure the total number of defects in a product. There is another technique you can use, but it requires expending additional effort. Wildlife biologists are often interested in measuring the size of animal populations. They trap, mark, and release animals. Then they trap (recapture) animals in the same area at a later time. You can determine estimates of the animal population based on the numbers of recaptured animals that are marked. There are two general classes of capture-recapture models. Open population models allow population gain (birth, recruitment) and population loss (death, emigration). Closed population models have no gain or loss during the study, and are most appropriate for examining defects from peer reviews.

The basic concept is to have two different reviewers examine the same work product. You analyze the defects discovered by each reviewer, and identify the defects that both reviewers found, and identify the following counts:

N_1 = Total defects found by reviewer 1
N_2 = Total defects found by reviewer 2
N_{12} = Total defects found by both reviewers

You calculate the total number of defects in the work product, N_{total}, using

$$N_{total} = N_1 * N_2 / N_{12}$$

The total defects remaining in the product is thus

$$N_{remain} = N_{total} - N_1 - N_2 + N_{12}$$

You can extend this calculation for more than two reviewers but the mathematics becomes complicated. For details, see [Otis, 1978].

25.11 Observing Defects During Actual Use

When development and testing are finished, users can directly observe failures in the actual operational setting. Observation has its own peculiar problems, however, which make it difficult to determine the actual number of defects. The two main challenges to counting defects are as follows:

- Multiple reports of the same problem.
- All reported "problems" are not due to software faults.

Chapter 6, "Estimating Annual Maintenance Costs," discussed the analysis of problem reports. Additional complications related to multiple reporting are that the users are using different versions of the product, or different configurations of the same (or different) version. (Identifying the installed version is essential because multiple versions are in use at any particular time.) Some reported "problems" are unrelated to software faults. They may arise from confusing documentation, user mistakes or misconceptions, invalid or corrupted data, or equipment problems. Users may also submit "problem reports" to suggest new features or enhancements.

Even for valid software failures, it may be difficult for analysts to identify the actual causes. They usually have incomplete information about the user's platform configuration, data values, error messages, and event sequences. Analyzing the information is hard because software exhibits complex behavior. Analysts must consider many variables, multiple states, and sequences of events.

If you use a reliability growth model to fit observed failures, measuring time is also difficult. Some devices, such as avionics, do not operate continuously, whereas others operate 24×7×52. If a product is operating at multiple sites, it is difficult to determine the total execution time. In an ideal world, all users install a new product version on the same day, and all have the same speed processors. Then the total execution time would be, say, eight hours per day times the number of copies in active use. In the real world, there are several problems. First, some sites may not install the product version at the same time, or may never install it. (Users may think that the corrections and enhancements are not needed for their organization. Other users fear that the new version will contain new bugs.) Second, the various user sites may use processors that run at different speeds. Third, the sites may have different operational profiles and workloads. Edward Adams discusses these problems in a classic paper [Adams, 1984].

25.12 Closing the Loop

Figure 25-6 shows the stages of quality estimation, measurement, and observation with calibration added. Calibration closes the loop from observation back to estimation and measurement. Calibration uses historical data to improve prediction capabilities for future projects. Calibration may refit model coefficients, or may even formulate new models.

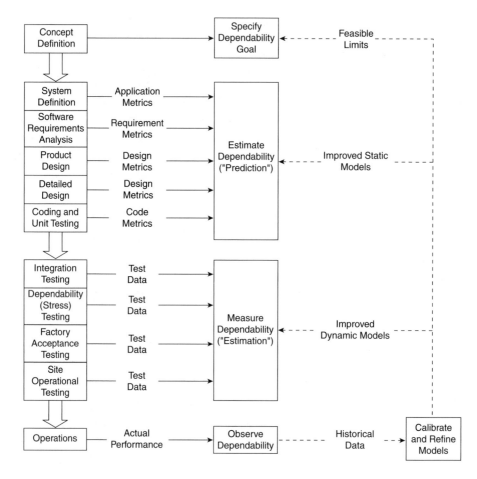

Figure 25-6 *Improving estimation ability*

25.13 Internal Measures of Software Quality

There are various measures of the internal quality of software. These measures include the average module size (in some units related to the implemented code), the logical complexity of a module in terms of the nesting of decisions and loops, and the structure of the program itself, measured in terms of the number of classes, depth of inheritance, the depth of the call tree, and the coupling between software components. Although there is no way to relate these measures to software reliability or other operational measures of operational dependability, you can use these measures to gauge the quality of existing software and to monitor the quality of successive software releases.

One measure that is easy to count is Thomas McCabe's *cyclomatic complexity*, which quantifies the control flow within a program by counting the number of independent paths on a control flow graph. (A simpler way is to count all of the conditional statements in a module or procedure, and add one. Complex conditions count as two.) Thomas McCabe defined cyclomatic complexity to gauge the difficulty of understanding the program. It also indicates the number of test cases needed. Other researchers have attempted to relate cyclomatic complexity to module defect density and development cost.

A number of tools analyze code and produce various quality measures, including cyclomatic complexity. You can use such tools to assess the quality of a large body of software code. For example, if you must estimate the costs to modify a software-intensive product containing several hundred modules, then you can use such measurement tools to gauge the quality of the software and the expected difficulty of performing the work. Figure 25-7 shows the distribution of 44 modules in a software product based on their cyclomatic complexity. You can use Excel's statistics functions to calculate measures such as the average, standard deviation, and median. Then you can set an acceptance threshold for the product. For example, in the figure, 86% of the modules have a cyclomatic complexity of 20 or less. If you consider a value of 20 to be acceptable, this body of code seems to be of high quality.[4]

Similarly, you could measure the "comment density" in each module, and prepare a similar histogram that indicates the difficulty of deciphering the total system. (The comment density is defined as the number of comments, divided by the total number of lines in the module, expressed in percent.)[5] Clearly, modules with no comments are bad. Also, modules that are 100% comments are not useful. You might choose to define "good" modules as ones with comment densities between 10% and 20%. You can compute the fraction of total modules that lie within these limits. (This could be a quick way to assess 400 KSLOC of code that your boss wants you to maintain!)

---

[4] There are actually different definitions of cyclomatic complexity. The original McCabe value counts each branch of a selection statement (i.e., a case or switch construct) as a decision point. Some analysts argue, however, that the use of structured programming makes a selection statement "easier to understand" and so it should be less complex. Some tools calculate an "essential cyclomatic complexity" by counting selection statements as a single decision regardless of the number of alternatives within the construct. If this were the definition of cyclomatic complexity in the figure, a more realistic threshold is a value of 10, and the code does not look well structured at all. Only 55% of the modules have a cyclomatic complexity of 10 or less. The threshold value depends on which definition you use.

[5] If lines can contain both code and comments ("mixed lines"), then comment density = (pure comments + mixed)/(total + mixed).

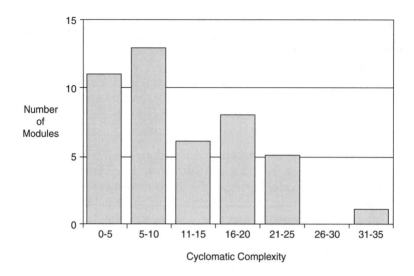

Figure 25-7 *Distribution of module complexity*

You should measure these statistics for new, modified, and unmodified code separately so that your developers are not penalized for "inherited code" that is of poor quality.

To monitor and control product evolution, you can plot a quality measure by release to see if quality is changing with time as shown in Figure 25-8. You would measure all modules "touched" in each release. (Touched means new code and modified code [repaired, perfected, adapted].) This plot illustrates that quality (average cyclomatic complexity) decreases through release 1.2, and increases thereafter. Controlling product complexity helps reduce the erosion of architectural and design integrity over the life of the product.

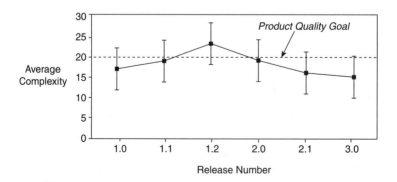

Figure 25-8 *Variation of average module complexity by release*

25.14 Measures of Document Quality

The most common measure of document quality is "readability." This section describes measures of readability, as well as other measures.

25.14.1 Measures of Readability

You can use readability measures to detect poorly written documents. Essentially, readability measures predict reading ease, but do not account for other factors that affect reader comprehension and retention of information such as the reader's educational level, prior knowledge of the subject, and interest in the subject. You may still find them useful as an objective measure of document quality. Use the various readability measures as indicators of document quality, and supplement the other measures such as defects found by peer reviews.

Most readability formulas use one semantic factor (the difficulty of words) and one syntactic factor (the difficulty of sentences). Words are either measured against a frequency list or are measured according to their length in characters or syllables. Sentences are measured for the average length in characters or words. There are many ways to gauge readability. Table 25-7 lists six of these formulas defined for English. Rudolf Flesch's Reading Ease rates text on a scale of 0 to 100 [Flesch, 1949]. The higher the score, the easier the text is to read. "Plain English" has a score of 60. Scores below 50 correspond to "college-level" material. Scores of 0 to 30 are "graduate level." The Flesch-Kincaid Grade Level Index represents the educational level that a reader needs to read the material [Kincaid, 1975]. The Gunning Fog Index also represents the years of education needed for a reader to comprehend text, and has a wider range [Gunning, 1968]. A Fog Index of 5 is very readable, and a rating of 20 is very difficult. (Note: The values given by the various formulas are not always consistent with one another.) You can also measure other characteristics that affect readability such as the average sentence length, average syllables per word, and the percentage of passive sentences.

Many word processing applications routinely calculate such measures. For example, Microsoft Word provides the measurements shown in Figure 25-9.[6] Automated tools make collection consistent and inexpensive, so you can easily collect several measures and use the data to establish norms for particular types of documentation in your organization.

---

[6] It appears that Microsoft Word caps the Flesch-Kincaid grade level at 12, which is too low for most technical documents. This means that the measure cannot distinguish "hard" documents from "very hard" documents.

Table 25-7 *Some Document Readability Measures*

Automated Readability Index	= 4.71*characters/words + 0.5*words/ sentences – 21.43
Coleman-Liau Index	= 5.89*characters/word – 0.3*sentences/(100*words) – 15.8
Flesch Index	= 206.835 – 84.6*syllables/words – 1.015*words/sentences
Fog Index	= 0.4*[words/sentences + 100*({words > = 3 syllables}/words)]
Kincaid Index	= 11.8*syllables/words + 0.39*words/ sentences – 15.59
SMOG Index	= 3 + SQRT[{words > 3 syllables}*sentences/30]

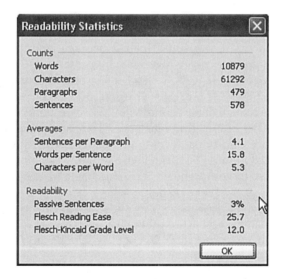

Figure 25-9 *Readability statistics provided by Microsoft Word*

25.14.2 Counting Word Frequencies

You can also count words in various categories. For example, NASA's Automated Requirements Measurement (ARM) tool[7] analyzes specification documents looking for specific words and phrases that indicate information content

---

[7] This tool is available for free from the NASA Software Assurance Technology Center at http://satc.gsfc.nasa.gov.

(or lack thereof). The ARM tool uses the categories in Table 25-8 to analyze individual requirements in a specification document. (It also collects structural information about the document.) The top half of the table defines "good" strings. An explicit specification usually has large numbers of imperative words. Continuances indicate how well requirements are organized and structured. Many continuances may indicate multiple, overly complex requirements. Many directives may indicate more precision in the requirements. The bottom half defines "bad" strings. Weak phrases may indicate that the requirement is defined elsewhere. They may also indicate that the requirement is open to subjective interpretation. Options loosen the specification, reducing the specification writer's control over the product. Incomplete flags indicate missing information.

Table 25-8 *Types of Strings Counted by the ARM Tool*

"Good" Strings
Imperatives. Words and phrases that command that something be provided: • *Shall* normally dictates a functional capability. • *Must/must not* establishes performance requirements/constraints. • *Are applicable* includes, by reference, standards and other documents. • *Will* indicates something provided from outside the specified product.
Continuances. Phrases that follow an imperative and precede low-level requirements: • Examples: *following, in particular,* and *below*
Directives. Point to information that illustrates or helps interpret requirements: • Examples: *Figure, Table,* and *for example*
"Bad" Strings
Weak phrases. Clauses that are open to multiple interpretations: • Examples: *adequate* and *as appropriate*
Options. Words that give developers latitude in implementing a requirement: • Examples: *can, may,* and *optionally*
Incomplete. Words that clearly indicate missing information: • Examples: *TBD* (to be determined) and *TBS* (to be supplied)

25.14.3 Other Measures of Readability

Peter Mosenthal and Irwin Kirsch propose a measure of document readability that is a function of the document's structure and the "density" of the information [Mosenthal, 1998]. They measure structure by counting four "primitive" types of lists: simple, combined, intersected, and nested, assigning a "complexity score" ranging from 1 to 4, respectively. A *simple list* is a group of items with some feature or attribute in common. The label of the list usually identifies the shared attribute. (Not all lists have labels, however. They may appear as a series of items in a sentence, separated by commas.) A *combined list* is two or more lists merged into one structure. The items are paired and the order is usually determined by the order of the first list (e.g., item identifier). For example, a catalog combines a list of items and a list of prices. An *intersecting list* occurs when the same key or identifier appears in two combined lists, and so the items in the first two lists serve as labels for items in the third, intersected list. A good example is the schedule of sessions at a conference presented as a matrix. The rows are time slots, and the columns are rooms. The intersections (cells) contain the name of the talk and the speaker's name. A *nested list* is a list that is broken into subcategories. For example, you can group a simple list of catalog items by product type: clothing, shoes, and furniture.

Of particular interest, Mosenthal and Kirsch also address graphic documents (pie charts, bar charts, line graphs, time lines), locative documents (maps), and data entry documents (forms, templates). They relate each of these to one of the four fundamental types. In some cases, they give additional weight based on specific features of the particular object. For example, although a bar chart is equivalent to an intersected list, it may receive a score of three or four. Data entry forms can be quite complex. They assign the complexity score based on the most complex structure that appears on the form. However, they provide rules to adjust the score on forms that use a number of the fundamental structural elements. They give an example in their paper where the form received a rating of 9. (They note that U.S. Internal Revenue Service documents are usually too complex. More than 50% of tax returns have to be corrected for reasons related to document complexity. See their paper for a reference.)

The work of Mosenthal and Kirsch is interesting because you can relate their structural elements to objects encountered in graphical user interfaces and computer-generated reports. A menu or a pick list is a simple list. Data entry forms can include menus, check boxes, radio buttons, and dialog boxes. This means that the PMOSE/IKIRSCH readability measure might be a way to measure software complexity, quality, or size.

25.15 Recommended Reading

Stephen Kan provides a broad overview of software quality [Kan, 2003]. His book covers possible quality metrics (product complexity, defects, and availability), defect estimation models, quality management models, and measures of customer satisfaction. Of particular interest, his book relates product quality to production processes and to process improvement. His book also contains a short chapter on measurement theory. If you can only buy one book on product quality, especially as it relates to process characteristics, this is the book.

Norman Fenton and Shari Pfleeger discuss software quality models in Chapter 9 of [Fenton, 1997]. They also provide a concise overview of software reliability measurement and prediction in Chapter 10 of the same book. Their book is very useful for all aspects of software measurement.

John Musa gives a non-technical treatment of software reliability engineering [Musa, 1999]. He covers all of the important concepts including definitions, operational profiles, testing, and how to use observed failure data to guide project decisions. His last chapter gives a non-technical overview of software reliability models. (This chapter is a reprise of the classic book by John Musa, Anthony Iannino, and Kazuhira Okumoto [Musa, 1987].)

Michael Lyu is the editor of a book that addresses software reliability engineering in detail, with chapters written by many noted experts [Lyu, 1995]. This is an excellent source if you want to estimate and measure software reliability.

Hoang Pham provides a shorter book on software reliability [Pham, 2000]. He defines measures of system reliability, discusses the process to assess reliability over the software development life cycle, and ranks environmental factors (essentially "quality drivers") that affect software reliability. He provides a concise summary of various software reliability models. Of particular note, he discusses several software cost models for products subject to reliability constraints. He also provides a brief discussion of reliability calculations for fault tolerant software.

For overviews of software reliability, see [Fenton, 1999] and [Littlewood, 2000c]. Brad Clark and Dave Zubrow give an overview of defect prediction techniques in [Clark, 2002]. Several authors address the limits to measuring and estimating software reliability. Recommended papers include [Littlewood, 2000a], [Littlewood, 2000b], [Littlewood, 1999], [Bertolino, 1996], [Littlewood, 1993], [Butler, 1993], [Butler, 1991], and [Adams, 1984].

NASA's Software Assurance Technology Center developed the initial error trending model used by John Fodeh. For further information, see [Waterman, 1994] and [Rosenberg, 1998]. Niels Svendsen describes the BK-MED error trending model and its use [Svendsen, 2000]. Marnie Hutchinson describes the use of S-curves to gauge test progress [Hutchinson, 1996].

The most complete article on using capture-recapture techniques for inspections of work products is [Briand, 2000]. A less mathematical treatment is in [Fuente, 2002]. David Otis et al. give the equations for more than two reviewers [Otis, 1978]. Some tools are available at: http://www.cnr. colostate.edu/~gwhite/software.html.

For more on measures of internal software quality, see [Fenton, 1997], [Hughes, 2000], and [Card, 1990]. ISO/IEC Standard 9126 defines quality characteristics to evaluate software products [ISO/IEC 9126, 1991]. It defines a quality model that is applicable to every kind of software. The model defines six product quality characteristics: functionality, reliability, usability, efficiency, maintainability, and portability. Each of these characteristics is decomposed into sub-characteristics, which may in turn be decomposed. The International Organization for Standardization (ISO) is revising the standard, and it appears that the new standard will have three parts: (1) quality characteristics and sub-characteristics, (2) external metrics, and (3) internal metrics. One source of additional information is: http://www.cse.dcu.ie/essiscope/sm2/9126ref. html.

For good descriptions of the NASA Automated Requirements Measurement (ARM) tool, see [Wilson, 1997] and [Rosenberg, 1998b].

25.16 Summary

Defining, measuring, and estimating the quality of software-intensive products is very difficult. Product quality has many possible definitions depending on the interests of particular stakeholders. Quality most commonly is associated with *defects*, but this term has no industry standard definition.

Over the development life cycle, emphasis shifts from estimating quality values, to measuring quality values during testing, and finally to observing the quality during actual operation. Each activity has its own particular challenges and requires different techniques and tools.

Static estimation models are parametric models and estimate defects based on characteristics of the product, process, project, and personnel. Static models are useful during early planning and development before you have any test data. The Rome Air Development Center model assumes that the estimator will acquire additional information as the development life cycle proceeds, and so the model adds parameters in each phase. The final model has nine parameters. (Software size is the tenth parameter.)

The COnstructive QUALity MOdel (COQUALMO) estimates the number of residual defects in three types of work products: requirements, documents, and code. The model first estimates the number of injected defects, and then estimates the fraction of defects removed. The nominal number of defects injected is estimated using the size of the work product (pages or lines of code). The model adjusts the nominal value using 21 multiplicative factors. The model multiplies the number of injected defects by factors that account for three different removal techniques: automated analysis, peer reviews, and testing.

Dynamic estimation models measure the quality of the product using observed failures. You can only use these models after the product is executing in a test environment. Reliability growth models (RGMs) quantify the increase in reliability as testing discovers and removes faults in a software product. To obtain a more accurate prediction with the limited data available, a reliability growth model makes assumptions about the product's defect density and the failure, testing, and repair processes and so derive the form of the underlying statistical distribution. Various assumptions give rise to literally hundreds of different reliability growth models. Sadly, no single model gives accurate results for all situations, and there is no way to identify *a priori* which particular model will provide the "best" predictions for a particular situation. The industry best practice for using reliability growth models is to fit several different models and then pick the one that seems to perform the best for your situation. Recalibration can improve the prediction accuracy of any reliability growth model. To measure the prediction accuracy of a statistical model, you compare the sequence of future predictions to the actual points measured at those future times. If you can assume that the sequence changes slowly with time (e.g., the developers are not making major changes to the software), you can approximate the correction function and "recalibrate" the raw model output to improve the prediction accuracy.

When development and testing are finished, users can directly observe failures in the actual operational setting. Observation has its own peculiar problems, however, which make it difficult to determine the actual number of defects. The two main challenges to counting defects are as follows:

- Multiple reports of the same problem.
- All reported "problems" are not due to software faults.

(Chapter 6 discusses several possible definitions.) Additional complications related to multiple reporting are that the users are using different versions of the product, or different configurations of the same (or different) version.

The next chapter describes process performance models. The staged defect removal models described there provide another way to estimate the defect density of delivered products.

Chapter 26

Measuring and Estimating Process Performance

A project assembles resources (people, tools, and facilities) for a finite time to produce and deliver products (and services) using a process. A production process is the "software" that humans "execute" during a project. The process consumes resources, and so affects project costs and duration. The process also affects product cost, performance, and quality. Thus, being able to measure, predict, and control process performance can be vitally important to any organization. This chapter describes the challenges and identifies possible approaches. This is still an area of active research so the models are primarily experimental and have limited practical utility.

26.1 Defining a Process

Before you can measure, estimate, and improve a process, you must define the process. A *(process) capability maturity model* defines and formally documents the requirements for a "good" process, using some structure or taxonomy. Process maturity models define how you "ought to" produce a product. (For one example, see note N39, "The SEI CMMI.") A *process architecture model (project life cycle model)* describes "how to" produce a product by identifying project activities at a high level, and the time dependencies of the activities. High-level process architecture models are adequate for planning and estimating. They provide a means to divide and conquer the problem, identifying an initial set of work packages used for planning, estimating, and scheduling (as well as for tracking). They lack adequate detail to direct and perform the actual work, however. A *defined process model* describes in detail how to produce a product, and consists of policies, artifacts, activities, roles, and responsibilities. Another name for the defined process (model) is the *organization's standard process (OSP)*.

A *process performance model* makes quantitative predictions about a particular process architecture or defined process (depending on the model's scope). Process performance models predict (estimate) quantities such as resource consumption, time delays, effectiveness, and efficiency.

Figure 26-1 shows how best practices, process models, and project plans are related. An organization starts by analyzing several sources of best practices, and selects those applicable to their business needs and product types. (Some customers may specify particular standards.) The organization's existing processes and the practical experience of its employees are also possible sources of best practices. (Existing organizational processes include policies, forms, templates, and procedures.) The organization defines a standard process (the OSP) that fits its needs, culture, and business objectives. (An organization may have multiple "standard processes.") Each project tailors the standard process to fit the needs of a particular customer, product type, and project giving a tailored process (model). *Tailoring* chooses a particular standard process (if your organization has more than one), and then selects procedures and standards from that standard process to fit the product type and your development approach.[1] For example, a process might have several procedures for configuration management of source code, one for prototypes, one for web applications, and one for safety critical applications. Tailoring may also revise a few existing procedures and, possibly, standards to make them fit project needs better.

The tailored process is the starting point for estimating project cost and schedule, and is the basis for the project's plans. Tailored processes are not identical, making comparison of process performance measurements from different projects difficult. Estimating process performance for these projects also requires different predictive models. You must balance tailoring versus standardization. More standardization increases the size of the sample for statistical analysis (number of similar projects) but generally restricts measurements to common, high-level characteristics. Many organizations measure and estimate subprocesses that are common to most or all of the tailored processes.

---

[1] U.S. DoD standards define "tailoring" as deleting text or requirements. This definition does not allow modifying or adding new sections of text.

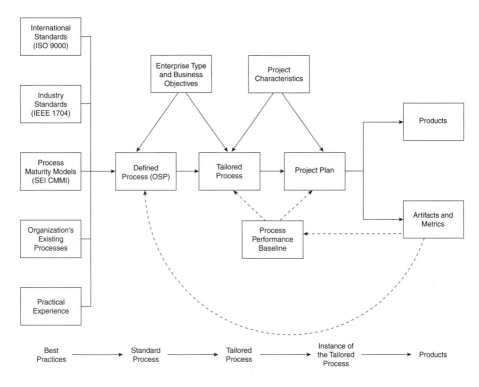

Figure 26-1 *From best practices to products*

Projects execute the plan(s), providing metrics used to calculate baseline process performance and to improve the defined process. The dashed lines in Figure 26-1 indicate these data flows, which occur after project completion.

26.2 Controlling Production Processes

The cheapest way to produce high-quality products is usually to improve the process, not the product. Rework effort can be especially high for projects using the "code and fix" software project life cycle described in Section 7.2 of [McConnell, 1996]. Agile methods perform a large amount of rework (including refactoring), but use a streamlined process to greatly reduce the associated effort. Even if a process is capable of producing acceptable products, it may still be inefficient or unpredictable. For example, the productivity of the process may be low.

Project managers must establish a closed-loop feedback control system because
there are errors in estimates and because things change during a project. *Quantitative process management* uses measurements and predictions to control product quality, service quality, and process performance. Figure 26-2 shows the
activities of quantitative process management.[2] Predictive process performance
models supplement measurements. Managers and engineers need both measurements and predictions to control and (especially) improve the process.
(They also need measurements to develop the predictive model.) The
"measurement/prediction" loop and the "improved process" loop are analogous to the two loops in the estimation process diagrammed in Figure 1-7.

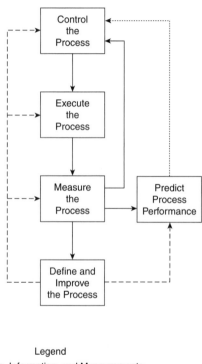

Legend
——— Data, Information, and Measurements
·········· Predictions
– – – – Defined (and Improved) Process

Figure 26-2 *Feedback loops for quantitative process management*

---

[2] This figure extends Figure 1.2 in [Florac, 1999]. William Florac and Anita Carleton discuss their
figure in Sections 1.2 and 1.3 of their book. I have added the activity that provides predictive
process models.

26.3 Measuring Process Performance

To plan, control, and improve processes, you must measure how well a process performs, and predict how process changes will affect the performance. Typical questions are these:

- What is the current performance?
- Is this value "good?"
- Is it changing?
- How can I make the value "better?"

The first three questions relate to the quantitative management of the process. The last question relates to improving the process.

William Florac and Anita Carleton identify five issues for process management [Florac, 1999, Section 1.4]. I have reordered and extended these to obtain six characteristics of "good" process performance:

- The process is defined (completeness, compatibility).
- The process is being followed (compliance, consistent use).
- The process is stable (repeatable, low variability).
- The process is effective (capable).
- The process is efficient (productivity, affordable).
- The process is predictable (future performance, effects of changes).

Table 26-1 identifies possible measures for each characteristic. Process performance measurements often involve a time dimension. You might track the amount of variation in some measured process characteristic versus time to determine process stability or the degree of improvement. Regardless of the process performance measure you choose, you compare the measured performance values to a target (goal) value to decide if the process is performing acceptably. The target value may be specified by a customer or it may represent some obvious criterion, such as the fraction of all branch instructions in a software product that are exercised by a set of test cases. A process must meet multiple goals, which often reflect business objectives, customer desires, and legal statutes. Each organization chooses particular measurements based on its business objectives.

Table 26-1 *Possible Measures of Process Performance*

Goal	Measure	Comments
Completeness (fit to organization's needs)	Number of waivers granted within a specified time interval	What fraction of projects receive waivers?
Completeness (fit to organization's needs)	The number of process elements added, changed, and deleted during tailoring	Is substantial tailoring needed for every project?
Completeness (growth)	Number of process elements added within a specified time interval	Count the number of standards and procedures added.
Completeness (coverage)	Fraction of unmapped WBS elements	A large fraction of WBS elements that are not tied to process elements (products, activities) indicates a poor fit.
Compliance	Number of discrepancy reports generated by Quality Assurance audits	The discrepancy reports are classified by severity, and are normalized by the number of workers assigned to the project.
Compliance	Fraction of staff who have completed the training required for their role(s)	If untrained, then it is likely the staff will be unable to use the process correctly, if at all.
Stability (volatility)	The number of process elements changed within a specified time interval	Count the number of standards and procedures that are revised. Also, are there a large number of change requests?
Stability	The rate of staff turnover	Loss of trained staff has the largest impact for "learned" processes: agile, and the least impact for well-documented processes.
Effectiveness	Product performance	This could be any of the measures described in Chapters 24, "Determining Product Performance," and 25, "Determining Product Quality."

Goal	Measure	Comments
Effectiveness	Product quality	One example is the estimated residual defect density (defects per source line of code) at the time the product is delivered.
Effectiveness	Test coverage	Low coverage may correlate to more defects reported during operational use.
Effectiveness	Defects discovered	Expressed as a fraction of the (estimated) total lifetime defects.
Effectiveness	Defect leakage to subsequent phases	Also called defect containment or the process defect profile.
Effectiveness	The total number of trouble reports and action items, classified by type	These indicate that exceptional events are occurring.
Effectiveness (of estimation process)	Estimating accuracy	This is the difference between the original estimate and the final actual values. The quantities estimated could be effort, cost, schedule, product quality, or product performance. If legitimate changes occur to the estimated quantity (adds, changes, or deletes), you must adjust the original estimated value and use the adjusted value as the reference point. Also, consider measures such as MMRE (mean magnitude of relative error), PRED, and EQF.
Effectiveness (for a subprocess under statistical process control)	Capability	In SPC, this is the number of values measured within a particular time interval that lie within specified performance limits. These limits indicate what is acceptable to the customer or the process owner.

(continues)

Table 26-1 *Possible Measures of Process Performance (continued)*

Goal	Measure	Comments
Effectiveness	Customer satisfaction (problem reports, complaints, canceled orders/subscriptions, failure to renew)	It is often hard to obtain data on why customers are unhappy. Some leave, so you cannot "measure" them. Also, many people dislike conveying bad news or confronting a vendor. Third-party surveys are one approach.
Effectiveness	Website performance (see Chapter 24)	Tracking site hits and visit ratios is a way to obtain information quickly, cheaply, and without confrontation. Tracking sales per visit ties directly to business objectives (revenues).
Effectiveness	Help desk performance	This is another way to gauge customer satisfaction. Besides obtaining problem reports and suggestions (a form of survey), you can use quantitative measures such as the average waiting time, service time, and fraction of callers that balk or renege.
Efficiency	Productivity (or production coefficient)	Remember to define this measure carefully!
Efficiency	Cycle time	The elapsed time between specified project life cycle milestones or process anchor points. Closely related to productivity.
Efficiency	Rework percentage	Expressed as a fraction of the total effort (or labor cost) expended on the project. Rework often has a large impact on productivity and cycle time.
Efficiency	The ratio of costs for defect prevention, defect removal, and useful work	Also see the cost of quality.

Goal	Measure	Comments
Efficiency	Defect removal costs	You usually classify these costs by product type, phase detected, phase injected, etc. (These are a refinement of the preceding two measures.)
Efficiency	Rework as a fraction of total effort	
Efficiency	Cost Performance Index (CPI) and Schedule Performance Index (SPI)	These are earned value performance indices for a project.
Predictability	MMRE, PRED, minimum/maximum range, and other measures of estimation accuracy	All predictability measures may depend on time if the estimates involve rates. You may be able to use process performance models to compute the effects of multiple factors on the estimation error.
Predictability	Probability distribution for an estimated quantity or related statistics	One statistic is the coefficient of variation. Another is the maximum error for X% confidence.

Many process performance measures depend on measurements of products and projects. For example, you use product size and project effort to compute process productivity. Similarly, you use the effort expended to perform peer reviews and the number of defects found to compute the productivity for defect removal. In addition, defect density equals the number of defects divided by the product size, and so you can consider it both a product characteristic and a process characteristic. Some attributes, such as size, appear in multiple measures. You cannot afford to measure everything. Chapter 4, "Measurement and Estimation," described the goal-question-metric method to select appropriate measures. A possible goal for a process improvement program might be to improve product quality, defined as the defect density at delivery. Table 26-2 shows an example of questions for this goal. Some of the measured quantities appeared in the estimation model for the maintenance process described in Chapter 6, "Estimating Annual Maintenance Costs." Measurement M4.2 indicates that two test cases found the same error, or that the error "re-appeared" after it was repaired (a symptom of poor configuration management).

Table 26-2 *GQM Example for Improving Product Quality*

Q1: What constitutes the product?

M1.1: Version number

M1.2: List of modules: name, type

Q2: What are the product's characteristics?

M2.1: Total number of modules

M2.2: Total size of release (SLOC)

M2.3: Total size added

M2.4: Total size modified

M2.5: Total size used unchanged

M2.6: Average cyclomatic complexity of the modules

Q3: What faults were detected prior to testing?

M3.1: How many modules were peer reviewed?

M3.2: What fraction of code was peer reviewed?

M3.3: How many unique faults were reported? (by type)

Q4: What failures were detected by testing?

M4.1: Number of valid, unique defects found (by type)

M4.2: Number of valid, unique defects reported twice; see text

M4.3: Total effort for initial testing

M4.4: Total effort for repairing defects (rework)

M4.5: Total effort for retesting fixes

M4.6: Total effort for general regression testing

M4.7: Total CPU execution time for initial testing

M4.8: Total CPU execution time for retesting fixes

M4.9: Total CPU execution time for regression testing

Q5: What failures were detected by users?

M5.1 Total valid software failures reported (by type and severity)

M5.2 Total valid unique software failures reported (by type and severity)

26.4 Measuring the Cost of Quality[3]

One measure of process performance is the *cost of quality (CoQ)*, which equals the costs incurred due to poor quality, plus the costs incurred to achieve good quality. Table 26-3 shows that each of these costs has two components. The fourth column in the table gives examples of each type of cost. Because software development is labor-intensive, the effort expended performing various activities is often a significant cost contributor.

---

[3] This section generally follows [Houston, 1996]. See the "Recommended Reading" section.

Table 26-3 *Cost of Quality Components*

Class	Component	Description	Examples
Costs due to poor quality (the cost of rework)	Cost of internal failures or faults	Faults and failures detected before product shipment	Effort for defect tracking, causal analysis, rework, retest, and temporary workarounds
	Cost of external failures	Faults and failures detected after product shipment	Effort for customer support, problem analysis, problem correction, and distributing patches
			Cost of warranty repairs and replacements, penalties (consequential and liquidated damages), litigation, and loss of future sales (due to loss of reputation and customer goodwill)
Costs to achieve good quality	Cost of appraisal	Measure the quality of implemented products	Effort for testing, parts inspection (product assurance), and independent validation and verification
			Cost of code analysis tools, test tools, and test facilities
	Cost of prevention	Activities to improve the quality of future products	Requirements elicitation and validation, design reviews, prototyping, code reviews, quality assurance audits, Configuration Management, measurement and analysis, process improvement, and staff training

Figure 26-3 shows that the costs due to poor quality and costs of achieving good quality vary inversely. In this simplified view, eliminating all defects requires an infinite amount of money, but it does drive the failure costs to zero. For manufacturing, increasing the defect prevention effort greatly reduces appraisal costs. This is not possible for software because testing is the only way to detect certain types of defects.

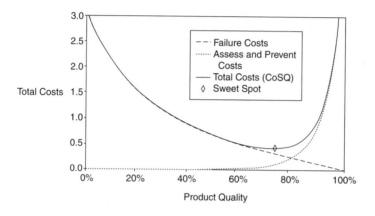

Figure 26-3 *The Cost of Quality model*

Stephen Knox developed a theoretical *Cost of Software Quality (CoSQ)* model tied to the SEI Software Capability Maturity Model (SW-CMM) [Knox, 1993]. His model estimates the costs for the four components shown in Table 26-3 at each CMM level. Figure 26-4 shows his estimates. For SW-CMM Level 3 organizations, Knox's model suggests that CoSQ is about half of the total development costs. (One way to view the cost of quality is that it represents the difference between the actual and ideal costs of producing a product.) Dan Houston and Bert Keats state that the CoSQ ranges from 20% to 70% of software development costs, compared to 5% to 25% of company sales for manufactured products [Houston, 1998]. (Note the different units of measure.)

Figure 26-5 shows a spreadsheet with sample cost of quality data. Column A identifies the type of cost, and column B shows the specific activities. This example represents activities for a simple consumer product that consists primarily of software. Columns E through I indicate the phases of the production process. To show the quality-related costs, the construction phase is split into two parts: Make the Product, and Integrate and Test the Product. Because this is a consumer product, beta testing occurs during the Transition phase, resulting in addition of some features and some rework. Columns J, K, and L indicate effort expended during the first 18 months after product release. (You would extend these if the product has a longer life.)

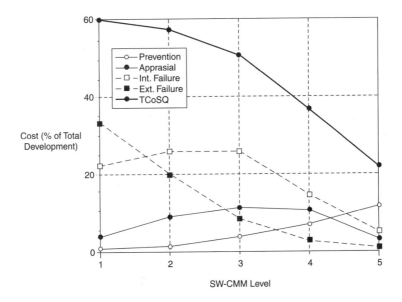

Figure 26-4 *The Software Cost of Quality model [Knox, 1993]*

Rows 7 through 20 show the effort by phase for each activity. During creation of the product, there is no effort to deal with external failures. This particular example assumes that the team adds no new features during the 18-month operational phase. Thus, there is no effort associated with internal failures and appraisals after Transition ends. Row 4 shows the fraction of effort expended by phase for the entire reporting period (analyze requirements through operational month 18). Testing constitutes the majority of quality-related costs (32% = 65,000/205,250). Overall, CoSQ equals 59% of the total development effort. The relative amounts of "normal" creation effort and quality-related effort vary by phase. This means that the apparent cost of quality, expressed as a percentage of total development costs (or total product life cycle costs), depends on the phases that you include. (This is the same problem discussed for defining productivity in Chapter 4.) Considering only the development phases, CoSQ = 49%. Considering the total for the product life (through the 18 calendar-month operational period) CoSQ = 53%. The value of CoSQ continues to increase as the operational period continues because the developer expends effort to deal with external failures, and to maintain configuration control of the code. (This also includes effort for peer reviews and quality assurance of repaired code.)

Note N40, "Collecting Cost of Quality Data," provides guidance for measuring the cost of quality.

Product: Consumer Product
Vendor: Model 1234

Cost Type	Activity	Percent of CoSQ	Cumul.	Analyze Reqmts	Design Product	Make Product	Integrate and Test	Transition	"Reporting Period" 0-6	7-12	12-18
	Effort (% of CoSQ)	100%		2%	6%	12%	50%	16%	5%	5%	4%
	Effort (phrs)	117130	117130	1775	7115	14045	59070	18445	6280	5540	4860
Activity											
Internal Failure	Log and Analyze Defects	0%	400	30	100	100	150	20			
	Rework	2%	1895	80	380	935	300	200			
	Re-review and Retest	0%	155	15	35	60	30	15			
External Failure	Log and Consolidate Problem Reports	9%	10500						4000	3500	3000
	Analyze Problem Reports	1%	1050						400	350	300
	Rework	2%	2450						900	800	750
	Retest	1%	1350						500	450	400
	Distribution of Patches	0%	400						160	120	120
Appraisal	Inspect Shipments from Suppliers	0%	350	50	200	100	0	0			
	Inspect Items Fabricated/Assembled	1%	650	0	0	550	90	10			
	All testing (Excludes Retest)	55%	65000	0	0	0	50000	15000			
Prevention	Peer Reviews	5%	6165	300	1200	3900	0	600	50	60	55
	Configuration on Management	14%	16325	800	3200	5400	5000	1600	120	100	105
	Quality Assurance	9%	10440	500	2000	3000	3500	1000	150	160	130
Creation	Analyze, Design, Code, and Fabricate		104800	8500	35000	58500	1700	1100			
	Total Development Effort by Phase		205250	10275	42115	72545	60770	19545			
	Development Effort by Phase (%)		100%	5%	21%	35%	30%	10%			
	CoSQ/ Total Development Effort (%)		49%	17%	17%	19%	97%	94%			

Figure 26-5 *Cost of software quality example*

26.5 Predicting Process Performance

Process performance models can estimate baseline process values to guide project managers, and to evaluate the potential benefits of improving various process activities. (These models support the goals of CMMI Maturity Levels 4 and 5.) Predictive models help answer questions such as these:

- How do process parameters affect project productivity, cost, and schedule?
- How do process performance parameters relate to product quality?
- How can we improve our process? (What is the increase in product quality if I invest more effort in design instead of testing?)

No single model can estimate all quantities of interest. Table 26-4 shows three types of predictive process models listed in order of increasing sophistication. The following paragraphs briefly describe each model.

Table 26-4 *Types of Predictive Process Models*

Type	*Handles Unstable Process*	*Representation of Process Mechanisms*	*Comments*
Statistical	No	None	Uses statistics to describe the variation of outputs of a stable process.
Functional	No	Explicit	Parametric models with inputs and algorithms based on causal mechanisms.
Dynamic (responsive)	Yes	Implicit (via propagation)	Systems of coupled equations embody the causal mechanisms. Solve numerically to obtain predicted behavior.

Statistical models assume that the underlying process is unvarying (stable), and use statistical techniques to predict future values of process performance measures. Statistical models provide no insight into the causal mechanisms responsible for the observed performance values, however.

Functional models represent casual relationships as algorithms with input parameters. The classic example is the parametric models used to estimate project effort and schedule. Another example is staged models. Staged models assume that the production process is operating in a steady state, and calculate the number of defects injected and removed in each phase, the number of defects propagating (leaking) into downstream phases, and the defect density of the product at delivery.

Dynamic models view processes as sets of activities or subsystems that influence one another, representing them using a set of coupled equations. Dynamic process models calculate the effects of changing conditions during a project, although the characteristics of the activities and their interactions remain constant over time. The models use numeric techniques to calculate the output quantities from the coupled equations. These models integrate a set of coupled first order differential equations that are integrated in discrete time steps. One characteristic of such models is that they tend to "blow up" exponentially. Model builders must carefully balance the equations to avoid this. The three main uses of dynamic quantitative process performance models are as follows:

- Research to identify key factors and understand interactions between factors
- A "project simulator" to train managers, engineers, and even customers
- A tool to plan and control actual projects

You can use a (validated) system dynamics model of software development like a parametric model before or during a project for estimation, planning, and control.

Table 26-5 identifies specific models of each type, including abbreviations often encountered in the literature for some of the models. Estimators have used all of these in some way. Later sections address the most important ones. (Previous chapters have discussed some already. I included them in the table to give a complete list.) Classifying the models into the three types (statistical, functional, and dynamic) is only an approximation because some models have characteristics of more than one type.

Table 26-5 *Models to Predict Process Performance*

Type	Name	Description	Examples
Statistical	Statistical process control (SPC)	Predicts statistics (mean, standard deviation) for a single process parameter.	Often used to predict peer review performance. See [Florac, 1999].
Functional	Parametric models (calibrate and then predict)	Provides a statistical prediction based on a function of multiple variables, calibrated using regression with historical data.	COCOMO, SLIM, RADC Defect Model.
Functional	COQUALMO (two-part parametric model)	Computes delivered defects using two parametric models to predict defects injected, and the defects removed.	Predicts requirements, design, and code defects. Models removal of defects by automated analysis, peer reviews, and testing.
Functional (algorithmic)	Case-based reasoning (CBR) (search and average)	Selects the historical data points that are "closest" in N-dimensional space to the point representing the process to be estimated. Averages the performance value(s) associated with these points to obtain the estimated value.	Essentially a function that estimates project effort based on a set of characteristics. The technique is applicable to other quantities. The ANGEL tool is an example [Scofield, 1995] and [Shepperd, 1997].
Functional	Neural net (NN) (train and then predict)	Calculates a single output value using multiple input values. The model is a predefined network of "neurons" that are trained using historical data. Predicting the accuracy of the output value is difficult.	Two stages: train and predict. The estimating function evolves during training. Researchers have built neural network models to estimate project effort and schedule, and product reliability.
Functional	Bayesian belief network (BBN)	A Bayesian belief network is an acyclic graph and an associated set of probability tables. The nodes are discrete directed or continuous variables. The arcs are causal or relevance relations between variables. The estimator sets input values, and the model uses rigorous mathematics to compute the output values.	Executes fixed rules to convolve conditional probabilities. To set the many probabilities needed, modelers may use data and even learning techniques (similar to neural network models, but usually must make subjective estimates. An estimate requires many calculations and, in this sense, these models are similar to

(continues)

Table 26-5 *Models to Predict Process Performance (continued)*

Type	Name	Description	Examples
			system dynamics models (described below). Bayesian belief networks explicitly account for uncertainty, however, while system dynamics models use Monte Carlo techniques.
Functional (staged)	Defect removal model (DRM)	Represents defect injection and removal for a fixed set of phases, predicting defects in later stages based on values measured in earlier stages.	Calibrated using measured efficiencies. For examples, see [Humphrey, 1989] and [Kan, 2003].
Functional (staged)	Remus and Zilles	A two-stage leakage model, which includes "bad fixes," that is solved in closed form.	Used for peer review and test data. See Secton 6.3.2 in [Kan, 2003].
Functional	Reliability growth (sequentially fit a predefined function)	Chooses a particular function to model the error detection (testing) process. Refits this function each time a data point arrives. The function's coefficient values represent the software quality.	A key concern is that hundreds of possible models exist, and no one can predict *a priori* which model will best represent a particular project. Requires integrated,working code to provide the necessary failure data.
Dynamic	System dynamics model (SDM)	Represents information flows within a process using coupled first-order differential equations. Coupling is based on analysis of the process. Rate equations and coefficients are based on historical data or guesses. Numerically integrates these equations forward in time, calculating many quantities (product, project, and process). During a run, the estimator can change the conditions and observe how the process responds.	Executes fixed rules derived from data and guesses. The rules are first order differential equations. Stability is sometimes a problem. Often lack detailed historical data to quantify the many relations, causing modelers to use heuristic models with subjective estimates of parameters.

26.6 Statistical Process Control

If your process is well defined, used correctly, and stable, you can predict its performance within certain limits using statistical process control techniques [Florac, 1999]. Statistical process control (SPC) works as follows. Engineers choose particular process performance measures that are observable and controllable (directly or indirectly). They collect and analyze measurements, track these measures over time, and then adjust the process to bring the performance measures within the desired limits. (Figure 26-2 showed the feedback loop used in process management.) Once the process is established (defined, used properly, and stabilized), it operates within known levels of variability. (The process is "under statistical control.") You can then predict process performance (within stated limits) for the process, providing realistic, achievable estimates of process-related quantities. (If the process performance is not acceptable, then you can either improve and restabilize the process, or you can renegotiate the criteria for acceptability.)

Stability and capability are important concepts for statistical process control. Suppose that you make many measurements of a process performance parameter, x. Because of variations in executing the process, the measured values are not identical. The variation arises from common causes and special causes. *Common causes* are intrinsic to the process itself, and are characterized by a stable probability distribution. In this sense, they are predictable. *Special causes* are unusual, unpredictable events that cause the measured value to deviate significantly from the majority of measured values, the ones characterized by the stable distribution. The development team, assisted by process engineers, tries to eliminate all special causes of variation. If an unexpected situation does occur, the team must identify when the unusual influence was active, and remove all measurements collected during this interval so that they do not affect the calculation of the parameters of the stable distribution.

A *stable process* is governed only by common causes, and a series of measurements typically produces a distribution like the one shown in Figure 26-6. Most of the measured values lie near the point x0, with tails extending in both directions. Using the measured data and standard statistical techniques, you can calculate statistics such as the average, median, and standard deviation for the set of measurements.[4] Most of the data points will lay between a *lower control limit (LCL)* and an *upper control limit (UCL)*. These limits are approximately plus or

---

[4] You can replace the continuous probability distribution function with a histogram for some analyses. Histograms group data into bins. Calculations of statistics using grouped data must adjust the values to account for the effects of bin size. W. F. Sheppard developed corrections for grouping of data [Sheppard, 1898]. These corrections apply only when the distribution is continuous, and the distribution tapers off in both directions. Sheppard's corrections are described in most statistics textbooks. One reference is [Arkin, 1967].

minus three standard deviations from the mean value.[5] The essential concept is
that you can characterize a process by a mean value (the centerline or CL) and
the calculated control limits (the *natural process limits*). The natural process limits are the *voice of the process*. You can use measurements of past performance to
determine the centerline and the control limits for a process. These values only
serve as reliable predictors of future process performance if the underlying
process is stable.

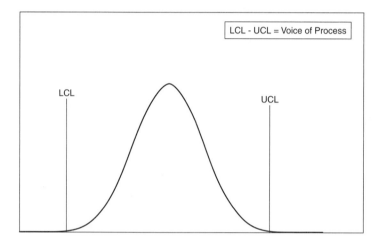

Figure 26-6 *Process variation with control limits*

Even though a process is stable, it may not be performing acceptably when
compared to customer requirements, project goals, or organizational objectives.
Figure 26-7 shows the same curve with two additional pairs of limits, called
specification limits. The first set of limits, LSL_1 and USL_1, are widely spaced and
lie outside of the control limits for the process so the process is acceptable. The
second pair of limits, LSL_2 and USL_2, is closely spaced, and lie inside of the
process' control limits. In this case, a large number of the data points will lie
outside of the specified limits. A *capable process* has a variation (of some
attribute) that is within specified limits. (Capable processes are always stable.)
Because the customer usually specifies the acceptable limits, the specification
limits are the *voice of the customer*. (Project engineers may also set specification
limits based on design constraints.) Bill Florac and Anita Carleton describe
quantitative measures of process capability in Section 7.3 of [Florac, 1999].

---

[5] You need to make some adjustments based on the type of data, the assumed distribution, and
small sample sizes. See Appendix A in [Florac, 1999]. Section 8.2 and Appendix B.2 in [Florac, 1999]
explain why three sigma is the appropriate choice.

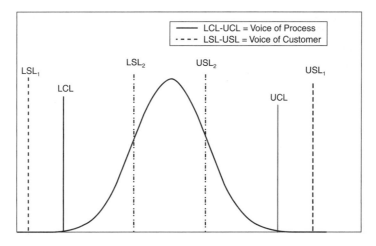

Figure 26-7 *Process variation with control and specification limits*

Summary of the Key Points

1. Common causes are inherent to the process and make the measured data points to vary randomly within the control limits.

2. Special causes arise due to unusual, anomalous events, which cause the measured data points to vary non-randomly. (The points often lie outside of the control limits.)

3. The voice of the process indicates the level of performance that is actually achievable.

4. The voice of the customer indicates the level of performance that is desired (the goal or target).

You use statistics to calculate control limits, but the details depend on the type of data. *Variables data* usually represents measurements of continuous phenomena such as physical quantities or amounts. *Attributes data* arises from counting objects that meet particular criteria such as faults of a particular type. Analysts treat some measured quantities as variables even though they are determined by counting because they represent the size of the total population. Examples are requirements, lines of code, and defects. Classifying data as either attributes data or variables data really depends on how the data is collected and used, not whether the measurement is discrete or continuous. For good discussion of this distinction, see Section 4.3.2 in [Florac, 1999]. To compute correct control limits, you must record when process changes occur, and then group the data based on these times. To control the process, you need to decide when you have enough data to calculate adequately accurate estimates of the natural process limits. For details, see Section 4.2 of [Florac, 1999].

Processes can exhibit various types of anomalous behavior over time:

- Cycles
- Gradual trends
- Rapid shift in level
- Unstable mixture (due to two or more error sources)
- Bunching of data values (near the centerline)
- Stratification

Florac and Carleton discuss each of these in Section 6.2 of [Florac, 1999].

The best way to detect time-dependent behavior is to use control charts, which plot measured values as a function of time. Figure 26-8 shows an example. The only requirement for the "time" variable is that it increases monotonically. Instead of time, you could use other measures such as the cumulative number of units produced or the number of trouble reports processed by a customer support department. The usual assumption is that time advances in equal increments.

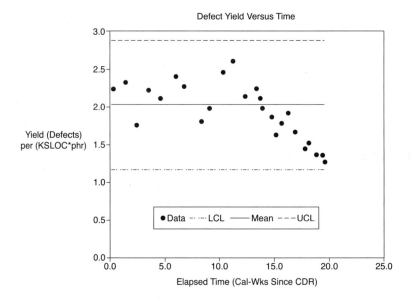

Figure 26-8 *Sample control chart*

You can obtain the values plotted on a control chart from any statistic that is defined for a sequence of individual measurements.[6] The values can represent individual data points, averages of several points in a subgroup, ranges of the values in a subgroup, moving averages, or moving ranges. Consequently, there are several different kinds of control charts, depending on the data type (variable or attribute), the sample size, the range of values (for variables data), or the type of distribution (for attributes data). Florac and Carleton explain how to choose the appropriate charts for a particular situation in Chapter 5 in [Florac, 1999].

Control charts work even if the variation in a process is not normally distributed. William Florac and Anita Carlton explain that the assumption of a normal distribution only affects the factors used to adjust the statistics for bias and to compute control limits [Florac, 1999, page 230]. In addition, they explain why choosing three sigma limits will never cause an excessive rate of false alarms, even if the process' underlying distribution is distinctly non-normal [Florac, 1999, pages 227–230].

Control charts provide an easy way to detect if a process is stable, is experiencing anomalies, or has changed its baseline performance. Section 7.1 in [Florac, 1999] gives a good discussion with examples showing how to use the various types of control charts to interpret process behavior. In particular, see Figure 7.2 on pages 160–161. Florac and Carleton discuss other ways to evaluate process stability in Section 4.2 of their book.

The value of statistical process control for estimators is that projects in the organization can set realistic, quantitative goals for product quality and process performance. The degree of variation of the chosen characteristics is predictable, and provides a known baseline for tracking.

26.7 Staged Defect Removal Models

Software engineers must build and integrate all parts before they can thoroughly test the product so they cannot measure the product's quality and performance until construction is completed.[7] It is then too late to make any process changes that would affect the product's quality. Project managers and software engineers need an "early warning system" to proactively manage the quality of software products and the software development process. Because software developers often execute a series of subprocesses over time, a possible approach is to use measurements from the early subprocesses to predict the performance of later subprocesses, the product quality, and project effort.

---

[6] A statistic is a single-valued function of observable random variables that is itself an observable random variable and that only contains known parameters [Mood, 1974].

[7] As explained in Chapter 25, even when testing is done, you will not precisely know the product's dependability and reliability. Some defects will remain after any specified amount of testing.

A *staged defect removal model* (DRM) predicts the number of defects injected and removed in specific development phases, and so gives more information for project planning and control than simple parametric models such as the RADC model and COQUALMO described in Chapter 25. The process is viewed as a series of activities that alternately inject and remove defects. Figure 26-9 shows how the number of remaining defects varies with time. For example, during coding, programmers create code, and inadvertently inject defects in the code. They then inspect the code to identify and remove these defects (faults). In the figure, the code inspection occurs at time 0.63, and the level of remaining defects is slightly less than 30. Then testing begins, progressing through integration testing, alpha testing, and beta testing. The programmers develop no code during the testing phase (except for implementing any minor features that were overlooked and correcting any faults discovered). Thus, each successive test phase reduces the number of remaining defects. Undetected defects propagate to later phases of the production process.

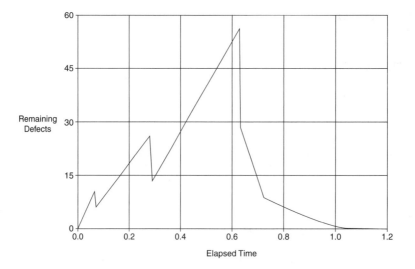

Figure 26-9 *Alternation of defect injection and removal*

If your production process is defined and stable, you can use measurements from past projects to determine the injection and removal rates for each stage, and so predict the defect discovery profiles for future projects (assuming that the product and the production process are similar to those of previous projects).

The number of predicted defects depends on whether defects are passive or active. A passive defect causes no additional defects downstream, while an active defect creates additional defects in subsequent work products. For example, a requirement defect may cause several errors in a design document, and each of these design errors may cause multiple errors in the code. The remainder of this section describes a staged defect removal model to study the multiplication ("expansion") caused by active defects.

This model estimates defects for three work products: requirements, design, and code, denoted by R, D, and C, respectively. The model assumes a simple life cycle with phases: analysis, design, code, integration test, alpha test, and beta test, abbreviated as A, D, C, IT, AT, and BT. It includes a simple time distribution to indicate the duration of each phase. Table 26-6 shows the phases, where "PR" denotes the peer review of the work product from the preceding phase. The model has seven parameters.

#	Description
3	Number of defects injected (added) when creating each work product
2	Expansion multiplier for defects into the following work product
1	Detection efficiency of all peer reviews for all defect types
1	Detection efficiencies of all tests for all defect types

Initially, the three work products (requirements, design, and code) have zero defects. The values added (injected) represent typical values for defects/KSLOC but you can use another measure if you desire. In this table, an undetected requirements defect causes three defects in the design, and an undetected design defect causes three defects in the code. This model assumes that peer reviews detect all defects with equal efficiency (60%) and that all tests detect all defects with equal efficiency (75%).

Table 26-6 *Process Model Parameters*

Phase	ADD			EXPANSION			DETECT		
	R	D	C	R	D	C	R	D	C
A	10.0								
A-PR							60%		
D		20.0		3.0					
D-PR							60%	60%	
C			40.0		3.0				
C-PR							75%	75%	75%
IT							75%	75%	75%
AT							75%	75%	75%
BT							75%	75%	75%

The model uses the preceding assumptions and parameters to calculate total defects in each work product at each stage. Table 26-7 shows the calculated defect densities (in defects per KSLOC). The three regions track defects in the three work products separately. This model predicts the (validated unique) defects that users will find during operational use by work product, normalized by the delivered size. The model assumes that reviewers and testers detect some defects in previous work products (e.g., by tracing back to find the root cause). This model assumes, however, that the developers must also find all of the "expanded" defects in the downstream work product as well. (This depends on how your detection and correction process works. If you can identify the root cause and then trace it downstream to locate all of its progeny, you can remove the "expanded" defects when you find the causal defect. If you lack traceability, however, you must find every instance of the "expanded" defect. The staged model can represent either process.)

Figure 26-10 shows the number of remaining defects versus time for two cases. For passive defects, the expansion multiplier equals zero. For active defects, the multiplier equals three. Each of the first three stages injects defects, and removes some of them. Then the three test phases successively reduce the number of defects. The figure illustrates, as expected, that a process that cannot trace "expanded" defects produces a poorer quality product.

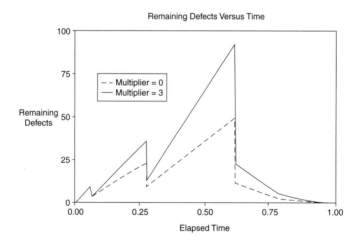

Figure 26-10 *Total defects versus elapsed time*

Table 26-7 *Calculated Defects by Work Product and Phase*

Phase	Requirements				Design				Code				Total
	Add	Expd	Det	Rem	Add	Expd	Det	Rem	Add	Expd	Det	Rem	
Start				0.00				0.00				0.00	0.00
A	10.0			10.00				0.00				0.00	10.00
A-PR			6.00	4.00				0.00				0.00	4.00
D				4.00	20.0	12.00		32.00				0.00	36.00
D-PR			2.40	1.60			19.20	12.80				0.00	14.40
C				1.60				12.80	40.0	38.40		78.40	92.80
C-PR			1.20	0.40			9.60	3.20			58.80	19.60	23.20
IT			0.30	0.10			2.40	0.80			14.70	4.90	5.80
AT			0.08	0.03			0.60	0.20			3.68	1.23	1.45
BT			0.02	0.01			0.15	0.05			0.92	0.31	0.36

To calibrate the model, you can count the defects for each root cause discovered at each process stage, and divide by the delivered software size to get the observed defect density. As a simple example, assume that there is no expansion of defects into other downstream work products. If so, then the defect model for each work product is independent of the models for the other work products. Define these model parameters.

Activity	Parameter	Meaning
Requirements definition	RI	Requirement defects injected per size unit
Requirements peer review	RR	Requirements peer review detection efficiency
Design peer review	DR	Design peer review detection efficiency
Code peer review	CT	Code peer review detection efficiency
Integration test	IT	Integration test detection efficiency
Alpha test	AT	Alpha test detection efficiency
Beta test	BT	Beta test detection efficiency

The density of requirements defects at the end of each sequential activity is

$$R_1 = RI$$
$$R_2 = RI*(1 - RR)$$
$$R_3 = RI*(1 - RR)*(1 - DR)$$
$$R_4 = RI*(1 - RR)*(1 - DR)*(1 - CR)$$
$$R_5 = RI*(1 - RR)*(1 - DR)*(1 - CR)*(1 - IT)$$
$$R_6 = RI*(1 - RR)*(1 - DR)*(1 - CR)*(1 - IT)*(1 - AT)$$
$$R_7 = RI*(1 - RR)*(1 - DR)*(1 - CR)*(1 - IT)*(1 - AT)*(1 - BT)$$

The observed densities are

$$O_1 = \text{None detected}$$
$$O_2 = RI*RR$$
$$O_3 = RI*(1 - RR)*DR$$
$$O_4 = RI*(1 - RR)*(1 - DR)*CR$$
$$O_5 = RI*(1 - RR)*(1 - DR)*(1 - CR)*IT$$
$$O_6 = RI*(1 - RR)*(1 - DR)*(1 - CR)*(1 - IT)*AT$$
$$O_7 = RI*(1 - RR)*(1 - DR)*(1 - CR)*(1 - IT)*(1 - AT)*BT$$

Suppose that you count requirements defects through beta testing for 10 projects. You can use Excel's Solver to compute the model's coefficients. Figure 26-11 shows the results using a minimum mean magnitude of relative error (MMRE) criterion. The gray bars with the error bars are the observed values. The striped bars are the values computed by the fitted coefficients. The MMRE was 13% for this particular case. (You can also fit using a minimum sum of squared residuals criterion. See the CD-ROM.)

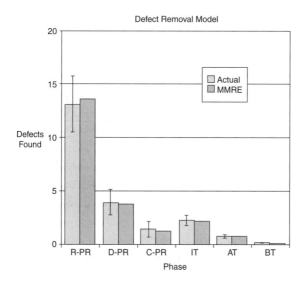

Figure 26-11 *Model predictions versus averages from 10 projects*

To estimate the total defects observed at each stage, you must use the estimated delivered size for the product, which introduces more uncertainty into the predicted values. (Either you use this value to multiply the predicted density to get the predicted defect counts for the different phases, or you use the estimated value to normalize the observed defect counts to obtain defect densities that you can compare with the model's predicted densities. Either way, you depend on the estimated delivered size.)

This model is on the CD-ROM, and you can enter separate detection efficiencies for the different types of defects and detection mechanisms. You can extend this model to handle "bad fixes."

One way to measure the capability of the development process is to see how many defects "escape" or "leak" into subsequent phases.[8] You define a matrix like the one in Table 26-8. The names of the rows and columns are the phases of the development process. Each row records the number of defects found in a particular work product. The matrix is triangular because you cannot find defects before you create the work product. The first pale-gray cell in each row is the number of defects injected when you create the work product. The following cells are the number of defects in that work product found in subsequent phases. This assumes that developers and testers discover the defects and that they identify the phase that each fault was injected (created). This matrix characterizes the performance of the process in terms of its defect removal capability. Large off diagonal values indicate a poor process, because the process does not promptly detect most defects.

---

[8] Some authors talk of "containing" defects or detecting them "in phase."

Table 26-8 *Sample Defect Leakage Matrix*

Phase Injected	Phase Detected					
	Analysis	Design	Code	Integ. Test	Alpha Test	Beta Test
Analysis	98.0	6.0	12.0	14.0	27.0	18.0
Design		142.0	38.0	23.0	17.0	8.0
Code			114.0	61.0	23.0	4.0
Integ. Test				16.0	2.0	1.0
Alpha Test					2.0	0.0
Beta Test						1.0

The matrix contains a large number of values. You can define an aggregate figure of merit to compare the performance (capabilities) of different processes [Stutzke, 1999]. The approach is to compare the total number of defects in the cells lying on the diagonal to the total number defects for the cells lying off the diagonal. Large numbers of defects lying off the diagonal indicate a poor process. A possible figure of merit is:

$$FOM = \frac{N_{prompt}}{N_{prompt} + N_{late}}$$

where N_{prompt} is the sum of the values in the cells lying on the diagonal, and N_{late} is the sum of values in all the off diagonal cells. The FOM is 100% if no leakage occurs (i.e., a perfect process). The problem with this measure is that you do not know how many defects will be detected in the future. Thus, you can only calculate this figure of merit after project completion (neglecting the defects discovered during operational use). This measure is adequate to analyze process capability and performance, and to compare processes, but provides no help in managing the process during a project.

You can also compute such values for each row. This gives insight into each phase and each activity. You can only sum across the rows, however, because the defects are in different work products. Table 26-9 shows the total and the numbers of prompt and late defects for each row in Table 26-8. The last column shows the Figure Of Merit for each work product. The row for Requirements shows that requirements peer review finds 56% (= 98/175) of the defects promptly. The peer reviews of the design documents and code find some additional requirements defects. Integration testing finds a few more. Alpha and beta testing finds the remaining 26% (= (27 + 18)/175). This indicates that the original requirements did not seem to match the users' expectations or needs. Figure 26-12 shows a category plot of the figure of merit based on the type of defect. The first three bars represent the work products (requirements, design, and code). The last three bars represent "bad fixes" that occurred repairing problems during the three types of testing. You could use a chart like this as a process performance profile.

Table 26-9: *Figure of Merit Calculation*

Phase Injected	Row Totals	Size Units	# Prompt	# Late	FOM (%)
Analysis	175.0	UCP	98.0	77.0	56%
Design	228.0	OP	142.0	86.0	62%
Code	202.0	FP	114.0	88.0	56%
Integ. Test	19.0	FP	16.0	3.0	84%
Alpha Test	2.0	FP	2.0	0.0	100%
Beta Test	1.0	FP	1.0	0.0	100%

As Figure 1-4 (Boehm's cost of repair chart) showed, finding defects later increases the cost to correct them. Thus, you might want to apply a weighting function to the numbers of defects that are found late. The weighting function increases monotonically to indicate the increasing cost of repair. For details, see [Stutzke, 1999]. For other related studies, see Chapters 4 and 6 in [Kan, 2003] and [Hudec, 1996].

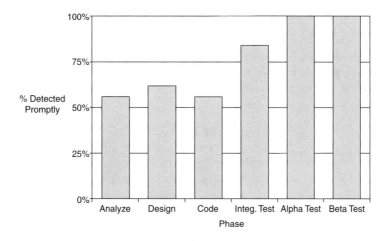

Figure 26-12 *Defect containment profile*

Staged models assume that the production process is operating in a steady state. In actuality, various factors change during the course of a project. The next section describes dynamic process models that represent the effects of these changes.

26.8 Dynamic Models

Dynamic simulations of software development processes allow investigators to study the effects of different development activities on characteristics such as software quality (effectiveness), and on project cost and development time (efficiency). Dynamic system simulation models help investigators do the following:

- Understand and validate the relationships within a complex system
- Examine sensitivity to assumptions, internal factors, and external factors
- Predict the consequences of proposed actions and options on the system

26.8.1 System Dynamics

One of the most popular approaches is system dynamics, which represents interactions among process activities using coupled equations, and then solves them using a computer to predict the dynamic behavior of the system [Forrester, 1961]. The modeler identifies entities of the software process such as activities, and describes their behavioral characteristics. The modeler also specifies influence (cause/effect) relationships between the entities. For example, work products and resources flow between entities. The quantities moving through the system are modeled as continuous quantities. Process activities cause the flows between states by creating, transforming, or destroying objects. (Some quantities [code, defects] do not enter the system, but are generated inside.) Feedback loops typically appear, and so an entity's actions (positively or negatively) affect another entity after a time delay. Figure 26-13 illustrates an influence diagram for software productivity. The signs at the arrowheads indicate if the influence increases or decreases the variable. (Rus and Collofello provide a nice example related to the cost of software quality [Rus, 2001].)

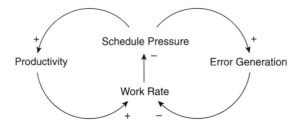

Figure 26-13 *Influence diagram for software productivity*

System dynamics derives its terminology from fluid flow, as illustrated in Figure 26-14. A *pool* collects a particular quantity (e.g., water). The *level* is the amount of fluid in a pool. (Modelers use the terms "pool" and "level" interchangeably.) Levels (pools) are shown by rectangles. The level is the net accumulation over time of flows entering and leaving a pool. The levels of all quantities jointly comprise the state of the system. Examples of quantities are people, expended effort, code, and defects. External *sources* and *sinks* are depicted as clouds. The *flow of fluid* between pools (levels), and between pools and external sources and sinks, is indicated using lines with arrows. Solid lines show flows of materials. Dashed lines show flows of information. (Some modeling tools and authors call information flows *connectors*.) Quantities having different units of measure (e.g., water and oil) have separate pools and flow over separate paths. The *rate of fluid flow* between levels, or between a level and a source or a sink, is controlled by a valve, shown as an X-shaped symbol. Feedback loops defined by the modeler adjust the flow rates. *Auxiliaries* are intermediate variables and functions used to calculate flow rates or other auxiliaries, and are shown as circles. Information and constants (shown as a horizontal line with a dot) flow into auxiliaries. Auxiliaries convert input quantities to internal units, store constants, calculate and store working values, or convert quantities to external units. Each object flows through the system along a *chain* of boxes, which represent different states of the object, and contain the amount of the object in that state at the current time, t. For example, employees could have states: newly hired, being trained, working productively, and terminated (quit, transferred, or fired).

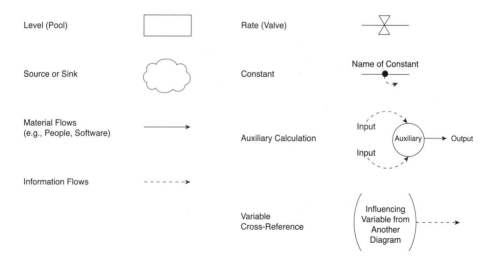

Figure 26-14 *Symbols used in system dynamics models*

Modelers use a description of the process, empirical data, and opinion to identify the quantities of interest, the flows, the links, and functions to calculate the
flow rates for the various quantities. The functions quantify the effects of the
various influences, and can depend on the amount in a pool, other rates,
endogenous (internal) events, exogenous (external) events, and auxiliaries.
Modelers base their functions on the best historical data available, supported
by any appropriate constraints on the functional form such as symmetry or
restriction to a range. The box "Failure Rate" gives an example. The modeler
usually lacks enough data to define all of the functions needed, however, and
so uses a mixture of empirical data plus heuristics. (The process is similar to
that used to define effort multipliers in a parametric effort estimation model.)
You may think that you should not define a mathematical model until you have
enough data to define the function accurately. Jay Forrester argues, however,
that omitting a significant factor just because you cannot define it precisely is
equivalent to saying that the factor has no effect [Forrester, 1961]. In addition,
Dietmar Pfahl and Günther Ruhe point out that building a dynamic simulation
provides insight into the type of measurements needed to understand a process
[Pfahl, 2003a] and [Pfahl, 2003b]. Note N41, "System Dynamics Models of Software Processes, " identifies some specific studies.

Failure Rate

After the programmers have written and integrated all of the required
code, testing and repairing the integrated product causes the failure rate
to decrease over time. Ioana Rus and James Collofello extend an exponential model [Musa, 1987] to represent the failure rate observed during
product testing, including process-specific effects [Rus, 2001]:

$$R(t) = R_0*(1 - N(t)/N_0) * F_1(\text{test effectiveness}) * F_2 (\text{test coverage})$$

where

$R(t)$ = Failure rate at time t

R_0 = Initial failure rate

$N(t)$ = Total failures observed up to time t

N_0 = Total failures observed over the entire product life

The function F_1 measures the capability of the test cases to uncover
defects. The function F_2 measures the number of test cases executed so far.
The particular form of these two functions depends on calibration data
for a particular organization and process. The modeler also needs to specify the initial failure rate, R_0. One approach is to use the Rome Laboratory
model that predicts the failure rate as a function of the defect density

(defects per source line of code) at the beginning of system integration testing:

R_0 = C * Defect density (at completion of code and unit test)

where C called the transformation ratio [McCall, 1987]. McCall et al. provide values of the transformation ratio for various types of applications.

26.8.2 Abdel-Hamid's Simulation of Software Development

Tarek Abdel-Hamid was the first to apply system dynamics to software development processes [Abdel-Hamid 1984]. Abdel-Hamid studied the effects of project management policies on software development (ignoring requirements gathering and analysis). Figure 26-15 shows the subsystems of his model.[9] Planning estimates the required effort, calculates the work force needed, and estimates the completion date. Planning updates the production schedule and directs the human resource management subsystem to hire more workers. Controlling measures and evaluates progress. Human resource management determines the number of workers available, hires additional ones, and accounts for attrition. Abdel-Hamid modeled the software production subsystem in detail, using four sectors (submodels): manpower allocation, software development, quality assurance and rework, and system testing.

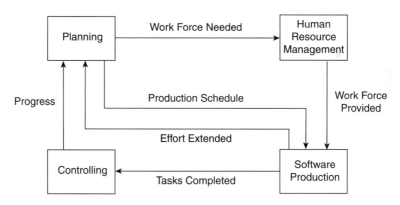

Figure 26-15 *Abdel-Hamid's four subsystems for software project management.*

---

[9] For more details, see Figure 2.3 in [Abel-Hamid, 1991].

26.8.3 Example: A Model to Study the Cost of Quality

Figure 26-16 shows a portion of a system dynamics model to study activities that affect the cost of software quality. This figure is a highly simplified consolidation of Abdel-Hamid's original model of the software development, quality assurance, and test sectors. (The box "Simplifications of Abdel-Hamid's Model" explains the major differences.) The key objects are software modules and errors (defects). Software development appears at the right side of the figure. (Abdel-Hamid calls software "tasks," but measures tasks in SLOC.) Tasks flow from top to bottom down the right side of the figure in a "chain," which corresponds to the progress of modules through a set of states. A similar chain for errors in the product appears near the center of the figure. The error chain is more complicated than the software (task) chain because of the possibility of bad fixes. The figure has two different error densities. The first represents the error density of the product when it enters inspection. The second represents the error density of the product when it enters test. The simplified model does not address repair of errors detected during testing or retesting of the repaired modules. You would model these similarly to the activities shown for repairing inspection defects. (You will have to add retesting.)

Simplifications of Abdel-Hamid's Model

Abdel-Hamid's original model distinguishes active and passive errors. (Active errors generate additional errors as time increases. An example is design errors that cause errors in the code based on the design.) Many of his rates depend on staff motivation, their ability to communicate, their experience, and other factors. For example, Abdel-Hamid assumes that productivity increases during a project as workers gain experience. I replaced the submodels associated with these effects with simple constants. For example, the inspection effort needed to detect an error really depends on several factors, but the figure shows it as a constant. (His original model uses *quality assurance* rather than *inspection*. I use the latter term to conform to modern usage.) Similarly, the testing effort needed per task depends on multiple factors, but the figure only shows dependence on the error density at test. The inspection rate is in a three-part rectangle because his model subdivides inspection into three parts having different delays. For additional details, see [Abdel-Hamid, 1991].

His model also ignores unit testing. Thus, once a module ("task") is developed, the team inspects it, performs necessary correction of errors that are discovered (rework), and passes the corrected modules to the test process. The original model ignores bad fixes to repair errors found by testing and retesting.

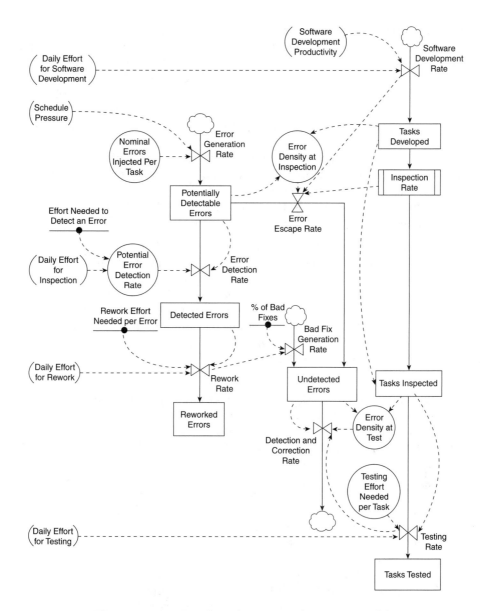

Figure 26-16 *Portion of a system dynamics model*

The far left side of the diagram shows four effort inputs that come from another part of the model, the planning subsystem. Three of these inputs correspond to components of the cost of software quality. (The model does not address the cost of external failures.) The fourth effort input corresponds to the cost of production. You can use these values to calculate process efficiency. The planning subsystem decides how to allocate available personnel to the tasks of software development, inspections, rework, and testing. The human resource management subsystem, also not shown, determines the number of personnel available. The human resource management subsystem determines whether the project needs more personnel based on the perceived backlog and rate of progress, and then hires new employees, and trains them. The human resource management subsystem includes a delay to assimilate the new employees. (This models the effects of Brooks's Law.)

The resulting model is a set of coupled first-order differential equations. (The rates are the derivatives.) The modeler or a programmer then enters the model into a simulation tool, which generates the dynamic behavior of the process integrating the equations over time in small steps. At each step, the model calculates the state of each entity, and then propagates the state to other entities. The model displays results as plots of the amount of each object (level) versus time. For software development processes, typical model outputs are effort consumption, defects injected and removed, staffing level, and completion times.

As an example, Figure 26-17 shows results from a system dynamics model of new software development. The abscissa is time measured relative to the final project duration. The ordinate is in arbitrary units. The quantities indicated with open symbols are estimates. Starting from the top, the estimated schedule ("end date") gradually rises, as does the estimated effort. The reason is that the size, shown lower in the figure, gradually increases until approximately halfway through the project. The other three curves with solid symbols represent actual values. The estimated effort increases approximately linearly during this project. Two lines show amount of software produced. The first (solid squares) is the amount of software coded but not tested. The second curve (solid diamonds) is the amount of software tested. One feature to note is that the size reaches its final value at time ~0.55, but the estimated schedule increase at this point is only half of what it will finally be. This is probably due to a delay in recognizing the true scope of the problem. In this case, the manager assigned personnel who were to do testing to write the extra code and did not hire additional personnel. This delayed the start of testing, slipping the schedule. The effort also increased due to the increase in estimated size.

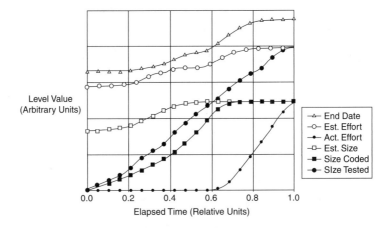

Figure 26-17 *Typical results from a system dynamics model*

You can use a closed-loop system dynamics model just like a parametric model to estimate project effort and duration. You can also couple it to other parametric cost models. Open-loop system dynamics models are well suited for planning a project and evaluating the potential impact of alternative courses of action in midstream. Several organizations have used them as a "flight simulator" to train software project managers. In this case, the fidelity of the model need not be very high. It is only necessary that the model react in a "reasonable" way to the decisions made by the manager.

26.9 Building Process Performance Models

In-process measurements and predictive estimating models are mutually supportive. Without valid data to provide a model's inputs, inaccurate predictions result. Without an accurate model, accurate input data will still not result in accurate predictions. The box "Tips on Building Process Performance Models" provides guidance on building and using such models.

Tips on Building Process Performance Models

The following steps are adapted from a 10-step process to define and use a dynamic simulation model defined by Alan Pritsker [Pritsker, 1986].

1. Formulate the objective of the study: What are the goals, questions, and measurements needed? The measurements include inputs and outputs (the independent and dependent variables). As you gain insight, you will refine these.

2. Understand the system *or* study the problem: Gather information and analyze it to understand the system structure and operations. Abstract the problem to extract the essential elements and interactions of the elements. Only include those that cause "significant influences" on the output variables of interest. (This is not easy to do. Experience helps, but it is still an art. For ideas, see Raj Jain's book [Jain, 1991].)

3. Define the model: Record the mathematical and logical relationships among the elements, external objects, plus scenarios and events (stimuli).

4. Acquire additional data: Identify, specify, and collect data to define the system configuration, characteristics, functions, and behavior (e.g., modes of operation). Also, collect data to describe external stimuli (exogenous events, workloads). Use this data to define, refine, calibrate, verify, and validate the model. (Steps 2, 3, and 4 overlap. Analysis generates new questions, causing you to collect additional data. Steps 6 and 7 use the data to verify and validate the model.) Collecting data for some characteristics may be costly, so you must evaluate the sensitivity of model outputs to the various characteristics.

5. Implement the model: Express the model in executable form (a computer program, commercial tool, or possibly a spreadsheet).

6. Verify the implementation: Test the executable model to ensure that it executes as intended. You can do peer reviews, manually check calculated values, or compare output values to results from known benchmark cases.

7. Validate the model: Establish that the model's outputs correspond to those of the real system with adequate accuracy for your intended purpose. You usually validate simulation models by using them to reproduce the results of known ("benchmark") results for the modeled system. Be sure to check configuration parameters, constants, coefficients, and units conversions. Also perform sensitivity analysis to provide insight into the uncertainty.

8. Design experiments: Design experiments to test the hypotheses under study and to produce the maximum confidence in the output data. (Raj Jain provides a good discussion in [Jain, 1991, Part IV].)

9. Conduct experiments: Execute the experiments and collect measurements.

10. Analyze results: Use statistical methods to draw inferences from the data. (Pritsker's Step 10 also implements the decisions that are based on the analyzed results.)

11. Prepare complete documentation: Describe the model, its use, and your findings.

Ioana Rus and James Collofello describe a similar five-step process for building and using system dynamics models [Rus, 2001].

Achieving predictable outputs for any process demands a degree of stability. To obtain predictions needed to control a process, you need to pick subprocesses that are performed early in the project and that influence the final outcome. You can use statistical process control to control the input parameters of a predictive process model to improve prediction accuracy. Stephen Kan points out that applying control charts and other SPC techniques to subprocesses is a piecemeal approach, however, and does not guarantee that the project team will achieve their final goals for the process, product, and project. (Only a part of the process is under SPC.) If you have validated predictive models, however, you can apply SPC in a limited sense [Kan, 2003, Section 19.4].

26.10 Recommended Reading

Joseph M. Juran defined the cost of quality measure in 1951 to help justify investments in process improvement [Hagan, 1986]. Many manufacturing and service industries use cost of quality techniques to balance their production activities and identify opportunities to reduce costs. In the late 1980s, researchers applied the concept to software quality [Daugherty, 1988]. Raymond Dion used the cost of quality model to interpret results of quality initiatives at Raytheon's Electronics Systems (RES) division [Dion, 1993]. Thomas Haley updated Dion's original study [Haley, 1995] and [Haley, 1996]. (This work won the IEEE Computer Society Software Process Achievement Award.)

William Florac and Anita Carleton focus on statistical process control techniques for software process improvement [Florac, 1999]. They describe selecting in defining measures, collecting data, and analyzing process behavior. They explain how to use control charts to evaluate process stability and capability, and how to use this information for process improvement and controlling processes. Their book is noteworthy because it provides practical guidance on selecting the correct type of control chart for particular types of data, grouping data, and interpreting patterns to draw conclusions about process performance. For additional details about the uses of control charts, see Chapters 5 and 6 in [Florac, 1999]. Stephen Kan gives a good explanation of control charts in Section 5.7 of [Kan, 2003]. For additional details in evaluating and improving process stability, see Chapters 4 and 7 in [Florac, 1999].

Various authors have proposed staged defect removal models, including [Humphrey, 1987], [Kan, 2003], and [Stutzke, 1999]. Stephen Kan provides a broad overview of software quality including possible types of product quality metrics, defect estimation models, and quality management models [Kan, 2003]. His book provides many practical examples based on his actual experience in managing software quality by controlling processes. Kan's Chapter 6 examines defect removal effectiveness and staged models, with additional material in his Section 4.2.3. He briefly discusses statistical process control. David Raffo, Warren Harrison, and Joseph Vandeville address the use of models and metrics to manage software projects [Raffo, 2000]. Also see [Kellner, 1991].

Marc Kellner, Raymond Madachy, and David Raffo provide an excellent overview of software process simulation modeling in [Kellner, 1999]. This article introduces an entire issue of the Journal of Systems and Software devoted to this topic. Papers in the issue address four modeling approaches: system dynamics (continuous simulation), general discrete event simulation, state-based process models, and rule-based languages.) Their article defines a model taxonomy, and then provides a characterization of past work in terms of these elements. This is an excellent place to start if you are interested in this field.

A project actually encompasses multiple processes. Process engineers need to decide which of these processes need to be measured and controlled based on customer requirements, business objectives, and affordability. Project management textbooks discuss ways to measure the performance of the overall project, an activity called "performance analysis." (Performance analysis in this context refers to the evaluation of how well a project meets its cost and schedule objectives.) A popular technique used for many large projects is earned value measurement. Although primarily intended for project management, some organizations have used various metrics based on earned value to assess the performance of their processes. Two good references are [Lipke, 2000] and [Lipke, 2002b].

26.11 Summary

Parametric estimation models, such as COCOMO and COQUALMO, estimate values using fixed values of the independent variables. (The same is true for parametric models that estimate product performance, product quality, and process performance.) Staged models represent the process as a static series of phases. Project, product, and process characteristics do change as a project unfolds, however. Typical changes are personnel turnover and reassignment, new or revised product requirements, and repetition of activities (rework to correct defects). Dynamic process performance models explicitly estimate changes in product quality, project performance, and process behavior arising from changes in model parameters over time.

Existing predictive process performance models are still relatively crude, but they provide information and insight for planning, controlling, and improving software production processes. Decision makers must consider the credibility of the simulation results, as well as other factors such as cost, schedule, legal constraints, and risks.

The ability of a model to predict accurately depends largely on the stability and maturity of the development processes. Organizations that do not collect consistent metrics data or do not follow the defined process, will find it difficult to build, calibrate, and use such models. Such organizations may still build reliable software, but they cannot do so predictably.

Chapter 27

Ranking and Selecting Items

Before you can estimate the size of a product or the resources required for a project or process, you must define the scope. Customers and designers often identify large lists of items (features, tasks, and services) to be implemented and delivered. Usually, the available resources (effort, time, money, and computer capacity) are not adequate to implement all of the items. To select the "best" items to implement, you need methods to help multiple individuals (the stakeholders) agree on a subset of the items.

This chapter covers the following techniques:

- Approval voting
- Nominal group technique
- Multivoting
- Multiple criteria decision making

The first three techniques all require multiple participants. Use of historical data is optional for these techniques. (Ranking and selection techniques estimate quantities that are measured using the nominal or ordinal scales.) There are powerful techniques that explicitly identify and quantify the effect of multiple attributes. Many of these techniques produce quantitative measures of the "separation" of the items. They are essentially ways of ranking alternatives, however, so I describe them here.

The following sections describe these techniques and also provide examples showing the use of each technique. You can easily implement the voting techniques using paper forms or templates. You can also implement the forms using a spreadsheet to provide dynamic data validation and error checking, thus making the form an active tool. Multiple criteria decision making uses more mathematical techniques. The book's CD-ROM provides spreadsheets for some of these. I provide references to computerized tools for the others. The box "Brainstorming" describes how to generate a list of items.

Brainstorming

There are many ways to generate a list of items. One is to examine documents, extract items, and make a list. (Many books on requirements analysis describe useful techniques.) Another is to interview users or other stakeholders to elicit their needs, requirements, and expectations. Some individuals are reticent to reveal /convey information, however.

Brainstorming is a useful technique to generate lists of items such as product features or project tasks. Brainstorming solicits ideas about a topic or problem anonymously from a group of people, and then the group organizes and prioritizes the ideas, identifying the best ones. You can use this technique for groups of any size. It usually requires only an hour or two. The group often develops a more complete list than any single individual could generate. In addition, the stakeholders tend to support the results because they contributed to producing the results.

A facilitator leads the group. The steps of the process are as follows:

1. The facilitator states the topic and objectives (the scope of the session).

2. The facilitator gives each person several blank cards and a pen.

3. The facilitator sets a time limit (15 to 30 minutes).

4. Each participant independently generates as many ideas as possible, writing one per card.

5. The facilitator collects the cards and summarizes the items on a whiteboard so that everyone can see them.

6. The group discusses each item, consolidates similar items, sharpens the item descriptions, and looks for useful associations, similarities, and trends.

7. The group rates and selects the "best" item(s) based on the session's objectives.

8. Use the rating and ranking techniques described in this chapter.

Two references are *Crawford Slip Writing* [Crawford, 1983] and *Mind Dumpster* [Hall, 1995, pp. 202–205].

27.1 Introduction

Software-intensive projects must make many kinds of decisions, as illustrated in Table 27-1. Decisions may involve product parameters, project cost and risks, and process performance.

Table 27-1 *Typical Decisions for Software-Intensive Projects*

Choose product features (with/without other constraints).
Identify the "best" design option (trade studies).
Decide whether to make, reuse, or buy.
Select a commercial off-the-shelf (COTS) component or tool.
Pick a vendor or subcontractor.
Choose a cost estimating method.
Select a risk mitigation approach.
Decide to bid or not.
Terminate software testing.
Modify work products that are already baselined.

Figure 27-1 illustrates the basic decision-making process. The process begins when the team recognizes they have a problem or issue to resolve and that there are multiple possible alternatives. Making any decision requires time and money. Thus, you must first decide whether the issue merits use of a formal decision method. If making a wrong decision will have significant impacts for the project, the team should use a formal decision method. Typical criteria to decide if a decision is "significant" are cost, delay, safety, and corporate liability. For example, if a particular component contributes 50% to the total cost of the system, careful analysis is warranted.

This chapter addresses two types of methods: voting and multiple-criteria decision making. Voting techniques allow a group to rank alternatives based on unstated criteria. Multiple-criteria decision making (MCDM) techniques allow a group of people to specifically identify important criteria, and then combine ratings of these criteria to identify the "best" alternative.

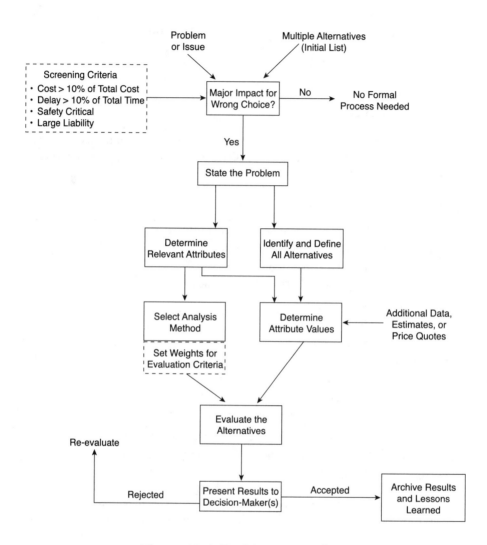

Figure 27-1 *Decision process flow*

27.2 Voting Techniques

A general problem faced by estimators is how to rank items on a list. This chapter describes three simple techniques to do this. After you have ranked (or prioritized) the items, you can select the N highest ranked ones. In some cases, you may only select a single item. For example, you can only choose one design from among several alternative designs since you can only build one design. Later sections describe other ways to address this problem.

27.2.1 Approval Voting[1]

Approval voting works as follows. Each voter can vote for (or approve of) as many items as he wants. Each voter can cast only one vote for each item however. The item with the most votes wins. (Alternately, you might decide to choose the N items with the largest numbers of votes as the winners.) Approval voting is simple to understand and use. Many governments and organizations around the world use it to elect officials.

Table 27-2 shows an example of approval voting used to select features from a list of five features, here identified as A through E. There are five voters (estimators or stakeholders) whose votes are shown by the X's in the table. The column on the right shows the total votes received by each feature. Feature D is the winner, with feature B the second choice.

Table 27-2 *Approval Voting Example*

Feature	Estimator					Total Votes
	1	2	3	4	5	
A		X				1
B		X	X		X	3
C						0
D	X	X	X	X	X	5
E	X					1
Total votes by voter	2	3	2	1	2	

The bottom row of the table shows the total votes cast by each voter. The number of votes cast varies. This means that stakeholders may not carefully consider their choices and so the result may not truly represent the best consensus.

---

[1] Several people independently proposed approval voting in the 1970s. Robert J. Weber is usually acknowledged as the person who originated and named "approval voting" in 1971.

(Section 27.2.4 discusses this issue.) To obtain a "better" result, you can use techniques that require voters to make a standardized commitment and so improve the sampling of the electorate (the stakeholders). Two ways to do this are the nominal group technique and multivoting.

27.2.2 Nominal Group Technique[2]

The nominal group technique produces a consensus of rankings. Table 27-3 lists the steps of the nominal group technique. Note that the originator of an item or idea can withdraw it prior to the start of voting. Assume that the number of items in the list is L. The facilitator allows each person to choose N items, where N is approximately the total number of items desired on the final list. (You might make N less than the final number desired to force the stakeholders to make careful decisions.) Each person must select the N most important items, ranking them from N (most important) to 1 least important. (This is a good choice since items receiving no votes will have a zero score. Scoring would be more complicated if 1 denoted the most important item. The sport of figure skating uses this convention, for example.) The facilitator collects the results and totals the values for each item. The item with the largest total wins.

Table 27-3 *Steps of Nominal Group Technique*

1. The facilitator asks each person to identify the N "best" items (N = L/5).
2. Each person chooses and ranks the N "best" items, ranking them from 1 … N. (N is the most preferred. 1 is the least.)
3. The facilitator records rankings for each item from all persons.
4. The facilitator totals the values for each item.
5. The items with highest totals are selected.
6. Optionally, discuss top few items, revise item descriptions, and repeat process.

Table 27-4 shows an example for five features (A through E) with five stakeholders (1 through 5). Each stakeholder was allowed to choose and rank the three most important items. The last column shows the total score. Feature B is best, with Feature D a close second.

---

[2] The nominal group technique (NGT) was developed by Andre L. Delbecq and Andrew H. Van de Ven in 1968 [Delbecq, 1971] and [Delbecq, 1975], and is a variation of the voting scheme proposed by Jean-Charles Borda [Borda, 1781].

Table 27-4 *NGT Example*

Feature	Estimator					Total Votes
	1	**2**	**3**	**4**	**5**	
A		1	2		2	5
B	3	2	1	3	3	12
C						0
D	2	3	3	2	1	11
E	1			1		2

Table 27-5 shows results for the same set of five features, but this time the stakeholders have ranked the items differently. Feature B is still the best, but now Features A and D are tied for second place. If only two features can be selected (due to limited resources, for example), the group will have to find some other way to break the tie to choose the second item.

Table 27-5 *NGT Example with Revised Rankings*

Feature	Estimator					Total Votes
	1	**2**	**3**	**4**	**5**	
A		3	2		2	7
B	3	2	1	3	3	12
C						0
D	1	1	3	1	1	7
E	2			2		4

27.2.3 Multivoting

In multivoting, each stakeholder is given a certain number of votes, V, to "spend" as he or she likes. V can be the number of items, N, that you want on the final list, or some fraction of the total number of items, L, in the initial list, e.g., V = L/3. A stakeholder can cast one, two, or even all V votes for a single item. Table 27-6 lists the steps for this technique. Table 27-7 shows an example for eight features (A through H) and six voters (estimators or stakeholders). Each voter is given three (3) votes to cast. The table shows the total votes for each feature and ranks the features based on these totals. Feature B is ranked first. Feature E is ranked second. Features C and D have the same total score, but Feature C was selected for third place because three stakeholders voted for it whereas only two voted for Feature D.

Table 27-6 *Multivoting Procedure*

1. Give each person V votes.
2. Each person allocates one, two, or even all votes to one or more items.
3. The facilitator asks each person for her vote.
4. The facilitator totals the votes.
5. The group eliminates the items with the fewest votes.
6. Optionally, discuss the top few items, and revise the item descriptions.
7. Repeat the process with the revised list if needed.

Table 27-7 *Example of Multivoting*

Feature	Estimator						Total Votes	Rank
	1	2	3	4	5	6		
A							0	—
B	3	1	1	1	1		7	1
C			1	1		1	3	3
D		1			2		3	4
E		1	1	1		1	4	2
F							0	—
G						1	1	5
H							0	—
Total votes cast	3	3	3	3	3	3		

You can use a Pareto histogram to see how close the scores of various items are. Figure 27-2 shows an example. Feature B is clearly preferred. Features E, C, and D are close together. A change of one vote from E to C (or D) would cause C (or D) to move into second place. Feature G is a distant fifth, and is only one vote away from obscurity (with Features A, F, and H). Such histograms help you evaluate the strength of the stakeholders' preferences.

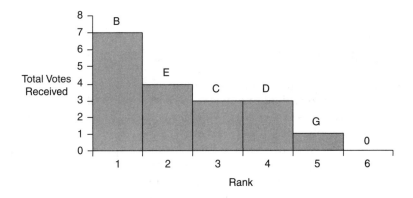

Figure 27-2 *Pareto ranking of the scores*

27.2.4 Other Voting Schemes

There are many types of voting schemes described in the literature. In *plurality voting*, each voter is allowed to cast a single vote for one item in the list (one of the candidates). Variations on plurality voting include the possibility of having a runoff election if two or more candidates have vote totals that are closely comparable. The Hare *Single Transferable Vote (STV)* system and the *Borda count* allow voters to rank candidates. The STV system has some undesirable properties. (See the article by Brams and Fishburn in [Maisel, 1991].) In the Borda count, each voter ranks all N candidates, giving the lowest candidate 0 points, the next lowest 1 point, and so on until the highest candidate receives M − 1 points. Sum the points by candidate for all voters, and the candidate with the most points wins. (The nominal group technique is a form of Borda voting.) *Cumulative voting* allows voters to allocate a fixed number of votes among candidates. (The multivoting technique is a form of cumulative voting.) These systems are designed to ensure proportional representation of different groups in the electorate. *Additional-member systems* allow extra seats to be given to parties that are underrepresented. *Approval voting* is a nonranked voting system that tends to help minority candidates.

Each voting scheme has particular advantages and disadvantages with respect to various criteria such as fairness, monotonicity, sensitivity to minor changes in the way the votes are cast, abstentions, insincerity, and susceptibility to manipulation. For example, the "fairness" of the voting system means that the results of the election represent the opinions and desires of the majority of the stakeholders. All voting systems are vulnerable to strategic manipulation, with the Borda count being the most manipulable.

27.3 A Technique to Handle Two Criteria

You can use a two-dimensional prioritization scheme to evaluate the relative merits of a set of proposed alternatives. You have a group of people individually rate the alternatives in terms of two criteria, such as cost versus benefit or difficulty versus importance. If the x-axis represents cost to implement and the y-axis represents the benefit, then the most attractive options are in the upper left quadrant of the plot. Options in the lower-right quadrant are the least attractive because they cost the most and provide the least benefit. Typically, the ratings range from 1 through 9, with 1 being the lowest and 9 the highest. (Nine values seem to be the practical limit for discriminating between options when doing subjective ratings.)

Figure 27-3 shows a plot of ratings from eight individuals. This spreadsheet calculates the mean and standard deviation for each dimension from the ratings submitted for an alternative. It uses these values to plot the one-sigma ellipse as shown. The size of the ellipse indicates the degree of consistency between the various people. A small ellipse indicates good agreement. A large ellipse indicates a wide range of opinions.

Figure 27-4 shows a plot from a spreadsheet that consolidates the ratings of several individuals. As with the wide-band Delphi process, you can have the individuals discuss each alternative, refine the descriptions of the alternatives, and then submit new ratings. For more information, see Note N42, "Designing the Two-Dimensional Rating Spreadsheet."

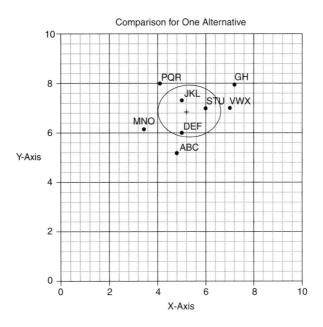

Figure 27-3 *Comparison of one alternative*

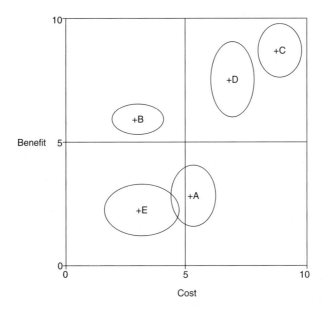

Figure 27-4 *Consensus of two-dimensional ratings for five alternatives*

27.4 Techniques to Handle Multiple Criteria

Estimation often involves ranking objects based upon multiple criteria. For example, you might need to choose the most important set of tasks to implement due to limited resources, or you may want to choose the "best" design from a set of possible designs.

Estimators and engineers are also involved in determining the value or utility of a particular product or process. Often, the value, or benefit, depends on many subjective factors that are difficult to quantify. The academic discipline of decision making deals with models (normative models) that help reason about such factors. The two main types of models are expected utility theory and multi-attribute utility theory (MAUT).

In *expected utility theory*, the value of a particular outcome is determined by estimating the probability of that outcome, and multiplying it by the estimated utility of that outcome. For example, suppose that you purchase a lottery ticket for $5. If you win the lottery, then you will receive $10,000. If your probability of winning the lottery is one part in one million, however, your expected return is $0.01 (= 10 – 6 * 104). In this case, the expected return does not justify the price of the ticket. Chapter 18, "Updating Estimates," uses this approach to estimate the impact of various risks and to calculate the appropriate size of a project's risk reserves. You can also use the technique to estimate risks associated with product performance.

Decision trees extend basic utility theory by allowing deterministic variables to be included. The basic idea is to build a tree whose branches correspond to different alternatives. Each of these branches is decomposed to show the contributors to its value (usually money). For example, to purchase a commercial off-the-shelf component there is a deterministic cost, the catalog cost quoted by the vendor. There may also be a random cost due to the possible delay in delivering the component. To calculate this, you could estimate the probability that the product will be delivered some number of days late and estimate the cost impact to the project should such a delay occur. The product of the probability times the cost impact gives the cost for this particular scenario. You could construct a table of probabilities and associated delay-related costs, and sum them to obtain the expected value for the delay. Adding this to the cost of the purchased component gives the total cost of this alternative to the project. You can perform similar calculations for each alternative. Then you can compare the total costs for each alternative to choose having the lowest cost.

Multi-attribute utility theory (MAUT) extends expected utility theory to decide between multiple alternatives that depend on many attributes. The usual approach is to calculate the expected utility for each attribute, and then to combine the utility values using a set of weights that indicates the importance of that particular attribute. (The Analytic Hierarchy Process (AHP), described in Section 27.6, essentially does this, too.) The next section describes the details of the MAUT technique.

27.5 Multi-Attribute Utility Theory (MAUT)

Multi-attribute utility theory (MAUT) maximizes a function of the values of various attributes. It assumes that one attribute can counterbalance another ("substitution"). For example, cost reductions or revenue increases can offset investment or implementation costs.

To define a MAUT technique, you must consider two things. First, how can you map the properties to an appropriate measurement scale that preserves the relations between the objects? (This is the *representation problem*.) A related issue is choosing properties that are orthogonal (no overlap in what each measures). Second, how should you define the function to maximize? (This is the *construction problem*.) A related issue is how to estimate the function's parameters (e.g., weights used to combine ratings for different criteria).

MAUT techniques use preference ratings, illustrated in Table 27-8, which are ordinal measurements. The ordinal scale only allows comparisons and equality. If you compare the values, X and Y, for some attribute, you can always guarantee that X = Y. (The criterion is called a *true criterion*.) You can also define a restricted ordinal scale that places objects into bins. Table 27-9 illustrates such a scheme. Many parametric estimation models use such rating scales.

Table 27-8 *Four Examples of Preference Ratings (Likert Scales)**

Strongly Disagree	Disagree	Neutral	Agree	Strongly Agree
Very low	Low	Nominal	High (average)	Very High
Never	Seldom	Sometimes	Often	Always
Hourly	Daily	Weekly	Monthly	

*Originated by Rensis Likert [Likert, 1932].

Table 27-9 *Restricted Ordinal: Programmer Experience*

Very low	≤ Four months
Low	> Four months and ≤ one year
Nominal	> One year and ≤ three years
High	> Three years and ≤ six years
Very high	> Six years

The usual approach for MAUT is to construct a linear function. You need to do the following:

1. Determine a measurement scale for each attribute, R_i.
2. Map the rating, R_i, to a (ratio scale) value, V_i.
3. Specify the relative weights of the attributes, W_i.

Compute the score using

$$\text{Score} = \sum_{i=1}^{N} W_i * V_i$$

where N is the number of attributes, properties, criteria, or factors. (This is a form of the additive model discussed in Section 5.2.1.) The CD-ROM contains a spreadsheet that implements the calculation. It allows you to define the factors, their rating scales, the mapping of the ratings to ratio scale values, and the relative weights.

For example, suppose that you want to evaluate four COTS components (named A, B, C, and D). You want to consider these factors:

- Functionality
- Integration effort (person-weeks)
- Cost (dollars)
- Vendor reputation
- Product maturity
- Developer toolkit available
- Training availability

The top half of Figure 27-5 lists the rating scale for each factor and its relative weight. (The weights sum to 1.0, but this is not necessary.) The bottom half of the table shows the (ratio scale) values assigned to each rating. Figure 27-6 shows the evaluator's ratings for each factor for each component, with the total weighted score shown in row 6. Component D is the best, with Components A and D nearly tied for second place. For details, see Note N43, "Designing the MAUT Spreadsheet."

	G	H	I	J	K	L	M
7	Factor Name	Weight	Ratings				
8	Functionality	0.30	VL	LO	NM	HI	VH
9	Integration Effort (Person-Weeks)	0.20	1	2	3	4	5
10	Cost (Dollars)	0.20	Below 500	500 to 1000	Above 1000		
11	Vendor Reputation	0.10	Poor	Unknown	Good	Excellent	
12	Product Maturity	0.10	VL	LO	NM	HI	VH
13	Developer Toolkit Available	0.05	No	Yes			
14	Training Availability	0.05	No	Some	Full		
15							
16							
17	Factor Name		Values				
18	Functionality		1.00	2.00	3.00	4.00	5.00
19	Integration Effort (Person-Weeks)		1.00	2.00	3.00	4.00	5.00
20	Cost (Dollars)		1.00	0.00	-1.00		
21	Vendor Reputation		-5.00	-3.00	0.00	9.00	
22	Product Maturity		1.00	2.00	3.00	4.00	5.00
23	Developer Toolkit Available		0.00	1.00			
24	Training Availability		1.00	2.00	3.00		
25							

Figure 27-5 *User-specified criteria and weights*

	A	B	C	D	E
1	Description:	Evaluation of Four COTS Products			
2	Prepared By:	Mary Smith			
3	Date Prepared:	14-Oct-04			
4					
5	Option =	A	B	C	D
6	Score =	1.80	1.30	1.75	2.30
7	Factor				
8	Functionality	HI	NM	LO	VH
9	Integration Effort (Person-Weeks)	1	2	3	4
10	Cost (Dollars)	500 to 1000	Below 500	500 to 1000	Above 1000
11	Vendor Reputation	Good	Poor	Good	Unknown
12	Product Maturity	NM	LO	HI	NM
13	Developer Toolkit Available	No	Yes	No	Yes
14	Training Availability	Some	No	Full	Full
15					

Figure 27-6 *Weighted scores for the COTS components*

27.6 The Analytic Hierarchy Process

The *analytic hierarchy process* (AHP) is a popular MAUT technique developed by Thomas Saaty [Saaty, 1977]. AHP addresses multiple criteria, including subjective criteria. AHP constructs a multilevel hierarchy, shown in Figure 27-7. The top level is the decision objective. The bottom level has the possible actions or alternatives. The intermediate levels represent factors that affect the preference or desirability of one alternative, or subfactors that contribute to a factor.

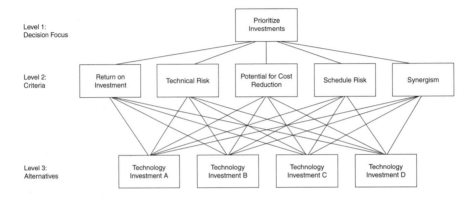

Figure 27-7 *A hierarchy for technology investment*

Figure 27-8 shows the steps of the AHP process. The decision maker identifies which factors are important, and defines how they influence one another. Then evaluators make pair-wise comparisons at each level, capturing these in "judgment matrices," one for each criterion or alternative. Figure 27-9 shows such a matrix. The rating matrix is triangular because complementarity is assumed. That is, if A >> B, then B << A. If A_{ij} denotes the rating of object i relative to object j for attribute A, the AHP model assumes that

$$A_{ji} = 1/A_{ij}$$

Because an object is identical (equal) to itself, $A_{ii} = 1$. For a single criterion having N alternatives, the evaluator must make $N \times (N - 1)/2$ comparisons. Table 27-10 shows Saaty's nine-value preference scale. (You can use others if desired.) For each criterion, the AHP method calculates a priority vector (a ratio scale preference vector) that ranks the alternatives based on that criterion. There are several ways to calculate the priority vector. Thomas Saaty computes matrix eigenvalues. Gordon Crawford and Cindy Williams describe a method using the geometric mean [Crawford, 1985]. (The next section describes an example for a single criterion: software size.) Then the method uses the weights to combine the priority vectors and obtain the final ranking of alternatives.

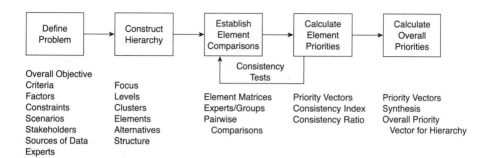

Figure 27-8 *Steps of the analytic hierarchy process*

Criterion C	A_1	A_2	A_3
A_1	1	a_{12}	a_{13}
A_2	$1/a_{12}$	1	a_{23}
A_3	$1/a_{13}$	$1/a_{23}$	1

Figure 27-9 *The comparison matrix*

Table 27-10 *Saaty's Nine Preference Ratings*

Verbal Scale	Numeric Value
Equally important, likely, or preferred	1
Moderately more important, likely, or preferred	3
Strongly more important, likely, or preferred	5
Very strongly more important, likely, or preferred	7
Absolutely more important, likely, or preferred	9

27.7 Estimating Module Size Using AHP

George Bozoki was the first to apply AHP to the problem of estimating the size of software modules. He reasoned that early in a project, estimates of relative sizes are more accurate than estimates of absolute sizes. Also, the expert's estimate of the relative magnitudes and the actual relative magnitudes are strongly correlated. Bozoki used AHP to convert the relative size estimates into size ratios. (Using only a single criterion (relative size) greatly simplifies Saaty's technique.) If you know the actual size of one or more modules, you can calculate the absolute sizes of all the remaining modules. (Bozoki's tool, the Software Sizing Model, actually combines estimates from four different methods to estimate module sizes.) Size can be in function points, screens, reports, and so forth. The only requirement is that all of the objects are measured using the same size unit.

Figure 27-10 shows how to use the (simplified) analytic hierarchy process to estimate module size. (This diagram was adapted from one in [Miranda, 2001].) First, identify the items to be sized. You should also provide a description of each item. A single estimator ranks the items from largest to smallest, and then estimates the relative sizes of each pair. Saaty provides a verbal scale to help standardize the comparison. Miranda interprets this scale for software modules, as shown in Table 27-11. The dashed lines in the figure indicate optional data you may use such as known module sizes or Miranda's verbal rating scale. You enter the ratings into a "judgment matrix," and the algorithm computes a vector of relative sizes, r_i. Using the vector of relative sizes, plus the known sizes of one or more "reference modules," you can compute the sizes of all the remaining modules. (See details below.)

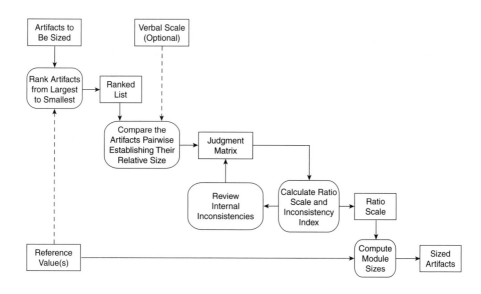

Figure 27-10 *AHP process diagram*

Table 27-11 *Verbal Scale for the Software Domain*

Definition	Explanation	Relative Value	Reciprocal
Equal size	$E_i/E_j \leq 1.25$ (0% to 25%)	1.00	1.00
Slightly bigger (smaller)	$1.25 < E_i/E_j \leq 1.75$ (26% to 75%)	1.25	0.80
Bigger (smaller)	$1.75 < E_i/E_j \leq 2.275$ (76% to 275%)	1.75	0.57
Much bigger (smaller)	$2.275 < E_i/E_j \leq 5.75$ (276% to 575%)	4.00	0.25
Extremely bigger (smaller)	$5.75 < E_i/E_j \leq 10$ (576% to 1,000%)	7.00	0.13

Table 27-12 lists the four steps of the algorithm. The pairwise ratings go in the upper or lower triangular sections of the matrix, depending on how you define the ratios. You can enter rating values in either section (and the values in the mirror image section are the reciprocals: $a_{ji} = 1/a_{ij}$). Saaty enters data in the upper section, and defines the value of a_{ij} as the size of i divided by the size of j. (If A_1 is three times larger than A_3, you enter 3 in element a_{13}.)

Table 27-12 *AHP Calculations*

1. Create an $n \times n$ judgment matrix of pair-wise comparisons. $$a_{ij} = \frac{Size_i}{Size_j}$$ $$a_{ii} = 1$$ $$a_{ji} = \frac{1}{a_{ij}}$$
2. Compute the geometric mean of each row. $$m_i = \left[\prod_{j=1}^{n} a_{ij} \right]^{\frac{1}{n}}$$
3. Compute the ratio scale. $$r_i = \frac{m_i}{\sum_{j=1}^{n} m_j}$$
4. Given the ratio scale $[r_1, \ldots ,r_n]$ and a reference module of known size, compute sizes. $$Size_i = Size_{REF} \times r_i / r_{REF}$$
5. Compute the Consistency Index: $$CI = \frac{\sqrt{\sum_{i=1}^{n} \sum_{j>i}^{n} \left(\ln a_{ij} - \ln \frac{m_i}{m_j} \right)^2}}{\left[\frac{(n-1) \times (n-2)}{2} \right]}$$

The fifth step shown in the table is optional. It computes a measure of "rating consistency." You enter $n*(n - 1)/2$ ratings but the algorithm only produces $(n - 1)$ ratios. The ratings are thus overdetermined provided that $n > 3$. Consistency arises because of the transitivity of the comparison operator. If $a < b$ and $b < c$, then $a < c$. The estimator enters all three comparisons and may perhaps rate $a < b$, $b < c$, and $a > c$, the latter being inconsistent. This seems like a stupid mistake, but inconsistencies appear when many items must be compared. (In practice, the list of items should not exceed 20 or so.) Table 27-12 shows one way to compute the *consistency index (CI)* for the matrix's values. Saaty's original work computes the consistency index using the maximum eigenvalue of the judgment matrix. Saaty also defines a *consistency ratio (CR)* by dividing CI by the value expected if all ratings were totally random. If $CR \leq 0.1$, then the rating matrix is considered to have "good" consistency. See [Saaty, 1980] for details.

Figure 27-11 shows an example for four modules. The judgment matrix is in columns D through G, rows 3 through 6. The estimator supplies the ratings in the six shaded cells. The geometric mean of each row is shown in column B, rows 3 through 6, and the final priority (preference) vector is in column A, rows 3 through 6. The results are on the left side so that you can easily expand the matrix to the right and down to handle more alternatives. (Note N44, "Designing the AHP Spreadsheet," provides additional details.) The resulting vector of relative sizes is (0.518, 0.245, 0.131, 0.108). If module 1 has a known size of 1,000 "size units" then

$Size_2 = 1,000*(0.245/0.528) = 473$
$Size_3 = 1,000*(0.131/0.518) = 253$
$Size_4 = 1,000*(0.108/0.518) = 208$

The total estimated total size of the unknown modules is 934 (= 473 + 253 + 208). The (assumed) total size of the same modules was 875 (= 500 + 250 + 125). The error is

$Error = (Estimated - True)/True = (934 - 875)/875 = 59/875 = 7\%$

The ratings shown in this example are not consistent (e.g., row 2 has M_4 50% larger[3] than M_3, but row 3 has them equal), but the method still gives about 7% accuracy in this case. The matrix shown in the figure has CI = 10%.

---

[3] Assuming transitivity of the size ratios, M3/M4 = $(M2/M3)^{-1}$ * (M2/M4) = (1/2.0)*(1.33) = 0.67.

	A	B	C	D	E	F	G
1	Priority Vector	Geometric Mean		Ratio = Row/Column			
2	(ratios)	5.8253	4	Module 1	Module 2	Module 3	Module 4
3	0.6535	3.8068	Module 1	1.000	4.000	7.000	7.500
4	0.1598	0.9306	Module 2	0.250	1.000	1.500	2.000
5	0.1134	0.6606	Module 3	0.143	0.667	1.000	2.000
6	0.0734	0.4273	Module 4	0.133	0.500	0.500	1.000

Figure 27-11 *Sample AHP calculation*

There are some practical considerations in using the AHP technique. First, the list of items should not be too long. Eduardo Miranda suggests dividing up a long list with n items among multiple judges, limiting the number of judges to less than $n/3$ so that each judge will have the opportunity to make multiple comparisons [Miranda, 2001]. Second, Saaty's method assumes that the various alternatives are "close" in each attribute. (He uses nine ratings.) If the attributes have a larger range, e.g., 100, the mathematics may not be accurate. Third, as Miranda notes, the choice of the reference value(s) can affect the results, especially if there is only one. Choosing a value at either end of the scale will tend to amplify any biases in the results. Miranda recommends choosing a reference value that will divide the population into two equally sized parts. Even better, you can use more than one reference value. See Note N45, "Analytic Hierarchy Process with Multiple Reference Values."

27.8 Recommended Reading

Voting schemes are intended for use in elections. However, the preceding sections show how you can use voting schemes to prioritize lists. The fields of political science, government, discrete mathematics, game theory, and economics have all studied voting schemes. Steven J. Brams and Peter C. Fishburn describe approval voting in [Brams, 1983]. Also see http://bcn.boulder.co.us/ government/approvalvote/center.html. Delbecq, Van de Ven, and Gustafson provide step-by-step procedures and examples for the Nominal Group Technique and the Delphi technique [Delbecq, 1975]. Brams and Fishburn provide a good overview of alternative voting schemes, and their advantages and disadvantages in [Maisel, 1991]. You can obtain their article from http://bcn.boulder.co.us/government/approvalvote/altvote.html. Donald Saari provides a nontechnical look at voting in [Saari, 2001].

Peter C. Fishburn laid out the foundation for expected utility theory in [Fishburn, 1970] and [Fishburn, 1982]. (Daniel Bernoulli first used the concept to solve the St. Petersburg Paradox [Bernoulli, 1738].) Steve Tockey discusses utility theory, Monte Carlo analysis, and decision trees in Chapter 24 of [Tockey, 2005]. A good reference on decision trees is [Schuyler, 2001]. John Goodpasture covers decision trees in Chapter 4 of [Goodpasture, 2004]. Roger Pressman has a short example showing the use of decision trees for software acquisition [Pressman, 1992, pages 117–119].

Many articles and books deal with multi-attribute utility theory and multiple criteria decision making (MCDM). The topics are part of operations research, which is now called management science. Dyer et al. provide a good summary article in [Dyer, 1992]. (One of the authors is the same Peter Fishburn who studied voting theories. This indicates the overlap between these fields of study.) James Corner and Craig Kirkwood also provide an overview in [Corner, 1991], with additional information in [Kirkwood, 1992]. Norman Fenton and Shari Pfleeger describe multi-criteria decision aids in Section 6.4.4 of [Fenton, 1997]. They briefly cover the MAUT and outranking methods. (Outranking also uses pair-wise comparison, but uses weaker assumptions than MAUT.) Phillipe Vincke also discusses these [Vincke, 1992]. Steve Tockey describes multi-attribute decisions in Chapter 26 of [Tockey, 2005]. Craig Kirkwood explains how to use spreadsheets for multi-objective decision analysis in [Kirkwood, 1997]. Some articles and tools (spreadsheets and Visual Basic) are available from http://www.public.asu.edu/~kirkwood. Several authors have applied AHP to estimate the sizes of software modules and task effort [Bozoki, 1993], [Barker, 1999], [Santillo, 2000], and [Miranda, 2001].

Thomas L. Saaty originated the analytic hierarchy process [Saaty, 1977] and has written several books on the subject, the first being [Saaty, 1980]. Many of his early books are now out of print. A recent summary for managers is [Saaty, 2000]. Saaty has extended AHP to create the analytic network process (ANP). ANP models have two parts: The first is a control hierarchy or network of objectives and criteria that control the interactions in the system under study; the second the subnetworks of influences among the elements and clusters of the problem, one for each control criterion. (AHP is a special case of the ANP.) Both the AHP and the ANP derive ratio scale priorities for elements and clusters of elements by making paired comparisons of elements on a common property or criterion. For more information, see [Saaty, 2001]. Software tools are available. See http://www.creativedecisions.net and http://www.expertchoice.com/software. You can find many references for decision making at http://www.logicaldecisions.com.

Another good source of information on decision making is Part III of [Boehm, 1981]. Boehm specifically addresses quantities of interest to software and system engineering. Part III of [Boehm, 1981] covers the following:

- Cost-effectiveness analysis:
    Performance and cost-effectiveness models
    Choosing among alternatives
- Multiple-goal decision analysis:
    Net value and marginal analysis
    Present value of future expenditures and income
    Figures of merit
    Constraints and optimization
    Irreconcilable and unquantifiable goals
- Uncertainties, risk, and the value of information:
    Risk analysis
    Statistical decision theory

The business community has extensively studied decisions involving financial analysis. Two references that address software-related business decisions are [Tockey, 2005] and [Reifer, 2001].

27.9 Summary

This chapter described simple techniques for ranking and selecting items, and ways to evaluate alternatives based on multiple attributes. There are many types of voting schemes, each having particular advantages and disadvantages. This chapter described three simple voting techniques to rank lists of items. Approval voting allows each individual to vote for as many items as he or she wants, but each person can cast only one vote for a particular item. The nominal group technique produces a consensus of rankings. Multivoting gives each individual a certain number of votes to cast. An individual can cast one, two, or even all of his votes for a single item.

You can use a two-dimensional plot to evaluate alternatives based on two criteria. You plot the paired ratings and can use a one-sigma ellipse to indicate the dispersion of the ratings. You can apply this technique to compare multiple ratings for a single alternative or to compare multiple alternatives. Such plots are useful to support the wide-band Delphi process.

The discipline of decision making provides various models to rank alternatives based upon multiple criteria. Expected utility theory calculates the value of a particular outcome by multiplying estimates of its probability of occurrence and its utility (e.g., benefit or cost). Decision trees extend basic utility theory by representing different alternatives as branches, decomposing each branch to show the contributors to the alternative's value. Multi-attribute utility theory (MAUT) extends expected utility theory by calculating the expected utility for each attribute, and then combining the calculated values using weights that reflect the relative importance of the attributes.

The analytic hierarchy process (AHP) has the capability to address problems involving multiple criteria, many of which are highly subjective. AHP systematically extracts subjective expert opinions on a set of criteria by means of pairwise comparison, and combines these opinions in a quantitative way. AHP enables decision makers to choose among several alternatives by identifying the factors and criteria that affect the desirability of an alternative. The factors and criteria can be concrete characteristics or can be intangible. The full method arranges the factors in a hierarchy (hence the name) to indicate their relative degrees of influence. One or more individuals provide judgments on the individual factors and criteria. The method uses mathematical techniques to combine the individuals' judgments to rank the alternatives.

These techniques all assume rational behavior on the part of the participants. Challenges in applying such techniques in practice include the following:

- People do not always make perfect decisions (due to ignorance, biases, or manipulative strategies).
- People may change their minds.
- You may not have enough resources (time, money) to assign good ratings to all the factors identified.
- You may fail to identify key factors that greatly affect the desirability of the alternatives (e.g., architectural compatibility of COTS software components).
- It may be difficult to identify orthogonal criteria. (This is not a serious drawback.)

Appendix A

Roles and Responsibilities for Estimation

This appendix defines standard terminology to eliminate possible confusion caused by overlapping names. I have tried to use these terms consistently in the book when referring to business processes, roles, and responsibilities. (You can use the definitions in this appendix to map my terms to the ones used by your organization.)

Defining business processes involves three types of entities. First, there are *organizations*: the customer, the producer of the products, and possibly suppliers (or subcontractors) that provide components to the (prime) producer. Each organization consists of multiple *departments*. Corresponding departments in the different organizations usually communicate with one another. (The departments in different organizations often have the same name or very similar names, making it unclear which organization's department is meant. For example, both the customer and the producer may have a legal department.) Third, individuals within the departments fulfill specific *roles*, with each role having an assigned set of *responsibilities*. Role names may also overlap. For example, some organizations call a purchasing agent a "buyer." Others refer to the customer as the "buyer." In addition, organizations may use different titles for a particular role. For example, some organizations refer to a costing analyst as a "pricer."

Table A-1 shows terms used for three different types of organizations, their departments, and the roles of the individuals working in the departments. The three organization types are purchaser, producer, and supplier. The second row of the table shows alternative terms (in italic) used for each type of organization. The same term appears in multiple columns, indicating potential sources of confusion. Every organization has a similar set of departments, shown here with the same name for all organization types. The bottom row of the table shows the primary roles that are involved with building or using a product.

Table A-1   *Organizations, Departments, and Their Associated Roles*

Organization	*Purchaser*	*Producer*	*Supplier*
Alternative Terms	*Customer* *Consumer* *Buyer* *End user*	*Contractor ("prime")* *Developer* *Seller (retailer, vendor)* *Buyer*	*Subcontractor* *Seller (wholesaler, vendor)*
Departments	Corporate management Legal Contracts Finance Procurement	Corporate management Legal Contracts Finance Purchasing Subcontracts	Corporate management Legal Contracts Finance Purchasing Subcontracts
Roles	Procurement official Project manager User Operator CM specialist QA specialist Cost analyst	Contracts manager Project manager Developer/engineer Tester CM specialist QA specialist Purchasing agent (buyer) Subcontracts manager Costing analyst (pricer) Finance manager Facilities manager	Contracts manager Project manager Developer/engineer Tester CM specialist QA specialist Purchasing agent (buyer) Subcontracts manager Costing analyst (pricer) Finance manager Facilities manager

From an estimating standpoint, the roles shown in the Producer column are of primary interest. The roles in the Supplier column are essentially a duplicate of those shown in the Producer column. (A supplier is a separate organization such as a subcontractor or product vendor, and employs individuals who perform similar functions to those of the producer.) The roles of interest for the "purchaser" are the procurement official who actually negotiates the payment for the product, the user, and the operator. The purchaser's cost analyst evaluates each producer's costs and prices for completeness, correctness, consistency, and fair market value. (Prior to awarding a contract, the producer is called a bidder.) The Producer's costing analyst converts resource estimates to cost, and applies loading factors.

A business organization is complex, and actually has more roles than the primary roles listed in Table A-1. You can group these roles by area:

- Management oversight
- Project leaders
- Production staff
- Support staff
- External individuals and organizations.

Table A-2 lists the responsibilities of each role. The name of each role is capitalized in the Responsibilities column to highlight the interactions between roles. Generally, the engineers, specialists, and administrators perform daily work on project tasks, whereas managers and supervisors typically spend some time on other duties besides project activities. For example, the subcontracts manager has overall responsibility for defining and negotiating subcontracts with various suppliers, whereas the subcontracts administrator handles the details and the day-to-day communications with the subcontractor's contracts manager.[1] This illustrates the complementary nature of some roles. Other roles, such as engineers and project managers, communicate with their direct counterparts. One person may perform multiple roles, depending on the size of the organization. There is no role called "customer." Instead, the table has purchaser, user, and operator because different individuals have these responsibilities in large organizations. For a consumer product, one person performs all three roles.

---

[1] The Contracts Manager and Subcontracts Manager focus on the legal aspects of contracts and subcontracts. They are familiar with contract law, statutory requirements, and regulations such as the U.S. Federal Acquisition Regulations (FAR) and the U.S. Uniform Commercial Code (UCC).

Table A-2 *Roles and Responsibilities by Area*

Position	Responsibilities
Management Oversight	
Senior Manager (Corporate Manager)	Sets overall business goals and objectives
	Defines and approves organization's policies
	Grants waivers for deviations from the policies
	Arbitrates unresolved issues
	Addresses any conditions adverse to quality or organizational performance
	Completes all training designated for this role
Proposal Manager (Business Manager, Sales Manager, Marketing Manager)	Identifies potential opportunities (programs, procurements, customers, markets) compatible with the organization's business objectives and capabilities
	Prepares a business case for senior management
	Assembles a team to pursue the opportunity
	Manages and leads preparation of the proposal (offer)
	Supports Contract Manager during negotiation with the Purchaser
	Completes all training designated for this role
Line Manager	Approves project plans prepared by their project teams
	Periodically reviews status of projects performed by their project teams
	Sponsors the training of their personnel
	Verifies training completions of their personnel
	Handles the hiring, transferring, and termination of personnel
	Completes all training designated for this role
Contracts Manager	Coordinates and controls all contractually binding communications between the organization and the Customer
	Prepares, coordinates, and negotiates agreements between multiple organizations participating in a project
	Prepares proposal and contractual documents that define the work to be performed (cost/price, assumptions, terms and conditions, deliverables, licenses, certifications)

Position	Responsibilities
Management Oversight	
Contracts Manager (*continued*)	Leads the negotiation of the offer with the Purchaser
	Monitors cost, schedule, and technical performance against contractual requirements
	Negotiates and resolves exceptional situations or change orders with the Purchaser
	Documents the contract history and maintains the proposal in contract files
	Requests payment from the Purchaser for all work performed
	Initiates actions to handle late payments or deliveries, defective goods, and other problems
	Identifies and coordinates the flow-down of requirements to Subcontractors
	Completes all training designated for this role
Subcontracts Manager	Writes subcontractor statement of work (SOW), describing tasks, deliverables, and Ts & Cs
	Selects qualified Subcontractors
	Assists Subcontract Administrators in negotiating subcontracts
	Reviews and approves the Subcontractors' plans for performing work
	Monitors the technical work performed by Subcontractors against the plan
	Resolves problems that may arise with the Subcontractors
	Completes all training designated for this role
Finance Manager	Authorizes and tracks payments to suppliers
	Authorizes and tracks billing of purchasers
	Monitors cash flow
	Helps Senior Managers prepare annual business plan
	Monitors progress against the business plan
	Completes all training designated for this role

(*continues*)

Table A-2 *Roles and Responsibilities by Area (continued)*

Position	Responsibilities
Management Oversight	
Quality Assurance Manager	Oversees quality verification activities
	Audits compliance to documented quality assurance process
	Reports significant conditions adverse to quality to Senior Manager
	Assists project managers to resolve quality-related issues
	Contacts the Purchaser and Users to determine customer satisfaction
	Completes all training designated for this role
Process Improvement Manager	Oversees the operation of the process improvement team
	Defines and manages the process improvement budget
	Prepares yearly training plan and schedules
	Reports process improvement status to Senior Manager(s)
	Completes all training designated for this role
Project Leaders	
Project Manager	Manages the overall technical, cost, and schedule aspects of a project (may delegate the responsibility for technical product acceptance to the Chief Engineer)
	Approves all changes to the project scope
	Approves the selected and tailored process and submits requests for any waivers
	Ensures that the process is followed on the project
	Defines budget and schedule for the project
	Defines the training needs for the project
	Defines the project's organizational structure, assigns roles, and manages staffing
	Interfaces with support elements within and external to the organization to obtain information and resources (equipment, people, lab space, etc.) needed by the project
	Defines work packages for Subcontractors

Position	Responsibilities
Project Leaders	
Project Manager (continued)	Oversees work performed by Subcontractors, and tracks progress, cost, and schedule
	Writes and maintains the project plan(s)
	Manages customer (Purchaser and Users) expectations
	Establishes and manages communications between the "project team" and the Purchaser
	Note: The "project team" comprises the project manager, engineers, testers, and all other personnel who support the project, full-time or part-time, direct or indirect.
	Maintains a file of all correspondence with the customer, Subcontractors, and Suppliers
	Provides status to upper management (Line Manager and Senior Manager)
	Responsible for gathering metrics data and project closeout reports
	Provides annual performance reviews for assigned individuals
	Completes all training designated for this role
Chief Engineer (Lead System Engineer)	Translates customer (Purchaser, User) requirements into engineering requirements
	Evaluates alternative solutions (especially ones involving the operational concept)
	Analyzes feasibility and performance of alternative designs and configurations
	Supports planning, cost analysis, and schedule analysis
	Defines the overall form of the product (operational concept, product requirements, product architecture, and design)
	Responsible for the technical acceptance of the product
	Defines, collects, and analyzes the technical performance measures for the product
	Defines test strategy, test methods, test tools, and test procedures
	Selects and tailors the standard process to fit the product

(continues)

Table A-2 *Roles and Responsibilities by Area (continued)*

Position	Responsibilities
Project Leaders	
Chief Engineer (Lead System Engineer) (*continued*)	Helps prepare specifications and statements of work for Subcontractors
	Helps the Subcontract Administrator monitor Subcontractors' technical performance
	Manages the technical baseline of the system (requirements, architecture, and design)
	Maintains the interface with the Purchaser (or the Purchaser's technical representatives) on the technical baseline
	Approves all build/buy decisions, including reuse of existing code or components
	Monitors releases of COTS components to identify whether and when upgrades will be made
	Is the focal point for the product's vision, features, performance, and planned upgrades
	Attends reviews of work products and project status
	Supervises assigned personnel
	Provides technical guidance to Subcontractor personnel
	Ensures that work products meet all appropriate requirements
	Manages the interfaces between all subsystems (hardware and software)
	Reports status of work performed to the Project Controller, the Project Manager, or to their supervisor [as designated in the project plan(s)]
	Completes all training designated for this role
Production Personnel	
Engineer (software or hardware)	Performs assigned technical work
	Analyzes, designs, "produces," and tests components to meet allocated requirements, using the approved process (includes architecture definition and build/reuse/buy decisions)
	Note: "Produce" includes buy, build (fabricate or code), configure, integrate, and assemble.
	Prepares all appropriate documentation

Position	*Responsibilities*
Production Personnel	
Engineer (software or hardware) (*continued*)	Participates in peer reviews of their work products or the products of others
	Reports technical problems to the Chief Engineer and Project Manager (possibly via a supervisor)
	Resolves problems and action items as assigned
	Reports status of work performed to the Project Controller, the Project Manager, or to their supervisor [as designated in the project plan(s)]
	Completes all training designated for this role
Engineering Analyst	Investigates operational concepts, technical feasibility, design tradeoffs, and system performance
	Analyzes, designs, implements, and tests mathematical or simulation models using either commercially available tools (including spreadsheets) or custom-built software
	Designs databases, loads and processes data, and analyzes the results
	Documents analysis models, tools, and databases
	Independently reviews and validates models, tools, and documents developed by others
	Participates in peer reviews of their work products or the work products of others
	Provides cost and schedule estimates for their assigned task to their supervisor
	Performs assigned technical work using the approved process
	Reports status of work performed to the Project Controller, the Project Manager or to their supervisor [as designated in the project plan(s)]
	Completes all training designated for this role
Resource Estimator	Identifies and estimates the effort, materials, consumables, and travel needed to perform specific WBS tasks (work packages)
	Locates relevant historical data
	Selects and calibrates estimation models
	Reviews estimates made by others
	Completes all training designated for this role

(*continues*)

Table A-2 *Roles and Responsibilities by Area (continued)*

Position	Responsibilities
Production Personnel	
Cost Analyst	Builds and uses cost analysis models
	Makes computations or solves data analysis problems using commercially available tools such as spreadsheets, databases, and documentation tools
	Documents analysis models and tools
	Independently reviews and validates models, tools, and documents developed by others
	Loads and processes data, and analyzes the results
	Provides cost and schedule estimates for their assigned task to their supervisor
	Performs assigned technical work using the approved process
	Reports status of work performed to the Project Controller, the Project Manager, or to their supervisor [as designated in the project plan(s)]
	Completes all training designated for this role
Test Engineer	Performs testing of products, subsystems, or components against allocated requirements (this person should be independent from the developer but on small projects this may not be possible)
	Writes test plans and procedures in accordance with test strategy developed by the Chief Engineer
	Performs test plans and procedures that are approved by the Chief Engineer
	Reports the test results to the Project Manager and Chief Engineer
	Verifies corrections by regression testing
	Reports status of work performed to the Project Controller, the Project Manager, or to their supervisor [as designated in the project plan(s)]
	Completes all training designated for this role
System Administrator (also see Operator)	Configures and maintains the development and test environment (SEE and STE)
	Installs upgrades of commercial products (operating system, compiler, tools, etc.) in a coordinated manner as directed by the Project Manager
	Maintains user accounts and access privileges

Position	Responsibilities
Production Personnel	
System Administrator (*continued*)	Assists personnel in using the system
	Performs backups as required by the project plan(s)
	Performs configuration control of engineering libraries and data during development
	Completes all training designated for this role
Peer Review Moderator	Schedules the reviews
	Arranges for the distribution of the work product to the reviewers
	Moderates the review meeting
	Records the results (defects, metrics) of the review and conveys these results to individuals as designated in the project plan(s)
	Arranges for identified defects to be corrected and verifies the corrections
	Reports status of work performed to the Project Controller, the Project Manager, or to their supervisor[as designated in the project plan(s)]
	Completes all training designated for this role
Configuration Management Specialist	Creates the configuration management plan and procedures for the proposal and the project (including tasks, schedules, and estimated resources)
	Maintains the project baseline (deliverables and nondeliverables [plans, code, data, documents, etc.]) as designated by the Project Manager in the project plan(s)
	Assists in tracking and configuring the hardware associated with the project
	Releases copies of baselined material to project personnel
	Periodically determines and reports status of project baselines to the Project Manager as specified in the project plan
	Works with System Administrator to prepare backups and arranges for offsite storage as directed by the project plan
	Reports status of configuration management work performed to the Project Controller, the Project Manager, or to their supervisor [as designated in the project plan(s)]
	Completes all training designated for this role

(continues)

Table A-2 *Roles and Responsibilities by Area (continued)*

Position	Responsibilities
Support	
Quality-Assurance Specialist	Creates the quality-assurance plan and procedures for the project (including tasks, schedules, and estimated resources)
	Reviews project plan(s) for their assigned projects
	Periodically performs independent audits of products and the process using the organization's policies, standards, procedures, and product requirements as specified in the approved project plan(s)
	Attends project peer reviews as specified in the project plans
	Inspects vendor deliveries to find missing, damaged, or noncompliant items
	Documents the results of all reviews and inspections
	Reports results of audits to the Project Manager and Quality Assurance Manager
	Reports unresolved problems to successively higher levels of management until resolved
	Performs or witnesses testing and retesting of all products, and approves release of products to the Purchaser
	Reviews deliverable documents and approves release of documents to the Purchaser
	Typically assigned on a part-time basis to multiple projects
	Reports status of work performed to the Project Controller, the Project Manager, the Quality Assurance Manager, or to their supervisor [as designated in the project plan(s)]
	Completes all training designated for this role
Documentation Specialist	Plans and manages the production of required documents (deliverables and optionally, nondeliverables) in accordance with approved standards and guidelines
	Produces documents (typing, proofing, editing, and copying)
	Distributes documents to all designated recipients
	Completes all training designated for this role

Position	Responsibilities
Support	
Administrative Staff	Performs activities needed to support the project team (these activities include facilities, security, personnel, finance, accounting, clerical, property management, etc.)
	Completes all training designated for this role
	Note: Individuals performing this role typically bill to overhead (indirect charge), and are normally not counted in the direct labor estimates for the project.
Project Controller	Develops plans, establishes, and maintains the contract cost and schedule baseline, and monitors performance against that baseline
	Prepares and maintains the detailed work breakdown structure (WBS) (task list, WBS dictionary, dependencies) for a project (based on the SOW and ECPs provided by the Contracts Manager and guidance from the Project Manager)
	Prepares and maintains the detailed schedule for the tasks in the WBS
	Defines and maintains the set of charge numbers for all tasks
	Allocates ("spreads") the project budget to the work packages (tasks)
	Enters the budgets for all tasks into the tracking tool
	Collects, enters, and proofs actual costs and completion status for all work packages
	Computes status (cost, schedule, earned value, overruns and trends), as directed by the Project Controller and/or the Project Manager
	Participates in project reviews
	Reports status (cost, schedule, earned value, overruns, and trends) to the Project Manager
	Helps collect, analyze, and maintain historical basis of estimate data
	Completes all training designated for this role
Purchasing Agent	Obtains quotes for catalog items and services
	Selects "best" Supplier (vendor) based on criteria (approved vendor, lowest price)

(continues)

Table A-2 *Roles and Responsibilities by Area (continued)*

Position	Responsibilities
Support	
Purchasing Agent (*continued*)	Issues purchase order to Supplier to purchase items and services
	Investigates past due deliveries (items not delivered when promised)
	Notifies Supplier of missing or damaged items received in shipments
	Handles return of items to Supplier
	Handles the replacement items received from the Supplier
	Maintains a log of orders, shipments, returns, and replacements
	Completes all training designated for this role
Subcontracts Administrator	Prepares a request for quote (RFQ) or request for proposal (RFP) using a SOW provided by the Project Manager and Chief Engineer
	Selects the appropriate contract type
	Coordinates the flow down of requirements to subcontractors and Suppliers with Project Manager and Contract Manager
	Solicits Supplier quotes
	Provides subcontractor and Supplier quotes and bills of material pricing to the Contract Manager (or Cost Analyst)
	Negotiates subcontract agreements, terms and conditions, and payment schedule
	Converts the project's purchase requests into purchase orders or subcontracts
	Issues contract modifications to Subcontractors and Suppliers
	Completes all training designated for this role
Facilities Manager	Obtains, operates, and maintains facilities
	Identifies, issues, and tracks all property and equipment
	Manages shipping and receiving
	Completes all training designated for this role

Position	Responsibilities
Support	
Process Librarian (PAL)	Organizes and maintains the process asset library
	Makes information available on request
	Helps collect, analyze, and maintain historical basis of estimate data and lessons learned
	Completes all training designated for this role
Measurement Analyst	Assigns and maintains unique project identifiers
	Manages all metrics data (receives and enters data from the Project Managers, prints and sends out the reports)
	Maintains the organizational metrics database
	Helps collect, analyze, and maintain historical basis of estimate data
	Completes all training designated for this role
Costing Analyst (Pricer)	Converts estimated effort to cost using approved base labor rates and loading rules
	Applies loading rates to labor, materials, subcontracts, travel, ODCs, and other costs in accordance with the organization's cost accounting rules, contract type and terms, and management directives
	Completes all training designated for this role
Training Program Administrator	Is the central point of contact for all training activities
	Responsible for the configuration management of all training materials
	Responsible for publishing training schedule and registering students
	Responsible for course operations
	Records student attendance and graduation in the organization's training database
	Analyzes and reports training data to the Process Improvement Manager
	Assists the Process Improvement Manager in estimating costs for training
	Completes all training designated for this role

(continues)

Table A-2 *Roles and Responsibilities by Area (continued)*

Position	Responsibilities
Support	
Project Mentor	Helps assigned projects implement the standard process
	Interprets tailoring guidance for the organization's standard process
	Assists in writing and reviewing project plan(s) and process documents
	Conveys issues to the Process Improvement Manager for resolution and disseminates decisions to project teams
	Completes all training designated for this role
Appraisal Team Member	Conducts appraisals for process improvement in accordance with specified process standards and maturity models
	Documents results and reports findings to the sponsor of the appraisals
	Completes all training designated for this role
External Individuals and Organizations	
Purchaser	Requests products and/or services
	Establishes requirements for the requested products and services
	Specifies constraints such as cost and schedule
	Accepts or rejects offers and proposals
	Provides funding for the project (or purchases the products and/or services)
	Participates in joint reviews
	Monitors status of the project
	Accepts or rejects products
Regulatory Agency	Reviews the product to ensure that it meets all regulatory requirements
	Grants license to operate the approved system (or sell the product)
Supplier (Vendor)	Provides technical data about items to Engineers
	Supplies prices and specifications for items as requested by the Purchasing Agent
	Delivers items ordered by the Purchasing Agent

Position	Responsibilities
External Individuals and Organizations	
Subcontractor	Provides requested information (consulting)
	Provides personnel possessing specified skills
	Designs, builds, or configures components (hardware or software) as specified in the statement of work (SOW)
External Test Facility	Provides the facilities/services to test the product
User	Uses product/system to perform activities directly related to the enterprise's mission
	Completes all training designated for this role
Operator (also see System Administrator)	Distributes copies of the product/system to Users (may include installation)
	Performs activities to ensure accurate, reliable, and efficient operation (periodic housekeeping, performance monitoring, and tuning)
	Safeguards operational data and software assets (periodic backups)
	Completes all training designated for this role

Appendix B

Measurement Theory and Statistics

The quantities used in estimation and measurement have an underlying mathematical basis. This appendix describes measurement scales and their implications for calculating values. It also reviews concepts in statistics useful for estimators. Measurement scales also affect the types of statistical tests that you can use to draw conclusions about a set of measurements.

B.1 Measurement and Scale Types

Measurement uses a specified mathematical model (a "mapping") to assign values (numbers or symbols) to *represent* properties of actual entities. If the mathematical model faithfully "captures the essence" of the property, you can use mathematics to manipulate the model's values and draw valid conclusions about the characteristics of the actual entities. *A particular mapping limits the manipulations to ones that preserve the underlying relationships in the data.*

There are five possible types of mappings or *measurement scales* [Stevens, 1946]. The *nominal scale* simply assigns names to categories, classes, groups, and sets. The rule to assign objects is that they possess some common set of characteristics. For example, you might group modules based on the programming language used to write their source code. The *ordinal scale* orders (or ranks) objects based on some criterion. For example, the winners of a race are identified as first, second, third, and so forth.[1] You use an ordinal scale to rank objects based on some characteristic, such as complexity or preference. (See the explanation of the Likert scale.) The *interval scale* gives numeric values representing the separation of objects in terms of some characteristic. A good example is pointer offsets used in memory addressing. A *ratio scale* preserves the *relative degree* of the property. For example, you can say that one object is twice as hot as another object. Most physical measurements use the ratio scale. The *absolute scale* is a ratio scale that has its reference point (zero value) fixed. (There is one and only one absolute scale for a given choice of units. The uniqueness of the measure is what distinguishes the absolute scale from the ratio scale.) Examples of absolute scale objects in software engineering are development effort and the number of observed failures.

Table B-1 shows the "abilities" of each scale type plus examples of software engineering quantities for each scale type. A ratio scale is appropriate for size in SLOC because there are many possible definitions for SLOC. Fenton and Pfleeger note that a common mistake is to assume that SLOC is an absolute scale measure because you obtain its value by counting. It is the empirical relations, however, that determine the scale type [Fenton, 1997, page 53]. For software engineering, the distinction between the ratio and absolute scales is not usually significant.

Table B-1 *Examples of Measured Quantities for Each Scale Type**

Scale Type	Abilities	Examples
Nominal	Determine membership	Application domain, cost type (direct, indirect), programming language used, operating modes
Ordinal	Compare relative sizes	Preference (Likert ratings), such as ease of use (low to high), complexity (VL to EH)
Interval	Preserve amount of separation	Numbers of months since product release, offsets used in relative memory addressing
Ratio	Preserve ratios	Percentage of comments in source code, defect density, size in SLOC
Absolute	Map uniquely	Number of COTS licenses, number of users, number of observed failures

*Adapted from Figure 2.5 in [Fenton, 1997].

---

[1] Robert Hughes distinguishes unrestricted and restricted ordinal scales [Hughes, 2000, page 31]. With unrestricted ordinals, every object is assigned a unique number (e.g., the winners of a race). With restricted ordinals, objects are placed into bands or groups based on the value of some characteristic. For example, you might place programmers into categories based on years of experience: ≤ 1, > 1, and ≤ 2, etc. You can place data points into bins for histograms, or map the bins to Likert ratings (described later in this section). The bands need not be of equal width.

Table B-2 shows the allowed transformations (mathematical operations) for each scale type. The first row shows the allowed operations. The second row shows the capabilities provided by each operation. The X's in the remaining rows indicate the allowed operations and capabilities for each scale type. The allowed operations *preserve the relations* between all of the measured objects of that type. For example, rescaling values by converting units can only be done for interval, ratio, or absolute scale measures.[2] Ratio scale measurements are useful for estimation and measurement. A ratio scale preserves certain relations between entities (ordering, relative sizes of the intervals between them), has a zero value, and has a linear scale of units. You can also apply the usual arithmetic operations to values measured using the ratio scale, and will obtain the expected results. (One example is scaling by a multiplicative constant.)

Table B-2 *Allowed Operations for Measurement Scales*

	Operations	Equality	Rank	Add, Subtract	Multiply, Divide	Unique Zero Element	
	Capabilities	Determine membership	Compare relative sizes	Preserve amount of separation	Preserve ratios	Map uniquely	Has units
Scale Type	Nominal	X					
	Ordinal	X	X				
	Interval	X	X	X			X
	Ratio	X	X	X	X		X
	Absolute	X	X	X	X	X	X

What about more complicated conversions? One example is memory offsets. Suppose that an operating system allocates blocks of contiguous memory to a process. The absolute address, A, in the processor, and the relative address, R, in the block are both interval scales. You can convert one to the other using linear relations (affine transformations) of the form $y = ax + b$. For this example, $a = 1$, and so

$$A = R + B$$

where B is the beginning address of the allocated memory block.

---

[2] Horst Zuse stresses the difference between a scale and a scale type. He defines a *scale* as a homomorphic mapping. A *scale type* is a scale with associated admissible transformations. See page 660 in [Zuse, 1997]. Zuse describes the measurement process in Section 4.6 of his book.

Nonlinear transformations of scale are often useful to fit data. Common functions are logarithms and powers. Nonlinear transformations can, however, distort the relation between the numbers and the properties that the numbers represent. In addition, some operations that can be applied to numbers in a particular measurement scale are not appropriate for the transformed values. When you transform a scale X into a scale ln(X), addition has no simple counterpart. *If you choose a particular scale transformation to simplify analysis, be careful that the scale transformation does not change the underlying relation of interest.*

B.2 Statistics and Scale Types

Statistics is a mathematical way to quantify the degree of understanding and confidence in hypotheses based on empirical data. Statistics allows you to draw quantitative conclusions about products and processes based on incomplete and noisy data. (Noisy data contains measurement errors.) Statistics addresses methods to collect, summarize, analyze, and present data. (The word *statistics* is also used to refer to the data or the numbers derived from measurement data.)

Statistics studies the characteristics of a *population* of similar objects.[3] You can often only collect measurements for a small number of objects. These measurements are called the *sample* (or the *data set*). The measured values comprising the sample are assumed to be representative of the object being measured (i.e., they are not anomalous data points). By analyzing the sample, you compute various measures that describe the characteristics of the entire population. The accuracy of the computed characteristics (called "estimates" of the population parameters by statisticians) depends on the sample size, the measurement errors, and assumptions about the shape of the functions representing the characteristics and the errors. The *probability distribution (or density) function (PDF)* gives the probability, denoted by the function P(x), that an object in the population has some particular value, x, of a characteristic. The probability may depend on several characteristics, P(x, y, z, ...).

You can also use such functions to describe the probability that a measured value has a certain amount of error. *Parametric statistics* makes statements about the probability of error in an assertion (hypothesis) or a trend (model). It assumes that the measured values use an interval, ratio, or absolute scale, with the errors normally distributed. Parametric statistics uses various mathematical functions (probability distribution functions) to represent the (assumed)

---

[3] You can also apply statistics to measurements of a single object made at different times. This set of points is called a *time series*. Analysis of such data reveals changes and trends over time.

distribution of errors. You can manipulate these functions and the measured data to draw conclusions about the properties of the observed system, and can quantify the degree of uncertainty in your conclusions. (There are some adjustments for small sample sizes, non-normal distributions, etc.) Estimators usually deal with parametric statistics.

Nonparametric statistics makes no assumptions about the distribution of errors, and so computes a weaker class of results. You can use nonparametric statistics with nominal and ordinal measurements, as well as with interval, ratio, and absolute scale measurements. Parametric statistics can only be used with interval, ratio, and absolute scale measurements. Thus, the appropriate statistical technique depends on the measurement scale. Choosing the wrong statistical technique can produce incorrect or misleading results. Because the choice of the measurement scale is often unclear for software development, Romeu and Gloss-Soler suggest that studies of software data should always use nonparametric statistics [Romeu, 1983].

To simplify analysis, you sometimes put data points that have measured values that are close to one another into a *group*. For example, all values lying between 0.2 and 0.3 might be counted as members of a single group or *bin*. If you normalize the counts in each bin by dividing by the sum of counts in all bins, you obtain an approximation to the probability density function. (Note N22, "Types of Plots, " explains how to use the FREQUENCY function to create such histograms.)

B.3 Statistical Measures

Table B.3 defines statistical measures used in this book. You can easily calculate these using built-in functions in ordinary spreadsheets. (In Microsoft Excel, look under Functions | Statistics.)

Each measure has certain advantages and disadvantages. (All are easy to compute using a spreadsheet.) The minimum and maximum values are easy to comprehend but their values are distorted by any extreme values ("outliers") in the sample. Both minimum and maximum are not defined if the distribution is "open-ended" (that is, the data has some points grouped as "over value X").

The *arithmetic mean* is the average of the n values in a sample. It is also called the *sample average*. The average for multiple groups of data equals the weighted average of the averages of the groups. The *law of large numbers* states that the sample average approaches the true mean of the distribution as n increases. The law of large numbers means that you can estimate the mean value of a quantity even though you do not know the exact form of the underlying probability distribution. All you have to do is to average a reasonable number of samples. For details, see [Goodpasture, 2004, pages 55 through 57].

Table B-3 *Useful Statistical Quantities*

Purpose	Name	Symbol	Definition
Characterize the data set	Size of sample	n	Number of data points in sample
	Minimum	MIN	Smallest value in the sample
	Maximum	MAX	Largest value in the sample
Measures of central tendency	Arithmetic mean	$\overline{X}$ or μ	$$\overline{x} = \mu = \frac{1}{n}\sum_{i=1}^{n} x_i$$
	Median	None	The value of the middle item when all items have been ranked in size order. If there is an even number of items, the median is the arithmetic mean of the two center items.
	Mode	None	The value that occurs most frequently in the sample.
	Geometric mean	G_m	$$G_m = \left(x_1 \cdot x_2 \cdot x_3 \ldots x_n\right)^{\frac{1}{n}}$$
	Quadratic mean	Q_m	$$Q_m = \sqrt{\frac{\sum x^2}{n}}$$
	Harmonic mean	H_m	$$\frac{1}{H_M} = \frac{1}{n}\left(\frac{1}{x_1} + \frac{1}{x_2} + \frac{1}{x_3} + \cdots + \frac{1}{x_n}\right)$$
Measures of dispersion and variability	Variance (x)	VAR(x)	$$VAR(x) = \frac{1}{n}\sum_{i=1}^{N}\left[x_i - \overline{x}\right]^2$$
	Standard deviation	s_x or $\sigma(x)$	$$\sigma = \sqrt{VAR(\overline{x})}$$
Relation between data pairs, or agreement of observed and predicted values	Sample correlation coefficient	r	$$r = \left(\frac{1}{n-1}\right) * \sum_{i=1}^{n}\left[\frac{(x_i - \overline{x})}{s_x}\right] * \left[\frac{y_i - \overline{y}}{s_y}\right]$$
	Coefficient of determination	r^2	Square of r

A disadvantage is that the mean value is distorted by extreme values ("outliers"). The mean is also not defined if a distribution is open-ended. The mean is only defined for interval, ratio, and absolute scales.

The *median* is not distorted by outliers, so its value better typifies the overall sample. You can compute it even if the class intervals are open-ended. Disadvantages are that you must first rank (sort) the items. The median has a larger standard error than the arithmetic mean. You also cannot combine grouped data. The median is defined for interval and higher scales.

The *mode* is the most typical value (the peak of the probability distribution) and is entirely independent of outliers. (More data points in the sample give better accuracy, of course.) The value is inaccurate if you have only a few data points. The mode does not exist if no values are repeated. The mode is defined for all measurement scales.[4]

The *geometric mean* is less affected by extreme values (outliers) than the arithmetic mean. If any single value is zero, the geometric mean is zero. It cannot handle negative values. You can manipulate it algebraically. (The calculations for the analytic hierarchy process, described in Chapter 27, "Ranking and Selecting Items," use it.) The geometric mean is not widely known and cannot be computed using inexpensive four-function pocket calculators. The *harmonic mean* is the reciprocal of the arithmetic mean of the reciprocals of the values. It is often used to average rates of change. The *quadratic mean* is the square root of the mean square of items. These means are defined for ratio and absolute scales. The arithmetic mean of a number of positive quantities is always greater than or equal to their harmonic mean.

TIP: Estimators should have a scientific calculator that can compute logarithms, exponentials, and powers of numbers.

The *standard deviation* is a measure of the dispersion of values in a sample relative to the arithmetic mean of the sample. The standard deviation is the quadratic mean of the squared differences of each data point from the mean of all data points. The standard deviation indicates the spread (width) of a frequency distribution. A small standard deviation means that most of the values lie close to the mean value. (When computing the "population mean" from a sample of n data points, replace n with $(n - 1)$ in the expression for the variance to obtain the *unbiased estimate* of the standard deviation. Most statistics packages routinely do this. The difference is not significant if n is large, of course.)

---

[4] For symmetrical distributions, the mean, mode, and median coincide. If the distribution is skewed to the left (more area below the mean) then Mode < Median < Mean. If it is skewed to the right, then Mean < Median < Mode. If the frequency distribution is unimodel (i.e., has a single peak) and is moderately skewed (asymmetrical), then empirical data shows that Mean – Mode ≈ 3*(Mean – Median).

You are also often interested in the relationship between two sets of data, for example pairs of points (x, y). The *Pearson product-moment correlation coefficient*, r, is often used to indicate the strength of the linear relationship between x and y:

$$r = \left(\frac{1}{n-1}\right) * \sum_{i=1}^{n}\left[\frac{(x_i - \bar{x})}{s_x}\right] * \left[\frac{y_i - \bar{y}}{s_y}\right]$$

where n is the number of data points, $\bar{x}$ and $\bar{y}$ are the sample means of x and y, respectively, and s_x and s_y are the sample standard deviations of x and y, respectively. (There are also other mathematical forms for r.) When x and y have a positive linear relationship (y = a + b*x with b > 0), then r = 1. If they have a negative linear relationship (b < 0), then r = –1. A value near zero indicates lack of a linear relationship. Some authors call the quantity the *sample correlation coefficient*. The square of r, r^2, is called the *coefficient of determination*, and indicates the percentage of variance of one quantity (e.g., y) that can be accounted for by the variation in the other quantity (e.g., x).[5] A strong correlation between two quantities does *not* necessarily imply a causal relationship between them. You must perform further analysis to decide whether a causal relation actually exists. These correlation measures are defined for interval, ratio, and absolute scale measurements.

To measure correlation for interval scale data, you use the Spearman rank correlation coefficient, defined as

$$r_{RANK} = 1 - \left[\frac{6}{n(n^2 - 1)}\right]\sum_{i=1}^{n}D_i^2$$

where D_i is the difference in the ranks for item i obtained using two different measurements. For example, two different individuals might each rank a list of product features. The value of r_{RANK} indicates the consistency of their rankings. There are some options on handling ties. See Chapter IX in [Arkin, 1970] for details.

There are many other statistical tests, each suited for some particular situation. For example, *chi-squared tests* are useful for data represented on a nominal scale (such as counts of defects by type). Fenton and Pfleeger provide a good summary in Section 6.5 of their book [Fenton, 1997]. Also see Table 2-3 in [Goodpasture, 2004, page 46].

---

[5] You can extend the concept to multiple variables using the *coefficient of multiple determination*, R^2. R^2 represents the amount of total variation in the sample that is accounted for by a multiple regression model. (Section 17.6 describes regression fitting.) To balance the complexity of using more parameters in the model function against the increase in the value of R^2, statisticians use the *adjusted coefficient of multiple determination*. Consult the statistics books referenced at the end of this appendix for details.

B.4 Recommended Reading

Several excellent books discuss measurement theory as it applies to software and system engineering. Norman Fenton and Shari Lawrence Pfleeger provide a good overview of the difficulties in defining software measurements in general in Chapter 5 of [Fenton, 1997]. Also see the books by Bob Hughes [Hughes, 2000], Martin Shepperd [Shepperd, 1995], and Sam Conte et al. [Conte, 1986]. Horst Zuse has the most comprehensive discussion [Zuse, 1997, Section 5.13]. Cem Kaner gives a short overview in an article [Kaner, 2000]. Stephen Kan provides a brief overview in Sections 3.1 and 3.2 of [Kan, 2003].

There are many books on statistics and analysis of experimental data. David Card gives a good overview in Appendix D of [Card, 1990]. Chapter 13 of [Devore, 1991] is highly recommended. Richard Wyskida describes statistical techniques for cost estimation in Chapter 3 of [Stewart, 1995]. Fenton and Pfleeger identify statistical measures that are appropriate for different scale types in Table 3.8 of [Fenton, 1997]. David Sheskin's handbook is very comprehensive and covers both parametric and nonparametric statistical procedures [Sheskin, 2000]. Sidney Siegel and John Castallan cover nonparametric statistics in [Siegel, 1988]. The U.S. National Institute of Standards and Technology publishes an online engineering statistics handbook, accessible at http://www.itl.nist.gov/div898/handbook/index2.html. John Goodpasture provides a concise description of probability distributions in [Goodpasture, 2004, pages 41–46]. He also provides a good description of statistical measures on pages 45 through 55 of the same book. William Press et al. give a short overview of statistics in Chapter 14 of [Press, 1992]. Sam Kachigan covers univariate and multivariate methods [Kachigan, 1986].

Appendix C

Measures of Estimation Accuracy

Two types of measures describe the accuracy of estimation models. The first deals with the characteristics of a set of estimates and uses statistics to describe the population. The second deals with the time history of estimates. You can apply these two types to any estimated quantity. All you need is a set of paired values. Each pair consists of the estimated value, E, and the actual (true) value, A. For the first type (set of values), these are the estimated and true values. For the second type (time series), these are the estimated value and the time that it was estimated, plus the (final) true value.

C.1 Statistics of a Set of Estimates

The *residual error*, R, is defined as

$$R_i = A_i - E_i$$

where i denotes the particular data pair. An error of a particular size represents a more serious error for a small quantity than for a large quantity, however, so it is better to normalize the value of the residual by the measured value to get the *relative error*, RE:

$$RE_i = R_i / A_i = (A_i - E_i) / A_i$$

The relative error measure is independent of scale. Residuals can be positive and negative, so just adding them may cancel out large errors, giving a false indication of accuracy. A better accuracy measure is the *magnitude of the relative error (MRE)*

$$\text{MRE}_i = |\text{RE}_i|$$

The *mean magnitude of the relative error (MMRE)* is defined as:

$$\text{MMRE} = \frac{1}{n}\sum_{i=1}^{n}\text{MRE}_i = \frac{1}{n}\sum_{i=1}^{n}\left|\frac{A_i - E_i}{A_i}\right|$$

where n is the number of samples.

Conte, Dunsmore, and Shen first defined the MMRE measure [Conte, 1986]. They also used MRE to define another measure called the *prediction level (PRED)*.[1] For a set of n estimates, let k denote the number of estimates for which MRE is less than or equal to some value q. Define:

$$\text{PRED}(q) = k/n$$

For example, PRED(0.25) = 0.75 means that the model estimated the quantity within ±25% of actuals 75% of the time. Conte, Dunsmore, and Shen consider a "good" estimating model to have MMRE ≤ 0.25 and PRED(0.25) ≥ 0.75.

MRE is used in MMRE and PRED. Recent work by Tron Foss, Ingunn Myrtveit, and Erik Stensrud indicate that MRE is larger for small projects than for large projects based on effort data from 81 projects [Foss, 2001]. The implication is that effort estimates for small projects will have more error (potential uncertainty) than would be indicated by the MMRE value computed for a sample of mixed size projects. MMRE tends to conceal the effect of underestimates because of an asymmetry in the value of RE for quantities that are constrained to be greater than or equal to zero such as size and effort. This constraint means that the value of RE has an upper limit of 1 for underestimates (for the worst case of E = 0), but has an infinite upper value for overestimates. Yukio Miyazaki and his colleagues therefore proposed the *balanced relative error (BRE)*:

$$\text{BRE} = |A - E|/\min(A, E)$$

See [Miyazaki, 1991].

Robert Hughes observes that the balanced relative error appears to involve two different measurements:

- The residual divided by the actual
- The residual divided by the estimate

---

[1] They also defined three other measures: the coefficient of multiple determination (R^2), the mean squared error (MSE), and the relative root mean squared error (RMS). The latter two are defined for regression models only. Most studies of estimation accuracy only use MMRE and PRED.

The first is essentially MMRE. The second considers the estimate to be a *target* for planning and managing the project, and measures how well the manager can hit the target. (Chapter 1, "Introduction," discussed estimates as targets.) The "goodness" of the initial estimate is important because an overestimate of the required resources might lead to a decrease in productivity because the staff has a lot of slack time. In contrast, an underestimate might pressure the team to deliver a product that has fewer features than desired or that has many defects.

To measure the "goodness" of a target estimate, Hughes proposes a measure called the *variation from estimate (VFE)* defined as

VFE = (Estimate – Actual)/Estimate = $(E - A)/E$

The *mean variation from estimate (MVFE)* is defined analogously to MMRE. Hughes and his colleagues argue that MVFE is a truer reflection of estimation accuracy *from a project manager's viewpoint*. They do *not* propose MVFE as a replacement for MMRE as a measure of estimating accuracy. MVFE really provides another view. (This is another example of how the definition of the measure depends on your measurement goals.) For details see [Hughes, 2000, page 161] and [Hughes, 1998].

C.2 Statistics of a Time Sequence of Estimates

Tom DeMarco defines a measure of estimating accuracy over time in Section 3.2 of his classic book [DeMarco, 1982]. He gauges estimation success based on how well the series of estimated values converges to the final actual value. He defines the estimation quality factor (EQF) as the reciprocal of the average discrepancy (the estimation error).

Figure C-1 shows a series of estimated values (solid line) versus (relative) time. The dashed line shows the final actual value. To calculate the value of EQF, compute the total area between the dashed line and the solid line. Call this the *weighted estimation error*. Then divide the total area under the dashed line by the weighted estimation error. For the data shown in the figure, the total area equals 3.5 and the weighted estimation error equals 0.40, giving EQF = 8.75 (= 3.5/0.4). DeMarco says this is not too bad. Larger values of EQF imply a more accurate estimate. (A perfect estimate has EQF = ∞.)

Unfortunately, you can only compute the value of EQF *after* the actual value is known. Still, you may find this measure useful for measuring the accuracy of the estimating process. Note, however, that EQF measures the *combined* effects of estimation errors *and* any changes in the scope of the project. Because the completed project is seldom the project that was estimated at the beginning, EQF might not be a useful measure of estimating performance for projects with significant growth and volatility. In addition, this means that EQF is a poor measure for long-duration projects. EQF should be a good measure if the project's scope does not change. This is a good assumption for agile methods.

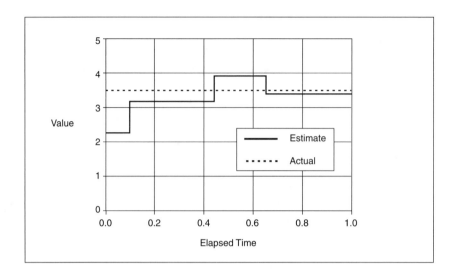

Figure C-1 *Estimated values versus time*

Another concept is to devise a functional form based on historical data that gives a correction factor versus time. The value of this factor starts at some finite value, and then decreases monotonically to zero as the project approaches completion. For examples of such functions, see [Stutzke, 2000]. You could possibly use such functions to correct their estimates made at any particular time, thereby achieving greater accuracy.

C.3 Choosing the "Best" Measure of Estimation Accuracy

Statistical analyses assume that the data points represent a random sample of a static population. In practice, this is seldom the case. Thus, some estimation models may fit certain data sets better than others, based on a particular accuracy measure, whereas the reverse may be true if another accuracy measure is used. The same holds true for time series data because the "project" evolves between measurements, and so trends may affect the data. (Section 3.5 in [Conte, 1986] provides an example of such behavior by evaluating the accuracy of four estimation models against the same set of data using six different accuracy measures. See Table 3.13 in [Conte, 1986].) *Always* use *multiple* accuracy measures and apply judgment to interpret the results.

C.4 Using Excel to Calculate Estimation Error

Figure C-2 shows a spreadsheet to compute the accuracy measures for 19 data points collected by J. W. Bailey and V. R. Basili, taken from Appendix B.3 in [Conte, 1986]. (Using the same data allows comparison of my results to those of Conte et al.) I used their Model 4 as the effort estimator, $\text{Effort} = 2.09 * \text{Size}^{0.95}$. The spreadsheet shows the usual notation and Conte's notation for each quantity. It also shows the units of measure under each quantity. For example, size is measured in KSLOC.

Evaluation of Estimation Accuracy
NASA SEL Data [Bailey, 1981]
Model 4 - Power Function: $2.09 * S^{0.95}$

Usual:	N	S	MA		ME	MRE	MMRE	MSE	MSA	RMS	Rel RMS	RSQ
Conte:	N	S	Not Defined		E-Bar	RE-Bar	MRE-Bar	SE-Bar	Not Defined	RMS	RMS-Bar	RSQ
	19		53.05		3.18	-0.05	0.27	414.33	5125.64	20.91	0.39	0.82
ID#	Size	E_act	E_est	Act-Est	RE	ABS(RE)	(Act-Est)^2	(E_act)^2	RMS	Rel RMS	RSQ
	(KSLOC)	(PM)	(PM)	(PM)	(Fraction)	(Fraction)	(PM^2)	(PM^2)	(PM)	(Fraction)	(Fraction)
1	90.157	125.5	150.5	-25.0	-0.199	0.199	622.56	15750.25			
2	46.211	104.0	79.7	24.3	0.233	0.233	588.74	10816.00			
3	46.458	85.6	80.1	5.5	0.064	0.064	29.80	7327.36			
4	54.531	98.4	93.3	5.1	0.052	0.052	25.84	9682.56			
5	31.144	36.7	54.8	-18.1	-0.493	0.493	327.94	1346.89			
6	12.754	20.5	23.5	-3.0	-0.145	0.145	8.82	420.25			
7	10.511	11.2	19.5	-8.3	-0.744	0.744	69.39	125.44			
8	21.508	30.9	38.6	-7.7	-0.248	0.248	58.65	954.81			
9	3.060	7.5	6.0	1.5	0.194	0.194	2.11	56.25			
10	4.233	9.8	8.2	1.6	0.160	0.160	2.46	96.04			
11	7.825	7.9	14.8	-6.9	-0.868	0.868	47.00	62.41			
12	2.052	5.4	4.1	1.3	0.234	0.234	1.59	29.16			
13	4.978	9.1	9.6	-0.5	-0.055	0.055	0.25	82.81			
14	78.580	107.0	132.0	-25.0	-0.234	0.234	626.81	11449.00			
15	9.736	16.9	18.2	-1.3	-0.075	0.075	1.59	285.61			
16	12.455	25.9	22.9	3.0	0.114	0.114	8.72	670.81			
17	49.468	139.5	85.1	54.4	0.390	0.390	2963.09	19460.25			
18	48.968	132.9	84.2	48.7	0.366	0.366	2366.95	17662.41			
19	12.112	33.3	22.3	11.0	0.329	0.329	119.99	1108.89			

Figure C-2 *Estimation accuracy—data and statistics*

To get PRED you could sort the points by their MRE value and plot a histogram or scatter plot. To show another method, I used the Excel COUNTIF function to compute the data plotted in Figure C-3. (The spreadsheet on the CD-ROM has seven columns above the plot that define the "bins.") I counted only the values of Abs(RE) having a value less than or equal to the bin limit (0.05, 0.10, etc.). I normalized the counts by the total number of points (19 in this case). The plot shows the PRED value versus accuracy. From the plot, PRED(0.25) is 68%. (Table 3.12 in [Conte, 1986] gives 63%.)

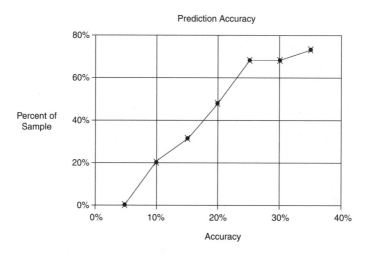

Figure C-3 *Plot of PRED value for estimation data*

Appendix D

Summation Formulas for Series

Series arise in estimating software product performance, for example, in queueing theory. This appendix collects some useful results.

Successive terms of the *arithmetic progression* differ by a constant amount, d. The sum of the first n terms is

$$a + (a + d) + (a + 2d) + (a + 3d) + \ldots + \{a + (n-1)d\}$$

$$= \sum_{i=1}^{n} (a + [i-1]d) = na + n(n-1)\frac{d}{2}$$

Successive terms of the *geometric progression* differ by a constant factor, r. The sum of the first n terms is

$$\sum_{i=1}^{n} ar^{i-1} = \frac{a(r^n - 1)}{r - 1} = \frac{a(1 - r^n)}{1 - r} = \sum_{i=0}^{n-1} ar^i$$

If $r^2 < 1$, then

$$\sum_{i=1}^{\infty} ar^{i-1} = \frac{a}{1 - r}$$

Also

$$\sum_{i=0}^{n-1} ir^i = \sum_{i=1}^{n-1} ir^i = \frac{r(1-r^n)}{(1-r)^2} - \frac{nr^n}{(1-r)}$$

If $r < 1$, then

$$\sum_{i=1}^{\infty} ir^i = \frac{r}{(1-r)^2}$$

You can replace the ratio, r, with any power of r. For example, using r^2 in a geometric progression with a=r gives

$$\sum_{i=0}^{n-1} r^{2i+1} = r\sum_{i=0}^{n-1}(r^2)^i = \frac{r(1-r^{2n})}{(1-r^2)}$$

Here are some other useful results for the sums of powers of the first n numbers

$$\sum_{i=1}^{n}(i) = 1+2+3+4+5+....+n = \frac{n(n+1)}{2}$$

The sum of the squares of the first n numbers is

$$\sum_{i=1}^{n}(i^2) = 1^2 + 2^2 + 3^2 + 4^2 + 5^2 + ... + n^2 = \frac{n(n+1)(2n+1)}{6}$$

The sum of the cubes of the first n numbers is

$$\sum_{i=1}^{n}(i^3) = 1^3 + 2^3 + 3^3 + 4^3 + 5^3 + ... + n^3 = \frac{n^2(n+1)^2}{4}$$

You can approximate the value of $n!$ using Stirling's Formula:

$$n! \approx e^{-n}n^n\sqrt{2\pi n}$$

Appendix E

Excel for Estimators

This appendix describes features of Microsoft Excel that are useful for estimators. It also describes tips and techniques that you can use to ensure that users obtain accurate, consistent results every time. Notes N42, N43, N44, and N49 provide specific examples that use these techniques. This appendix also identifies books and websites where you can find more information.

E.1 Introduction

For every spreadsheet, I provide user instructions, data validation, standard labeling, and a consistent appearance. I take the time to specify labels, pagination, and print areas. If appropriate, I force calculations to occur at certain times. Although you can do many of these actions "on-the-fly" (e.g., selecting and then printing an area), this is time-consuming and error prone, especially when users make multiple runs in rapid succession. Investing extra effort in constructing a spreadsheet will pay big dividends later.

E.1.1 Contents

It was difficult to decide what to include because Excel has many features. Many people know some of the features. Few people know all of the features. In addition, different people often know different subsets of Excel features. There are many good books describing Excel's features, but these are often very large, making it hard for estimators to locate information that is relevant to their needs.

I did not want to duplicate material in Excel textbooks but I did want to pro-vide enough basic information to get you started.[1] I decided to focus on describing the basic features that estimators will use. I used all of these in the book. I will also post updates and new Excel tips on my website.

I organized material so you can locate what you need quickly. (Skip over the topics you already know.)

1. Introduction and References
2. Basic Concepts
3. Labeling
4. Helping Users and Maintainers
5. Printing
6. Plotting
7. Advanced Features
8. Macros and Visual Basic for Applications

Warning: These instructions work for Excel 2003. The instructions and menus may be located on different menus on your version. I ask readers to send me updates for their versions so I can post them on the book's website.

E.1.2 Reference Books

This section identifies books I used in preparing the spreadsheets described in this book. Features change with each release of Excel, however, so you should check for recent releases or new editions. You can also find much useful infor-mation in Excel's Help Wizard and on the Web.

No single book covers all of Excel's features. No matter which book you con-sult, the best book is the *third* book. (By then you are starting to understand it!) I found the following books useful:

[Frye, 2003]   *Microsoft Office Excel 2003 Step by Step*, Curtis Frye, book and CD-ROM, Microsoft Press, 2003, ISBN 0-7356-1511-X. For beginners.

---

[1] Another potential drawback of providing a lot of detail is that the text will become obsolete sooner.

[Stinson, 2004]   *Microsoft Office Excel 2003 Inside Out*, Craig Stinson and Mark Dodge, book and CD-ROM, Microsoft Press, 2004, ISBN 0-7356-1518-7. Covers all features and is well organized. Good for intermediate to advanced users.

[Walkenbach, 2003]   *Excel 2003 Bible*, John Walkenbach, book and CD-ROM, John Wiley & Sons, 2003, ISBN 0-7645-3967-1. Very complete.

[Blattner, 2003]   *Special Edition Using Microsoft Office Excel 2003*, Patrick Blattner, book and CD-ROM, Que, ISBN 0-7897-2953-9. For seasoned users.

The following books are useful if you plan to write Excel VBA:

[Webb, 1996]   *Special Edition Using Excel Visual Basic for Applications, 2nd Edition*, Jeff Webb, Que, 1996, ISBN 0-7897-0269-X.

[Roman, 2002]   *Writing Excel Macros with VBA, 2nd edition*, Steve Roman, O'Reilly and Associates, 2002, ISBN 0-596-00359-5.

For more on the problems of end-user programming, see [Harrison, 2004].

[Harrison, 2004]   *The Dangers of End-User Programming*, Warren Harrison, IEEE Software, v. 21, n. 4, July/August 2004, pages 5–7.

William Orvis describes numerical techniques that may be of interest for some estimators:

[Orvis, 1996]   *Excel for Scientist and Engineers, 2nd edition*, William J. Orvis, Sybex, 1996, ISBN 0-7821-1761-9.

E.1.3 Websites

Many websites provide information about Excel. For a tutorial, just enter "Excel tutorial" in any search engine. One such site is http://www.ce.memphis.edu/1112/excel/xlweb.htm.

You can also search on "Excel tips" for lots of advice. Microsoft maintains pages of Excel tips submitted by users, but there are many other sites as well. Sites dealing specifically with Visual Basic for Applications include the following:

http://www.excel-vba.com/excel-vba-contents.htm

http://www.j-walk.com/ss/excel/tips/

E.2 Basic Concepts

This section reviews terminology and explains how to calculate using a spreadsheet.

E.2.1 Worksheets and Cell Addresses

A *workbook* is a single Excel file containing worksheets and charts. (The words *spreadsheet* and *workbook* are synonymous.) Each worksheet and chart has a name, shown in the tab at the bottom of the screen. A *worksheet* consists of cells arranged in rows and columns. The rows are numbered, beginning with 1. The columns are lettered, beginning with A. You can specify a particular cell by giving its address. A *relative address* refers to a cell in relation to the currently selected cell (e.g., B3 refers to the cell three rows below and two columns to the right). An *absolute address* specifies position relative to the upper-left corner of a worksheet (e.g., $A$1 is the cell in the upper-left corner). A *Row-Column reference* (also call an *R1C1 address*) uses numbers for both rows and columns (e.g., R10C3 is equivalent to C10). You will use the relative and absolute addresses most often. The Row-Column reference style is useful when you use loops to index through multiple cells. (See Section E.8 on macros.) You can optionally address cells on another worksheet by putting the name of the worksheet before the address and including an exclamation mark. For example, Data!A1 references cell A1 on the worksheet named Data.

A *range* is a single cell or a group of cells, which need not be contiguous. (An *area* is a contiguous group of cells. A range can consist of multiple areas.) You specify a range with a colon. For example, A1:C1 specifies three cells (A1, B1, and C1). You can also reference a range of cells on another worksheet: Data!A1:C1.

Cells contain data or formulas. You can specify the type of data and how it is displayed in the cell. For example, you can specify the number of digits for a numeric value. A formula calculates the value of a cell, usually by referring to other cells. To enter a function you select the cell, and enter the equals sign (=) followed by the desired calculation. For example, to add the contents of cells A1 and B1, type the following:

= A1 + B1

If you click the lower-right corner of a cell, you can drag formulas to adjacent cells. (You can also copy and paste formulas, formats, etc.) Excel automatically updates addresses. For example, if you drag the preceding formula right one cell, it becomes

= B1 + C1

If you instead drag it down one row, it becomes

= A2 + B2

To prevent this automatic indexing, enter a dollar sign ($) before the coordinate you want to keep fixed. For example, $A1 locks the cell in column A, but dragging the formula down will increment the row number. Typing $A$1 locks both the row and column.

E.2.2 Calculating: Formulas and Functions

You can compute/manipulate the contents of a cell using a formula. For numbers you can add (+), subtract (–), multiply (*), divide (/), divide and truncate to integer (\), and exponentiate (^). You can concatenate text strings using the & operator (e.g., "High" & D7). You must enclose strings within double quotes in formulas or in the arguments of functions and subroutines. To enter text lines beginning with the equals sign (=), you must precede it with an apostrophe (').

You can compare numbers (or strings) using these operators:

=	Equal
<>	Not equal
<	Less than
>	Greater than
< =	Less than or equal to
> =	Greater than or equal to

There are additional operators. Consult Excel's Help or consult one of the books cited previously. For example, Table 3.3 in [Webb, 1996] lists all operators and their order of precedence.

Excel has many built-in functions that you can use in formulas to perform complicated calculations. For example, the SUM function adds the values in ranges of cells containing numbers:

= SUM(A1:C1, F7:H7)

To view the list of built-in functions, select a cell. The formula bar at the top of the sheet (below the tool bars) opens. To the left is the symbol f_x. Clicking this symbol causes the Insert Function window to pop up. Select a category and then a function. You can also ask for help on each function, which includes detailed examples showing how to use the function. The categories of Excel's built-in functions are as follows:

- Financial
- Date & Time
- Math and Trig
- Statistical
- Lookup and Reference
- Database
- Text
- Logical
- Information
- User Defined

For example, you have functions to select portions of a string (LEFT, MID, and RIGHT), and to CONCATENATE strings. You can use these to construct cell addresses used by other functions. (Note N49 describes some examples.)

Use the IF function to perform actions based on some condition. The format is

= IF(condition, action if true, action if false)

For example, you might write

= IF(A1 > 0, B1 + C1, D1 + E1)

which puts the sum of B1 and C1 in the cell if the value in A1 is greater than zero; otherwise, it loads the sum of D1 and E1. You can construct more complex conditions using the logical operators NOT, AND, and OR in the conditions:

NOT (A1 > 0)
AND (A1 > 0, H1 < 6)
OR (A1 > 0, H1 < 6)

You can also combine these with built-in functions. The formula

= IF(COUNT(A1:C1, "X") > 0, D1, E1)

counts cells A1:C1 containing the letter X. If the count is greater than zero, it loads the value of cell D1; otherwise, it loads the value of E1.

TIP 1: Place the totals at the *top* of pages so you can add more rows by simply dragging the formulas down. (Click the lower-right corner of the cell and drag it down.)

TIP 2: Mark the last row in a worksheet to show where the formulas end. Otherwise, users might enter values past the last row, and they would not be included in totals, averages, or other calculations. Some writers just drag formulas down a thousand rows or so, "larger than any user would conceivably need." Users do strange things, however, so I prefer to mark the last row across all columns with a gray or yellow background, optionally typing "End of Formulas" in one of the cells. (You can use the MATCH function to detect the end of data. See Note N49, "Designing the CLEF2PA Spreadsheet." AHP.xls also provides an example.)

You can display the formulas in all cells by simultaneously pressing the Ctrl and back single quote (`) keys. You can then print the spreadsheet to obtain a hard copy. (If the formulas are long, you will have to widen the columns to see the entire formula.) This is useful for debugging and documenting formulas. Pressing the same two keys again toggles back to the view of the values in each cell.

E.2.3 Example: Functions for Population Statistics

Measured values often have significant errors. Appendix B, "Measurement Theory and Statistics," defines basic statistical measures that describe a collection of data points (a "population sample"). You can use Excel's statistical function to compute these measures. (Appendix C, "Measures of Estimation Accuracy," describes how to use Excel to calculate various measures of estimation error.)

Figure E-1 shows a spreadsheet illustrating the use of these functions. The X and Y data shown in columns A and B is fictitious. Column C, rows 2 through 8, lists some common statistical measures. Columns D and E show the values of these measures for X and Y, respectively. Column D, rows 11 and 12, show the values of r and r^2. All of these values are obtained from built-in Excel functions as shown in Figure E-2.

	A	B	C	D	E
1	X	Y		X	Y
2	1.3	9.2	Count =	8	8
3	1.3	8.7	Minimun =	1.30	8.60
4	1.7	9.8	Maximum =	2.80	12.40
5	1.9	8.6	Arith. Mean =	2.03	10.24
6	2.2	10.9	Median =	2.05	10.35
7	2.4	10.9	Mode =	1.30	10.90
8	2.6	12.4	Std. Dev. =	0.57	1.37
9	2.8	11.4			
10			Correlation of X and Y		
11			r =	0.861	
12			r^2 =	0.742	
13					

Figure E-1 *Examples of the basic population statistics*

	A	B	C	D	E
1	X	Y		X	Y
2	1.3	9.2	Count =	= COUNT(A2:A20)	= COUNT(B2:B20)
3	1.3	8.7	Minimun =	= MIN(A2:A20)	= MIN(B2:B20)
4	1.7	9.8	Maximum =	= MAX(A2:A20)	= MAX(B2:B20)
5	1.9	8.6	Arith. Mean =	= AVERAGE(A2:A20)	= AVERAGE(B2:B20)
6	2.2	11	Median =	= MEDIAN(A2:A20)	= MEDIAN(B2:B20)
7	2.4	11	Mode =	= MODE(A2:A20)	= MODE(B2:B20)
8	2.6	12	Std. Dev. =	= STDEV(A2:A20)	= STDEV(B2:B20)
9	2.8	11			
10			Correlation of X and Y		
11			r =	= PEARSON(A2:A20,B2:B20)	
12			r^2 =	= RSQ(A2:A20,B2:B20)	
13					

Figure E-2 *Excel formulas for previous figure*

To measure correlation for interval scale data, you use the Spearman rank correlation coefficient. For example, two individuals might each rank a list of product features. The value of r_{RANK} indicates the consistency of their rankings. Figure E-3 shows an example for nine features, A through I. Figure E-4 shows the formulas used.

	A	B	C	D	E
1	*Spearman Rank Correlation*			r_RANK =	0.850
2				n =	9
3				Sum(D^2) =	18
4					
5	Feature	Person #1	Person #2	D	D^2
6	A	1	3	-2	4
7	B	2	1	1	1
8	C	3	4	-1	1
9	D	4	5	-1	1
10	E	5	2	3	9
11	F	6	6	0	0
12	G	7	7	0	0
13	H	8	9	-1	1
14	I	9	8	1	1
15					
16					

Figure E-3 *Spreadsheet to calculate the Spearman rank correlation coefficient*

	A	B	C	D	E
1				r_RANK =	= 1-6*$E$3/($E$2*($E$2^2-1)
2				n =	= COUNTA(A6:A20)
3				Sum(D^2) =	= SUM(E6:E20)

Figure E-4 *Formulas for Spearman rank correlation*

E.3 Labeling Spreadsheets and Documents

You will produce and update many spreadsheets for a large project. Updates occur rapidly when you are preparing estimates for a proposal. To help you keep track of the printed copies that accumulate, you need a way to label spreadsheets and documents *automatically* to identify versions.

You need to record the following:

- Workbook or document name and version (filename)
- Worksheet name (for workbooks)
- Date and time (last updated)
- Page X of Y

You will probably want a systematic way to capture other information such as project identifier, run identifier, author's name, and company name.

You can use filenames to capture some of this information. If you use Microsoft Excel and Word, you can capture other information using headers and footers. This section gives suggestions.

E.3.1 Choosing Filenames

You should devise a filenaming scheme that suits your project, preferably *before* you generate a lot of files. Use short filenames that include a version number. I put the version number in parentheses (e.g., Project X Est (v1).xls). For a new project, you will want to copy and rename the file. You can type the name and version of the original source in the "Notes" worksheet, type it into the header or footer, or use the SetFooter macro described in Section E.8. Naming is more complicated if you need spreadsheets for multiple variants (e.g., for three distinct product designs). Suppose that you have three versions, A1, A2, and B0. You could construct names such as Project X Est A1 (v2).xls, for example.

E.3.2 Labeling Microsoft Word Documents

Although this appendix focuses on Excel spreadsheets, you will want to track Word documents too. (This is actually easier to do in Word than in Excel.) My usual convention is as follows:

Left header:	Filename
Right header:	SaveDate
Center footer:	Page (or Page X of Y)

(Using "Page X of Y" allows you to detect missing pages at the end of a document.) If you like, you can put information on multiple lines:

Left header:	Filename
	Author
Right header:	SaveDate
	Page (or Page X of Y)

I use the date/time saved, not the date/time printed so that all copies, whenever printed, will have the same date/time value.

To set up headers for Microsoft Word, click View | Header and Footer. Dashed rectangles appear at the top and bottom of each page, and the Header and Footer toolbar appears. You can move the cursor to either rectangle and click to select it. (Alternatively, toward the right on the toolbar is an icon to select header or footer. Placing the cursor over the icons displays their name.)

For the left header, click Insert Auto Text on the toolbar, and then select File-name. (You can also select Pathname to get the full path if desired.) Tab to the right header. In the *top* (Word) toolbar, click Insert | Field, then select Date and Time, and then SaveDate. Then pick a format showing the date and time to the nearest second. (For Microsoft Word, selecting Date and Time on the Insert Auto Text menu gives the last date *printed*, which will be *different* on every copy that you print, even if you have not altered the document in any way. This creates confusion in tracking updates to the document. To avoid this, always use the SaveDate or the EditDate, which you can only select from the Insert | Field menu.)

To set page numbers, position to the desired location, and either click Insert Auto Text, or click the icons on the toolbar, or use Insert | Numbering and select Page. (The Pages item equals the total pages and is under Document Information for some reason.)

E.3.3 Labeling Microsoft Excel Worksheets

I put all information at the top of the worksheet. I do not use the footer. My recommended settings are as follows:

Left header:	Filename and Worksheet Name
Center header:	Date and Time
Right header:	Page X of Y

I only include the page numbers if I expect multiple pages. If appropriate, also include your name, and the name of your company, department, project, and so forth. Always label *every* worksheet in your spreadsheet.

To create a header for an Excel worksheet, click View | Header and Footer, and then click Custom Header. The Header dialog box appears with three areas: Left, Center, and Right. Click an area to set it. The toolbar has icons you can select. Picking an icon inserts a variable name in the field. The conventions are as follows:

Object	*Icon*	*Variable Name*
File	Sheet icon with green X	&[File]
Worksheet	Sheet icon with tiny tabs at bottom	&[Tab]
Date	Calendar icon	&[Date]
Time	Clock icon	&[Time]
Page	Sheet icon with #	&[Page]
Total pages	Sheet icon with ++	&[Pages]

To enter "Page X of Y" you must type "Page ", click the page number, type " of ", and then click total pages. Click OK twice to accept the values you enter. Figure E-5 illustrates a spreadsheet with a header.

| Good Header (v1) | | | 2/1/2005 |
| Data | | | 12:58 PM |

	A	B	C	D
1	**First**	**Last**	**ID Number**	**Role**
2	Mary	Smith	011	Engr
3	John	Brown	314	Engr
4	Frank	White	278	Mgr
5	Susan	Jones	987	Engr
6	Bill	Green	023	Mgr
7	Jill	Black	057	Engr
8				
9		End of Formulas		

Figure E-5 *Spreadsheet with a header*

One shortcoming of Microsoft Excel is that the date and time that appear on the sheet is when it was *printed*. If you reprint a copy of the spreadsheet, it will have a different date and time, which can lead to confusion. Excel has no option to insert the date and time that the spreadsheet was last saved in the header or footer. However, you can use the SaveDate macro described in Section E.8. This makes configuration control a lot easier, but requires a macro in every spreadsheet.

E.3.4 Using Templates

You can use headers and footers to label every page of a document, and every page of every worksheet. Unfortunately, setting headers and footers in every document is not automatic. You can, however, define *templates*, special files that serve as a model for new documents (DOT file) or new worksheets (XLT file). Templates standardize forms and reports, and protect the original version (because users must specify a new name when they create a new object using the template). You can use any Word document or Excel workbook as a template. You add templates to a special folder. Then you can select a template from a list when you create a new document or worksheet. For more information, see any of the Excel books identified in Section E.1.2.

E.3.5 Setting and Using Properties

You *can* set certain fields for a Word document or Excel spreadsheet by right-clicking the document or spreadsheet icon and selecting Properties. You can set the author's name on the Summary tab. The Custom tab provides fields such as Subject and Keywords. You can convey most of these to headers or footers by selecting Insert | Field and picking the item from the list. (Some items are not on the list, however, and so are not easily accessible. You can access them using macros, however.)

E.4 Helping Users

Problems arise when someone besides the original author uses a spreadsheet or needs to modify the spreadsheet (often months later). This section describes features you can use to help users of your spreadsheets.

E.4.1 Notes

The original author of a spreadsheet should always provide a brief description, usage instructions, and some design rationale. The rationale should explain the sequence of computation, logic for data validation, conditional formatting, control of computations, the sources or derivations of key equations, unusual features, and any key assumptions or nonobvious programming tricks. (References to specific pages in books are often useful.) You can also provide additional information describing the project, assumptions, and conditions as appropriate. I include a Notes worksheet that contains this information in every workbook. Anyone who modifies the spreadsheet should update this information.

E.4.2 Comments

You can attach a comment to any cell. Click to select the cell, and then right-click to get the drop-down menu. Then select Insert Comment. A box with shaded edges appears containing the name of the registered user of the copy of Excel you are using. (This is usually your name.) Select the name by holding down the left mouse button and dragging the cursor over the text. Press the Delete key. Then enter your message. Use a carriage return to insert blank lines. Keep your message short. (You can enter several lines of text, but the box only displays 5 lines of approximately 20 characters each. There is no scrollbar.) Click another cell when you are done entering text. A small red triangle appears in the upper-right corner of a cell to indicate that it has an attached comment. Moving the cursor into the cell causes the comment to appear.

E.4.3 Coloring

I use consistent colors in all worksheets to indicate the purpose of the cell. For example, I shade cells requiring user input light green. To set colors, first click the cell(s) to change. A drop-down list appears. Click to select Format Cells. The Format Cells dialog box appears with the following tabs:

- Number
- Alignment
- Font
- Border
- Patterns
- Protection

To set the background color, click the Patterns tab. Then click the desired color in the palette, and then click OK. You can also specify a pattern by clicking on Pattern. To set the font color, click the Font tab, and click Color to get the color palette. (You can also set font style, emphasis, and point size.)

E.4.4 Conditional Formatting

Conditional formatting changes the appearance of a cell based on values in the cell or values in other cells. I use conditional formatting to highlight cells and to suppress unneeded or distracting information. For example, if the user answers "Yes" to a question, you might want the user to enter additional data in other cells. You can indicate this by highlighting these cells. To do this, select the cell(s) requiring the additional data. Select Format | Conditional Formatting. On the left drop-down list, select Formula. In the center area, enter the desired condition using the two other cells at the right if needed. (See the following examples.) Then click the Format button, and select the desired format. For input values, select the Patterns tab, and click the light-green color. Here are examples of formulas for conditional formatting to shade a cell if

Cell A1 contains a "Y":	= ($A$1 = "Y")
Cell A1 contains a number between 2 and 9:	= AND($A$1 > 2, $A$1 < 9)
Cell A1 is not empty:	= NOT(ISBLANK($A$1)

An empty cell is not the same as a cell with a blank (""). Cells with conditional formatting or formulas are not empty, even though you may see nothing on the screen. The cells referenced in the condition for conditional formatting must be on the same worksheet as the cell being formatted.

E.4.5 Data Validation

Data validation can validate an entry against a specified condition (text, number, date, list, etc.). If you use a list (specified by a range), it can also display the list as a drop-down menu. The list (cell range) must be on the same worksheet as the cell being validated.

To validate data, select a cell and click Data | Validation. The Data Validation dialog box appears. Choose the Settings tab. Choose your condition by clicking the drop-down icon under Allow. Click your choice. Depending on the choice, you will be prompted for values, a range, or a formula. (The cells referenced in the condition must be on the same worksheet as the cell being validated.) Then click OK. You can also specify whether blanks are ignored.

You also can use data validation to provide help to users. Select the Data Validation dialog box. Select the Input Message tab. Then enter your instructions. This text appears whenever the cursor is in the associated cell. Select the Error Alert tab and enter information about errors. This text appears each time the user enters an invalid value in the cell. To alert the user that a value is needed, you can also use conditional formatting to change the cell's background color if the cell's value is invalid. Note N49 provides examples.

E.4.6 Viewing Data (Freeze Panes)

If a worksheet has many columns or rows, you cannot view everything at once. You can use the Freeze Pane option to keep headings in rows and columns visible as the user scrolls through the other rows and columns.

You specify the rows and columns to freeze by placing the cursor in the cell just past the last row and column you want to freeze and then click. For example, if you want to freeze columns A through D and rows 1 and 2, you select cell E3. Then select Window in the Excel toolbar and click Freeze Panes. (To unfreeze panes, click Window and uncheck the Freeze Pane entry.) You can only freeze the leftmost columns and topmost rows, so you must lay out your headings with this in mind.

E.5 Printing

Excel's Print Setup feature enables you to specify orientation, page size and margins, coloring, and print order; add gridlines, row and column numbers; and specify rows and columns that will appear on every printed page.

E.5.1 Setting Print Options

Select File, and then Page Setup. On the Page tab, you can set orientation (portrait or landscape), and can also force a spreadsheet to fit on a specified number of pages. You can either Adjust to X% of normal size, or you can choose the number of pages wide and/or tall.

Select File | Print Setup. On the Sheet tab, you can mark check boxes for Gridlines, Black and White, and Label Rows and Columns (useful for debugging formulas). If you select Black and White, all colored and/or patterned cells print as white.

E.5.2 Setting Page Breaks

Use the Page Break Preview to manually set page breaks. Select View | Page Break Preview. The default page breaks appear as dashed blue lines. You can click and hold a line, and then drag it to the column (or row) you want. When you release it, it becomes a solid blue line.

TIP 1: Choose page breaks to fit related data on a single page for viewing and printing.

TIP 2: Choose the number of rows to reduce the printing of blank pages.

E.5.3 Repeating Headings

You can freeze rows and columns on printed pages using File | Page Setup and selecting the Sheet tab. When the Sheet dialog box appears, specify the rows and columns to repeat. For example, if you want to repeat columns A through D and rows 1 and 2, for example, enter 1:2 for the rows to repeat and A:D for the columns to repeat.

E.6 Plotting ("Charting")

Excel provides many types of plots and many options to control their appearance. (Note N22, "Types of Plots," gives instructions and examples for many types of plots.)

E.6.1 Removing the Gray Background in Plots

To remove the gray background, right-click the chart itself to get the Format Plot Area dialog box. Under Area, click the button for None.

E.6.2 Formatting and Rotating Text

To format any text (e.g., the y-axis label), right-click the text. You get a dialog with two choices: Format <object> and Clear. Click Format, and you get several tabs for Font, Alignment, and so forth. Choosing Font allows you to choose the font type, point size, and emphasis (bold, italic). Use a large point size if you must project the chart in a large room. Avoid light pastel colors. Orient all text horizontally so it is easy to read. To do this, select Alignment to obtain a window with orientation on the left. There is a semicircle with several diamonds. The red diamond indicates the current orientation. For the y-axis, the top diamond is red and the y-axis label is vertical. Just click the diamond at "3 o'clock." It turns red, and the y-axis label rotates to a horizontal position. Figure E-6 shows a well-formatted chart.

E.6.3 Setting Colors and Patterns

To set colors, right-click a line to obtain the drop-down box. Select Format Data Series and click to get the dialog box. Select the Patterns tab. Then set the Line and Marker parameters. For Lines, set the Style, Color, and Weight. For the Marker, select None or Custom to set the Style, Foreground and Background colors, and Size.

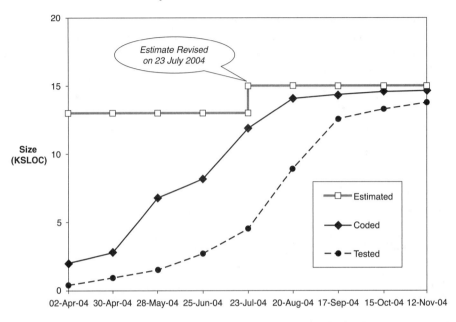

Figure E-6 *A well-formatted chart*

E.6.4 Adding Text Boxes to a Chart

Go to View | Toolbars and select Drawing. A toolbar appears at the very bottom of the frame (below the worksheet tabs). Select the text box icon (a box that has the letter *A* and a few horizontal lines). Click this icon. Then move the cursor to the location in your plot where you want to place the box. Right-click and a box having broad, fuzzy lines appears. You can type the text in this box. Right-click and select Exit Edit Text. The box is still highlighted with the fuzzy lines. While it is still highlighted, you can use commands in the upper toolbar to select bold, italics, to center the text, and so forth. It is very important to right-click the box again and then select Bring to Front. This forces the text to appear in the chart. (Otherwise, it is behind the chart and invisible.) Exit the text box by positioning the mouse to some other portion of the plot and clicking. This causes the fuzzy border to disappear. Now go back to the box and click again to obtain the drop-down menu. Then right-click and select the menu choice Format Textbox. (I do not know why you must exit the box and return. If you do not, the only tab you will see in the format text box is Font. If you do this correctly, you should have seven different tabs.) Select the tab Colors and Lines. This allows you to put a border around the box and select its background color. Under Fill, there is an entry called Color. Selecting the drop-down menu allows you to set the background color. Under the Color choice, there is a drop-down menu. Initially this is set to No Line. If you right-click, you can select a color. Other options also "unghost" at this point, allowing you to set the weight of the line and whether it is dashed.

The trick in selecting is to position the cursor on the edge of the box, not on the inside. If you select with the cursor on the inside you only get the tab related to the font characteristics. Clicking on the fuzzy border of the box brings up the full Format Text Box dialog box with the seven tabs. When the cursor is on the edge of the box the cursor changes from a thin vertical line with a short line transversely on each end (looking like a capital *I*) to a small plus sign (+) with arrowheads on the ends of each of the four lines.

You can reposition the box by moving the cursor until you get the + icon, and then drag the box to the location you want. You can also resize the box by positioning the cursor until you get a line with an arrowhead on each end (↔); then you can click and drag to resize the box.

E.6.5 Adding Error Bars

You can add error bars to data series plotted as area, bar, column, line, and xy (scatter) charts in Excel. You can specify error bars for the x values, y values, or both values. You can specify the error amount using one of these options:

- Fixed value
- Percentage of the point's value
- Some multiple of the sample's standard deviation
- Standard error for the values in the sample
- Custom

The standard deviation and standard error options use the same error amount for every point, and are useful for showing outliers in control charts. There is no option to *compute* the error bars for a point based on the value of the point.

To select an option, perform the following steps:

1. Plot the data points in a separate worksheet.
2. Click a data point. (The Format Data Series dialog box appears.)
3. Select the Y Error Bars (or X Error Bars) tab.
4. Select the desired option, entering any values needed.

The Custom option is the most useful for estimators. You must first calculate the error amount for each point in the spreadsheet, and then reference the values. For example, if the data value is in cell $C2 and you want to use a three standard deviation value for the error bars, then you might use the formula = 3.0*SQRT($C2) in row 2.[2] Suppose this formula is in cell $E2. If so, click cell $E2. Position the cursor on the lower-right corner, click the left mouse button and hold it, dragging the formula down the rows in column E. This computes the error amounts in the cells $E2:$E12. Now select the Custom option on the plot worksheet. To use the computed amounts for the + error bar, position the cursor in the + box and click. Now enter the string =MyDataSheet!$E2:$E12, where MyDataSheet is the name of the worksheet containing your data. (If the worksheet name has blanks you must enclose it in single quotes: ='My Data Sheet'!$E2:$E12.) Now (the trick) press Crtl+Shift+Enter. The formula is stored, and Excel surrounds it with curly brackets to indicate that it is an *array formula*. Repeat the process for the lower error bar.[3]

E.6.6 Fitting Trendlines

Trendlines graphically display trends in a set of data points. Excel fits a curve using regression analysis to the data in a chart and then draws the curve on the chart. You can specify the type of function to use. Microsoft Excel provides these choices: linear, logarithmic, polynomial, power, exponential, and moving average. By displaying the R-squared value (the coefficient of determination), you can decide which type of function best fits a set of data. This helps to characterize the data, and is useful when constructing parametric estimation models. You can also fit trendlines to histograms to get a crude probability distribution function. You can develop functions that fit the data in a table, and can then use this function instead of interpolating. (This is a means of functional approximation.) You can extend the trendline forward in time to forecast or predict future values. Forecasting is one technique for estimating.

To create a trendline, select a worksheet that has a plot. Select Chart | Add Trendline to obtain the Add Trendline dialog box. The Type tab allows you to select the type of function fitted: You can choose the type of function based on the following:

- Some assumed model (e.g., $y = ax^b$)

---

[2] For the square root function, you use SQRT in Microsoft Excel formulas but you use SQR in Microsoft Visual Basic for Applications code.

[3] To plot error bars, you first have to compute the error amounts on the data sheet. It would be more convenient to compute the error amounts by specifying an array function in the X Data Bars or Y Data Bars tabs. For example, you would like to be able to enter an array function using a string such as = 3.0*SQRT(MyDataSheet!$E2:$E12) to define the limit amount. Unfortunately, SQRT is not an array function. This forces you to calculate each of the values on the spreadsheet and then reference them.

- The shape or asymptotic behavior you expect (e.g., exponential decay for large x values)
- The pattern of the plotted data points
- The highest r^2 value (see text) among several fitted functions

You can specify the degree of the polynomial and the number of points to include in the moving average. The Options tab allows you to do the following:

- Set the intercept to zero (for linear, polynomial, or exponential plots)
- Display the equation for the fitted curve (except for a moving average)
- Display the r^2 value on the chart
- Extrapolate ("forecast") the fitted curve forward, backward, or both for some specified distance along the x-axis

As an example, consider the two data sets shown in Table E-1. Figure E-7 plots the points in Data Set 1 and shows the trendline. Choosing a second order polynomial gives the equation shown with an r^2 value of 1. (Surprise!) You can use this equation to predict the value of y at other values of x. For example, y = 1.512 at x = 3.5. Extrapolating to x = 6 gives y = 1.20.

Table E-1 *Sample Data Sets Used to Illustrate Interpolation*

Set 1		Set 2	
X	Y	X	Y
1	1.2	1	1.2
2	1.4	2	1.4
3	1.5	3	1.6
4	1.5	4	1.5
5	1.4	5	1.4

Data set 2 is similar to data set 1, differing only in the value at x = 3 (1.6 instead of 1.5). Figure E-8 shows the plot of data set 2 and the second-order polynomial fit, which has an r^2 value of 0.94. Using the fitted equation gives y = 1.557 at x = 3.5, and y = 1.119 at x = 6. Assuming that data set 1 is the true function, the two errors in the predictions using the equation based on the "experimental" data are 3.0% and 6.7%, respectively. This illustrates a general result: *Interpolated values are more accurate than extrapolated values.* Press et al. stress the dangers of extrapolation and note that the values will typically "go berserk" when the value of *x* lies outside the range $[x_{min}, x_{max}]$ by more than the average spacing of the tabulated points.

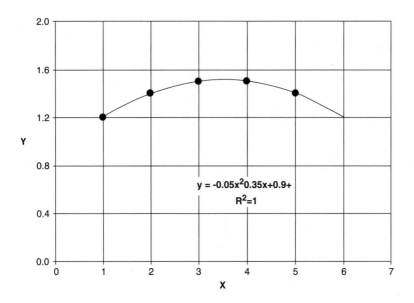

Figure E-7 *Plot of data set 1*

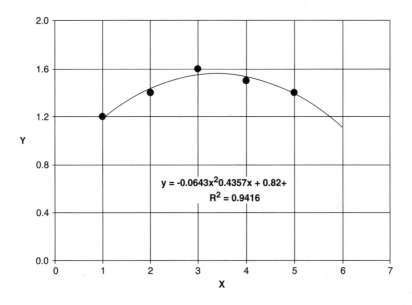

Figure E-8 *Plot of data set 2*

E.7 Advanced Features

This section mentions Excel features that you will find most useful to manipulate sets of data.

E.7.1 Sorting

You can use Excel to sort data in a range of cells. Select Data | Sort, and the Sort Dialog box appears. The first time you sort the list, the box has default options. If you have sorted the range before, the dialog box contains your previous settings. You can specify up to three sort parameters (columns), choosing ascending or descending for each. Excel usually realizes whether the range has a header that should remain in place. If it does not, click the appropriate box at the bottom of the dialog box (header row or no header row). If your selection does not include adjacent columns, Excel asks whether you want to expand the range to include them. For example, if you choose employee last names in column B, Excel asks if you also want to sort (move) the associated data in Column A (first name) and column C (employee ID).

When sorting a range that contains blank fields, Excel places the blank rows at the top. To force empty cells to the bottom, I insert "zzz" in empty cells in the sort column, and then use conditional formatting to color the text white, making the "zzz" invisible. (For testing, first choose another color such as pale blue.)

E.7.2 Filtering

Excel's filtering function allows you to selectively view data within a table. This is useful when you have many rows and are only interested in a subset of them. Suppose you have a table of employees with columns for first name, last name, employee ID, and role. Click any cell in this table. Clicking Data | AutoFilter causes Excel to create a drop-down list for each column, based on the unique entries in that column. For example, if column D has the roles Engineer and Manager, the drop-down list will have several entries, including Engineer, Manager, and All. Selecting Manager causes the other entries to disappear, leaving only the rows with managers. Clicking the icon again and selecting All causes the entire list to reappear. See the spreadsheet Filter Demo.xls on the CD-ROM. To remove the drop-down lists, click Data | Filter again. The Filter item has a check box to the left. Click this check box to remove the lists. You can use the Advanced Filter option to sort a list and remove duplicate entries. Click Data | Filter | Show All to restore all of the names, including the duplicates.

E.7.3 Excel Add-Ins (Analysis ToolPak)

Excel comes with add-in programs ("add-ins") that provide additional features. You must install these, however. Table E-2 lists the add-ins supplied with Excel. To install these, click Tools | Add-Ins and click the appropriate check boxes. See Excel's Help Wizard for more information about these. Many third-party vendors provide add-ins as well. For information, see the Microsoft Office Marketplace home page at http://office.microsoft.com/en-us/marketplace or http://office.microsoft.com/ and click Office Marketplace.

Table E-2 *Excel's Add-Ins*

Name
Analysis ToolPak
Analysis ToolPak VBA
Conditional Sum Wizard
Lookup Wizard
Solver
Internet Assistant VBA
Euro Currency Tools

The Analysis ToolPak has several tools for data analysis, including analysis of correlation, covariance, and variation (ANOVA). It also provides a tool to create histograms. (Note N22, "Types of Plots," describes how to build your own histograms.) Solver is a tool that finds a combination of variables that maximize or minimize the contents of a cell. For example, suppose you have a set of project data, and have defined a parametric estimation model. To determine the values of the coefficients, you can define a cell that calculates the sum of the squared residuals (or MMRE or PRED). You can also specify constraints on the solution. For example, some coefficient must be positive. The TRENDX spreadsheet uses Solver. You can find tips on using Solver at http://www.solver.com/suppstdvba.htm.

Support and troubleshooting help is at http://www.solver.com/suppstdsolver.htm.

E.7.4 Pivot Tables and Other Excel Features

Although there is not time to explain them here, you should be aware of the Excel features in Table E-3. See the books cited in Section E.1.2 for more information.

Table E-3 *Other Excel Features*

Purpose	Feature
Data analysis	Pivot tables and pivot charts
Protection	Locking cells and worksheets
Visibility	Hiding cells and worksheets
Comparisons using different sets of input values	Scenarios: A set of input values applied to a spreadsheet model

A pivot table allows you to instantly summarize a table of data in different ways. For example, you could use a pivot table to view calibration data in terms of project size, product type, programming language, year of completion, and other characteristics. You can also construct pivot charts to display the information pictorially. Given a table of data (not necessarily contiguous), you specify the fields (rows and columns) containing the data you want to analyze, how you want the table or chart organized, and the calculations to perform (e.g., summing values meeting certain criteria). After you have built the table, you can rearrange it to view your data in different ways. (You "pivot" the rows and columns of the table to obtain different views.) For instructions on using pivot tables and charts, see the books cited in Section E.1.2.

E.8 Macros and Visual Basic for Applications

A *macro* is a series of actions that Excel can execute upon command or when certain events occur. You can use macros to perform repetitive tasks quickly and accurately. Macros also provide a way to perform actions that cannot be done using Excel's built-in functions. The spreadsheets included on this book's CD-ROM provide examples that you can study and modify to meet your own needs. This section explains how to enable, record, view, edit, and invoke macros.

E.8.1 Enabling Macros

Excel has a security level to prevent macros from executing. To set your security level, do this:

1. Select Tools | Options.
2. Select the Security tab.
3. Click the rectangle Macro Security in the lower-right corner.

4.   Select the Security tab.

5.   Click the Medium button. (Never pick the Low button.)

Selecting Medium causes Excel to alert you each time you open a workbook that contains macros by displaying the Security Warning dialog box. It has three options:

- Disable Macros
- Enable Macros
- More Information

If you do not expect the spreadsheet to have macros, choose Disable Macros. If you know the spreadsheet has macros, choose Enable Macros. The XLS List.doc lists all the spreadsheets on this book's CD-ROM, and has a column indicating whether a spreadsheet contains macros.

E.8.2 Recording Macros

The simplest way to create a macro is to record a series of user actions as follows:

1.   Click Tools | Macro | Record New Macro. A screen titled Record Macro appears.

2.   Type a name for the macro and (optionally) assign it a keystroke shortcut. (Keyboard shortcuts are case-sensitive.)

3.   Perform the sequence of desired actions just as you normally would.

4.   Stop recording by clicking Tools | Macro Stop Recording.

You can now execute the macro by typing the keyboard shortcut (the Ctrl key plus some other key), or you can choose Tools | Macro | Macros and obtain a dialog box showing the available macros. Double-clicking invokes the macro. You can also select the filename and choose Run.[4] If you assigned the macro to the Tools menu when you recorded it, you can also run it by selecting it from the drop-down list under Tools.

---

[4] If you select ThisWorkbook when you record a macro, you can only access the macro when the workbook is in use. To make macros available when you are working in other workbooks, you can either copy the macro code to the other workbooks, or you can create a Personal Macro Workbook and store the macros there. The second option makes the macros visible to all workbooks. This is not always a good idea. For more information about macros, see the Excel Help Wizard or the textbooks cited in Section E.1.2.

The CD-ROM has Macro Demo.xls that sorts a list of names. I created this using the preceding steps. I selected a range of cells, and then clicked on Data | Sort to sort the cells based on the last names in column B.

Macros are stored within the workbook, and are only accessible within that workbook. (If you want to share macros with other workbooks, there are ways to do this. Consult the reference texts mentioned earlier.)

The Microsoft suite of office applications (Excel, PowerPoint, Word, and Access) use *Visual Basic for Applications (VBA)* to record macros. VBA has many useful features. The real power, however, is that you can edit recorded macros or even write your own code ("scripts") to perform more complicated actions.

TIP: Capture valid, working code for an Excel subroutine or function by first recording a macro and then editing the code to fit your needs. (This is handy because argument lists are sometimes lengthy.)

E.8.3 Editing Macros

You use the Visual Basic Editor to view and edit macros. To access the VBA Editor, go to Tools | Macro | Visual Basic Editor. (You can also press Alt plus F11). To return to the Excel spreadsheet, you can click View | Microsoft Excel (or press Alt plus F11 again to toggle back to Excel.) Figure E-9 shows a picture of the VBA Editor. The left window is the Project Explorer that lists all the sheets in the workbook and any modules. All can contain macro code. The right screen shows the code for a selected object (worksheet, chart, ThisWorkbook, or module). The left drop-down menu at the top of this window indicates the scope of the macro: General means that it applies to all the worksheets in the workbook, and Worksheet (or Workbook) means it applies to the specific workbook. The right side, Declarations, allows you to define variables, and select predefined subroutines from a drop-down list. (See example later in this section.)[5] The toolbar across the top gives the usual features plus some additional items. Help is at the right and provides information about using the Visual Basic Editor. For instructions on using the Debug and Run commands, see the books on VBA cited in Section E.1.2.

Another way to invoke the editor is to press Alt+F8. This gives a list of macros. Select the macro you want, and then press the Edit button. This will take you into the Visual Basic Editor. The Visual Basic Editor provides context sensitive help (e.g., it identifies allowed choices for arguments of a function). This helps you write code without referring to a reference manual.

---

[5] You can activate additional windows in the VisualBasic Editor to set specific properties of objects and to aid debugging. See the books on VBA cited in Section E.1.1.

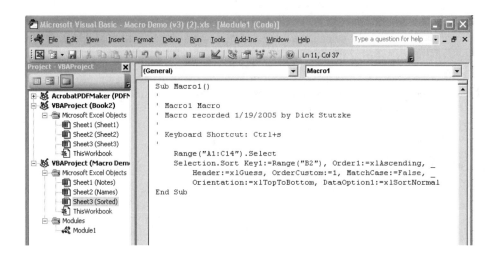

Figure E-9 *Visual Basic Editor screen*

The right window in Figure E-9 shows the VBA code for the recorded macro that performs the sort in Macro Demo.xls. If a statement extends over more than one line, include the underscore (_) character at the end of the line to indicate that the line is continued. Comments are preceded by an apostrophe. When you record a macro, VBA inserts comments giving the name of the macro, who recorded it, and when that person recorded it.

VBA provides all the features of a typical programming language. You can declare variables of a particular type and perform calculations, branching, and looping. You can also format data and manipulate the cells in a worksheet. Each version of VBA has extensions that apply to the host application. For example, Excel has many extensions that deal with workbooks, worksheets, charts, ranges of cells, and individual cells. Excel also provides objects to enable you to reference the active sheet, the one where the cursor is located. (Other methods enable you to access other sheets as well.)

E.8.4 Using Events

You can invoke a macro every time a particular event occurs. Table E-4 shows some events for worksheets and workbooks. The SetFooter and SaveDate macros described later use some of these events.

Table E-4 *Useful Excel Events*

Worksheet Events	Workbook Events
Activate	BeforeClose
BeforeDoubleClick	BeforePrint
BeforeRightClick	BeforeSave
Calculate	NewSheet
Change	Open
Deactivate	SheetActivate
SelectionChange	SheetChange

Suppose that you have a workbook consisting of multiple worksheets, and one of these worksheets has data copied from another worksheet that you would like to sort. You can record or write a sort macro, and then you can use the Visual Basic Editor to invoke the macro. Use the sort macro described previously. First, pick the name of the worksheet where you want the sort to occur from the list in the Explorer window at the left. For this example, it is Sorted. The screen on the right will be blank. In the upper-left drop-down, click Worksheet. This creates skeleton code for a subroutine:

```
Private Sub Worksheet_SelectionChange(ByVal Target As Range)

End Sub
```

To select another event, click the right drop-down. Selecting Activate gives the following code:

```
Private Sub Worksheet_Activate()

End Sub
```

Then switch to Module1 and copy the text of the sort macro (Ctrl+C), return to the worksheet where your want the sort to occur, and paste (Ctrl+V), inserting the code between the beginning and end of the subroutine. You have now created a sort routine that will execute every time that the sheet is activated. (I added message boxes that display text each time the macro is invoked. Use double quotation marks to enclose literal strings. I also changed the descriptive comments.) The working code is as follows:

```
Private Sub Worksheet_Activate()
'
' Sort by last name
' Written 1/19/2005 by Dick Stutzke
'
    MsgBox ("Sorting the names")
    Range("A1:C14").Select
    Selection.Sort Key1:=Range("B2"), Order1:=xlAscending, _
        Header:=xlGuess, OrderCustom:=1, MatchCase:=False, _
        Orientation:=xlTopToBottom, DataOption1:=xlSortNormal
    MsgBox (" Sort is finished")
End Sub
```

Figure E-10 shows the resulting list. Note that blanks sort to the top of the list. To prevent this, you can insert a string such as "zzzz" that sorts to the end of the list, and then use conditional formatting to set the font to the background color so the "zzzz" disappears.

First	Last	ID Number
Jill	Black	057
John	Brown	314
Bill	Green	023
Susan	Jones	987
Mary	Smith	011
Frank	White	278
End of Formulas		

Figure E-10 *Employees sorted by last name*

E.8.5 Creating Functions

Excel distinguishes functions from subroutines. Functions return values. Generally, it is a good idea for functions to have no side effects. That is, functions should not manipulate worksheet objects. Functions provide a good way of performing specific types of complicated calculations. You invoke functions using formulas within cells. For example, suppose you defined a macro called RatioAverage that operates on a range of cells. You would invoke this function in a cell by entering

= RatioAverage($C$3:$C$22)

E8.6 Using Forms and Controls

You can also enable users to invoke a macro by clicking a button or entering a command sequence. Excel enables you to draw forms, drag and drop *controls* onto the form, and then "connect" the code to the controls. The following controls are available:

- Label or text box (displays instructions or information to users)
- Radio button (user picks a single option)
- Check box (user picks one or more options)
- Button (user initiates an action)
- List box (user picks one or more items from scrollable list)
- Drop-down list (user picks one item from scrollable list)
- Combo box (user picks or types one or more items from scrollable list)

In practice, the terms *list box*, *drop-down list*, and *combo list* are used somewhat interchangeably. The TRENDX spreadsheet on the CD-ROM uses a form with controls.

You can also use macros to have spreadsheets retrieve data from sources on the Web, or to post results to the Web. For details, see the books on Excel VBA cited earlier in Section E.1.1.

Tips for Writing VBA

1. Be careful of capitalization. (VBA is case sensitive.)

2. Be careful of plurals. (Excel VBA interprets ROW and ROWS differently.)

3. Always enter `Option Explicit` in the first line of your code. This helps detect typographical errors and ensures that every variable is correctly defined.

E.8.7 Debugging Macros

Tools for debugging include the following:

- Single-step execution
- Watches
- Immediate window
- Breakpoints

For example, breakpoints allow you to run the code from the beginning but have it stop when it reaches a certain line of code. Then you can observe the situation at that point. This is good when an error does not occur until you have done a substantial amount of processing. See the Excel VBA books for additional guidance.

E.8.8 Printing a Version Number (SetFooter)

The spreadsheet SetFooter records information such as a version number in the left footer just before a worksheet is printed. Writing the information just before printing overwrites any information the user might have put in the footer. This guarantees you will know what version was used. (The only way to remove the information is to remove the macro.) This enables you to determine which version of a spreadsheet someone was using in order to locate bugs. You can also record other information such as copyrights and author. To insert multiple lines in one field, insert a carriage return, CHR(10), in the string. Here is an example:

```
Private Sub Workbook_BeforePrint(Cancel As Boolean)
'    Inserts version information in the footer
'    of a worksheet just before it is printed.

    With ActiveSheet.PageSetup
        .LeftFooter = "Version 2.3" & Chr(10) & "18OCT04)" _
                           & Chr(10) & "R. Stutzke"
        .CenterFooter = "Center" & Chr(10) & "Field"
        .RightFooter = "Right" & Chr(10) & "Field"
    End With
End Sub
```

To set only a single field in the footer you can use

```
ActiveSheet.PageSetup.RightFooter = "Separate Field"
```

You insert this code in the module ThisWorkbook. The preceding code produces this text for the left footer on the printed page :

Version 2.3 (01FEB05)

(c) 2005 by R. Stutzke

E.8.9 Printing the Date Saved (SaveDate)

If the user has not altered the spreadsheet, you want the same date and time values to appear whenever pages are printed. Microsoft Word allows users to set the SaveDate to do this. You must use a macro to do this in Excel.

The spreadsheet SaveDate has a macro that records the current date and time in every worksheet of a spreadsheet (workbook) every time that a user *saves* the workbook. This macro records the filename and worksheet name in the left header, and the save date and time in the center header. To insert multiple lines in one field, insert a carriage return, CHR(10), in the string. Also, see SetFooter, which shows how to record other information such as version identifier and copyright date in the footer.

```
Private Sub Workbook_BeforeSave(ByVal SaveAsUI As Boolean, Cancel As
Boolean)

'    This subroutine inserts the current date/time in the center
'    header of every worksheet of a workbook before it is saved.
'    The file name in the header is the new name, even though this
'    subroutine is executed BEFORE you enter the new file name in
'    the "Save As" dialog box.

     Dim TheDate
     Dim TheTime

     TheDate = Date
     TheTime = Time

     For Each wk In Worksheets
         'MsgBox ("Opening worksheet " & wk.Name)
         wk.Select
         With ActiveSheet.PageSetup
             .LeftHeader = "&F" & Chr(10) _          'File Name and
                               & "&A"                'Worksheet Name
             .CenterHeader = TheDate & Chr(10) & TheTime
         End With
     Next 'end of For loop
End Sub
```

Acronyms

3GL	Third-generation language
AA	Assessment and assimilation. Size increase (%) to reflect extra effort for reused code. (COCOMO II sizing model)
AAF	Adaptation adjustment factor (COCOMO sizing model)
AAM	Adaptation adjustment multiplier (COCOMO II sizing model)
ACA	Application characteristics adjustment (used in function point counting)
ACAP	Analyst capability (COCOMO cost driver)
ACWP	Actual cost of work performed
AD	Architectural design (activity); see PD
AEXP	Applications experience (COCOMO cost driver)
AFP	Adjusted function points (software size measure)
ASIZE	Adapted size; existing code that must be modified (sizing model)
AT	Automated translation; percentage of existing code that will be automatically translated (COCOMO sizing model)
BAC	Budget at completion
BAFO	Best and final offer; bidder's final price and related terms and conditions
BCR	Baseline change request
BCWP	Budgeted cost of work performed (= earned value)
BCWS	Budgeted cost of work scheduled
BOE	Basis of estimate
BOM	Bill of materials
CASE	Computer-aided software engineering; see also ICASE, SEE, and STE
CCB	Configuration control board or change control board
CDR	Critical design review (process milestone)
CDRL	Contract data requirement list (identifies documents to be delivered)
CFI	Customer-furnished information or item

CLEF	Component-level estimating form; a template for performing microestimation (Intermediate COCOMO 1981)
CLIN	Contract line item number (U.S. government contracts)
CM (1)	Configuration management (activity); (2) percentage of existing code that must be modified (COCOMO sizing model)
CMM	Capability Maturity Model
CMU	Carnegie Mellon University; host organization for the SEI
COCOMO	COnstructive COst MOdel; a set of equations to estimate software development effort and time
CONOPS	Concept of operations; same as OPSCON
COTS	Commercial off-the-shelf; denotes a purchased product
CP	Cost plus (contract type)
CPA	Critical path analysis
CPAF	Cost plus award fee (contract type)
CPFF	Cost plus fixed fee (contract type)
CPI (1)	Cost Performance Index, (2) continuous process improvement
CPIF	Cost plus incentive fee (contract type)
CPLOE	Cost plus level of effort (contract type)
CPLX	Product complexity (COCOMO cost driver)
CPM	Critical path method; used in task scheduling
CPU	Central processing unit or, more generally, a computer
CTC	Contract target cost
CUT	Code and unit test (activity)
CV	Cost variance
DACS	Data and analysis center for software
DATA	Database size (COCOMO cost driver)
DBMS	Database management system
DD	Detailed Design (activity)
DFAR	Defense Federal Acquisition Regulations (U.S. government)
DI	Degree of influence; rating of a general system characteristic (FPA)
DID	Data item description (defines content and format of a document)
DL	Direct labor
DM (1)	Percentage of design that must be modified to reuse existing code (COCOMO sizing model); (2) data management (activity)
DOCU	Documentation to match life cycle needs (COCOMO II cost driver)
DoD	Department of Defense (U.S. government)
DSIZE	Delivered size; equals NSIZE + RSIZE (sizing model)

DT&E	Development test and evaluation (activity or product life cycle phase)
EAC	Estimate at completion
EAF	Effort adjustment factor; a variable in the COCOMO model
ECP	Engineering change proposal; a formal document specifying a proposed change to job requirements
EMD	Engineering, manufacturing, and development (phase in product life cycle)
ESIZE	Equivalent size; equals AAM*ASIZE (sizing model)
ETC	Estimate to complete
EV	Earned value; same as BCWP
EVM	Earned value measurement (a process)
FAR	Federal Acquisition Regulations (U.S. government); see also DFAR
FAT	Factory acceptance test (activity); completion is a process milestone
FCA	Functional configuration audit (activity); completion is a process milestone
F-F	Finish-to-finish; timing constraint used in task scheduling
FFP	Firm fixed price (contract type)
FLEX	Flexibility of requirements, process, etc. (COCOMO II scale factor)
FOC	Final (or full) operational capability (process milestone)
FP (1)	Function points (software size measure); (2) fixed price (contract type)
FPA	Function point analysis
FPLOE	Fixed price level of effort (contract type)
FQT	Formal qualification test; equivalent to FAT (activity or process milestone)
F-S	Finish-to-start; timing constraint used in task scheduling
FSP	Full-time staff person; same as FTE
FTE	Full-time equivalent person; same as FSP
FW	Firmware; software recorded in read-only memory
FY	Fiscal year
G&A	General and administrative
GFE	Government-furnished equipment
GFI	Government-furnished information or item
GFY	Government fiscal year
GLA	General ledger account
GROW	Growth in size (%) over entire project (sizing model)
GSC	General system characteristic (FPA)

GUI	Graphical user interface
HLL	High-level language
HMI	Human machine interface
HOL	High-order language (sometimes "high-level language")
HW	Hardware
I&T	Integration and test (activity); also written as IT
I/O	Input/output; also IO
ICASE	Integrated computer-aided software engineering (refers to the tools used to develop software)
ICD	Interface control document (or drawing)
IDIQ	Indefinite delivery, indefinite quantity (contract type)
IEEE	Institute for Electrical and Electronic Engineers
IFPUG	International Function Point Users Group
IM	Percentage of nominal integration and test effort needed for reused code (COCOMO sizing model)
INCOSE	INternational Council On Systems Engineering
IOC	Initial operational capability (process milestone)
IPR	In-process review (process milestone)
IR&D	Independent research and development; also written as IRAD
IRR	Inception readiness review (MBASE/RUP process milestone)
ISO	International Organization for Standardization
IT (1)	Integration test (activity), also called functional testing; (2) information technology, term referring to business-related data processing; see MIS
IV&V	Independent verification & validation (activity)
JAD	Joint application development (development process)
KSLOC	Thousands of source lines of code (COCOMO II sizing model)
LAN	Local area network
LCA	Life cycle architecture review (MBASE/RUP process milestone)
LCC	Life cycle cost
LCL	Lower control limit
LCO	Life cycle objectives review (MBASE/RUP process milestone)
LEXP	Programming language experience (COCOMO 1981 cost driver)
LOE	Level of effort
LSLOC	Logical source lines of code; a measure of software size obtained by counting the statements in a particular programming language; see PSLOC
LTEX	Language and tool experience (COCOMO II cost driver)

M&A	Management and administrative
M&S	Materials and subcontracts
MBASE	Model-based (system) architecting and software engineering (development process similar to RUP)
MIL-STD	Military standard
MIS	Management information system; IT is a more modern term
MOA	Memorandum of agreement
MoD	Ministry of defence (British equivalent of U.S. DoD)
MODP	Modern programming practices (COCOMO 1981 cost driver)
MOU	Memorandum of understanding
MR (1)	Modification request; (2) management reserve
MSF	Microsoft Solutions Framework (development process similar to MBASE/RUP)
MTBF	Mean time between failures
MTTF	Mean time to failure
MTTR	(1) Mean time to repair; (2) mean time to recovery
NASA	National Aeronautics and Space Administration
NCSS	Non-comment source statement (a software size measure)
NDS	Non-developed software; existing software reused either "as is" or adapted
NIST	National Institute of Standards and Technology
NSIZE	New size; code developed from scratch (sizing model)
OBS	Organization breakdown structure
ODC	Other direct costs; trips, equipment, and consumables
OH	Overhead
OPSCON	Operational concept (same as CONOPS)
OS	Operating system
OT&E	Operational test and evaluation (activity or product life cycle phase)
PAR	Product acceptance review (MBASE/RUP process milestone)
PC (1)	Personal computer; (2) project control (activity: tracks budgets and costs)
PCA	Physical configuration audit (activity); completion is a process milestone
PCAP	Programmer capability (COCOMO cost driver)
PCON	Personnel continuity (COCOMO II cost driver)
PCR	(1) Problem/change request; (2) project closeout report
PD	Product design (activity); see AD; may also refer to a design document

PDL	Program design language
PDR	Product design review (not "preliminary"); (process milestone)
PERT	Program evaluation and review technique
PEXP	Platform experience (COCOMO II cost driver)
PM (1)	Person-month(s), the effort expended by one person working for one calendar-month; (2) project manager (role); (3) project management (activity); (4) COCOMO II variable name denoting computed effort
PMAT	Process maturity (COCOMO II scale factor)
PMO	Project management office
PO	Purchase order
POP	Period of performance
PPL	Project products list
PR	Problem report
PREC	Precedentedness (COCOMO II scale factor)
PRR	(1) Plans and requirements review (process milestone); (2) product release review (MBASE/RUP process milestone). Cutover to new system is completed at key sites. Equivalent to FOC. Also see SAT.
PSIZE	Processed size; proportional to development effort (sizing model)
PSLOC	Physical source lines of code; a measure of software size obtained by counting line terminators
PSP	Personal software process
PVOL	Platform volatility (COCOMO II cost driver)
QA	Quality assurance (activity)
R&D	Research and development (activity; sometimes RAD or IRAD)
RA	Requirements analysis (activity)
RAD	Rapid application development (development process)
RAM	(1) Random access memory; (2) reliability and maintainability; (3) responsibility assignment matrix
RDT&E	Research, development, test, and evaluation (phase of product life cycle)
RELY	Required software reliability (COCOMO cost driver)
RESL	Architecture/risk resolution (COCOMO II scale factor)
REVIC	Revised Enhanced Version of Intermediate COCOMO 1981
RFP	Request for proposal
RFQ	Request for quote (or quotation)
RLN	Resource loaded network
ROI	Return on investment

ROM	(1) Rough order of magnitude; (2) read-only memory
RSIZE	Reused size; equals ASIZE + TSIZE (sizing model)
RUP	Rational unified process (development process); see also MBASE
RUSE	Required reusability (COCOMO II cost driver)
RVOL	Requirements volatility; a parameter in some estimation models
SAIC	Science Applications International Corporation
SAT	Site acceptance test (activity); completion is a process milestone
SCCB	Software Change (configuration) Control Board
SCED	Required development schedule (compared to the nominal schedule) (COCOMO parameter)
SCM	Software configuration management (activity)
SDP	Software development plan
SDR	System design review (process milestone)
SEE	Software engineering environment
SEI	Software Engineering Institute
SEMP	Systems engineering management plan
S-F	Start-to-finish; timing constraint used in task scheduling
SITE	Multi-site operation (COCOMO II cost driver)
SLOC	Source lines of code; a measure of software size. Lack of standardization can greatly affect the apparent value. See LSLOC and PSLOC.
SOW	Statement of work or scope of work
SPC	(1) Statistical process control; (2) Software Productivity Consortium
SPI (1)	Schedule Performance Index; (2) software process improvement
SQA	Software quality assurance (activity)
SQL	Structured Query Language
SRR	System requirements review (process milestone); sometimes *software* requirements review
S-S	Start-to-start; timing constraint used in task scheduling
SSR	Software specification review (process milestone)
STE	Software test environment; may be part of the SEE; also see ICASE
STOR	Main storage constraint (COCOMO cost driver)
STR	(1) Software trouble report; (2) software test report
SU	Software understanding; size increase (%) to reflect extra effort for reused code; Zero if DM = 0 and CM = 0 (COCOMO II sizing model)
SV	Schedule variance
SW	Software

SWIT	Software integration and test (activity); same as IT
T for C	Termination for convenience
T for D	Termination for default
T&E	Test and evaluation (activity)
T&M	Time and materials (contract type)
TAB	Total allocated budget
TBD	To be determined
TCPI	To Complete Performance Index
TDEV	Time to develop the product (development schedule); (COCOMO parameter)
TDP	Technical data package
TEAM	Team cohesion (COCOMO II scale factor)
TIME	Execution time constraint (COCOMO cost driver)
TOOL	Use of software tools (COCOMO cost driver)
TPM	Technical performance measure
TR (1)	Trouble report, same as PCR and PR; (2) test report
TRR	Test readiness review (process milestone)
Ts & Cs	Terms and conditions; contract clauses specifying rights and obligations of buyer or seller
TSIZE	Translated size; code automatically translated by a tool (sizing model)
TURN	Turnaround time (on development platform) (COCOMO 1981 cost driver)
UCL	Upper control limit
UFP	Unadjusted function points (software size measure)
UNFM	Programmer unfamiliarity with software to be reused (COCOMO II sizing model)
UTC	Unit test complete (process milestone)
V&V	Verification and validation
VDD	Version description document
VEXP	Virtual machine experience (COCOMO 1981 cost driver)
VIRT	Virtual (target) machine volatility (COCOMO 1981 cost driver)
VOLA	Volatility of size (%) over entire project (sizing model)
VUPR	Validated unique problem report
VUSTR	Validated unique software trouble report (the software defects)
WAN	Wide area network
WBS	Work breakdown structure

Glossary

Introduction

Estimation spans many disciplines, each with their own specialized vocabulary. This glossary collects terms defined for various disciplines to provide a consolidated glossary for all readers, regardless of their background and knowledge. I consulted the following sources:

I consulted the following sources:

- CMMI Glossary, contained in [Chrissis, 2003, page 611 ff]. This particular glossary encompasses 13 different sources but focuses primarily on process-related terminology.
- IEEE Standard Glossary of Software Engineering Terminology [IEEE Std 610.12, 1990], Institute of Electrical and Electronics Engineers Standards Association (IEEE-SA), 1990, ISBN 1-5593-7067-X. (Corrected edition issued February 1991. Reaffirmed in 2002. The IEEE disclaims any responsibility or liability resulting from the placement and use of in the described manner.)
- Glossary of Defense Acquisition Acronyms and Terms, 11th edition, Department of Defense, Defense Acquisition University, Center for Program Management, Fort Belvoir, Virginia, September 2003.
- The National Estimating Society Dictionary, as adapted in [Stewart, 1995, pages 657–710].
- The International Function Point Users Group (IFPUG) Glossary, Release 1.0, January 1994, published by IFPUG, Westerville, Ohio.

I have supplemented these sources with definitions gleaned from other textbooks and from web searches. When I use a definition unchanged or with slight modifications, I cite the original source. In many cases, I have revised or extended the published definitions to make them consistent with the concepts described in this book. If so, I do not cite the original source.

Other online sources that readers might find useful include the following:

- [PEH, 2003], the "Parametric Cost Estimating Handbook," defines many estimating terms in Appendix A.
- [IEEE-CSDP, 2003] provides a compilation of software engineering terms from existing sources, primarily ANSI/IEEE Std 610.12-1990.
- [Pressman, 2004] provides an abbreviated software engineering glossary.
- [Wideman, 2002] provides an extensive glossary of project management terms.
- Although not accessible online, [Fleming, 2000] has a glossary of terms for earned value management.

Terms

acceptance   The act by which the buyer, through an authorized representative, assents to ownership of existing or identified items or approves specific services rendered, as partial or full completion of a contract.

acceptance testing   Formal testing conducted to enable a user, customer, or other authorized entity to determine if a product or product component satisfies its acceptance criteria. See also *formal acceptance test, site acceptance test, integration testing*.

accounting   Measuring the money that has been spent.

accuracy   A quantitative measure of the magnitude of error. Indicates how closely a measured or calculated value matches the actual or correct value. Contrast with *precision*.

acquisition   The process of obtaining products and services through a contract.

action item   A description of a task to handle an exceptional event that might jeopardize project success. Action items are tracked until they are completed.

activity   A series of purposeful actions performed to achieve specific objectives. Activities use and produce artifacts, and consume resources. One or more roles are responsible for performing an activity.

activity duration   The length of time in work-days that it takes to complete an activity. Activities with zero durations are milestones.

actual cost of work performed (ACWP)   The dollar value of resources consumed in the accomplishment of work performed. This includes actual direct costs, such as the incurred costs for labor, material, and other direct costs (ODCs), plus the related indirect costs (overhead, fringe, and general and administrative [G&A]). Actual cost of work performed can also be expressed in terms of person-hours.

actual costs   Costs actually incurred by a project (actuals). These costs should also include committed amounts (commitments).

actual dates   The dates that activities really started and finished as opposed to planned or projected dates.

actuals   See *actual costs*.

adapt   The activity of modifying a component, and possibly its design, so it will fit or interface with other components of a system. This occurs when reusing software not originally designed to be configurable. See *configure*.

agile method   A software development process (life cycle model) that evolves a product in a series of rapid iterations (several weeks or less) using continuous involvement with end user representatives. Several variations exist.

algorithm   A set of rules for the solution of a problem in a finite number of steps; for example, a complete specification of a sequence of arithmetic operations for calculating a numeric value to a given precision.

allocation   (1) Distributing requirements, resources, or other entities among the components of a system or the tasks of a project. (2) The result of the distribution in (1).

analysis   The activity of determining the requirements for a product. To create a totally new product, a specification is either provided by the buyer or is written by the developer (sometimes jointly with customer representatives). To modify an existing product, changes to the existing (baseline) product are defined by analyzing baseline change requests (BCRs) and software trouble reports (STRs). When requirements for an existing product are not recorded, they are reconstructed by reverse engineering the source code and/or by analyzing existing documentation. For large projects, this activity ends with the system requirements review (SRR) or the software requirements review (SSR).

anomaly   Anything observed in the documentation or operation of a product or system that deviates from expectations based on documented requirements or previous experience.

application software   Software designed to fulfill specific needs of an end user; for example, preparing paychecks or controlling a vehicle. Contrast with *support software, system software*.

architectural design   The activity to identify the major hardware and software components of a system, and their relationships and interfaces. This includes analyzing design alternatives and estimating timing and sizing of the system or its components. Refinement of the architecture gives the top-level (product) design where components are named and their nature and scope are described. Also called product design. (2) The result of this activity.

architecture   See *software architecture.*

artifact   A tangible object produced by an activity. Examples are specifications, design documents, audit records, code, data, reports, plans, schedules, and training courses. The object can be a product component or a work product.

attributes   Characteristics of products, services, and project tasks used to help in estimating project resources, product performance, and process performance. These characteristics include items such as size, complexity, weight, power consumption, and functionality. They are typically used as one input to deriving other project and resource estimates (e.g., effort, cost, and time).

audit   An independent examination of work products or work processes to assess compliance with defined processes, procedures, standards, specifications, or other criteria.

availability   The fraction of time that a system or component is operational and ready for use. Availability = MTTF/MTBF.

backward scheduling   A scheduling technique where the schedule is computed starting with the due date for the product and worked backward to determine the required start date.

baseline (1) A specification, document, software element, hardware item, or product that has been formally reviewed and approved by designated stakeholders at a specific time during the configuration item's life cycle. Thereafter, it serves as the basis for further development and can be changed only through formal change control procedures. (2) The action of placing any product under formal configuration control.

baseline change request (BCR) A request submitted by an end user or purchaser for a new or modified capability. The BCR defines additional requirements and/or modifies existing (baseline) requirements. BCR is a general name. Often such requests arrive as change requests, trouble reports, and so forth.

baseline item or product See *baseline* (noun).

basis of estimate (BOE) The documentation and supporting rationale that explains how a specific estimate was developed, why a particular estimating method or technique was selected, why a specific cost history was selected, how a given task or job is similar or dissimilar to past efforts performed by the bidder, and why the estimate is realistic and credible.

bill of material (BOM) A complete list of materials, parts, and components required to produce a particular product. It includes each item's description, quantity, and price. Sometimes called a purchase list.

breakage The amount of previously delivered code that must be modified when adding more functionality to a software product. Used in COCOMO II for incremental development.

budget The amount of resources needed to accomplish some objective, organized by category and (usually) time. Usually, the resource is money, and the objectives

are tasks identified in a work breakdown structure. The budget may also show sources of funding. Engineers sometimes prepare budgets for allocating computer resources.

budget at completion (BAC) The sum of all incremental budgets (budgeted cost for work scheduled [BCWS]) planned to accomplish the specified work.

budgeted cost for work performed (BCWP) The sum of the budgets for completed work packages and completed portions of open work packages, plus the appropriate portion of the budgets for level of effort (LOE) and apportioned effort (AE). Budgeted cost for work performed is the earned value. Budgeted cost for work performed can be expressed in terms of dollars and/or person-hours.

budgeted cost for work scheduled (BCWS) The sum of the budgets for all work packages and planning packages scheduled to be accomplished (including in-process work packages), plus the amount of level of effort and apportioned effort scheduled to be accomplished within a given time period. Budgeted cost for work scheduled can be expressed in terms of dollars and/or person-hours.

budgeting Allocating money to the performers of the tasks. See also *work authorization*.

build (1) A working version of a software product providing some or all of the product's required capabilities. It shows tangible progress (e.g., that certain functions work or certain problems have been solved). Engineering builds are often demonstrated to the buyer to show progress (and maybe to obtain feedback). If it is delivered to the end user, it is usually called a release or a version. Some authors use "version" to refer to a product with major enhancements and "release" to refer to products with minor changes, especially corrections to defects found in the preceding version. So, each version is followed by one or more releases. (2) The activity of linking and testing verified software components to produce an executable program.

burden Overhead expenses (labor, material, and other) not conveniently chargeable directly to a specific task or activity and, therefore, distributed over the appropriate direct labor, other direct cost (ODC), and/or material base.

business objectives Goals and strategies designed to ensure an organization's continued existence and enhance its profitability, market share, and other factors influencing the organization's success. Defined by senior management.

business process The sequence of activities "enclosing" the production process. These activities are common to all types of products and services, and include defining the job, negotiation with the customer, and reporting project status.

business risk An adverse impact on the developer's business organization due to the occurrence of a product or project risk. The business risk can arise directly from contract terms and conditions (e.g., warranties or consequential damages) or indirectly from loss of future business or reputation. Buyers use terms and conditions to protect their organizations in the event that the developer fails to deliver acceptable products and services on time. Thus, terms and conditions place the developer at risk.

buyer (1) The purchaser of a product or service. (2) The customer's employee or department responsible for the contractual and financial issues in buying a product. This is usually the project management office for systems built by the government.

capability maturity model (CMM) A formal document describing the requirements for a "good" process, using some structure or taxonomy. Process maturity models define how you "ought to" produce a product, and typically require that the process be defined, documented, taught, practiced, measured, improved, and enforced. Capability maturity models differ from other types of process standards because they define ratings, called maturity or capability levels, based on sets of required practices, and so provide a "yardstick" to measure process capability. These levels help organizations characterize the maturity of their process, establish goals for process improvement, and set priorities.

capable process A process that can satisfy its specified performance objectives. These objectives may relate to product quality, service quality, efficiency, or effectiveness. See also *stable process*, *defined process*, and *quantitatively managed process*.

cash flow An accounting measure showing how much of the cash generated by a business remains after both expenses (including interest) and principal on financing are paid. Equals cash receipts minus cash payments over a given period of time; or equivalently, net profit plus amounts charged off for depreciation, depletion, and amortization. A measure of a company's financial health.

causal analysis The analysis of defects to determine their cause.

change request Any request submitted by a customer (buyer or users) for a change to alter the system. These appear in various forms and include software trouble reports (STRs) and baseline change requests (BCRs). BCRs request changes to the system's specification.

channel capacity The maximum amount of data that can be transferred on a channel per unit of time. Syn. *data transfer rate*. See also *memory capacity, storage capacity*.

charge number A cost accumulation point where labor, other direct costs (ODCs), materials and subcontracts (M&S), and indirect costs are captured in the organization's cost accounting system.

chart of accounts A formally maintained and controlled identification of cost elements (labor by type, material, overhead, etc.).

code (1) Computer instructions and data definitions expressed in either a programming language (source code) or an intermediate form directly related to actual computer instructions (object code). See also *computer instruction, source code, object code*. (2) The action of writing a computer program in a programming language.

code and unit test (CUT) The activity of generating working code (manually or using various tools) to record the data structures, algorithms, and control logic defined during detailed design. Source code modules are compiled, linked, and executed in small units to verify their correct operation. (Test procedures and tools for integration testing and acceptance testing are typically developed concurrently with code and unit test.)

comment Textual information included in a computer program, job control script, or data set to assist human readers, but which is ignored by the computer.

commercial off-the-shelf (COTS) A standard item that is purchased from a commercial vendor without any changes in specification.

commitments Estimated costs for items and services ordered, but not yet invoiced to the buyer. Also called estimated actuals.

common cause of process variation The normal and expected variation of a process that arises from the inherent characteristics of the process itself. See also *special cause of process variation*.

complexity (1) The degree to which a system or component has a design or implementation that is difficult to understand and verify. (2) Pertaining to any of a set of structure-based metrics that measure the attribute in (1). (IEEE Std 610.12-1990)

component One of the parts that make up a system. A component may be software or hardware, and may be subdivided into other components. For software, the terms *component, module*, and *unit* are often used interchangeably, or may refer to different hierarchical levels of decomposition. For hardware, the terms *component, assembly*, and *unit* are often used interchangeably, or may refer to different hierarchical levels of decomposition. The relationship of these terms is not standardized.

computer instruction A single action, consisting of an operator and operands, performed by a computer. Usually refers to machine language instructions, but may also refer to instructions in object code, or even to an executable statement in the source code of a computer program.

computer program An organized set of data definitions and instructions that directs a computer to perform a particular task. See also *software, source code, object code, computer instruction*.

computer resources Processor time, main memory, input/output ports, and auxiliary storage needed by a computer program in order to operate.

computer-aided software engineering (CASE) The use of computers and software tools to aid software engineering activities such as requirements tracing, software design, code production, testing, and document generation. See also *support software*.

concept of operations See *operational concept*.

concept phase The initial phase of a development project that evaluates, defines, and documents user needs. Typical work products may include a statement of need, feasibility study report, preliminary operational concept, or system specification. See also *inception*.

configuration control The evaluation, coordination, approval or disapproval, and implementation of changes to configuration items.

configuration control board A group of designated stakeholder representatives that is responsible for reviewing and approving changes to the configuration baseline.

configuration item A hardware and/or software component with associated documentation that is identified and treated as a single entity for the purpose of configuration management.

configuration management The process of identifying and defining the configuration items in a system, controlling the release and change of these items throughout the system life cycle, recording and reporting the status of configuration items and change requests, and verifying the completeness and correctness of configuration items.

configure The activity of selecting and adapting a hardware or software component so it will fit into or interface with other components of a system. The component ("configurable item") is specifically designed to facilitate such reconfiguration. Contrast this to *adapt*.

construction The third phase of the Rational Unified Process (RUP). It itera-

tively builds and tests the product, evolving the vision and updating plans as necessary. It ends with the initial operational capability (IOC) milestone when a "usable subset" of the product's functions is available to users.

context diagram A diagram that depicts the boundary and external interfaces of a system. It is drawn as a single circle, labeled with the name of the system, with directed lines (arrows) on the exterior of the circle indicating data flows to and from external entities, which are shown as rectangles (called "terminators"). Context diagrams are used in structured analysis as the starting point for stepwise decomposition of the system's data flows.

contract A mutually binding relationship enforceable by law, expressing the mutual assent of two or more legally competent parties to do something they are not otherwise required to do, or not to do something they would otherwise have a right to do, and specifying the exchange of a consideration (something of value, usually money).

contract data requirements A contractual form that provides pertinent information regarding specific documents ("data") to be delivered. These are assigned sequence numbers and itemized on the contract data requirements list. Each item is identified with a work breakdown structure (WBS) element. The delivery schedule for each document is normally stated in the data item description (DID).

contract line item number (CLIN) Supplies and services that appear as itemized entries in a U.S. government contract.

contracting The actions associated with obtaining supplies, services, and construction from business and industry, from initial requirement description through contract completion.

convert To translate a software product from one programming language to another. This may also involve moving the product to a new computing environment. See *port*, *rehost*.

correctness (1) The degree to which a work product's specification, design, and implementation are free from faults. (2) The degree to which a work product meets its specified requirements. (3) The degree to which a work product meets user needs and expectations, whether specified or not.

cost The expenses incurred to obtain the labor and materials for a project.

cost driver Attributes that affect productivity, cost, and schedule for projects. Typically these encompass product, computer, personnel, and project characteristics.

cost driver rating The subjective rating assigned by an estimator to a cost driver attribute. In COCOMO, ratings range from very low to extra high.

cost element Cost elements are types of costs: labor, material, and other direct costs (ODCs). Synonymous with elements of cost (EOC).

costing Computing the monetary amounts (costs) needed to obtain required resources.

COTS product Items that can be purchased from a commercial vendor "off the shelf." (COTS stands for commercial off-the-shelf.) The product or item is specifically designed to meet the needs of a broad spectrum of users, who individually purchase copies of the product. The product developer is responsible for defining the requirements for the product (usually based on customer feedback and market trends).

critical design review (CDR) A review to verify that the detailed design is complete, correct, internally consistent, satisfies all requirements, and is a suitable basis for subsequent coding or fabrication. See *product design review*.

customer The party (individual, project, or organization) responsible for accepting products and services, or for authorizing payment. The customer is external to the project (except possibly when integrated product teams are used), but not necessarily external to the organization. The customer may be a higher level project. Customers are a subset of stakeholders. See also *end user*, *purchaser*, and *stakeholder*.

customer-supplied materials Materials needed for a project that the customer will provide. These can reduce costs, but are a potential source of risk because they may not be fit for use, may arrive late, or both.

data (1) A representation of facts, concepts, or instructions suitable to permit communication, interpretation, or processing by humans or by automatic means. (2) Used as a synonym for documentation in U.S. government procurement regulations. See also *operational data*.

defect A detected fault or an observation of incorrect behavior caused by a fault (a failure).

defect density Number of defects per unit of product size (e.g., validated unique software problem reports per thousand lines of code).

defined process (model) A detailed description of how to produce a product, which includes policies, artifacts, activities, roles, and responsibilities. Another name for the defined process (model) is the organization's standard process (OSP).

delivery (1) Release of a system or work product to a customer or end user. See also *software life cycle, system life cycle*. (2) Formal transfer of products and services to the buyer. The buyer either assumes ownership of the product or receives a license to use the product.

dependability A general term for product characteristics including access security, operator safety, data integrity, or the capability to provide service at a desired time or during a specified time interval. (See *reliability* and *availability*.) The characteristics of interest depend on the particular application.

deployment The process of "putting the product into service." Delivering a new or updated product to users. This can be as simple as shipping magnetic media or posting files for downloading. It can involve installing the product at each user site, training the users at the sites, and activating a unique or very complex system, usually because the user lacks the skills and knowledge to do these activities. Also called *fielding*.

derived measure Data obtained from two or more base measures by mathematical calculations.

derived requirements Requirements not explicitly stated by the customer that are inferred (1) from the environment (e.g., applicable standards, laws, policies, and management directives), or (2) from constraints associated with the product architecture. See also *product requirements*.

design (1) The activity of identifying and defining the architecture, components, interfaces, and attributes of a system or product. See also *architectural design*. (2) The result of the process in (1).

design phase The period of time in the project life cycle during which the product architecture and the designs for hardware and software components and interfaces are created, documented, and verified to meet requirements. See also *elaboration* and *construction*.

design review A process or meeting during which a system, hardware, or software design is presented to stakeholders for comment or approval.

detailed design (DD) (1) The activity of refining and expanding the product design to obtain designs of components that are sufficiently complete to be implemented. For software components, this activity defines the data structures, algorithms, and control logic that meet the functional and performance requirements allocated to a component or module and which comply with the constraints of the software architecture. For hardware components, this activity produces complete blueprints and assembly drawings, which are approved at the critical design review (CDR). (2) The result of the process in (1).

developer The organization that builds and tests the product, and delivers associated services.

development environment The software (including operating system, software tools, test software, drivers, analyzers, etc.), hardware (including computers, printers, chip programmers, interfacing equipment, power supplies, simulators, and test equipment) and other environmental assets (power, cooling, and physical security) used by the project team to build and test the products. This term encompasses the software engineering environment (SEE) and the software test environment (STE).

direct labor The engineering labor expended to design, build, and test a product, and to provide services such as installation and user training. "Direct labor" means that personnel charge their labor hours (effort) directly to the cost of production. Some projects also consider the support staff, such as configuration management and administrative personnel, to be direct labor.

document (1) A collection of data, regardless of the medium on which it is recorded, that generally has permanence and can be read by humans or machines. (2) The activity of writing a document.

documentation (1) Any information (text, diagrams, etc.) used to procure, develop, test, operate, and maintain a product or system. Examples include specifications, designs, plans, procedures, standards, reports, and manuals. (2) A collection of related documents dealing with a particular subject such as a product, project, or process. (3) The activity of generating or revising a document.

domain engineering Activities to characterize a set of similar products and generate a reference architecture.

duration Days that the project staff actually works on project tasks. Measured in work-days (also called project-days). Ignoring holidays, a week has five work-days and seven calendar-days.

dynamic analysis The process of operating a system or component under controlled conditions to collect measurements to determine and evaluate the characteristics and performance of the system or component. See also *testing*. Contrast with *static analysis*.

earned value The budgeted cost of work performed (BCWP) for a work breakdown structure element (or "task") or a group of related elements.

earned value measurement (EVM) A method that compares the amount of work that was planned with what was actually accomplished to measure a project's cost and schedule performance. See also *actual cost of work performed, budgeted cost for work scheduled, budgeted cost for work performed*, and *schedule*.

efficiency A measure of the degree to which a system or component performs designated functions with respect to the resources it consumes to perform those functions.

effort Labor expended to perform some activity. Measured in person-hours.

effort adjustment factor (EAF) In COCOMO, the product of the effort multipliers corresponding to ratings assigned to cost driver attributes.

elaboration The second phase of the Rational Unified Process (RUP). It specifies the main features of the product (the primary use cases), and implements an executable architecture prototype that addresses critical use cases (identified in the inception phase) that represent key technical risks (functionality or performance). The project manager plans the activities and estimates the resources needed to complete the project. It ends with the life cycle architecture (LCA) milestone.

embedded computer system A computer system that is an integral part of a larger system and performs some of the system's functions; for example, controlling fuel injection in an automobile engine.

embedded system A system comprised of hardware and software, in which hardware performs the primary functions, with software providing data processing and control. Embedded systems usually operate in real time. Embedded systems are often safety critica; for exampl, a fly-by-wire aircraft. See also *software-intensive system*.

end user The person or department in the customer organization who will use a product. See also *customer, purchaser*, and *stakeholder*.

engineering The application of a systematic, disciplined, quantifiable approach to analyze, design, and build structures, machines, products, systems, or processes.

engineering change proposal (ECP) A proposed change to an approved baseline (hardware, software, documentation) that is described, justified, and submitted to a configuration control board for formal approval.

engineering release A version of a software product that is prepared for a special purpose, and is usually shipped to a single site. (Contrast this to a normal release, which is shipped to all user sites.) An example is an instrumented version of software used to support field testing.

engineering staff The technical personnel (e.g., analysts, programmers, and engineers) who perform development and test activities.

error (1) The difference between a computed, observed, or measured value or condition and the true, specified, or theoretically correct value or condition. For example, a difference of 30 meters between a computed result and the correct result. (2) A human action that causes an incorrect result. See discussion under *failure*. See also *defect, fault, mistake, problem*. (IEEE Std 610.12-1990)

escalation The increase of costs and financial rates with time.

estimate (1) (verb) To determine the approximate amount of some quantity or the value of some attribute. (2) (noun) The amount or value produced by (1).

estimating Identifying the resources needed to perform project tasks. Resources are typically labor, computer time, and materials.

evolutionary A development process used when the complete design or requirements are not known when the project begins but "evolve" as the project progresses.

execute (1) To perform the tasks of a plan or the activities of a process. (2) To perform the actions dictated by the instructions of a software program within a computer.

execution time The amount of elapsed time or processor time used when executing a computer program. Processor time is usually less than elapsed time because the processor may be idle (awaiting needed computer resources) or may be performing other tasks. Syn: *run time*.

failure The inability of a system or component to perform its required functions within specified performance requirements. The fault tolerance discipline distinguishes between a human action (a *mistake*), its manifestation (a hardware or software *fault*), the result of the fault (a *failure*), and the amount by which the results are incorrect (the *error*). (IEEE Std 610.12-1990) Stated another way, a fault is a potential failure, which can cause an incorrect result (failure) in the future, or may have already caused one. The failure may not have observable consequences, however, and so may not be reported as a problem. See also *defect, mistake, problem, root cause*.

fault An incorrect instruction or data definition in a computer program, or a manufacturing flaw (bad solder joint) or a broken wire in a hardware component, which could cause a product to fail. An omitted requirement in a specification is a fault. However, faults (errors) in user documentation do not directly cause a program to fail and so are not usually counted as faults in the sense the word is defined here. (Incorrect documentation can indirectly cause failures by causing users to make mistakes.) See discussion under *failure*.

fee The percentage applied to total project costs to estimate the profit for a project. The fee value reflects the seller's risk, the competitive environment, and customer expectations.

field test (FT)   A test conducted outside the developer's facility to verify correct operation under field conditions. See also *site acceptance test*.

fielding   See *deployment*.

fielding plan   A plan that describes how a product will be put into the "field" where it will be used operationally. It addresses the required activities, who is responsible for each activity, schedule, resources needed, and potential risks.

fielding strategy   A description of how a project will deliver and install products and provide associated services at user site(s). Also called deployment strategy.

final operational capability (FOC)   A process milestone. All necessary product features and supporting documentation exist. The customer formally accepts the completed product.

firmware   Computer programs stored in a solid state memory device (such as a chip) so that they are retained when electrical power is removed.

first article   The first item completed and accepted by the Customer. Typically refers to hardware. Production of duplicate articles can begin once the first article and its technical data package have been accepted.

flaw   See *fault*.

formal acceptance test (FAT)   A test conducted in the developer's facility to verify that the product meets its acceptance criteria. *Formal* means that a documented procedure is executed in the presence of customer witnesses. Also called formal qualification test (FQT) or factory acceptance test (FAT).

formal qualification test (FQT)   See *formal acceptance test*.

formal review   A formal meeting at which work products are presented to the end user, customer, or other interested parties (stakeholders) for comment and approval. It can also review technical activities and project status.

formal testing   Testing conducted in accordance with test plans and procedures that have been reviewed and approved by a customer, user, or designated level of management. (IEEE Std 610.12-1990)

function point   A software size measure originally defined by Allan Albrecht to quantify the information processing functionality of a software product. Based on "counting rules" for inputs, outputs, queries, internal logical files, and external interface files.

function point analysis (FPA)   A standard method for measuring software functionality from a user's point of view. FPA distinguishes delivered functionality (which reflects value or utility) from added and modified functionality (which reflects programmer effort).

functional baseline   Approved documentation describing a system's function, interoperability, and interface characteristics and the verification required to demonstrate the achievement of those specified characteristics.

functional configuration audit (FCA)   A formal examination of a completed configuration item to confirm that it is satisfactory. The audit covers the item's functional and performance requirements and its operational and support documents. See also *configuration management, physical configuration audit*.

functional testing   Testing that ignores the internal mechanism of a system or component and focuses solely on the outputs generated in response to selected inputs and execution conditions. Also called black-box testing.

funding (1) The activity of authorizing or appropriating money for a project. (2) Money authorized or appropriated to cover the costs of a project. (3) A designated amount of money to be expended for a specific purpose, as authorized by law or management.

Gantt chart A chart that represents project activities as horizontal lines whose length shows the time span of each activity. The ends of each line correspond to the start and finish milestones, indicated by triangles. Progress is indicated by filling in the triangles when milestones are completed. Gantt charts are useful for simple schedules, but do not show task dependencies. Resource loaded networks (RLNs) should be used for projects with many interdependent tasks.

general and administrative Costs incurred to maintain the organization's infrastructure. These include senior management and departments for contracts, legal, finance, and personnel.

hard deliverables Products and services whose requirements are defined by the purchaser. Usually, these requirements are very specific and impose demanding constraints that are difficult to satisfy.

hardware The physical components of a system or product. Examples include sensors, actuators, computers, cables, and housings.

high-order language (HOL) A programming language that provides features to express data structures and program logic without detailed knowledge of the computer on which a program will run. Examples include Ada, COBOL, FORTRAN, C, and Java.

host machine A computer used to develop software intended for another computer. Contrast with *target machine*.

implementation (1) The process of translating a design into hardware components, software components, or both. Includes detailed design, coding (for software), fabrication and inspection (for hardware), and unit (component) test. For software, detailed design and coding are usually combined. (2) The result of the process in (1). Also called construction.

inception The first phase of the Rational Unified Process (RUP). It specifies the product vision, the critical use cases and scenarios that drive design trade-offs, the business case for the product, and the scope of the project to develop the product. It ends with the life cycle objectives (LCO) milestone.

inception readiness review (IRR) The milestone at the start of the MBASE/RUP process. The customer identifies a user or business need, identifies relevant stakeholders, and assembles the stakeholders to define the product and project.

increment A working version of the product providing some or all of the required capabilities. See *build*.

incremental development A process that develops the product in parts (increments), typically divided along functional lines. These increments may be delivered to the customer (incremental delivery) or they may be treated as demonstrations of developed capability (staged development).

independent verification and validation (IV&V) Review, analysis, and evaluation of a set of work products performed by an organization that is technically, managerially, and financially independent of the developer of the work products.

initial operational capability (IOC) A process milestone. A "usable subset" of the product's functions is available to users. For commercial products, the product is ready for beta testing by users.

inspection   Visual examination of work products to detect errors, violations of development standards, and other problems. See also *peer review* and *static analysis*.

integration and test (IT)   The activity of combining unit-tested components into larger subsystems (and eventually into the entire system) to verify correct operation. The testing emphasizes system-level functions and interfaces between components, and is usually performed by an independent test team (i.e., by people who did not develop the software being tested). Syn *integration testing*.

integration testing   Testing of combined components (hardware and/or software) to confirm that the individual components function together as an integrated unit. Syn. *functional testing, integration and test(ing)*. See also *unit testing*.

interface   (1) A shared boundary between two or more hardware or software components that conveys power and/or information from one to the other (2) To connect two or more components for the purpose of passing power and/or information from one to the other.

interoperability   The capability of two or more systems or components to exchange usable information.

labor estimate   The estimated labor hours, subdivided by skill level or labor category, for the activities required to accomplish a project.

labor grade breakdown   A decomposition of estimated labor hours into categories (grades) based on criteria

such as experience or education. The grades have different pay scales and so affect the estimated cost.

legacy system   A system in operational use that must be sustained. Sustainment is challenging for such systems due to obsolete technology, poor structure, out-

dated and incomplete documentation, and lack of people with the necessary knowledge and skills.

life cycle architecture (LCA)   The milestone at the end of the elaboration phase of the MBASE/RUP process. Work products include a stable architecture, buy/build/reuse decisions, and prototypes of critical components. Similar to the product design review for plan-driven processes.

life cycle model   A logical flow of activities representing an orderly progression. See also project life cycle and product life cycle.

life cycle objectives (LCO)   The milestone at the end of the inception phase of the MBASE/RUP process. Completed work products include an operational concept, a product vision, critical use cases, risks, a rough estimate of development effort and time, and a business case. Similar to the system (or software) requirements review in plan-driven processes.

list of deliverables   A list of the items (documents, hardware, software, etc.) that are to be delivered to the customer by a project.

maintenance   (1) The process of modifying a software system or component after delivery to correct faults, improve performance, or adapt to a changed environment. Also called sustainment. (2) The process of servicing and repairing a hardware system or component so that it can perform its required functions See also *preventive maintenance*.

materials   Items that are purchased and are incorporated in the product that is ultimately delivered to the buyer. Materials are defined in a document prepared by the engineers called a bill of materials (BOM). Materials are standard items available "off the shelf," typically as stock items listed in a vendor catalog.

MBASE The model-based (system) architecting and software engineering process model is an extension of the Win-Win Spiral Model. It is equivalent to the Rational Unified Process (RUP).

mean time between failures (MTBF) The estimated or measured average time between consecutive failures in a system or component. MTBF = MTTF + MTTR.

mean time to failure (MTTF) The estimated or measured average time elapsed from activating a system or component and the instant that it first fails.

mean time to repair (MTTR) The estimated or measured time required to repair a system or component and return it to normal operation.

measure (1) A mapping from empirical properties to quantities in a formal mathematical model called a measurement scale. (2) To obtain a measurement.

measurement (1) An instance of a measurement (a "data point"). (2) The activity or process of making a measurement; for example, mapping empirical values to numbers or symbols of a measurement scale.

measurement scale A formal mathematical model that correctly represents relations between objects defined in the model, and only those relations. The relation may be generally accepted (defined, proven) or proposed (hypothetical). Possible scales are nominal, ordinal, interval, ratio, or absolute. Some mathematical operations are undefined in certain measurement scales. Measures for interval, ratio, and absolute scales are represented with numbers and have associated dimensional units ("units of measure").

memorandum of agreement (MOA) Binding documents of understanding or agreements between two or more parties. Also known as a memorandum of understanding (MOU).

memory capacity The maximum amount of data that can be stored in a particular computer memory device; usually measured in bytes. Syn. *storage capacity*. See also *channel capacity*.

metric (1) The degree to which a product, process, or project possesses some attribute of interest. See *measure*. (2) A measured quantity (such as size, effort, duration, or quality). (3) The distance between two points in a vector space.

middleware A general term for any software that allows two separate and usually already existing programs to exchange data without the need for custom coding.

milestone The end of a phase, defined by a set of artifacts that stakeholders formally review and approve. (The approved artifacts are "baselined," and all stakeholders must review and approve all future changes.) Each project life cycle is characterized by a set of phases and milestones. A schedule assigns calendar dates to milestones.

mistake A human action that causes a failure or incorrect result. Software engineers include programmer mistakes in defects, but generally exclude user/operator mistakes. See discussion under *failure*.

module (1) A program unit that is discrete and identifiable with respect to compiling, linking, and loading. (2) A logically separable software design element. The terms "module," "component," and "unit" are not standardized and are interpreted differently by different individuals. See *unit*.

object code   Program logic, instructions, and data definitions expressed in a form close to actual computer (machine) instructions. A compiler or assembler produces object code. A linker maps object code to actual machine instructions. Contrast with *source code*.

offer   A bid to meet the purchaser's request. Provided to the purchaser for approval. Information includes the deliverables, cost, schedule, and terms and conditions. Also called a proposal.

operating system   The collection of software and firmware residing within a computer that controls the execution of other computer programs. The operating system schedules and controls jobs, allocates computing resources, controls data transfer, and manages data.

operation and maintenance phase   The period of the product life cycle during which a product is used operationally, serviced, repaired, modified, and upgraded as necessary to correct problems or to respond to changing requirements.

operational concept   A description of a system's (or product's) purpose, intended operational and support environments, primary functions, and how people will operate the system. It is written from a user standpoint and is nontechnical. The operational concept should clearly identify the functions performed manually (by the operators) from functions performed automatically (by the system). This allocation of system requirements determines the size and complexity of the product (implemented with hardware, software and data), the skill level of the operators, and the type and amount of operator training, and so affects the cost to develop, test, and operate the system. Also called the concept of operation (CONOPS), although this term is also used to denote the technical principles of operation of a

device. Hence, the term operational concept is preferred.

operational data   Enterprise-specific data needed by a software-intensive system in order to function. Examples include customer lists, price lists, financial rate tables (schedules), routing tables, and configuration parameters.

operational scenario   A sequence of events that describes the interactions of a system with its environment, users, and external systems, as well as interactions among system components. Operational scenarios are useful to evaluate system requirements and design and to verify and validate the system. See also *use case*.

organization   An administrative structure in which people perform one or more projects, in accordance with a common set of standard policies.

organization's measurement repository   Actual measurement data on projects, products, and processes and related information needed to understand and analyze that data.

organizational chart   A chart showing how the organizational structure is set up for a project. It shows all members of the project team, as well as the next higher level of management, and all administrative support personnel. Also called the organizational breakdown structure (OBS).

organizational standard process (OSP)   A defined and documented business and engineering process used by all projects in an organization to build and deliver products, provide services, and to plan and manage these activities. It consists of a process architecture and associated policies, procedures, standards, templates, tools, and tailoring guidance. The project team tailors the OSP when defining the approach for a particular project.

other direct cost (ODC) A cost incurred for resources consumed during the production process. Examples are diskettes, office rent, shipping and postage, telephone charges, and travel expenses. (Travel is often itemized separately since it is often a major contributor to the total project cost.) The acronym ODC is also used to refer to the consumed resource itself. For example, "Postage is an ODC." These items are not delivered to the customer.

overhead Costs (or rates) associated with a person's salary (taxes, pension, insurance), and production facilities (offices, furniture, and telephone).

peer review A formal review of a complete work product performed by a group to identify defects for removal, and to collect metrics. See also *inspection*.

performance A measure of the degree to which a system or component accomplishes designated functions within given constraints, such as accuracy, time, or resource usage.

Petri net A technique to model concurrent, asynchronous, distributed, parallel, nondeterministic, and/or stochastic systems developed by Carl Adam Petri. The elements of a Petri net are places, transitions, arcs that connect places and transitions, and tokens that reside within places. The type and number of tokens in each of the places jointly constitute the state ("marking") of the system. Although often represented as a graph, it is possible to define a Petri net using algebraic equations and other mathematical models. Adding time delays makes it possible to study system performance and dependability.

phase A set of activities performed concurrently to achieve some process milestone. Each phase includes a verification and/or validation (V&V) activity to identify any problems with the artifacts being produced during the phase. See *validation, verification,* and *independent verification and validation.*

physical configuration audit (PCA) A formal examination conducted to confirm that a configuration item, as built, conforms to the technical documentation that defines it. See also *functional configuration audit.*

plan A document that identifies the activities and their sequence of execution to accomplish some desired end, such as making a product. A plan describes what is to be done, by whom, and how the project manager intends to organize the work, deploy the resources, and control the performance of the tasks. Plans can have different levels of detail. Large projects may have several related plans addressing portions of the work (e.g., testing, configuration management, quality assurance, and fielding).

plan-driven process A development process that uses carefully planned iterations, extensive process documentation, and detailed measurements for project tracking and control. The process assumes that the requirements and architecture are known and essentially stable. The focus is on repeatability and predictability. Examples are the Waterfall Model and its derivatives. More flexible processes include the Rational Unified Process and the Microsoft Solutions Framework, which use a series of plans developed prior to the start of the next phase.

planning Identifying all tasks needed to make products and provide services. Products and services may be deliverable (software, data, documents) or nondeliverable (e.g., custom tools).

policy A guiding principle established by senior management to influence and determine decisions with an organization.

port   (1) To transfer a software product to a new computing environment. The hardware and operating system change, but the source code remains in the same programming language, although changes may be necessary. Synonymous with rehost. See *convert*. (2) A hardware component or fixture used to implement an interface.

precedented system   A system for which (1) the requirements are consistent and well understood, (2) a system architecture capable of satisfying the requirements is known, and (3) all project stakeholders have worked together previously to develop a similar system [Sylvester, 1994].

precision   The degree of detail used to state a numeric quantity; for example, writing a value to two decimal places instead of five decimal places. Contrast with *accuracy*.

preliminary design review (PDR)   See: *product design review.*

preventive maintenance   Maintenance performed for the purpose of preventing problems before they occur. Usually applies to hardware components to combat wear and corrosion. For software, includes disk defragmenting and file purging.

price   The revenue received from the sale of the product.

problem   A user's report of a program's unexpected behavior. "Problems" may be due to a defect, failure, misuse, or misunderstanding, or may even be a desired capability. Some problems may be reported by multiple users.

procedure   A written description of actions to be taken to perform a given task. Usually expressed as a sequence of steps.

process   The logical organization of people, policies, procedures, and standards into work activities designed to achieve a specified end result such as delivering a product or service. Often identifies additional intermediate work products, techniques, and tools.

process architecture (model)   A high-level description of "how to" produce a product. It identifies the production activities (analyze, design, code, test), their relationships, and time phasing, and the artifacts that these activities produce and consume, plus rules and guidelines for customizing (tailoring) these to the needs of a specific product and project. Also called a project life cycle (model). Such models help to identify work packages used for planning, estimating, scheduling, and tracking, but they lack adequate detail to direct and perform the actual work. Contrast with *process model*.

process assets   Artifacts that relate to describing, implementing, and improving processes (e.g., policies, process descriptions, guidance, examples, aids, checklists, project closeout reports, metrics data, and training materials). The artifacts meet the organization's business objectives, and represent investments expected to provide current and future business value.

process capability   A quantitative statement of expected process performance. See also *process performance* and *process performance baseline*.

process capability baseline   A range of expected results that would normally be achieved by following a defined process. Often expressed in terms of the process control limits defined by the discipline of statistical process control.

process improvement   (1) A program of activities designed to improve the performance and maturity of an organization's processes. (2) The results of such a program.

process model A formal, detailed description of a process that covers policies, activities, work products, roles, and responsibilities. Typically contains standards and procedures and identifies methods and tools as well. Contrast with *process architecture*.

process performance Quantitative results obtained by actually following a process, which may include process measures (e.g., effort, cycle time, and defect removal efficiency) and product measures (e.g., reliability, defect density, and response time).

process performance baseline Documented process performance values used as a reference to compare actual and expected process performance. See also *process performance*.

process performance model A model that makes quantitative predictions about a particular process architecture or process model. Typical predicted quantities include resource consumption, time delays, effectiveness, and efficiency.

process tailoring Making, altering, or adapting a process description to meet the objectives, constraints, and environment of the project.

product (1) Any tangible item or service that is delivered to a customer or end user. Examples are software, documents, databases, or hardware items. See also *artifact*, *product component*, and *work product*. (2) An item acquired from a supplier and then incorporated into a deliverable product.

product architecture See *software architecture*.

product baseline The approved documentation describing all the functional and physical characteristics of a product, and those functional and physical characteristics selected for its acceptance testing.

product component A "piece" (module, part, subassembly) that is integrated with other pieces to build the product. There may be multiple levels of product components. A product component is any work product that must be engineered (requirements defined and designs developed and implemented) to enable the delivered product or service to achieve its intended purpose throughout its life, and that is delivered to the customer. Examples are specifications, designs, code, operational data, user manuals, and training courses. See also *product* and *work product*. (Adapted from CMMI)

product design (PD) (1) The activity of choosing (and possibly modifying) the architecture for a product, populating ("instantiating") the architecture with named components, and allocating requirements to the components. For large projects, this activity ends with the product design review (PDR). For sustainment, the architecture is already defined, and so the Product Design activity just identifies modules to be modified and/or added to the product, and allocates the new/modified requirements to these modules. (Any new modules comply with the existing architecture.) The product design activity also defines the formal acceptance test strategy. This includes (a) defining test cases to test the new and modified modules, and (b) selecting existing test cases to verify the integrity of the modified product (regression tests). (2) The documented results of this activity. See also *top-level design*.

product design review (PDR) A formal buyer/developer review to verify that the top-level design of the product is consistent with defined requirements and adequate to allow implementation to proceed. The review also evaluates the compatibility of the physical and functional interfaces among the product components and with other external equipment, preliminary operational and support documents, and risk resolution. PDR corresponds to the life cycle architecture (LCA) milestone in the MBASE/RUP development process model.

For a software-intensive product, this review freezes the software architecture and identifies specific COTS components to be purchased. Software construction commences after PDR. In contrast, for hardware, PDR approves preliminary hardware designs. Detailed design of hardware commences after PDR, concluding with a critical design review when final blueprints are approved, allowing fabrication to start. In addition, the PDR for hardware may evaluate selected manufacturing methods and processes. Modern software development projects have no CDR milestone.

product development life cycle The period of time that begins with the decision to develop a product and ends when the first article is accepted by the buyer or, for manufactured products, approval is granted to begin producing copies. This cycle typically includes phases for requirements analysis, design, implementation, and test. For custom systems, development often includes an installation and checkout phase. The phases may overlap or be performed iteratively, depending on the development approach used. Contrast with *product life cycle*.

product life cycle The period of time that begins when a product is conceived and ends when the product is no longer available for use. This cycle typically includes phases for concept definition (verifies feasibility), full-scale development (builds and optionally installs the initial version of the system), production (manufactures copies of the first article), transition (transfers the responsibility for product upkeep to another organization), operation and sustainment (repairs and enhances the product), and retirement (removes the product from service). Full-

scale development may be divided into subphases to facilitate planning and management such as requirements analysis, design, implementation, integration and test, installation and checkout. For mass-market commercial products, installation and support are replaced by sales, distribution, and user support. Contrast with *product development life cycle*. See also *process architecture*.

product line A group of products addressing the needs of a particular market or mission that share a common, managed set of features. One example is a family of cell phones based on a particular technology.

product release review (PRR) An MBASE/RUP process milestone. Synonymous with final operational capability.

product requirements A refinement of the customer requirements into the developers' language, making implicit requirements into explicit derived requirements to guide the design and building of the product. See also *derived requirements*.

product risk An undesirable event which, if it occurs, can jeopardize the capabilities or performance of a product.

product trouble report (PTR) Another (and more general purpose) name for software trouble report.

product vision A short document, written from a user perspective, that bounds the scope of the product. It defines what the product is, and what the product is not. It defines the purpose and essential features of the product, recording the developer's understanding of the customer's requirements.

production process The sequence of engineering activities performed to specify, build, and test a product. This process is the heart of the project life cycle.

productivity Size divided by effort. Precise definitions of size and effort are essential.

profit The negotiated selling price (or the sales revenue) minus the production costs. The reward for risk.

program (1) An organized collection of people, facilities, and processes assembled to produce products and deliver associated services. A program usually contains several projects and it is run strategically. A program typically lasts for several years. (2) An executable collection of software components designed to accomplish some specified purpose.

project A collection of people equipment, tools, and facilities assembled to achieve specific objectives within specified cost and schedule constraints. A project typically operates according to a documented plan, which specifies the products and services to be delivered, the resources and funds to be used, the tasks to be done, and a schedule for doing the tasks.

project estimates Detailed estimates of software size, task effort, materials, schedule, and product quality. These are prepared by the project team and are used to prepare the offer to the customer.

project glossary One or more short documents that records acronyms, abbreviations, and terms encountered in a project's environment. These may refer to the application domain, design objects, implementation objects, products, or process activities. The project glossary facilitates precise, concise communication among all project stakeholders. Information is added as the project proceeds to capture and share "discoveries" made by the team.

project goals A short list stating the success criteria for a project. These include expectations and business objectives, and are written from a developer viewpoint.

These goals guide the team and maintain focus during planning and executing the project. Typical items included in the project goals are start and completion dates, negotiated cost, contract type (e.g., time and materials, cost plus a fee, or firm fixed price), constraints (e.g., hard launch date, "politics," process maturity level), major risks ("technical showstoppers," regulatory approvals or certifications, indemnification, and liquidated damages).

project life cycle A set of activities organized to produce a product and/or deliver services. A project life cycle partitions the activities of a project into a sequence of phases to assist planning and management. The early phases gather and analyze information about user needs, product requirements, and alternative designs. Later phases elaborate and implement the design. Some life cycles are iterative, performing certain activities multiple times. Same as project life cycle model.

project manager The person responsible for planning, directing, and controlling a project.

project plan A document that identifies project tasks, and describes how an organization intends to perform and control these tasks. The plan typically describes the tasks, the schedule, the production and management processes, the resources required, organization and responsibilities of the participants, and potential risks. For large projects, project plan(s) are usually split into several separate plans covering development, configuration management, quality assurance, risk management, and so forth.

project planning The process of defining the activities needed to deliver products and services to the project's customer. It includes determining the attributes of work products and tasks, estimating the resources needed, producing a schedule, identifying and analyzing project risks, and negotiating commitments. These activities are usually performed iteratively.

project profile   Summary information about a project's characteristics collected to aid planning and estimating, and interpretation and retrieval of metrics data. Typical information includes customer name, application domain, scope, technology used (platform, COTS components, languages) and the production process (methods, tools).

project risk   An undesirable event which, if it occurs, can jeopardize the success of the project. These risks may affect cost or schedule.

project schedule   The set of project milestones and their planned dates of accomplishment. The actual dates of accomplishment are also usually recorded as the project proceeds.

project team   The group of individuals who build and deliver a product or service. Each individual has one or more assigned roles, and belongs to the organization (e.g., a prime contractor or a subcontractor).

project's defined process   The documented process that the project team follows in performing project tasks. The project's defined process is tailored from the organization's set of standard processes. See also *defined process*.

prototype   Software program, hardware assembly, or mockup built to assess feasibility or risks, validate requirements, demonstrate critical features, quantify (measure) performance, or evaluate alternative designs.

purchase order   A legally binding document sent by an organization to a vendor to purchase items.

purchaser   The party (individual, project, or organization) responsible for accepting products and services and authorizing payment. The purchaser is external to the project (except possibly when integrated product teams are used), but not necessarily external to the organization. The purchaser may be a higher level project. Customers are a subset of stakeholders. See also *customer, end user,* and *stakeholder*.

quality   The degree to which a system, component, or process meets specified requirements, user needs, or stakeholder expectations.

quality assurance (QA)   (1) Activities to ensure that an item or work product conforms to established requirements and standards. Also called product assurance. (2) Activities to ensure that defined standards, procedures, and processes are applied.

quantitatively managed process   A defined process that is measured and controlled using statistical and other quantitative techniques throughout a project [Chrissis, 2003, page 626].

queue   (1) A sequence of work objects (customers) that are waiting to be processed by a server (or machine). The server selects a customer for service based on some policy (the queue discipline or service policy). Some authors refer to the customers plus the server(s) as a queueing system or a service center. (2) A mathematical model of a system comprised of one or more servers that process requests. See *queueing theory, queueing network modeling*.

queueing network modeling   A branch of mathematics that models a system as a network of service centers to predict its performance.

queueing theory A branch of mathematics that studies the properties and performance of a single service center. The model of a service center consists of the arrival distribution, service time distribution, number of servers, system capacity (buffer size), population size, and service discipline.

Rational Unified Process (RUP) A process model that focuses on developing a commercial product. Development occurs in four sequential phases: inception, elaboration, construction, and transition. Also called the Unified Process. See also *inception readiness review*, *life cycle objectives*, *life cycle architecture*, *initial operational capability*, *final operational capability*, and *product release review*.

re-engineer The process of analyzing a legacy system and producing a new, more maintainable system. See *reverse engineer* and *refactoring*.

refactoring Revising software design and code to improve their structure, without changing the functions and behavior of the software, in order to facilitate future modification and enhancement of the software. Used in many agile methods. Refactoring is a broader term than code restructuring.

regression testing Selective retesting of a modified system or component to verify that faults have not been introduced or exposed as a result of the changes, and that the modified system or component still meets its requirements.

rehost See *port*.

release (1) A working version of the product that is delivered to the user. The key difference between a release and a build is that the developer must support the release after it is delivered (e.g., run a help desk, answer questions, etc.) and so

expends more effort and money. (2) The activity of delivering a product. See *deliver*.

reliability The capability of a system or component to perform its required functions under stated conditions for a specified period of time. See also *availability*, *mean time between failures*. (IEEE Std 610.12-1990)

reliability growth The increase in reliability that results from correcting faults in a complete and stable software product.

request for proposal (RFP) A document from a potential customer asking for companies to submit an offer or bid to deliver products and services described in a statement of work.

requirement (1) A capability needed by a user to solve a problem or achieve an objective. (2) A characteristic that a system or product must have, or a capability that it must provide, to satisfy a contract, standard, or specification. (3) A documented representation of a characteristic or capability as defined in (1) or (2).

requirements analysis The process of studying, refining, documenting, and verifying the functional and performance characteristics of a system, product, or component thereof. This process considers customer needs, expectations, and constraints; the operational concept; measures of effectiveness; and sometimes the capabilities and limitations of the developer and the degree of risk.

resource calendar A list of time intervals in which activities or resources can or cannot be scheduled. A project usually has one default calendar for the normal work week (Monday through Friday), but may have other calendars as well, each with its own holidays and extra workdays.

resource loaded network (RLN) A diagram showing all activities necessary to accomplish a project's objectives, generally arranged in increasing time order from left to right. Each activity in the network is characterized by scope, logical relationships, specified or desired duration, needed (estimated) resource amounts, and assigned resources. The RLN integrates activities and resources to reveal the timing of critical project activities.

resources The labor, materials, and consumables used to build products and provide services. These include people, tools, equipment, facilities, and process assets.

response time The time following a user's query or command to an interactive computer system and the beginning of the system's response. See also *think time*.

responsibilities A short list of activities to be performed by a particular person. The list indicates the nature and scope of that person's work activities. See *role*.

retirement Permanent removal of a system or subsystem from operational use. Also called *decommissioning*. See also *software life cycle*, *system life cycle*.

return on investment The amount of additional profit, revenue, or cost savings, divided by the costs incurred to obtain the additional amount. Used to measure the benefit from performing some course of action.

reverse engineer The process of analyzing existing software code and associated documentation to recover its architectural design and specification [Sommerville, 1996, page 711]. This is often the initial activity for re-engineering. See *reengineering*.

review A process or meeting during which a work product or set of work products is presented to stakeholders for verification or approval. See also *peer review*.

risk An undesirable event that, if it occurs, may jeopardize project success, product capabilities, or product performance.

risk analysis The process of identifying, characterizing, and prioritizing risks.

risk management The organized, analytic process to identify future events (risks) that might cause harm or loss, assess and quantify the identified risks, and decide if, how, and when to prevent or reduce the risk. Also includes the implementation of mitigation actions at the appropriate times.

role Specified responsibilities that identify a set of related activities to be performed by a designated individual (e.g., a project manager).

root cause A source of a defect that, if removed, decreases or removes the defect. See *fault, failure*.

scenario A sequence of events that might occur when using a product. Scenarios help to make the needs of stakeholders (especially users and operators) explicit [Chrissis, 2003, page 475]. Analysts use a set of scenarios, plus information about the available technology, the structure of the user organization, and other constraints to define the operational concept for a product, and so the product's architecture and functionality. Scenarios are also the basis for workload scenarios that are used to estimate and measure product performance.

schedule (1) A document showing the tasks for a project and specific calendar dates when each task will be started and completed. (See *milestones*.) (2) The total time elapsed to build a product (calendar days).

scheduling Organizing tasks into a logical time sequence based on their dependencies and constraints.

scope of work See *statement of work*.

service An activity specified as a project deliverable. Examples are training users and installing equipment. Delivery of services consumes resources such as labor and ODCs.

setting price (activity) Choosing the monetary amount to quote to the customer. This is strictly a business decision. Usually, price = cost*(1 + fee), where fee is in percent. The fee reflects the seller's risk.

simulator A device, computer program, or system that represents certain characteristics of interest (size, weight, behavior) of a given system.

site acceptance test (SAT) A (usually formal) test conducted after a product has been installed at a user site to verify the correct operation of the installed product. See also *field test*.

size The amount of product produced or consumed. Some software size measures are source lines of code, statements, or function points.

soft deliverables Products and services whose acceptance is based only on general, high-level criteria. Examples are trade studies and technical reports.

software Computer programs, associated operational data, and (usually) the associated design and user documentation. See also *application software, support software, system software*. Contrast with *hardware*.

software architecture A framework defining key elements of a product that includes the hardware (platform) and software components, their partitioning (structures, arrangement, and relations), and the rules governing the interactions (data transfer, control, error handling) between these components, and between these components and external entities (users and other systems). Partitioning describes the (static) structure and relations between the components, including (a) which software components reside on which hardware components, and (b) the nature and scope of each component (i.e., the functions and data allocated to each component). The rules for the dynamic interaction of the components include error detection, propagation, and handling; interprocess communication and synchronization; human/machine interactions ("look and feel"); fundamental data elements (definition, allowed values, range, precision, default value, internal representation, units of measure; standard coordinate systems; internal units of measure; and physical models. May optionally define design and construction constraints (e.g., specific COTS components to be used).

software baseline A set of configuration items (software documents and software components) that has been formally reviewed and agreed upon, that thereafter serves as the basis for future development, and that can be changed only through formal change control procedures.

software development life cycle Same as product development life cycle.

software development process The set of activities, methods, practices, and tools that people use to develop and maintain software and associated products (e.g., plans, design documents, code, operational data, test cases, and user manuals). Same as *software process*. See also *product development life cycle*.

software engineering (1) The disciplined and systematic application of methods, techniques, and tools to the development, operation, and maintenance of software and software-intensive systems. (2) The building of large, complex software-intensive systems by teams of engineers and programmers. (3) The study of the activities defined in (1) and (2).

software engineering environment (SEE) The collection of computer equipment, tools, and documentation used to modify, compile, link, and test software for a system. See also *software test environment.*

Software Engineering Institute (SEI) A federally funded research and development center sponsored by the U.S. Department of Defense and operated by Carnegie Mellon University. The SEI is chartered to advance the state of the practice of software engineering to improve the quality of systems that depend on software.

software life cycle Same as product life cycle. Contrast with *software development life cycle.*

software process Same as software development process. The set of activities, methods, practices, and tools that people use to develop and maintain software and associated products (e.g., project plans, design documents, code, test cases, and user manuals). See *product development life cycle.*

software process improvement (SPI) The organized activity of defining, infusing, and improving the processes used by individual projects and organizations to develop software.

software requirements The subset of the system requirements that are to be implemented in the software components of the system.

software specification review (SSR) Formal review by the customer, developer, and other stakeholders to ensure that software requirements have been sufficiently defined to support the design of the system, and to ensure that the project team has correctly interpreted and captured the customer's needs.

software test environment (STE) The collection of computer equipment, tools, and documentation used to integrate and test software for a system. For some systems, the STE and the software engineering environment (SEE) are identical. For other systems, the STE has additional equipment, tools, and so forth. to perform stress testing, verify interfaces to other systems (interoperability), and so forth.

software trouble report (STR) A report submitted by an end user describing a problem with a fielded product. Also called product trouble report (PTR).

software-intensive system A system in which software, databases, computers, and networks provide most of the system's functionality. An example is an organization's management information system. Contrast with *embedded system.*

source code Computer instructions and data definitions expressed in a form readable by humans and suitable for input to an assembler, compiler, or other translator. Contrast with *object code.* See also *computer program.*

special cause of process variation A cause of a defect that is specific to some transient circumstance or anomaly, and is not inherent to the underlying process itself. Contrast with *common cause of process variation.*

specification A document used in procurement or development that describes the technical requirements for products, components, or services, usually including the procedures to be used to determine that the requirements have been met. Large systems may have multiple levels of specifications. Some specifications are common to multiple systems or products (e.g., interface definitions). See also *product requirements.*

stable process   A process from which all special causes of process variation have been removed and prevented from recurring so that only the common causes of process variation remain. See also *capable process, common cause of process variation, special cause of process variation, defined process*, and *statistical process control*.

staffing profile   A table, graph, or document showing how many people of each labor type will be required during each phase of a project.

stakeholder   A group or individual affected by, or in some way accountable for, the outcome of an activity or process. Stakeholders may include the project team, suppliers, customers, purchasers, end users, and others.

standard   (1) A documented description of an artifact, giving its purpose, intended audience, content, and (optionally) a format. (2) An approved, documented, and available set of criteria used to determine the adequacy of a product.

statement   A syntactically complete expression in a programming language that defines data, specifies program actions, or directs the assembler or compiler.

statement of work (SOW)   A customer's description of contracted work required to complete a project. This usually consists of a list of tasks or deliverables, and terms and conditions, describing payment arrangements, data rights, and other legal provisions. Also called a scope of work.

static analysis   Use of tools to evaluate the structure, completeness, and correctness of a software component without actually executing the code. The tools may be simple (e.g., statistics on module size and comment density) or sophisticated (e.g., call trees, setting and use of variables, fan out metrics). Contrast with *dynamic analysis*. See also *inspection, regression testing, stress testing*.

statistical process control   Statistical analysis of process performance to identify common and special causes of variation and to quantify the amount of variation in the process. Used to define operational limits on performance parameters to monitor and maintain process performance within limits. See also *common cause of process variation, special cause of process variation*.

storage capacity   The maximum amount of data that can be held in a particular storage device; usually measured in bytes. See also *channel capacity, memory capacity*.

stress testing   Testing that evaluates a system or component at or beyond its specified performance limits.

subcontract   A legal document between one contractor (the prime developer) and another supplier, obligating the supplier to produce and deliver a portion of the total product.

subcontracted item   A distinct subsystem, component, or a service defined in a documented statement of work prepared by engineers. Subcontracted items are not standard off-the-shelf items. The subcontractor "adds value" to materials in some way by producing a customized product or service. The subcontractor expends labor to design and produce the item, or may just customize, configure, or assemble the item. Contrast to *materials*.

subcontractor   A separate firm that configures, develops, or builds a customized product; uses its own management structure; and is usually not collocated with the primary developer. See *subcontracted item*.

supplier   An individual, company, or other organization that provides items to an acquirer (buyer) under the terms of a written agreement (contract or purchase order). The supplier may provide commercial-off-the-shelf items, may configure or modify COTS items, or may design and manufacture custom items. The supplier may also provide services such as installation, user training, and maintenance.

support   The activities performed during operations to ensure that a system or product continues to meet its requirements. These activities include preventive maintenance, repair, upgrade, and user training. See also *product life cycle, maintenance, sustainment.*

support software   (1) Software used to develop or maintain other software; for example, compilers, linkers, and CASE tools. (2) For some products and systems, the application software is distinguished as mission software (primary functions) and support software (ancillary functions such as diagnostic tests, instrument calibration, and infrequent data conversion). Both types are deliverable and used by the operational staff. The support software for such systems may or may not include software development tools. See also *application software, operating system* and *computer-aided software engineering.*

support task   A task done to facilitate or enable the activities of product developers and project managers.

sustainment   The processes used to ensure that a delivered system or product can be used operationally throughout its service life. Engineers correct errors, add functions, and improve performance, releasing a sequence of versions. Also called maintenance.

system   A collection of interrelated components that operate together to achieve some desired function, and support organizational mission or business objectives. A system may include software, hardware, and operational data. A system is operated by people. The word *system* often connotes a large product designed to meet the needs of a particular group of users. See also *product.*

system development life cycle   See *product development life cycle.*

system life cycle   See *product life cycle.*

system requirements review (SRR)   A review to evaluate the completeness and adequacy of the requirements defined for a system. See also *software requirements.*

system software   Same as operating system. Contrast with *application software.* See also *support software.*

systems engineering   A structured, interdisciplinary activity to define the total technical approach to transform customer needs, expectations, and constraints into a viable product solution. System engineering addresses the complete problem, including operations, performance, testing, manufacturing, deployment, user training and support, maintenance, upgrade, and disposal. System engineering also considers technical feasibility; costs and schedules for development, operation, and maintenance; and risks. Systems engineering focuses on methods and processes to integrate and coordinate the work of various engineering disciplines, which actually solve the specific technical problems. At the start of a project, systems engineering determines the business and technical needs of all system users, defines the required functionality, documents system requirements, synthesizes alternative design concepts, and evaluates these concepts to validate the requirements and to select the best design. At the end of development, systems engineering tests and validates the completed system.

tailoring   Selecting and customizing activities and artifacts of an organization's standard process to meet the objectives and constraints of a project.

target machine   The computer on which a completed program is intended to execute during operational use. Contrast with *host machine*.

task order contract   A contract where a basic contractual arrangement is established setting a general scope, rate structure, a process for defining and managing individual task orders, and a process for reporting task status and costs. Work is then assigned and negotiated during the contract as separate tasks (task orders).

technical data package (TDP)   A collection of information that provides everything needed to re-create, reproduce, or modify a product. Depending on the type of product, various items may be included in a technical data package. Typical contents of the TDP include engineering documents, drawings, and diagrams. Sometimes the TDP includes information on production and fabrication processes. For software, this usually includes a style guide with naming conventions and coding rules. For more information, see [Chrissis, 2003, page 630].

test bed   An environment containing the hardware, instrumentation, simulators, software tools, and other support elements needed to conduct a test. (IEEE Std 610.12-1990) Syn. *software test environment (STE)*.

test case   A set of test inputs, execution conditions, and expected results used to verify compliance with a specific requirement or to demonstrate a particular capability.

test plan   A document describing the scope, approach, characteristics and features to be tested, necessary tasks, resources, task schedule, responsibilities, and risks.

test procedure   (1) Detailed steps for running a test case, including the activities of setup, execution, and analysis of results. (2) A document containing the steps for running one or more test cases.

test readiness review (TRR)   (1) A review to evaluate the results of functional and integration tests for one or more hardware or software components to verify that the acceptance test procedures for the product or system are complete and correct, and comply with test plans. (2) A process milestone indicating that formal testing can proceed.

test report   A report describing the test(s) run and the results of the test(s).

test strategy   A brief description of the scope of and approach for product testing used to support initial planning and estimation, and provide a basis for later detailed test planning. It covers the types of tests (e.g. functional, interface, performance, stress, endurance, regression), the test configuration (product, equipment, test tools, dummy data), risks, and organizational responsibilities. The test strategy must cover product acceptance testing. The integration test strategy is usually closely tied to the build sequence (specified by the project team) and the delivery sequence (specified by the customer).

testing   The process of operating a system or component under controlled conditions to collect measurements needed to determine if the system or component meets its allocated requirements. See also *dynamic analysis*.

think time   The time following the display of a prompt or message generated by an interactive system and the beginning of the human user's response. See also *response time*.

third party   An organization outside the control of the developer or the customer, such as a licensing or regulatory agency that certifies that a product is safe to operate. These organizations usually have no financial stake in the project or the product and so are not motivated to act in an expedient or efficient manner.

thrashing   An undesirable operating condition in which a computer system is expending most of its resources on housekeeping (e.g., swapping data between memory and disk), rather than on useful processing.

throughput   The amount of work performed by a computer system within a specified time interva; for example, the number of transactions of a certain type that can be processed per second. See also *response time, workload, channel capacity.*

top-level design (TLD)   (1) The activity of identifying and naming specific instances of the architectural components, and allocating specific requirements to each of these components. Top-level design "instantiates" the architecture for a specific system or product. For example, in a client/server architecture, a specific communications protocol, say open system interconnect (OSI), may be chosen for the communications manager module and so the module would be named "osi_comm_manager". (2) The documents produced by the top-level design activity. See also *product design.*

tracking   Comparing actual costs to the planned budget (and especially to the amount of useful work performed).

trade study   An evaluation of alternatives, based on defined criteria and systematic analysis, to select the best alternative from among a set of candidate alternatives for achieving specified objectives. (Also called a trade-off analysis.)

training   Providing workers with the knowledge and skills needed to adequately perform the responsibilities of their role(s). Learning options may include in-class training, mentoring, web-based training, guided self-study, and on-the-job training. The learning options selected depend on the type of knowledge needed, the student's current ability, and cost.

transition   (1) The process of transferring responsibility for the maintenance of a product from the original developer to a sustaining organization. Transition is the complement of fielding (deployment). (2) The fourth phase of the Rational Unified Process (RUP). It develops, tests, and documents all remaining product functions. It corrects all defects found by beta testers. It also performs activities needed to deploy the product to users, train users, and provide user support. It ends with the final operational capability (FOC) or the product release review (PRR) milestone, which are synonymous.

unit   A logically separable software design element such as a function, procedure, module, or package. Units partition the product into meaningful entities to aid understanding and to manage production. (A unit is typically sized so that a single person can implement it.) The terms *module, component,* and *unit* are not standardized and are interpreted differently by different individuals. See also *module* and *units.*

unit development folder   A collection of material pertinent to the development or support of a component (subsystem, module, class, or assembly). Contents typically include (directly or by reference) allocated requirements, design considerations and constraints, design documentation and data, schedule and status information, test requirements, test cases, test procedures, and test results. Called the software development folder for software components.

unit testing   Testing of individual hardware components or assemblies, or software modules or groups of related modules. See also *integration testing*.

units   Refers to the units of measure used to express measurements. Examples include feet for length, radians for angles, bytes for storage, and SLOC for code size. See also *unit*.

unprecedented   Any product or system that violates one or more of the three criteria for a precedented system. See *precedented system*.

upper management   The persons responsible for supervising the activities of project managers and for maintaining the organization's overall infrastructure.

use case   A set of possible sequences of interactions (scenarios) between systems and users (actors) in a particular environment and related to a particular goal. The use case and goal are sometimes considered to be synonymous. Use cases capture the intended behavior of the system, without specifying how that behavior is implemented. Use cases can be employed to identify, clarify, and organize system requirements, and, during later stages of software development, to validate design, create test cases, and create online help and user manuals.

utilization   A measure used in computer performance evaluation, equal to the amount of time a system or component is busy divided by the time it is available.

validation   Confirmation that the product, as provided (or as it will be provided), will fulfill its intended use. Validation ensures that "you built the right thing." See also *verification* and *independent verification and validation*.

verification   Evaluating the products of a given activity to determine correctness and consistency with respect to the products and standards provided as input to that activity. Verification ensures that "you built it right." See also *validation* and *independent verification and validation*.

version   A product that has a unique identifier and whose performance requirements and design have been documented.

version description document (VDD)   A document that accompanies and identifies a particular version of a system or product. Typical contents include a list of component parts, the changes incorporated, and installation and operating instructions unique to the version (e.g., a README file).

virtual machine   The combination of hardware and software (OS, DBMS, etc.) that provides the underlying environment that supports the operation of a software product. Also called the platform.

Waterfall Model   A product development process that follows the sequence of analyze, design, code, and test. The underlying assumption is that each phase does not begin until the preceding phase is complete. There are no overlaps or iterations.

work authorization   (1) The activity of assigning responsibility and resources to accomplish work defined by a work package. (2) Administrative documents used to record the assignment.

work breakdown structure (WBS)   An arrangement of work elements and their relationship to each other and to the end product. The work elements are numbered to indicate their relation to each other. For large projects, the high-level work elements correspond to hardware and software components, services, and support activities. The lower level work elements are tasks that must be performed to produce and deliver the items identified in the higher levels. A WBS is the basis for Bottom-Up estimation, project scheduling, and project tracking. See *resource loaded network* and *earned value*.

work product (1) An artifact produced by a process that is not part of the delivered product. Examples are plans, schedules, audit records, and measurement data. Work products are not usually engineered. (One possible exception is custom-built test tools.) See *artifact* and *product component*. (2) In the CMMI model, any artifact produced by a process.

workload A defined mix of tasks used to estimate or measure the performance of a software-intensive computer system. Usually specifies the types and amount of computation and associated input/output activities.

Bibliography

The text and appendixes in this book cite more than 450 sources where you can find additional information. (The Notes cite additional sources.) Printing these sources would have required over 30 printed pages. I decided that readers would prefer access to an extensive list of sources over rapid access to these sources. Consequently, I provide a comprehensive "electronic bibliography" on the CD-ROM in both Microsoft Word and Rich Text Format. This bibliography contains the complete list of references that I consulted when researching and writing the book. I cited most of these in early drafts. As I condensed the text, however, I deleted some of them. You can use Microsoft Word's Find command to search the bibliography to locate topics, authors, and journals.

Index

W-Z